CAMBRIDGE LIBRAR**

Books of enduring schol

British and Irish History, Nineteenth Century

This series comprises contemporary or near-contemporary accounts of the political, economic and social history of the British Isles during the nineteenth century. It includes material on international diplomacy and trade, labour relations and the women's movement, developments in education and social welfare, religious emancipation, the justice system, and special events including the Great Exhibition of 1851.

A History of the Criminal Law of England

Sir James Fitzjames Stephen (1829–94) published this three-volume account of the English criminal law's historical development in 1883, four years after his appointment as a judge of the High Court. It is a revision and expansion of the second chapter in Stephen's 1863 *General View* (also reissued in this series). At first sight, it is ironic that the author of this classic of legal historical scholarship was himself a Benthamite who favoured and promoted the codification of the common law and worked on codes of criminal law and procedure for India and for England. Volume 1 contains a short preliminary account of Roman criminal law and pre-Conquest English criminal law; a survey of courts exercising criminal jurisdiction; a historical account of the development of the main elements of criminal procedure; a history of criminal punishments; and a general comparative view of the differences between English and French criminal procedure.

Cambridge University Press has long been a pioneer in the reissuing of out-of-print titles from its own backlist, producing digital reprints of books that are still sought after by scholars and students but could not be reprinted economically using traditional technology. The Cambridge Library Collection extends this activity to a wider range of books which are still of importance to researchers and professionals, either for the source material they contain, or as landmarks in the history of their academic discipline.

Drawing from the world-renowned collections in the Cambridge University Library and other partner libraries, and guided by the advice of experts in each subject area, Cambridge University Press is using state-of-the-art scanning machines in its own Printing House to capture the content of each book selected for inclusion. The files are processed to give a consistently clear, crisp image, and the books finished to the high quality standard for which the Press is recognised around the world. The latest print-on-demand technology ensures that the books will remain available indefinitely, and that orders for single or multiple copies can quickly be supplied.

The Cambridge Library Collection brings back to life books of enduring scholarly value (including out-of-copyright works originally issued by other publishers) across a wide range of disciplines in the humanities and social sciences and in science and technology.

A History of
the Criminal Law
of England

VOLUME 1

JAMES FITZJAMES STEPHEN

CAMBRIDGE
UNIVERSITY PRESS

CAMBRIDGE
UNIVERSITY PRESS

University Printing House, Cambridge, CB2 8BS, United Kingdom

Published in the United States of America by Cambridge University Press, New York

Cambridge University Press is part of the University of Cambridge.

It furthers the University's mission by disseminating knowledge in the pursuit of
education, learning and research at the highest international levels of excellence.

www.cambridge.org
Information on this title: www.cambridge.org/9781108060714

© in this compilation Cambridge University Press 2014

This edition first published 1883
This digitally printed version 2014

ISBN 978-1-108-06071-4 Paperback

A HISTORY

OF

THE CRIMINAL LAW OF ENGLAND.

VOL. I.

A HISTORY

OF

THE CRIMINAL LAW

OF ENGLAND.

BY

SIR JAMES FITZJAMES STEPHEN, K.C.S.I., D.C.L.,

A JUDGE OF THE HIGH COURT OF JUSTICE, QUEEN'S BENCH DIVISION.

IN THREE VOLUMES.

VOL. I.

London:

MACMILLAN AND CO.

1883.

LONDON :
R. CLAY, SONS, AND TAYLOR,
BREAD STREET HILL.

PREFACE.

THIS work, which attempts to relate the history of the Criminal Law of England, has a history of its own.

In 1863 I published what in one sense may be called the first edition of this work under the title of *A General View of the Criminal Law.* In 1869 I became Legal Member of the Council of the Viceroy in India, and held that office for about two years and a half, during which time my attention was strongly directed, from the legislative point of view, to the subject of Criminal Law, and particularly to its codification. Amongst other things, I drew and carried through the Legislative Council the Code of Criminal Procedure, Act X. of 1872, which, with some slight alterations and variations has just been reenacted and extended to the High Courts by Act X. of 1882.

In 1873 or 1874 I was informed that a second edition of my *General View* was wanted. I began to prepare one, but I found myself hampered at every page by the absence of any authoritative statement of the law to which I might refer. It then occurred to me that as there was no such statement in existence I might write something which at all events would express my own views as to what the law was, to which I might refer in discussing its provisions historically and critically. Acting on this I wrote my *Digest of the Criminal Law* which was published in 1877, and of which a third edition is just coming out. The *Digest* does not deal with the subject of Procedure. In order at once to complete it and to enable the readers of the present work to see the law of Criminal Procedure as well as that of crimes and punishments stated systematically, I have (with the help of my eldest son) written as a companion to the earlier *Digest* a *Digest of the Law of Criminal Procedure*, which is published contemporaneously with the present work.

When the *Digest of the Criminal Law* was written it occurred to me that with a little alteration it would make a Draft Penal Code. I communicated this view to Lord Cairns (then Lord Chancellor) and to the late Lord Justice Holker (then Attorney-General), and under their authority I drew the Draft Criminal Code of 1878, which was introduced into Parliament by Sir John Holker in the session of that year. Thanks to a great extent to the admirable skill with which Sir John Holker brought forward a measure which he appreciated with extraordinary quickness, for I think his attention had never before been directed to the subject of codification, the bill was favourably received, but Parliament had not time to attend to it. A commission, however, was issued to Lord Blackburn, Mr. Justice Barry, Lord-Justice Lush, and myself, to inquire into and consider and report upon the Draft Code. It was accordingly considered by us for about five months, namely from November, 1878, to May, 1879.[1] We sat daily during nearly the whole of that time, and discussed every line and nearly every word of every section. The Draft Code which was appended to the Report speaks for itself. It differs slightly from the Draft Code of 1878. The particulars of the differences are stated in the Report prefixed to the Draft Code of 1879. I did not discover, in the course of the searching discussions of every detail of the subject which took place, any serious error or omission

---

[1] The Report was signed June 12, 1879.

in the *Digest* upon which both measures were founded. Our report was presented too late for the Code to be passed in 1879. In 1880 there was a change of ministry, but in 1882 the part of the Code which related to Procedure was announced in the Queen's Speech as a Government measure. It had, however, to be postponed, like many other things, to matters of a more pressing nature. For reasons stated at length in the present work I should deeply regret the division of the Code into separate parts. Such a course would in my opinion produce confusion and deprive the measure of much of its value. If it is said that the Code taken as a whole is too extensive a measure to be disposed of in a single session, it may be replied that it is not longer than other single acts—for instance, the Merchant Shipping Act of 1854; and it may be added that by far the greater part of the Act is mere reenactment, and would in all probability give rise to no discussion. At all events, if the Bill is divided into two parts, it would be desirable to suspend the operation of the one first passed till the other could be enacted. They are so interwoven that it would be inconvenient to bring one into operation alone. To give a single instance. How can you retain the distinction between felony and misdemeanour as a part of the substantive law, and yet remove it from the law of procedure? How, if it is removed from the law of procedure, retain it as part of the substantive law? There is no hurry about the matter. The law as it stands is perfectly well understood and in substance requires little alteration. The use of codification would be to give it literary form, and so to render it generally accessible to all whom it concerns. Surely it would be unwise to perform the operation in such a way as to deprive the result of its principal value.

As soon as the sittings of the Criminal Code Commissions

were over I returned to the work which the preparation and
revision of the Draft Codes of 1878 and 1879 had forced
me to lay aside.

On turning back to the book published in 1863 I found
that though the experience collected in the manner already
stated had confirmed large parts of what I had written, the
book was in many places crude and imperfect, and that in
some respects it no longer represented my views. It seemed,
accordingly, that if the work was to be republished it must
be rewritten, and the present work is the result. I am conscious of many defects in it for which my best apology is
that it has been written in the intervals of leisure left by my
judicial duties. It is longer and more elaborate than I
originally meant it to be, but, until I set myself to study the
subject as a whole, and from the historical point of view, I had
no idea of the way in which it connected itself with all
the most interesting parts of our history, and it has been
matter of unceasing interest to see how the crude, imperfect definitions of the thirteenth century were gradually
moulded into the most complete and comprehensive body of
criminal law in the world, and how the clumsy institutions
of the thirteenth century gradually grew into a body of
courts and a course of procedure which, in an age when everything is changed, have remained substantially unaltered, and
are not alleged to require alteration in their main features.
Much has been said and written of late years on the historical
method of treating legal and political matters, and it has no
doubt thrown great light on the laws and institutions of
remote antiquity. Less has been done in investigating
comparatively modern laws and institutions. The history of
one part of our institutions has, under the name of constitutional history or law, been investigated with admirable skill
and profound learning. Comparatively little has been done

towards writing the history of other branches of our law which are perhaps more intimately connected with the current business of life. Of these the criminal law is one of the most important and characteristic. No department of law can claim greater moral importance than that which, with the detail and precision necessary for legal purposes, stigmatises certain kinds of conduct as crimes, the commission of which involves, if detected, indelible infamy and the loss, as the case may be, of life, property, or personal liberty. A gradual change in the moral sentiments of the community as to crime in general and as to each separate crime in particular, displays itself in the history of legislation on the subject, and particularly in the history of legal punishments. The political and constitutional interest of the subject is not inferior to its moral interest. Every great constitutional question has had its effect both on criminal procedure and on the definition of crimes. I may instance the history of impeachments, the history of the criminal jurisdiction of the Privy Council, the history of the gradual development of the modern system of trial, the history of the law relating to treason, and that of the law relating to libel. Subjects of even more vital interest than politics have their bearing upon the criminal law. Any history of it which omitted the subject of religious offences would be incomplete, but that history involves a sketch of the process which has, in the course of about five centuries, changed a legislative system, based upon practically unanimous belief in the doctrines of the mediæval church, into a system which, according to some, is based upon the principle that for legislative purposes many religions are to be regarded as about equally true (which is probably what is meant by the principle of religious equality), and according to others on the principle that all religions are untrue.

The subject of criminal responsibility and the relation
of madness to crime cannot be discussed without saying
something on subjects forming the debateable land between
ethics, physiology, and mental philosophy.

Again, the different views of social and political economy
which have prevailed at different times have left traces,
amongst others, on the laws which punish offences against
trade, and on ·the laws against vagrancy and on the game
laws.

Even the history of crimes which are crimes and nothing
else, such as homicide in its two forms, and theft, is full
of interest, partly because it illustrates the unexpressed
views of many different ages upon violence and dishonesty,
and partly because it is perhaps the most striking illustration to be found in any part of the law of the process
by which the crude and meagre generalities of the early
law were gradually elaborated into· a system erring on the
side of over luxuriance and refinement, but containing materials of the highest value for systematic legislation.

Lastly, the Criminal Law, like every other important branch
of the law, connects itself with other systems, and that in
several ways. First, the question of its local extent has
much to do with questions connected with International
Law. Secondly, it has been the parent of other systems,
one of which at least (the Criminal Law of India) is on
its own account a topic of great interest, whilst it becomes
doubly interesting when it is regarded, as it ought to be,
as a rationalised version of the system from which it was
taken. Thirdly, it is difficult to criticise the system properly
or to enter into its spirit except by comparing it with
what may be described as the great rival system,—that
which is contained in the French and German Penal Codes,
both of which may be regarded to a certain extent as

rationalised versions and developments (though in each case at several removes) of the Criminal Law of Rome.

I have tried to deal with these matters in such a manner as to write a hitherto unwritten chapter of the history of England, and at the same time to explain one of the most important branches of the existing law, and to show on what foundations rests the Code in which it is proposed to embody it.

J. F. STEPHEN.

ANAVERNA,
    RAVENSDALE,
        Co. LOUTH,
Oct. 19, 1882.

CONTENTS.

CHAPTER I.

PAGE

STATEMENT OF THE SUBJECT OF THE WORK 1

CHAPTER II.

ROMAN CRIMINAL LAW 9

CHAPTER III.

EARLY ENGLISH CRIMINAL LAW 51

CHAPTER IV.

THE ORDINARY CRIMINAL COURTS—QUEEN'S BENCH DIVISION OF THE
HIGH COURT, THE COURTS OF ASSIZE, THE COURTS OF QUARTER
SESSIONS, COURTS OF SUMMARY JURISDICTION, FRANCHISE COURTS,
WELSH COURTS 75

CHAPTER V.

THE CRIMINAL JURISDICTION OF PARLIAMENT AND THE COURT OF THE
LORD HIGH STEWARD 145

CHAPTER VI.

PAGE

THE CRIMINAL JURISDICTION OF THE PRIVY COUNCIL 166

CHAPTER VII.

HISTORY OF THE LAW OF CRIMINAL PROCEDURE.—PROCEDURE DOWN
TO COMMITTAL FOR TRIAL OR BAIL 184

CHAPTER VIII.

HISTORY OF THE LAW OF CRIMINAL PROCEDURE CONTINUED.—FORMS
OF ACCUSATION AND TRIAL—APPEALS—ORDEALS—TRIAL BY JURY 244

CHAPTER IX.

HISTORY OF THE LAW OF CRIMINAL PROCEDURE CONTINUED.—LEGAL
INCIDENTS OF A CRIMINAL TRIAL—INDICTMENT AND INFORMATION
—ARRAIGNMENT, TRIAL, AND VERDICT 273

CHAPTER X.

HISTORY OF THE LAW OF CRIMINAL PROCEDURE CONTINUED.—PROCEED-
INGS BY WAY OF APPEAL 308

CHAPTER XI.

HISTORY OF CRIMINAL TRIALS IN ENGLAND FROM 1554—1760 319

CHAPTER XII.

DESCRIPTION OF MODERN CRIMINAL TRIALS 428

CHAPTER XIII.

PAGE

HISTORY OF LEGAL PUNISHMENTS 457

CHAPTER XIV.

MANAGEMENT OF PROSECUTIONS 493

CHAPTER XV.

GENERAL AND COMPARATIVE VIEW OF ENGLISH AND FRENCH CRIMINAL

PROCEDURE 504

⁎ For List of CASES named, STATUTES cited and GENERAL INDEX,
see end of VOLUME III.

ERRATA AND CORRIGENDA.

Vol. I.

P. 56, *last line, omit* "[? culpam]" *and add the following note to the word* "colpum :"—"Colpus Gallis *coup* Italis *colpo* diminutivum ex colaphus."—*Ducange, sub voce.*

P. 70, *note 2, for* "Hen. 8," *read,* "Hen. 1."

P. 71, *line 20 from top, for* "theoir," *read,* "theow."

P. 98, *last line, for* "goal," *read,* "gaol."

P. 116, *last line of note 1, for* "c. 79," *read* "c. 76."

P. 126, *The passage quoted from Bracton is in* Vol. II., p. 538.

P. 127, *note 2, for* "Sir H. Twiss," *read,* "Sir T. Twiss."

P. 241, *add to note 4 the following :*—"The &c., to which this note is made is a misprint in Sir T. Twiss's edition for vic.,' the abbreviation of vicecomites, which makes the passage clear."

Vol. II.

P. 17, *note 1, line 2, for* "Horace," *read* "Travers."

P. 187, *line 5 from the bottom, for* "cur," *read* "eas."

Vol. III.

P. 15, *line 8 from bottom, dele* "who."

P. 21, *line 17 from top, dele* "two."

P. 29, *line next below the table, for* "Horace," *read* "Travers.'

P. 152, *note 1, for* "Shaw," *read* "Show."

P. 179, *line 17, for* "actions," *read* "sections."

P. 321, *line 6 from top, for* "they," *read* "he."

CRIMINAL LAW.

CHAPTER I.

STATEMENT OF THE SUBJECT OF THE WORK.

A COMPLETE account of any branch of the law ought to consist of three parts, corresponding to its past, present, and future condition respectively. These three parts are—

(1) Its history.

(2) A statement of it as an existing system.

(3) A critical discussion of its component parts with a view to its improvement.

My *Digest of the Criminal Law* and the *Digest of the Law of Criminal Procedure* now published as a companion volume to it are attempts to state the most important parts of the criminal law as it is systematically. The present work is intended to relate its history, and to criticise its component parts with a view to their improvement. The criticism is for the most part interwoven with the history.

Before undertaking either of these tasks I must endeavour to define what I mean by the Criminal Law. The most obvious meaning of the expression is that part of the law which relates to crimes and their punishment—a crime being defined as an act or omission in respect of which legal punishment may be inflicted on the person who is in default either by acting or omitting to act.

CHAP. I.   This definition is too wide for practical purposes. If it were applied in its full latitude it would embrace all law whatever, for one specific peculiarity by which law is dis-tinguished from morality is, that law is coercive, and all coercion at some stage involves the possibility of punish-ment. This might be shown in relation to matters altogether unconnected with criminal law, as the expression is commonly understood, such as legal maxims and the rules of inheritance. A judge who wilfully refused to act upon recognised legal maxims would be liable to impeachment. The proprietary rights which are protected by laws punishing offences against property are determined by the application of those laws. If there were no such crimes as theft, forcible entry, malicious mischief, and the like, and if there were no means of forcing people to respect proprietary rights, there would be no such thing as property by law.

This is no doubt a remote and abstract speculation. The principle on which it depends may be displayed by more obvious and important illustrations. It would be a violation of the common use of language to describe the law relating to the celebration of marriage, or the Merchant Shipping Act, or the law relating to the registration of births, as branches of the criminal law. Yet the statutes on each of these subjects contain a greater or less number of sanctioning clauses which it is difficult to understand without reference to the whole of the acts to which they belong. Thus, for instance, it is felony to celebrate marriage otherwise than according to the provisions of certain [1]Acts of Parliament passed in 1823 and 1837, and these provisions form a connected system which cannot be understood without reference to the common law on the subject. These illus-trations (which might be indefinitely multiplied) show that the definition of criminal law suggested above must either be considerably narrowed or must conflict with the common use of language by including many parts of the law to which the expression is not usually applied.

For all practical purposes a short description of the subject-matter to which the expression " criminal law " is commonly

[1] *Dig. Crim. Law*, 259, 260.

applied is more useful than any attempt to sum up in a few words the specific peculiarity by which this is distinguished from other parts of the law. The following is such a description : The criminal law is that part of the law which relates to the definition and punishment of acts or omissions which are punished as being (1) attacks upon public order, internal or external; or (2) abuses or obstructions of public authority; or (3) acts injurious to the public in general; or (4) attacks upon the persons of individuals, or upon rights annexed to their persons; or (5) attacks upon the property of individuals or rights connected with, and similar to, rights of property.

The laws which relate to these subjects may again be classified under three heads; they are—

First, general doctrines pervading the whole subject. These doctrines might be called collectively the conditions of criminality. They consist partly of positive conditions, some of which enter more or less into the definition of nearly all offences, the most important being malice, fraud, negligence, knowledge, intention, will. There are also negative conditions or exceptions tacitly assumed in all definitions of crimes, which may be described collectively as matter of excuse.

Secondly, the definition of crimes and the apportionment to them of punishments.

Thirdly, the procedure by which in particular cases criminals are punished according to those definitions.

All the laws which would commonly be described as forming part of the criminal law of this country might be classified under one or other of these heads.

The description of criminal law which I have substituted for a definition in the stricter sense of the word is intended to exclude two large and important classes of laws which might perhaps be included not only with theoretical propriety, but in accordance with popular language, under the phrase "criminal law." These are, first, laws which constitute summary or police offences, and secondly, laws which impose upon certain offenders money penalties, which may be recovered by civil actions, brought in some cases by the person offended, in others by common informers. Summary offences have of late years multiplied to such an extent that the law relating to them may be regarded as forming a special head of the law of England. Such offences differ in many important particulars from those gross outrages against the public and against individuals which we commonly associate with the word crime. It would be an abuse of language to apply such a name to the conduct of a person who does not sweep the snow from before his doors, or in whose chimney a fire occurs. On the other hand, many common offences against person and property have of late years been rendered liable to punishment by courts of summary jurisdiction, and such cases and the courts by which they are tried fall within the scope of the subject of this book, and are dealt with in their place.

Penal actions by which private persons may in particular cases protect rights of a peculiar kind are still further removed from the associations which commonly connect themselves with a criminal prosecution.[1] If a lecture is published without the lecturer's leave, he has power, after taking certain precautions, to seize all published copies, and to recover a penalty in respect of each of them; but a proceeding to enforce such a right is a civil action, and differs in many ways from a criminal proceeding, though it has the practical effect of imposing a heavy fine on the person in default. I have not, however, left entirely unnoticed either the law relating to offences dealt with in a summary way or the law relating to penal actions.

I have intentionally substituted this short description of the contents of an actually existing body of law for any definition attempting to sum up the characteristics of criminal law in a more abstract way, because the only abstractions which in any degree correspond with existing facts in reference to law are too wide in their sweep to furnish materials for such a definition.

Austin's definition of a law leaves room for no other definition of a crime than an act or omission which the law punishes, and the reasons already given show that for practical purposes this definition is inconveniently wide. I do not think that this result in any way discredits Austin's definition of a law, which is nothing more than the

[1] 5 & 6 Will. 4, c. 65.

recognition and record of the fact that there are in all human societies rules of conduct, differing from other rules of conduct in the circumstance that obedience to them is in some cases, and may be in all cases, enforced by the collective strength of the society in which they exist. To confine the word "law" to such rules, and to apply it to them irrespectively of their goodness or badness and of their origin is, I think, the first condition of clearness in all speculations on the subject. The only alternative is to attempt to embody goodness or wisdom in the definition of law, one effect of which must be to introduce into all legal questions the uncertainty which belongs to all discussions upon morality. In the common use of language, however, the word "crime" and "criminal" no doubt connote moral guilt of a more serious character than that which is involved in a bare infringement of law as defined by Austin. The effect of this difference between the popular meaning of the words "crime" and "criminal," and that broader signification which it would be natural to attach to it in connection with Austin's definition of law, is given by restricting the meaning of the expression "criminal law" in the manner already stated.

Much discussion has taken place on subjects connected, or supposed to be connected, with criminal law, which I leave on one side, because it seems to me at once idle and interminable. The subject in question is usually called the [1] Right to Punish. On what ground, it is asked, and under what limitations, has Society a right to punish individuals? These questions appear to me to be almost entirely unmeaning, and quite unimportant. Societies are stronger than their individual members, and do as a fact systematically hurt them in various ways for various acts and omissions. The practice is useful under certain conditions, and injurious under other conditions. What these conditions are is a question for legislators. If, all matters being duly considered, the legislature consider it expedient to punish a given action in a given way, I think they would be guilty of weakness if they did not punish that action in

---

[1] Rossi's *Traité du Droit Criminel* is occupied principally by discussions on this subject.

that way although they had no right to do so. If they considered it inexpedient that the act should be punished, they would be cruel if they punished it, however good a right they might have to do so. On this account the whole of the discussion as to the right to punish appears to me superfluous. I think indeed that from the nature of the case any conclusion as to any right alleged to exist antecedently to and independently of some law from which it is derived must be arbitrary and fanciful.

Taking this view of the elements of which the criminal law is composed, the next question is in what manner its history should be related.

In writing the history of a body of law, a difficulty presents itself which is inherent in the nature of the subject, and which reduces the writer to a choice between two modes of procedure, neither of which can be regarded as altogether satisfactory.

The law of England as a whole, or even the criminal law as a whole, can scarcely be said to have a history. There is no such series of continuous connected changes in the whole system as the use of the word "history" implies. Each particular part of the law, however, has been the subject of such changes. The law as to perjury and the definition of the crime of murder have each a history of their own, but the criminal law regarded as a whole is like a building, the parts of which have been erected at different times, in different styles and for different purposes. Each part has a history which begins at its foundation and ends when it reaches its present shape, but the whole has no history for it has no unity. How then is the history of the whole to be related ? If an account of each successive change affecting any part is given in the order of time, the result is that it is impossible to follow the history of any one part, and the so called history becomes a mass of unconnected fragments. If, on the other hand, the history of each part is told uninterruptedly, there is a danger of frequent repetitions. After much consideration of the subject the second course has appeared to me on the whole to be the least objectionable of the two.

I have accordingly dealt with the subject in the following order :—First, I have given some account of the Criminal Law of Rome, which has in many ways exercised an influence on our own law. I have then described both the substantive law and the criminal procedure of the English before the Conquest. Passing to the history of the existing English Criminal Law I have given, first the history of the Courts. Under this head I have traced, first the history of the ordinary criminal courts, namely, the Queen's Bench Division of the High Court, the Assize Courts, the Courts of Quarter Sessions, the Courts of the Franchises, and the Welsh Courts. I have next given the history of the extraordinary criminal courts, namely, Parliament and the Court of the Lord High Steward. Lastly, I have given the history of the criminal jurisdiction of the Privy Council.

From the Courts I pass to the procedure followed in them, describing in successive chapters, first, the history of the procedure for the apprehension, examination, and committal or bail of a suspected person ; secondly, the history of the various forms of accusation and trial, especially that of trial by jury and its incidents ; thirdly, I have given the history of the development of trial by jury from the reign of Mary to that of George III., when the present system may be said to have been established ; fourthly, I have given an account of our existing method of trial ; fifthly, I have given the history of legal punishments ; sixthly, I have given an account of the way in which prosecutions are managed and paid for. In conclusion, I have made some general observations on our system of criminal procedure viewed as a whole, and in particular I have given some account of the part of the Draft Code of 1879 which relates to procedure, and of the changes proposed by it in the existing law. I have also made a comparison between our own system and that of the *Code d'Instruction Criminelle* which prevails in France.

The second volume begins with a subject which has been little considered, and which is intermediate between criminal procedure and the substantive criminal law, namely, the limits of the criminal law in respect of time, place, and person.

I next proceed to treat of the substantive criminal law,

including, first, the theory of criminal responsibility, and the exceptions to the general rule that men are responsible for their actions; secondly, the leading points in the general history of the law of crimes, considered as a whole; thirdly, the history of the principal classes of offences into which the criminal law may be divided.

These topics comprise all that need be said on the criminal law of England taken by itself, but the law of England resembles that of Rome in many ways, and perhaps in nothing so much as in the fact that it prevails in a great number of countries other than that of its origin, and this is perhaps more strikingly true of the criminal law than of any of its other departments. I have accordingly added to my account of the criminal law of England an account of the system adapted from it established in India, and some notices of other systems founded upon it.

The work concludes with detailed accounts of several trials, chosen as fair specimens of the practical results of English and French procedure.

As to the order in which some of these matters are discussed, I may observe that in a systematic exposition of an existing body of law it is natural to state first the substantive law, and then the law as to procedure by which it is applied to particular cases; but in treating the subject historically it seems more proper to begin with an account of Courts and other Officers of Justice, as the substantive law is to a great extent, perhaps mainly, developed by their decisions and by their tacit adoption of rules and principles before they are reduced to an express written form.

CHAPTER II.

ROMAN CRIMINAL LAW.

THE oldest part of the Roman Criminal Law was contained CHAP. II. in the twelve tables. The twelve tables have been reconstructed by various authors, of course more or less conjecturally, from the remaining fragments of them. The following is M. Ortolan's [1] reproduction of what he numbers as the eighth table "*de delictis*":—

1. Libels and insulting songs to be punished by death.

2. Breaking a limb, unless settled for, to be punished by retaliation.

3. Breaking the tooth or bone of a free man, 300 asses; of a slave, 15 asses.

4. For insulting another, 25 asses.

5. For [2] damage to property caused unjustly . . . . If it is accidental, it must be repaired.

6. For damage caused by a quadruped, repair the damage or give up the animal.

7. An action lies against a man for pasturing his flock in the field of another.

8. [3] Whoever injures crops by enchantments or conjures them from one field into another . . . . (punishment unknown).

9. Whoever by night furtively cuts or causes to be grazed crops raised by ploughing, shall be devoted to Ceres and

---

[1] Ortolan, *Explication Historique des Instituts*, i. 114–118. The references to Pothier are to Pothier's *Pandectæ Justinianeæ*. 4 vols. Paris, 1818. This work contains all the texts of the Roman Law, arranged by Pothier in what he regards as their natural order. It is extremely useful.
[2] The fragment here is "Rupitias . . . Sarcito."   [3] Pothier, i. cxx.

CHAP. II. [1]put to death if he is an adult, or if he is under the age of puberty shall be flogged at the discretion of the prætor and made to pay double value as damages.

10. Whoever burns a house or a stack of corn near a house knowingly and maliciously (*dolo*) shall be bound, beaten, and burnt. If by accident, he must pay damages. If he is too poor he must be [2]slightly flogged.

11. A man who wrongfully cuts another's trees must pay twenty-five asses for each tree.

12. If a man is killed whilst committing theft by night he is lawfully killed.

13. If a thief is taken by day he may not be killed unless he resists with a weapon.

14. A thief taken in the fact (*fur manifestus*) must be beaten with rods, and adjudged (as a slave) to the person robbed. If he is a slave he must be beaten with rods and thrown from the Tarpeian rock. Youths are only to be beaten with rods at the discretion of the magistrate, and condemned to repair the damage.

15. A thief [3]discovered by plate and girdle is to be deemed to be taken in the fact.

A thief discovered in possession of the stolen property (not by plate and girdle), and a thief who hides the stolen property in the house of a third person must restore three times the value of the property.

16. When an action is brought for a theft not manifest, the thief must pay twice the value of the money stolen.

17. Stolen property cannot be acquired by usucaption.

18. [4]The interest of money is $8\frac{1}{3}$ per cent. per annum. A usurer who lends at a higher rate forfeits fourfold.

19. Breach of trust with a deposit is punished by double damages.

20. A guardian who appropriates the property of his ward forfeits double the amount.

---

[1] Pothier (i. cxxi.) says by hanging.   [2] *Levius castigator.*

[3] "*Lance licioque conceptum*"—a solemn search made with certain symbolical solemnities.

[4] "Si quis unciario fœnore amplius fœnerassit quadruplione luito." Unciarium fœnus is 1 per cent. per annum according to Pothier, $8\frac{1}{3}$ according to Ortolan. See also an account of the controversy as to the meaning of the phrase in the *Dictionary of Antiquities*, art. "Fœnus."

21. A patron who cheats his client is devoted to the gods [1](and may be killed by any one).

22. A person who, having been a [2]witness in any business or contract, afterwards refuses to give his evidence, becomes infamous and incapable of making a will.

23. Whoever gives false evidence must be thrown from the Tarpeian rock.

24. Whoever knowingly and maliciously kills a free man must be put to death. [3]Let him who uses wicked enchantments, or makes or gives poisons, be deemed a parricide.

25. [4]If a man kills his parent, veil his head, sew him up in a sack, and throw him into the river.

26. No one is to make disturbances at night in the city under pain of death.

The excessive curtness of these provisions implies the existence of an all but unlimited discretion in those who had to administer the law. We know, indeed, from other sources, that in ancient Rome the courts and magistrates practically made their own laws to a great extent.

The laws of the Twelve Tables were of less importance in the history of the development of Roman law than the institutions by which they were carried into execution.

Criminal jurisdiction was originally in the hands of the Comitia Centuriata, or Tributa, and in some cases in those of the Senate. [5]The Comitia Centuriata could sentence to death; the Comitia Tributa to exile. The Senate had an ill-defined jurisdiction which did not usually extend to capital cases. In cases of importance the Comitia and the Senate exercised their powers directly; but in other matters they delegated their powers to quæstors (inquirers, commissioners), who were appointed at first for particular cases, and afterwards for particular classes of cases. [6]In very early times there are traces of standing quæstores parricidii. In later, though still in early times, [7]we hear of a quæstio de conjurationibus, a quæstio de veneficiis, a quæstio de homicidiis established to deal with particular offences which happened to be common at a particular period. This led in time to the

[1] Pothier, i. cxxvii.   [2] Libripens.   [3] Pothier, i. cxxix.
[4] Ib. cxxxi.   [5] Ortolan, i. 216.   [6] Ib. 182-3.   [7] Ib. 217.

CHAP. II. establishment of standing commissions (quæstiones perpetuæ), for the purpose of dealing with particular classes of offences. Each of them was established by a special law, and consisted of a prætor chosen annually, assisted by a sort of jury, consisting sometimes of as many as 100 judices, who were summoned for each particular case.

These courts, the Roman legislative assemblies, and afterwards the emperors, produced, in the course of centuries, a body of law, the comments upon or fragments of which fill the 47th and 48th books of the *Digest*, and the 9th book of the *Theodosian Code*. From these authorities we can acquire a knowledge of the Roman law relating to the definition of crimes and also of the procedure for their punishment.

The Roman lawyers in the days of Justinian divided crimes into three classes, according to the manner in which they were prosecuted, namely, Publica Judicia, Extraordinaria Crimina, and Privata Delicta. These I shall notice in their order.

I. PUBLICA JUDICIA.

The Publica Judicia were the representatives of the old "quæstiones perpetuæ." They related to crimes which were specifically forbidden by particular laws under defined penalties, capital (death or exile) or not.

Extraordinaria Crimina were offences for which no special quæstio, and no specific punishment, were provided. The punishment was (within limits) at the discretion of the judge, and the injured party might prosecute, though he was considered in doing so to protect rather the public interest than his own.

Privata Delicta were offences for which a special action was set apart involving a definite result for the injured party, such, *e.g.*, as the actio furti or actio injuriarum.

The classification is a little like a classification of English crimes, as being either (1) Treason or felony; (2) Misdemeanours at common law; or (3) Torts; and there is something of a resemblance between the way in which, in the course of ages, the Publica Judicia and the Extraordinaria Crimina came to be formed into a single class of offences, as to all of

which the punishment was more or less discretionary, and the
gradual legislative removal in our own country of nearly every
substantial distinction between felony and misdemeanour.
The crimes included under the head of Publica Judicia
were those which were forbidden by the following laws :—
[1] Lex Julia Majestatis, [2] Lex Julia de Adulteriis, [3] Lex Julia
de Vi Publica et [4] Privata, [5] Lex Cornelia de Sicariis et Veneficiis, [6] Lex Pompeia de Parricidis, [7] Lex Cornelia de Falsis,
[8] Lex Julia Repetundarum, [9] Lex Julia de Annona, [10] Lex
Julia Peculatus et de Sacrilegiis et de Residuis, [11] Lex Julia
Ambitus, [12] Lex Fabia de Plagiariis.

The text of these laws has not in any instance been preserved, though the style of the comments made upon them
by the different jurists quoted in the *Digest* looks as if they
had given in several instances the very words of the law.
In the main, however, the *Digest* consists of observations,
and of notes of decisions upon them ; and in other clas-
sical authors there are passages which enable us to form
some sort of estimate, or at least reasonable conjecture, as
to the position which they held in the history of Roman
law. They seem to have been not altogether unlike our
modern Consolidation Acts, and their very words seem to
have been as carefully noted and insisted upon as the wording of our own acts of Parliament. I should think it very
doubtful whether they defined the fundamental terms which
occur in them, any more than the Consolidation Acts of
1861 define murder and theft.

[13] Thus, for instance, the Lex Julia Majestatis had been preceded by a provision in the Twelve Tables, the Lex Gabinia,
the Lex Apuleia, the Lex Varia, and the Lex Cornelia, just
as the Offences Against the Person Act was preceded by the
statute of Stabbing, the Coventry Act, the Waltham Black
Act, the Consolidation Act of George IV., and many others.

Roman Criminal Law does not appear to have been reduced to any very definite form by those who are treated as
authorities by the compilers of the *Digest*. The titles follow

[1] Dig. xlviii., Tit. 4.   [2] *Ib.* 5.   [3] *Ib.* 6.   [4] *Ib.* 7.
[5] *Ib.* 8.   [6] *Ib.* 9.   [7] *Ib.* 10.   [8] *Ib.* 11.
[9] *Ib.* 12.   [10] *Ib.* 13.   [11] *Ib.* 14.   [12] *Ib.* 15.
[13] Pothier, iv. 407—8.

CHAP. II. each other in no particular order, and the contents of the titles are arranged as far as can be judged at random. I notice the offences in the order in which they stand. THE LEX JULIA MAJESTATIS.—[1] "Majestas," says Cicero, " residet proprie in populo Romano. Hanc minuere dicitur, " qui de dignitate aut amplitudine aut potestate Populi " Romani, aut eorum quibus populus potestatem dederit " aliquid derogat." The offence of Majestas was divided into " perduellio" and "læsa majestas." Perduellio included offences closely resembling treason by levying war or assisting the Queen's enemies, and inciting to mutiny. It also included the offence of governors refusing to give up their provinces, or the command of their forces, and some other matters which with us would be dealt with under the Mutiny Act.

Læsa Majestas included every kind of act by which public authority was resisted, or usurped by a private person, or by which any sort of disrespect was shown to the Emperor. The interpretation put upon the law on this subject varied according to the temper of the different emperors. It reached at times a depth of servility of which it is difficult in our days to form an estimate. For instance, [2] " Non con- " trahit crimen majestatis qui statuas Cæsaris vetustate cor- " ruptas reficit," which implies that some one thought other- wise. On the other hand, they sometimes rose to a theatrical magnanimity. [3] " Si quis," wrote Theodosius, " modestiæ " nescius et pudoris ignarus, improbo petulantique maledicto " nomina nostra crediderit lacessenda ; ac temulentia turbu- " lentus, obtrectator temporum nostrorum fuerit ; eum pœnæ " nolumus subjugari neque durum aliquid nec asperum " volumus sustinere ; quoniam si id ex levitate processerit " contemnendum est, si ex insania miseratione dignissimum, " si ab injuria remittendum." The case that the emperor might deserve what was said of him does not suggest itself.

By the law of the Twelve Tables Majestas was punished by flogging to death. Under the republic it was punished by exile. Afterwards by death.

LEX JULIA DE ADULTERIIS.—The Lex Julia de Adulteriis

---

[1] Pothier, iv. 408.   [2] Dig. xlviii. 4, 5.   [3] Cod. ix. 7.

appears to have been directed against sexual crimes of every sort. It punished adultery (on the part of the wife but not on the part of the husband), fornication (stuprum) in certain cases, incest, polygamy, unnatural offences, and pimping. It is unnecessary to say much on this subject, but one or two points may be mentioned on account of a possible connection between them and part of our own law. A father had a right to kill both his married daughter and her accomplice if she was taken in adultery either in his house or in her husband's. The husband had no such right as to his wife in any case, and no such right as to her accomplice unless he was [1] an infamous person or a slave, taken not in his father-in-law's house, but in his own. If, however, the husband did kill the adulterer irregularly he was less severely punished than in other cases of homicide. [2] " Si legis auctoritate cessante, inconsulto dolore adulterum "interemit quamvis homicidium perpetratum sit, tamen, " quia et nox et dolor justus factum ejus relevant potest " in exilium dari." By one of the Novels (cxvii.) a man might kill as an adulterer any person whom he found in his wife's company either in that person's house or in the husband's house, or in an inn or "in suburbanis," after being thrice warned in writing and in the presence of three witnesses not to see her.

The father's right to kill (jus occidendi) was rather wider, but was narrowly limited. "Permittitur patri tam "adoptivo quum naturali, adulterum cum filia cujuscumque "dignitatis, domi suæ, vel generi sui deprehensum suâ "manu occidere." If the father was not himself emancipated he had not the right in question. It was to be exercised in respect of an offence committed in his own house or in that of his son-in-law only. [3] The offenders

[1] Pothier, iv. 427. "Infames et eos qui corpore quæstum faciunt." They are elsewhere enumerated pimps, showmen, dancers, and singers, persons convicted by a *publicum judicium*, the freedman of the husband, the wife, the father, mother, son, or daughter.

[2] Pothier, iv. 428.

[3] The text is very curious. "Quod ait lex INCONTINENTI FILIAM OCCIDAT ; " sic erit accipiendum, ne occiso hodie adultero reservet, et post dies filiam " occidat ; vel contra. Debet enim prope uno ictu et uno impetu utrumque " occidere æquali ira adversus utrumque sumpta. Quod si non affectavit sed " dum adulterum occidit profugit filia, et interpositis horis apprehensa est a " patre qui persequebatur Incontinenti videbitur occidisse." Dig. xlviii. 5 23, 4.

must be taken in the fact. It must be done at once. It was immaterial which was killed first, but if the adulterer only was killed and the daughter spared, the father was guilty of murder under the Lex Cornelia. If, however, the adulterer was killed and the adulteress having been wounded with intent to kill recovered, "verbis quidem legis non "liberatur" (pater) "sed Divus Marcus et Commodus rescrip-"serunt impunitatem ei concedi." [1] The reason for the greater latitude given to the father is thus stated : "Plerumque pietas "paterni nominis consilium pro liberis capit. Cæterum mariti "calor et impetus facile decernentis fuit refrænandus." This is a reason against killing at all. It hardly seems probable that any legislator should have devised such a law entirely on its merits, and it probably requires some historical explanation. Perhaps it is a relic of the ancient law which regarded the wife as her husband's daughter, and which gave every father power of life and death over his children. This power would, while it was in force, give the husband the right to kill the adulterous wife, but he would do so in his paternal character, and thus in later times the right would be restricted to the natural father. I mention this law because of its analogy to our own law as to one species of provocation which reduces murder to manslaughter. [2] The punishment of adultery was "relegation" to an island, the woman losing half her dower and a third of her goods, and the man half his goods.

LEX JULIA DE VI PUBLICA ET PRIVATA.—The Lex Julia de Vi Publica consolidated several earlier laws which punished acts of violence not falling within the law against Majestas on the one hand or the law "De Sicariis et Veneficiis" on the other. There is no trace of any specific definition of these vague expressions having been contained in the law, and it does not appear whether there was only one law on the subject divided into two heads, or two distinct laws ; but the different texts illustrating "Vis Publica" suggest some such definition as—Illegal violence not otherwise punishable, in which the public are interested either by reason of the character of the offender or by reason of the

---

[1] Dig. xlviii. 5, 22, 4.　　　　　[2] Pothier, iv. 425.

character of the person injured, or by reason of the purpose CHAP. II. for which it is employed.

The following were cases of the offence :—

A public officer inflicting death or any other corporal punishment on a Roman citizen pending an appeal.

Assaults upon or insults to ambassadors.

Levying new taxes without authority.

The acts which, under our mediæval law would have been described as maintenance or would have fallen under the statutes against badges and liveries were " Vis Publica." Thus, [1]"qui dolo malo fecerit quominus judicia tuto exer- " ceantur, aut judices ut oportet judicent." [2]"Qui turbæ " seditionisve faciendæ consilium inierint, servosve aut liberos " homines in armis habuerit," and the extent of the rule is proved by the exceptions made to it. " Exceptus est qui propter " venationem habent homines qui cum bestiis pugnent minis- " tros enim ad ea habere conceditur." Vis Publica also included what we should call forcible entry by armed men. [3]" Qui homi- " nibus armatis possessorem domo agrove suo aut navi sua de- " jecerit, expugnaverit concursu." It also included many kinds of riots. [4] " Qui cœtu . . . incendium fecerit . . . quive fecerit " quominus sepeliatur"—[5]"qui convocatis hominibus vim " fecerit quo quis verberetur et pulsetur neque homo occisus."

Rape was punished as Vis Publica, and not under the Lex Julia de Adulteriis.

Vis Privata was a milder form of Vis Publica, indeed it is doubtful whether one at least of the texts quoted above does not refer to it. The characteristic feature of Vis Privata seems to have been taking the law into one's own hands. Marcus Antoninus in an imperial rescript says :—[6] " Tu vim putas " esse solum si homines vulnerentur ? vis est et tunc quoties " quis id quod deberi sibi putat, non per judicem reposcit."

The punishment of Vis Publica was exile, and in some cases death ; the punishment of Vis Privata confiscation of the third of the offender's property and loss of certain civil rights.

THE LEX CORNELIA DE SICARIIS ET VENEFICIIS.—The Lex Cornelia de Sicariis et Veneficiis was passed by Sylla

---

[1] Dig. xlviii. 6, 10.   [2] Pothier, iv. 436.   [3] Dig. xlviii. 6,
[4] Ib. 6, 5.   [5] Ib. 6, 10.   [6] Ib. 7, 7.

and had thus been in force about 600 years when the *Digest* was compiled. It was extended to incendiaries, and also in the time of Diocletian to astrologers and similar impostors. The main subject of this law is homicide. The great extension given to it by commentators, and the want of any sort of systematic arrangement of the texts of the *Digest*, as well as the title of the law which might be literally translated, [1] "Stabbers and poisoners," make it probable that the original law itself was very curt and general. It seems never to have been elaborated with any system, but the principal points which long afterwards presented themselves to English lawyers presented themselves to the various jurists and emperors, and received at their hands solutions which, however fragmentary and hesitating, have a resemblance to those of the English courts.

As to the persons to whom the law extended, it seems to have applied in the time of the Antonines to slaves as well as freemen. [2] "Qui hominem occiderit punitur, non habitâ " differentia cujus conditionis hominem interemit." The moment at which a child became a human being for this purpose seems to have been a moot point.

The curious points which English lawyers have considered with so much care as to the nature of the connection necessary to constitute homicide between the act causing death and the death caused by it do not seem to have occurred to the Roman lawyers, but there are various passages in the *Digest* which state the principal cases in which the intentional infliction of death was considered justifiable. They are all reducible to the cases of self-defence and the arrest or punishment of criminals.

The Roman doctrine as to the degrees of homicide is shortly summed up in a rescript of Hadrian's. The rule was that the degree of guilt depended on the offender's intention as displayed by the circumstances of his offence. [3] "Eum " qui hominem occidit, si non occidendi animo hoc admisit " absolvi posse. Et qui hominem non occidit sed vulneravit

---

[1] " Sicarii proprie sunt latrones cultellis utentes recurvis ad similitudinem " eorum quos Romani *sicas* dixere qui ita breves erant ut occultari sinu vestis " possent."—Pothier, iv. 489.
[2] Dig. xlviii. 8, 1, 2.   [3] *Ib.* 8, 1, 3.

" ut occidat pro homicida damnandum. Et ex re constitu-
" endum hoc. Nam si gladium strixerit et in eo percusserit
" indubitate occidendi animo id eum admississe, sed si clavi
" percussit aut cuccuma " (an iron-bound stick) " in rixa,
" quamvis ferro percusserit tamen non occidendi animo
" leniendam pœnam ejus qui in rixa casu magis quam
" voluntate homicidium admisit."

Killing by negligence was not within the Lex Cornelia,
though it might subject the offender to an " extraordinarium
" judicium." The only form of provocation which seems to
have been recognised as affording grounds for diminishing
the punishment was the case of adultery already referred to.
[1] Special provision was made for the offence of poisoning, as
to which the law was extremely severe, applying to every
one " qui venenum necandi hominis causa fecerit, vel ven-
" diderit." Poisoning is naturally an object of excessive
dread in an age in which physical science is at a low ebb, and
when belief in witchcraft and other " maleficia " prevails.
The famous case of the cook who was boiled to death by
Act of Parliament in Henry VIII.'s time, and Sir E. Coke's
account of the " Great Oyer of Poisoning," are parallel
instances. [2] In the French Code Penal poisoning is distinguished as a special offence.

LEX POMPEIA DE PARRICIDIIS.—Parricide was killing any
relation nearer than or in the degree of a first cousin.

Parricide as well as poisoning must have fallen under the
Lex Cornelia de Sicariis, but the distinction is not without
an analogy in English law. It may be compared to petty
treason, which ceased to be distinguished from murder only
in 1828, by the operation of 9 Geo. 4, c. 31, s. 52.

Homicide under the Republic was punished by confiscation of goods and imprisonment in an island; under the
Antonines by death, [3] " Nisi honestiori loco positi fuerint ut
" pœnam legis sustineant." Common people were thrown
to the beasts. There was no special punishment for poisoners, or apparently for parricides, unless the person killed

---

[1] Dig. xlviii. 8, 3.
[2] Art. 301. " Est qualifié empoisonnement tout attentat à la vie d'une personne
" par l'effet de substances qui peuvent donner la mort plus ou moins prompte-
" ment, de quelque manière que ces substances aient été employées ou adminis-
" trées, et quelles qu'en aient été les suites." [3] Dig. xlviii. 8, 3, 5.

CHAP. II. was a father or mother, in which case the offender was burnt,
that punishment having been substituted for the ancient one
of drowning with a cock, snake, and dog. Burning was also
the punishment of incendiaries.

LEX CORNELIA DE FALSIS.—The Lex Cornelia De Falsis
was divided into two heads, namely, the *lex testamentaria*,
the main subject of which was forging and suppressing
wills, and *nummaria*, the main subject of which was counterfeiting money. [1] Paulus's statement of the effect of the
law, seems as if he had preserved its very words, "Qui
" testamentum amoverit, celaverit, eripuerit, deleverit, inter-
" leverit, subjecerit, resignaverit, quive testamentum falsum
" scripserit, signaverit, recitaverit dolo malo, cujusve dolo
" malo id factum erit." This branch of the law was afterwards extended to other offences. A provision was made
either by the Emperor Claudius, or by a decree of the
senate in the time of Tiberius, subjecting to the penalties
of the Lex Cornelia, every one who when drawing up the
will or codicil of another inserted in his own hand a
legacy to himself, or (as the law was interpreted) to any
person under his power. [2] Passages in the code seem to imply
that this was meant as a precaution against fraud, and that
even the testator's order was no excuse. "Senatus consulto
" et edicto Divi Claudii prohibitum est eos qui ad scribenda
" testamenta adhibentur *quamvis dictante testatore* aliquod emo-
" lumentum ipsis futurum scribere. Et pœna legis Corneliæ
" facienti irrogata est, cujus veniam deprecantibus ob ignoran-
" tiam et profitentibus a relicto discedere, amplissimus ordo
" vel divi principes veniam raro dederunt." The same inference
seems to follow from texts which show the effect of a special
and general ratification by the testator in particular cases.

The Lex Cornelia Testamentaria came in process of time
to be extended to every sort of instrument other than
wills. [3] Ulpian says generally, "Pœna legis Corneliæ

---

[1] Dig. xlviii. 10, 2. Compare the language of 24 & 25 Vic. c. 98, s. 2 :
"Whoever, with intent to defraud" (*dolo malo*), "shall forge, or alter"
(*interleverit*), "or shall offer, utter, dispose of, or put off" (? *recitaverit*),
"knowing the same to be forged or altered, any will, testament, codicil,
" or testamentary instrument." The 24 & 25 Vic. c. 96, s. 29 makes it penal
to "cancel" (*deleverit*), "obliterate, or conceal" (*celaverit*) "any will," &c.
[2] Cod. ix. 23, 3, and compare laws 4 6.   [3] Dig. xlviii. 10, 9, 3.

"irrogatur ei qui quid aliud quam in testamento sciens
"dolo malo falsum signaverit signarive curaverit." And
Paulus and Marcian say the same as to all who falsify
accounts, registers, contracts, or other writings, sealed
or not. A man might indeed commit the "crimen falsi" in a [1]genuine
document if he dated it falsely, or otherwise made it appear
to be what it was not. The law was also extended to giving
and suborning false evidence, and to the corruption of judges.
Modestinus extends it still further. He says: [2]" De impudentia
" ejus qui diversa duobus testimonia præbuit cujus ita anceps
" fides vacillat quod crimine falsi teneatur nec dubitandum
" est."

The law indeed applied to certain fraudulent contracts, to
the fraudulent assumption of a false name, and as Paulus
says, by a constitution of Adrian to one "who sells the
" same thing to two different people."

The punishment of "falsum" under the Antonines was,
in the case of a person of low rank, imprisonment in the
mines, in the case of a person of higher rank, forfeiture of
goods, and relegation to an island.

The Lex Cornelia Nummaria, like the Lex Testamentaria,
is referred to in terms which resemble those of the parallel
English enactments. [3]" Qui nummos aureos argenteos
" adulteraverit, laverit, conflaverit, raserit, corruperit vitia-
" verit." I do not find express mention in the *Corpus Juris*
of the offence of passing bad money, but a characteristic
provision occurs as to the refusal of good money. It was put
on the same footing as coining on account of the disrespect
shown to the image and superscription of the prince. The
text quoted above concludes, " vultuve signatam monetam
" præter adulterinam reprobaverit." Constantine said :
[4]" Omnes solidi in quibus nostri vultus ac veneratio una
" est, uno pretio estimanda sunt. . . Nec enim qui

---

[1] This is also the law of England—see R. *v.* Ritson, L.R. 1 C.C.R. 200.
[2] Dig. xlviii. 10, 27, 1.
[3] Pothier, iv. 455. Cf. 24 & 25 Vic. c. 99, s. 4 : "Impair, diminish, or lighten
" any of the Queen's gold or silver coin ;" and s. 3 : "Wash, case over, or
" colour any piece of gold or silver."
[4] Pothier, iv. 456.

" majore habitu faciei extenditur majoris est pretii ; aut qui
" angustiore expressione concluditur minoris haberi credendus
" est quum pondus idem existat."

The use of false measures, the assumption of marks of
dignity, and changing children, were regarded as species of
" the crimen falsi," or as analogous to it.

LEX JULIA REPETUNDARUM.—[1] The Lex Julia Repetundarum punished every sort of official extortion, being a sort
of Consolidation Act replacing five earlier enactments.
The law provided that no one was to receive anything
whatever, either for giving or for withholding any judicial
or official order. "Tenetur qui, quum aliquam potesta-
" tem haberet, pecuniam ob judicandum discernendumve
" acceperit."

The Lex Julia is also supposed to have contained provisions not altogether unlike those of certain Acts of Parliament relating to British officers in India. By the rules of
the Indian Civil Service a civilian may not hold land in his
own district, and by Act of Parliament it is unlawful for any
one whatever to make any present to him. By the Lex
Julia Repetundarum, [2] "Quod a præside sui procuratore vel
" quolibet alio in ea provincia in qua administrat, licet
" per suppositam personam comparatum est, infirmato con-
" tractu vindicatur, et æstimatio ejus fisco infertur. Nam
" et navem in eadem provincia in qua quis administrat
" ædificare prohibetur."

The offence of "repetundarum" became in the time of
the Antonines an "extraordinarium crimen," instead of a
" publicum judicium," except indeed in cases in which the
order corruptly given involved consequences of extreme
importance, as, for instance, when a judge was bribed to have
a man put to death. In such instances the punishment was
capital. In others it was fourfold damages.

LEX JULIA DE ANNONA.—[3] This was a law against what
was formerly called forestalling and regrating in English

---

[1] Dig. xlviii. 11, 3. Marcian. He gives elsewhere a much longer enumeration : "Ne quis ob judicem arbitrumve dandum mutandum juben-
" dumve ut judicet ; neve ob non dandum non mutandum non jubendum
" ut judicet," &c. ; and see Pothier, iv. 457-
[2] Pothier, iv. 458.   [3] Dig. xlviii. 12.

law—anticipating and so raising the price of food in the market.

LEX JULIA PECULATUS, ET DE SACRILEGIIS ET DE RESIDUIS. —These three offences were different forms of the offence of public dishonesty. [1] The law against "peculators" forbad "ne quis ex pecuniâ sacrâ, religiosâ, publicâve auferat, " neve intercipiat, neve in rem suam vertat, neve faciat quo " quis auferat, intercipiat, vel in rem suam vertat, nisi cui " utique lege licebit. Neve quis in aurum, argentum, æs " publicum quid indat, neve immisceat, neve quo quid indatur " immisceatur, faciat sciens dolo malo quo id pejus fiat." In other words it was theft of, or injury to, anything which was either consecrated to the gods, or was public property. The following illustrations are given of cases of peculation. Workmen in the mint coining too much money and carrying off the surplus; [2] carrying off title-deeds to state lands, and fraudulently altering them, and various frauds and irregularities as to the public accounts.

The punishment of peculation was the mines, or exile and forfeiture of property, according to the rank of the offender.

Sacrilege was the stealing of something at once public and sacred, but as appears from [3] a passage in Quintilian, the definition was not free from doubt. Sacrilege was punished with death, sometimes by burning, often by throwing to the beasts. Parts of the temples were peculiarly sacred. [4] "Qui sacrarium ingressus interdiu vel noctu sacrarium " aliquid inde aufert excæcator; qui vero extra sacrarium " e templo reliquo aufert verberatus et tonsus exilio mulc- " tator," says Ulpian, which seems inconsistent with what he had said before as to capital punishment.

[1] Dig. xlviii. 13, 1.
[2] " Qui tabulam æream legis formamve agrorum aut quid aliud continentem " refixerit vel quid inde inmutaverit."—Dig. xlviii. 13, 8.
[3] " Qui privatam pecuniam de templo surripuit sacrilegii reus est. Culpa " manifesta. Quæstio est an huic crimini nomen quod est in lege conveniat. " Ergo ambigitur an hoc sacrilegium sit. Accusator quia de templo sit surrepta " pecunia utitur hoc nomine. Reus quia privatam surripuerit negat esse sacrile- " gium sed furtum. Actor ergo ita finiet sacrilegium est surripuere aliquid de " sacro. Reus ita finiet sacrilegium est surripere aliquid sacri."—Quintilian, *Inst.* vii. 3.
[4] Pothier, iv. 462.

CHAP. II.   Theodosius and others assimilated heresy to sacrilege.
They put on the same footing, doubting the decisions of
the Emperor, and (very strangely) the attempt to get appointed governor of the province in which a man was
born.

The law "De Residuis" applied to those who, being accountable to the public, did not fully account for what they
had received.

LEX JULIA AMBITUS.—[1] The Lex Julia Ambitus seems
to have consolidated the provisions of ten previous laws. It
was passed by Augustus. It was probably a sort of Corrupt
Practices Act, but when popular election was replaced by
the appointment of officers by the Emperor, the law became
obsolete.

LEX FABIA DE PLAGIARIIS.—[2] Plagium was the crime of
manstealing—selling a free man as a slave. The punishment
was at first fine, but afterwards the mines or death.

II. EXTRAORDINARIA CRIMINA.

The second class into which crimes were divided were
"extraordinaria crimina," in translating which expression it
must be remembered that "crimen" means accusation and
not offence, and that "extraordinarium" refers to the nature
of the procedure, and not to the quality of the offence. The
expression indicates, in fact, a less formal mode of procedure
than had originally been appropriated to the Publica Judicia,
though, as I shall have occasion to explain more fully under
the head of Procedure, the distinction between the two
classes was of hardly any practical importance when the
Pandects were compiled. The "extraordinaria crimina"
noticed in the 47th book of the *Digest* are as follows:—

FAMILY OFFENCES.—[3] " Sollicitatores alienarum nupti-
" arum, itemque matrimoniorum interpellatores "—persons
who attempted to seduce or procure the divorce of a married
woman. Also those who corrupted youths of either sex.

---

[1] Dig. xlviii. 14 ; Pothier, iv. 463.   [2] *Ib.* 15.
[3] *Ib.* xlvii. 11, 1.   These come under the general head of " extraordinaria
crimina " in the *Digest.*

INTRODUCING NEW RELIGIONS.—[1] " Si quis aliquid fecerit
" quo leves hominum animi superstitione numinis terre-
" rentur." "Qui novas, et usui vel rationi incognitas
" religiones inducunt ex quibus animi hominum moveantur."
These and the laws against unlawful societies were the
laws by which the Christians were persecuted. This was
probably the law to which the Philippians appealed against
Paul and Silas. "These men being Jews do exceedingly
" trouble our city, and teach customs which are not lawful
" for us to observe nor to receive, being Romans " (Acts xvi.
20, 21).

ENGROSSING.—[2] To raise the price of corn was an "extraordinarium crimen." It does not appear where the line
was drawn between this offence and that which fell under
the Lex Julia de Annona.

ABORTION.—[3] A woman who procured her own miscarriage
was liable as for an "extraordinarium crimen," but not
under the Lex Julia against homicides. An unborn child
was not regarded as a human being.

VAGABONDS.—[4] An extraordinary prosecution lies against
vagabonds who carry about snakes and show them, if any
one is injured by the fear they cause. This is a little
like our law against rogues and vagabonds.

SPECIAL OFFENCES IN PARTICULAR PROVINCES.—[5] Of
offences of this kind two are mentioned in the *Digest*,
namely, in Arabia σκοπελίσμος, which consisted in laying
stones on an enemy's ground as a threat that if the owner
cultivated the land " malo leto periturus esset insidiis
" eorum qui scopulos posuissent "—a sort of primitive threatening letter, not unlike letters still occasionally delivered in
Ireland to prevent the occupancy of lands from which a
tenant has been ejected.

[6] In Egypt the breach of *chomata*, dykes of the Nile, was
a special offence.

Scopelismus was punished by death. The breach of banks
by the mines, at first, and afterwards by burning alive. It
is rather singular that these and no other local offences

---

[1] Pothier, iv. 375. [2] Dig. xlvii. 11, 6. [3] *Ib.* 11, 4.
[4] *Ib.* 11, 11. [5] *Ib.* 11, 9. [6] *Ib.* 11, 10.

CHAP. II. should be mentioned in the *Digest*. It would have been natural to expect that in so vast an empire many local laws must have been in force which would be deserving of notice. OFFENCES RELATING TO TOMBS.—The texts given in the 12th title of the 47th book of the *Digest* mix up inextricably the civil remedies relating to the violation of tombs, with provisions as to criminal prosecutions. [1] Tombs were violated by burying other bodies in them, by using them as habitations, and in various other ways, and the offender was in most cases liable to an action for a penalty sometimes of 100 and sometimes of 200 aurei. Those who plundered dead bodies were punished capitally, or by the mines, especially if they committed their crime in armed bands.

CONCUSSIO.—[2] Concussio is defined by Cujas, "terror in-"jectus pecuniæ alteriusve rei extorquendæ gratiâ." It answers in fact to our extortion by a public officer. A text from Macer shows that the offence bordered, so to speak, on the "publicum judicium" of the "crimen falsi."

[3] "Concussionis judicium publicum non est, sed si ideo "pecuniam quis accepit, quod crimen minatus sit, potest "judicium publicum esse ex senatus consultis quibus pœnâ "Legis Corneliæ" (*i.e.* Falsi) "teneri jubentur qui in accusa-"tionem innocentium coierint, quive ob accusandum vel non "accusandum, denuntiandum vel non denuntiandum testimo-"nium pecuniam acceperint." No reference is made to the Lex Julia Repetundarum, which is stated by Macer somewhat less widely than by Marcian who belongs to the same period. Macer's statement of the Lex Julia Repetundarum reads like a word for word quotation: [4] "Præcipit ne quis ob judicem "arbitrumve dandum mutandum jubendumve ut judicet, "neve ob non dandum non mutandum non jubendum ut "judicet; neve ob hominem in vincula publica conjiciendum "vinciendum vincirive jubendum, exve vinculis dimittendum; "neve quis ob hominem condemnandum absolvendumve; "neve ob litem æstimandam, judiciumve capitis pecuniæve "faciendum vel non faciendum aliquid acceperit."

---

[1] "Prætor ait . . si quis in sepulchro dolo malo habitaverit."—Dig. xlvii. 12, 3.
[2] Pothier, iv. 379. [3] Dig. xlvii. 13, 2. [4] *Ib.* xlviii. 11, 7.

Upon the whole it may be that "concussio" and "repetundarum" may be likened to common extortion and judicial corruption respectively.

ABIGEI.—Theft in general was treated as a tort, but some particular kinds of thieves were subject either to "publica "judicia," or to "extraordinaria crimina." Amongst the latter were "abigei" "drivers," or cattle thieves : [1] "qui "pecora ex pascuis, vel ex armentis subtrahunt et quo- "dammodo deprædantur; et abigendi studium quasi artem "exercent, equos de gregibus vel boves de armentis abdu- "centes. Cæterum si quis bovem aberrantem, vel equos in "solitudine relictos abduxerit, non est abigeus sed fur potius." The stealing of a single horse or ox might make a man an abigeus, but it seems that [2] the crime could not be committed on less than four pigs or ten sheep. They need not however be all taken together. In such a state of the law one would expect thefts of three pigs or eight sheep to become abnormally common. By a law of Hadrian this offence was punished by the mines, or if the thieves were armed, capitally.

PREVARICATION.—[3] Prevarication was a crime connected with the administration of justice.

"Prevaricator," says Ulpian, "est quasi varicator" (a man with bandy legs) "qui diversam partem adjuvat proditâ "causâ suâ." The name was strictly applied to accusers who favoured the accused in a "publicum judicium." An advocate who betrayed his client was more properly called "proditor," a traitor. The prevaricator was punished as a false accuser.

RECEIVERS.—The receivers of robbers were punished like robbers. [4] "Pessimum genus est receptatorum sine quibus "nemo latere diu potest. Et præcipitur ut perinde puniantur "atque latrones. In pari causa habendi sunt qui quum appre- "hendere latrones possent pecunia accepta vel subreptorum "parte demiserunt." Indulgence, though not complete impunity, was extended to those who were connected with the robber. "Eos tamen apud quos adfinis vel cognatus latro

---

[1] Dig. xlvii. 14, 1, 1.   [2] *Ib.* 14, 3.   [3] *Ib.* 15, 1.
[4] Paulus. *Ib.* 16, 1.

CHAP. II. "conservatus est, neque absolvendos neque severe admodum "puniendos."

AGGRAVATED THEFT.—[1] Thieves who stole under certain aggravated circumstances were subject to "extraordinaria "crimina." The aggravations were as follows :—

(a) Balnearii, those who stole the clothes of bathers in the public baths.

(b) Those who stole by night (there is no definition of night) or who defended themselves by arms.

(c) Housebreakers (effractores).

(d) "Expilatores qui sunt atrociores fures." It is not certain what was their special characteristic. Some say (fantastically), "expilatores dici quod ne pilum quidem "relinquunt in corpore spoliatorum." Others described them as, "eos qui noctu viatoribus pallia et vestes diripiunt."

(e) Saccularii, thieves who stole by tricks such as pretended magic.

(f) Directarii. "Hi qui in aliena cœnacula se dirigunt "furandi animo."

All these were punished at the discretion of the judge, the severest punishment being flogging and the mines.

CRIMEN EXPILATÆ HÆREDITATIS. — [2] A stranger who plundered the property of a deceased person was liable to be proceeded against as upon an "extraordinarium crimen."

STELLIONATUS.—Stellionatus is defined by [3] Pothier as "omnis atrox dolus qui proprio nomine caret." It is strangely said to be derived from "Stellio," a spotted lizard, of which Pliny strangely observes, "Quo nullum animal fraudulentius "invidere homini tradunt." The difficulty of giving an adequate definition of fraud has been felt at all times. One mode of avoiding the difficulty is the invention of a conveniently vague term of abuse like "stellionatus" or "dolus." Another is the plan of annexing the character of a crime to the combination of two things neither of which is criminal, as in our own conspiracy to defraud. The difficulty exists in the very nature of human conduct. The following are instances of "Stellionatus":—[4] "Si quis merces supposuerit,

---

[1] Dig. xlvii. 17 and 18.   [2] Ib. 19.
[3] iv. 384.   [4] Dig. xlvii. 20, 3, 1.

"vel obligatas averterit, vel si corruperit"—delivering goods
different from those sold, or removing goods pledged, or in-
juring them. By our own law, two persons who conspired
together for such a purpose would be guilty of an indictable
conspiracy, but if one person did it alone he would commit
at most an actionable fraud.

DE TERMINO MOTO.—[1]Moving or defacing landmarks was
a criminal offence, partly on account of the great importance
attached to them by the agrarian laws.

UNLAWFUL ASSOCIATIONS. — [2]No associations whatever
(with some slight exceptions) were allowed to exist unless
they were specially authorised either by the Emperor or by
the Senate. Those who formed such associations were
punished in the same way as persons "adjudged to have
"occupied in arms public places or temples." Meetings for
religious purposes were permitted in the case of religions
which were authorised by the State, but in no other cases.
This was one of the principal laws under which Christianity
was prohibited.

III. PRIVATA DELICTA.

Many of the commonest and, in practice, most important
of the offences against person and property which fall within
what I have described as the Criminal Law were treated by
the Roman lawyers as mere private wrongs, "privata delicta,"
though as time went on they seem to have come to be regarded as crimes. Two passages of Ulpian set this in a clear
light. [3]He says in his 2nd book (*De Officio Proconsulis*) :
"Si quis actionem quæ ex maleficiis oritur velit exsequi
"si quidem pecuniariter agere velit ad jus ordinarium re-
"mittendus erit: nec cogendus erit in crimen subscribere.
"Enimvero si extra ordinem ejus rei pœnam exerceri velit,
"tunc subscribere eum in crimen oportebit." [4]In another
passage (in his 38th book on the Edict) Ulpian says that in
his time thefts were generally prosecuted as crimes : "Memi-
"nisse oportebit nunc furti plerumque criminaliter agi, et
"eum qui agit in crimen subscribere : non quasi publicum

---

[1] Dig. xlvii. tit. 21.　　　　　[2] *Ib.* tit. 22, 1, 1.
[3] Dig. xlvii. 1, 3.　　　　　　[4] *Ib.* 2, 92.

CHAP. II. " sit judicium sed quia visum est temeritatem agentium etiam
          " extraordinaria animadversione coercendam.   Non ideo
          " tamen minus si qui velit poterit civiliter agere." One
obvious cause for this would be that thefts would usually
be committed by persons unable to pay damages.

The " privata delicta " mentioned in the *Digest* are as follows :—

FURTUM.—Theft is thus defined by Paulus :—[1] " Furtum
" est contrectatio rei fraudulosa, lucri faciendi gratia, vel
" ipsius rei, vel etiam usus ejus possessionisve, quod lege
" naturali prohibitum est admittere." The definition omits
the element which from other passages of the *Digest* it
obviously ought to have contained of " invito domino." The
manner in which the subject of theft is treated in the *Digest*
has considerable resemblance to the manner in which it is
dealt with in our own law, though there are also many differences between them.   Nearly every question which has presented itself to English judges and courts at different times
appears also to have presented itself to the Roman lawyers.
A comparison between them will not be without interest.

[2] By the Roman law the offence of theft could be committed
on anything which either was at the time or could be made
movable.   The Sabinians at one time held that land and
buildings fraudulently sold were stolen, but the Proculeians
were of the opposite opinion, and their view prevailed.   It
was always admitted that theft could be committed on
things forming part of or growing from the soil, such as trees,
stones, sand, and fruits.   The Roman lawyers knew nothing
apparently of the strange rules of the common law as to the
things which are not the subject of larceny.   Perhaps these
rules were made to evade the severity of the common law
punishment of theft.   The most objectionable of all the
common law rules (that by which things in action, as *e.g.*
notes and bills, were not capable of being stolen) [3] was diametrically opposed to the Roman law.   " Qui tabulas aut
" cautiones amovit, furti tenetur non tantum pretii ipsarum

---

[1] Dig. xlvii. 2, 1, 3.   In the same passage the word is derived from
" furvo, id est nigro . . . quod clam et obscuro fiat, et plerumque nocte."
Other fantastic derivations are given.
[2] Pothier, iv. 327.   [3] Dig. xlvii. 2, 27.

" tabularum, verum ejus quod interfuit, quod ad æstimationem
" refertur ejus summæ quæ in his tabulis continetur." This
resembles 24 & 25 Vic. c. 96, s. 27, by which a person who
steals a valuable security is punishable as if he had stolen
a chattel of the like value.

As to the nature of the crime itself the Roman law was in
one important particular far more severe than the common
law. Theft as defined by the common law includes an intent
to deprive the owner permanently of the stolen goods. The
Roman law applied also to an intent to steal its use or possession. Thus: [1] "Si pignore creditor utatur furti tenetur,"
[2] "fullo et sarcinator" (a tailor), "qui polienda vel sarcienda
" vestimenta accepit si forte his utatur, ex contrectatione
" eorum furtum fecisse videtur quia non in eam causam ab
" eo videntur accepta." [3] "Qui jumenta sibi commodata
" longuis duxerit alienâve re invito domino usus sit furtum
" facit." Perhaps, as the severity of the common law
led to the various subtleties by which its operation was so
much restricted, the principle that theft was in common cases
only a civil injury may have led the Roman lawyers to extend
the definition of it. The "contrectatio" of the Roman lawyers
was somewhat wider than the "taking" which enters into
the English definition of larceny. According to English law,
if the first taking is lawful no subsequent unlawful dealing
with the thing taken amounts to theft, special exceptions
excepted. This does not seem to have occurred to the Roman
lawyers, though they also regarded an actual touching of the
stolen goods as essential to theft ([4] "Hoc jure utimur ut furtum
" sine contrectatione non fiat," says Ulpian), but if there was
such a touching it was immaterial whether it took place before or after the offender got possession of the thing stolen.
[5] Thus, barely to deny the receipt of a thing intrusted to one
was not theft. To conceal it after receiving it with intent
to convert it to one's own use (intercipiendi causa) was theft.
So, [6] "Qui vendit rem alienam sciens, ita demum furtum
" committit si eam contrectaverit."

[1] Dig. xlvii. 2, 54.   [2] Ib. 2, 82.
[3] Ib. 2, 40, and see Pothier, iv. 329.   [4] Dig. xlvii. 2, 52, 19.
[5] Ib. 2, 12.   [6] This is Pothier's inference ; see iv. 321.

CHAP. II.   This view of the subject would avoid the distinction
between theft and some of the forms of fraudulent breach of
trust which went unpunished at common law. It would take
away one of the impediments by which English lawyers were
prevented from treating embezzlement as theft. This doctrine
also leads, by a shorter and plainer route, to the conclusion
at which the Court for Crown Cases Reserved lately arrived
in the case of [1] R. v. Middleton. It was decided in that
case that if *A* gives *B* a sovereign instead of a shilling, and
B knowingly accepts and keeps the sovereign, *B* is guilty
of theft. The case presented great difficulties, as may be
seen by the judgment, but by the Roman lawyers it was
very naturally decided: [2] "Si rem meam quasi tuam tibi
" tradidero scienti meam esse, magis est" (it is the better
opinion) "furtum te facere si lucrandi animo id feceris."
The difficulty with the Roman lawyers in such a case
was not as to the "contrectatio," but as to the "invito
domino."

It does not appear from the *Digest* that the Roman lawyers
found as much difficulty as our own in determining on the
precise moment at which theft is completed. Probably this
arises from the different view taken of theft in the two systems·
In a system which when it was formed regarded theft as a
capital crime, it was obviously necessary to distinguish with
perfect accuracy the moment at which the crime began. In
a system in which theft was regarded as a civil injury this
was immaterial, because no one would sue another for a mere
formal theft. Another application of the same principle is,
perhaps, to be found in the circumstance that one highly
technical branch of the Roman law on the subject is not
represented at all in English law. The *Digest* contains many
texts turning on the question how much of a given article
was stolen by a given act. [3] A man who cut off part of a
piece of plate (qui lancem rasit), was considered as having
stolen the whole plate. It was a moot point whether a man
who stole a bushel of corn from a heap or a cargo, stole the
whole heap or cargo or only the bushel. This is one of the

----

[1] L. R. 2 C. C. R. 38.   [2] Dig. xlvii. 2, 44, 1.
[3] Ib. 22, 2.

points which [1] Gibbon notices as illustrating the influence of
the Stoic philosophy on the Roman law. May not the question of the measure of damages have been connected with it? The result of an "actio furti" was double or quadruple damages according as the theft was "nec manifestum" or "manifestum." The amount due could obviously not be ascertained unless the value of the stolen goods was known, and that again must depend on the question as to how much was stolen. A passage of Ulpian on this subject deserves to be quoted as a good instance of that mode of argument by illustration and analogy which from the nature of the case must always be a favourite with lawyers. [2] "Si de navi
" oneratâ furto quis sextarium frumenti tulerit utrum totius
" oneris, an vero sextarii tantum furtum fecerit? Facilius
" hoc quæritur in horreo pleno. Et durum est dicere totius
" furtum fieri. Et quid si cisterna vini sit? Quid dicet?
" Aut aquæ cisterna? Quid deinde si [de] nave vinaria ut
" sunt multæ, in quas vinum effunditur? Quid dicemus
" de eo qui vinum hausit, an totius oneris fur sit? Et
" magis est et ut hic non totius dicamus."

The definition of theft according to Roman as well as according to English law included a mental element. By English law the taking in order to be felonious must be with intent to deprive another of his property permanently, wrongfully, and without claim of right. By Roman law the "contrectatio" must be "fraudulosa et lucri faciendi gratiâ." Of course a person who takes what does not belong to him, intending to deprive the owner of it, acts *primâ facie* fraudulently. The cases in which such a taking is innocent must under any system be exceptional. The exceptions in Roman law were much the same as they are in English law. By English law a claim of right excludes a felonious intent. Thus in Roman law, [3] "recte dictum est qui putavit se domini
" voluntate rem attingere non esse furem." [4] "Qui re sibi
" commodata, vel apud se depositâ, usus est aliter atque
" accepit, si existimavit se non invito domino id facere furti
" non tenetur." [5] "Si quis ex bonis ejus quem putabat

---

[1] Gibbon, ch. xliv.   [2] Dig. xlvii. 2, 21, 5.   [3] *Ib.* 2, 46, 7.
       [4] *Ib.* 2, 76.   [5] *Ib.* 2, 83.

" mortuum qui vivus erat, pro herede res apprehenderit, eum
" furtum non facere."

The principle in all these and other cases is the same;
there is no theft where there is a claim of right.

The rule of the Roman law that misappropriation must be
"lucri faciendi causâ" in order that it might amount to theft
has been on several occasions rejected expressly from the
English definition of theft. It is, indeed, obviously inexpedient and hardly capable of being applied. The *Digest*
does not supply many illustrations of it, and the texts which
bear upon it are not quite consistent. [1] " Verum est," says
Ulpian, "si meretricem alienam ancillam rapuit quis vel
" celavit furtum non esse; nec enim factum quæritur sed
" causa faciendi, causa autem faciendi libido fuit non furtum."
Paulus, however, says, [2] " Qui ancillam non meretricem libi-
" dinis causa surripuit furti actione tenebitur." An attempt
has been made to reconcile these texts, but they appear to
me clearly inconsistent. Possibly the "lucri faciendi causâ"
may have been inserted in the definition mainly with the
view of drawing a line between mischief and theft.

The Roman law at all events, regarded the question
whether the thief or some one else was to profit by the
offence as a matter of indifference. [3] " Si quis de manu
" alicujus nummos aureos vel argenteas vel aliam rem ex-
" cusserit, ita furti tenetur si ideo fecit ut alius tolleret
" isque sustulerit."

The doctrine that theft must be "invito domino," against the
will of the owner of the property stolen, is common to Roman
and English law, though the two systems apply it somewhat
differently. According to the law of England it is theft to
take goods with the owner's consent if the consent is obtained
by fraud, and if the owner intends to part with the possession
only; but it is not theft to take goods with the owner's
consent if he is persuaded by fraud to part not only with the
possession but with the property.

By Roman law the line between theft and obtaining goods
by false pretences turned not upon the question whether the

---

[1] Dig. xlvii. 2, 39.   [2] *Ib.* 2, 82, 2.   [3] *Ib.* 2, 52, 14.

owner consented to part with the property or with the possession only, but upon the question as to the means by which he was deceived. If a man deceived another by personation, or by means regarded as equivalent to it, and so obtained his property, the offence was theft. [1] "Falsus creditor," says Ulpian, "hoc est is qui se simulat creditorem, si quid " acceperit furtum facit, nec nummi ejus fiunt." He also says, [2] " Cum Titio honesto viro pecuniam credere vellem, subjecisti " mihi alium Titium egenum, quasi ille esset locuples, et num- " mos acceptos cum eo divisisti, furti tenearis quasi ope tuâ " consilioque furtum factum sit, sed et Titius furti tenebitur." On the contrary, [3] " Si quis nihil in personâ suâ mentitus est, " sed verbis fraudem adhibuit, fallax est magis quam furtum " facit, utputa si dixit se locupletem, si in mercem se collo " caturum quod accepit, si fideiussores idoneos daturum, vel " pecuniam confestim se soluturum." It must be observed that none of these cases, except perhaps the first, quite comes up to a false pretence of an existing fact. Perhaps if the case of a complete deception as to some existing fact other than that of the identity of a person had presented itself, the Roman lawyers would have held it to be theft. If so, their law and ours would be nearly coextensive, though they would not make the distinction which is made by us between theft and false pretences. The case of obtaining possession only by fraud and then converting the property (as where a man gets leave to mount a horse to try him and rides away) would present no difficulty to a Roman lawyer, as the riding the horse away would be clearly "fraudulosa contrectatio," though the mounting was not "invito domino."

It must be observed that the words "invito domino" were construed so strictly by some Roman lawyers, that the question was raised at all events, Whether, if a man gave up his property to a robber upon threats, the property was stolen? Labeo says, [4] " Si quis cum sciret quid sibi surripi non pro- " hibuit non potest furti agere. Paulus imo contra. Nam si

---

[1] Dig. xlvii. 2, 43.   [2] Ib. 2, 52, 21.
[3] Ib. 2, 43, 3.   [4] Ib. 2, 91.

" quis scit sibi rapi, et quia non potest prohibere quievit furti
" agere potest."

The Roman and the English law on the subject of the
possession of stolen property is not dissimilar, though many
of the fictions which have been introduced into English law
in order to evade the consequences of the rule, that
a wrongful taking is always necessary in larceny, are dispensed
with in Roman law by the more reasonable doctrine of
" contrectatio."

In order that a thing might be stolen it was necessary by
Roman law that it should be in the possession of some person,
or that some one should intend to possess it. Things which
had been abandoned by the owner, or which had never been
reduced into possession, could not be stolen. [1] "Quodsi dominus
" quid dereliquit furtum non fit ejus, etiamsi ego furandi
" animum habuero. Nec enim furtum fit nisi sit cui fiat?"
" [2] Si apes feræ in arbore fundi tui apes fecerint, si quis eas
" vel favum abstulerit eum non teneri· tibi furti, quia non
" fuerint tuæ; easque constat captarum terrâ mari cœlo
" numero esse."

The Roman and the English law agree in some particulars
as to the persons by whom theft can be committed.

Married persons could not steal from each other, nor was a
married person guilty of theft who helped some one else to
steal from his wife or husband.

[3] Joint owners could by the Roman law steal from each
other, " Si socius communis rei furtum fecerit (potest enim
" communis rei furtum facere) indubitate dicendum est furti
" actionem competere." This is the precise equivalent of
Mr. Russell Gurney's Act, 31 & 32 Vic. c. 116, s. 1.

The English rule of evidence as to recent possession was
also recognised by the Romans. Thus in the Sixth Book of
the Code Tit. ii. v., it is said, " Civile est quod [a te] adver-
" sarius tuus exigit: ut rei quod apud te fuisse fateris
" exhibeas venditorem, nam a transeunte et ignoto te emisse
" dicere non convenit volenti evitare alienam bono viro sus-
" picionem." " You ought to produce the person who you
" say sold you what you own you had, for no one who has

---

[1] Dig. xlvii. 2, 43, 5.   [2] Ib. 2, 26.   [3] Ib. 2, 45.

" any regard for his character for honesty will say he bought
" it from a man in the road whom he did not know." This
statement is often made in English courts, but as a rule by
those who can hardly expect " evitare alienam bono viro
" suspicionem."

Besides the common action of theft there were several
subordinate actions which provided for analogous wrongs.
They were as follows :

DE TIGNO JUNCTO.—[1] This was an action as old as the laws
of the Twelve Tables providing a special remedy in the case
of materials stolen and used up in erecting buildings, or
scaffolds for vines. A distinction was made between this and
other cases, " ne vel ædificia sub hoc prætextu diruantur, vel
" vinearum cultura turbetur."

SI QUI TESTAMENTO LIBER.—This was a special action
to provide for the case of a slave whose master had left him
his liberty, and who, in the interval between the testator's
death and the heir's succession fraudulently disposed of
anything to which the heir would have a right when he
succeeded to the inheritance. The necessity for such an
action arose from the singular doctrines of the Roman law
as to slavery and as to inheritance. During the interval
after his master's death the slave was the property of the
fictitious person, the inheritance itself. As soon as the
heir succeeded the slave became free under the will. On
attaining his freedom he was no longer punishable as a
slave, and till he attained it he was not punishable as a
free man. He could not therefore be punished in any way
for what he did whilst he was a slave to the inheritance. The
prætor's edict remedied this defect, [2] " Naturâ æquum est non
" esse impunitum eum qui hac spe audacior factus est quia
" neque ut servum se coerceri posse intelligit, spe imminen-
" tis libertatis, neque ut liberum damnari, quia hereditati
" furtum fecit, hoc est dominæ. Dominus autem dominave
" non possunt haberi furti actionem cum servo suo quamvis
" postea ad libertatem pervenerit."

The necessity which formerly existed for laying the property of the goods of a deceased person in the bishop of the

[1] Dig. xlvii. 3.   [2] Ib. 4, 1.

CHAP. II. diocese, and now in the judge of the Court of Probate, in prosecutions for stealing such goods before administration was taken out, has a sort of vague similarity to this proceeding.

FURTI ADVERSUS NAUTAS, CAUPONES, STABULARIOS.— [1] This was an action which lay against ship-masters, inn-keepers, and stable-keepers, for thefts committed by persons in their employ. " The master ought to answer for " what is done by his sailors, whether they are free or slaves." This is right because he employs them at his own risk, but he is answerable only for injuries done by them on board his ship ; if they do injury elsewhere he is not answerable for it. If he says beforehand that each of the passengers is to look after his own property, and that he (the master) will not be answerable for loss, and if the passengers agree he is not answerable. The master might free himself from responsibility as regarded the acts of his slave by giving up the slave in satisfaction (noxæ dedendo), but his responsibility for the fault of a free man employed by him was absolute. Ulpian speculates on the reason of this. [2] " Cur ergo non exercitor " condemnetur qui servum tam malum in nave admisit ? Et " cur liberi hominis nomine tenetur in solidum, servi vero " non tenetur ? Nisi forte idcirco, quod liberum quidem " hominem adhibens, statuere debuit de eo qualis esset, in " servo vero suo ignoscendum sit ei quasi in domestico malo, " si noxæ dedere paratus sit. Si autem alienum adhibuit " servum quasi in libero tenebitur."

[3] The title " Si familia furtum fecisse dicitur," throws further light on the responsibility of masters for the thefts and other offences of their slaves. The title goes into considerable detail, but it will be enough to say that masters were allowed as a matter of privilege to pay for damage done by their slaves, instead of being obliged to give them up by way of compensation, unless the injury done was done with the master's assent.

ARBORUM FURTIM CÆSARUM.—[4] This was a special action for damage short of theft to growing trees.

VI BONORUM RAPTORUM ET DE TURBA ET DE INCENDIO. RUINA, NAUFRAGIO, RATE, NAVE EXPUGNATA.—[5] These

---

[1] Dig. xlvii. 5.   [2] Ib. 5, 5.   [3] Ib. 6.   [4] Ib. 7.   [5] Ib. 8 & 9.

titles relate to civil remedies for acts which amounted to the CHAP. II.
crime of "vis publica" or "privata," and of arson ("incendium"). Incidentally, however, several Senatus Consulta are
mentioned which treat particular acts connected with wrecks
and fires as crimes. Some of these are very like English
Acts of Parliament. Thus: [1] "Senatus consulto cavetur eos
"quorum fraude aut concilio naufragi suppressi per vim
"fuissent ne navi vel iis periclitantibus opitulentur legis
"Corneliæ quæ de sicariis lata est pœnis afficiendos." Compare with this 24 & 25 Vic. c. 100, s. 17, which renders
liable to penal servitude for life every one who "prevents or
"impedes any person being on board of, or having quitted
"any ship or vessel in distress, wrecked, stranded, or cast on
"shore, in his endeavour to save his life, or prevents or im-
"pedes any person in his endeavour to save the life of any
"person so situated."

INJURIA.—The 10th title of the 47th book of the *Digest*
is headed "De injuriis et libellis famosis." The expression
"injuria" in Roman law was nearly as vague a word as the
expression "wrong" or "tort" in our own, for, in the wider
sense, it included [2] "omne quod non jure fit," and in the
narrower "contumelia," or "damnum culpâ datum." There
are, however, four special heads of "injuria" referred to in
the *Digest*, namely, injuries to the person, to dignity, to reputation, and to liberty. Injuries to the person consisted not
only in blows, but in threatening gestures, and included the
case of administering anything hurtful to the mind, [3] "si quis
"mentem alicujus medicamento aliove quo alienaverit."

An injury to "dignity" was apparently confined to a single
case: [4] "Ad dignitatem cum comes matronæ abducitur."
According to Roman manners, matrons were always accompanied in public by some person who acted the part, as we
should say, of a chaperon. To cause such a person to
desert his mistress was "injuria ad dignitatem pertinens."
If the offender went a step further his act was "injuria ad
infamiam pertinens," that is to say, if he paid attentions
to any person the object of which was [5] "ut ex pudico

---

[1] Dig. xlvii. 9, 3, 8.   [2] *Ib.* 10, 1.   [3] *Ib.* 10, 1, 2.
[4] *Ib.* 10, 15.   [5] *Ib.* 10, 10.

CHAP. II. impudicus fiat." The special example given is, "Si
quis mulierem appellaverit," and the word "appellare"
is defined thus: ¹ "blandâ oratione alterius pudicitiam
"adtentare." "Hoc," observes Ulpian, "non est con-
"vicium facere sed adversus bonos mores attentare." The
offence seems to have been rather more extensive than the
solicitation of chastity, which was, and theoretically still is,
an ecclesiastical offence in England. Mere following a
woman about was "injuria." "Quum quis honestam
"mulierem adsectatur. . . . Assectatur qui tacitus frequenter
"sequitur." Such attentions, however, must be "contra
"bonos mores." Ulpian is careful to explain that a man "non
"statim in edictum incidit, Si quis colludendi gratia id facit."
The law of libel and slander was in a very imperfectly
developed state at the time when the *Digest* was compiled.
The following texts show that defamation, whether written or
verbal, was regarded as an instance of "injuria," and that
the truth of a defamatory statement was a justification for
it. ³ "Si quis librum ad infamiam alicujus pertinentem scrip-
"serit, composuerit, ediderit, dolove malo fecerit quo quid
"eorum fieret, etiam si alterius nomine ediderit vel sine
"nomine, uti de ea re agere liceret."
"Convicium" was a form of "injuria." "Convicium" is said
to exist in the "collatio vocum." "Cum enim in unum
"complures voces conferuntur convicium appellatur quasi
"convocium."
In order, however, to be a "convicium," the "vociferatio"
must be "adversus bonos mores," and "ad infamiam vel in-
"vidiam alicujus." Not only he who himself vociferated, but
he who stirred up others to vociferation, committed the
offence, and if the defamatory matter was uttered publicly
"in cœtu" it was "convicium," whether it was said by one
person or by more persons than one. Defamatory matter
spoken in private, ⁵ "convicium non proprie dicitur, sed in-
"famandi causa dictum."
The commonest form of defamation at that time appears to
have been by symbolical actions, ⁶ as by wearing mourning, or

---

¹ *Dig.* xlvii. 10, 15, 20.   ² *Ib.* 10, 15, 22, 23.   ³ *Ib.* 10, 15, 9.
⁴ *Ib.* 10, 15, 4.   ⁵ *Ib.* 10, 15, 12.   ⁶ *Ib.* 10, 15, 27.

going about unshorn, or with loose hair, as a protest against CHAP. II. the oppression of the person defamed.

The question of justification is dealt with in these few very inadequate words of Paulus : [1]" Eum qui nocentem infamavit " non esse bonum æquum ob eam rem condemnari, peccata " enim nocentium nota esse et oportere et expedire."

" Injuria " might in some cases be committed by trespassers on property, as for instance by breaking into a dwelling-house, or entering upon land. [2]" Divus Pius aucupibus ita " rescripsit: non est (rationi) consentaneum ut per aliena " prædia invitis dominis aucupium faciatis." So it was " injuria" to make your neighbour's room smoke. [3]" Si " inferiorum dominus ædium superioris vicini fumigandi " causâ fumum faceret," but as to this there was some doubt.

IV. CRIMINAL PROCEDURE.

It would be foreign to my purpose to try to describe the criminal procedure of the Romans under the Republic, or to specify the numerous changes which were made at different times in the constitution and powers of the various tribunals of a criminal jurisdiction. The only form in which the system can have influenced our own criminal law, is that which it assumed under the Empire. It is still possible to give a pretty full outline of the system which probably prevailed there when Britain was a Roman province.

[4] In the days of Constantine the Empire was divided as follows :—

1. There were four prætorian præfects, namely, the præfect of the East, who governed Eastern Africa, Syria, and Asia Minor ; the præfect of Illyricum, who governed the whole of the South-East of Europe ; the præfect of Italy, who governed Italy, the South-West of Germany, and Western Africa; and the præfect of the Gauls, who governed Gaul, Spain, and Britain. Rome and Constantinople, with their respective territories, were excluded from these præfectures, and were under municipal præfects of their own.

These præfectures were divided into thirteen dioceses,

[1] Dig. xlvii. 10, 18.   [2] Pothier, iv. 363.
[3] Dig. xlvii. 10, 44.   [4] Gibbon, ch. xvii.

CHAP. II. namely, 1. The East; 2. Egypt; 3. Ariana; 4. Pontica; 5. Thrace; 6. Macedonia; 7. Dacia; 8. Pannonia; 9. Italy; 10. Africa; 11. Gaul; 12. Spain; 13. Britain. Each of these was under a vicar or vice-præfect, except Egypt, the ruler of which was called the Augustal Præfect, and the East, the præfect of which was called the Count of the East. The dioceses were divided into 116 provinces, of which 3 were governed by proconsuls, 37 by consulars, 5 by correctors, and 71 by presidents. They are commonly called by the name of *præses* in the *Digest*. Each province was composed of a number of cities greater or less with their *territoria*. The cities were of different ranks, some being colonies and others *municipia*, but each had their own magistrates. Through the *territoria* were distributed *stationarii milites* or policemen, who were under military organization, the superintendents being called centurions or *centenarii*. The *stationarii* were subject to a superior officer called *princeps pacis*, or *eirenarcha*—a word which it is impossible not to translate by justice of the peace. This organization of the Roman Empire corresponds with curious exactness to the organization of the British Empire in India, and especially in Northern India. India would have constituted a fifth præfecture, much larger than either of the others, or indeed than any two of them, but governed in much the same way. The Prætorian Præfect would answer precisely to the Governor-General, the Vicars to the Governors, Lieutenant-Governors, and Chief Commissioners of the different Indian provinces. The rulers of the Roman provinces would answer to the commissioners of divisions. The *civitas* with its *territorium* would correspond to a district. The officers of the *civitas* differed widely from the Indian magistrate of the district and his subordinates, as they were natives of their city, and permanent residents in it; but the *eirenarcha* or *princeps pacis* discharged some of the duties of the magistrate of the district, and the *milites stationarii*, with their decurions and centurions, answered precisely to the thannahdars, or officers in charge of police stations.

There were two modes of prosecuting crimes, public prosecutions and private prosecutions. Of these the private prosecutions have left the strongest traces in history, as the Chap. II. great political cases which occur in the early history of Rome, and of some of which the speeches of Cicero are monuments, were for the most part prosecuted in this manner. Public prosecutions as carried on under the Empire were no doubt the ordinary course for the administration of justice, and as the trials which took place attracted comparatively little attention, and left no monuments behind them, the whole subject has fallen into oblivion. As, however, if any part of the Roman system influenced our own institutions it must have been this, I will consider it first.

PUBLIC PROSECUTIONS UNDER THE EMPIRE.—[1] When a crime was committed which disturbed the public peace, it was the duty of the *milites stationarii* to apprehend the suspected persons, and to carry them before the eirenarcha, whose duty closely corresponded to that of an English justice of the peace, as may be gathered from the following remarkable passage of Marcian. [2] "Hadrian wrote to Julius "Secundus, and there are rescripts to the same effect that "the [3] letters of magistrates who send prisoners to the "president as if they were already convicted are not to be "taken as conclusive. A chapter of an order is still extant, "by which Antoninus Pius when President of Asia, enacted "in the form of an edict, that the eirenarchas, when they "apprehended robbers, should question them about their "accomplices and receivers, and send their examination "inclosed in a letter" (also called *elogium*), "and sealed up "for the information of the President. Persons sent up "with an "elogium" are to have a full trial" (*ex integro* *audiendi*), "although they have been sent with a letter from "the eirenarcha, or even brought by him. So too, both Pius "and other princes ordered that even those who were "reported for punishment [4] are to be tried, not as if they "were convicted, but from the beginning if there is any one

---

[1] The chief authorities for this are Pothier's preface to the 47th book of the *Digest*, and Godefroy's *Paratitlon to the Ninth Book of the Theodosian Code.*
[2] Dig. xlviii. 3, 6.
[3] They were called "elogium," "notoria," or "notaria."
[4] "Qui requirendi annotati sunt."

CHAP. II. "to accuse them. Therefore, whoever tries them ought to
"send for the eirenarcha and require him to prove the
"contents of his report. If he has done it diligently and
"faithfully he must be [1] commended; if he has acted hastily
"and [2] without careful inquiry, it must be officially noted that
"the eirenarcha acted hastily, but if it appears that he ques-
"tioned" (probably tortured) "the defendant maliciously,
"or reported what was not said as if it had been said, the
"eirenarcha, is to be punished for the sake of example, so as
"to prevent other things of the same sort in future."

This remarkable passage provides us with an outline of
the procedure adopted in common cases of crime. The
miles stationarius or his inferior officer arrests. The eirenarcha holds a preliminary investigation (probably with the
aid of torture) and commits for trial (as we know from other
texts referred to below) to the prison of the civitas, which
may perhaps be described as the county town, of the territorium in which the offence was committed. He acts to
some extent as a public prosecutor, as English justices did
in the days of the Stuarts, and as Indian magistrates still
do in many cases. The trial took place before the
præses, who, like Indian Commissioners of Divisions in some
parts of India, and till lately throughout all Northern India,
exercised the powers of a judge of assize, and made a circuit
to the different civitates in order to dispose of the business.
The præses, as the passage under consideration shows, had
before him the eirenarcha's report, and copies of the depositions just as an English judge of assize has the depositions
taken before the magistrate. The præses seems to have
exercised over the eirenarcha and his preliminary procedure
a greater degree of discipline and superintendence than is
exercised by any one over an English justice, or even over
an Indian magistrate, subject though the latter is to an
exceedingly strict system both of appeal and supervision.

PRIVATE PROSECUTIONS UNDER THE EMPIRE.—Crimes
might be prosecuted under the Empire as well as under
the Republic by a private prosecutor. In such cases the
procedure closely resembled that which was pursued in

---

[1] Qy. "confirmed."   [2] Non exquisitis argumentis.

purely civil actions, indeed, the action for a *privatum delictum*
—for instance, a prosecution for a common theft differed
from other civil actions only as such actions differed from
each other.

With regard to accusations of public crimes by private
persons, the system was as follows :—

Any one might act as an accuser except women, minors,
soldiers, persons convicted of crime, and some others. These
excepted persons however, might prosecute in cases in which
they were interested. " Si suam injuriam exequantur mortemve
propinquorum defendant ab accusatione non excluduntur."

All persons [1] except the præses of the province during his
tenure of office, and [2] magistrates absent in good faith on
public duties, were liable to accusation.

Under the Empire the accusation was made at Rome before
the præfect of the city, and in the provinces before the præses.
In each case the judge took cognizance of crimes committed
within his district.

[3] The accuser cited the accused before the præses, and
obtained the leave of the præses to prosecute. The parties
appeared before the judge. The accuser took an oath that
his accusation was not calumnious, and stated the nature of
his accusation. If the accused did not deny its truth he
was held to have pleaded guilty. If he denied it his name
was entered on a register of accused persons, and the
accuser filed an indictment—*libellus.* The form was thus:
[4] " Consul et dies. Apud illum prætorem vel proconsulem
" Lucius-Titius professus est se Mæviam lege Julia de Adul-
" teriis ream deferre, quod dicat eam cum Gaio Leio in
" civitate illâ, domo illius, mense illo, consulibus illis, adui-
" terium commississe." It was we are told necessary to state
the place, person, and month of the offence, but not the day
or hour. Aggravations of the offence were to be stated in the
libel, and it was to be signed by the accuser, who was liable
to the penalty of retaliation if his accusation failed. If this
provision was acted upon it must practically have put a stop to
private accusations, [5] but there is some evidence that the *pœna*

---

[1] Dig. xlviii. 2, 11.   [2] *Ib.* 2, 12.   [3] Pothier, iv. 397.
[4] Dig. xlviii. 2, 3.   [5] Coote's *Romans in Britain,* 307, 308.

CHAP. II. *talionis* was practically only a penalty which might be reduced by the judge in his discretion to a money fine.

The indictment might apparently be amended if an extension of time was allowed by the judge for that purpose.

The accuser was also bound over to prosecute, and if he did not appear he was not only liable to be punished in the discretion of the judge, but had to pay all the defendant's costs, including his travelling expenses.

A day was then fixed for the *judicium*, and under the Republic *judices* were appointed, a proceeding which had some resemblance to the appointment of a jury. It is difficult to say how long this system lasted, or who the judices were, especially under the Empire.

THE TRIAL.—The court being constituted, a certain time was allowed for the production of witnesses and documents, the witnesses being liable to be both examined in chief and cross-examined. It is difficult to say whether each side was allowed to call witnesses to facts. Pothier's opinion, founded on a passage of [1] Quintilian, is that both sides might call witnesses, but that the prosecutor only could compel their attendance. The following is the passage from Quintilian :—

"Duo genera sunt testium, aut voluntariorum, aut eorum
" quibus judex in publicis judiciis lege denuntiari solet,
" quorum altero utraque pars utitur, alterum accusatoribus
" tantum concessum est."

That either party to a criminal prosecution should be debarred from calling witnesses is so repugnant to our conceptions of justice, that it seems at first difficult to imagine that such could ever have been the rule under any moderately civilized system. It will, however, be shown [2] hereafter that trial by jury in its original form dispensed with witnesses altogether; that under the civil law as administered all over the Continent down to recent times the prosecutor only could call witnesses; and that in England the prisoner's right to call witnesses upon equal terms with the Crown was not established till the reign of Queen Anne. [3] After the examination of the witnesses was

---

[1] Inst. v. 7.   [2] See pp. 349-53, *infra*.
[3] Mr. Trollope, in his interesting *Life of Cicero*, observes that the prisoner

complete, the parties or their counsel (*patroni*) made speeches, of the character of which much may be learnt from Cicero's orations, and from Quintilian's *Institutes*, but of which nothing need be said here. [1] The accused was allowed to call witnesses to character (*laudatores*). Finally, the decision was given, at the time when judices were appointed, by the vote of the judices by ballot, afterwards probably, or in cases where there were no judices, by the præses.

If the accused was acquitted the accuser might be convicted of calumny if the judge thought he had brought his accusation from improper motives. [2] "Non utique qui non "probat quod intendit protinus calumniari videtur. Nam "ejus rei inquisitio arbitrio cognoscentis committitur qui reo "absoluto, de accusatoris incipit consilio quærere qua mente "ductus ad accusationem processit et si quidem justum "errorem reperirit absolvit eum ; si vero in evidenti calumniâ "eum deprehenderit legitimam pœnam ei irrogat." The original punishment for calumny was branding the offender with a K on the face. Constantine enacted that instead of the face the hands and calves of the legs should be branded. The calumniator was also subjected to retaliation.

TORTURE.—The only further observation I have to make upon the Roman criminal procedure, relates to the use of torture. It formed an essential part of the procedure under the Empire, though the *Digest* contains passages which show that it was used with caution, and reserved in most cases for slaves. An edict of Augustus still remains which lays down a general principle on the subject : [3] "Quæstiones neque " semper in omni causâ et personâ desiderari debere arbitror. " Et quum capitalia et atrociora maleficia non aliter ex- " plorari et investigari possunt quam per servorum quæstiones; " efficacissimas eas esse ad requirendam veritatem existimo " et habendas censeo." The commonest case for the application of torture was that

---

was not allowed to call witnesses. He allows me to say that his opinion, formed after a careful study of Cicero's orations, is that, whatever the law upon the subject may have been, there are no traces in the orations of any accused person having actually done so. I have not myself studied them from this point of view.

[1] Pothier, iv. 399. [2] Dig. xlviii. 16, 3, 1. [3] *Ib.* 18, 8.

of slaves who were liable to be tortured when their owners were suspected of offences. [1]" Ad tormenta servorum ita " demum venire oportere cum suspectus est reus, et aliis " argumentis ita probationi admovetur ut sola confessio " servorum deesse videatur." The accused himself might however be tortured, and that repeatedly, if the evidence against him was strong, but not otherwise. [2]"Reus eviden- " tioribus argumentis oppressus repeti in quæstionem potest, " maxime si in tormenta animum corpusque duraverit. In " eâ causâ in quâ nullus reus argumentis urgebatur tormenta " non facile adhibenda sunt: sed instandum accusatori ut id " quod intendat comprobet atque convincat." [3]The torturer was not to ask leading questions, " Qui quæstionem habiturus " est non debet specialiter interrogare an *Lucius Titius homi-* " *cidium fecerit,* sed generaliter quis id fecerit, alterum enim " magis suggerentis quam requirentis videtur." The evidence obtained by torture was to be received with caution, [4]"Quæs- " tioni fidem non semper nec tamen nunquam habendam: " constitutionibus declaratur. Etenim res est fragilis et " periculosa et quæ veritatem fallat. Nam plerique patientia " sive duritia tormentorum ita tormenta contemnunt ut ex- " primi iis veritas nullo modo possit: alii tanta sunt " impatientia ut quovis mentiri quam pati tormenta velint; " ita fit ut etiam vario modo fateantur ut non tantum " se verum etiam alios comminentur."

Such was the Roman law as to the definition of crimes, and the procedure for their punishment. It exercised greater or less influence on the corresponding part of the law of every nation in Europe, though in all it was far more deeply and widely modified by legislation than any other part of the Roman jurisprudence. Perhaps it was preserved with less alteration in Holland than elsewhere, as may be seen by reference to Grotius and Voet's commentary. It still retains a sort of vitality in the colonies conquered by England from the Dutch, though in Holland, as in other parts of the Continent of Europe, it has been superseded by more modern legislation.

---

[1] Dig. xlviii. 18, 1, 1.   [2] *Ib.* 18, 18, 1.   [3] *Ib.* 18, 1, 21.
[4] *Ib.* 18, 1, 23.

How far the system described in the *Digest* was ever in CHAP. II.
force in England is a problem which I suppose can never be
solved. The German conquest took place in the fifth century,
the Roman forces having been finally withdrawn in 409
(Gibbon, ch. xxxi.). The *Theodosian Code* was compiled
not long afterwards, and the *Digest* as we have it, between
530 and 533. As, however, they were both founded on the
existing law of the Roman Empire, and as there is no reason
to suppose that Britain was treated differently from the other
provinces, it is natural to suppose that the system described
above obtained here as well as elsewhere. Whether any
portion of it survived the German conquest, and so influenced
the earlier and ultimately the existing English law is a
question of purely antiquarian interest. In the laws made
before the Conquest some expressions occur which have been
taken from the Roman Law, but the important influence
of Roman upon English law was exercised through the
founders of the English common law long after the Norman
conquest. Glanville and Bracton, but especially Bracton, are
full of references to it, and indeed derived most of their
definitions and principles directly from it, although it had
little or no assignable influence on the modes of procedure.
These were derived from other sources.

It is observed with great truth by [1]Rossi that there is a close
analogy between the manner in which Roman and English
laws were developed. In each the system in its origin consisted of crude and vague definitions gradually manipulated
into a sort of system by legislation, especially by judicial
legislation. The English system has at the present day had
a history of about 600 years, if we take Bracton as the
earliest writer who can now be regarded as in any sense an
authority. The interval between the Twelve Tables and the
compilations of Justinian was about a thousand years; but
legislation was resorted to much more extensively, and at a
much earlier date in the history of the Roman criminal law
than in the history of our own. The various *leges Juliæ* may
be not at all unfairly compared to the Consolidation Acts of
1861, and they were passed about three centuries after the

[1] *Traité du Droit Pénal*, p. 49.

CHAP. II. legislation contained in the Twelve Tables. I do not think
that the Roman criminal law, as stated in the autborities
from which the preceding account has been extracted, contains anything which can justify the loose popular notion
that Roman law is peculiarly complete and scientific. In
the absence of the text of the laws themselves, it is difficult
to form an opinion on the subject; but it would be idle to
compare the heap of extracts collected in the *Digest*, and
thrown together with no arrangement whatever, even with so
clumsy a compilation as *Russell on Crimes*. It is infinitely
less copious. It does not go into anything like such full detail,
and it is certainly not better arranged, though *Russell on Crimes*
is arranged exceedingly ill. The notion of extracting from
the works of the jurists a set of definite, well stated, and
duly qualified principles, and arranging them in their natural
order in a complete coherent system, does not appear to
have presented itself to Tribonian and his assistants, any
more than it has to the great mass of writers on English law.
There is a close resemblance between the two systems, and a
resemblance all the more curious and interesting because the
direct effect of the earlier on the later system, though still
traceable, was small, but the resemblance is to be traced at
least as distinctly in the defects of the two systems as in
their merits.

CHAPTER III.

EARLY ENGLISH CRIMINAL LAW.

IT is a matter of great difficulty, indeed I think it would CHAP. III.
be impossible, to give a full and systematic account of
the criminal law which prevailed in England in early
times. The original authorities are scanty, and all presume
the existence of the very knowledge of which we are in
search. Both the laws of the early kings and our own
statute book presuppose knowledge of an unwritten law. Our
own unwritten law can still be ascertained, but such parts
of the earlier law as were not written have absolutely
disappeared. The collection of *Ancient Laws and Institutes
of England*, published by Mr. Thorpe, under the direction of
the Record Commissioners, contains in all forty-seven sets of
laws, or partly ecclesiastical, partly secular statutes, bearing
the names of [1] fourteen different rulers. Of these the *Leges
Henrici Primi*, though the least authentic, are, perhaps, the
most instructive. They are obviously a compilation made in
the time of Henry I., by some private person, of the laws then
in force, or supposed to be in force, among the English. They
form a sort of digest, collecting into one body many things to
be found in the earlier enactments, as well as a good deal of
matter which is not to be found there, but is, at all events in
many places, extracted from the Civil and Canon law. It also
contains several express references to the Salic Law, and the

---

[1] 1. Æthelbirht. 2. Alothhære and Eadric. 3. Wihtræd. 4. Alfred. 5.
Ina. 6. Edward (the Elder). 7. Ethelstan. 8. Edmund. 9. Edgar.
10. Ethelred. 11. Cnut. 12. Edward the Confessor. 13. William the
Conqueror. 14. Leges Henrici Primi. The references to Thorpe are to the
8vo edition in two volumes.

CHAP. III. law of the Ripuarian Franks. It is a slovenly composition, full of inconsistencies, repetitions, and distinctions unnecessary in themselves, and forgotten as soon as they are made. With all its defects, however, the work probably gives us better means than any other now extant of forming an opinion as to the nature of law amongst the early English. [1] The general impression which it makes is that they had an abundance of customs and laws sufficiently well ascertained for practical purposes, but that when anything in the nature of a legal principle or definition was required they were quite at the mercy of any one whom they respected as a learned man, and who was prepared to lay down any such principle or definition upon or without any authority whatever. Roman law must have been the source from which such definitions and principles were drawn, because no other was then in existence. At what time, by whom, in what degree these principles and definitions were first introduced, how far locally they extended, how far they varied, are questions which will probably never be answered, and are of no importance.[2]

The laws of the different kings closely resemble each other in their general outline. Indeed, they are, to a great extent, re-enactments of each other, with additions and

[1] The laws of Edward the Confessor were collected, as their title states, in the fourth year after the Conquest, when William "Fecit summoniri per "universos patriæ comitatus Anglos nobiles sapientes, et in lege suâ "eruditos ut eorum consuetudines ab ipsis audiret."

[2] There is a work called the *Mirror*, which has been regarded as throwing light on the principles and definitions of the early English laws, and as showing that they were of Roman origin. It certainly is a curious book, but I cannot myself attach much importance to it. It was written not earlier than 13 Edw. 1 (A.D. 1285), as it refers to a statute passed in that year, but it contains all sorts of assertions about Alfred, and in particular a specification of forty judges, whom he is said to have hanged as murderers, for putting different people to death unjustly. It also contains a number of what profess to be indictments, or rather appeals, as the author calls them. It is difficult, to me at least, to understand how the assertions of a writer of the end of the thirteenth century, who gives no authorities, can be regarded as of any weight about the details of transactions said to have occurred 400 years before, and which are noticed by no one else. Alfred's laws do not even mention judges, nor do they in any respect confirm the strange assertions of the *Mirror*. My conjecture would be that the part of the *Mirror* which relates to the laws of Alfred, &c., is simply an invention. One of the author's objects was to protest against judicial corruption and other abuses of his time, and his assertion that Alfred executed forty specified judges for specified offences was probably made as a suggestion as to what ought to be. See some remarks on this book by Sir F. Palgrave, ii., cxiii.

variations; and most of them contain a greater or less ad-
mixture of moral and religious exhortation. The laws of
Alfred, for instance, begin with the Ten Commandments,
an adaptation of considerable parts of Exodus, extracts
from the Acts, and a historical statement as to the diffusion
of Christianity.

To extract anything complete or systematic from such
materials is obviously impossible. There is, indeed, an
abundant supply of modern literature upon the subject, but
it is impossible to read it without perceiving that the results
arrived at are, to a great extent, conjectural, and that the
most learned and acute writers have frequently given to the
public rather proofs of their own learning, industry, and in-
genuity, than definite information. Moreover, questions
about the early English, which bear upon the origin of the
popular parts of our government, parliament, and trial by
jury, have been debated with no small share of the heat
which attaches to all political controversy.

I. EARLY ENGLISH CRIMES.

Pursuing the division of the subject already adopted, I will
first describe, as well as I can, the early English doctrines
on the subject of crimes, and next the system of criminal
procedure then in force.

So far as I have been able to discover there are hardly
any definitions of crimes in the early laws, but they
contain provisions of one sort or another about a large
proportion of the offences which would be defined in a
modern criminal code.

The following are the principal offences against the Government referred to in the laws. [1]"Plotting against the
"king's life, of himself, or by harbouring of exiles or of
"his men." [2]"Plotting against a lord." [3]Fighting in a
"church, or in the king's house." [4] "Breaking the king's

---

[1] Alfred 4 ; Thorpe, i. 63.   [2] Ethelstan 4; Thorpe, i. 203.
[3] Ethelred, vii. 9 ; Thorpe, i. 331 ; Cnut, 60 ; Thorpe, i. 409.
[4] This is mentioned in nearly all the laws, e.g. Ethelred, vii. 11 ; Thorpe,
i. 331 ; Cnut, 12 ; Thorpe, i. 383.

CHAP.III.   " peace (*frith*, or *grith*) or protection (*mund-bryce*)." [1] In
several of the laws there is mention of *overseunesse* or
oferhynes.   This seems to have been a general expression, including whatever we should call contempt, and
also disobedience to lawful authority, especially by public
officers.   [2] Thus, "Qui justum judicium ordinabiliter habi-
" tum et legitime redditum improbaverit overseunesse Ju-
" dicetur L. sol. in Westsexa, si erga comitem XL. sol., &c."
" [3] Si quis a justicia regis implacitatus ad consilium exierit,
" et ad inculpacionem non responderit XX. marce vel over-
" seunesse regis culpa sit."
Of offences against public justice [4] perjury is mentioned on
several occasions.   Offences against religion and morals are
dealt with at length in the ecclesiastical ordinances, but they
are also mentioned frequently in the secular ordinances.
Heathenism is thus defined : [5] "Heathenism is that men wor-
" ship idols, that is, they worship heathen gods and the sun
" or the moon, fire or rivers, water-wells or stones, or forest
" trees of any kind."   Many of the laws contain provisions
as to different forms of unchastity, adultery, incest and even
simple fornication.   [6] By a law of Cnut's a woman was to
"forfeit both nose and ears " for adultery.   [7] Procuring abortion seems to have been regarded as an ecclesiastical offence
only.   [8] Some provisions occur as to witchcraft, and "making
" offerings to devils."   The only offence at all resembling a
public nuisance which I have noticed is *Stredbreche*, which is
thus defined in the *Leges Henrici Primi :* [9] "Stredbreche est si
" quis viam frangat concludendo, vel avertendo, vel fodiendo."
Offences against the persons of individuals are most
minutely provided for by some of the laws, which contain
provisions as to homicide, different kinds of wounds, rape,
and indecent assaults.   The definitions of these offences
are assumed, but there are a few passages which to
some extent recognize a distinction analogous to ours

---

[1] Thorpe, i. 537 ; Hen. 1, xxxiv. 3 ; Thorpe, i. 551, 593 ; Hen. 1, liii. 1 ;
lxxxvii. 5.
[2] Thorpe, i. 537.   [3] Thorpe, i. 538 ; Hen. 1, xlviii. 1.
[4] Edw. 3 ; Eth. v. 25 : vi. 28, &c.   Hen. 1, xi. 6 ; Thorpe, i. 521.
[5] Cnut, 5 ; Thorpe, i. 379, and see Edward and Guthrum 2 ; Thorpe, i. 169.
[6] Cnut, 54 ; Thorpe, i. 407.   [7] Hen. 1, lxx. 16 ; Thorpe, i. 574.
[8] Wiht. 12, 13, &c. ; Thorpe, i. 41.   [9] lxxx. 5 ;   orpe, i. 586.

between murder and killing by negligence. The distinction between murder and manslaughter, as we now
understand it, is, I think, much more modern. The laws
of Alfred embody the provisions of Exodus xxi. 12—15.
They also provide for cases of accident or negligence. [1] " If
" at their common work one man slay another unwilfully,
" let the tree be given to the kindred, and let them have
" it off the land within xxx. days, or let him take
" possession of it that owns the wood "—a provision which
assumes that the commonest case of accidental death
was the felling of timber. [2] "If a man have a spear over
his shoulder and any man stake himself upon it that he "
(the man with the spear) "pay the were " (compensation to
the party) " without the wite " (the fine to the king). [3] So in
the laws of Henry I. it is laid down as a general principle that
"qui inscienter peccat scienter emendet," for which reason,
if any one accidentally kills another in any game or exercise,
or frightens a person so that he runs away and falls and so
is killed, the person causing the death is to pay the *were*.
Some obvious cases of justifiable homicide are also mentioned.
One is remarkable because it affords a clear instance of the
process by which Roman law found its way in particular cases
into English law. [4] " Pugnare potest homo contra eum quem
" cum desponsata sibi uxore post secundam et tertiam pro-
" hibitionem clausis hostiis et sub una coopertura inveniet."
[5] This is obviously adopted from the provision in the novel
cxvii. already noticed. A vague attempt is made in the *Leges
Henrici Primi* to define homicide, but the writer arrives only
at a tolerable classification of the degrees of guilt involved.
The passage is a good specimen of the work in which it
occurs: [6] " Homicidium fit multis modis, multaque distancia
" in eo est in causâ et in personis. Aliquando autem fit per
" cupiditatem, vel contencionem temporalium, fit etiam per
" ebrietatem, fit per jussionem alicujus, fit etiam pro defen-

---

[1] Alf. 13 ; Thorpe, i. 71.
[2] Alf. 36 ; Thorpe, i. 85. I omit some obscure expressions as to the shape of
the spear. The same law is given more fully, but in several parts indistinctly,
in Leg. H. 1, c. lxxxviii. ; Thorpe, i. 595.
[3] Hen. 1, lxxxviii. 6 ; Thorpe, i. 595.   [4] Hen. 1, lxxxii. 8 ; Thorpe, i. 591.
[5] See *ante*, p. 15.   [6] Hen. 1, lxxii. 1 ; Thorpe i. 577.

CHAP. III. " sione et justicia, de quibus ita meminit beatus Augustinus,
—————   "' Si homicidium est hominem occidere, potest aliquando
              "' accidere sine peccato; nam miles hostem, et judex
              "' nocentem, et cui forte in vita vel imprudenti telum manu
              "' fugit, non mihi videntur peccare cum hominem occidunt.'
              "¹ . . . 'Fit etiam homicidium casu consilio.' "

The crime of inflicting bodily harm is described in some
of the laws with almost surgical minuteness. Of the
seventy-seven laws of Alfred, no less than thirty-four
define the different injuries which may be inflicted by unlawful violence. Here is one specimen: ² "If the great toe
" be struck off let twenty shillings be paid him as *bot*. If
" it be the second toe, fifteen shillings. If the middle-most
" toe, nine shillings. If the fourth toe, six shillings. If the
" little toe be struck off let five shillings be paid him."

Of offences against property theft is the one most commonly referred to. I have found no definition of it in any
of the laws, though I think it may be said to be the subject
to which they refer most frequently. Some aggravated
forms of the offence are, however, distinguished. Robbery,
roberia, is frequently mentioned; but I think no definition
of it is given. *Forestel* and *hamsocna* are defined: ³ "Forestel
" est si quis ex transverso incurrat vel in via expectet et
" assalliat inimicum suum." It is distinguished from a
challenge to fight: "Si post eum expectet vel evocet ut ille
" revertatur in eum, non est forestel si se defendat."
Hamsocna was, no doubt, the earlier form of burglary.
⁴ "Hamsocna quod domus invasionem Latine sonat fit
" pluribus modis. Hamsocna est si quis alium in suâ vel
" alterius domo cum ⁵ haraido assailiaverit vel persequatur,
" ut portam vel domum sagittet vel lapidet vel colpum
" [? culpam] ostensibilem undecunque faciat. Hamsocna est

---

¹ Here follow quotations from Jerome and the Bible.
² Alf. 64 ; Thorpe, i. 97.
³ Hen. 1, lxxx. 4 ; Thorpe, i. 586, derived in Thorpe's *Glossary* from *fore*,
before, and *stellan*, to leap or spring.
⁴ Hen. 1, lxxx. 10 ; Thorpe, i. 587.
⁵ *Haraidum = heri reita.* The Bavarian laws took a distinction between
here reita and *heimzucht*. For *here reita* there must be at least forty-two
armed men. If there were less it was *heimzucht* (Thorpe's *Glossary*). In
Ina's laws (13 Thorpe, 48) it is said, "Thieves we call as far as 7 men ; from
vii. to xxxv. a *hloth;* after that it is a *here*."

" vel hame fare si quis premeditate ad domum eat ubi suum
" hostem esse siet, et ibi eum invadat in die vel nocte hoc
" faciat; et qui aliquem in molinum vel ovile fugientem
" prosequitur hamsocna adjudicatur. Si in curiâ vel domo
" seditione orta bellum eciam subsequatur et quivis alium
" fugientem in aliam domum infuget, si ibi duo tecta sint
" hamsocna reputatur. Infiht vel insocna est quod ab ipsis
" qui in domo sunt contubernales agitur."

Of mischievous offences against property *bernet* or arson
is [1] several times mentioned, but with no detail.

Of fraudulent offences the only one of much importance
or interest is coining. In nearly all the laws the offences of
moneyers are referred to in general terms, and as if they were
well understood.

Such were the crimes known to Anglo-Saxon law. The
punishments appointed for them were either fines or corporal
punishment, which was either death, mutilation, or, in some
cases, flogging. Imprisonment is not, I think, mentioned in
the laws as a punishment, though it is [2] referred to as a way
of securing a person who could not give security. The
fines were called *wer*, *bot*, and *wite*. The *wer* was a price
set upon a man according to his rank in life. If he was
killed the *wer* was to be paid to his relations. If he was
convicted of theft he had in some cases to pay the amount
of his *wer* to his lord, or to the king. If he was outlawed
his sureties (*borhs*) might have to pay his *wer*.

Bot was compensation to a person injured by a crime. It
might be either at a fixed rate (*angild*), or at the market
price of the stolen goods (*ceaf-gild*).

Wite was a fine paid to the king or other lord in respect
of an offence.

Speaking generally, all crimes were, on a first conviction,
punishable by *wer*, *bot*, and *wite;* the *wer* being sometimes
the measure of the *bot*, or compensation, as where a man
was murdered and compensation had to be made to his

---

[1] Hen. 1, lxvi. 9 ; Thorpe, i. 570, and elsewhere.
[2] " If a friendless man or a comer from afar be so distressed through want
" of friends that he has no *borh* (surety) at the *fiumtihtle* (first accusation)
" let him then submit to prison, and there abide till he goes to God's ordeal,
" and here let him fare as he may."—Cnut, ii. 35 ; Thorpe, i. 397.

CHAP. III. relations; and at other times the measure of the *wite,* as when the thief, being outlawed, his sureties had to pay his *wer* to the king or lord. A great part of many of the laws is taken up by provisions fixing the amount of the *wer* of different classes of people, and the *bot* due in particular cases. [1] The *wer* is mentioned both in the laws of the Conqueror and in the [2] *Leges Henrici Primi,* and it also appears in [3] Henry I.'s Charter to the citizens of London.

After a previous conviction *bot* might no longer be made.

[4] "At the first time let him make *bot* to the accuser, and to "the lord his *wer,* and let him give true *borhs* that he will "hereafter abstain from all evil. And at the second time let "there be no other *bot* than the head."

A certain number of cases were *bot*-less or inexpiable—and the punishment for them was death or mutilation on the first offence.

A passage in the [5] *Leges Henrici Primi* gives a classification of crimes according to their punishment. The laws of Cnut say : [6] "Housebreaking and arson, and open theft, and "open-morth, and treason against a lord are by the secular "law *bot*-less." [7] This is repeated in the *Leges Henrici Primi* with the addition of "effraccio pacis ecclesia vel manus regis "per homicidium."

The punishment upon a second conviction for nearly every offence was death or mutilation. [8] In Ethelred's laws it is said of the accused when ultimately convicted—"let him be "smitten so that his neck break."

The laws of Cnut lay down the principles on which punishment should be administered, and also regulate the practice of the court. The principle is thus stated: "Though any one sin,

---

[1] " De were ergo pro occiso soluto primo viduæ x. sol. dentur et residuum " liberi et consanguinei inter se dividant. Poterit autem quis in were " solvendo equum masculum non castratum pro xx. sol. dare et taurum pro " x. sol. et verrem pro v. sol." (Will. 1, 7, 9 ; Thorpe, i. 471.)

[2] Hen. 1, lxxvi. is headed "De precio cujuslibet," and begins thus : "Si " homo occidatur sicut natus erit persolvatur." (Thorpe, i. 581.)

[3] " Et homo hundoniarum non judicetur in misericordia nisi ad suam were " scilicet ad c. solidos, dico de placito quod ad pecuniam pertineat."—Stubbs, *Charters,* 108.   [4] Ethel. vi. 1 ; Thorpe, i. 281.

[5] Hen. 1, xii.; Thorpe, i. 522.   [6] Cnut, ii. 65 ; Thorpe, i. 411.   "Open morth" is a contradiction in terms, as the meaning of "morth" is secret killing. It may perhaps mean a murder after discovery.

[7] Hen. 1, xii.; Thorpe, i. 522.   [8] Ethel. iii. 4 ; Thorpe, i. 295.

"and deeply foredo himself, let the correction be regulated so
"that it be becoming before God and tolerable before the world.
"And let him who has power of judgment very earnestly bear
"in mind what he himself desires when he thus says: 'Et
"'dimitte nobis debita nostra sicut et nos dimittimus.' And
"we command that Christian men be not on any account
"for altogether too little condemned to death; but rather
"let gentle punishments be decreed for the benefit of the
"people; and let not be destroyed for little God's handy-
"work, and His own purchase which he dearly bought."
The practice of the courts is regulated by the following
enactment: — "That his hands be cut off, or his feet, or
"both, according as the deed may be. And if he have
"wrought yet greater wrong, then let his eyes be put out,
"and his nose, and his ears, and his upper lip be cut off,
"or let him be scalped; whichever of these those shall
"counsel whose duty it is to counsel thereupon, so that
"punishment be inflicted, and also the soul be preserved."

Capital punishment would seem to have been common
after Cnut's time, notwithstanding his cautions against the
abuse of it, as William the Conqueror found it necessary
to forbid it. His principles differed from Cnut's, though
the practical result seems to have been much the same. [1] He
says: "Interdicimus etiam ne quis occidatur vel suspendatur
"pro aliquâ culpâ sed enerventur oculi et abscindantur pedes,
"vel testiculi, vel manus, ita quod truncus remaneat vivus
"in signum proditionis et nequitiæ suæ."

II. EARLY ENGLISH CRIMINAL PROCEDURE.

The early English Criminal Procedure was of two kinds;
namely, the law of infangthief, a procedure so summary as
hardly to deserve the name, and the law of purgation and
ordeal (*urtheil*), a system which formed the first step towards
our modern law. It is natural to suppose that the more civilised
system gradually encroached upon and superseded the other. In
order to explain their relation, it should be remembered that in

---

[1] Will. 3, 17; Thorpe, i. 494.

CHAP. III. early times the really efficient check upon crimes of violence was the fear of private vengeance, which rapidly degenerated into private war, blood feuds, and anarchy. The institution of the *wer* in itself implies this. I have described it in connection with the subject of punishment, but it belongs properly to a period when the idea of public punishment for crimes had not yet become familiar; a period when a crime was still regarded to a great extent as an act of war, and in which the object of the law-maker was rather to reconcile antagonists upon established terms than to put down crimes by the establishment of a system of criminal law, as we understand the term.

A few authorities will show the importance of private war in reference to the laws of the early English. In the laws of Alfred it is enacted, [1] "That the man who knows his foe to " be home-sitting fight not before he demand justice of him. " If he have such power that he can beset his foe and " besiege him within let him keep him within for seven " days and attack him not if he will remain within." Several other delays having been provided for, the law proceeds, "if " he will not deliver up his weapons then he may attack " him." Liberal exceptions are allowed to the restrictions imposed by the law upon private war. " With his lord a man " may fight *orwige* (*i.e.* without committing war) if any one " attack the lord: thus may the lord fight for his man."

In nearly all the laws provision is made for the breach of the king's, the lord's, or the Church's peace or protection (*frith-bryce, mund-bryce*) in such a way as to show that peace was an exceptional privilege, liability to war the natural state of things. The King's Peace was extended to particular times and places, or conferred as a favour on particular persons. [2] "Some time after the Conquest all " these special protections were disused : but they were " replaced by a general proclamation of the 'King's Peace,'

---

[1] Alf. 42 ; Thorpe, i. 91.
[2] Palgrave i. 285. A curious instance occurs in the laws of the Conqueror (xxvi. ; Thorpe, i. 479). "In tribus stratis regiis, id est Wateling Street, " Ermonge Strete et Fosse" (the French version says "quatre chemins," adding "Hykenild") "qui hominem per patriam transeuntem occiderit " vel insultum fecerit, pacem regis infringit."

" which was made when the community assented to the " accession of the new monarch: and this first proclamation " was considered to be in force during the remainder of his " life, so as to bring any disturber of the public tranquillity " within its penalties. So much importance was attached " to the ceremonial act of the proclamation that even in the " reign of John, offences committed during the interregnum " or period elapsing between the day of the death of the " last monarch and the recognition of his successor were " unpunishable in those tribunals whose authority was " derived from the Crown."

When trial by combat was introduced by William the Conqueror the language used expressly treats it as a modified form of private war. [1] " Si Anglicus homo compellet aliquem " Francigenam per bellum, de furto, vel homicidio, vel aliquâ " re pro qua bellum fieri debeat vel judicium inter duos " homines, habeat plenam licentiam hoc faciendi." Indeed trial by battle was only private war under regulations.

Strongly as these instances illustrate the importance of crime, and the space which it filled in early times, I am not sure that the same inference may not be drawn even more plainly from some isolated rules of the early laws. The laws of Ina establish what we should call a presumption of law as follows: [2] " If a far-coming man or a stranger " journey through a wood out of the highway, and neither " shout nor blow his horn, he is to be held for a thief, either " to be slain or redeemed." Several of the laws provide that if a stranger stayed three days in his host's house the host was to be answerable for him, [3] " Nemo ignotum vel " vagantem, ultra triduum absque securitate detineat." These rules are precisely analogous to the [4] ancient identification between a stranger and an enemy as " hostes."

THE LAW OF SUMMARY EXECUTION OR INFANGTHIEF.— A single step, but still a step, however short, from private

---

[1] "Carta Regis Willelmi de appellatis pro aliquo maleficio. Franco ve l Anglico." (Will. 3, 1 ; Thorpe, i. 488.)
[2] Ina, 20 ; Thorpe, i. 117.   [3] Hen. 1, viii. 5 ; Thorpe, i. 516.
[4] " Hostis enim apud majores nostros is dicebatur quem nunc peregrinum " dicimus."—*Cicero de Officiis*, i. 12.   " Hostis " was itself a euphemism for " perduellis."

CHAP. III. war and blood feuds is made when people are invested by law with the right of inflicting summary [1]punishment on wrongdoers whose offences injure them personally. To recognise the right of the injured husband, or owner of property, to put the adulterer or thief to death there and then, is a nearer approach to law than to leave them to fight out their quarrel subject to a compulsory arbitration ending in the payment of a prescribed sum.

Of this right of summary execution the Saxon laws are full, as the following extracts show: " If a thief be seized let " him perish by death, or let his life be redeemed according " to his *wer*," say the laws of [2]Ina, meaning apparently that the thief's fate was to be in the discretion of his captor. [3]Another of Ina's laws says, " He who slays a thief must " declare on' oath that he slew him offending [4]not his gild " brethren." A very obscure law of Ethelstan's begins thus: [5]" That no thief be spared who may be taken *hand-* "*hæbbende* above xii. years and above eight pence." The rest of the law implies that in some cases the thief may be imprisoned. Another law of the same king [6]implies that the natural and proper course as to thieves was to kill them. " If any thief or robber flee to the king or to any church and " to the bishop, that he have a term of nine days. And if " he flee to an ealdorman, or an abbot, or a thane, let him

---

[1] A curious modern example of this is to be found in Burnes's *Travels into Bokhara :* " In one of our rides about Peshawur " (then, in 1831, an Afghan city) " we had a specimen of justice and Mohammedan retribution. As we " passed the suburbs of the city we discovered a crowd of people, and on a " nearer approach saw the mangled bodies of a man and woman, the former " not quite dead, lying on a dunghill. The crowd instantly surrounded the " chief and our party, and one person stepped forward and represented, in a " trembling attitude, to Sultan Mohammed Khan that he had discovered his " wife in an act of infidelity, and had put both parties to death ; he held the " bloody sword in his hands, and described how he had committed the deed. " The chief asked a few questions, which did not occupy him three minutes ; " he then said, in a loud voice, ' You have acted the part of a good Moham- " medan, and performed a justifiable act.' He then moved on, and the crowd " cried out ' Bravo ' (*Afreen*). The man was immediately set at liberty. We " stood by the chief during the investigation, and when it finished he turned " to me and carefully explained the law. ' Guilt,' added he, ' committed on " ' a Friday is sure to be discovered.' "—Burnes's *Travels into Bokhara,* i. 93, 94.
[2] Ina, 12 ; Thorpe, i. 111.   [3] Ina, 16 ; Thorpe, i. 113.
[4] These obscure words are supposed by Mr. Thorpe to mean that the slayer must not himself be a thief (" Thieves we call as far as vii. men," says Ina, 13). The slayer must not be one of the other six.
[5] Ethelr. 1 ; Thorpe, i. 199.   [6] Ethel. iv. 4 ; Thorpe, i. 223.

" have a term of three days. And if any one slay him
" within that term then let him (*i.e.* the slayer) make *bot* the
" *mund-byrd* of him whom he before had fled to " (*i.e.* pay a
fine for the breach of the protection of the person to whom
the thief had fled). " And flee he (the thief) to such *socn*
" as he may flee to " (*i.e.* in whatever jurisdiction he takes
" refuge) " that he be not worthy of his life but as many days
" as we here above have declared, and he who after that
" harbours him (the thief) let him (the harbourer) be worthy
" of the same that the thief may be, unless he can clear
" himself that he knew no guile nor any theft in him."

[1] The *Judicia Civitatis Lundoniæ* begin by declaring
" that no thief be spared over xii. pence, and no person over
" xii. years whom we learn according to folkright that he is
" guilty and make no denial; that we slay him and take all
" he has." Many provisions are made as to following thieves
and tracking them, and in the 7th rule it is provided " that
" he who should kill a thief before other men that he be
" 12 pence the better for the deed and for the enterprise
" from our common money." There are to be monthly
meetings, at which the persons present are to dine together,
and if it then happened that any men be so strong and so
great " . . . that they refuse us our right, and stand up in
" defence of a thief . . . that we all ride thereto, and avenge
" our wrong and slay the thief, and those who fight and
" stand with him, unless they be willing to depart from him."
[2] In the laws of Edward the Confessor elaborate provisions
are made for trying the question whether a person killed as
a thief " injuste interfectus sit, et injuste jacet inter latrones."
If it appears that this is the case the body is to be taken up
and reburied " sicut Christianum," with proper ecclesiastical
ceremonies.

The law of *infangthief* comes very near to this. It may
indeed be viewed as a particular case of summary execution.

---

[1] See on this document some curious and interesting remarks of Mr. Coote,
intended to show that it contains some rules of a Roman collegium, the object
of which was the recovery of stolen stock and slaves, and the indemnification
of the owners if they could not be recovered.—*Romans in Britain*, 394, &c.
For the document, see Thorpe, i. 229—243.
[2] Edw. Conf. xxxvi.; Thorpe, i. 460.

CHAP. III. It was one of the franchises usually conceded to the lords of townships, and is thus defined in the laws of Edward the Confessor: [1] "Justicia cognoscentis latronis sua est, de " homine suo si captus fuerit super terram suam." [2] *Infangthief* long survived the Conquest, though the exertion of the right was put under restrictions. [3] In the Hundred Rolls which record the results of an inquiry into the whole state of government in England at the beginning of the reign of Edward I. a return is made of the franchises exercised by lords of manors in most of the counties in England, hundred by hundred. These returns show that at that time the franchise of *infangthief* was common. It soon, however, disappeared. Sir Francis Palgrave says, [4] "In England the " records and annals of the law have not furnished any " instances of the exercise of *infangthief* after the reign of " Edward III., except in one northern borough, Halifax, " where a judicature grounded upon the Anglo-Saxon custom " subsisted until a comparatively recent era." Of these modes of punishing crime, Sir F. Palgrave well observes, [5] "Perhaps the name of legal procedure can scarcely be " given with propriety to these plain and speedy modes of " administering justice : they are acts deduced from the mere " exercise of the passions natural to man, and the law consists " only in the restrictions by which the power of self-protec- " tion and defence were prevented from degenerating into " wanton and unprovoked cruelty."

POLICE ORGANISATION, PURGATION, ORDEAL.—[6] Side by side with the rough, indeed barbarous, institutions just described, the early laws contained provisions which formed the foundation on which a more enlightened system was gradually constructed. The best order in which to consider them will be to speak first of

---

[1] Ewd. Conf. xxii.; Thorpe, i. 452.   [2] Palg. i. 210.   [3] See *infra*, p. 125.
[4] Palg. i. 213.   [5] Palg. i. 211.
[6] The whole subject of the early English courts and the territorial divisions of the country has been examined with so much labour and with such a profusion of learning by Mr. Stubbs, that I have felt it safer as well as easier to adopt his conclusions upon the matters treated of in this section than to undertake the arduous task of examining the original authorities for myself. Though he has added much to what is stated in the earlier works of Palgrave, Hallam, and Kemble, I do not think he has altered their principal conclusions.

the local distribution of the country for purposes of police, CHAP. III.
and also for the purposes of criminal jurisdiction, and
then to pass to the modes of trial, and to the infliction of
punishment in cases in which punishments proper in our
sense of the word were inflicted.

[1]The territorial divisions known to the early English, and
bearing on the subject of the administration of criminal justice, were the kingdom, the shire or county, the hundred or
wapentake, and the tithing, which it does not seem easy to
distinguish from the township or parish. The greater townships were called *burhs*. The administration of justice
was one of the great prerogatives of the king. For each
shire there was an earl or alderman, and a sheriff or viscount.
Whether there was or was not a chief officer for every
hundred is doubtful; but such officers did exist in some
cases. Each township or tithing was on all occasions represented by a body of five principal inhabitants, namely, the
reeve and four men.

[2]Under the later kings, and in the days of William the
Conqueror and his sons, laws were enacted whereby " all
" men were bound to combine themselves in associations of
" ten," each of whom "was security for the good behaviour
" of the rest," and had to produce him if he were charged
with any offence, and if they failed to do so to make good
any mischief he had done. These associations were called
tithings or *frith-borhs*, or frank-pledges. How far they
were connected with the local tithings is not clear.

[3]" The 'view of frank-pledge,' the business of seeing that
" these associations were kept in perfect order and number,
" and of enforcing the same by fine was one of the *agenda*
" of the local courts, and became ultimately, with the
" other remunerative parts of petty criminal jurisdiction,
" a manorial right exercised in the courts-leet, where it
" still exists."

Besides the tithings and hundreds there were also liberties or
franchises within which prevailed all or some of the privileges
comprised under the words " *Sac* and *soc, toll* and *team*, and
" *infang-thief*." These were simply hundreds or tithings

[1] Stubbs, i. 101.   [2] *Ib.* 87.   [3] *Ib.* 88.

granted as a privilege to private persons, and standing outside the general organisation.

This organisation still exists in name. We have still shires with their sheriffs (the earl's office having become merely titular), hundreds which till 1869 had their high bailiffs, chief constables, or other officers; and parishes, townships, and tithings which till 1872 had their parish constables, borsholders, and tithing-men, though the police functions of these officers had within living memory been superseded by more modern arrangements. We have still also liberties with their ancient names. The Soke of Peterborough may stand as one amongst many instances.

In early times these institutions formed the police system of the country, and in that capacity had various duties, of which the most important was that of raising in case of need the hue and cry, and tracking thieves and stolen cattle. The early laws are full of provisions on this subject, the substance of which is that if the track of stolen cattle is followed into land it must either be followed out or paid for. In the *Judicia Civitatis Lundoniæ* the following passage occurs: [1] "And if any one trace a track " from one shire to another, let the men who there are next " take to it, and pursue the track till it be made known to " the reeve; let him then with his *manuncy* (the people of " his district) take to it and pursue the track out of his shire " if he can, but if he cannot let him pay the *angylæ* (the " fixed price analogous to the *were*) of the property, and let " both reeveships have the full suit in common, be it where- " ever it may, as well to the north of the march as to the " south, always from one shire to another, so that every reeve " may assist another for the common *frith* (peace) of us all " by the king's *oferhyrnes* " (*i.e.* under pain of being guilty of a neglect of duty, and so liable to a fine).

Upon the whole the early police may be thus shortly described. The sheriffs of counties, the bailiffs of hundreds, the reeves and four men of townships, were its officers. Their duty was to arrest criminals and recover stolen property. In this they were assisted by the institution

---

[1] Thorpe, i. 237.

of frank-pledge, which made every one accountable for all his neighbours. CHAP. III.

The next step in tracing out the early procedure is to describe the Courts of Justice. [1] In the later period of our early history the administration of justice was regarded as the great prerogative of the king, who, after a long series of struggles, had become [2] " the source of justice, the " lord and patron of his people, the owner of the public lands." Though he occasionally discharged this office either personally or by the officers in immediate attendance upon him, the regular and stated method of doing so was through the local courts which were held before his officers, [3] the ealdorman, and the sheriff, or before landowners to whom he had granted jurisdiction (*sac* and *soc*) in their own bounds. These officers may roughly be described as the judges of the courts, though it is probable that there was little in common between their duties and those of a judge of the present day. The courts themselves corresponded to the police organisation, and were as follows :—

(1) The township officers, who could scarcely be said to form a court, but were rather the executive officers of the superior courts.

(2) The Hundred Courts.

(3) The County Courts.

(4) The Courts of Franchises, which were, so to speak, hundreds in themselves.

Each of these Courts was in the nature of a public meeting, attended by specified "suitors," or members, just as the Courts of Quarter Session in our own days are meetings of the county magistrates, and form a court of which the magistrates might be called the suitors. The suitors at the hundred court were the parish priest, the reeve, and the four men of each township in the hundred ; at the county court the same persons from each township in the county, all lords of lands, and all public officers were also suitors. Each court had jurisdiction in both civil and criminal cases. On the criminal side the court was called the

---

[1] Stubbs, i. 90.   [2] Stubbs, i. 207.

[3] The bishop also sat in the County Court, but I shall refer to this part of the subject elsewhere.

CHAP. III. Sheriff's *tourn* (or circuit). There appears to have been no distinction for purposes of criminal jurisdiction between the hundred court and the county court, as the sheriff's *tourn* was simply the county court held in and for a particular hundred. [1]The court consisted of the suitors collectively, but "a representative body of twelve seem to have been insti-"tuted as a judicial committee of the court."

Such were the early courts. The next question is as to their procedure. [2]According to Sir Francis Palgrave it was wholly oral. The court was summoned by verbal messages sent through the district, or perhaps by a token. "All the proceedings in these assemblies participated of their "native rudeness and simplicity. Scribes, or registrars, were "not required to attend the meeting of the hundred or the "shire: the memorials of the court were entrusted to the "recollections of the *Witan*, the judges by whom the "decrees were pronounced . . . Legal archives, in the proper "sense of the words, did not exist among the Anglo-Saxons. "On rare occasions the verdicts of the hundred or the shire "might be written in the blank leaves of the missal belong-"ing to some neighbouring minster; but though this mode "of preserving the history of the transactions might be "adopted, the document had no legal effect. It could not "be pleaded, and the strict and proper mode of legal proof "was by appealing to living testimony. If evidence was "required of judicial transactions, the proof was given by "the hundred or shire, in its corporate capacity, the suitors "bearing witness to the judgments which they or their "predecessors had pronounced."

The procedure itself appears to have consisted of accusation and trial.

[3]Accusation might be made either by the committee mentioned above, who possibly may have been the predecessors of the grand juries of later times, or by the four men and the reeve of the township, or lastly by a private accuser. This appears as to the twelve thanes from the laws of [4]Etheldred:—

---

[1] Stubbs, i. 103. See more particularly *Leges Henrici Primi*, v. De causarum preprietatibus. Thorpe, i. 505.   [2] Palg. i. 143.
[3] *Ib.* 213.   [4] Ethel. iii. 3 ; Thorpe, i. 294-295.

"and that a gemot be held in every wapentake, and the
" twelve senior thanes go out, and the reeve with them, and
" swear on the relic that is given to them in hand, that they
" will accuse no innocent man, nor conceal any guilty one."
That the four men and the reeve had also a power of
accusation is inferred by Sir Francis Palgrave from a passage
in the laws of Cnut :—[1] " And if any man be so untrue to the
" hundred, and so *tiht-bysig* (ill-famed), and three men
" together then accuse him, let there be no other (course) but
" that he go to the threefold ordeal ; " also from one of the
laws of William the Conqueror :—[2] " Si quis in hundredo
" inculpatus fuerit et a iv. hominibus rettatus (accused) purget
" se manu xii." Several passages in the laws seem to show
that a single person could accuse another. The most important occur in one of the laws of [3] Ina, which is interesting
because it implies that a person accused might be bailed, and
if he could not get bail, be imprisoned till trial :—" When a
" man " (A) " is charged with an offence, and is compelled to
" give pledge, but has not himself aught to give for pledge,
" then goes another man " (B) " and gives his pledge for
" him, as he may be able to arrange, on the condition that
" he " (A) " give himself into his " (B's) " hands until he "
(A) " can make good his " (B's) " pledge. Then again a
" second time he " (A) " is accused and compelled to give
" pledge ; if he will not continue to stand for him who
" before gave pledge for him " (if B will no longer go bail for
A) " and if he " (the last accuser) " then imprison him " (A),
" let him " (B) " then forfeit his pledge who had before
" given it for him " (A). This wilderness of pronouns seems to
have the following meaning :—A is accused of a crime, B gives
bail upon condition that A will put himself into B's custody
till A appears to answer the accusation. A second accusation is then made against A. B refuses to give further
security, and A is imprisoned by his second accuser. B
forfeits the security he gave for A's appearance on the first
charge. This must refer to charges before two different
courts. A is accused in London, and B gives bail for his
appearance in London. If A is accused and imprisoned in

[1] Cnut, 30 ; Thorpe, i. 393. [2] Thorpe, i. 487. [3] Ina, 62 ; Thorpe, i. 141-142.

respect of that accusation at Bristol, B forfeits his recognisance in London, if by reason of the imprisonment at Bristol A does not appear in London.

[1] Several forms of the oaths of accusation taken by individual accusers are still preserved, which implies that private accusations were common:—"By the Lord before " whom this relic is holy, I my suit prosecute with full folk " right, without fraud and without deceit, and without any " guile, as was stolen from me the cattle N, that I claim, and " that I have attached with N. By the Lord I accuse not N " either for hatred, or for envy, or for unlawful lust of gain; " nor know I anything so other, but as my informant to me " said, and I myself in sooth believe that he was the thief of " my property."

The form of the oath would no doubt vary according to the nature of the crime imputed.

The mode in which the trial was conducted can still be traced with reasonable distinctness from the enactments of [2] several kings which repeat each other with variations, the most complete types being those of Ethelred and Cnut.

The accused person denied in general terms and upon oath what was imputed to him. [3] His oath was:—"By the " Lord I am guiltless, both in deed and counsel of the charge " of which N accuses me."

This being done, the question of his guilt was to be decided, according to the character of the accused, by the *lad*, *i.e.* by compurgation, or by ordeal. If he was of good character he was entitled to the *lad*, or "oathworthy." If the *lad* failed, or in the expressive words of the law, "if the oath burst," or if he was *tiht bysig*, *i.e.* a man of bad character, he was obliged to go to the ordeal.

The first question accordingly at the trial was as to his character, which was decided by the system of *borhs* or sureties, which was as follows:—

[4] "Ethelstan enacted that the lord or the lord's steward " should answer for all his men." "Omnis homo" (obviously

¹ Thorpe, i. 179-185.
² Ethelred, i. 1 ; Thorpe, i. 283 ; Cnut, ii. 30 ; Thorpe, i. 393 ; Hen. 8, xli. 6 ; lix. 6 ; lxiv. 9 ; lxv. 3 ; Thorpe, i. 515-541.
³ Th. i. 181.   ⁴ Æthelstan ii. ; Thorpe, i. 217.

·every lord) "teneat homines suos in fidejussione suâ· contra
"omne furtum. Si tunc sit aliquis qui tot homines habeat
"quod non sufficiat omnes custodire præponat sibi singulis
"villis præpositum unum qui credibilis sit ei, et qui concre-
"dat hominibus. Et si præpositus alicui eorum hominum
"concredere non audeat inveniat xii. plegios cognationis suæ
"qui ei stent in fidejussione."

"That every freeman have a true *borh*, that the *borh*
"may present him to every justice if he should be acᴄused."

[2] Cnut enacted, "We will that every freeman be brought
"into a hundred and into a tything who wishes to be entitled
"to *lad* or *wer* in case any one shall slay him after he is
"twelve years of age. Let him not afterwards be entitled
"to any free rights be he *heath-fœst* [3](living in his own
"house), be he follower. And that every one be brought
"into a hundred and in *borh*, and let the *borh* hold
"and lead him to every plea. Many a powerful man will
"if he can and may defend his man in whatever way it
"seems to him that he may the more easily defend him,
"whether as a freeman or a *theoir*. But we will not
"allow that injustice." Later enactments developed this
into the law of frank-pledge (*frith-borh*—peace-pledge) already
referred to.

The accused then being "led to the plea" by his *borh*,
the *borh* had to swear that the accused had not been
convicted since a certain period. The oath to be taken
under Ethelred's law was [4]"that he has not failed neither
"in oath nor ordeal since the gemot was at Bromdun."
In [5]Cnut's time, "since the gemot was at Winchester."
Under each of these laws the oath was to be made not
only by the lord of the accused (if he had one,) but by
"two true thanes of the hundred or the reeve," who were
also to swear that the accused had not paid *thief-gild*.
This being done the accused was entitled to choose whether
he would have a "single ordeal" or a "pound-worth oath
within the three hundreds for above xxx. pence." [6]The

---

[1] Ethelred, i. 1 ; Thorpe, i. 281.
[2] Cn. ii. 20 ; Thorpe, i. 387.
[3] Thorpe's note.
[4] Ethelred, i. 1 ; Thorpe, i. 281.
[5] Cnut. ii. 30 ; Thorpe, i. 393.
[6] Edgar, 9 ; Thorpe, i. 261.

CHAP. III. single ordeal was handling a piece of red-hot iron of a pound's weight or plunging the hand up to the wrist into boiling water. [1] How many witnesses were "a pound-worth" does not appear, nor do I think that it appears clearly how it was determined who the witnesses were to be, and in particular whether the accused might call whom he would, or whether the sheriff summoned the persons whom he believed to be most likely to know the facts, subject to some right of challenge on the part of the prisoner; but however this may have been the *lad* or compurgators swore not to particular facts, but in general terms to their belief in the innocence of the accused. This appears from the form of the oath, which is as follows:—"His" (the accused) "companion's oath who stands with him" (the accused)—"By the Lord, the oath is clean and unperjured "which N has sworn."

Whether any evidence at all was given of particular facts, and if so, at what stage of the proceedings, and in what manner, it is now impossible to say. It is hardly conceivable that the necessity for it should not have been perceived at a very early time, and it is not unlikely (though this is of course a mere conjecture) that the compurgators might have a right to have witnesses to facts examined before, to use an expression which often occurs in the laws, they "dared" to swear. All that can be positively affirmed is, that [2] witnesses are mentioned in the laws of Henry I. and that [3] a form of oath has been preserved, which implies that evidence in our sense of the word, was, or might be, given at some stage of the proceedings. "How he shall swear that stands with "another in witness. In the name of Almighty God as I "here, for N in true witness, stand unbidden and unbought, "so I with my eyes oversaw, and with my ears overheard that "which I with him say."

---

[1] In many parts of the laws there are provisions about the relative value of the oaths of people of different ranks and professions, *e.g.* "A mass priest's "oath and a secular thane's are in English law reckoned as of equal value, "and by reason of the seven church degrees that the mass priest, through the "grace of God, has acquired, he is worthy of thane right." "A twelf-hynde "man's oath stands for six ceorls' oaths, because if a man should avenge a "twelf-hynde man he will be justly avenged on six ceorls, and his *wer-gild* "will be six ceorls' 'wer gilds.'"—Thorpe, i. 183.

[2] Hen. 5, i. ; Thorpe, i. 505.   [3] Thorpe, i. 181.

However this may have been, if the oath succeeded the accused was acquitted. If it failed or "burst," that is, if the witnesses could not be found, or would not swear, or if the accused were a man of bad character, he had to go to the triple ordeal (*urtheil*), that is [1] to handle red-hot iron of three pounds weight, or to plunge his arm into boiling water to the elbow.

It is unnecessary to give a minute account of the ceremonial of the ordeals. They were of various kinds. The general nature of all was the same. They were appeals to God to work a miracle in attestation of the innocence of the accused person. The handling of hot iron, plunging the hand or arm into boiling water unhurt, were the commonest. The ordeal of water was a very singular institution. Sinking was the sign of innocence, floating the sign of guilt. As any one would sink unless he understood how to float, and intentionally did so, it is difficult to see how any one could ever be convicted by this means. Is it possible that this ordeal may have been an honourable form of suicide, like the Japanese happy despatch? In nearly every case the accused would sink. This would prove his innocence, indeed, but there would be no need to take him out. He would thus die honourably. If by any accident he floated, he would be put to death disgracefully.

If the ordeal failed, the accused was convicted, the consequences of which were provided for as follows:— [2] Ethelred says, "If he be guilty at the first time, let him "make *bot* to the accuser twofold, and to the lord his *wer*, "and let him give true *borhs* that he will thereafter abstain "from every evil. And at the second time let there be no "other *bot* than the head. But if he run away and avoid "the ordeal, let the *borh* pay to the accuser his *ceap-gild* "(the market price of the thing stolen) [3] and to the lord his "*wer* who is entitled to his *wite*. If any one accuse the

---

[1] Edgar, 9 ; Thorpe, i. 261. The fullest description of an ordeal by fire is in the laws of Ethelstan, iv. 7 ; Thorpe, i. 227.

[2] Ethelred, i. 1, Thorpe, i. 282-283 ; and Cnut, ii. 30, Thorpe, i. 393-394.

[3] *i.e.* the *were* of the offender is to be paid to the lord who is entitled to the *wite* (or fine) due in respect of the offence. The *were* meant both the price to be paid to a person's relations if he was killed, and the price to be paid in respect of him if he committed an offence.

CHAP. III. "lord that he (the man) ran away by his (the lord's) counsel "and that he (the lord) had previously acted unlawfully, let "him (the lord) take to him five thanes and be himself the "sixth, and clear himself thereof. And if the purgation "succeed, let him (the lord) be entitled to the *wer*. And if "it do not succeed let the king take the *wer* and let the "thief be an outlaw to all people." The law of Cnut is to the same effect, but the punishments differ, as I have already said.

CHAPTER IV.

THE ORDINARY CRIMINAL COURTS—QUEEN'S BENCH DIVISION
OF THE HIGH COURT, THE COURTS OF ASSIZE, THE COURTS
OF QUARTER SESSIONS, COURTS OF SUMMARY JURISDIC-
TION, FRANCHISE COURTS, WELSH COURTS.

[1] CRIMINAL justice is in the common course of things ad- CHAP. IV.
ministered in the present day by the Queen's Bench Division
of the High Court of Justice, the Assize Courts, the Central
Criminal Court, and the County and Borough Courts of
Quarter Sessions. I propose to relate the history of these
courts and that of the courts which they superseded in the
present chapter. I shall relate in other chapters the history of
Parliament considered as a court of criminal jurisdiction, the
history of the criminal jurisdiction of the Privy Council and
that of the Court of Star Chamber. [2] The history of the Admiralty Jurisdiction will be considered under a different head.

In a very few words the history of the ordinary courts is
as follows : Before the Conquest the ordinary criminal court
was the County or Hundred Court, but it was subject to the
general supervision and concurrent jurisdiction of the King's
Court. The Conqueror and his sons did not alter this state
of things, but the supervision of the King's Court and the
exercise of his concurrent jurisdiction were much increased
both in stringency and in frequency, and as time went on
narrowed the jurisdiction and diminished the importance of
the local court. In process of time the King's Court developed
itself into the Court of King's Bench and the Courts of the
Justices of Assize, Oyer and Terminer and Gaol Delivery,

---

[1] For the constitution of the existing criminal courts stated systematically,
see *Dig. Crim. Proc.* pp. 9-16.   [2] See *post*, Ch. XVI. Vol. II. p. 1.

or to use the common expression, the Assize Courts; and the County Court, so far as its criminal jurisdiction was concerned, lost the greater part of its importance.

These changes took place by degrees during the reigns which followed the Conquest, and were complete at the accession of Edward I.

In the reign of Edward III. the Justices of the Peace were instituted, and they, in course of time, were authorised to hold Courts for the trial of offenders, which are the Courts of Quarter Sessions. The County Court, however, still retained a separate existence, till the beginning of the reign of Edward IV., when it was virtually, though not absolutely, abolished. A vestige of its existence is still to be traced in Courts Leet.

The Courts of summary jurisdiction have been established within the last few years.

The courts above mentioned formed and form the regular provision for the administration of criminal justice throughout England, but besides them the right of administering justice within particular local limits was granted by way of franchise to particular persons, either in their individual or in their corporate capacity. The leading features of their history are shortly these: The judicial authority annexed to manors has long since dwindled to almost nothing, though some traces of it may be discovered. A few of the greatest of all the franchises (especially the Courts of the Counties Palatine, Chester, Durham, and Lancashire), were annexed to the Crown and survived as mere names till very modern times.

The franchise of the City of London was merged in the Central Criminal Court established in 1834. The franchises of the other cities and towns corporate were of an extremely varied character. Most of them were regulated as far as the question of criminal jurisdiction is concerned by the Municipal Corporations Act of 1834, and many others to which that Act did not apply have become obsolete and are forgotten, although they have never been formally abolished.

Lastly, Wales became a part of England by several successive steps, from the reign of the Conqueror, downwards.

This is the outline of the history which I now propose to relate more fully.

THE COUNTY COURTS.

Nothing can be more definite than the image which the CHAP. IV.
words "court of justice" raise in our minds. We associate
with the expression a large room arranged in a particular
way. The proceedings follow a well-known prescribed
routine, and terminate in a definite result.
Such associations would be misleading if they were
allowed to influence our conception of the courts of the
early kings, and their subjects and officers. The courts
of those days supplied the means by which every kind of
business was transacted, and had probably a greater resemblance to a public meeting than to a court of justice in
the modern sense of the term. This was true of all courts
whatever, but especially of the County Court, which was in
the earliest times of our history, and continued to be down to
the reign of Edward I., if not later, [1] "the Folkmoot,
"or general assembly of the people," in which were transacted all the more important branches of public business,
judicial, financial, and military. [2] The sheriff was in
early times "the king's steward and the judicial president
"of the shire, the administrator of the royal demesne, and
"the executor of the law." It is impossible to determine
precisely the relation which he bore to the Ealderman, and
the extent to which the Bishop took part in or controlled
his proceedings. Such questions have in a practical point of
view no importance, as from the Conquest at all events the
Ealderman's office merged in the titular dignity of an earl,
and the Bishop acquired a separate court with a jurisdiction of
its own by the charter of William I. It is equally difficult to
give a perfectly clear account of the nature of the sheriff's
functions in criminal trials. He convened the court. He no
doubt had considerable influence over its decisions, [3] but the
suitors and not the sheriff were, properly speaking, the judges.
Whatever his functions may have been and whatever may

[1] Stubbs, ii. 205.   [2] *Ib.* i. 113.   [3] *Ib.* 393-4.

CHAP. IV. have been the nature of the procedure observed, the court itself appears to have been a representative assembly composed of the lords of lands in the county or their stewards, the parish priest, and the reeve and four men from each township. The character of the court, its great importance, and the fact that the king and his officers had concurrent jurisdiction in it with the sheriff, its ordinary president, may be gathered from the few remaining reports of its proceedings.

[1] "The great suit between Lanfranc as Archbishop of " Canterbury, and Odo as Earl of Kent, which is perhaps " the best reported trial of the Conqueror's reign, was tried " in the County Court of Kent, before the king's representa-" tive Gosped, Bishop of Coutances, whose presence, and that " of most of the great men of the kingdom, seem to have " made it a Witenagemot. The Archbishop pleaded the " cause of his Church in a session of three days on Pennenden " Heath ; the aged South-Saxon Bishop Ethelric was brought " by the king's command to declare the ancient customs of " the laws, and with him several other Englishmen, skilled " in ancient laws and customs. All these good and wise men " supported the Archbishop's claim, and the decision was " agreed in, and determined by, the whole county."

Of course the cases which present features of exceptional interest or solemnity, are those which are reported by historians. It is only by accident that we can get a glimpse at the common course of business, by which ordinary thieves or murderers were brought to justice. I have however been fortunate enough to be referred to what may stand for a report of the trial of a common thief, in the reign of Henry II. It occurs in the *Materials for the Life of Thomas Becket*, [2] and is one of an immense number of stories of miracles, said to have been worked by his intervention after his murder. It probably has the same sort of relation to actual fact as an account of a trial by a modern novelist would have to what actually passes in courts of justice. It relates to the miraculous cure of one Ailward, whose eyes

[1] Stubbs, i. 277.
[2] Published by the Master of the Rolls, i. 155-7. My friend Mr. Froude directed my attention to this curious story. It is also printed in Mr. Bigelow's *Placita Anglo-Normannica*.

and other organs were said to have been reproduced after he CHAP. IV.
had been mutilated by the sentence of the County Court
of Bedford. The story is as follows: "Ailward's neighbour
" owed Ailward a debt, and when he was asked to pay it,
" refused ; whereupon Ailward, in a rage, broke open the
" house of his debtor, which his debtor, [1]who had gone to the
" public house, had left fastened with a lock hanging down
" outside. Ailward took, as a security, the lock, a whetstone
" hung from the roof of the house, a gimlet and tools, and
" went away. The children who were playing in the house,
" where they had been locked up by their father, told him
" how the house had been broken open, and how the thief
" had carried off the things. The father followed him, caught
" him, and, wresting the whetstone from his hand, as he
" sauntered, wounded his head with it. He then drew his
" knife, stabbed him through the arm, and taking him to the
" house into which he had broken, bound him [2]as an open
" thief, with the stolen goods upon him. A crowd collected,
" one of whom was Fulco the apparitor, who suggested,
" that as a man cannot be mutilated for stealing under the
" value of a shilling, the stolen goods should be increased by
" other goods alleged to be stolen. Accordingly there were
" laid by the prisoner, a bundle, a *pellium*, linen, gowns, and
" the iron tool commonly called *volgonum*.

"Next day he was taken with the aforesaid bundle,
" which was hung round his neck, before one Richard
" the sheriff and other knights. Lest however, in a matter
" of doubt, the sentence should be hurried, judgment was
" deferred. He was kept for a month in the prison at
" Bedford." [3]

---

[1] "Ad tabernam digressus."
[2] "Quasi furem manifestum cum concepto furto." The use of the technical terms of the Roman law is noticeable.
[3] The account of the way in which he passed his time in prison is curious,
though not relevant to the matter in hand. "Interim clam vocato pagano pres-
" bytero suos excessus omnes ab ineunte ætate confessus est, et monitus est
" suffragia beatæ Mariæ sanctorumque omnium, et maxime beati Thomæ
" quem Dominus virtutum et signorum indiciis glorificare dignatus est
" suppliciter implorare, omnem iram et incentivum odiorum ab animo
" secludere, de Dei misericordiâ non diffidere, et quicquid pati cogeretur
" æquanimiter in remissionem peccatorum continere, et eo attentius quod
" vigilia Pentecostes ipse parvulus regeneratus aquâ submergi vel igne cre-
" mari non posset sicut vulgaris habuit opinio, si judicium alterutrum subi-

After this, "it happened that he was taken to Leighton
" Buzzard where the magistrates met (*magistratibus con-*
" *venientibus*). There he demanded to fight Fulco his accuser,
" or to undergo the ordeal of fire, but [1] with the assent of
" Fulco who had received an ox for it (*ob id ipsum bovem*
" *acceperat*) he was condemned to the ordeal of water, so
" that he might by no means escape. Thence he was taken
" back to Bedford, where he passed another month in prison.
" The judges met there (*convenientibus judicibus*), and when
" he was given up to be examined by the ordeal of water,
" [2] he received the melancholy sentence of condemnation,
" and being taken to the place of punishment, his eyes
" were pulled out and he was mutilated, and his members
" were buried in the earth, in the presence of a multitude
" of persons." The rest of the passage describes their
miraculous restoration.

This story sets in a vivid light the procedure of the old
County Court in a common case of theft. The thief is
arrested with the goods in his possession. He is taken
before the sheriff and other knights, and committed to
Bedford gaol. Two tourns or adjournments of the County
Court are held in successive months, one at Leighton,
the other at Bedford. They are described as a meeting
of magistrates or judges. The words " magistratus " and
" judices " being probably used in a popular way, and no
doubt denoting the stewards and other persons of local
importance who were present at the County Court. The
defendant claims the trial by combat, but, [3] (no doubt

" turus esset, virgamque dedit quâ quinquies in die susceptâ disciplinâ Dei
" misericordiam in se provocaret. Qui monita libenter audiens circumducto
" filo corpori suo martyri se devovit, emendationem vitæ promittens, timens-
" que sibi panniculos suos diripi in dextro humero calido ferro signum crucis
" impressit."

[1] Perhaps at the suggestion *annuente Fulcone*. It is difficult to understand why Fulco should require a bribe to consent to his enemy being sent to
the kind of ordeal which appears to have been regarded with most fear.

[2] "Damnationis suæ tristem excepit sententiam." This probably means
that the ordeal went against him. Can it mean that he shrank from the
ordeal and pleaded guilty? The whole passage implies that the ordeal of
water was more dreaded than that of fire, probably because it gave less opening for fraud.

[3] The chronicler obviously wishes to make the best of his hero at the
expense of the apparitor Fulco and the person robbed, but we have not their

because his guilt was considered to be obvious), is adjudged
to the ordeal of water. Hereupon he is either found guilty
or confesses his guilt, and is there and then blinded and
mutilated. When we remember that at the County Courts
or meetings held in this manner all sorts of financial and
military business was transacted, that it was in them
that [1] charters were read, and other proclamations made,
that in them, [2] the military orders of the sheriff were
published, and the obligations incident to military tenure
enforced, and finally, that in them, the local assessment and
collection of taxation took place, it is obvious that the
sheriffs who presided over them were at the head of the
two great branches of government, namely, the financial
and the judicial branch, and that if they had been altogether
independent of the king and his representatives, they would
have been petty kings, each in his own county.

In the reigns of the Conqueror and his sons they seem in
fact to have held some such position, as [3] there are many
instances in which the office of a justiciary of the King's
Court was united with that of the sheriff of a county.
This led to abuses both by way of oppression and corruption
which caused the [4] "Inquest of the Sheriffs" held in 1170
by the orders of Henry II. On that occasion all the sheriffs in
England were displaced and an inquiry was made into their conduct by a body of justices specially appointed for that purpose.
This however was only an isolated measure, and does not
appear to have changed the legal position of the sheriffs.

The judicial authority of the old county courts has been
so completely superseded by other tribunals that it is
difficult to form a clear notion of the manner in which it
was exercised, nor has the inquiry any practical importance.
It seems however that the court was held monthly for
general purposes, probably at the county town, and twice
a year under the name of the sheriffs' tourn or circuit
in every hundred of the county for criminal trials. It
also appears that by royal grants many districts such as

account of the matter, and if the prisoner really was innocent, it is not easy
to understand the extreme penitence ascribed to him.
[1] Stubbs, 576.   [2] Stubbs, ii. 212, 3.
[3] Stubbs, i. 192, 3.   [4] Stubbs, *Charters*, 147.

CHAP. IV. towns, manors, &c., were exempted from the tourn and
           provided with a tourn of their own called the leet, which
           was held not before the sheriff but before the lord of the
           franchise or his steward. Many of these leets are still in
           existence, and their proceedings perhaps give a better notion
           of the ancient criminal procedure than is to be got from books.
           I shall return to them in connection with that subject.

           The steps by which the criminal jurisdiction of the
           County Court became all but obsolete can still be traced
           with fair completeness. In the very earliest times the
           kings when they granted jurisdiction, reserved to themselves
           particular classes of cases. Such at least is the interpretation
           put by [1] Mr. Stubbs on a law of Cnut's. [2] "These are
           "the rights which the king enjoys over all men in Wessex
           "that is *mund-bryce* (breach of the king's peace or special
           "protection), and *ham-socn* (burglary), [3] *forstal* (premedi-
           "tated assault), *flymena-firth* (outlawry), and *fyrd-wite*
           "(fines for neglect of military duty), unless he will more
           "amply honour any one and concede to him this worship."
           Mr. Stubbs supposes these were the original "pleas of the
           "Crown." However this may be, it is certain that when
           Glanville wrote (in the days of Henry II.) the distinction
           between the pleas of the Crown and the pleas of the sheriff was
           well known. He states it at the beginning of his first book.

           [4] "Placitorum aliud est criminale, aliud civile. Item
           "placitorum criminalium aliud pertinet ad Coronam domini
           "Regis, aliud ad Vicecomites provinciarum." He then enu-
           merates the pleas of the Crown as treason, concealment of
           treasure trove, breach of the king's peace, homicide, arson,
           robbery, rape, crimen falsi, "Et si quæ alia sunt similia:
           "quæ scilicet crimina ultimo puniuntur supplicio aut mem-
           "brorum truncatione." The crime of theft (although punished
           by death or mutilation) belongs to the sheriffs, and to them
           also it appertains to take cognisance of frays (*medletis*) strokes
           and wounds "*pro defectu dominorum*" (I suppose this means
           where there is no franchise), "unless the accuser lays the
           "offence to be against the king's peace."

           ---

           [1] Stubbs, i. 187.   [2] Thorpe, i. 383 ; Cnut, *Secular Laws*, 12.
           [3] *Ante*, p. 56.   [4] Glanville, p. 1.

By the assize of Clarendon [1] it was provided that when CHAP. IV. any one was accused before the sheriff of being a "robator " vel murdrator vel latro vel receptor eorum" he should be sent to be finally disposed of before the justices or if the justices were not soon to come into the county, then the sheriffs were to send word to the nearest justice, and send the prisoners to such place as the justice should appoint.

The 12th article of the assize of Northampton [2] (A.D. 1176) also provides that a thief (*latro*) when taken is to be in the custody of the sheriff, or, in his absence, of the nearest *castellanus*, but the justices are to take assizes "de "latronibus iniquis et malefactoribus terræ" (art. 7). The language of the rest of the assize seems to imply that the justices were to try prisoners accused of all serious offences except "minutis furtis et roberiis quæ facta fuerunt tempore "guerræ sicut de equis et bobus et minoribus rebus." These provisions lay down no distinct proposition as to the powers of the sheriff, but they imply that the most important cases were reserved for the justices.

The 24th article of Magna Charta is as follows :—" Nul-" lus vicecomes constabularius coronatores vel alii ballivi " nostri teneant placita coronæ nostræ." What the "placita " coronæ" meant, in 1215, it is impossible to say precisely. They must, at least, have meant serious crimes, and this enactment cannot have had a less effect than that of depriving the Sheriff's Court of all criminal jurisdiction of importance. The sheriff's tourn, however, was not expressly abolished by Magna Charta. It was held for centuries; not for the sake of trying prisoners, but for the sake of taking indictments which were anciently presented before the sheriff in his tourn in the way in which an inquisition is now made before a coroner. A man can, as the law still stands, be put on his trial for murder or manslaughter on a coroner's inquisition. Long after the sheriffs had ceased to be judges they continued to be the presidents of a number of small local courts which could accuse though they could not try. Indeed, till justices of the peace were established, the sheriffs and coroners, and the grand juries at the courts of the justices, must have

[1] Stubbs, *Charters*, p. 143.   [2] *Ib.* 157.

CHAP. IV. discharged the duties of committing magistrates. Several traces of their proceedings in this respect are to be found in the Statute Book. Thus, by the Statute of Westminster 2nd, 13 Edw. 1, c. 13 (1285), it is enacted, that whereas sheriffs have frequently extorted money by imprisoning persons not lawfully indicted before them in their tourns on the pretence that they were so indicted, such indictments shall, for the future, be taken by lawful men, and by twelve, at least, who are to put their seals to the inquisition. By the statute 1 Edw. 3, st. 2, c. 17 (1330), it is provided that the indictments are to be in duplicate, " so that the indictments shall " not be embezzled as they have been in times past, and so " that one of the inquest may show the one part of the inden- " ture to the justices when they come to make deliverance."

In the course of the following century the jurisdiction of the sheriffs both as judges and as committing magistrates, having been practically altogether displaced by the Courts of the Justices of Assize and Quarter Sessions, and by the justices of the peace, the tourns became a mere engine of extortion. "[1] Inordinate and infinite indictments and presentments as well " of felony, trespasses, and offences as of other things," were taken before sheriffs and their subordinates "at their tourns, or " law days," which indictments were " oftentimes affirmed by " jurors having no conscience, and little goods, and often by " the said sheriff's menial servants and bailiffs." The persons indicted were then arrested and imprisoned, and " constrained " to make grievous fines and ransoms " to procure their liberty, and then the indictments were withdrawn. To remedy these evils the sheriffs and their bailiffs were forbidden to arrest any person on any such indictments or presentments, and were required to carry them before the next Court of Quarter Sessions.

From this time the sheriff's tourn became practically obsolete, as it could neither try nor accuse, and the only remnant of the ancient criminal jurisdiction of the County Court which still survived was to be found in the leet, already referred to.

I now pass to the courts by which the County Court was

[1] 1 Edw. 4, c. 2.

superseded, and which still continue to administer the CHAP. IV.
Criminal Justice of the country in all common cases. These
are the High Court of Justice, and especially the Queen's
Bench Division of it; the Courts of Assize; and the Courts
of Quarter Sessions.

THE QUEEN'S BENCH DIVISION OF THE HIGH COURT OF JUSTICE.

The kings of England had, from a period much earlier
than the Conquest, claimed and exercised the prerogative of
being the fountain of justice, and their courts had been the
centres in which all the most important of the national
affairs were transacted. In particular, in one way or another, the whole administration of justice was derived from
the royal authority. As has been shown above, the king
sat, or appointed special representatives to sit for him, in the
County Courts whenever he thought proper to do so, and in
granting judicial powers to particular courts or persons, he
made such reservations as to particular classes of cases as he
thought fit. [1] "In the later laws," says Mr. Stubbs, "the
" king specifies the pleas of criminal justice which he retains
" for his own administration and profit; such a list is given
" in the laws of Canute; breach of the king's protection,
" house-breaking, assault, neglect of the 'fyrd' (military
" service), and outlawry. These were the original pleas of
" the Crown, and were determined by the king's officers in
" the local courts."

Under the Norman kings the importance and influence of
the King's Court, the Curia Regis, was greatly increased. It
seems to have contained the germ of all the great institutions of our present system of government, though, as yet,
they were not distinguished from each other. In order to
form a distinct conception of the Curia Regis as it was under
the Norman and Angevin kings, we must bear in mind two
points in which it differed widely from more modern institutions known to us as courts, whether the word is applied
to courts of justice or courts held for purposes of State.

[1] Stubbs, *Charters*, 147.

CHAP. IV. The first point is that the Curia Regis was the great centre not only of business but of society. In an often quoted passage, the author of the *Saxon Chronicle* says of the Conqueror: [1]"Thrice he wore his crown each year, as oft as he " was in England. At Easter he bare it in Winchester, at " Pentecost at Westminster; at midwinter at Gloucester; and " there were with him all the rich men over all England, " archbishops and diocesan bishops, abbots and earls, thanes " and knights."

The following description of the Curia Regis is given by Madox, [2]who has collected from various sources nearly every notice which can be found of the Court and its proceedings :—

"At the King's Court, and more especially at some solemn " times of the year he held his great councils, and ordinarily " transacted such affairs as were of great importance or re-" quired pomp and solemnity according to the custom of the " times. There he was attended by his barons and knights " who were to accompany him in his wars and expeditions. " There coronations, marriages, and knighthoods of the king's " children, and solemnities of great festivals were celebrated. " There was placed the throne or sovereign ordinary court of " judicature, wherein justice was administered to the sub-" jects either by the king or his high justicier. There was " the conference of the nobility and prelates who used to be " near his royal person ; and there the affairs of the royal " revenue were managed by the king himself or (most usually) " by his justicier barons and prelates employed therein by his " command.

[1] p. 294. The following passage from an early chronicler gives a vivid picture of the social side of a Court:—"Henricus Rex Junior" (the son of Henry II.) "ad natale fuit a Bur Juxta Baiocum, et quia tunc primum tenebat " curiam in Normanniâ voluit ut magnifice festivitas celebraretur. Interfuerunt " episcopi, abbates, comites, barones, et multa multis largitus est. Et ut " appareat multitudo eorum qui interfuerunt, cum Willermus de Sancto " Johanne Normanniæ procurator et Willermus Filius Hermonis senescallus " Britanniæ qui venerat cum Gaufrido duce Britanniæ domino suo come-" derunt in quâdam camerâ, prohibuerunt ne quis miles comederet in eadem " camerâ, qui non vocaretur Willermus, et ejectis aliis de camerâ remanserunt " 117 milites qui omnes vocabantur Willermi exceptis plurimis aliis ejusdem " nominis qui comederunt in aulâ cum rege." (R. de Monte, 520.) See too Froissart's account of the Court of the Count of Foix in the third volume of the *Chronicles*.

[2] *Hist. Exch.* i. p. 1–153, chapters i. ii. iii. See also Stubbs, *Cons. Hist.* i. xi.

" This may serve for one view of the King's. Court. To
" vary the prospect, let us take a view of it another way. The
" realm of England was anciently deemed one great seigneury
" or dominion, of which the king was sovereign or chief lord ;
" having under him many barons or great lords, and many
" knights and military tenants, besides soccagers, burgesses,
" and others. In order to survey the court of this chief lord
" of the regnum, or terra Angliæ, we may consider him as
" residing in his palace and surrounded by his barons and
" officers of state. The baronage attending on his royal person
" made a considerable part of his court. They were his
" homagers. They held their baronies of him. He was
" their sovereign or chief lord, and they were his men as to
" life, limb, and earthly honour. They were called Pares or
" Peers, as they were peers or convassales of his court, peers
" to one another, and all of them liege-men to their chief lord
" the king. As peers they had an immediate relation to his
" court. In that respect they are styled his *fideles* and *fami-*
" *liares*, his liege-men and domestics, and *barones curiæ regis*.
" With them the king consulted in weighty affairs, and did
" many solemn acts in their presence and with their concur-
" rence. They or such of them as ordinarily attended in the
" King's Court, by his command were (together with some
" of the bishops and prelates) concerned in managing the
" affairs of the revenue and in distributing public justice in
" causes brought into the King's Court: and came in process
" of time to be called the *conciliarii* or *concilium regis*, the
" King's Council, and some of them held and executed the
" respective *ministeria*, or great affairs of the King's Court."
Another point which ought not to be forgotten in relation
to the King's Court is its migratory character. The early
kings of England were the greatest landowners in the country,
and besides their landed estates [1]they had rights over nearly
every important town in England, which could be exercised

---

[1] "In Hereford in the time of Edward the Confessor, for instance, when
" the king went to hunt, one person went from each house to the stand or
" station in the wood. Other tenants not having entire masures found three
" men to guard the King when he came into the city." " Six smiths made
" 120 nails from the King's iron." There were seven moneyers, and "when
" the King came to the city they were bound to coin as much of his silver
" into pence as he demanded."—Ellis's *Introduction to Domesday*, ii. 195.

CHAP. IV. only on the spot. They were continually travelling about from place to place, either to consume in kind part of their revenues, or to hunt or to fight. [1] Wherever they went the great officers of their court, and in particular the Chancellor with his clerks, and the various justices had to follow them. The pleas, so the phrase went, "followed the person of the " king," and the machinery of justice went with them.

Two remarkable illustrations of this feature in the old courts and of their consequences to suitors may be given. Sir Thomas Hardy has prepared from the Patent Rolls an ephemeris of King John's reign, from which it appears that between May 23 and the end of December, 1213, his movements were as follows :—May 23, Ewell; 26, Wingham; 28, Dover; 30, Wingham; June 3, Chilham; 5, Ospring; 6, Rochester; 10, Ospring; 11, Chilham; 13, Battle; 16, Porchester; 17, Bishopstoke; 21, Corfe; 25, Camford; 27, Beer Regis; 29, Corfe; 30, Bishopstoke. In July he was in Dorchester. In August, amongst other places, at Marlborough, Clarendon, Winchester, and Northampton. In September at Nottingham, Southwell, York, Darlington, Durham, Knaresborough and Pontefract. In October at Westminster Rochester, and Clarendon, and in the course of November and December at Oxford, Gloucester, Reading, Guildford, St. Albans, Waltham, and the Tower. On Christmas Day he was at Windsor. He was then at the Tower again, and on the 30th December again at Waltham.

The effect of this mode of life upon the suitors and the administration of justice is shown by the [2] history of the plea of Richard d'Anesty in the King's Court. It begins "These are the costs and charges which I, Richard de Anesty " bestowed in recovering the land of William my uncle," and it proceeds to enumerate the various journeys which he took to get writs, to get " days " given him by the king and the justices, and to keep the days so given. The history fills

---

[1] So late as the year 1300 it was enacted (28 Edw. 1, c. 5) that the Chancellor and the Justices of the King's Bench should " follow him so that he " may have at all times near unto him some sages of the law which he may be able " only to order all such matters as shall come unto the Court at all times " when need shall require." Indian magistrates and commissioners on tour in their districts and divisions are at times followed by pleas like the early English kings.   [2] Palgrave, *Commonwealth*, ii. ix.—xxvii.

nearly nineteen 4to pages. The litigation lasted more than
five years (1158-1163). It involved journeys by d'Anesty and
others to the following amongst other places, Normandy, Salis⊥
bury, Southampton, Ongar, Northampton, Southampton,
Winchester, Lambeth, Maidstone, Lambeth, Normandy,
Canterbury, Avinlarium (supposed by Sir F. Palgrave to
be Auvilar on the Garonne), Mortlake, Canterbury, London,
Stafford, Canterbury, Wingham, Rome, Westminster, Oxford,
Lincoln, Winchester, Westminster, Rumsey,[1] Rome, London,
Windsor, and at last Woodstock. The principal question
in d'Anesty's case was whether a marriage was void
by reason of a precontract. This was regarded as a
matter of ecclesiastical cognisance, and involved questions
in the spiritual courts and an appeal to Rome, but the
different steps in the case strongly illustrate the meaning
of "following" a plea. Here is a specimen of the narrative.
[2] " After I had fined with the King, my Lord Richard de
" Lucy by the king's precept gave me a day for pleading
" at London at mid-Lent; and there was then a Council; and
" I came there with my friends and my helpers; and because
" he could not attend to this plea on account of the king's
" business I tarried there for four days and there I spent fifty
" shillings. From thence he gave me a day on the clause of
" Easter, and then the King and my Lord Richard de Lucy
" were at Windsor; and at that day I came with my friends
" and helpers as many as I could have. . . And because my
" Lord Richard de Lucy could not attend to this plea on
" account of the plea of [3] Henry de Essex, the judgment was
" postponed until the King should come to Reading, and at
" Reading in like manner it was postponed from day to day
" until he should come to Wallingford. And from thence
" because my Lord Richard was going with the King to Wales,
" he removed my plea into the court of the Earl of Leicester
" at London; and there I came . . . . and because I could not

---

[1] The Pope had directed his first writ to the Bishop of Chichester and the
Abbot of Westminster, of which the King disapproved, requiring one directed
to himself. D'Anesty sent a messenger for it, "and in that journey the
" messenger spent fifty shillings."
[2] P. xxii.
[3] This is the trial of Henry de Essex for treason. It is referred to in Mr.
Carlyle's *Past and Present*.

" get on at all with my plea I sent to the Lord Richard in
" Wales to the end that he might order that my plea should
" not be delayed; and then by his writ he ordered Ogerus
" Dapifer and Ralph Brito that without delay they should
" do justice to me : and they gave me a day at London. I
" kept my day. . . . From thence my adversaries were sum-
" moned by the king's writ and also by the Lord Richard's
" writ that they should come before the king : and we came
" before the king at Woodstock and there we remained for
" eight days, and at length, thanks to our lord the king and
" by judgment of his court, my uncle's land was adjudged
" to me." The history concludes with an account of the money
which Anesty had to borrow from Jews for the expenses—
mostly travelling expenses—of his plea, usually at the rate
of a groat a week for the pound, which is nearly 87 per cent.
per annum.

The King's Court which led this wandering life, and which
at intervals brought together all the most powerful and
brilliant members of the community, had its standing officers
and organisation. It was divided into two great departments,
the Curia Regis and the Exchequer, which may be compared
to the different sides or departments of one court. In the
Curia Regis justice was administered, matters of state were
debated, and public ceremonials of all kinds were celebrated.
In the Exchequer were managed all affairs relating to the
revenue. [1]It seems to have been stationary, at least many
of its officers were stationary, and the treasure itself was kept
in one place. The Exchequer had an organisation of its own
which I need not describe. The two departments however
were intimately connected. All the great officers of the
Curia Regis had seats in the Exchequer and were described
as Barons of the Exchequer. Moreover the administration
of justice, particularly the functions of the Justices in Eyre,
not only contributed largely to the revenue by fines and
amercements but were the means by which some branches
of the revenue were collected. Hence the Curia Regis and
the Exchequer, though separate in name, and to some extent

---

[1] See the *Dialogus de Seaccario*, printed in Madox, vol. ii., and also in
Stubbs's *Select Charters*.

different in their functions may be considered as forming CHAP. IV.
collectively one great institution.

[1] The great officers who held the most conspicuous places
both in the Exchequer and in the Curia Regis were seven
in number, namely the Chief Justiciar, the Constable, the
Marshal, the High Steward, the Chamberlain, the Chancellor,
and the Treasurer. Besides them there were an indeterminate number of justices distinguished by no particular
title.

"The Chief Justiciar was the first and greatest officer
" of the King's Court." " When the king was beyond sea
" he governed the realm like a viceroy." "Next to the
" king he presided in the Curia Regis as chief judge both
" in criminal and civil causes." " He presided likewise in the
" King's Exchequer, having the superior care and guidance
" of the Royal Revenue."

This great office was held by [2] Odo of Bayeux and William
Fitz Osborne under the Conqueror, by [3] William Flambard
(for many years) under William Rufus, by Roger of Salisbury under Henry I., by Richard de Lucy under Stephen
and Henry II., and by Ranulf de Glanville also in Henry
II.'s time. The last of the Chief Justiciars was Hubert de
Burgh in the reign of Henry III.

In the Curia Regis the Norman kings exercised as
well in criminal as in civil cases, the original and appellate
jurisdiction which had been perhaps the greatest of the
prerogatives of their predecessors, and many trials of the
greatest importance took place in it. For instance,
[4] Waltheof was condemned to death at the court held at
Westminster by the Conqueror at Christmas 1074.

[5] In 1096 William Rufus held his court at Windsor.
" There Godfrey Bainard accused William de Ou, the king's
" kinsman, of treason and vanquished him in single combat ;
" whereupon the king commanded William de Ou to be
" blinded and otherwise mutilated, and his dapifer (one
" William by name) to be hanged; and there Euda, Count

---

[1] Madox, *Hist. Exch.* chap. ii. pp. 30—80.　　[2] *Ib.* p. 31.
[3] *Ib.* p. 32.　　[4] Stubbs, i. 371.
[5] Mad. i. 89, quoting Hoveden and Saxon Chronicle.

CHAP. IV.   " of Champagne, the king's son-in-law, and many others
"were deprived of their lands, and others were taken to
" London and there executed." [1]In the reign of Henry I.
the famous Robert Belesme was tried in the King's Court
upon no less than forty-five charges of outrages of various
kinds.

[2]In 1184 (30 Hen. 2) Gilbert de Plumtun Knight was
accused before the king by Glanville the high justiciary of a
rape, and, according to Hoveden, would have been hanged if
the king had not pitied him, suspecting Glanville's motives.

Other instances are to be seen in Madox of the exercise
of the jurisdiction of the Curia Regis. I will now proceed to trace the steps by which nearly all the most important of our existing courts of justice were derived from
it. The industry of Madox [3]has collected evidence that the
expression "Common Bench" or "Bank" is older than
the reign of King John, and it is highly probable that
some distribution of the business of the Curia Regis whereby
civil actions might be assigned to one division of the court
might take place during the reign of Henry II., when its business increased so much, and when the spirit of judicial and administrative reform was so active; but however this may be,
there is no doubt that a great and indeed decisive step in this
direction was made by the 17th Article of Magna Charta
in 1215, which is in these words, " Communia placita
" non sequantur curiam nostram sed teneantur in aliquo loco
" certo." The reasons of this enactment, and the evils which
it was intended to remedy are sufficiently illustrated by the
account already given of the plea of de Anesty and of the

---

[1] Mad. i. 93; Stubbs, i. 371. Robert de Belesme is one of the most prominent characters in the history of Ordericus Vitalis, and his career supplies
an excellent specimen of the sort of disorders which the royal power had at
that time to deal with.

[2] Eodem anno cum Gilbertus de Plumtun miles nobili prosapia ortus
ductus esset in vinculis usque Wigorniam et accusatus esset de raptu coram
Domino Rege a Ranulfo de Glanvilla Justiciario Angliæ, qui eum condem-
nare volebat, injusto judicio judicatus est suspendi in patibulo, &c. Rex
pietate commotus consilioque suorum præcepit sic (custoditum) eum manere
donec ipse aliud de eo fieri præcepisset. Sciebat enim quod per invidiam
fecerat hæc illi Ranulfus de Glanvilla, qui eum morti tradere volebat propter
uxorem suam, &c. Sic itaque miles ille a morte liberatus usque ad obitum
regis fuit incarceratus per R. de Glanvilla. Hoveden, quoted by Madox,
i. 20.

[3] *Hist. Exch.* vol. i. chap. xix. pp. 787—801.

travels of King John. This was the origin of the Court of CHAP. IV.
Common Pleas which from that day to this (1882) has been
held in Westminster Hall.[1]

The Court of Exchequer was always, as I have already
observed, to some extent separate from the rest of the Curia
Regis, and was also to some extent stationary. It gradually
became a separate court.

The Court of King's Bench represented so much of the ordinary jurisdiction of the Curia Regis as was not appropriated
to the Common Pleas and the Exchequer. It had no definite
known beginning as a separate institution, but the following
points in relation to it may be noticed. The name "Curia
Regis" begins, according to Madox, to cease to be used in the
Records after the enactment of Magna Charta, and the pleas
which would have been described as being held in the *Curia
Regis* are said to be held *coram ipso rege*. This form of
expression corresponds to the style which belonged to the
Judges of the Court of Queen's Bench down to its abolition,
"the Justices of our Lady the Queen assigned to hold pleas
"before the Queen herself." It also corresponds to the
singular [2] legal fiction which supposed the king to be in
some mystical way personally present in the Court of
Queen's Bench (it may be in all the superior courts) which
was the reason assigned for the extreme severity with which
contempts of such courts might be punished.

It is also to be observed that Hubert de Burgh, the famous
minister of Henry III., was the last person who held the
office of Chief or High Justiciar. The powers of the office

---

[1] Madox observes that even after Magna Charta there were some exceptions to the rule which it laid down, but these are of no practical importance.

[2] "However, it is certain that by the common law which continues to
"this day, striking in Westminster Hall, where the king is only present as
"represented by his judges and by their administration, distributing justice
"to his people, is more penal than any striking in another place in his actual
"presence; for the latter is not punished with the loss of hand unless some
"blood is drawn, nor even then with the loss of lands or goods; but if a
"person draw his sword on any judge in the presence of the Court of King's
"Bench, Chancery, Common Pleas, or Exchequer, or before the justices
"of assize, or oyer and terminer, whether he strike or not; or strike a juror,
"or any other person with or without a weapon, he shall lose his hand and
"his goods, and the profits of his lands during his life, and suffer perpetual
"imprisonment, if the indictment lay the offence as done *coram domino
"rege.*" . 1 Hawkins, p. 62 (edition of 1824), and see on this subject R. *v.*
Lord Thanet and others. 27 *State Trials*, 822.

CHAP. IV. indeed were so exorbitant that they were too great for a
subject, and it is a not improbable conjecture (though there
seems to be a complete absence of positive historical evidence
on the matter) that the offices of Lord Chief Justice of the
King's Bench, Lord Chief Justice of the Common Pleas,
and Lord Chief Baron of the Exchequer were instituted in
order to discharge the different duties which had formerly
belonged to the Chief Justiciar. The exact date at which
these changes were made is uncertain,[1] but the three courts
were distinguished from each other before the accession of
Edward I. The lists of the Chief Justices of the King's
Bench and the Common Pleas, go back to the beginning of the reign of that king. The lists of the Lord Chief
Barons to the middle of the reign of Edward II.

We have thus arrived at the Court of King's Bench.
From the reign of Edward I. to the year 1875 it continued
to be the Supreme Criminal Court of the Realm, with no
alterations in its powers or constitution of sufficient importance to be mentioned except that during the Commonwealth
it was called the Upper Bench.

In 1875 the Judicature Act of 1873 was brought into
operation, and the Courts of Common Law and of Equity,
all of which had been originally derived from the Curia
Regis, or the powers of one of its members, the Lord Chancellor, were reunited under the name of the High Court of
Judicature. The Court of Queen's Bench thereupon lost
its ancient title, which however survives in the name of
the Queen's Bench Division, and its Chief Justice became
the Lord Chief Justice of England, a title which almost
literally reproduces that which was borne by Lucy, Glanville,
and de Burgh. The High Court of Judicature, and more
particularly the Queen's Bench Division of that Court,
is thus the representative of the Curia Regis in its capacity
of a Court of Criminal Justice. It will be interesting to
enumerate shortly the particulars of the jurisdiction which
it thus inherits.

In the first place the Curia Regis had original jurisdiction
in all cases whatever. The same is the case with the High

---

[1] Stubbs, *Cons. Hist.* ii. 266-7.

Court of Judicature. There is no offence, from the most CHAP. IV.
serious to the most trivial, from high treason to a petty
assault, which the High Court is not competent to try.

In the second place the High Court has succeeded to what
I have described in general terms as the appellate jurisdiction of the Curia Regis. This jurisdiction is of two kinds.
The High Court may issue, hear, and determine (subject
to a further appeal to the House of Lords) writs of
error. A writ of error is an order for the production of the
record of proceedings before an inferior court founded upon an
allegation on the part of a person aggrieved, that the record
will show that the proceedings were erroneous, for which
reason they ought to be quashed. This proceeding in the
present day affords a mode of trying questions of law relative to procedure, but not questions as to the correctness of
the judge's direction to the jury or as to the admissibility of
evidence, or as to errors of fact committed by the jury.

In the third place the High Court may in its discretion
issue a writ of *certiorari*, by which it can direct any inferior
court to send to the High Court any indictment which may
be found before the inferior court, in order that it may be
tried either before the High Court or before a judge of the
High Court either in London or on the circuit. This power
is in some particular cases regulated by statute, but it is
perfectly general, and is in continual use in cases in which for
any reason a trial in the ordinary course appears likely to be
unsatisfactory.

The writ of error and the writ of certiorari are both as old
as the common law, and their very form and the nature of
their contents distinctly show that they are the stated established way of exercising that superintendence over inferior
courts, which, as I have pointed out, formed one of the most
important branches of the Royal Prerogative ages before the
Norman Conquest, and was exercised by the Curia Regis
after that event and down to the time of the institution
of the Court of King's Bench.

It is a curious question, though perhaps the solution would
not be worth the trouble necessary to arrive at it, how far, at
different periods of its history, the Court of King's Bench was

in practice as well as in theory a court for the trial of common criminal cases. Till the year 1872 the grand jury of Middlesex used to be summoned every term, but indictments were so very seldom preferred before them, that in that year an Act (35 & 36 Vic. c. 52) was passed providing that it should no longer be necessary to summon the grand jury unless the master of the Crown Office has notice of bills to be sent before them, in which case they may still be summoned. It has been usual to present such bills in cases of great public interest and importance only. The last instance of the kind which occurs to me was the prosecution of Governor Eyre, in 1866, for misdemeanour in sending Mr. Gordon for trial to Morant Bay, in Jamaica, in order that he might be tried before a Court-martial. Criminal cases are not very unfrequently removed by *certiorari* into the High Court, and tried at the sittings at Nisi Prius; but these are almost always misdemeanours partaking more or less of the character of private wrongs, as indictments for libel, conspiracy to defraud, or the like. Proof, however, still exists that in ancient times the criminal business of the Court was exceedingly important, and came from all parts of England. In the Second Appendix to the Third Report of the Deputy Keeper of the Public Records (Sir F. Palgrave) are a considerable number of calendars and records, showing the amount of criminal business done in the Court of King's Bench in various terms between 1477 (17 Edw. 4) and 1547 (37 Hen. 8). It appears from these that the Court was largely occupied at that time by trying all sorts of criminal cases arising in every part of the country. To give a few instances. In Trinity Term, 1477 (April 29 to June 20), sixteen writs of *certiorari* issued, to bring up for trial cases which had occurred in other parts of England. Of these four were murders from Stafford, Warwick, Nottingham, and London, respectively. There were five cases of robbery, two complicated with forcible entry; two forcible entries; a conspiracy; two thefts, and two assaults. In Easter Term, 1501 (16 Hen. 7), twelve cases were brought into court by *certiorari*, including cases of theft, burglary, riot, and forcible entry. It thus appears that the criminal trials held in the Court in those

days must have formed a considerable branch of its business. CHAP. IV.
Those trials which were held in the term were as they still are
called trials at Bar. Those which were held after term and put
in a list with civil causes were said to be tried at Nisi Prius.

[1] THE COURTS OF ASSIZE.

I come now to consider the history of the Courts of Assize.
These courts are not so much derived from, as of equal antiquity with the Curia Regis, and appear to me to be the
means by which the king exercised that concurrent jurisdiction with the County Courts which, as I have already
observed, formed one of the most important and ancient
branches of his prerogative. This concurrent jurisdiction
seems from the very first to have been exercised most
frequently not by calling the suitors to the King's Court,
but by sending representatives of the King's Court to
preside in the local tribunal. The king himself in very
ancient times, as appears from the instances already given,
sat on particular occasions in the County Court, but it
is natural to suppose that he would more frequently dele-
gate such a function to others. Sufficient evidence to show
that in fact he did so is still in existence. [2] Mr. Stubbs mentions many persons besides the chief Justiciars who acted
as "Justiciarii," during the reign of Henry I. and other instances are mentioned by Madox. [3] Thus:—" In the year
" 1124, the King (Henry I.) being in Normandy between St.
" Andrew and Christmas, Ralf Basset and the King's thanes
" held a council of the nobles at Hundhoge in Leicestershire
" and caused execution to be done on many malefactors."
The Pipe Roll of 1130 mentions (according to Mr. Stubbs) ten
justices of whom Ralph and another Basset were two. These,
however, are matters which need not detain us, as Bracton
in his third book gives an account of the office of the justiciar

---

[1] *Dig. Crim. Proc.* art. 23.
[2] Stubbs, *Cons. Hist.* ii. 388-9.
[3] Madox, i. 12. Quoting from Hoveden. " suspenderunt ibi tot fures quot
" antea nunquam scilicet in parvo temporis spatio omnino quatuor et
" quadraginta viros, sex item viros privarunt oculis et testiculis, admodum
" gravis fuit hic annus."

in the reign of Henry III. so full and precise as to render any other authority superfluous.

[1] He mentions as distinct the " Aula regia," and its " Justi-" tiarios capitales qui proprias causas regis terminant," and the " curiam et justitiarios in banco residentes," but upon the whole it appears from his work that whatever special titles they might have on particular occasions, the justices were a body of royal officers of uncertain, or at least, of unspecified number, who were capable of being and habitually were employed upon a great variety of different duties according to the commissions directed to them from time to time. After giving many different forms of writs he concludes thus : [2] " Et infiniti sunt casus et formæ infinitæ quibus con-" stituuntur justitiarii, secundum quod inferius videri poterit " in multis locis.   Sed hæc ad præsens sufficiant exempli " causâ." He gives many forms of the commissions which were issued to particular justices in particular cases.   The king, he says, [3] " Habet justitiarios itinerantes de comitatu " in comitatum quandoque ad omnia placita, quandoque ad " quædam specialia, sicut assisas novæ disseisinæ et mortis " antecessoris capiendas, et ad gaolas deliberandas, quandoque " ad unicam vel duas et non plures " (causas).   In [4] another place he says that the power of the justices depends on their commission, but that it is complete in regard to the whole of the cause or causes to which the commission extends down to judgment and execution.   Various forms of writs are given which invest the justice with a jurisdiction more or less extensive according to circumstances. [5] In one case the words are, " Ad itinerandum per comitatum talem, vel comitatus " tales A. de omnibus assisis et placitis tam coronæ nostræ " quam aliis."   In another the power is limited to the pleas, " quæ emerserint postquam justitiarii nostri ultimo itiner-" averunt in comitatu illo."   In some cases the commission would authorise a goal delivery, in others not.

---

[1] See Bracton, *De Legibus*, iii. (*De Actionibus*) vii. 2 (*De diversitate Justi-tiariorum*) vol. ii. pp. 160—207 in Sir H. Twiss's edition.   [2] P. 206.
[3] P. 160, and see p. 180, where this is repeated in substance.
[4] " Est autem eorum potestas quod ex quo lis commissa est causa una vel " plures licet simpliciter extenditur eorum jurisdictio ad omnia sine quibus " causa terminari non potest, quantum ad judicium et executionem judicii." —P. 182.   [5] P. 184.

It is, I think, commonly supposed that the Court of the Chap. IV.
Justices in Eyre, first brought into prominence by Henry II.
though not originally established by him, was a special institution differing in kind from the courts of the other
justices.[1] I think that this view is mistaken, and that
it has introduced an appearance of confusion and obscurity into what is really a simple matter. There was never
any standing institution, known as the Court of the
Justices in Eyre or the Court of the Justices of Gaol
Delivery. The difference lay in the commissions which
the king issued in different terms to the same persons
as occasion required. From the very earliest period of
English history the king exercised his prerogative of justice
locally by the agency of commissioners authorised to try
particular causes or classes of causes in particular places.
The cases to be tried and the local limits of the jurisdiction were determined by the terms of the commission.
These commissions were issued by the Conqueror and his
sons, and by Henry II. his sons and grandson to their
"justitiarii," just as they are issued by Her Majesty
in the present day to the Judges of the High Court of
Judicature. At the present day the judges act under
three commissions (Assize and Nisi Prius, Oyer and
Terminer, and Gaol Delivery) if Civil as well as Criminal
business is to be taken at the Assizes; under two only
(Oyer and Terminer and Gaol Delivery) if all criminal
business is to be taken; and under one only (Gaol
Delivery) if a particular gaol is to be delivered, but
prisoners on bail are not to be tried. In the days of
Henry I., Henry II., and Henry III., the authority of the
justice was limited by the extent of his commission in precisely the same manner. As to the eyre, every justice deputed
to a particular place was "in eyre," or as we should say,
"on circuit." No doubt there were justices who by way
of pre-eminence were described as the Justices in Eyre, and
there can also be no doubt that Henry II. first systematised

---

[1] See e.g. fourth *Institute*, ch. 27, 28, 30, 33, 34. There is a full history
of all matters connected with the Courts of Assize in the judgment of
Willes J., *ex parte* Fernandez, 10 C.B., N.S. 42-57.

CHAP. IV. these eyres, and divided the country into circuits each of which was allotted to one set of judges, and he may thus be described as the founder of the system of circuits. He was not, however, the founder of the system of the local administration of justice by Royal Commissioners appointed to take Assizes, to hear and determine pleas, and to deliver gaols. This system was probably as old as the doctrine that the king is the fountain of justice. That it was older than the establishment of the circuits is certain. The establishment of the circuits is usually dated from 1176, [1] when Henry II. divided the country into six parts and appointed eighteen itinerant justices for them, but [2] Madox quotes from the Exchequer Rolls a long series of the names of justices errant from 1170, of whom some were appointed " for pleas of the Crown or common pleas, and for imposing " and setting the assizes or tallages on the king's demeans," and others "for pleas of the Crown and common pleas" only. Moreover the language of the Assize of Clarendon (1166) implies that in all parts of England justices either came (no doubt on circuit and with commissions of gaol delivery or oyer and terminer), or were accessible at short intervals. After providing for the arrest of robbers and murderers, the Assize goes on to say, that when persons are arrested for robbery or murder, "if the justices are not to come soon " into the county in which the prisoners are in custody, the " sheriffs are to send to [3] the nearest justice by some intelligent " person to say that they have taken such prisoners, and the " justices are to send back to the sheriffs to say where they " wish the prisoners to be brought before them, and the " sheriffs shall bring them before the justices." This implies that even if it was not intended to send justices into any given county at a particular time, there would always be a justice in the neighbourhood, and this implies that at least ten years before the institution of regular circuits, the practice

---

[1] "Communi omnium concilio divisit regnum suum in sex partes ; per " quarum singulas tres justitiarios itinerantes constituit quorum nomina hæc " sunt, &c."—Hoveden, quoted in Madox, *Ex.* i. 18, and see 1 Stubbs, *Cons. Hist.* 602.

[2] i. 123-140.

[3] The words are *propinquiori justitiæ* (in the singular) in this phrase.

of issuing commissions for the local administration of criminal CHAP. IV
justice by the king's justices was common.

The great peculiarity of the circuits, established by Henry II.,
and continued for a great length of time after his death, was
the multiplicity of business imposed upon the justices.
They were not only to dispose of the civil and criminal litigation of their circuit, but to preside over many branches of
the king's revenue, and see to the enforcement and preservation of all his rights. This is clearly shown by the articles of
the general summons given in Bracton, whose[1] treatise "De
"Corona" may be regarded as the foundation to a considerable extent of English criminal law. [2]A general summons to
sheriffs of the counties on the circuit was issued, requiring
them to summon by good summoners all archbishops, bishops,
abbots, priors, counts, barons, knights, and freeholders of
their entire bailiwick, and of each vill four lawful men and
the reeve, and of each borough twelve lawful burgesses
"et omnes alios qui coram justitiariis itinerantibus venire
"solent et debent." In a word, the sheriff was to convene
the full county court for the transaction of all the business
committed to the justices. The first business done was the
criminal business, according to a mode of procedure which I
shall describe fully hereafter. After this, inquiry was to be
made as to the king's wards, as to marriages, advowsons,
escheats, serjeanties, purprestures (encroachments), measures,
wines, franchises, Christian usurers, the chattels of Jews
slain, coinage, outlaws, markets, new tolls, and a great many
other particulars relating to the revenue and other rights of
the king. [3]Their enumeration fills several pages of Bracton,
and I think the only adequate way of describing them is by
saying that their collective effect is to require the justices to
undertake a general review of the whole administration of
the country. The articles apparently were varied from time
to time and to suit particular circumstances.

[4]Thus Bracton gives the form of a summons, convening
a Court at Shipwey, before justices for the liberty of

[1] 2 Bracton, by Twiss, p. 234-581.
[2] See the form, 2 Bracton, 188.
[3] Pages 241-53 (half of them are an English translation by Sir T. Twiss).
[4] ii. 253.

CHAP. IV. the Cinque Ports. It authorises them to inquire, amongst
other things, "de navibus captis in guerra et traditis, per
" ¹ Wil. de Wroteham, et quis illas habeat vel quid de illis
" actum sit."

What further process was to be had upon the returns made
by the justices I am unable to say, as Bracton is silent on
the subject; but probably the records of the eyre would be
made up and forwarded to the exchequer, and form the basis,
or at all events part of the materials, for the strict account
which, as appears from the *Dialogus de scaccario*, the sheriff
of every county had to pass every year. This, however,
does not fall within my subject.

It is enough for me to point out that, on the circuits instituted by Henry II., and commonly distinguished as "eyres"
by way of pre-eminence, the administration of criminal
justice was treated, not as a thing by itself, but as one
part, perhaps the most prominent and important part, of the
general administration of the country, which was put to
a considerable extent under the superintendence of the
justices in eyre. Nor is this surprising when we consider
that fines, amercements, and forfeitures of all sorts were
items of great importance in the royal revenue. The rigorous
enforcement of all the proprietary and other profitable rights
of the Crown which the articles of eyre confided to the
justices was naturally associated with their duties as adminis-
trators of the criminal law, in which the king was deeply
interested, not only because it protected the life and property
of his subjects, but also because it contributed to his revenue.

The transition from the eyres, described by Bracton, to
the assize courts of our own days may still be traced. As
I have already shown, the commissions under which civil and
criminal justice was administered were distinct from the
articles of the eyre, and were probably much more ancient.
The eyres were converted into circuits, in our sense of the

---

¹ Sir T. Twiss says that he was a famous sea-captain and Keeper of the
King's ports, who died in the second or third year of Henry III. He had
been Archdeacon of Taunton in 1204, and was Keeper of the King's Galley
during the reign of King John. Sir T. Twiss supposes the writ to have
been the first issued to the barons of Hastings after the conclusion of the
general war at the commencement of Henry III.'s reign.

word, simply by confining the commissions issued to the
justices to those which are still issued (assize and nisi prius
for civil business, oyer and terminer and gaol delivery for
criminal business), and by dropping the financial and administrative matters contained in the articles of eyre. It would
be a waste of labour to attempt to ascertain precisely by
what steps this change was carried out, but the nature and
reasons of the process are obvious in themselves and have
left traces by which they are sufficiently explained.

It is obvious that such an inquiry as would be necessary to
execute fully the articles of eyre given in Bracton would be
cumbrous in the extreme, and would be burdensome to the
public in direct proportion to the degree in which it was
profitable for the Crown. So obvious was this that the eyres
became septennial early in the thirteenth century, and continued to be so throughout the reign of Henry III. and into that
of Edward I. In the Parliament Rolls a variety of references
to the subject occur, which prove that the holding of the
eyre was regarded as a great public burden. Edward III.
and Richard II. upon the petition of the Commons agreed to
suspend it on various occasions for a greater or less period.
The following references suffice to prove this:—In A.D. 1348
(22 Edw. 3), the Commons make it a condition of an aid
for the war in France that [1] " Eyres des justices en le meen
" temps, si bien des forestes come des communes Pleez et
" general enquerrez par tote la terre cesse." The petition
connected with this grant marks the distinction between
financial and judicial business. " Que nul Eyre des Forestes
" le roi ni de la roigne, ne de prince soit duraunt la guerre,
" ne autres Eyres, n'Enquerrez fors la justice de la pees en
" chescun pays de mesme le pays d'oyer et terminer come au
" drein parlement estoit priez." The petition is continued on
the same page. " Prie la commune que les commissions de
" generals Enquerrez et tous maners des Eyres des justices
" cessent de tut durant les trois aunz tan que l'eide a vous a
" ceste parlement grauntez soit levez." (Answer.) " Il
" semble eue conseil que tieux Enquerrez cessent en ecse du
" poeple s'il plest au roi, si sodeigne necessite ne surveigne."

[1] 2 *Rot. Par.* 200, *a.*

CHAP. IV. [1]In 1371 (45 Edw. 3), a petition was granted that the king would issue no commission. of eyre or trailbaston during the war, " fors qe en horrible cas." [2]There is a similar petition in 1377 (1 Rich. 2), that there may be no eyre nor trailbaston for the war, or for twenty years, but this was refused, [3]and another in 1382 (6 Rich. 2) which was granted for two years. The fullest and most instructive notice of the subject which I have found in the Parliament Rolls occurs in the [4]Parliament Roll of 1362 (36 Edw. 3). The Commons had asked for a general pardon of " all manner of articles " of eyre except pleas of land, quo warranto, treason, robbery, " and other felonies punishable by loss of life or member." The Council had said that they regarded the petition as prejudicial to the king, and the Commons thereupon explain that they did not wish the king to give up anything which would injure his Crown permanently, such as " escheats, " wardships, marriages, fees, advowsons, serjeanties, rents, " services, lordships," and many other matters, but that they wished him to pardon " trespasses, misprisions, negligences, " and ignorances " committed before the then parliament, and all " articles of eyre, the punishment of which would involve " fine or ransom or other money punishments, amercements " of counties and towns, and charges upon the heirs of " coroners, sheriffs, and other royal officers." [5]A general pardon, of all such articles of eyre was granted in 1397 (21 Rich. 2).

I have not taken the trouble to try to ascertain precisely the history of the gradual disuse of these commissions. In Coke's [6]fourth *Institute*, they are spoken of as things of the past, and in the first *Institute* it is said that [7] " as the power of the " justices of assize by many acts of parliament and other com- " missions increased, so these justices itinerant by little and " little vanished away." I think it much more probable that, as the king came to depend more and more upon parliamentary grants of money, and less and less on his land revenue and casual profits, the commissions of Oyer and Terminer, gaol

[1] 2 *Rot. Par.* 305, a.
[2] 3 *Rot. Par.* 24, *a*, and see pp. 90-96.
[3] *Ib.* 138, *b.*
[4] 2 *Rot. Par.* 272, *a*, *b.*
[5] 3 *Rot. Par.* 369.
[6] Fourth *Inst.* 184.
[7] *Co. Litt.* 514.

delivery, assize and *Nisi Prius* superseded the commissions CHAP. IV.
containing fiscal articles.

The history of the commissions of gaol delivery is as
follows : Their origin is matter of conjecture. They are
probably as ancient as the gaols [1] themselves, and as the
local administration of justice by royal officers. At all
events they are repeatedly mentioned by Bracton. The
systematic periodical issue of such commissions was, however, a consequence of the establishment of the periodical
issue of Commissions of Assize. The word "Assize" was
used in a great variety of senses. In some cases it meant a
law, as in the expressions "The Assize of Clarendon," "The
"Assize of Jerusalem." It also meant a jury, as in the
expression "The Great Assize," which is employed by
Glanville, and to which I shall have to return. It also
meant the form of action in which trial by a jury took place,
as in the expression, "The Assize of Novel Disseisin,"
"The Assize of Mort d'Ancestor." These actions, which
were mostly for the recovery of land or rights connected
with land formed the most important part of the litigation
of early times, and the first Commissions of Assize were
commissions for the trial of such actions. They formed an
independent part of the business of the justices in eyre, and
were to be held much more frequently. [2] It was provided by
the 18th Chapter of Magna Charta, that the king or in
his absence abroad his Chief Justiciar should send two
justices into every county four times a year to take assizes
of novel disseisin, mort d'ancestor, and darrein presentment.
This, says [3] Mr. Stubbs, was in the following year altered to
once a year. I am not aware of any enactment in very early
times as to the degree of frequency with which assizes were
to be held, but it was enacted by 13 Edw. 1, c. 30 (A.D.
1285), [4] that they should be held three times a year at most.
And in 1299, it was enacted by 27 Edw. 1, c. 3, that justices

---

[1] A gaol, properly speaking, is a cage. See 2 Palgrave's *Commonwealth*,
clxvi. The Assize of Clarendon (ch. vii.) provides for the making of gaols
where they do not exist, the wood being provided out of the royal forests.
See Stubbs's *Charters*, p. 144.
[2] Stubbs, *Charters*, 299. [3] *Ib.* 141.
[4] "Capiant assisas predictas et attinctas ad plus ter per annum."

CHAP. IV. appointed to take assizes should also "deliver the gaols of
—   " the shires as well within liberties as without of all manner
" of prisoners after the form of gaol deliveries of those
" shires beforetime used." This statute shows that commissions of gaol delivery were well known in 1299; and it
would secure their being issued as often as the Commissions
of Assize were issued according to the 13 Edw. 1, that is to
say, not more than three times a year.

The next statute relating to them is 2 Edw. 3, passed
in 1328, which provides that "good and discreet persons,
" others than of the places, if they may be found sufficient
' shall be assigned in all the shires of England to take
" assizes, juries, and certifications, and to deliver the gaols,
" and that the said justices shall take the assizes, juries, and
" certifications, and deliver the gaols at the least three times
" a year, and more often if need be."

From that time to the present commissions of gaol delivery
have regularly been issued, and form one of the authorities
under which the Judges of Assize now execute their office.

The commissions of Oyer and Terminer are found in existence at the same time as the commissions of gaol delivery,
though I am not prepared to cite, either from Glanville or
from Bracton, any instance in which the expression is used.

The first express mention of them with which I am acquainted is in the statute 13 Edw. 1, c. 29 (A.D. 1285), which
taken in connection with some subsequent authorities throws
considerable light on their nature. They were either general
or special. General when they were issued to commissioners
whose duty it was to hear and determine all matters of a
criminal nature within certain local limits, special when the
commission was confined to particular cases. Such special
commissions were frequently granted at the prayer of particular individuals. They differed from commissions of gaol
delivery principally in the circumstance that the commission
of Oyer and Terminer was "ad inquirendum, audiendum, et
" terminandum," whereas that of goal delivery is [1] "ad gaolam
" nostram castri nostri de C. de prisonibus in eâ existentibus
" hac vice deliberandam," the interpretation put upon which

[1] Fourth *Inst.* 161, 167.

was that justices of Oyer and Terminer could proceed only CHAP. IV.
upon indictments taken before themselves, whereas justices of
gaol delivery had to try every one found in the prison which
they were to deliver. On the other hand, a prisoner on bail
could not be tried before a justice of gaol delivery, because he
would not be in the gaol, whereas if he appeared before justices
of Oyer and Terminer he might be both indicted and tried.

These differences, however, seem so slight and technical
that I am inclined to think that the commission of Oyer and
Terminer must originally have been used rather for special
than for general purposes, and that it was granted in particular cases to particular persons who had been injured by
some special offence by an offender not arrested by the public
guardians of the peace. It would be natural to give a
general commission of this kind to justices of gaol delivery,
in order that any such cases not brought before them in their
other capacity of justices of gaol delivery might be disposed
of at the same time. In later times such cases were usually
dealt with by the Court of Star Chamber.

This is suggested both by the statute 13 Edw. 1, c. 29, and
by some later authorities. The words of the statute are " a
" writ of trespass, to hear and determine, from henceforth
" shall not be granted before any justices, except justices of
" either bench and justices in eyre, unless it be for an heinous
" trespass where it is necessary to provide speedy remedy, and
" our lord the king of his special grace hath thought it good to
" be granted." This of course implies that the practice had
previously been different. The exception made in the statute
left in existence if it did not introduce great abuses. This
appears from a petition in the Parliament Rolls of 1315
(thirty years after the statute.)

The petition says: [1] " Great evils and oppressions against
" law are done to many people by granting commissions of
" Oyer and Terminer more lightly and commonly than is
" proper against the common law. For when a great lord or
" powerful man wishes to injure another, he falsely accuses
" him of a trespass" (*il forge trespas vers luy*), " or maintains
" some one else on whom he " (his enemy) " has trespassed,

[1] 1 *Rot. Par.* 290, *a*.

" and purchases commissions of Oyer and Terminer to people
" favourable to himself and hostile to the other side, [1] who
" will be ready to do whatever he pleases, and will fix a day
" of which the other side will either receive no notice from
" the sheriff and his bailiffs (who are procured to take part
" in the fraud), or else such short notice that he cannot
" attend ; and so he is grievously amerced, namely £20, or
" 20 marcs, or £10, at the will of the plaintiff. [2] And then
" he has another day appointed him in some upland incon-
" venient village in which his adversary is so powerful that
" the defendant dares not go there for danger of his life, and
" can have no counsel for fear of the same power. And thus
" he is [3] fined three or four times the value of his chattels,
" that is to say, a common man, [4] £26 for a day, or 100 marcs,
" or £40, more or less according as the plaintiff is urgent "
(_postive_). " And if the defendant keeps his day, he will
" either receive bodily harm, or he will have to agree to do
" more than is in his power, [5] or a jury from distant parts will
" be procured which knows nothing of the trespass, by
" which the defendant will be convicted of the trespass,
" though he may not be guilty, and the damages taxed at the
" will of his adversary, that is to say, for a trespass for which
" [6] 20_d._ would be enough at £200, £400, sometimes 1,000
" marcs. And if the party convicted is caught " (_trapee_), " he
" will be imprisoned, and remain there till he has paid every
" penny, or till he agrees to sell his land; or till his friends
" pay, if he is ever to get out. And if he cannot be taken
" he will be put in exigent and exiled for ever " (by being
outlawed).

The answer to this petition is : " As for writs of Oyer and
" Terminer they shall for the future be granted only for
" enormous trespasses " (_pro enormis transgressionibus_) " ac-
" cording to the form of [7] the statute, and for this shall be
" assigned justices sworn discreet and not suspected."

---

[1] " Se dorront a faire tut ceo qil voet."
[2] " Et avera aultre jour en ville Duppelond ne mie convenable."
[3] " Mis as issues," fined for non-appearance and entered by the Sheriff on
the roll, which led to the issue of a writ of distringas. See 2 Madox, 234.
[4] xxvi. li.
[5] " Ou serra procure une jure d'estrange pays qui rien soit du trespas."
[6] " xx sontz." Perhaps shillings.   [7] _i.e._ 13 Edw. 1, c. 29.

This petition sets in a striking light the occasional individual character of the administration of justice even at so late a period as the reign of Edward II., and the great oppressions incidental in those days to trial by jury. It clearly shows that the septennial eyres and the more frequent commissions of gaol delivery did not provide sufficiently for the administration of criminal justice, especially as regarded offences which were regarded (to use the language of our own day) rather as torts than crimes.

The subject is so curious that it may be well to illustrate it further by a few specimens of the cases in which after the petition referred to private commissions of Oyer and Terminer were issued.

In the same Parliament in which the petition was presented [1] certain persons were appointed justices of Oyer and Terminer, as to " all complaints which any one wished to " make of prises, [2] carriages, and other trespasses done by " John de Segrave and his servants by reason of his custody " of the forest beyond Trent, and the castles of Nottingham " and Derby."

A similar commission [3] was issued at the same time to different persons with reference to the conduct of Gerard de Salveyn, as escheator beyond Trent and sheriff of Yorkshire.

In 1320 [4] (14 Edw. 2), Ralph de Draiton, the parson of the parish of Luffenham, asked for a commission of Oyer and Terminer, to inquire into the conduct of Robert de Veer, Simon de Draiton, and John de Clifton, who, he said, by the orders of Gilbert de Middleton, Archdeacon of Northampton, imprisoned him till he resigned his living, and took and carried away his goods and chattels, and cut out the tongue and pulled out the eyes of one Agnes de Aldenby, and he said that a commission had already been issued on the subject at York. The answer is that the petitioner must produce the former commission in the Chancery where he will be answered.

[5] In the year 1321 or 1322 Robert Power asks for a com-

---

[1] 1 *Rot. Par.* 325, *a.*
[2] Taking supplies and compelling people to carry.
[3] 1 *Rot. Par.* 325, *b.*   [4] *Ib.* 376, *a.*   [5] *Ib.* p. 410, *a.*

CHAP. IV. mission of Oyer and Terminer against various persons who, during the siege of Tickhill Castle, came to take him prisoner, and hold him to ransom, and destroyed a quantity of his property. The answer is "Adeat legem communem."

Various other instances are given in the Parliament Rolls.

The abuse complained of in the petition above quoted still continued, as appears from [1] a petition presented in 1328 (2 Edw. 3) complaining of the irregular and illegal conduct of one Robert de Scoresburgh, who was a Commissioner of Oyer and Terminer at Scarborough, on the writ of one Alisandr' de Berwiz. The petition was granted, and the result was the statute of 2 Edw. 3, c. 2, which enacts "that the "Oyers and Terminers shall not be granted but before jus-"tices of the one bench or the other, or the justices errants, "and that for great hurt or horrible trespass, and of the "king's special grace, after the form of the statute thereof "ordained in time of the said grandfather, and none "otherwise."

The result of this statute was that the criminal jurisdiction of the justices of assize and *Nisi Prius* was put on its present footing. They were to be commissioners of gaol delivery under 27 Edw. 1, and might be commissioners of Oyer and Terminer under 2 Edw. 3. The practice now is to issue both commissions to the judges on each circuit, though occasionally commissions of gaol delivery only are issued.

Besides the ordinary commission of Oyer and Terminer a commission which, according to Coke, was a species of Oyer and Terminer, and which bore the odd name of [2] Trailbaston, was issued under Edward I., and some of his successors. Its form is given in 1 *Rot. Par.* 218-9 (35 Edw. 1, A.D. 1306). It tells us nothing except that certain justices were to "en-"tendre les busoignes de traillebaston" on five circuits, including 38 counties. Certain articles are annexed to the commission, which look as if they were intended to define the duties of the justices. They read like a short abridgment of the articles of the eyre.

---

[1] 3 *Rot. Par.* 28, *b.*

[2] Sir Francis Palgrave says that the word refers rather to the crime than to the court. A "trailbaston" was a clubman, one who carried a bludgeon—the Indian "latthiar"—from "lathi" a club.

"Et qe vostre poyne aide et consail a tot vostre poair CHAP. IV.
" dorrez et mettrez as droitures le Roi et de la Corone garder
" meintenir sauver et repeler par la ou vous purroz sanz tort
" faire.   Et la ou vous saverez les choses de la Corone et le
" droitz ' le Roy concellez, ou a tort alienez, ou soustrez, qe
" ' vous le frez saver au Roi.   Et que la Corone arrestrez a
" ' votre poair et en loais manere.' "

The Commission says nothing of criminal jurisdiction, but
Coke asserts that the Commissioners possessed it, and instances
might be cited from the Parliament Rolls which support
this.   In 1347 [1](25 Edw. 3), the Commons petition that
" comunes Trailbastoneries ne courgent come autre foitz fut
" assentuz en Parlement; car eles furent tout a destruction
" et anientissement du Poeple et a moult petit ou nul amende-
" ment de la ley ou de la Pees ou punissement des felons
" ou tresspassours."

The commissions of Trailbaston are mentioned in most of
the passages already cited as to the remission of the eyres for
a longer or shorter time, and the two were probably more or
less closely connected.   Whatever their nature may have
been they have long since become obsolete, and inquiries into
their nature have only an antiquarian interest.   We have
thus arrived at the establishment of the second of the ordinary superior criminal courts, the courts of the Justices of
Assize.   They can hardly be said to have had any later history.   Some small variations in the number of the circuits,
and as to the places in which they were to be held, have
been made especially within the last few years, but the
circuits have altered but little, and the constitution of
the Courts has hardly altered at all since the reign of
Edward III.

THE COURTS OF QUARTER SESSIONS.

I now come to the history of the Courts of Quarter
Sessions for counties.   In order to explain their origin and
constitution it is necessary to refer shortly to the origin of

[1] 2 *Rot. Par.* 174.

CHAP. IV. the office of Justices of the Peace. [1] Keeping the peace
was one of the chief prerogatives of the Crown, and it was
exercised both by some of the great officers of the Crown
throughout England, and by sheriffs, coroners, and constables
in their various counties and smaller districts. [2]The judges
of the Court of King's Bench were, and the judges of the
High Court of Justice are, conservators of the peace all
over England, and though a judge in the present day seldom
if ever acts as a justice of the peace, it was customary for
them to do so for centuries. When the Supreme Courts were
first established in India, the judges were expressly made
justices of the peace, and they used to sit as such regularly.
Besides those who were conservators of the peace by virtue of
their offices, there were evidently others who were elected for
particular districts as coroners now are. At the beginning of
the reign of Edward III., and no doubt in order to enable him,
or rather his mother, Queen Isabel, and her advisers to keep
order and support their authority, it was enacted in 1327
(1 Edw. 3, c. 16) that "in every county good men and
"lawful which be no maintainers of evil or barretors in the
"country should be *assigned* to keep the peace." This put
an end to the election of conservators, and was the beginning
of the legislation relating to the officers who afterwards
became justices of the peace. At first their authority was
simply executive, being limited probably to suppressing disturbances and apprehending offenders, so that they were little
more than constables on a large scale. Three years afterwards,
in 1330, it was enacted (4 Edw. 3, c. 2) that there should be
three gaol deliveries in every year, and that at the time of the
assignment of the keeper of the peace "mention shall be made
"that such as shall be indicted or taken by the said keepers
"of the peace shall not be let to bail or mainprise by the
"sheriffs," and that the justices of gaol delivery should

---

[1] Lambard, *Eirenarcha*, pp. 3-22. Lambard is the foundation of Blackstone
(Book i. c. 9) and other writers. See also *Dig. Crim. Proc.* chap. v. arts.
28—36.
   [2] Lambard, fo. 13. As to judges acting as justices, see Campbell's *Chief
Justices*, iii. 11 (life of Holt) ; and see Spencer Cowper's case, in which Holt
took depositions, 13 *State Trials*, 1142. As to India, see 13 George 3,
c. 63, s. 38. In Sir William Jones's *Life*, mention is made of his holding
evening sittings as justice of the peace for Calcutta.

deliver the gaols of the persons indicted or taken by the keepers of the peace. The powers of the keepers of the peace at this time therefore extended to receiving indictments. In 1344 (18 Edw. 3, st. 2, ch. 2) it was enacted that " two or three of the best of reputation in the counties shall " be assigned keepers of the peace by the King's Commis- " sion, and at what time need shall be the same with others " wise and learned in the law shall be assigned by the " King's Commission to hear and determine felonies and " trespasses done against the peace in the same counties, " and to inflict punishment reasonably." This was the first act by which the Conservators of the Peace obtained judicial power. Apparently some of them were to be associated with the Commissioners of Oyer and Terminer and Gaol Delivery, but they were not themselves to form a complete court.

In [1] 1350 the Statute of Labourers required the justices to hold sessions four times a year to enforce that statute.

After a further interval of ten years, namely, in 1360, a statute was passed (34 Edw. 3, c. 1) which not only author-ised the keepers of the peace to arrest offenders, but gave them authority to " hear and determine at the King's suit " all manner of felonies and trespasses done in the same " county." Lambard conjectures that it was upon the passing of this statute that the Conservators of the Peace first ac-quired the higher title of Justices. He also says that some words in the beginning of the statute, " In every county in " England shall be assigned," &c., had the effect of providing a separate Commission for every county, a Commission for several counties having, at all events in earlier times, been given to particular persons. This statute is still the foundation of the jurisdiction of the Courts of Quarter Sessions for counties.

In 1388 a further statute was passed fixing the number of justices at six for every Commission of the Peace, besides the Justices of Assize. They were to keep their sessions four times a year for three days if need be. The statute adds that if a judge of either bench or a serjeant-at-law is in the Commission, he is not to be required to sit as the other Commissioners, the which be continually dwelling in

[1] 25 Edw. 3, st. 1, c. 7 ; and see 2 *Rot. Par.* 234.

the country, but that "they shall do it when they may best "attend." Several later statutes are to much the same effect, though they have been interpreted as removing the restriction as to the number of justices. They are 13 Rich. 2, st. 1, c. 7, 2 Hen. 5, st. 2, c. 1 and c. 4, which last statute again prescribes the dates at which the sessions are to be held.

Many statutes have been passed relating to various matters connected with justices of the peace, but the constitution of the [1]Court of Quarter Sessions has never been materially altered from its first establishment to the present day. The time at which it is to meet is now regulated by 11 Geo. 4, and 1 Will. 4, c. 70, s. 35.

The jurisdiction of the Court depends partly on statute and partly on the Commission issued under the earlier statutes, [2]the form of which was first settled in Michaelmas Term, 1590, by Lord Chief Justice Wray and the other judges, and which has been in use ever since, though some of its terms are sufficiently antiquated. [3]It provides that the justices are to "hear and determine all felonies, poisonings, enchant-"ments, sorceries, arts magic, trespasses, forestallings, re-"gratings, engrossing, and extortions, and all other crimes "and offences of which such justices may or ought lawfully "to inquire," subject to this caution, "that if a case of diffi-"culty shall arise they shall not proceed to give judgment "except in the presence of some justice of one of the benches "or of assize."

The jurisdiction of the Court of Quarter Sessions thus extended nominally to all felonies and indeed to all crimes except treason, subject only to the condition that in cases of difficulty a judge of the superior courts ought to be present.

All through the sixteenth century the Quarter Sessions did in fact sentence to death large numbers of people, who were executed upon their sentence. This appears from Mr. Hamilton's *History of the Quarter Sessions*, compiled from records at Exeter Castle; but they seem to have confined themselves principally to cases of theft and the like. As time went on their jurisdiction was in practice greatly narrowed, and

---

[1] *Dig. Crim. Proc.* p. 23, ch. vi.
[2] Lambard, p. 43 ; 2 Stephen's *Com.* 646.   [3] Chitty, 138.

Chitty, writing in 1826, says, "It is now the common practice Chap. IV "to try only petty larcenies and misdemeanours in this "court." It was not thought proper that they should deal with capital offences even when they were entitled to the benefit of clergy. It was a singular indirect effect of the old law as to capital punishment that it thus came to narrow and cripple the powers of the Court of Quarter Sessions. Their jurisdiction as regards crimes is now determined by [1] 5 & 6 Vic. c. 38, passed in 1842, soon after the law relating to the punishment of death had been reduced nearly, though not quite, to its present condition. This Act provides negatively that the Court shall not try prisoners accused of treason, murder, or any capital felony, or for any felony for which on a first conviction an offender may be sentenced to penal servitude for life, nor for any one of eighteen other specified offences, which include all the offences in relation to which legal or constitutional questions of importance are likely to arise. All offences except these they can try under the statute above referred to, and under the terms of their Commission.

The only point which remains to be noticed in connection with the Quarter Sessions for counties is the local limits of their jurisdiction. This depends upon the Commissions by which the justices are appointed, and which assign the limits within which they are to act. [2] There are in England and Wales the following Commissions:—

One for each county in England and Wales, except York and Lincoln 50
One for each Riding of the county of York . 3
One for each of the three parts (Lindsay, Holland, and Kesteven) of the county of Lincoln 3
One for each of the following Liberties:— Cawood, Cinque Ports, Ely, Haverfordwest, Peterborough, Ripon, St. Albans, Tower of London, Westminster 9
                                           ——
                                           65

---

[1] There have been one or two small variations by subsequent legislation.
[2] My friend, Mr. Godfrey Lushington, was so good as to obtain from the Home Office this information for me.

CHAP. IV.   There are also separate Commissions for each of the
[1] eighteen counties of cities and towns, and for many
municipal boroughs.

[2] BOROUGH QUARTER SESSIONS.

I now pass to the Borough Quarter Sessions, the history of
which is more complicated than that of the Quarter Sessions
for counties.

The history of the growth of towns in England has
been considered from a constitutional point of view by
[3] many writers of high authority. It is enough for my
present purpose to observe that from the time when Henry I.
granted its first existing charter to the City of London
down to our own days, charters of incorporation have been
granted to a great number of towns and cities. These
charters, from the earliest times, contained grants of courts
of various degrees of importance. The mayor and aldermen
were, in some cases, made magistrates *ex officio*, and authorised to hold Courts of Quarter Sessions; and these grants
were accompanied or not, as the case might be, by a clause
called the "non intromittant clause," which ousted the jurisdiction of the county magistrates. In some cases towns were
made counties of themselves. Such towns usually appointed
their own sheriffs. Occasionally particular officers were to
be put upon all commissions of Gaol Delivery and Oyer and
Terminer issued for such counties of towns. For instance
in London, by a series of charters from the days of Henry I.
downwards, the Lord Mayor, the Aldermen, and the Recorder,
were to be put into all commissions of Gaol Delivery for the
gaol of Newgate, and all commissions of Oyer and Terminer
for the City of London. In some cases there was no limitation
at all upon the extent of the town jurisdiction. They might

---

[1] Bristol, Canterbury, Chester, Coventry, Exeter, Gloucester, Lincoln,
Lichfield, Norwich, Worcester, and York, and the towns of Caermarthen,
Haverfordwest, Hull, Newcastle-on-Tyne, Nottingham, Poole, and Southamp-
ton (5 & 6 Will. 4, c. 79, s. 61, and see Schedule A).

[2] *Dig. Crim. Proc.* arts. 31, 38, 41.

[3] Hallam, *Middle Ages; Cons. Hist.;* Brady, *History of Boroughs;*
Stubbs, *Const. Hist.*

try all crimes and inflict any punishment up to death. In other cases they were confined within narrower limits. I am not aware of any case in which the grant ousted the concurrent jurisdiction of justices of Gaol Delivery or commissioners of Oyer and Terminer appointed for the county in which a corporate town not being a county of itself was situated, or in which it prevented the king from issuing such a Commission to his own justices to be executed within the limits of a county of a city or town corporate. In nearly every instance in which any such charter was granted, the corporation were authorised to appoint a judicial officer, generally a recorder, who held his office during good behaviour, and acted as judge in the criminal court, and usually in the civil court also, if there was one.

The counties of cities and towns, the boroughs, and the towns corporate continued to exercise the jurisdiction thus conferred upon them from the date of their respective charters and according to their tenor down to the year 1834. In that year a Commission was issued to inquire into their various constitutions. It made several reports, the first of which was printed in 1835. These reports give in minute detail an account of every charter known to have been granted to every town in England and Wales. They formed the basis upon which was founded the [1]Municipal Corporations Act (5 & 6 Will. 4, c. 76). The effect of this measure would hardly be apparent to any one who read it without reference to other matters, particularly to the reports of the Commissioners, but it was as follows :—

The Commissioners "found satisfactory reasons for believ-"ing that there were in England and Wales" in all 246 corporate towns. Of these 178 are mentioned in two schedules to the Act, and to them only the Act applies. The 178 do not include either the City of London on the one hand, or on the other 88 small places which had been incorporated at various times, but had declined in importance. Other towns of very great importance are also absent from the list (*e.g.*,

---

[1] On January 1, 1883, the Municipal Corporations Act of 1882 (45 & 46 Vic. c. 50) is to come into force. It repeals, re-enacts, and consolidates all the older Acts.

CHAP. IV. Manchester and Birmingham), because at the time when the
Act passed they were not incorporated. Manchester and
Birmingham, and a considerable number of others, have since
been incorporated, either under [1] 7 Will. 4, and 1 Vic. c. 78,
s. 49, or under 40 & 41 Vic. c. 69, by which the enactment
previously mentioned is repealed and re-enacted in a more
elaborate form, and to all boroughs so incorporated the provisions of the Municipal Corporations Act are, I believe,
extended.

The English towns may thus be classified as follows :—

1. London.

2. Eighty-eight small corporate towns not affected by the
Municipal Corporations Act.

3. The 178 towns to which the Municipal Corporations Act
applies.

4. The towns which have been incorporated since the
Municipal Corporations Act, but to which its provisions have
been extended.

Upon each of these classes separate observations arise :—

1. London is, by charter, a county of itself; and by
various charters, the Lord Mayor, the Recorder, and the
Aldermen, were entitled to be put upon all commissions
to deliver the gaol of Newgate, and all commissions of
Oyer and Terminer for the City of London. By what
precise authority they tried Middlesex prisoners also, I am
unable to say, and it is now of no importance, but, in fact,
they did try them. Under their charters they hold Quarter
Sessions both for the City of London and for the Borough of
Southwark.

[2] The provisions of the charters by which they sat as Commissioners of Oyer and Terminer and Gaol Delivery, are now
merged in the Central Criminal Court, which was established
by 4 & 5 Will. 4, c. 36. This Court consists of the Lord
Mayor for the time being, the Lord Chancellor, all the Judges
of the High Court, [3] the Judge of the Provincial Courts of

---

[1] In the preamble to 45 & 46 Vic. c. 50, it is stated that the act of 1835
applies to all the bodies constituted after it passed. Sec. 210 of the act of
1882 is now substituted for 40 & 41 Vic. c. 69.

[2] *Dig. Crim. Proc.* art. 25.

[3] I suppose this is the effect of the Judicature Act of 1873. Before that

Canterbury and York, the Aldermen of the City of London, the Recorder, the Common Serjeant and the Judge of the Sheriff's Court, and of every one who has held the office of Lord Chancellor, Lord Keeper, or a Judge of the High Court, and of such other persons as Her Majesty appoints. In practice, the judicial duties of the Court are discharged by the Judges of the Queen's Bench Division and the three judicial officers of the City.

A Commission of Oyer and Terminer as to all offences committed within the district of the Central Criminal Court and a Commission to deliver the gaol of Newgate issues from time to time to the persons above mentioned. The district over which the court has jurisdiction, includes the City of London, the County of Middlesex, and certain parts of the Counties of Kent, Essex, and Surrey. The Court has also Admiralty jurisdiction.

2. The small towns which were not affected by the Municipal Corporations Act are numerous, but in a large number of cases their jurisdiction has become obsolete. In some cases it extended, and still extends, theoretically, to the infliction of capital punishment. [1]Several small villages in Kent have charters by which they might, apparently, still try people for their lives, but as the county justices and the assizes had always concurrent jurisdiction, the power has been forgotten and has become, practically, obsolete. A considerable number of these small towns have either no criminal jurisdiction at all, or a very small one, and many have no recorders.

3. The 178 towns which are mentioned in the two schedules to the Municipal Corporations Act are divided into two

Act passed the judges of the Courts of Equity were not judges of the Central Criminal Court. The Judge of the Court of Admiralty and the Dean of the Arches were members of it. Under 37 & 38 Vic. c. 85, s. 85, the judge appointed under the Public Worship Regulation Act is *ex officio* Dean of the Arches.

[1] This seems to be the effect of s. 107, taken in connection with the interpretation of the word "Borough" in s. 142. By s. 107 it is enacted that after May 1, 1836, all jurisdiction to try treasons, capital felonies, and all other criminal jurisdictions whatever, granted or confirmed by any law, &c., or charter, &c., to any mayor, &c., "in any borough" shall cease. By s. 142 " 'borough' shall be construed to mean city, borough, port, cinque port, or "town corporate, named in one of the schedules (A and B)," *i.e.* the 178 places referred to.

CHAP. IV. classes. The first class (Schedule A) contains 128 towns, as to which it is enacted, that they are to have separate commissions of the peace. The second class (Schedule B) are to have separate commissions of the peace if the Crown is pleased, upon the petition of the Council thereof, to grant them.

[1] Every borough, whether in Schedule A or Schedule B which wished to have a separate Court of Quarter Sessions was to petition for one, stating what salary they were willing to pay their recorder, and the Crown was empowered to grant that a separate Court of Quarter Sessions should be thenceforward held in and for the borough. The right to appoint the recorder which had previously been vested in most cases in the Corporation was by this Act transferred to the Crown. [2] The recorder is to hold his court four times a year or oftener, if he thinks fit, or if the Crown thinks fit to direct him to do so; [3] and he is the sole judge of the court. In all cases in which a separate Court of Quarter Sessions is granted to a borough in either schedule, the jurisdiction of the county justices is excluded if the borough was exempt from their jurisdiction before the passing of the act. In scheduled boroughs in which a separate Court of Quarter Sessions was not granted before May 1, 1836, the county justices are to have concurrent jurisdiction, although there may be a separate commission of the peace.

It would not be worth while to ascertain the precise effect of these curiously qualified provisions, but by comparing the list of recorders given in the *Law List* with the list of 128 boroughs in Schedule A, it appears that eighty-five have recorders, and that forty-three have not. Of the fifty towns in Schedule B, forty-one have not, and nine have, recorders.

By s. 107, all the towns in both schedules which have not a separate Court of Quarter Sessions have lost all their criminal jurisdiction, and even if they have a

---

[1] s. 103. As to borough courts and recorders, see 45 & 46 Vic. c. 50, part viii. ss. 154-169.

[2] s. 105.

[3] s. 111. Even in cases where he used to be assessor only   See 7 Will. 4, and 1 Vic. c. 78, s. 34.

separate commission of the peace (which all the towns
in Schedule A have), the county justices have concurrent
jurisdiction.

No town in either schedule can have a separate Court of
Quarter Sessions unless it has both a separate commission of
the peace and a recorder, but the converse is not true. Many
towns have recorders which have no separate Court of Quarter
Sessions, and I think that some towns have both a recorder
and a separate commission of the peace, and yet no separate
Court of Quarter Sessions. In such cases the recorder's
office is merely honorary.

Upon the whole, I think it will be found that
about 85 of the 178 boroughs specified in the Municipal Corporations Act have separate Courts of Quarter
Sessions.

4. In the course of the forty-three years which have
passed since 1836, a considerable number of new charters
have been granted ; some to towns of the first importance,
as for instance to Manchester and Birmingham. In some
of these cases a separate Court of Quarter Sessions and a
separate Commission of the Peace has been granted, and in
others not.

The intricacy of all this, and the difficulty of spelling it
out from the acts of parliament and other authorities relating to the matter, is a good instance of some of the causes
which make our law obscure and repulsive. [1] No one could
understand the true nature and effect of the Municipal Corporations Act without acquiring a great deal of knowledge as
to which the act itself does not even contribute a suggestion ;
and even when that knowledge is acquired, the application of
it to the wandering arrangement and clumsy phraseology of
the act is a matter of much difficulty.

The jurisdiction of the Borough Quarter Sessions over
crimes is the same as that of the County Quarter
Sessions.

---

[1] Since this was in type, all the acts on the subject have been consolidated
by 45 & 46 Vic. c. 50, which is much better drawn and arranged, but a knowledge of the history of the subject is still necessary to understand it.

COURTS OF A SUMMARY JURISDICTION.

CHAP. IV. The last set of criminal courts still existing are the courts of a summary jurisdiction. Their history is short, but it is highly characteristic.

From the first institution of justices of the peace to our own times a number of statutes have been passed authorising sometimes one justice, and in other cases two, to inflict in a summary way penalties of different kinds upon a great variety of offenders. These penalties have in most cases consisted in the infliction of fines of a greater or less amount, and sometimes in imprisonment, and occasionally in setting the offender in the stocks. Most of the offences created by legislation of this sort have consisted in the violation of rules laid down for some administrative purpose, and so belong rather to administrative law than to criminal law as usually understood. The Statute of Labourers was the first act of the sort, and the Poor Laws supply another illustration. Sometimes, however, the offences subjected to summary punishment were offences properly so called—acts punished not in order to sanction any part of the executive government, but because they were regarded as mischievous in themselves. Nearly the oldest act of this sort still in force (though, I believe, it is practically obsolete) is 19 Geo. 2, c. 21 (1745-6), "An Act more effectually to prevent profane cursing and swearing." This act empowers and requires justices of the peace to fine profane swearers. If the offender does not pay, he may be sent to the house of correction with hard labour for ten days, or, if he is a common soldier or sailor, set in the stocks.

The next act, 19 Geo. 2, c. 27, supplies another illustration. It enables justices to inflict a penalty of £5 to 50s. on masters of ships who throw out ballast in such a way as to injure ports or navigable rivers. Many acts (which, I believe, have never been expressly repealed) punish workmen in various trades who dishonestly appropriate to themselves ("purloin" is a word frequently used) goods entrusted to them in their trade in a manner not amounting to theft at common law.

Speaking very generally, it may, I think, be said that the CHAP. IV.
general character of statutes giving summary jurisdiction to
magistrates was for a great length of time to enable them to
deal with matters of small importance, more particularly with
offences in the nature of trifling nuisances or disturbances of
good order, jurisdiction in cases of serious crime being reserved
for juries. Besides this, it was the common characteristic of
these acts to leave the subject of procedure unprovided for,
or provided for only in a very general and insufficient manner.
For instance, the 19 Geo. 2, c. 21, says nothing of the right
of the defendant to defend himself, or even to have the
evidence given in his hearing. Nor does it contain any
provision as to the way in which the defendant is to be
"caused to appear" before the magistrate, nor as to the
attendance of witnesses, or a variety of other matters essential
to the regular administration of justice. It was probably
considered best to leave all such questions to the discretion of
the justice. This vagueness led in course of time to a
variety of questions both as to the jurisdiction and as to the
procedure of the magistrates. These were raised upon writs of
certiorari, which issued from the Court of King's Bench, to
call up and quash convictions, and many convictions were
quashed accordingly. It became usual in consequence to put
into acts giving summary jurisdiction to magistrates [1] a clause
taking away the writ of certiorari, but new questions arose as
to the effect of such enactments and the cases to which they
applied. A variety of acts which need not be specifically
mentioned were passed which affected the procedure in such
cases, but the subject was at last comprehensively dealt with
by 11 & 12 Vic. c. 43, which, though open to various objections, may by a combination of study and practice be understood, and by this act, and others amending it, the procedure
before magistrates has been regulated since the year 1848.

The procedure was thus reduced to system before the
courts to which it applied were formally constituted as
courts. The magistrates acting under these statutes formed
in fact criminal courts, though they were not so described by
statute till very lately. But the extent of their jurisdiction

---

[1] *e.g.* 24 & 25 Vic. c. 97, s. 69, but innumerable examples might be given.

CHAP. IV. was increased by modern legislation and as a formal procedure was established they came to be invested with the name
of courts of summary jurisdiction. The following is the history
of the gradual introduction of the name and of the reasons
which led to its introduction.

In 1828 the Courts of Quarter Sessions were authorised
by [1] 6 Geo, 4, c. 43, to divide their counties into divisions
for holding special sessions.

In 1847 justices " in petty sessions assembled and in open
" court" were empowered to try offenders under fourteen
years of age for simple larceny. The expression "petty
" sessions" must at that time have been rather popular than
legal, as the preamble of 12 & 13 Vic. c. 18 (1849), recites that
" certain meetings of the justices called petty sessions of the
" peace are holden in and for certain divisions of the several
" counties of England and Wales called petty sessional
" divisions," and that important duties have lately been
assigned to the justices attending at such petty sessions. It
then goes on to enact that " every sitting and acting of
" justices of the peace or of a stipendiary magistrate shall
" be deemed a petty sessions of the peace, and the district in
" which the same shall be holden shall be deemed a petty
" sessional division." Enactments follow to the effect that
places shall be provided for holding such petty sessions out
of the county or borough rate.

The summary powers of magistrates in cases of serious crime
were considerably enlarged by several later acts. The first
of these was 18 & 19 Vic. c. 126, commonly known as the
Criminal Justice Act, 1855, which (as amended by 31 & 32
Vic. c. 116) gives justices summary jurisdiction over theft
and embezzlement of things of the value of less than five
shillings if the party accused consents, and power, if they
think fit to do so, to take a plea of guilty in cases where
the value of the property exceeds five shillings. This was
followed by the Criminal Law Consolidation Acts of 1861,
each of which (except the Forgery Act) contains many provisions conferring jurisdiction on justices in what would

[1] Amended by 6 & 7 Will. 4, c. 12.

commonly be described as criminal cases, such jurisdiction CHAP. IV.
being in some cases (as, for instance, in the case of an assault)
concurrent with that of the superior courts, and in other
cases supplementary to it.

Ten years later the Prevention of Crimes Act, 1871
[1] (34 & 35 Vic. c. 112), conferred upon justices many powers
in connection, amongst other things, with the system of police
supervision then established, and introduced (I am not sure
whether for the first time) the expression "Court of Sum-
"mary Jurisdiction," [2] defining it for the purposes of the act
only. It may have been used in some later acts, but however this may be, the courts of summary jurisdiction are
now regularly constituted and their jurisdiction is defined,
and their procedure prescribed by the Summary Jurisdiction
Act, 1879 (42 & 43 Vic. c. 49). [3] Under the provisions of
this act a "court of summary jurisdiction means any justice
"of the peace or other magistrate, by whatever name called,
"to whom jurisdiction is given by or who is or are authorised
"to act under the Summary Jurisdiction Acts, or any of
"such Acts." These acts are defined as being 11 & 12 Vic.
c. 43, the Summary Jurisdiction Act itself, and all acts past
or future amending either of them.

[4] The courts may try all children under twelve for any
offence except homicide, unless the parent or guardian
objects.

[5] They may try persons between twelve and sixteen, if
they consent, for larceny, and cognate offences, and adults, if
they consent, for a somewhat more restricted class of crimes.

[6] They may also receive a plea of guilty from an adult
for an offence for which a person between twelve and sixteen
might plead guilty.

The limit of their power of inflicting punishment is in
most cases three months' imprisonment and hard labour.
In the case of adults pleading guilty, it is six months' imprisonment and hard labour. In the case of children under

---

[1] This replaced a similar Act, 32 & 33 Vic. c. 69, the Habitual Criminals
Act, 1869.
[2] See s. 17. The definition is very elaborate.
[3] s. 50.   [4] s. 10 (1).   [5] s. 11 (1).   [6] s. 13.

CHAP. IV. twelve, one month's imprisonment, and in the case of boys
under sixteen and twelve, whipping to the extent of twelve
and six strokes of a birch respectively.

THE COURTS OF THE FRANCHISES.

I now pass to the courts of which the interest is only
historical. From the earliest period of English history, the
King claimed and exercised the right of granting jurisdiction
of greater or less extent to his subjects. It would be impossible in such a work as this to treat the subject of the extent
and nature of this branch of the prerogative fully, or to give
anything like a detailed history of the manner in which it
has in fact been used. It will be sufficient for my purpose
to refer to three principal classes of franchises; that is to say
(1) grants of courts to manors, castles, &c., and grants of courts
leet; (2) grants of Jura Regalia and Counties Palatine; and
(3) Forest Courts.

The way in which in the very earliest times property in
land was accompanied by jurisdiction is fully treated (amongst
other writers) by Sir Francis Palgrave and Mr. Stubbs, and I
will content myself with a reference to their writings on the
subject. Whatever may have been the precise nature and
origin of manors and manor courts, there can be no doubt
that they formed an important element in the judicial institutions of the country before and at the time of the formation of the common law. The following passage from Bracton gives a full account of the state of the franchise courts
in his time. " There are certain barons and others who have
" franchise, to wit, sock and sack, toll and team, infangenthef,
" and utfangenthef. They may judge in their court if any
" one is found within their liberty in actual possession
" of stolen goods; [1] that is to say (sicut), handhabend or
" bakbarend, and if he is pursued by the [2] saccabor " (the
person entitled to the goods), " for if he is not in actual
" possession of the goods, although he may be followed as a

---

[1] "Seysitus de aliquo latrocinio manifesto."   [2] 1 Stubbs, *Cons. Hist.*

" thief" (probably by hue and cry), "[1]it shall not pertain to CHAP. IV.
" the court (*i.e.* the franchise court), to take cognizance of
" such a theft, or to inquire by the country, whether the
" person not so possessed was guilty or not."

" Now infangenthef means a thief taken on the ground of
" another, [2]being one of his own men, and being in actual
" possession of the stolen property. Utfangenthef is a foreign
" thief coming from elsewhere from the land of another, and
" taken in the land of the lord of the franchise. But it does
" not follow that he (the lord) can bring back into his franchise
" his own man taken out of his franchise and there judge
" him by reason of such franchise. For a man must abide
" the law of the place where he offends. The lords of
" franchises may judge their own robbers and foreign
" robbers taken in their franchise. They can also take
" cognizance of medleys and assaults and woundings, unless
" felony or breach of the king's peace or the sheriff's is
" charged."

It so happens that we have the means of measuring with
accuracy the nature and extent of these franchises. The
troubles of the reign of Henry III. led to the assumption by
the nobility of all sorts of authority, and especially to the
exercise by them of an immense amount of criminal jurisdiction. Edward I., on his return from the crusade in the
second year of his reign, issued a commission to justices,
in the nature of justices in eyre, to inquire into the state
of the demesnes, the rights and revenues of the Crown,
the conduct of the sheriffs, and in particular into all franchises. The articles drawn up for their guidance are very
similar to those which were issued to the justices in eyre.
One of them which has special reference to franchises is thus

---

[1] "Non pertinebit ad curiam hundreda vel wapentakia cognoscere de
" hujusmodi furtis." I do not understand the words *hundreda vel wapentakia*. Sir Horace Twiss translates it "shall not pertain to the court, nor
" the hundred, nor the wapentake, to take cognizance," &c. This can
hardly be right, as it would imply that a thief within a franchise not taken
in possession of the goods would not be liable to be tried at all. Besides,
this does not seem to be the meaning of the words. Can it mean " it does
" not appertain to the court in the hundred or wapentake, *i.e.* acting as a
" hundred court, to take cognizance," &c. ?

[2] "De hominibus suis propriis," Sir H. Twiss translates "by his own
" men," which I think is not consistent with what follows.

CHAP. IV. worded, "Qui etiam alii a rege clamant habere retornum
" brevium et qui teneant placita de vetito namio, et qui cla-
" mant habere wreccum maris quo waranto et alias libertates
" regias ut furcas assisas panis et cerevisiæ et alia quæ ad
" coronam pertinent et quo tempore."

The commissioners went through every county in England,
and took inquisitions as to every hundred showing in detail,
in reference to each what franchises existed in it and under
what warrant they were claimed. Their returns are called
the Rotuli Hundredorum, and they furnish as complete and
authentic a picture of one part of English life in the years
1275–8, as Domesday Book affords of another about two
centuries earlier.

The returns made by the Commissioners were the occasion
of the [1] Statute of Gloucester, the effect of which was to
declare that all who claimed franchises must appear before
the king or the justices in eyre and prove their title to them,
and that if they failed to do so the franchises should be
seized into the king's hands. [2] This statute creates the writ
Quo Warranto, which still affords a remedy for excesses of
jurisdiction of whatever nature.

The Hundred Rolls deserve a far more careful examination
than could properly be given to them in this place, but I will
give a few illustrations of that part of their contents which
bears upon the history of the courts granted by charter. The
general impression which they convey is that the usur-

---

[1] 6 Edw. 1 (1278).

[2] The note made by Coke in his second *Institute* (p. 280) on the Statute of
Gloucester, quotes from Polydore Virgil a passage treating the Act as most
tyrannical. "The king wanting money," says Coke, paraphrasing his
authority, "there were some innovators in those days that persuaded the
" king that few or none of the nobility, clergy, or commonwealths that had
" franchises of the grants of the king's predecessors had right to them, for
" that they had no charter to them for the same, for that in troth most of
" their charters, either by length of time, or injury of wars and insurrections,
" or by casualty, were either consumed or lost : whereupon (as commonly
" new inventions have new ways) it was openly proclaimed that every man
" that held those liberties or other possessions by grant from any of the
" king's progenitors should before certain selected persons thereunto appointed
" show 'quo jure quove nomine illi retinerent,' &c. Whereupon many that
" had long continued in quiet possession were taken into the king's hands.
" Hereat the story says, 'Visum est omnibus edictum ejusmodi post homines
" 'natos longe asperrimum : qui fremitus hominum ? quam irati animi ?
" 'quanto in odio princeps esse repente cœpit.'" Perhaps if Coke had been
acquainted with the Hundred Rolls (which he does not mention) he would
have been of a different opinion.

pation of franchises had gone to an extraordinary length.
In every county there are numerous entries of "*habet furcas ;*"
"he has a gallows." Thus in Bedfordshire there were eight,
in Berkshire thirty-five, of which no less than twelve are
mentioned in the hundred of Newbury alone, nor were these
"*furcæ*" left idle, as the following entry (there are many
others) sufficiently shows : [1] "Hundr', de Toltyntre. The Arch-
" bishop of Canterbury has return of writ, wreck of the sea,
" gallows, assize of bread and beer, and pleas of wrongful dis-
" tress, they (the jurors) knew not by what warrant. Also Lord
" William de Monte Canis has a gallows at Swaneschamp in
" his barony, and there three thieves were hung, and the
" monks hospitallers took them to the monastery where one of
" them was found to be alive, and he stayed in that church as
" long as he pleased, and left it when he pleased, and is still
" alive. Also they say that nine years ago Adam Toxkemale
" was hung in the same place, on an oak, by the judgment of
" the court of Hertleye, and he was taken there by the suitors
" of the whole court, and they found the gallows fallen down
" and they will not put it up. The jurors knew not by what
" warrant."
    The following illustration of the same right is found in the
[2] Parliament Rolls. In 1290 (18 Edw. 1), "Bogo de Knowell
" the King's bailiff of Montgomery complains that whereas one
" of the King's men of Montgomery slew one of the men of
" the Bishop of Hereford and fled to the land of Edmund
" Mortimer of Wigmore,—Edmund though often asked by
" Bogo to give up the said felon to be tried in the King's
" Court tried him on the suit of the relations of the slain
" man in his own court at Wigmore, and hanged him to the
" injury of the franchise of the said castle of Montgomery."
Mortimer confessing the fact, the liberty of Wigmore was
adjudged to be forfeited, but the King allowed him to retain
it on condition " quod idem Edmundus in signum restitu-
" tionis libertatis Domini Regis prædictæ, reddat predicto
" Bogoni Ballivo Domini Regis, quandam formam hominis
" nomine et loco prædicti felonis. Et præceptum est eidem
" Ballivo quod formam illam admittat et loco prædicti

" felonis suspendere faciat, et suspens', quam diu poterit " pendere permittat," &c. Mortimer made difficulties about delivering the effigy, and his franchise was seized till he did so.

Innumerable entries in the Rolls show the nature of the franchise courts and the reason why they were so much valued. They were a regular source of income to the lord of the franchise, and were by him farmed out to bailiffs or stewards who made their profit by fines and amercements, which were often exorbitant and must always have been vexatious. The power to hold courts frequently, to require the attendance at them of all who owed suit and service, and to levy fines for every default must have been extremely liable to abuse. The effect of it was to establish in every liberty a person who was at once a common informer and a judge in his own cause. [1] In regard to the town of Pontefract for instance, the return is that the Earl of Lincoln and his bailiffs abuse their franchise by forcing the suitors to attend daily or weekly, and to [2] swear as often as they please, and if any one objects they imprison him and keep him imprisoned till he answers any sort of plea.

The bailiffs, moreover, had many ways of extorting money by the abuse of their power. [3] In the hundred of Tenterden the jurors present that one Hugo de Wey, who was probably bailiff or chief constable, "took of Josiah de " Smaldene 12d., for removing him from an assize. Also he " impounded the mare of Gunnilda de M'skesh'm by virtue of " his office, and would not give her up till he got half a marc, " which was not due to him. Also, by virtue of his office, he " took ten shillings from Henry Miller, falsely alleging that a " prisoner who had been attached in Tenterden hundred had, " by Miller's means escaped. Also he forced Joseph Askelin " of Emsiden, and William his son and his daughter to come " to the house of William de la Feld, in the same hundred, " and they came. And because they had been bound by " robbers in their own houses in the hundred of Ralwinden " and could not say by whom they were bound he took from

---

[1] 1 *Rot. Hund.* 119. [2] *i.e.* to serve on juries.
[3] 1 *Rot. Hund.* 217.

" them half a marc. Also Hugh took a marc unjustly from
" Henry Smith of Tenterden, because the said Henry threw out
" of his own close a linen gown and towels which a female
" neighbour of his hung there without his knowledge and on
" an unlawful (*falsa*) occasion. Also Hugo charged the said
" Henry, while he lay ill in bed, with being an usurer, whereby
" the said Henry promised the said Hugh twenty shillings and
" paid him, and paid forty shillings for the use (*ad opus*) of
" Lord William de Hevre, the then sheriff, that he might have
" an inquisition from seven hundreds to see whether he was a
" usurer or not, which inquisition acquitted him. And, by
" virtue of his office he (de Wey) took one Nicholas Mason of
" the parish of Lamberhurst on account of a quarrel which
" Mason's sister, Beatrix, had against him, to wit, that she had
" lent Nicholas £20 of her money which he would not pay
" her. And Hugh kept the body of the said Nicholas in the
" hundred of Tenterden till he unjustly received the aforesaid
" money and kept it for himself, and Beatrix has got, and
" can get, none of it," &c.

The hundred of Tenterden, which was in the king's hands,
paid the king, with seven other hundreds, £10 a year at Dover
Castle. De Wey's extortions came in [1] all to £27 4s. 4d. or
nearly three times as much as had to be paid to the king.

The Hundred Rolls supply various illustrations of the
spirit which these local jurisdictions fostered, one of which I
will quote. [2] In the wapentake of Stayncliff, in Yorkshire,
the return says : " Gilbertus de Clifton ballivus de Stayn-
" cliff" (which was in the hands of the Earl of Lincoln by
" grant from Henry III.), "verbis turpessimis (*sic*) insultavit
" Willielmum de Chatterton Justiciarium assignatum ad istas
" inquisitiones capiendas et minas intulit pro eo quod sug-
" gessit juratoribus patriæ quod non omittent veritatem dicere
" de ballivis comitis Lincolniæ propter aliquem timorem et
" dictus Gilbertus dixit ei quod si præsens fuisset ubi hæc
" verba predicasset ipsum traxisset per pedes, et adjecit quod
" ante dimidium annum noluisset inquisitiones istas fecisse
" pro totâ terrâ suâ.

---

[1] I have omitted several for the sake of brevity.
[2] 1 *Rot. Hund.* 111.

K 2

" Item cum Reginald Blanchard de Wadinton comparuisset
" coram duodecem juratores istius wapentakiæ ostensurus
" transgressiones sibi et aliis de patriâ per ballivos comitis
" Lincolniæ illatas, dictus Gilbertus hæc percipiens cepit
" averia sua ; et retinuit nec propter mandatum justiciari-
" orum ad inquisitiones illis partibus capiendas assignatos ea
" deliberare curavit, sed dixit quod si ipsi infra libertatem sui
" domini venissent corpora eorum et omnia bona sua arestasset
" nisi venisse se [1] ——— nomine comitis domini sui."

[2] The use made of these inquisitions seems to have been
that after the passing of the Statute of Gloucester, the inquisitions or copies of them were given to the justices on their
next eyre, and in every case in which the return "nesciunt
" quo warranto" appeared on the Hundred Roll, the person
in possession of the franchise was required to show his title,
and if he failed to do so was deprived of it.

These proceedings must have struck a. heavy blow at the
Franchise Courts, but it appears from the Parliament Rolls
that the practice of granting out hundreds to private persons
continued long afterwards. The effect of this was that the
fines and amercements of the Hundred Court went to the
grantee for his own use, subject to a fixed payment to the
king. The practice however was avowedly a bad one. In
[3] 1306 (35 Edw. 1), the following entry appears on the
Parliament Roll : " The king has said and commanded that
" after the grant which he has made to the Earl of Lincoln to
" have return of writs in two hundreds for his life, he will
" grant no such franchise to any one else as long as he lives,
" except his own children. And the king's will is that this be
" enrolled in the Chancery, the Wardrobe, and the Exchequer."

In 1328, by the Statute of Northampton (2 Edw. 3, c. 12),
it was enacted that hundreds and wapentakes let to farm
should be rejoined to the counties to which they belonged,
and not be so let in future.[4]

---

[1] There is here an abbreviation which I cannot read ; the word must mean
" proved," or the like.
[2] See Mr. Illingworth's introduction to the *Rotuli Hundredorum*.
[3] 1 *Rot. Par.* 111.
[4] In 1376 (50 Edw. 3) there occurs an entry on the Parliament Roll
which shows that this statute was not always observed, and which illustrates
in detail the effect of the grant of a hundred. 2 *Rot. Par.* 349.

The decline in the importance of the Hundred Courts, and the effect of the writ of *Quo Warranto* and of the Statute of Northampton, must have been to put an end to a large number of the Franchise Courts, though as I have already said, the courts leet, which are still attached to particular manors or other places, still remain as a vestige of them.

A minute inquiry into the history of all the Franchise Courts would, of course, be out of the question on this occasion, but I may refer shortly to a few of the most important of them which survived in name till very lately, though they had for a long time been practically absorbed into the general system.

The most important of these courts were the courts of the three Counties Palatine, Cheshire, Durham, and Lancashire.

According to [1] Coke the County Palatine of Chester being a County Palatine by prescription, was " the most ancient and " most honourable County Palatine remaining in England " in his time. It was originally granted by the Conqueror to his nephew Hugh Lupus, and came afterwards to be one of the honours of the Prince of Wales.

The County Palatine of Durham came next in antiquity. There are several records in the Parliament Rolls which set out its history and privileges at considerable length.

In the Rolls of Parliament, 21 & 22 Edw. 1 (A.D. 1292), there is a curious record of a presentment, made under the Statute of Gloucester, as to the privileges of the Bishop of Durham, from which it appears that the Bishop " solet per " ballivos suos obviare justic' itineratur' hic in adventu suo " infra com' istum apud Chylewell vel apud Fourstanes vel " apud Quakende brigge, videlicet per quam illarum partium " contingeret justic' venire. Et postea venire coram eis hic " apud Novum Castrum primo die itineris et tam in obviatione " justic' quam hic petere a præfatis justic' articulos coronæ " placitandos hic in itinere." It also appears, however, that the Bishop had " Cancellarium suum et per brevia sua et " justiciarios suos proprios placitat" in certain parts of the county. The later history of the County Palatine may be collected from a record in the Parliament Rolls, iv. 426—

---

[1] *4th Inst.* p. 211.

CHAP. IV. 31, 11 & 12 Hen. 6, A.D. 1433. In this record Durham is said to have been a County Palatine before the Conquest. The subject is also discussed at length in the preface to *Registrum Dunelmense,* published by order of the Master of the Rolls and edited by Sir T. D. Hardy. The County Palatine was vested in the Bishop of Durham in the year 1836, when by [1] 6 & 7 Will. 4, c. 19, the palatine jurisdiction of the Bishop of Durham was transferred to the Crown.

As to the County Palatine of Lancaster, Coke says :—" In " full parliament aº. 50 Edw. 3 (1376), the king erected " the county of Lancaster a County Palatine, and honoured " the Duke of Lancaster (John of Gaunt) therewith for term " of his life," and he quotes from the Patent Rolls a grant to that effect, saying that the Duke was to hold as freely as the Earl of Chester. The Duchy was held by Henry V. and Henry VI., and was the subject of a remarkable act, in 1 Edw. 4 (1461), [2] by which it is " ordeigned and stab- " lished " that certain lordships, &c., said to be forfeited " by " Henry late called King Henry the Sixt make and be " called the said ' Duchie of Lancaster Corporate ' and be " called the ' Duchy of Lancaster,' and that the County of " Lancaster be a County Palatine, with a real chancellor, " judges, and officers there for the same, and over that " another seal called the seal of the Duchy of Lancaster." The Duchy was by this act permanently annexed to the Crown.

Anciently [3] " the power and authority of those that had " Counties Palatine was king-like, for they might pardon " treasons, murders, felonies, and outlawries thereupon. They " might also make justices of eyre, justices of assize, of gaol " delivery, and of the peace. And all original and judicial " writs, and all manner of indictments of treason and felony " and the process thereupon were made in the name of the " person having such Counties Palatine. And in every writ " and indictment within any County Palatine it was supposed " to be *contra pacem* of him that had the County Palatine."

[1] See also 21 & 22 Vic. c. 45.　　　　　[2] 5 *Rot. Par.* 478.
　　　　　　　　[3] *4th Inst.* 204.

These powers were greatly diminished by the act 27 Hen. 8, c. 24 (A.D. 1535), which enacted that no one but the king should have power to make any justice of assize, of the peace, or of gaol delivery, in any County Palatine or other liberty, and that all writs and indictments should be in the king's name and laid as against the king's peace. It was, however, provided that commissions to the county of Lancaster should be under the king's usual seal of Criminal Courts of Lancaster. This put the Durham and Lancashire Assizes and Quarter Sessions on the same footing as those of the rest of the country, except that the Lancashire commissions were under a different seal. Chester had till 1830 a local Chief Justice and Second Justice, who, however, were appointed by the Crown. These offices were abolished, and it was enacted that Assizes should be held in Chester and in Wales, in the same way as in other places, by 11 Geo. 4, and 1 Will. 4, c. 70, ss. 14 and 20. Lastly, it was provided by the Judicature Act of 1873 (36 & 37 Vic. c. 66, s. 99), that "the " Counties Palatine of Lancaster and Durham shall respec- " tively cease to be Counties Palatine as regards the issue " of Commissions of Assize or other like commissions but no " further."

Thus all the greater Franchise Courts have by degrees been turned into Courts of Assize and Quarter Sessions like the rest.

THE FOREST COURTS.

The Courts of the Forests were at one time important, and their procedure was curious. A forest was one of the highest of royal franchises. It was thus defined by [1] Manwood: "A forest is a certain territory of woody " grounds and fruitful pastures, privileged for wild beasts " and fowls, fowls of forest chase and warren, to rest and " abide in the safe protection of the King." Within these territories the forest laws prevailed, and were administered by the Forest Courts. It must not be supposed that the forests were mere wildernesses, or that the soil was the king's property. On the contrary, the soil was private property, and

[1] *Forest Laws*, p. 40.

CHAP. IV. the population might be considerable, and these were the circumstances which made the forest laws so great a hardship as they undoubtedly were. The principal object of the forest laws was to subordinate within the forests all the rights of the proprietors to the exercise of the King's right of hunting. " The laws of the forest do restrain every man from cutting " down of his woods within his own freehold in the forest " is the general title of ch. viii. 2, of Manwood, and though this rule was subject to exceptions it must have acted most harshly; for instance, [1] an owner wishing to cut down a wood had to "repair to the Lord Chief Justice of the Forest and " show his honour what his request is," and get "a writ of " ad quod damnum " addressed to the Warden of the Forest, who was to summon a jury, who were to certify to the King in Chancery upon oath "these ten points following." Many other acts of ownership, e.g. [2] ploughing up ancient meadows amounted to waste, which was a forest offence. [3] An "assart" was worse than a waste. It was where a man cut down woods and tilled the ground. A [4] purpresture or encroachment was even worse than an assart, and many other offences might be committed,—by keeping dogs, by surcharging the forest, by poaching, or by unauthorised taking of various casual profits.

The system of courts by which these offences were dealt with was elaborate. The officers of the forest were the Verderers, elected like the Coroner in the County Court; the Regarders; the Foresters. The foresters resembled constables; the regarders were inspectors who from time to time visited the forest; and the verderers were the judges of the local courts and heads of the forest to which they were attached. Above all these was the Lord Chief Justice in Eyre of the Forests. There were three separate courts by which the forest law was enforced. Once in every forty days was held a court of attachment; three times a year a Court of Swanimote (the mote or meeting of the swains); and at uncertain intervals a Court of Justice Seat, presided over by the Lord Chief Justice in Eyre of the Forests. When an offence was committed and came to the knowledge of the

---

[1] *Forest Laws*, viii. 3.   [2] *Ib.* viii. 5.   [3] *Ib.* ix. 2.
[4] *Ib.* xi.

forester, it was his duty to attach the suspected offender,
i.e., to take steps to secure his appearance to answer for his
offence. [1] This might be done according to circumstances,
either by seizing " his cows, his horse, or any other goods
" that he had within the forest," or (if he was " taken with the
" manner " " trespassing in vert ") by attaching his body subject to the right of being bailed or mainprised, or if taken in
the manner in certain other cases, by attaching his body
without bail or mainprise, *i.e.*, by imprisoning him. At the
Court of Attachments all such attachments were presented
and enrolled under the direction of the verderers, and both
things and persons so attached might be replevied. [2] At the
Court of Swanimote, held three times a year, the verderers
were judges, and they and all the officers of the forest, and
four men and the reeve from every township in the forest, had
to attend and receive indictments for forest offences, especially
in respect of the persons attached by the foresters at the
Courts of Attachment. The Swanimote Court either convicted or acquitted as it seems on their local knowledge.
[3] Manwood says : " All the presentments of the foresters for
" any offence in the forest, either in vert or venison, are there
" delivered to the jury which are sworn for that purpose to
" inquire the truth of those matters ; and if the jury do find
" those presentments that the foresters have presented be true,
" then the offender against whom they are presented doth
" stand convicted thereof in law, and shall not per assisas
" forestæ traverse any such indictment."

The Court of Swanimote, however, could not give judgment.
This power was vested exclusively in the Court of Justice
Seat, which was held, when the King issued a commission
for that purpose, by an officer of great dignity, called the
Lord Chief Justice of the Forest in Eyre. The charges
given at the Swanimote and at the Court of Justice Seat [4] are
printed in Manwood, and enumerate all the offences which
could be committed, either against the forest laws by the
public, or by officers of the forest against the public.
They are most elaborate, the first containing forty-five, and

---

[1] *Forest Laws*, xxii. 5.   [2] *Ib.* xxiii. 2.
[3] *Ib.* xxiii. 6.   [4] *Ib.* xxiii. 7, and xxiv.

CHAP. IV the second eighty-four heads. The Court of Justice Seat
———   passed judgment on the offenders presented at the Court of
Attachments and convicted at the Court of Swanimote, and
from its decision there was no appeal. [1] "The Lord Chief
" Justice of the Forest hath an absolute authority appointed
" unto him to determine of offences that are committed and
" done within the King's Majesty's forests, either in vert or
" venison, and the same offences are to be determined before
" him, and not before any other justice." Of these courts
Blackstone says : "These Justices in Eyre were instituted by
" Henry II. A.D. 1184," "and their courts were formerly
" very regularly held; [2] but the last Court of Justice Seat of
" any note was that holden in the reign of Charles I. before
" the Earl of Holland ; the rigorous proceedings of which are
" reported by Sir William Jones. After the Restoration
" another was held, *pro formâ* only, before the Earl of
" Oxford, but since the era of the Revolution in 1688, the
" forest laws have fallen into total disuse, to the great ad-
" vantage of the subject."

THE WELSH COURTS.

So far I have considered the criminal courts of England.
The same system now prevails in Wales, but the Welsh courts
have a history of their own.

It consists of four stages. (1) The institutions of Edward I.
(2) The jurisdiction of the Lords Marchers. (3) The institutions of Henry VIII. (4) The changes made in the reign
of William IV.

Edward I., after the conquest of the greater part of Wales,
passed an act known as the *Statutum Walliæ* (12 Edw. 1,
1280), which is one of the most remarkable monuments still
remaining of the methods by which in that age justice was
administered. It may be described as a code of criminal and
revenue procedure prepared specially for Wales, and may be
compared to the codes prepared under the direction of Lord
Lawrence for the government of the Punjab on its annexation,

---

[1] Manwood, p. 489.
[2] On this, see Gardiner's *Fall of the Monarchy*, i. 71, and referring to personal government of Charles I., ii. 73, 76, 172, 182.

or to the regulations which having been already enacted for Lower Bengal were re-enacted for what are now known as the North-West Provinces upon their conquest in 1801. To borrow the language of Indian administration, the *Statutum Walliæ* converted a considerable part of Wales into a regulation province. It recites that Divine Providence has annexed and united the land of Wales, which had previously been subject to the King by feudal law, to the Crown of England as part of the body of the same. It also recites that Edward had inquired into the laws and customs of Wales, allowed some, amended others, and made some additions, and it then goes on to enact that they are to be held and observed in the manner under written.

The statute lays down a complete scheme of government setting forth first the divisions of the country, then the powers of the courts and officers, especially the sheriffs and coroners by whom it was to be governed, and then giving the forms of writs in all actions to be brought. This last enactment of course introduced into Wales the English Common Law of which the writs in question are the foundation.

The part of this memorable document which concerns the present purpose is that which relates to the organisation of the Courts. It provides as follows: "We provide and decree "that the justice of Snowdon (*Snaudon*) shall have the "custody and rule of our royal peace in Snowdon and our "adjacent lands of Wales, and shall administer justice to all "according to the royal original writs, laws and customs "under written."

"We also will and ordain that there be sheriffs, coroners "and bailiffs of [1] commotes in Snowdon and in our lands in "those parts." It then proceeds to provide that there shall be a sheriff for each of six counties, namely, Anglesea, Caernarvon, Merioneth, Flint, Caermarthen, and Cardigan.

The effect of this was to introduce a justice, sheriffs, coroners, and courts similar to those of England into the six counties above named. The remainder of Wales, which till the reign of Henry VIII. included Monmouthshire and

---

[1] The commote was a division like a hundred. It was a sub-division of a cantred.

part of the present counties of Shropshire, Hereford, and Gloucester, was then, and till the reign of Henry VIII., continued to be, divided into districts called "Lordships Marchers," which were subject to the authority of hereditary rulers called Lords Marchers. These Lords Marchers exercised what can hardly be described otherwise than as a despotic authority; though by 28 Edw. 3, c. 2 (1354) it was "accorded and es-"tablished that all the Lords of the Marches of Wales shall be "perpetually attending and annexed to the Crown of England, "as they and their ancestors have been at all times past, and "not to the principality of Wales, in whose hands soever the "principality be or hereafter shall be." [1] Lord Herbert of Cherbury in his history of Henry VIII. gives the following account of the Lordship Marchers : " As the Kings of England hereto-"fore had many times brought armies to conquer that country "(Wales), defended both by mountains and stout people, "without yet reducing them to a final and entire obedience, "so they resolved at last to give all that could be gained "there to those who would attempt it, whereupon many "valiant and able noblemen and gentlemen won much land "from the Welsh, which as gotten by force was by permission "of the kings then reigning held for divers ages in that "absolute manner as *Jura Regalia* were exercised in them by "the conquerors. Yet in those parts which were gotten at "the King's only charge (being not a few) a more regular "law was observed. Howsoever, the general government "was not only severe, but various in many parts; insomuch, "that in about some [2] 141 Lordships Marchers which were "now gotten many strange and discrepant customs were "practised." Lord Herbert's statement is no doubt true as to parts of South Wales, especially the counties of Pembroke and Glamorgan, but a large part of the Lordships Marchers must have been in the hands of native Welsh princes, who had never been conquered at all, but represented the original rulers of the country.

A full account of the jurisdiction of the Lords Marchers

---

[1] P. 369. When I was at the Bar I was once asked to advise upon certain claims of a gentleman of very ancient family, who believed himself to be the last Lord Marcher.

[2] In 27 Hen. 8, c. 26, 137 lordships are enumerated.

is to be found in [1] Coke's entries. In the precedents of
proceedings by way of *Quo warranto* he gives at length
the pleadings in a proceeding on a *Quo warranto* in the
42 Eliz. (1600) against Thomas Cornewall of Burford, in
Shropshire. The information alleges that Burford without
warrant uses in the manor of Stapleton and Lugharneys in
the county of Hereford, the franchise of taking the goods
and chattels of felons.

To this the defendant pleaded that before and up to
the statute of 27 Hen. 8, and from the time of legal
memory [2] Wales was governed by Welsh laws and Welsh
officers in all matters, whether relating to lands and tenements,
or to life and limb, and all matters and things whatever.
Also at the passing of the statute of 27 Hen. 8, divers
persons were seized of divers "several lordships, called in
" English Lordships Marchers in Wales, and held in them
"[3] royal laws and jurisdiction as well of life and limb as of
" lands and tenements and all other things, and they could
" pardon and had full and free power . . . of pardoning all
" treasons, felonies, and other offences whatever, and also
" to do and execute all things whatever within their separate
" lordships aforesaid, as freely and in as ample a manner and
" form as the King may in his aforesaid dominions; and that
" moreover the King ought not and could not interfere in
" any of the said Lordships belonging to any other person for
" the execution of justice." The plea further states that the
Lords Marchers were entitled to all forfeitures, goods of
felons, deodands, &c., according to the laws and customs of
Wales without any grant. It was further pleaded that up to
the date of the statute the King's writ did not run in the
Lordships Marchers. The plea then goes on to aver that
the manors in question were Lordships Marchers, to which
Cornewall and his ancestors had been entitled at the passing
of the statute 27 Hen. 8, c. 26, and that neither that

---

[1] Coke's *Entries*, 549-551, No. 9, *Quo Warranto*.

[2] "Dominium Walliæ ac omnia dominia . . . ejusdem fuerunt ordinat' et
" gubernat' per Wallicas leges . . . ac omnes Principes Walliæ inde seisiti
" existentes tenuerunt eadem secundum leges Wallicas, ac usi fuerunt in
" eisdem per seperales officiarios suos eorundem dominiorum leges Wallicas
" eorundem dominiorum et nullas Anglicanas leges," &c.

[3] "Regales leges et jurisdictiones."

CHAP. IV. statute, nor the statute of Philip and Mary, c. 15, deprived
—— him of the particular franchise in question, but confirmed it
to him. To this plea the Attorney-General demurred, thereby
admitting the truth of its averments. Shortly, the pleadings
came to this, that so much of Wales as had not been brought
under the *Statutum Walliæ* by Edward I. continued till the
27 Hen. 8 (1535) to be governed by a number of petty
chiefs called Lords Marchers—chiefs who might be compared
to the small Rajahs to whom much of the territory of the
Punjab and the North-West Provinces still belongs. [1]

In 1535 and 1543 two Acts were passed by Henry VIII.
(27 Hen. 8, c. 26, concerning the laws to be used in Wales,
and 34 & 35 Hen. 8, c. 26, an Act for certain ordinances in
the King's dominion and principality of Wales) which were
the complements of the Statutum Walliæ, and introduced
the English system for the administration of justice with
some slight modifications into every part of Wales. The
first of these Acts (27 Hen. 8, c. 26) abolishes (s. 1) all
legal distinctions between Welshmen and Englishmen, and
after reciting the disorders arising from the Lordships
Marchers enacts that some of the said Lordships shall be
annexed to adjacent English counties and others to adjacent
Welsh counties, and that the remainder shall be formed into
five new counties, namely, Brecon, Radnor, Montgomery,
Denbigh, and Monmouth, the first four of which are to be
Welsh counties and the last an English county. The Act
then proceeds to give the details of this arrangement (ss. 4–19
inclusive). It provides (s. 26) for a commission to divide
all Wales except Anglesea, Flint, and Carnarvon, into hundreds, and (s. 37) empowers the King to erect such Courts of
Justice in Wales as he thinks proper.

The second Act (34 & 35 Hen. 8, c. 26, A.D. 1543) com-

---

[1] There are a number of small states in the neighbourhood of Simla which
might well be compared to Lordships Marchers in point of size and importance,
though the government of India exercises much more careful supervision over
their proceedings, especially in the matter of the administration of justice, than
the English kings from Edward I. to Henry VIII. exercised over the Lordships
Marchers. See *Punjab Administration Report*, 1878-9, p. 29, and Mr. Lepel
Griffin's *Chiefs of the Punjab.* One of these petty chiefs, the Rajah of
Sirmur, sent 200 men to the war in Afghanistan, and many others offered
contributions in money, camels, &c.

pletes the provisions of the first. [1] It enacts (s. 2) that thenceforth there shall be twelve shires in Wales, whereof eight ([2] Glamorgan, Caermarthen, [2] Pembroke, Cardigan, Flint, Caernarvon, Anglesea, and Merioneth) are old, and four (Radnor, Brecknock, Montgomery, and Denbigh) were new, the latter having been formed out of such of the Lordships Marchers as were not annexed to other English or Welsh counties. The limitations of the Hundreds made under commission were confirmed (s. 4). It was enacted that there should be great sessions to be called "the King's Great Sessions in Wales," held twice a year in each of the twelve shires, as follows:—

The Justice of Chester . . . . . (s. 6).	$\left\{\begin{array}{l}\text{Denbigh.}\\ \text{Flint.}\\ \text{Montgomery.}\end{array}\right.$
[3] The Justices of North Wales . . (s. 7).	$\left\{\begin{array}{l}\text{Caernarvon.}\\ \text{Merioneth.}\\ \text{Anglesea.}\end{array}\right.$

[1] "And forasmuch as there are many and divers Lordships Marchers within " the said country or dominion of Wales lying between the shires of England, " and the shires of the said country and dominion of Wales, and being no " parcel of any other shires where the laws and due correction is used and had, " by reason whereof hath ensued and hath been practised, perpetrated, com- " mitted, and done manifold and divers detestable murders, burnings of " houses, robberies, thefts, trespasses, &c., &c., the offenders making their " refuge from Lordship to Lordship were and continued without punishment " or correction," &c. (s. 3.)

[2] These shires are not mentioned in the Statutum Walliæ. The county of Glamorgan is the most ancient county in Wales. One of the companions of William the Conqueror, Fitz Hamon, originally conquered the district and established there a Lordship Marcher which was a county in itself, containing eighteen castles and thirty-six and a half knights fees. He had his own Chancery and Exchequer in Cardiff Castle, and there were eleven other Lordships Marchers, each of which was a member of the county. As to Pembrokeshire William the Conqueror authorised Arnulf Montgomery, son of the Earl of Shrewsbury, to conquer what he could, and he conquered Pembroke and some of the neighbouring districts. "Neither he nor his " immediate successors appear to have held their possessions with such ample " powers as were exercised by the Lords Marcher for the King's writs issuing " out of the courts at Westminster were current in the conquered territory of " Pembroke." Parts of Pembroke (in particular Tenby and Haverfordwest) were colonised by Flemings under Henry I. In 1109 Gilbert de Clare, surnamed Strongbow, was created Earl of Pembroke by Henry I., and in 1138 he was invested with all the powers of a count palatine over the country from which he derived his title, so that Pembroke became a county palatine. Its character as such, however, seems to have been taken away by 27 Hen. 8, c. 26, s. 37, which added certain towns and districts to it. See Lewis's *Topographical Dictionary of Wales*, articles "Glamorgan" and "Pembroke," and as to Pembroke, 4th Inst. 22.

[3] These I suppose had replaced the "justice of Snowdon," mentioned in the *Statutum Walliæ*.

A person learned in the law of the realm of England to be appointed by the King to be Justice of these shires (s. 8).

$\left\{\begin{array}{l}\text{Radnor.}\\\text{Brecknock.}\\\text{Glamorgan.}\end{array}\right.$

Another such person . . . . . (s. 9).

$\left\{\begin{array}{l}\text{Caermarthen.}\\\text{Pembroke.}\\\text{Cardigan.}\end{array}\right.$

The jurisdiction of the Justices was to include all matters civil and criminal which were disposed of by the English Superior Courts (ss. 11-52), and there were in addition to be Courts of Quarter Sessions, held by Justices of the Peace, who were to be appointed in the same manner as in England (ss. 53-60), and Sheriff's tourns (s. 75) and other County and Hundred Courts as in England (s. 73). [1] By s. 119 the King received an unlimited power of legislation for Wales. This section, though afterwards alleged to have been personal to the King himself, whose successors are not mentioned in the Act, was repealed by 21 Jas. 1, c. 10, s. 4.

Of this statute [2] Barrington (himself a Welsh judge) observes that it was so well drawn " that no one clause of it " has ever occasioned a doubt or required an explanation," though Serjeant Runnington points out a few limitations upon this remark. At all events the Courts established by this statute continued to administer justice in Wales till the year 1830, when the Welsh Courts and Judges and the Palatine Jurisdiction of the County of Chester were abolished. An additional judge was added to each of the three superior Courts at Westminster, and it was provided that their jurisdiction should be extended to Wales and Chester, and that assizes should be held there in the same manner as in other parts of the country.[3]

---

[1] Compare the power vested by various Acts of the Government of India in the Governor-General, and even in some cases in Lieutenant-Governors, to declare what laws should be in force in particular non-regulation districts. The validity of such legislation has been doubted, but was affirmed in R. v. Burah L. R. 5 Ind. App. 178.

[2] See Hale's History of the *Common Law*, by Runnington (ed. 1779). p. 203, quoting Barrington's observations, 324-329.

[3] 11 Geo. 4, and 1 Will. 4, c. 70, ss. 1 and 2, and ss. 13-34.

CHAPTER V.

[1] THE CRIMINAL JURISDICTION OF PARLIAMENT AND OF THE
COURT OF THE LORD HIGH STEWARD.

HAVING described the history of the courts in which the CHAP. V. common routine of criminal justice is carried on, I come to the courts which are called into activity only on rare occasions and for special purposes. These are the High Court of Parliament and the Court of the Lord High Steward.

The criminal jurisdiction of Parliament is probably derived from the powers of the Curia Regis. Speaking of the reign of John Mr. Stubbs says, [2] "As a high court of justice they had " heard the complaints of the king against individuals, and " had accepted and ratified his judgments against high " offenders." Speaking of Henry III.'s time he says, [3] "Their " judicial power was abridged in practice by the strengthened " organisation of the royal courts, but it remained in full " force in reference to high offenders and causes between " great men ; the growth of the privileges of baronage gave " to the national council as an assembly of barons the " character of a court of peers for the trial and amercement " of their fellows."

The character of the judicial functions of Parliament in Edward I.'s reign may be gathered from the "Placita " coram ipso domino rege et concilio suo in Parliamento" printed in the first volume of the Parliament Rolls. It is not however my object to enter upon this subject further

---

[1] *Dig. Crim. Proc.* arts. 16-21.   [2] Stubbs, ii. 236, 237.   [3] Stubbs, ii. 37.

CHAP. V. than is necessary to trace the history of the present law as to impeachments.

That law may be stated as follows :—

1. The House of Lords is a court of justice in which peers may be tried for any offence, and commoners for any offence not being [1] treason or felony upon an accusation or impeachment (*impetitio*) by the House of Commons, which is the grand jury of the whole nation.

2. When such an impeachment is once made it is not abated either by a prorogation or by a dissolution of Parliament, but must go on from session to session and from parliament to parliament till it is determined.

3. A pardon by the Crown cannot be pleaded in bar of an impeachment.

This is the net result of a long process, the nature of which can be understood only by a study of the judicial proceedings of successive parliaments.

The earliest case to be referred to is one which perhaps hardly deserves the name of a parliamentary proceeding at all. This was the trial of David the brother of Llewellyn for treason against Edward I. The trial took place at Shrewsbury at a sort of parliament which met Sept. 30, 1283. [2] " The sheriff of each county was to return two elected " knights, and the governing bodies of twenty cities and " boroughs were to return two representatives for each " Eleven earls, ninety-nine barons, and nineteen other men " of note, judges, councillors, and constables of castles, were " summoned by special writ." " At Shrewsbury accordingly " David was tried, condemned, and executed ; his judges were " a body chosen from the justices of the Curia Regis under " John de Vaux : the assembled baronage watched the trial as " his peers, and the Commons must be supposed to have " given a moral weight to the proceedings."

A few years later, 21 & 22 Edw. 1 (A.D. 1291), a prosecution occurred which is recorded in the Parliament Rolls.

[3] The Archbishop of York was " coram ipso domino rege et

---

[1] There may be some doubt as to treason. See note in 8 *St. Tr.* 236, in FitzHarris's case.   [2] 1 Stubbs, 116.

[3] 1 *Rot. Par.* 120. The archbishop denied the purchase of the debt, but admitted that its existence came to his knowledge when he visited a monastery

" consilio suo arrenatus " for buying a debt due to a Jew who CHAP. V.
had been banished and whose debts had been forfeited to the
king.   In 33 Edw. 1 (A.D. 1304) Nicholas de Segrave was
accused in parliament by the king of having brought an
accusation against John Crumbwell whilst both were serving
in the army against the Scotch, of having waged battle
against Crumbwell, of having afterwards " adjourned " Crumbwell before the King of France, and of having gone to France
to prosecute Crumbwell leaving, for that purpose, the king's
army whilst still in danger and against the king's express
command,   thereby "subjiciens   et   submittens   dominium
" regis et regni Angliæ subjicioni domini regis Franciæ."
To this charge Segrave pleaded guilty, and the king
required the advice of parliament or rather of his great
Council ("volens habere avisamentum Comitum Baronum
"Magnatum et aliorum de Consilio suo") as to the punishment to be inflicted.   They replied, "quod hujus modi
" factum meretur pœnam amissionis vitæ,[1] &c."   Segrave
however was pardoned on the terms of giving security
to go to prison [2]"ubi et quando et quotiens dominus rex
"voluerit."

In 4 Edw. 3 (1350) a remarkable though anomalous
proceeding took place in regard to Sir Thomas Berkeley,
charged with the murder of Edward II.   [3] The record throws
light not only on the functions of parliament but on its
procedure and on the early form of trial by jury.   It is as
follows : "Sir Thomas de Berkeley came before the king in
" full parliament and being asked " (allocutus de hoc)

at Burlington, from which it was due, and that he told the prior and convent,
" Quod pecuniam illam sana conscientia retinere non possent, et quod sic
" facerent quod animas suas salvarent, sed quod nunquam eis injunxit quod
" pecuniam illam sibi aut alii nomine predicti Judei solverent."   He further
owned that he had seen the Jew at Paris, who begged him for God's sake to
get him his money.   The archbishop was amerced because he concealed the
existence of the debt, and because " contra fidem quam Regi tenetur injunxit
" præfato Priori et conventui quod animas suas salvarent ; quod tantum
" valuit.quantum si dixisset quod Judeo satisfacerent."   This seems to admit
that the proclamation which required the debtors of Jews to pay their debts
to the king could be obeyed only at some risk to the debtor's soul.
   [1] ‘The " &c." probably means forfeiture.
   [2] 1 Rot. Par. 172,   In the pleadings mention is made of " Nicholas de
" Warrewyk qui sequitur pro ipso domino rege," the style of the Attorney-
General of later times.   [3] 2 Rot. Par. 57.

CHAP. V. how he could acquit himself of the death of Edward II.
who had been delivered to his custody and to that of John
Maltravers, and had been murdered in the castle of
Berkeley? he said he did not consent to it or know of
it till this parliament. He was asked how he could excuse
himself, seeing that the castle was his, and the king was
delivered to him for safe custody? He replied that the
castle was his, and that the king was delivered to him
and Maltravers for safe custody, but that at the time of
the murder he was lying so ill at Bradley that he could
remember nothing (*quod nichil ei currebat memoriæ*). He
was then asked how he could excuse himself when he
had guards and officers under him? He replied that he
put under him guards and officers in whom he trusted
as he did in himself, and that they with Maltravers had
charge of the king, and that he was in no way guilty of
the death of the king or of being accessory to or procuring
it. Then follows, " et de hoc de bene et malo ponit se super
" patriam. Ideo venerunt inde jurat' coram domino rege
" in parliamento suo." Then follow the jurors' names, and
their finding, " Dicunt quod predictus Thomas de Berkle
" in nullo est culpabilis " . . . . " et dicunt quod tempore
" mortis ejusdem Domini Edwardi Regis patris domini Regis
" nunc fuit ipse tali infirmitate gravatus apud Bradeleye extra
" castrum suum predictum quod de vitâ ejus desperabatur.
" Ideo idem Thomas inde quietus."

The record implies, First that in this instance at least jurors
were introduced into parliament. Next that the accused
was questioned till a specific defence resting on a particular
alleged fact was set up by him; and lastly, that the jurors
gave their verdict on the special defence as well as generally
on his guilt or innocence.

. Towards the end of the reign of Edward III. in what was
known as the Good Parliament (50 Edw. 3, A.D. 1376) occurred a celebrated series of proceedings which are regarded
both by Hallam and by Mr. Stubbs as the earliest impeachment in the full sense of the word known in English
history. This is no doubt true if by an impeachment is
meant a trial by the Lords upon an accusation made by the

Commons, though, as the cases already referred to show, criminal proceedings in parliament were of much greater antiquity. The persons impeached were Richard Lyons, William Ellis of Yarmouth and John Peake of London (the agents and accomplices of Lyons) William Lord Latimer and John Lord Neville. [1]All of these were charged with different kinds of frauds and malpractices connected with the revenue. There is a petition in the Parliament Roll of this parliament which throws some light on the character of these proceedings and to some extent anticipates points long afterwards decided. [2] The Commons prayed that all articles of impeachment with the matters put forward by the Commons which had not then been tried for want of evidence (*par défaut de prove*) or any other cause should be heard and determined by commission by the judges and other lords in London and other suitable towns (*autres lieux busoignables*). The king promised to assign suitable justices.

[3] In the following parliament the result of one proceeding under this clause is recorded. A petition sets forth that Hugh Fastolf had " by malice and hatred of some of his " neighbours both by bills previously delivered and by clamour " made at the end of the last parliament" been impeached for various oppressions and misdeeds, that a commission of Oyer and Terminer had accordingly been sent to Suffolk and Norfolk " et les copies des ditz Billes issint baillez en " Parlement si furent envoiez a mesmes les justices souz " le grant seal." Fastolf was tried by no less than seventeen inquests and acquitted by all of them.

This shows that in Edward III.'s time the theory of impeachment as afterwards understood was far from complete. It never would have occurred to the parliament which impeached Warren Hastings that at the end of the session the case might be sent before a special commission and tried by a jury.

In the reign of Richard II., criminal proceedings in Parliament were frequent and important. Thus, in the

---

[1] 2 *Rot. Par.* 323—326, and 329.   [2] *Ib.* 385.
[3] 51 Edw. 3 (1376—7), 2 *Rot. Par.* 375.

CHAP. V. beginning of the reign [1] several persons were impeached for
losing towns and other military misconduct in France. [2] In
1386 Michael de la Pole, Lord Chancellor, was impeached
for misconduct in his office, and judgment was given that
certain grants made to him should be set aside, and charters
and letters patent declared void. There is nothing on the
face of any of these proceedings which calls for special
remark. The accusations are specific, and so are the
answers, which sometimes go into great detail; and it
appears that in particular cases witnesses were called and
fully examined.

The most remarkable instance of this is to be found in
the case of [3] Alice Perrers, who was accused on the part of
the King, and not, as far as appears, by the Commons, for
breaking an ordinance by which women in general and she
in particular had been forbidden to do business for hire and
by way of maintenance in the King's Court. The charge was
that she nevertheless had persuaded Edward III. to counter-
mand the appointment of Sir Nicholas Dagworth to go on
a certain commission to Ireland, and had persuaded him
to pardon Richard Lyons as to part of his punishment.
Dagworth was to go to Ireland to inquire into the official
conduct there of William of Windsor the husband of
Alice Perrers, and she objected to this on the ground that
Dagworth was Windsor's enemy. Many witnesses were
examined on the subject, one of whom said, " he never heard
" Dame Alice speak to the King on the subject, but he had
" heard her greatly complain in the King's palace and say
" that it was neither law nor reason that Dagworth, who was
" William de Windsor's enemy, should go to Ireland and in-
" quire and do justice against him." Twenty witnesses in
all were examined on the occasion, and the principal depositions are entered on the Roll.

[1] Case of John de Gomenys and William Weston, 3 *Rot. Par.* 10—12
(1377); Cressingham and Spykesworth, p. 153 (1383); Bishop of Norwich,
p. 153 (1383); Elmham and others, p. 156 (1383).
[2] 3 *Rot. Par.* 216—219.
[3] *Ib.* 12. " Alice Perrers fuist fait venir en mesme le Parlement devant les
" prelates et seigneurs pur y repondre sur certains choses quelles pur lors
" serroient surmises envers elle de par le Roi. Monsr. Richard le Scrop
" Chivaler seneschal de l'hostel n̄r̄e S̄r̄ le Roi y rehercea en Parlement," &c.

The most remarkable feature in the criminal .proceedings in parliament in the time of Richard II. is that it was the regular course for private persons, even persons who were not members of parliament, to bring accusations of a criminal nature in parliament, upon which proceedings were had. [1] Thus, for instance, in 1384, one John Cavendish, a fishmonger of London, impeached Michael de la Pole, the Chancellor, for taking a bribe, namely, £40, three yards of scarlet cloth, worth thirty-two shillings, given to Otter the Chancellor's clerk, and a quantity of herring, sturgeon, and other fish, delivered free at his house. The Chancellor swore that he was absolutely innocent, that whatever took place between Cavendish and Otter was without his knowledge, and that he ordered the fish to be paid for as soon as he heard they were delivered. After examining witnesses the Lords acquitted the Chancellor, and Cavendish was convicted of defamation.

[2] So, in 1381, Clyvedon brought a bill of appeal or accusation in Parliament against Cogan for a riot at Bridgewater, and for forcing the master of the Hospital of St. John there to pay money and execute deeds. The bill concludes by saying that if Cogan denies the charge Clyvedon is ready to prove it by his body according to the law of arms or as the court pleases, otherwise than by jury (*sinoun per verdit des jurrours*) " for he says, the said William (Cogan) is rich and " he poor, whereby he could never make a jury go against " the said William although his cause is as true as that God " is in heaven."

Cogan said he would put himself on a jury, and the parties were left to the course of the common law.

These cases throw some light on the memorable proceedings which took place in the later part of the reign of Richard II., and which appear not only to have caused his deposition, but to have established the law of impeachment on its present basis. I refer to the three sets of " appeals "

---

[1] 3 *Rot. Par.* 168. "Johan Cavendish de Londres pessoner soi pleignast " en le Parlement premerement devant la Coe en lour assemble en presence " d'aucuns Prelatz et Seignrs temporelx illocqoes lors estant et puis apres " devant tous les Prelatz et Seignrs esteantz en ce Parlement."
[2] *Ib.* 106.

CHAP. V. or accusations brought against each other by the ministers
of Richard II.

[1] The first set of appeals took place in 1387-8, when the
Duke of Gloucester (the King's uncle) and several other
"lords appellants" accused the Archbishop of York, Robert
de Vere Duke of Ireland, the Earl of Suffolk, Tressilian
Chief Justice, and Sir Nicholas Brember, Lord Mayor of
London of high treason. The substance of the charge
against them was that they had led Richard II. to misgovern
in various ways, and in particular that they had induced him
to resist or evade an act passed in 1386 which practically
put the Royal Power in commission, and that they had procured an opinion from five judges and a serjeant-at-law that
the commission so issued was void, and that those who procured it were liable to be punished as traitors. This was
elaborated into thirty-nine charges. [2] The king referred the
charges " to the judges, serjeants, and other sages of the law
" of the realm " (*i.e.* of the common law) " and also to the
" sages of the civil law, who were charged by the king
" to give their opinion to the Lords of Parliament, to
" proceed duly in the cause of the said appeal. The said
" judges, serjeants, and sages of the common law and also of
" the civil law took the matter into consideration, and avowed
" to the Lords of Parliament that they had seen and heard
" the tenor of the appeal, and that it was not made ac-
" cording to the requisitions of either law. Upon which the
" Lords of Parliament considered the matter, and with the
" assent of the king, and by their common assent, it was
" declared that in so high a crime as is alleged in this appeal
" which touches the person of our lord the king and the
" state of his whole realm, and which is said to be committed
" by peers of the realm and others, the cause must not be
" decided elsewhere than in parliament, nor by any other
" law than the law and course of parliament, and that it
" appertains to the Lords of Parliament and to their franchise

---

[1] 3 *Rot. Par.* 229—244.
[2] P. 236. This passage is quoted by Mr. Stubbs. I think he overlooks
the opposition between the common and the civil or Roman law. He seems
to take "civil " in the sense of ordinary law as opposed to parliamentary
privilege. I do not think this can be the meaning of the passage.

" and liberty by the ancient custom of parliament to be
" judges in such cases, and to adjudge them with the king's
" assent. And that so it shall be done in this case by award
" of parliament because this realm of England never was and
" it is not the intent of the king or the lords that it ever
" should be ruled or governed by the Civil Law. Moreover
" they do not mean to rule or govern so great a case as this
" appeal, which as aforesaid is not to be tried or determined
" out of parliament, by the course, process and order used in
" any inferior court or place in the realm, which courts and
" places are only to execute the ancient laws and customs of
" the realm and the ordinances and establishments of par-
" liament." The appeal was accordingly held good, and
fourteen out of the thirty-nine charges contained in it were
held to amount to treason. The appellees were convicted,
and some executed as traitors, and others banished for life
and deprived of their property. Other persons besides the
original appellees were implicated in the matter, and in
some cases condemned and executed, but this belongs rather
to the general history of the time than to the history of impeachments. [1] A sum of £20,000 was voted to the lords
appellants for their costs and charged on the subsidy granted
at the end of the session.

After an interval of ten years, the king's party in their
turn, appealed or accused of treason by " accroaching " the
royal power, the Duke of Gloucester, and the Earls of
Arundel and [2] Warwick. The Earl of Arundel was convicted and executed. The Duke of Gloucester was murdered
at Calais, and the Earl of Warwick was tried and sentenced
to be hung, drawn, and quartered, though his sentence was
changed into one of imprisonment for life in the Isle of Man.
The principal point urged against him was, that on the
trial of Sir Simon Burley and others, who were appealed
by the original Lords Appellants, " Warwick with others,

---

[1] 3 *Rot. Par.* 245. " Vint mille livers de meme le subside, pur lour
" custages, travails et despenses faites a devant pur l'onour profit, et salvation
" de Roi et de tout le roialme." The costs were principally military, as the
Lords Appellant had raised troops to support their cause. See Stubbs, *Cons.
Hist.* ii. 476—482, 494—497, and iii. 19, 20, on the transactions here referred
to.   [2] *Ib.* 377.

CHAP. V.   "made the king come to a secret place at Westminster,"
and there forced him against his own judgment to say that
Burley was guilty, though he thought, and had previously
said, he was not. This looks as if on these trials, at all
events, the king personally acted as one of the judges.

In the course of another two years, Richard was deposed,
and in the first parliament of Henry IV. (1399), the second
set of appellants [1] were impeached by the Commons for
their appeal. They were accordingly questioned about the
appeals, and gave answers which threw light on the nature
of the proceeding. They all said that they acted under
compulsion, and one of them (the Earl of Gloucester)
gave a lively account of his conduct. He said that, "on
" St. Oswald's day, as the late king sat at meat in the great
" hall of Nottingham Castle, and he, the Earl, also sat at
" meat at a side table in the same hall, the late king sent
" him a message to get up and come to him. Thereupon the
" Earl went to his room in the keep of the said castle, and
" put on a habergeon and his sword, and took with him
" about six men (vadletz), supposing he would have to arrest
" some one; and when he came outside the gate, he found
" there the other appellants, and amongst them William Le
" Scrop, reading the bill of appeal, the greater part of which
" was read before he came, and just then the late king sent
" to tell them to come on, and asked why they waited so
" long. And thus came the name of the Earl of Gloucester
" to be put into the appeal, but he heard nothing of it from
" any person; but for fear of death, he durst not oppose the
" orders of the late king as to the prosecution of the appeal."

Sir William Thyrning, the Lord Chief Justice, made a
speech which is entered [2] in the Parliament Rolls, to the
effect that the proceedings of the appellants had been so
irregular, that the common law had made no provision
for them, and that their misdoings must accordingly be

---

[1] 3 *Rot. Par.* 449. "Les Communes du Parlement monstrerent au
" Roy," &c.

[2] *Ib.* 451. It is in English, and is a curious specimen of the transition
state of the language. "The Lords . . . deme and ajuggen and decreen
" that the Dukes of Aumarle, Surr, and Excestre, that bene here present
" lese and forgo fro hem and her heirs," &c.

dealt with specially by the king in parliament. He then declared the judgment of parliament to be, that they should be degraded from their rank, and incur other forfeitures. These proceedings took place on the 6th October, 1399. [1] On the 3rd November, [2] the Commons by a petition, " showed to the king, that judgments in parliament belong " only to the king, and the Lords, and not to the Commons " unless the king, of his special grace, pleases to show them " the judgment," (this they said) " for their ease, that no " record should be made in parliament against the Commons, " that they are or shall be parties to any judgments given, " or to be given afterwards in parliament. To which it " was answered by the Archbishop of Canterbury by com- " mand of the king, that the Commons are petitioners and " demanders " (plaintiffs or accusers), " and that the king " and the Lords from all time have had, and still have by " right judgment in parliament as the Commons have shown. " But in making statutes, and granting aids and subsidies " and such things for the common profit of the realm, the " king's special will is to have their advice and consent ; " and this order is to be observed for all time to come."

In the same parliament was passed, [3] the statute 1 Hen. 4, c. 14, which provides, that all appeals of things done in the realm, shall be tried and determined by the laws of the realm (*i.e.*, at common law), that all appeals of things done out of the realm, shall be tried by the constable and marshal, and " that no appeals be from henceforth made, or " anywise pursued in parliament in any time to come."

I have noticed these proceedings in detail because they throw light upon the manner in which the present theory of the power of parliament as to impeachments came to be legally settled—a point which historians more interested in political events than in legal history have not I think altogether cleared up. Told shortly the history seems to be this.

---

[1] " Le Lundy en le Fest de Seinte Feye la Virgine." 3 *Rot. Par.* 449.
[2] *Ib.* 427.
[3] This statute was repealed by the Statute Law Revision Act, 1863 (26 & 27 Vic. c. 125). I think that a great constitutional and historical landmark might have been spared. The Act is only fourteen lines in length. The repeal, however, does not revive the power of appealing in Parliament, as all appeals in criminal cases were abolished by 59 Geo. 3, c. 46.

CHAP. V. The judicial powers of the Curia Regis survived when parliament assumed its present character. They were exercised in no very regular way throughout the reigns of Edward I. and Edward III. In the later part of the reign of Edward III. the House of Commons by assuming the position of accusers imposed a severe check on the proceedings of what we should now describe as ministers of state, but concurrently with this development of their powers there arose a practice of "appeal" or private accusation which enabled any one to bring any one else to trial for any offence before parliament. In some cases this practice appears to have worked worse than the unlimited power of private accusation which exists at the present day, and in the hands of a fierce and turbulent feudal nobility who could enforce their accusations by armies of retainers it became an abuse which largely contributed to the revolution by which Richard II. was deposed and Henry IV. set on the throne. This in its turn led to the Wars of the Roses, the destruction of the feudal nobility, and the establishment of the semi-despotic authority of the Tudors. It is not surprising that this should have been the case when we read the account given in the Parliament Rolls of the principles on which Parliament proceeded in such cases. The Lords in 1388 distinctly repudiate the authority of all law whatever except "the Law of Parliament" a phrase for that which parliament judging *ex post facto* might consider reasonable. In other words their claim was to be at once accusers, judges, and *ex post facto* legislators with regard to the exigency, real or supposed, of the particular case before them. The practical effect of this was that in the course of ten years accusers and accused changed places, the survivors and representatives of those who had been put to death for accroaching royal power, succeeding in putting to death for the same offence those who had destroyed their predecessors.

The statute 1 Hen. 4, c. 14, put an end to this great evil, and went a great way towards establishing the later view of parliamentary impeachment according to which there must be an accusation by the Commons and a trial before the Lords. From that time there is a marked change in the character of the prosecutions which took place in parliament. Several such proceedings occurred, some of which cannot be reckoned as impeachments in the full and proper sense of the word. [1]Thus in 1409 Thomas Erpyngham accused the Bishop of Norwich of some offence, it does not appear what, but the King ordered them to be reconciled, forgiving the Bishop, who he said had erred negligently, and thanking Erpingham and assuring him that he believed him to have acted from zeal to his service. It is not at all unlikely that the King thought that the proceeding was opposed to the statute of the previous year. In the case of the Percies (7 & 8 Hen. 4, A.D. 1406) for the rebellion in the north, ending with the Battle of Shrewsbury, there was a question as to the manner in which proceedings were to be taken, and the peers upon deliberation determined that they should be " *solonc la ley et usage d'armes.*" The record then sets forth the offences charged, proclamations made for the appearance of the parties, and the non-appearance of [2]Henry Percy and Bardolf, and proceeds to convict them of treason and subject them to the penalties for that offence.

In [3]1450 the Duke of Suffolk was impeached for high treason, and one [4]Tailboys for an attempt to murder Ralph Lord Cromwell. [5]Lastly, in 1459 Lord Stanley was impeached for not sending his troops to the Battle of Bloreheath.

All these impeachments appear to have been conducted according to what would now be recognised as the regular course of proceeding. I may, however, observe that in 1399 or 1400 a case occurred which contradicts the principle subsequently established as to pardons. [5]It appears

---

[1] "Le Roi seant en son see Roiale de son bouche propre monstra et dist a " dit Mōns Thomas coment meme celuy Mōns Thomas devant ces heures " avoit baillez a n̄re dit Sr̄ le Roy une Bille de certeines empeschementz " touchantz le dit Evesque, du quel fait meme n̄re Sr̄ le Roy remercia le dit " Mōns Thomas et dist qu'il savoit bien q̄ ceo q̄ meme celuy Mōns Thomas " avoit fait a cell temps feust fait pur les grantz zele chierte et tendresse " queux il avoit a sa persone," &c. The record ends by saying that the archbishop took the hands of the bishop and Erpingham, and "les fist prendre " l'un l'autre par la magne et leur baiser ensemble en signe d'amour perpetuel " entre eux en tout temps advenir." 3 *Rot. Par.* 456. Compare Shakspeare's mention of Erpingham in *Henry V.*

[2] Thomas Percy was killed at Shrewsbury but his father survived the battle for three years.

[3] 5 *Rot. Par.* 176. This is Shakspeare's Suffolk in *Henry VI.*

[4] *Ib.* 200.   [5] *Ib.* 369.   [5] 3 *Rot. Par.* 458.

CHAP. V. from a petition of 1400 that one Bagot had been impeached
by the Commons of "pleuseurs horribles faits et mespri-
"sions." He was put to answer before the Lords and produced a "chartre generale de pardon" on which the Lords
considered "q le dit Monrs William ne deust etre empesche
"ne mys a response par la loie."

It appears from all this that, with insignificant exceptions,
the present law and practice as to parliamentary impeachments was established as the result of the transactions above
referred to, which took place in the latter part of the reign
of Edward III. and the reign of Richard II.

From 1459 to 1621, a period of 162 years, no impeachment
appears to have taken place, at least none is mentioned either
in the Parliament Rolls or the Lords Journals, so far as
appears from the elaborate [1]indices to those collections. It
is not quite easy to give a full explanation for this, though
some of the reasons are obvious. The greatly increased
judicial power of the Privy Council which was vested in the
Star Chamber affords one reason. Such cases as those of
Cogan were no doubt more easily and speedily dealt with
there than by an impeachment.

The immense increase of royal power during the Tudor
period would supply another reason. It was not till parliament reasserted itself under James I. and Charles I. that
it became natural or perhaps possible to use impeachments
for the punishment of ministers considered corrupt or oppressive. If the King himself wished to punish a minister a
bill of attainder was more convenient than an impeachment
because it superseded the necessity for a trial; and though our
accounts of the earlier impeachments are imperfect, enough
remains to show that in many cases at least witnesses were
examined and some proceedings in the nature of a trial had.

Whatever the reasons may have been the fact is that
the next [2]regular impeachment to Lord Stanley's, in 1459,
was that of Sir Giles Mompesson in 1621. From that
date to the present day there have been fifty-four impeach-

---

[1] The index to the Parliament Rolls is a folio volume of 1036 pages. The
calendar to the Lords' Journals fills two folios.

[2] Articles of accusation were presented in Parliament in the cases of
Wolsey, Lord Seymour of Sudeley, and perhaps some others.

ments, so far as I have ascertained from the calendar to the
Lords' Journals. A list of them will be found in the footnote.[1] The proceedings under some of them have been
amongst the most memorable events in our general history, but little need be said of them in reference to our
judicial history. They represent for the most part the

[1] 1621.

Sir Giles Mompesson.
Lord Bacon.
Sir F. Mitchell.
Sir H. Yelverton.

1625.

The Earl of Middlesex.

1626.

The Earl of Bristol.
The Duke of Buckingham.

1640.

The Earl of Strafford.
The Lord Keeper Fynch.
Sir R. Barkly and other judges.

1641.

Sir G. Ratcliffe.

1642.

Archbishop Laud.
Dr. Cosens.
Bishop Wren.
Daniel O'Neale.
Sir E. Herbert.
Sir E. Dering.
Mr. Strode.
Mr. Spenser.
Nine Lords.
Sir R. Gurney.
Mr. Hastings.
Marquis of Hertford.
Lord Strange.
Mr. Wilde.
Mr. Broccas.

1661.

Mr. Drake.

1666.

Lord Mordaunt.

1667.

Lord Clarendon.

1668.

Sir W. Penn.

1678.

Lord Stafford and four other Roman
    Catholic lords.
Lord Danby.

1680.

Edward Seymour.
Sir W. Scroggs.
Earl of Tyrone.

1681.

Fitz-Harris.

1689.

Sir A. Blair and others.
Lord Salisbury.
Earl of Peterborough.

1695.

Duke of Leeds.

1698.

John Goudet and others.

1701.

Lord Portland.
Lord Somers.
Lord Halifax.

1709.

Dr. Sacheverell.

1715.

Lord Oxford.
Lord Bolingbroke.
Duke of Ormond.
Earl of Strafford.
Lord Derwentwater.

1724.

Lord Macclesfield.

1746.

Lord Lovat.

1787.

Warren Hastings.

1805.

Lord Melville.

CHAP. V. working of a regular and well understood institution. Twice
in the reign of Charles I. attempts were made to break in
upon the established theory of impeachment, once in the
case of the Earl of Bristol, whom the king attempted to
accuse of treason in the House of Lords without any impeachment by the Commons or any indictment found by a grand
jury, and once in the famous case of the five members. The
list given in the note shows that the really important period,
in the modern history of impeachment, was the seventeenth
century, and particularly the reign of Charles I. The
power of impeachment was the weapon by which the
parliament fought their battle from 1640 to 1642. In the
eighteenth century its importance declined, and it became a
subject rather of constitutional and antiquarian curiosity
than of practical importance. [1] The impeachment of Warren
Hastings is, I think, a blot on the judicial history of the
country. It was monstrous that a man should be tortured, at
irregular intervals, for seven years, in order that a singularly
incompetent tribunal might be addressed before an excited
audience by Burke and Sheridan, in language far removed
from the calmness with which an advocate for the prosecution
ought to address a criminal court. The acquittal of the defendant shows conclusively that if a guilty man did not
escape, an innocent man was cruelly oppressed.

It is hardly probable that so cumbrous and unsatisfactory
a mode of procedure will ever be resorted to again. The full
establishment of popular government, and the close superintendence and immediate control exercised over all public
officers whatever by parliament, make it not only unlikely
that the sort of crimes for which men used to be impeached
should be committed, but extremely difficult to commit them.

In order to complete what I have to say on the subject of
the criminal jurisdiction of Parliament I ought to notice bills
of attainder and of pains and penalties. Such a bill is an

---

[1] Pitt's India Bill, 24 Geo. 3, sess. 2, c. 25 (amended by 26 Geo. 3, c. 57),
provided a special court for the trial of offences committed in India. It was
to be composed of three judges, five members of the House of Lords, and seven
members of the House of Commons. The court has never sat. It was constituted before Warren Hastings was impeached, and indeed before his return
from India. I suppose the act was considered not to be retrospective, or
Hastings might have been tried under it.

act of parliament for putting a man to death or for otherwise CHAP. V.
punishing him without trial in the usual form. I am unable to say what was the first act of this kind, but the first
that I am prepared to refer to is the [1] act of attainder of
the Duke of Clarence, passed in 1477 (17 Edw. 4). It is
very long and oratorical, and after setting out at length the
offences imputed to Clarence, enacts " that the said George
" Duke of Clarence be convicted and atteynted of high
" treason." The act is followed by the appointment of the
Duke of Buckingham as lord high steward for that occasion
to do execution. Bills of attainder were, in the reign of
Henry VIII., used instead of impeachments ; as for instance
in the cases of Wolsey, Thomas Cromwell, Queen Katharine
Howard, the Duke of Norfolk, and the Earl of Surrey. They
have occurred occasionally in our later history. The most
memorable case is that of Lord Strafford. Other instances
are those of Lord Danby, the Duke of Monmouth, and Sir
John Fenwick. As instances of a bill of pains and penalties
I may refer to the bill against Bishop Atterbury, and to the
bill against Queen Caroline, which will probably long continue
to be referred to as the last instance of such legislation.

Thus far I have considered the extent of the criminal
jurisdiction of Parliament, when set in motion by an impeachment by the Commons who are said to be, for that
purpose, the grand jury of the whole nation. I proceed now
to consider the special criminal jurisdiction which the House
of Lords possesses over Peers of Parliament. It extends only
to felonies, for in cases of misdemeanour a peer may be tried
like a commoner. When Parliament is sitting the tribunal
is the House of Lords, which is usually, though not necessarily, presided over by a Lord High Steward appointed for
the purpose. In this case the peers themselves are the
judges, the Lord High Steward being only the president of
the court.

If Parliament is not sitting the court is the Court of the
Lord High Steward, who is the only judge of it, such other
peers as may attend the court acting as a jury, under the
name of the " Lords Triers."

[1] 6 *Rot. Par.* 193.

CHAP. V.   These courts are of the most remote antiquity, and may
indeed be regarded as remnants of the old Curia Regis, which
have survived without material alteration the vicissitudes of
eight centuries. The courts can hardly be said to have any
history, though it will be worth while to mention a few
points connected with them.

I have sufficiently illustrated the judicial functions and
powers of the Curia Regis itself. [1] The famous passage in
Magna Charta about the "legale judicium parium suorum"
appears to me to refer to the trial of peers in the King's
Court rather than to trial by jury. The 21st Article of
Magna Charta has a similar expression: "Comites et barones
"non amercientur nisi per pares suos et non nisi secundum
"modum delicti." I do not think that the expression "trial
"by jury" would have been used, or would have been intelligible, in King John's time. It would have been described rather as the taking of an inquisition by an assize,
or by lawful men, and is I think referred to by the words
"vel per legem terræ." These would include not only
inquests taken by jurors on the execution of commissions of
eyre, gaol delivery and oyer and terminer, but also trials by
combat or by ordeal, each of which was part of the lex
terræ at the date of Magna Charta. In short, I should be
inclined to construe "nullus liber homo" distributively—

---

[1] "Nullus liber homo capiatur vel imprisonetur aut dissaisiatur, aut
"utlagetur, aut exuletur, aut aliquo modo destruatur nec super eum ibimus
"nec super eum mittemus, nisi per legale judicium parium suorum vel per
"legem terræ." Stubbs, *Charters*, 301. The following observation on this
passage is made in the *Report on the Dignity of the Peer* (i. 450). "The
"right to the *judicium parium* asserted by that charter was probably the
"ancient law of the kingdom, and therefore when a person of rank was
"accused of any offence for which the law required trial by his peers, it was
"necessary that the King should summon to the Court of Justice by which
"the person accused was to be tried the peers of the accused. The persons
"attending on such occasions are sometimes described by the general words
"*proceres*, or 'magnates,' and sometimes more particularly as Archbishops,
"Bishops, Abbots, Priors, Earls, and Barons, with the addition also some-
"times of the general words *proceres*, or 'magnates.' It is probable that
"many persons answering the several descriptions attended on extraordinary
"occasions which required their presence." This most elaborate report is
occupied almost entirely with the legislative functions of the peerage, and
says hardly anything of their judicial functions. The expression "judicium
parium" is however older than Magna Charta. In the leges Henrici Primi
xxxi. 7 (Thorpe i. 534), this passage occurs: "Unusquisque per pares suos
"judicandus est, et ejusdem provinciæ." This however appears from
xxix. i. to apply to "barones comitatus." See too in reference to this matter
the trial of Hugo in 1303, p. 260, *post*.

"no free man shall be taken, &c., except (if he is one of the
" vassals of the King's Court) by the lawful judgment of his
" peers, or (if he is not such a vassal) by the law of the land,
" *i.e.* the ordinary course of justice." However this may have
been, the right of the peers to be tried by their peers for
treason or felony has never at any period of English history
been either questioned or invaded, or modified in any way,
with some slight exceptions.

I will give one or two instances of its solemn recognition.
[1] In 1322 Thomas of Lancaster was put to death in a summary way by Edward II. In 1327 the judgment against
him was reversed upon a writ of error, one of the principal
errors assigned being "quod cum predictus Thomas comes
" fuisset unus Parium et Magnatum regni, et in Magna
" Cartâ de Libertatibus Angl' contineatur quod" (the well-
known passage is here quoted) "predictus Thomas comes .
"   morti adjudicatus est absque arenamento seu respon-
" sione seu legali judicio parium suorum." [2] In 4 Edw. 3
(1330) Roger Mortimer and his accomplice Simon de Bereford were charged in Parliament with treason. The "earls,
" barons, and peers" examined the articles alleged against
Mortimer, convicted him of treason, and sentenced him to
death. As to Bereford, "our lord the King charged the
" said earls, barons, and peers, to give right and lawful
" judgment as appertains to them on Simon de Bereford,
" Knight" . . . . " And the earls, barons, and peers re-
" turned to the King, and said all with one voice that the
" said Bereford was not their peer, wherefore they were not
" bound to try him as a peer; nevertheless, as he was a
" notorious traitor, they sentenced him to be drawn and
" hung."

The right of peers to be tried in Parliament was affirmed
by [3] statute in the year 1341 (15 Edw. 3), which recited
that peers of the realm had been arrested, imprisoned, subjected to forfeitures, and in some cases to death without
judgment of their peers, and enacted that for the future

---

[1] 2 *Rot. Par.* 5, 6.
[2] *Ib.* 53. See some remarks on the irregularity of this proceeding in *Report
on Dignity of a Peer*, i. p. 299, and further remarks on the case of Berkeley
(mentioned above) at p. 301.   [3] *Ib.* 132.

" no peer of the realm, officer, or other, on account of his " office, or for things touching his office," should be liable to be tried or punished " except by award of the said peers in Parliament ; " and that if any peer submitted to be judged or to answer elsewhere, that was not to prejudice the rights of other peers or his own rights on other occasions.

This statute was repealed in 1343, [1] but with this singular reservation : " as some of the articles comprised in the statute " are reasonable and in accordance with law and reason, those " articles and the others agreed upon in this Parliament are " to be made into a new statute." Whatever may have been the effect of the repeal, it does not affect the recognition of the principle made by the statute. It must be observed, however, that the statute went far beyond what has ever since been recognised as the law, for it applies to all offences whatever, and is not confined to treason and felony. I am unable to give the history of the limitation of the privilege of peers to cases of treason and felony. It is, however, apparently as old as 1442, for in that year an act (20 Hen. 6, c. 9) was passed, which recites that although Magna Charta provides that " nullus liber *homo* " shall be punished except by judgment of his peers, " n'est my mention fait coment fem- " mes, dames de graunde estate par cause de leurs barons " peres de la terre covertez or soulez," are to be tried upon indictments of treason or felony, and it provides that they shall be tried like other peers of the realm. It seems clear from this that a peer was not at that time entitled to be tried by his peers for a misdemeanour.

The Court of the Lord High Steward is probably a rem- nant of the Curia Regis, which has survived unimpaired from the Conquest at least, and probably from earlier times. The Lord High Steward was one of the great officers of the Curia Regis, and in [2] Madox may be seen a collection of a great number of records and notices by historical writers relating to the different holders of the office, and to similar offices in Normandy, France, and Spain. The steward of Arragon had " a great judicial power, for he had cognizance of all causes " and quarrels, except in certain cases reserved to the King's

---

[1] 2 *Rot. Par.* 139.   [2] 1 *Hist. Exch.* 48.

" own cognizance, and when he was present in any city or CHAP. V.
" town whatever, all causes before any other judge were to
" cease, if he so commanded." The judicial officer in all the
manor courts was, as indeed he still is, called the Steward.

According to [1] Coke the office of High Steward was hereditary till the time of Henry IV., after which it was granted
hâc vice when an occasion arose for the services of such
an officer either at the trial of a peer or at a coronation.

The only legislative enactment which has taken place
in relation to these courts is 7 & 8 Will. 3, c. 3, which
provides that upon the trial of any peer or peeress for
treason or misprision, all the peers who have a right to sit
and vote in Parliament shall be duly summoned, twenty days
at least before every such trial, to appear at every such trial,
and that every peer so summoned, and appearing at such
trial, shall vote in the trial.

The object of this statute was to remedy an abuse which
formerly existed in the case of trials before the Court of the
Lord High Steward. The Lord High Steward summoned such
and so many Lords Triers as he thought fit, and no one who
was not so summoned had a right to take part in the trial.

Indictments upon which the House of Lords or the Court
of the Lord High Steward proceed may be and are found,
like other indictments, either in the Queen's Bench division
or on circuit, and I suppose they might be found at the
Quarter Sessions, if a peer committed an offence cognizable
there. When so found they are removed by certiorari into
the Court before which they are to be tried.

There have been four trials of peers in the House of Lords
since the end of the reign of George II., viz., Lord Ferrers for
murder in 1760; Lord Byron for murder in 1765; the
Duchess of Kingston for bigamy in 1776; and Lord Cardigan
in 1841. The trial of Lord Delamere for treason in 1686,
before Jeffreys, is, I believe, the last instance of a trial in the
Court of the Lord High Steward.

[1] Coke, *4th Inst.* 58. The derivation of the office according to Coke was
thus :—The Earls of Leicester were High Stewards till Simon de Montfort
forfeited the office to Henry III. Henry granted the office and the earldom to
his second son, Edmond, whence it descended to Henry of Bolingbroke, son and
heir of John of Gaunt, and afterwards Henry IV.

CHAPTER VI.

THE CRIMINAL JURISDICTION OF THE PRIVY COUNCIL.

CHAP. VI. THE growth of the Courts of Equity forms one of its most important chapters in the history of our law. These courts supplied the defects of the crude and meagre system which constituted the common law, by the introduction of remedies unknown to it, and by the enforcement of obligations which it did not recognize. To describe the steps by which this was done does not fall within the scope of this work, but it illustrates an analogous process with reference to the criminal law, which, after making much progress, was brought to an abrupt conclusion by the legislature in consequence of the way in which it was abused. I refer to the criminal jurisdiction of the Council as exercised by the famous Court of Star Chamber. Several other analogous courts exercised a similar jurisdiction in particular places. The most important of these were the Court of the President of the North and the Court of the Marches of Wales. They have not, however, left such traces either in the law itself or in history as to make it worth while to treat of them at length. The case is different with respect to the judicial authority of the Privy Council. Not only did its decisions leave deep traces both on our law and on our history, but it is closely connected with the body which to this day holds the position of the Supreme Court of Appeal in all criminal cases arising in any of Her Majesty's dominions beyond the seas—the Judicial Committee of the Privy Council. [1] The history is as follows:—

---

[1] The authorities for what follows are Hallam, *Middle Ages*, iii. 138-147 (ed. 1855) ; Hallam, *Const. Hist.* i. 48-55, 230-233, &c., and ii. 29-31, &c. ;

I have already described the constitution of the Curia Chap. VI. Regis and the manner in which the Courts of Common Law were derived from it. Its relation to Parliament has been traced by others, and need not be mentioned here. It also (as I have said) falls outside of my subject to give any account of the origin or gradual development of the judicial authority of the Lord Chancellor, who was one of its great officers ; but I must add to what has already been said that, after throwing off the great branches already enumerated the Curia Regis still continued to occupy a position corresponding to that of the Cabinet or rather of the Ministry of our own day, but of greater importance, as it had judicial as well as executive functions. In this capacity it was called the Council, and as time went on three several bodies so called came to be distinguished by different titles, namely (1) the Great Council of the Nation or Parliament ; (2) the Council ; (3) the Privy Council. It is a matter of great difficulty to distinguish these three bodies from each other in the early stages of their history. I need say nothing as to the difficulty of distinguishing between councils and parliaments ; nor is it necessary to my present purpose to go beyond a mere mention of the difficulty of discriminating between the body called the Council and the House of Lords on the one hand, and the Privy Council on the other. A full collection of all that is known on these subjects will be found in the works of the writers already referred to.

The leading points in the history of the judicial authority of the Council are these : It took from the earliest times a part in the administration of justice, which was viewed with great suspicion by Parliament, and was made the subject of remonstrance by them on various occasions in the course of

Palgrave's *Essay on the Original Authority of the King's Council* ; Hudson's "Treatise on the Star-Chamber," in *Collectanea Juridica*, vol. ii. The passages referred to in Hallam are little more than an abstract of what is said by Palgrave and Hudson. A note in the last-mentioned treatise says that a MS. copy of it contains a memorandum purporting to be signed by J. Finch, Chief Justice of the Court of Common Pleas, and afterwards Lord Keeper, which says, " This Treatise was composed by William Hudson, of Gray's " Inn, Esquire, one very much practised, and of great experience in the Star " Chamber, and my very affectionate friend." The note in question also refers to a reference made to it by Lord Mansfield in Wilkes's case, 4 Burr. 2554. The treatise is singularly well written and full of curious information.

CHAP. VI. the fourteenth and fifteenth centuries. Notwithstanding these remonstrances, and also notwithstanding the provisions of several statutes on the subject, the jurisdiction of the Council continued and increased, and it ultimately established itself as one of the recognised institutions of the country.

The Council when acting in its judicial capacity [1] "held its " sittings in the 'Starred Chamber,' an apartment situated " in the outermost quadrangle of the palace, next to the " bank of the river, and consequently easily accessible to the " suitors, and which at length was permanently appropriated " to the use of the Council. The lords sitting in the Sterre " ' Chamber' became a phrase . . . . and we can hardly " doubt that this circumstance contributed to assist the " Council in maintaining their authority."

The Court of Star Chamber had become an established institution by the reign of Henry VII. Early in that reign a statute was passed (3 Hen. 7, c. 1), which, though it did not, as has been sometimes supposed, create the court, conferred special powers on some of its members.

The court rose to the height of its influence under Elizabeth. It was regarded under James I. and Charles I. as oppressive, and was finally abolished in 1640, by 16 Chas. 1, c. 10. This celebrated Act recites the different statutes bearing on the subject, declares that the proceedings, censures, and " decrees of the court have by experience been " found to be an intolerable burden to the subjects, and the " means to introduce an arbitrary power and government," and enacts that the Court of Star Chamber, and all similar courts, and particularly the Courts of the Council of the Marches of Wales, the President and [2] Council of the North, the Duchy of Lancaster, and the Court of Exchequer of the County Palatine of Chester, shall be abolished, and that no similar court shall be established for the future.

---

[1] Palgrave, 38.

[2] The words of the Act (s. 4) are : "The like jurisdiction now used and " exercised " in the courts named "shall be also repealed and absolutely " revoked and made void." The Court of Star Chamber was dissolved (s. 3), but the other courts were not dissolved in terms. The "Court holden before " the President and Council of the Marches of Wales" seems to have survived for forty-eight years, as it was abolished in 1688 by 1 Will. & Mary, c. 27.

It is unnecessary to dwell in this place upon events which CHAP. VI. fill so large a space in the general history of the country, but the earlier history of the Council is less well known than the events which led to its fall.

[1] " It seems," says Sir F. Palgrave, " that in the reign of " Henry III. the Council was considered as a Court of Peers " within the terms of Magna Charta ; and before which, as a " court of original jurisdiction, the rights of tenants holding " *in capite,* or by barony, were to be discussed or decided ; " and it unquestionably exercised a direct jurisdiction over all " other the King's subjects." " Great transgressions against " the public peace were heard before the Council." In a note to this passage Sir F. Palgrave refers to the arraignment of Segrave, Constable of the Tower, for permitting the escape of Mortimer, and quotes a curious record, in which Sir John Dalton is summoned, " sub forisfacturâ vitæ et " membrorum et omnium aliorum quæ nobis forisfacere " poteris" to bring before the Council one Margeria de la Beche, the wife of Gerard De L'Ile, whom Dalton had forcibly abducted, and to do and receive (*ad faciendum et recipiendum*) such orders as the Council shall give.

No opposition appears to have been made to this jurisdiction till the 25th Edw. 3 (1350), when the [2]Commons petitioned " qe nul franc homme ne soit mys a respondre de " son franc tenement ne de riens que touche vie et " membre fyns ou redemptions par apposailles (informa- " tions) devant le conseil n̄r̄e seignur le Roi, ne devant ses " ministres quecumques sinoun par proces de ley de ceo en " arere use." The answer is, " Il plest a n̄r̄e seignur le " Roi q̄ les leies de son Roiaume soient tenuz et gardez en " lour force, et q̄ nul homme soit tenu a respondre de son " fraunk tenement sinoun par processe de ley ; mes de chose " que touche vie ou membre contemptz ou excesse soit fait " come ad este use cea en arere."

This seems to be an express recognition of the fact that for at least 135 years after Magna Charta the criminal jurisdiction of the Council was undisputed. [3]Either in the

---

[1] P. 34.

[2] 2 *Rot. Par.* 228, and see Palgrave, 25.
[3] 2 *Rot. Par.* 239.

CHAP. VI. same or in the next Parliament a similar petition was granted without any reservation, and this led to the statute printed as 25 Edw. 3, st. 5, c. 4. Similar statutes were passed in 1354 (28 Edw. 3, c. 3) and in 1368 (42 Edw. 3, c. 3).[1] On two occasions in the reign of Richard II., three in the reign of Henry IV., two in the reign of Henry V., and one in the reign of Henry VI., petitions were made by Parliament with a view to limit the powers of the Council, but none of them passed into a statute, the answers given by the King being either unfavourable or qualified. Some of these petitions and the answers show that the ground on which the jurisdiction of the Council was defended was the difficulty in many instances of obtaining redress for injuries at the common law. [2] Thus in 1399 (1 Hen. 4) the Commons petition that personal actions between party and party may not be tried by the Council, to which the answer is, " Soit l'Estatut ent fait tenuz et gardez, la ou l'une " partie est si graunt et riche, et l'autre partie si povre " qu'il ne purra autrement avoir recoverer." The word " except " (supplied by [3] Sir F. Palgrave after " gardez ") appears to be wanted.

Upon the whole, the legal position of the Court of Star Chamber in 1640 seems to have been this. It had existed for 135 years after Magna Charta without being supposed to be illegal or to be in any way opposed to Magna Charta. In 1350, 1354, and 1368, three successive acts of Parliament were passed, which, at first sight, seem to be intended to abolish it. From 1368 to 1640 (272 years) it continued to exist, notwithstanding parliamentary petitions which did not become statutes, the last of which was made in 1422, 218 years before 1640. On the other hand, the statute 3 Hen. 7, c. 2, if it did not exactly recognise the powers of the old court, at all events established a new one composed of several of its members and with a jurisdiction which, as far as it went, was identical with it.

It would seem natural under such circumstances to suppose that some other interpretation ought to be put upon the statutes of Edward III. than that which was given to them

[1] See too 11 Rich. 2, c. 10.   [2] 3 *Rot. Par.* 446.   [3] p. 47.

in 1640. [1] Hudson suggests " that these statutes did not
" extinguish the power of the court, but the abuse of appre-
" hending men's persons to answer suggestions." The words
of the statutes are " no man shall be put to answer before
" the King or his Council without presentment before his
" justices, matter of record, or writ original according to
" the ancient laws." [2] Hudson argues that the letter of
privy seal, by which proceedings were, at least in many
cases, commenced before the Star Chamber was an original
writ, and that the abuse intended to be remedied was the
arrest of a defendant by a pursuivant on a bare suggestion
by a plaintiff. The phrase " no man shall be put to answer
" before the Council, unless " certainly seems to imply that
there was some legal way of proceeding before that body.
Be this as it may, it is to be observed that even the Act of 1640
did not declare the Court to be in itself illegal and its powers
to be usurped. On the contrary, it recites that the matters
examinable there are all capable of being duly remedied at
common law, and that " the reasons and motives inducing
" the erection and continuance of that court do now cease."

I shall have to return to the subject of the Star Chamber
in connection with the history of the definitions of crimes
and the history of legal procedure. I will conclude what I
have to say at present by some observations on the general
character and functions of the court.

The praises of trial by jury as a bulwark of individual
liberty are a familiar topic. It is less commonly known,
but it is certainly no less true, that the institution
opened a wide door to tyranny and oppression by men of
local influence over their poorer neighbours. [3] In feudal

---

[1] P. 12.　　　　　　　　　[2] P. 4 ; see too Coke, *4th Inst.* 63.
[3] Sir F. Palgrave (pp. 103, 289, &c.) gives some curious illustrations of this.
The following are verses from a "ballad or libel " of the time of Edward I. :—

　　" Mes *le male doseynes* dount Dieu n'est ja pieté,
　　Parmi lur fauce bouches me ont enditée,
　　De males robberies e autre mavestée,
　　Qe je n'ose entre mes amis estre receptée.

　　" Si ces *maveis jurours* ne se vueillent amender,
　　Qe je pus a mon pais chevalcher e aller,
　　Si je les pus ateindre la teste lur froi voler,
　　De touz lur manaces ne dorroi un dener.

CHAP. VI. times the influence of a great landowner over the persons who were returned as jurymen to the assizes was practically almost unlimited, and the system of .indictment by a grand jury which merely reported on oath the rumours of the neighbourhood might, and no doubt often did, work cruel injustice. The offence which was long known to the law as maintenance, or perverting justice by violence, by unlawful assemblies and conspiracies, was the commonest and most characteristic offence of the age. One of its commonest forms was the corruption and intimidation of jurors. Signal proof of this is supplied by the repeated legislation against this offence. The nature of the offence itself, and the

> " Vous qui estes endité je lou venez ci moi,
> Cit vert bois de Belregard, la n'y a nul ploy,
> Forsque beste savage e jolyf umbroy,
> Car trop est dotouse la commune loy.

The following passage is from the *Dance of Death*, and gives a conversation between Death and a juror :—

> " Master jurrour, which that at assizes,
> And at sheres quests didst embrace
> Deper didst lond like to thy devises,
> And who most gave most stood in thy grace,
> The poor man lost both lond and place,
> For gold thou couldest folk disherite,
> But now let see with thy pale face,
> Tofore the judge how canst thee quite ? "

The jurrour maketh answer :—

> " Whilom I was cleped in my countrey,
> The belweather, and that was not alight ;
> Nought loved but drad of high and low degree,
> For whom the best by craft I could endite,
> Hengen the true and the thef respite,
> All the countrey by my word was lad,
> But I dare sein shortly for to write,
> Of my death many a man is glad."

The case of Cogan, quoted above, from the Parliamentary Rolls is an illustration of the same thing. He offered to make good his case in any way, "sinoun par verdit de jurrours." I cannot say, however, that the introduction of such phrases into popular ballads proves very much. The writers may have been great rogues. In my youth a ballad used to be sung which was said to be a genuine product of the hulks. It began—

> " My curse rest on you, Justice Bayley,
> And gentlemen of the jury also,
> For transporting me from the arms of my Polly,
> For twenty long years as you know."

This is very like the "males doseynes dount Dieu n'est ja pieté." The defects of trial by jury in early times rest, however, on better evidence than this.

manner in which it was to be corrected by the Court of Star CHAP.VI.
Chamber, are fully described in the preamble and first section
of 3 Hen. 7, c. 1, " The King our said sovereign lord remem-
" bereth how by unlawful maintenance, giving of liveries, signs,
" and tokens, and retainders by indentures, promises, oaths,
" writings, or otherwise embraceries of his subjects, untrue
" demeanings of sheriffs in making of panels and other un-
" true returns, by taking of money by juries, by great riots
" and unlawful assemblies, the policy and good rule of this
" realm is almost subdued, and for the not punishing of these
" inconveniences, and by reason of the premises, little or
" nothing may be found by inquiry " (*i.e.* by inquests or
juries), " whereby the laws of the land in execution may take
" little effect, to the increase of murders, robberies, perjuries,
" and unsureties of all men living, and losses of their lands
" and goods to the great displeasure of Almighty God."
" Therefore it is ordained for Reformation of the Premisses
" by authority of the said Parliament, that the Chancellor
" and Treasurer of England for the time being, and Keeper
" of the King's Privy Seal, or two of them, calling to them
" a bishop and a temporal lord of the king's most honour-
" able Council, and the two chief justices of the King's
" Bench and Common Pleas for the time being, or two other
" justices in their absence, upon bill or information put to
" the said Chancellor for the king or any other against any
" person for any misbehaviour before rehearsed, have authority
" to call before them by writ or by Privy Seal the said misdoers,
" and them and other by their discretion, by whom the truth
" may be known, to examine, and such as they find therein
" defective to punish them after their demerits, after the
" form and effect of statutes thereof made, in like manner
" and form as they should and ought to be punished as if
" they were thereof convict after the due order of the
" law."
It is extremely difficult to say what was the precise object
or effect of this statute. Coke seems to attribute to it
no other effect than that of varying the procedure of the
Star Chamber by enabling them to examine defendants, but
this seems impossible, both because (according to Hudson)

CHAP. VI. such was the regular procedure of the Court, and because
that procedure does not appear to have been confined after
the statute to cases which fell within it.

[1] Hudson refers to the subject in such a way as to show
that at one time it was a moot point whether the Council
had any criminal jurisdiction other than that which this
statute conferred upon them, but that the court held that it
had. [2] Lord Bacon says of the statute that "the authority
" of the Star Chamber which before subsisted by the ancient
" common laws of the realm was confirmed in certain cases
" by it." A very indefinite remark, accompanied by no explanation of the reasons for such an enactment. [3] Mr.
Hallam's opinion, founded upon an elaborate examination of
the authorities, is as follows :

1. The Court erected by the statute of Henry VII. was
not the Court of Star Chamber.

2. The Court by the statute subsisted in full force till
beyond the middle of Henry VIII.'s reign. but not long
afterwards went into disuse.

3. The Court of Star Chamber was the old concilium
ordinarium, against whose jurisdiction [4] many statutes had
been enacted from the time of Edward III.

4. No part of the jurisdiction exercised by the Star
Chamber could be maintained on the authority of the
statute of Henry VII.

On so very obscure a subject it is impossible now to go
beyond conjecture. My conjecture, offered with very little
confidence, is that the statute was meant to give an indis-

---

[1] P. 80. "It is a received opinion that the court should meddle with no
" other causes than are expressed in the statute 3 Hen. 7, and I well re-
" member that the Lord Chancellor Egerton would often tell that in his time,
" when he was a student, Mr. Serjeant Lovelace put his hand to a demurrer in
" this court for that the matter of the bill contained other matters than were
" mentioned in the statute 3 Hen. 7, and Mr. Plowden, that great lawyer,
" put his hand thereto first, whereupon Mr. Lovelace easily followed. But
" the cause being moved in court, Mr. Lovelace being a young man, was
" called to answer the error of his ancient Mr. Plowden, who very discreetly
" made his excuse at the bar that Mr. Plowden's hand was first unto it, and
" that he supposed he might in anything follow St. Augustine. And although
" it were then overruled, yet Mr. Serjeant Richardson, thirty years after, fell
" again upon the same rock, and was sharply rebuked for the same." See also
the case of Chambers, 3 St. Tr. 380.

[2] History of Henry VII., Bacon's works, by Spedding, vi. 85.

[3] Cons. Hist. i. 55, note.   [4] This is rather an overstatement.

putable statutory authority to that part of the Star Chamber jurisdiction which appeared at the date of the statute most important, but that as it was found that the wider authority of the old court was acquiesced in, the statute fell into disuse. This conjecture is strengthened by the circumstance that the statute of Henry VII. is silent as to the jurisdiction of the court over several offences which, at the end of the fifteenth century, were probably of comparatively little importance, but which in the sixteenth and the beginning of the seventeenth century gave the court its principal value in the eyes of the government. Of these, libels are the most important.

Whatever may be the true explanation of these matters there can be no doubt at all as to the nature and functions of the court itself. The jurisdiction of the Chancellor in civil matters, and the jurisdiction of the Council or Star Chamber in criminal matters, grew up side by side. Lord Bacon, after mentioning the common law courts,[1] says, " There was nevertheless always reserved a high and pre- " eminent power to the king's counsel in causes that might " in example or consequence concern the state of the Com- " monwealth; which if they were criminal, the counsel used " to sit in the chamber called the Star Chamber; if civil, " in the White Chamber or White-hall. And as the Chancery " had the prætorian power for equity, so the Star Chamber " had the censorian power for offences under the degree of " capital."

[2] In early times the Council was accustomed to grant to individuals the special commissions of Oyer and Terminer under the Privy Seal, which I have already referred to. When such commissions were forbidden by statute, the Council heard such cases themselves, they compelled appearance by [3] writs of premunire, and afterwards by the writ of [4] subpœna, which was invented in Edward III.'s time by Sir

---

[1] Works, vi. 85.   [2] Palgrave, pp. 27-38.
[3] " Edwardus, &c., Vice comitibus London, salutem.   Quibusdam certis de " causis vobis mandamus firmiter injungentes quod præmunire faciatis " H. C. &c., quod . . . sit . . . . coram consilio nostro, &c."   Palgrave, note 11, p. 131.
[4] " Edwardus, &c., R. S. salutem.   Tibi præcipimus quod sis coram consilio " nostro, &c.   Et hoc sub pœnâ centum librarum nullatenus ommittas." Palgrave, p. 41.

CHAP. VI. John de Waltham (afterwards Bishop of Salisbury). Sir Francis Palgrave compares the authors of these writs to the forgotten inventors of the writs of [1] Latitat and Quo Minus, by which the Courts of King's Bench and Exchequer usurped civil jurisdiction. The Star Chamber proceeded by bill and answer, and administered interrogatories to the accused party, whom they examined upon oath. [2] Hudson gives several instances in which, without exactly trying people for common offences, such as treason and murder, they inflicted heavy penalties for acts which might have been punished at common law under those denominations. The Earl of Rutland, for instance, was fined £30,000 for being concerned in the Earl of Essex's insurrection. [3] "And "there are above a hundred precedents where persons that "gave countenance to felons were here questioned." In cases "pending upon felony" the party was not examined upon oath.

These, however, were not the cases which commonly employed the Star Chamber. They are thus enumerated by [4] Hudson : Forgery, perjury, riot, maintenance, fraud, libelling, and conspiracy. Besides these [5] he ascribes to the court power to punish offences not defined or punishable at common law, and [6] he enumerates some instances in which jurisdiction was conferred on the court by statutes long since forgotten.

To some of these matters I shall have to return in another part of this work. It is enough for the present to say that the tyrannical proceedings for political offences which ultimately caused the abolition of the court ought not to make us forget the great services which it rendered, not only to the cause of good order but to the law of the country.

---

[1] The writ of Latitat affirmed that the defendant ought to be in the custody of the Marshal of the King's Bench, to answer for a trespass, suggested in what was called a Bill of Middlesex, instead of which he "latitat et discurrit" in some county other than Middlesex. The writ of Quo Minus stated that the defendant being a Crown debtor owed money to the plaintiff, whereby he was less able than he would have been to pay his debt to the Crown—a matter for the Exchequer. (3 Black. *Com.* 284-286.)

[2] P. 62.   [3] P. 64.

[4] P. 71. Bacon (vi. 85) mentions four "forces, frauds, crimes various of "stellionate, and the inchoation or middle acts towards crimes capital or "heinous not actually committed or perpetrated."

[5] P. 107.   [6] P. 113.

The common law was in all ways a most defective system.
It was incomplete. Its punishments were capricious and
cruel. Its most characteristic institution, trial by jury, was
open to abuse in every case in which persons of local influence
were interested. Juries themselves were often corrupt, and
the process of attaint, the only one by which at common law
a false verdict could be impeached or corrupt jurymen be
punished, was as uncertain and as open to corrupt influences
as other forms of trial by jury. [1] "When a corrupt jury,"
says Hudson, "had given an injurious verdict, if there had
" been no remedy but to attaint them by another jury, the
" wronged party would have had small remedy, as is mani-
" fested by common experience, no jury having for many
" years attainted a former. As also at this day in the Prin-
" cipality of Wales, if a man of good alliance have a cause
" to be tried, though many sharp laws have been made for
" favourable panels, yet it is impossible to have a jury which
" will find against him, be the cause never so plain : or if
" arraigned for murder he shall hardly be convicted, although
" the fear of punishment of this court carries some awful
" respect over them."

According to our modern views, the proper cure for such
defects would be intelligent and comprehensive legislation as
to both crimes and criminal procedure, but for many reasons
such an undertaking as a criminal code would have been
practically impossible in the Tudor period. In these circumstances, the Star Chamber, not merely exercised a control
over influential noblemen and gentlemen which put a stop
to much oppression and corrupt interference with the course
of justice, but supplied some of the defects of a system
which practically left unpunished forgery, perjury, attempts
and conspiracies to commit crimes, and many forms of fraud
and force.

In the later stages of its history no doubt the Court of
Star Chamber became a partisan court, and punished with
cruel severity men who offended the King or his ministers.
Nothing can be said in excuse of such proceedings as those
against Prynne or Lilburne; but it is just to observe that the

[1] P. 14.

CHAP. VI. real objection made was to the punishment of the acts themselves, rather than to the cruelty of branding or whipping.
The punishments inflicted by the common law were in many
cases more cruel than those of the Star Chamber, yet they
seem to have excited no indignation. There is also some
reason to believe that the cruel punishments inflicted under
Charles I. were at least to some extent an innovation on the
earlier practice of the court.

It is curious to observe the degree to which the Court of
Star Chamber impressed the imagination of several observers,
one of whom at all events was unlikely to flatter it at the
expense of the courts of common law, though it may
certainly be observed of all that they seem to protest too
much to be quite sincere. Bacon [1] describes it as " one of
" the sagest and noblest institutions of this kingdom." [2] Coke
says, " It is the most honourable court (our parliament
" excepted) that is in the Christian world, both in respect of
" the judges of the court, and of their honourable proceeding
" according to their just jurisdiction, and the ancient and
" just orders of the court." . . . " This court, the right
" institutions and ancient orders thereof being observed, doth
" keep all England in quiet." [3] Hudson becomes quite
enthusiastic on the subject. " Since the great Roman senate
" so famous to all ages and nations as that they might be
" called *jure mirum orbis*, there hath no court come so near
" them in state honour and judicature as this; the judges of

---

[1] *Works*, vi. 85.　　　　　　　　　　[2] *4th Inst.* p. 65.

[3] P. 17.　His enthusiasm is displayed in an amusing way in his discussion
of the origin of the name of the court (p. 8).　" I confess I am in that point
" a Platonist in opinion that ' *nomina naturâ fiunt potius quam vagâ imposi-*
" *tione*,' for assuredly Adam before his fall was abundantly skilful in the nature
" of all things ; so that when God brought him all things to name he gave
" them names befitting their natures.　And so I doubt not but Camera
" Stellata . . is most aptly named ; not because the Star Chamber is so
" adorned with stars gilded, as some would have it, for surely the chamber is
" so adorned because it is the seal (? seat) of that court ; . . . and it was so fitly
" called because the stars have no light but what is cast upon them by the sun,
" by reflection being his representative body ; and as his royal majesty himself
" was pleased to say,"—in short he said that he was the sun and the judges the
stars, but his majesty and Hudson between them spin out this conceit much
as Lady Margaret Bellenden spun out the history of Charles II.'s breakfast
at Tillietudlem.　The favourite derivation of the name of the court is from
the starrs or Jewish charters anciently kept there. (See Madox, *Exch.* i. 237.)
The Jews were expelled in Edward I.'s reign, and the meaning of the word
" starra " would naturally be forgotten, though the name might survive.

"this court being surely in honour, state, and majesty, learn-
"ing, understanding, justice, piety, and mercy equal, and in
"many exceeding the Roman senate by so much, by how
"much Christian knowledge exceedeth human learning."
After giving a long and curious account of the authority
of the Chancellor as chief judge of the court, [1] he says:
"As concerning the great and eminent officers of the king-
"dom, the Lord Treasurer, Privy Seal, and President of the
"Council, their places or voices in this court when the
"superior sitteth are of no more weight than any other of
"the table; so that the displeasure of a great officer cannot
"much amaze any suitor, knowing it is but one opinion, and
"the court is not alone replenished with noble dukes,
'marquises, earls, and barons, which hereby ought to be
"frequented with great presence of them, but also with
"reverend archbishops and prelates, grave counsellors of
"state, just and learned judges, with a composition for
"justice, mercy, religion, policy, and government, that it
"may be well and truly said that Mercy and Truth are met
"together, Righteousness and Peace have kissed each other."
He adds that in the reigns of Henry VII. and Henry VIII.
the number of members present was at times thirty or
even forty, as also in the time of Elizabeth, "but now
"much lessened since the barons and earls not being privy
"councillors have forborne their attendance." He also
remarks that in the time of Henry VII. and Henry VIII.
the punishments were far less severe than afterwards, the
fines being imposed with due regard to the " *salvo contenemento
suo*" of Magna Charta, and [2] "the slavish punishment of
"whipping" not having been introduced "till a great
"man—of the common law and otherwise a worthy justice
"forgot his place of session, and brought" (? it) "in this
"place too much in use."

This curious passage seems to show that under the Tudors
the Star Chamber was a numerous and comparatively mild

---

[1] P. 35.
[2] The words in the printed book are "the slavish speech of whispering,"
which is nonsense. Hallam makes the emendation given in the text upon
the authority of a MS. in the British Museum. (See Hallam, *Cons. Hist.* ii.
p. 34, ed. 1855.)

CHAP. VI. body, resembling in its constitution and proceedings a deliberative council rather than an ordinary court of justice, and that the proceedings which led to its abolition and made its name infamous were carried on at a time when it had come to consist of a small number of what we should call cabinet ministers, who abused its powers to put down opposition to their policy. It is unnecessary to refer in detail to the well-known instances of this abuse which led to the abolition of the court, though I have noticed some of them [1] elsewhere.

Although the Court of Star Chamber, and with it the most important judicial powers of the Council, were abolished in 1640, one degree of criminal jurisdiction still remained in and is actually exercised at this day by the Privy Council. Whatever may be the law as to the power of the sovereign to establish new courts of justice in England by charter— a power which if it exists is never exercised or likely to be exercised except under the provisions of acts of parliament (as for instance, when a borough is created with a new Court of Quarter Sessions under the statutory provisions already referred to), it is the undoubted prerogative of the crown to establish courts of justice in any possessions which it may acquire beyond the realm, either by conquest or by settlement, and an appeal lies from such courts to the sovereign, unless it is taken away either by statute or charter. An appeal to the King also lay from all ecclesiastical courts, and from the Court of Admiralty. These last mentioned appeals were made by virtue of 25 Hen. 8, c. 19, and 8 Eliz. c. 5, to "the King's Majesty in the King's Court of Chancery," and were heard by a body of delegates named by commission for that purpose. By 2 & 3 Will. 4, c. 92, the appeal in such cases has to be made to the King in Council, and by 3 & 4 Will. 4, c. 41, all such appeals, and also all appeals "from various Courts of "Judicature in the East Indies, and in the plantations, "colonies, and other dominions of his Majesty abroad" were to be heard before a body called the Judicial Committee of the Privy Council, which was constituted by the act

[1] See p. 338, *post.*

in question in place of a committee of the whole of the CHAP. VI.
Privy Council, before which it had up to that time been
customary (as the act recites) to hear such appeals.

The right to hear appeals in criminal as well as in civil
matters from all Her Majesty's dominions beyond the seas,
in all cases in which that right has not been expressly taken
away, has been solemnly affirmed and exercised in a series
of very modern cases. The principle is laid down in the
case of [1] R. *v.* Bertrand in which Sir J. T. Coleridge in
delivering judgment said : " Upon principle and reference to
" the decisions of this committee it seems undeniable that
" in all cases, criminal as well as civil, arising in places from
" which an appeal would lie, and where, either by the terms
" of a charter or statute, the authority has not been parted
" with, it is the inherent prerogative right, and on all proper
" occasions the duty of the Queen in Council to exercise an
" appellate jurisdiction. . . . . But the exercise of this
" prerogative is to be regulated by a consideration of
" circumstances and consequences ; and interference by Her
" Majesty in Council in criminal cases is likely in so many
" instances to lead to mischief and inconvenience that in them
" the crown will be very slow to entertain an appeal by its
" officers on behalf of itself or by individuals. The instances
" of such appeals being entertained are therefore very rare."
Many cases are referred to in this report, by which the
conclusion quoted is fully established. It is remarkable
that the [2] earliest of them was decided so lately as in the
year 1835, and it does not appear from the report that the
question, Whether the court had any such jurisdiction or not
was raised on that occasion; the jurisdiction has been
exercised sparingly no doubt, but on several very recent
occasions.[3] This jurisdiction is so narrowly limited, and
so rarely exercised that it has been little noticed by writers

---

[1] L.R. 1 P.C. 529. In this case the question was discussed whether a new
trial in cases of felony could be granted at common law.

[2] Pooneakhoty Modeliar *v.* The King, 3 Knapp, 348.

[3] See *e. g.* R. *v.* Burah, L.R. 3-App. Cases, 889, in which the question was
as to the extent of the legislative powers of the government of India; R. *v.*
Mount, L.R. 6 P.C. 283, in which the question was as to the sentence to be
passed by an Australian court in its Admiralty jurisdiction.

CHAP. VI. on criminal procedure. In a historical point of view it is one of the most remarkable parts of the whole system, for it connects the common administration of justice in our own days with the Curia Regis through the Court of Star Chamber.

In a few words the result of the history just related at length is as follows:

From the most remote antiquity the administration of justice was the highest or one of the highest prerogatives of the sovereigns of this country, and his council or court was the organ by which that prerogative was exercised.

The original council or court was divided in course of time into the Court of King's Bench, the Court of Common Pleas, and the Court of Exchequer, each of which had originally its own peculiar province but each of which contrived to intrude to some extent upon the province of the other two, the three between them administering the known and well recognised law of the land.

By the side of this comparatively well-defined jurisdiction, grew up by degrees the equitable jurisdiction (as it came to be called) of the Lord Chancellor, and the judicial authority, both civil and criminal, of the Council itself or Court of Star Chamber. The jurisdiction of the Chancellor being by experience found to be beneficial, and being wisely and justly used, was the foundation of the great Court of Chancery and of that part of our law or jurisprudence which goes by the name of equity. The judicial authority, civil and criminal, of the Council or Star Chamber being used oppressively for political purposes, was destroyed. After its destruction, however, the authority of the sovereign extended itself over a vast empire, including the whole of India, a great part of North America, Australia, New Zealand, the Cape, and many other places. [1] The ancient prerogative of

---

[1] The extreme difficulty of saying precisely how far the prerogative of the sovereign as fountain of justice extends, and at what point the power of the King to erect courts of justice ends, is well illustrated by the discussions which arose some years since as to the validity of those clauses in the patents of certain colonial bishops, which purported to give some of them jurisdiction over others. The question was fully argued before the Judicial Committee of the Privy Council in the matter of the Bishop of Natal. One point raised during that argument was as follows: It was urged that the view contended for by

the crown as the fountain of justice was held to vest in
it the ultimate appeal in all cases, civil and criminal, from
all courts in these vast territories, and a committee of the
Privy Council, which is the direct descendant of the old
Curia Regis, is to this day the organ by which that prerogative
is administered.

In concluding this account of the criminal jurisdiction of
the Privy Council I must mention their powers as committing magistrates. From the earliest times they have exercised
the power of inquiring into criminal charges and committing
suspected persons for trial.   "The power of the Privy
"Council," says Blackstone, [2] "is to inquire into all offences
"against the government and to commit the offenders
"to safe custody, in order to take their trial in some of
"the courts of law." For a great length of time this was
the common course in regard to all political offences, but
now it is usual to send even political offenders before a
magistrate to be dealt with in the ordinary way. When
Oxford shot at the Queen he was examined in the first
instance before the Privy Council but was afterwards sent
before a police magistrate. Maclean, who committed the
same offence in 1882, was not brought before the Privy
Council at all, but was committed in the common way by
the borough magistrates at Windsor.

the counsel for the Bishop of Natal involved the absurd conclusion that he
was subject to no jurisdiction at all. To this his counsel answered that the
crown could issue a commission to try him. It was replied that this would be
contrary to the statute (16 Chas. 1, c. 11, s. 5) by which the High Commission
Court was abolished and the foundation of similar courts forbidden for the future.
It was rejoined that such a construction of the statute would involve the
absurd result that if the Archbishop of Canterbury were to commit an ecclesiastical offence he could not be tried at all, for he could not try himself in
his own court, and there was no other to try him, unless the Queen could issue
a commission for that purpose. The counsel against the Bishop of Natal
attempted to rebut this argument in different ways. Sir Robert Phillimore
suggested that in such a case the archbishop might be tried by a general
council of the church (which was directly opposed to the royal supremacy)
and Lord Cairns (then Sir Hugh Cairns) suggested that he might be impeached
in parliament, which again seems a singular mode of proceeding in an ecclesiastical case, though no doubt there were precedents for it in the reign of
Charles I.
[2] 1 Black. *Com.* 230.

CHAPTER VII.

HISTORY OF THE LAW OF CRIMINAL PROCEDURE.—PRO-
CEDURE DOWN TO COMMITTAL FOR TRIAL OR BAIL.

CH. VII.   HAVING in the last chapter traced the history of the
courts of a criminal jurisdiction, I now proceed to the history
of the procedure followed for the punishment of criminals.
I shall give the history of each step in the procedure separately, and I intend in the present chapter to treat of the
procedure from the arrest of the offender to his discharge or
committal for trial.   This consists of two stages, namely, the
apprehension of the offender, closely connected with which is
the law as to the suppression of offences, and the preliminary
investigation before a magistrate, which results in the discharge,
or committal for trial, or bailing of the supposed offender.

In each case, the law itself was as a matter of fact subsequent to the establishment of the officers or courts by
which it was carried into execution.   Also, in each case, after
the practice of the officers or courts had gradually formed
the law, alterations were made by statute both in the law
itself and as to the officers and courts by whom it was
to be administered.

[1] THE APPREHENSION OF OFFENDERS AND SUPPRESSION OF
OFFENCES.

I have described above the system for the apprehension of
offenders and the prevention of crime which existed down
to the time of William the Conqueror and his sons.

The foundation of the whole system of criminal pro-

---

[1] As to existing laws of arrest, see *Dig. Crim. Proc.* ch. xii. arts. 96-98.

cedure was the prerogative of keeping the peace, which is CH. VII.
as old as the monarchy itself, and which was, as it still is,
embodied in the expression, "The King's Peace," the legal
name of the normal state of society.   This prerogative was
exercised at all times through officers collectively described
as the [1] Conservators of the Peace.   The King and certain
great officers (the chancellor, the constable, the marshal, the
steward, and the judges of the King's Bench) were conservators of the peace throughout England, but the ordinary
conservators of the peace were the sheriff, the coroner,
the justices of the peace, the constable, each in his own
district.   During the reigns of Henry II., Richard I., John,
Henry III., and Edward I., the system administered by these
authorities (with the exception of the justices of the peace,
who were not established till the reign of Edward III.) was
elaborated and rendered more stringent than it had been
before the Conquest by a long series of enactments.

The first of these was the [2] Assize of Clarendon issued by
Henry II. in 1166, just 100 years after the Conquest.   It
was re-issued as the [3] Assize of Northampton in 1176, in the
form of instructions to the six "committees of judges who
" were to visit the circuits then marked out."   The provisions
of the Assize of Clarendon bear more directly on the present
subject than those of the Assize of Northampton.

[4] The Assize provided that the sheriffs and justices should
make inquiry upon the oath of twelve men from every hundred
and four men from every township whether any man in any
township was [5] a robber, murderer, or thief, or a receiver of
robbers, murderers, or thieves ; that every person so accused
should be taken and brought before the sheriffs and by them
before the justices, and that no lord of a franchise [6] "nec in
" honore etiam de Wallingeford" should interfere to prevent
the sheriff from entering his franchise either to arrest accused

---

[1] On the conservators of the peace, see FitzHerbert, *Justices of the
Peace*, 6 B. ; Coke, *2nd Inst.* 538 ; a large collection of authorities in Burn's
Justice, title "Justices of the Peace ;" Hawkins, *Pleas of the Crown*, bk. ii.
ch. viii. vol. ii. p. 38, edition of 1814 ; but the best and most instructive
account of the matter is to be found in the celebrated judgment of Lord
Camden in Entick *v.* Carrington (the case of the seizure of papers),
19 *St. Trials*, 1030.   See also *ante*, p. 110, &c.
[2] Stubbs, *Charters*, 140-146.   [3] *Ib.* 150-153.   [4] Arts. 2, 4.
[5] "Robator vel murdrator vel latro."   [6] Arts. 9-11.

CH. VII. persons or to examine the frank pledges and see that every one was a member of a frank pledge. The Assize of North-hampton [1] enacts amongst other things that every robber on being taken is to be delivered to the custody of the sheriff, and in his absence to be taken to the nearest " castellanus " to be kept by him till he is delivered to the sheriff. The Assize also provides (art. 2) that no one is to be allowed to entertain any guest in his house, either in a town or in the country (neque in burgo neque in villâ), for more than a night unless the guest has some [2] reasonable excuse which the host is to show to his neighbours, and when the guest leaves, he must do so in the presence of neighbours and by day.

By the [3] Assize of Arms, issued in 1181, every one was bound to have certain arms according to his property. The justices, on their eyre, were to make the representatives of all hundreds and towns swear to give in a return showing the property of all persons in the neighbourhood, and which of them had the arms which, according to their property, they were bound to have. Those who had not such arms were to be brought before the justices to swear to have them by a given day, and "justitiæ facient " dici per omnes comitatus per quos ituræ sunt, quod qui " hæc arma non habuerint secundum quod prædictum est, " dominus rex capiet se ad eorum membra et nullo modo " capiet ab eis terram vel catallum."

The main object of these provisions no doubt was to provide a military force; but they were also intended to give the local authorities the means of suppressing violent crimes, for the persons so armed formed the power of the county (*posse comitatus*), which it was the duty of the sheriff in case of need to raise by hue and cry.

This is set in a striking light by a [4] passage in Bracton, which describes the steps to be taken on opening a commis-sion of eyre by the justices in eyre. The representatives of the county having been convened, the justices were to make

---

[1] Art. 12; Stubbs, *Charters*, 152.
[2] "Essonium," this is the technical word for the excuses given for not taking a step in procedure, *e.g.* for not appearing on being summoned in an action.   [3] Stubbs, *Charters*, 154.
[4] Bracton, iii. 1, vol. ii. p. 235-237 (Twiss's edition).

a speech to them. " In the first place, concerning the peace
" of our Lord the King, and the violation of his justice by
" murderers, robbers, and burglars, who exercise their malice
" by day and by night, not only against men travelling from
" place to place, but against men sleeping in their beds, and
" that our Lord the King orders all his faithful subjects, by
" the faith which they owe to him, and as they wish to
" preserve their own, to give effectual and diligent counsel
" and aid to the preservation of peace and justice and to the
" taking away and repression of the malice of the aforesaid."
The principal persons are then to be taken apart, and are to
be privately informed " that all persons of fifteen years of
" age and upwards, as well knights as others, must swear
" that they will not receive outlaws, murderers, robbers, or
" burglars, nor consent to them, nor to those who receive
" them, and that if they know of such persons, they will
" cause them to be attached, and give information to the
" sheriffs and bailiffs, and, if hue and cry is raised upon
" them, will, as soon as they hear the cry, follow with their
" households and the men of their land." If the criminal
is not taken on the spot, he is to be tracked. " Let them
" follow the track through their own land, and at the end
" of their own land show it to the lord of the next land, and
" thus let pursuit be made from land to land " (township
to township) " with all diligence till the criminals are taken,
" and let there be no delay in following the track unless a
" difficulty arises by the coming on of night, or by other
" reasonable cause, and they must, according to their power,
" arrest those whom they suspect without waiting for the
" orders of the justice or the sheriff, and must inform the
" justices and sheriffs of what they have done. They must
" also swear that if any one comes into any village or town
" or elsewhere to buy bread or beer or other victuals, and is
" suspected of doing so for the use of criminals, they will
" arrest him and deliver him, when he is arrested, to the
" sheriff or his bailiffs. They must also swear that they
" will take in no one as a guest in their houses by night,
" unless he is well known, and that if they entertain any
" unknown person they will not permit him to leave on the

" morrow before it is clear daylight, and that in the presence
" of three or four of their nearest neighbours."

Bracton wrote in the reign of Henry III. In the time
of Henry's son and successor the system embodied in these
enactments reached its highest point of strictness. This
appears from the provisions of the Statute of Winchester
(13 Edw. 1, st. 2, c. 1, 2, 4, 5, 6), passed in 1285. ¹ This
statute enacts (ch. 2) that when a robbery is committed
the hundred shall be answerable unless the robbers are
apprehended within forty days, that in all walled towns the
gates shall be shut from sunset to sunrise, that a watch
should be set at each gate, and " that no man do lodge in
" suburbs from nine of the clock until day without his host
" will answer for him." All strangers passing the watch at
night are to be arrested till morning. All roads are to be
cleared, " so that there be neither dyke, underwood, nor
" bush whereby a man may lurk to do hurt" within 200
feet on each side of the road. Lastly, every man is to "have in
" his house harness to keep the peace after the ancient assize"
(the Assize of Arms). The arms were to be viewed twice
a year by constables chosen for that purpose, who were to
present defaulters to the justices. The sheriffs and bailiffs
were to follow the cry with proper horses and armour
whenever it might be raised.

By this time frank pledge must have become obsolete.
The Statute of Winchester makes no mention of it, nor
does the Statutum Walliæ, nor indeed does any other
statute with which I am acquainted treat it as an actually
existing institution for keeping the peace. The name indeed continued and still exists. The view of the frank
pledge, that is to say, the verification of the fact that the
frank pledges were in full efficiency, and that every one
belonged to such a body, was anciently one of the most important duties of the county and hundred courts and the
courts leet. Hence, as the county and hundred courts

---

¹ This enactment was followed by others, *e.g.* 9 Geo. 1, c. 22, s. 7 (the
Black Act), which in particular cases rendered the hundred liable for damages
inflicted by criminals. They were all repealed by 7 & 8 Geo. 4, c. 27.
There are, however, still one or two cases in which such a liability is imposed
by 7 & 8 Geo. 4, c. 31. These relate to damages caused by rioters.

were disused, the expression "the view of frank pledge" came to be synonymous with "court leet." The chief business transacted in these views of frank pledge or courts leet was the presentment of petty nuisances, and especially the "assiza panis et cerevisiæ," violations by bakers and brewers of rules as to the quality of their bread and beer. It is in this sense that frank pledge is referred to in the [1] Parliament Rolls, and that the expression is used by Coke. The "Statute for View of Frank Pledge" (18 Edw. 2, A.D. 1325) specifies thirty-four such articles as to which stewards were to inquire in their leets.

Shortly the system just described was as follows. Upon the commission of a felony any one might arrest the offender, and it was the duty of any constable to do so. If the offender was not arrested on the spot, hue and cry might and ought to be raised. The sheriff and constables from the earliest times, the justices of the peace from the beginning of the reign of Edward III., were the officers by whom the cry was to be raised. In order to render the system effective, every one was bound to keep arms to follow the cry when required, all towns were to be watched and the gates shut at night, and all travelling was put under severe restrictions.

The Assize of Arms and the [2] Statute of Winchester fell into disuse, but the right of summary arrest in cases of felony continues to this day to be the law of the land, and though the sheriff's personal intervention in the matter has practically fallen into disuse, the justices, and the constable are still the authorities by whom the system is worked.

One great alteration was made in the system just described between the fourteenth and the seventeenth centuries. During that period, summonses and warrants superseded

---

[1] See e.g. a petition in 1377 (1 Richard II.) : "Item suppliont les ditz com-"muns q les Srs qui ount letters et viewe de frank plegg' q'ils faient due "punissement as Taverners de vins si avant come des autres vitailles." The answer is, "Il n'est mye article de veue de frank plegge mais en soit usee "come ad estee fait resonablement avant ces heures." 3 Rot. Par. 19 ; and sce 4th Inst. 261.

[2] The Statute of Winchester is not mentioned in Coke's 2nd Institute, and though it was not repealed till 1828, it had for centuries before that time been greatly neglected. See Barrington's Observations on the Statutes, p. 146.

Ch. VII.   the old hue and cry which practically fell into disuse. The
———   history of this substitution is curious.

Justices of the peace were first instituted in 1326.   Their
duties were described in the most general terms.   They were
by 1 Edw. 3, c. 16, "assigned to keep the peace."   By
34 Edw. 3, c. 1 (1360), they were empowered "to take and
"arrest all those they may find by indictment or suspicion
"and put them in prison."   But neither in these nor any
other early statute with which I am acquainted is there any
provision which enables them directly to take an information
as to the commission of a crime and issue a summons or
warrant for the apprehension of the suspected person.

The statutes above quoted give them no other authority
for the apprehension of offenders than was by the common
law inherent in every constable and indeed in every private
person.   By degrees, however, the practice of issuing
warrants came into use.   The general authority of the
justices in all matters relating to crime and indeed to the
whole internal government of the country was firmly established by a great variety of statutes, and it would be natural
that their directions should be taken when a crime was committed.   It would also be more natural for the justice to
authorise the constable to undertake the actual arrest of the
offenders than to do it himself, and it might often be convenient, if a suspected person was to be searched for in more
directions than one, to give written authority to various persons
for the purpose.

This would be specially convenient in the case of a
hue and cry.   If offenders were to be followed from township
to township, the different constables of each being required to
join, a written authority from a known public officer like a
justice of the peace would be a great convenience.   The
phrase [1] "grant a hue and cry" was apparently in common use
in the seventeenth century for granting a warrant but the
granting of warrants was afterwards recognised by [2] various

---

[1] "At eleven o'clock the same night, as I was going into bed, Mr. Thynne's
"gentleman came to me to grant a hue and cry" (on his master's murder by
the friends of Count Coningsmark).—*Sir J. Reresby's Memoirs*, p. 235 (edition
of 1875).

[2] See *e.g.* 9 Geo. 1, c. 7, s. 3 ; 13 Geo. 3, c. 31 ; 44 Geo. 3, c. 92.

statutes, and was finally set upon an [1] indisputable statutory
foundation in 1848 by 11 & 12 Vic. c. 42, ss. 1, 2, 8, &c.
The effect of these provisions is that, where a complaint is
made to any justice that any person has committed any indictable offence, the justice may issue a summons to such
person, or, if he thinks it necessary, and if the charge is made
on oath, and in writing, a warrant for his apprehension.

The power of the justices to issue such process was however
disputed for centuries. In [2] Hawkins's *Pleas of the Crown*,
many authorities upon the subject are referred to, and a very
qualified and hesitating conclusion is reached, that "perhaps
" it is the better opinion at this day that any constable or
" private person to whom a warrant shall be directed from a
" justice of the peace to arrest a particular person for felony
" or any other misdemeanour within his jurisdiction may law-
" fully execute it, whether the person mentioned in it be in
" truth guilty or innocent, and whether he were indicted of
" the same offence or not, and whether any felony
" were in truth committed or not." This hesitation is explained by the difference of opinion between Coke and Hale
upon the subject. [3] Coke maintained that, before the statutes
of Philip and Mary authorising justices to examine witnesses
when a person was arrested for felony, "a justice of the peace
" could not make a warrant to take a man for felony unless he
" be indicted thereof." He also maintained that the only
warrant which the statutes of Philip and Mary could be taken
to authorise by implication (they say nothing at all about
warrants) were warrants to constables to see the king's peace
kept upon the occasion of the apprehension of the person
suspected by the person having suspicion. Coke goes so far
as to maintain that upon such a warrant the constable would
not be justified in breaking open a door, "for it is in law the
" arrest of the party that hath the knowledge or suspicion."

[4] Hale referring to this passage, says that Coke "hath
" delivered certain tenets which, if they should hold to be
" law, would much abridge the power of justices of the peace,

---

[1] *Dig. Crim. Proc.* arts. 99-108.
[2] Bk. ii. ch. xiii. vol. ii. pp. 129, 130, edition of 1824.
[3] *4th Inst.* 176, 177.   [4] 2 *P. C.* 107-110.

"and give a loose to felons to escape unpunished in most
"cases." He then proceeds to refer to the statutes of
Edward III., and argues in substance that as at common
law a private person might and a constable ought to arrest
supposed felons upon suspicion without warrant, the justice
might do so *à fortiori*, in virtue of the general terms of the
statutes, and that he might also "issue a warrant, to appre-
"hend a person suspected of felony though the original
"suspicion be not in himself, but in the party that prays his
"warrant, and the reason is because he is a competent judge
"of the probabilities offered to him of such suspicion." This
opinion prevailed in practice long before any necessity arose for
inquiring whether it was well founded in theory. That it
was highly expedient that justices of the peace should act
judicially in issuing warrants admits of no question at all.
That it was intended that they should do so when the statutes
under which they were first appointed were enacted seems to
me unlikely. If such had been the intention of the legislature, it is probable that they would have been authorised
and indeed required to proceed in the same manner as
coroners, namely, by summoning inquests; but, however this
may be, the whole subject is now set on a perfectly plain
foundation by the statutes already referred to.

Whilst the duties of private persons, constables, and justices
were being gradually ascertained, the law as to the circumstances which would justify an arrest for felony was being
elaborated. In an earlier chapter I have given some illustrations of the manner in which all sorts of criminals, and
especially all thieves, were regarded in very early times as
enemies to be put to death almost like wild animals. It would
not be worth while to trace minutely the steps by which
this general and crude view of the subject was gradually
reduced to the shape in which it now stands. Questions continually arose as to whether a person who had killed another
in resisting apprehension was guilty of any offence at all, and,
if guilty, whether the offence of which he was guilty amounted
to murder or manslaughter. These cases were decided from
time to time according to a variety of distinctions suggested by the circumstances of each particular case, a long

detail of which may be found in [1] Hale's *Pleas of the Crown*   Ch. VII.
which is still the leading authority as to the general principles
of the subject, though subsequent decisions and enactments
have to some extent modified Hale's conclusions. [2] The result
of his inquiry may be thus stated :—

1. Any person may arrest any person who is actually
committing or has actually committed any felony.

2. Any person may arrest any person whom he suspects on
reasonable grounds to have committed any felony, if a felony
has actually been committed.

3. Any constable may arrest any person whom he suspects
on reasonable grounds of having committed any felony,
whether in fact any such felony has been committed or not.

The common law did not authorise the arrest of persons
guilty or suspected of misdemeanours, except in cases of an
actual breach of the peace either by an affray or by violence
to an individual. In such cases the arrest had to be made not
so much for the purpose of bringing the offender to justice as
in order to preserve the peace, and the right to arrest was
accordingly limited to cases in which the person to be arrested
was taken in the fact or immediately after its commission.

As to the degree of force which may be used in order to
arrest a criminal, many questions might be suggested which
could be answered only by way of conjecture. Two leading
principles, however, may be laid down with some confidence,
which are also to be collected from Hale. The first is [3] that
if a felon flies or resists those who try to apprehend him, and
cannot otherwise be taken, he may lawfully be killed. [4] The
second is that a person who makes an arrest because it is his
legal duty to do so is more readily justified in using violence
for the purpose than a person who is under no such duty.

---

[1] 2 Hale, 72-105.
[2] As to present law of summary arrest, see *Dig. Crim. Proc.* ch. xii. arts.
96-98.
[3] 1 Hale, 481, 489 ; and see Foster, 271. This rule seems to overlook the
distinction between taking a man prisoner and taking possession of his dead
body, for it is difficult to see in what sense a pickpocket can be said to be
taken if he is shot dead on the spot. The rule would be more accurately expressed by saying that a man is justified in using any violence to arrest a felon
which may be necessary for that purpose, even if it puts, and is known and
meant to put, his life in the greatest possible danger, and is inflicted by a
deadly weapon, and does in fact kill him.   [4] 1 Hale, 490 ; Foster, 418.

CH. VII.   If A kills B, whom he suspects on probable grounds of having committed a felony, though in fact he has not, and whom he cannot otherwise arrest, it appears probable that A is guilty of manslaughter if he is a private person, but if A is a constable following a hue and cry, his act is justifiable because he acts in the discharge of a legal duty.

The common law as to the arrest of prisoners remained substantially unaltered for a great length of time. It is indeed in force at this day with some few modifications, to be stated immediately; but since it reached the state of development just described, changes of the greatest importance have been made in the position of the officers by whom it is put in force. These changes I now proceed to notice.

From the earliest times to our own days, there were two bodies of police in England, namely, the parish and high constables, and the watchmen in cities and boroughs. [1] The parish constables, under various names (borsholders, headboroughs, tithingmen, chief pledges, &c.), were probably the successors of the old reeves, who with their four men represented the township on all occasions at the beginning of our legal history. In each hundred and in many franchises there were also high constables, or similar officers with other names, who were to the hundred or franchise what the parish constables were to the township. These officers continued to be appointed till within the last few years. The duties of the high constables came to be almost nominal, consisting principally in issuing various notices under different statutes, and they were relieved of them almost entirely in 1844 by the 7 & 8 Vic. c. 33, ss. 7 & 8. The office itself was practically abolished in 1869 by 32 & 33 Vic. c. 47. The parish constables continued to be appointed till 1872, when their appointment was rendered unnecessary (except in some special cases) by 35 & 36 Vic. c. 72; but from the time when the Statute of Winchester and the Assize of Arms became obsolete till the year 1829, they were the only body of men, except the watchmen in cities and boroughs, charged with the duty of apprehending criminals and preventing crimes.

---

[1] Dalton's *Justice*, p. 3 ; Burn's *Justice*, title " Constable." A tithingman seems to have been subordinate to the constable.

The watchmen in towns were first established by the
Statute of Winchester, and the powers of the town magistrates depended originally upon their charters, which were
often silent on the subject of watchmen. At a time which
I am not able to fix with precision, but which from [1] expressions in the Report of the Municipal Corporation Commission
I think must have been in the latter part of the last century,
it became customary to pass Local Improvement Acts, by which
the management of matters connected with the police of towns
was usually vested in a body of trustees or commissioners
distinct from the corporation itself. There were great differences in the manner in which these powers were allotted.
The following passage occurs in the report already quoted :—
[2] " In a very great number of towns there are no watchmen
" or police officers of any kind except the constables, who are
" unsalaried officers. They are sometimes appointed at a
" court leet, more frequently by the corporate authorities.
" The police, and the powers conferred by local acts for
" paving, lighting, and watching the town, are seldom ex-
" clusively in the jurisdiction of the corporation; sometimes
" they are shared by the corporate authorities and commis-
" sioners ; sometimes they are vested in commissioners alone."
A striking illustration of the confusion thus produced is
given in [3] Colquhoun's *Treatise on the Police of the Metropolis.*
He observes :—" At present the watchmen destined to guard
" the lives and property of the inhabitants residing in near
" 8,000 streets, lanes, courts, and alleys, and about 152,000
" houses, composing the whole of the metropolis and its
" environs, are under the directions of not less than above
" seventy different trusts, regulated by perhaps double the
" number of local acts of parliament (varying in many shades
" from one another), under which these directors, guardians,
" governors, trustees, or vestries, according to the title they
" assume, are authorised to act, each attending only to

[1] 1st Report, p. 17.   [2] P. 29.
[3] Published in 1796. In the *Report of a Select Committee on the Police of
the Metropolis,* published in 1838, the Committee says of this work, "The
" merit of being the first to point out the necessity and practicability of a
" system of preventive police upon an uniform and consistent plan is due to
" Mr. Colquhoun, the author of the treatise *On the Police of the Metropolis.*"

CH. VII.   " their own particular ward, parish, hamlet, liberty, or
———   " precinct."

Nothing could exceed the inefficiency of the constables
and watchmen. Of the constables, Dalton (in the reign of
James I.) observes that they " are often absent from their
" houses, being for the most part husbandmen, and so most
" of the day in the fields." The charge of Dogberry shows
probably with no great caricature what sort of watchmen
Shakespeare was familiar with. In the work already quoted,
[1] Colquhoun observes of the watchmen of his time that the
pay was so bad that " the managers have no alternative but
" to accept of such aged and often superannuated men living
" in their respective districts as may offer their services." . . .
" What can be expected from such watchmen ? Aged in
" general; often feeble ; and almost on every occasion half
" starved from the limited allowance they receive, and
" without any claim upon the public or the least hope of
" reward held out even if they performed any meritorious
" service " . . . " and, above all, making so many parts of
" an immense system, without any general superintendence,
" disjointed from the nature of its organisation, it is only a
" matter of wonder that the protection afforded should be
" what it really is."

The defects of this state of things were slightly, but very
slightly, mitigated by the institution of a number of small
bodies of constables under the direction of particular magistrates. In the year 1796 there were eight such constables at
Bow Street (known as Bow-Street runners), and six others
at each of seven other police offices in London, making in all
fifty constables who gave their whole time to their business.
There were also sixty-seven mounted police, forming what was
called the horse patrol, who patrolled the roads near London
for the suppression of highwaymen. Probably there may
have been arrangements more or less resembling these in other
large towns. This system continued practically unaltered till
the year 1829, although [2] various parliamentary inquiries into

---

[1] Colquhoun, p. 232.
[2] Parliamentary committees reported on the subject in 1816, 1817, 1818,
1822, and 1828. The evidence given before them fills several bluebooks, and is
curious and instructive.

the subject took place.   In 1829 was passed the first of a   CH. VII.
series of acts which put the administration of the law as to
the apprehension of offenders upon quite a new footing.
This was the 10 Geo. 4, c. 44.   Under this act, as amended
by the [1] later acts referred to in the notes, the following system
was established, and still exists, in the neighbourhood of
London.   The city of Westminster and certain parts of the
counties of Middlesex, Surrey, Hertford, Essex, and Kent are
constituted into a district called "The Metropolitan Police
District."   [2] Her Majesty is empowered to appoint a "Commissioner of the Police of the Metropolis," with two Assistant
Commissioners, who in certain cases may act as his deputies
and in other cases act under his orders.

[3] The Commissioner and assistants are during their tenure
of office justices of the peace for Middlesex, Surrey, Hertford, Essex, Kent, Berkshire, and Buckinghamshire, but
they must not sit at quarter sessions, nor act except
for the preservation of the peace, the prevention of crimes,
the detention and committal of offenders, and the execution
of the acts by which they are appointed.

[4] A sufficient number of fit and able men are from time to
time by the direction of the Home Secretary to be sworn in
before the Commissioner to act as a police force for the whole
district, and throughout the counties of Middlesex, Surrey,
Hertford, Essex, Kent, Berkshire, and Buckinghamshire,
and [5] on the Thames, and the members of the force are
throughout those counties to have all the powers which constables duly appointed have within their constablewick at
common law.

[6] The Commissioner may, subject to the approbation of the

---

[1] 10 Geo. 4, c. 44, s. 4.   The schedule to the act constitutes certain
parts of Middlesex, Surrey, and Kent into the Metropolitan Police District.
S. 34 gives the Secretary of State power to extend it to places within twelve
miles of Charing Cross, and this is extended to fifteen miles by 2 & 3 Vic.
c. 47, s. 2.
[2] There were at first two justices, 10 Geo. 4, c. 44, s. 1.   They were to
be called Commissioners of Police by 2 & 3 Vic. c. 47, s. 4.   One Commissioner and two Assistant Commissioners were substituted by 19 & 20 Vic.
c. 2.
[3] 10 Geo. 4, c. 44, s. 1; 2 & 3 Vic. c. 47, s. 4; 19 & 20 Vic. c. 2, s. 1.
[4] 10 Geo. 4, c. 44, s. 4.   [5] 2 & 3 Vic. c. 47, s. 5.
[6] 10 Geo. 4, c. 44, s. 5.

CH. VII.   Home Secretary, frame orders and regulations for the government and regulation of the force.

[1]The expenses of the force are paid by a rate not exceeding
8*d.* in the pound which the Commissioner is empowered to
lay upon parishes in the Metropolitan Police District, and
which is to be collected with the poor rate. [2]It is received
and administered by an officer called the Receiver for the
Metropolitan Police District, who receives, expends, and accounts for the moneys in a manner prescribed in the various
acts referred to below. [3]A sum not exceeding £20,000 a
year may be contributed by the Treasury to the expenses of
the Thames police.

These provisions are the essential part of the acts by which
the metropolitan police were established. They contain
besides numerous important provisions as to police courts
and police offences.

The next general measure relating to the appointment of
police constables was embodied in the [4]Municipal Corporations
Act. By this act the councils of the boroughs were empowered to appoint a sufficient number of their own body
to be, together with the mayor, the watch committee of the
borough. The watch committee are to appoint a sufficient
number of fit men (to be sworn in before a borough justice)
as constables. The constables are to act as such, not only
within the borough, but also within the county in which such
borough or part of it is situated, and also within every
county within seven miles of any part of the borough. The
watch committee are to make such rules as they think
expedient for preventing neglect or abuse and for rendering
the constables efficient in the discharge of their duties.

These provisions were, I believe, generalised from those
which were usually inserted in the Local Improvement Acts
already referred to, [5]and it was accordingly provided that, as

---

[1] 10 Geo. 4, c. 44, s. 23.
[2] 10 Geo. 4, c. 44, ss. 10-17, 25-29 ; 2 & 3 Vic. c. 71, ss. 7, 8, 47 ; 20 &
21 Vic. c. 64, ss. 13-15 ; 24 & 25 Vic. c. 124 ; 34 & 35 Vic. c. 35.
[3] 2 & 3 Vic. c. 47, s. 5.
[4] 5 & 6 Will. 4, c. 76, ss. 76-86 ; see also 45 & 46 Vic. c. 50, ss. 190-200.
[5] S. 84. This section does not appear to have been re-enacted by 45 & 46
Vic. c. 50. Improvement Acts are still passed for towns and populous districts
which are not incorporated, and in order to provide generally for such cases

soon as constables have been appointed by the watch committee, and a notice given as specified in the act, other acts relating to the subject shall cease.

The expenses of the borough police are payable out of the borough rate.

The next step towards the provision of a general system of police was taken in 1839 by the Act 2 & 3 Vic. c. 93. This act permitted a body of police to be established for a county, with the consent of [1] the Secretary of State for the Home Department, on a representation from the magistrates at quarter sessions. [2] The Home Secretary makes rules as to the government, pay, clothing, and accoutrements of the constables. [3] The justices appoint for the county a chief constable or in certain cases more chief constables than one. [4] The chief constable (subject to the approval of at least two justices in petty sessions) appoints the other constables for the county, and a superintendent to be at the head of the constables of each division of the county, and can dismiss all or any of them at pleasure. He has the general disposition and government of the constables so appointed, subject to such lawful orders as he receives from the justices in sessions, and to the rules established for the government of the force.

[5] The constables have all the powers of a constable at common law throughout every part of their own and of all adjoining counties, [6] and are subject to the same provisions as to notice, neglect of duty, and the like, as those which have been already noticed in reference to the metropolitan police.

[7] The expenses are paid by a police rate made by the justices and received and expended by the county treasurer; [8] but one fourth of the expense of the pay and clothing of the constables is, if they are certified by the Secretary of

an act called "The Town Police Clauses Act, 1847" (10 & 11 Vic. c. 19) was passed, which contains provisions similar to those already referred to, and is usually embodied by reference in the special acts.

[1] In all these acts the expression is "one of her Majesty's principal Secretaries of State." In practice this means the Secretary of State for the Home Department.

[2] 2 & 3 Vic. c. 93, s. 3.   [3] 2 & 3 Vic. c. 93, s. 3, and see 20 Vic. c. 2.
[4] 2 & 3 Vic. c. 93, s. 60.   [5] S. 8.
[6] 2 & 3 Vic. c. 93, ss. 10-14.   [7] 3 & 4 Vic. c. 88, ss. 3-13, 25.
[8] 19 & 20 Vic. c. 69, s. 16.

Cʜ. VII.   State to be in a state of efficiency in point of numbers and discipline, to be paid by the Treasury out of the general taxation of the country.

[1] The Secretary of State for the Home Department has power to appoint three inspectors to inquire into the state and efficiency of the county and borough police and to see that the provisions of the Police Acts are properly carried out.

In 1856, after an experience of seventeen years in the working of the Act 2 & 3 Vic. c. 93, an act (19 & 20 Vic. c. 69) was passed which made compulsory the establishment of county police in all parts of England in which they had not been already established.

The result is that a disciplined force in the nature of a standing army for the suppression of crime and the apprehension of offenders has been provided throughout every part of England by four successive steps, namely, (1) the establishment of the metropolitan police in 1829, (2) that of the borough police in 1836, (3) the partial establishment of the county police by the permissive act of 1839, and (4) its complete establishment by the compulsory act of 1856.

Extensive additions to the powers of summary arrest which were vested in constables by common law have been made with respect to particular offences. I do not propose to enter at length upon this subject, but the [2] references given below will enable any one to do so who is so disposed.

SUPPRESSION OF OFFENCES BY MILITARY FORCE.—So far I have dealt with the provision made by law for the apprehension of offenders in common cases, but there are other cases which occur less frequently, and for which it is necessary to make special provision as they arise.

These are offences committed by large numbers of persons and with the strong hand. They may vary in gravity from

---

[1] 19 & 20 Vic. c. 69, s. 15.

[2] See 14 & 15 Vic. c. 19, as to persons committing indictable offences at night; 24 & 25 Vic. c. 96, s. 103, as to persons found committing offences against the Larceny Act; s. 104, as to arrest of persons found loitering in yards, &c.; 24 & 25 Vic. c. 97, s. 57, as to offences against the malicious injuries to Property Act; 24 & 25 Vic. c. 100, s. 66, as to offences against the person; 24 & 25 Vic. c. 99, as to offences relating to the coinage; 5 Geo. 4, c. 83. s. 4, as to offences against the Vagrant Act, and in 34 & 35 Vic. c. 112, s. 15, which amends it. As to police offences in the metropolis see 2 & 3 Vic. c. 47. s. 55. See too *Dig. Crim. Proc.* arts. 96 98.

an ordinary riot up to high treason by waging war against the Queen, and they may either be suppressed immediately or may grow into civil wars.   The law on this subject has considerable historical and constitutional interest.

The definition of the various crimes by which the peace may be disturbed will be considered hereafter, but I propose at present to state the effect of the law as to their suppression.

The common law right and duty not only of the conservators of the peace but of all private persons (according to their power), to keep the peace and to disperse and, if necessary, to arrest those who break it, is obvious and well settled, but it is also obvious that it can hardly be discharged to advantage without special statutory power.   In the earlier stages of our history the power and turbulence of the nobility was so great that private war was all but continual, and the preservation of the peace by force of arms was the first duty of all rulers.   Violence in all its forms was so common, and the suppression of force by force so simple a matter, that special legislation did not appear necessary in very early times.   [1] The earliest express recognition by statute of this state of things to which I can refer occurs in the Statute of Treasons.   After defining treason positively, the statute proceeds to say what shall not be held to be treason.   " And " if percase any man of this realm ride armed covertly " (it should be translated " openly," the French is "descovert") " or secretly with men of arms against any other to slay " him, or rob him, or take him, or retain him till he hath " made fine or ransom for to have his deliverance, it is not " the mind of the king nor his council that in such case it " shall be judged treason, but shall be judged felony or " trespass according to the laws of the land of old time " used and according as the case requireth."   In other words, private war, whatever else it may be, is not treason.

The first definite legislation as to the suppression of riots dates from 1393 (17 Rich. 2, c. 8).

This statute recites that, notwithstanding the prohibition

[1] See, however, 7 Edw. 1, st. 1, A.D. 1279, as to coming armed to Parliament, and 33 Edw. 1, st. 2 (1304), a definition of conspirators.

CH. VII of riots which had been made twelve years before (in 1381, the date of Wat Tyler's insurrection), great disturbances had been made in Chester, Lancashire, and elsewhere (probably in connection with the Lollards), and enacts that in cases of riot the sheriffs are, "with the strength of the county and " counties to set disturbance against such malice with all " their power and shall take such offenders and them put in " prison." This act was supplemented by many others. By 13 Hen. 4, c. 7 (A.D. 1411), it is enacted that, when a riot happens, two justices at least and the sheriff or under-sheriff "shall come with the power of the county and shall " arrest them," and shall have power to record "that which " they shall find so done in their presence," and either try the offenders within a month or "certify the deed and " circumstances thereof" to the king and his council, "which " certificate shall be of like force as the presentment of " twelve," and the offenders are to be punished according to the discretion of the king and his council. By the 2 Hen. 5, st. 1, c. 8, it was added that, if the sheriffs and justices made default, any party aggrieved might have a commission from the chancellor to the coroners to inquire both into the riot and into the default of the justices and sheriffs. The justices suppressing the riots were, on the other hand, to be paid their expenses. The next chapter (ch. 9) of the same statute provides that, if the rioters fly, they may be proclaimed, and shall be liable to conviction if they do not come in upon the proclamation. [1] Under the Tudors, acts were passed which made it felony for twelve persons or upwards to continue together riotously for an hour after they had been ordered by a justice to disperse, but none of these acts provided any special force beyond the power of the county which could be used by the sheriff or justices.

Throughout the seventeenth century, [2] Parliament was little disposed to legislate against riots, but at the beginning of the eighteenth century was passed the famous Act, 1 Geo. 1, st. 2, c. 5, still in force and commonly known as the Riot Act. It increases the severity of the Tudor Acts (which expired at

---

[1] 3 & 4 Edw. 6, c. 5 ; 1 Mary, sess. 2, c. 12 ; 1 Eliz. c. 16.
[2] See, however, the act for suppressing seditious conventicles, 22 Chas. 2, c. 1.

the death of Elizabeth) by making it felony without benefit CH. VII. of clergy, for twelve rioters to continue together for one hour after the making by a magistrate of a [1] proclamation to them to disperse. It then requires the magistrates to seize and apprehend all persons so continuing together, and it provides that, if the persons so assembled, or any of them, " happen to " be killed, maimed, or hurt in dispersing, seizing, or appre- "hending, or endeavouring to disperse, seize, or apprehend " them," the magistrates and those who act under their orders shall be indemnified. As a standing army had come into existence before this act passed, the effect of it was that after making the proclamation and waiting for an hour the magistrates might order the troops to fire upon the rioters or to charge them sword in hand. To say so in so many words would no doubt have given great offence, but the effect of the indirect hint at the employment of armed force given by the statute was singular. It seems to have been generally under- stood that the enactment was negative as well as positive ; that troops not only might be ordered to act against a mob if the conditions of the act were complied with, but that they might not be so employed without the fulfilment of such conditions. This view of the law has been on several occasions decided to be altogether erroneous. The true doctrine on the subject was much considered, both in the case of Lord George Gordon's Riots in 1780, and in the case of the Bristol Riots in 1831. It may be shortly stated as follows. The fact that soldiers are permanently embodied and subjected by the Mutiny Act to military discipline, and bound to obey the lawful orders of their superior officers, does not in any degree exempt them from the obligation incumbent on all her Majesty's subjects to keep the peace and disperse unlawful assemblies. On the contrary, it gives them special and peculiar facilities for discharging that duty. In a case of extreme emergency they may lawfully do so

---

[1] "Our sovereign Lady the Queen chargeth and commandeth all persons " being assembled immediately to disperse themselves and peaceably to depart " to their habitations or to their lawful business, upon the pains contained " in the Act made in the first year of King George for preventing tumults " and riotous assemblies. God save the Queen." The making of this pro- clamation is commonly, but very incorrectly, called reading the Riot Act.

Ch. VII. without being required by the magistrates. [1] In the words of Lord Chief Justice Tindal, in his charge to the grand jury at Bristol, 2nd January, 1832 :—"The law acknowledges no "distinction between the soldier and the private individual. " The soldier is still a citizen, lying under the same obligation " and invested with the same authority to preserve the peace " of the King as any other subject. If the one is bound to "attend the call of the civil magistrate, so also is the other. " If the one may interfere for that purpose when the occasion " demands it without the requisition of the magistrate, so " may the other too. If the one may employ arms for that " purpose when arms are necessary, the soldier may do the "same. Undoubtedly, the same exercise of discretion which "requires the private subject to act in subordination to, "and in aid of, the magistrate rather than upon his own " authority before recourse is had to arms ought to operate in " a still stronger degree with a military force. But where the " danger is pressing and immediate ; where a felony has " actually been committed or cannot otherwise be prevented "and from the circumstances of the case no opportunity is " offered of obtaining a requisition from the proper au- " thorities, the military subjects of the King, like his civil " subjects, not only may but are bound to do their utmost of " their own authority to prevent the perpetration of outrage, " to put down riot and tumult, and to preserve the lives and " property of the people. Still further by the common law " not only is each private subject bound to exert himself to " the utmost, but every sheriff, constable, and other peace "officer is called upon to do all that in them lies for the " suppression of riot, and each has authority to command all " other subjects of the King to assist them in that "under the King."

The result of this view of the subject is to put soldiers acting under the orders of their military superiors in an awkward position. By the ordinary principles of the common law they are, speaking generally, justified only in using such force as is reasonably necessary for the suppression of a riot. By the Mutiny Act and the Articles of War they are bound to

[1] 5 C. & P. 261, &c.

execute any lawful order which they may receive from their CH. VII. military superior, and an order to fire upon a mob is lawful if such an act is reasonably necessary. An order to do more than might be reasonably necessary for the dispersion of rioters would not be a lawful order. The hardship upon soldiers is, that if a soldier kills a man in obedience to his officer's orders, the question whether what was done was more than was reasonably necessary has to be decided by a jury, probably upon a trial for murder; whereas, if he disobeys his officer's orders to fire because he regards them as unlawful, the question whether they were unlawful as having commanded something not reasonably necessary would have to be decided by a court-martial upon the trial of the soldier for disobeying orders, and for obvious reasons the jury and the court-martial are likely to take different views as to the reasonable necessity and therefore as to the lawfulness of such an order.

I do not think, however, that the question how far superior orders would justify soldiers or sailors in making an attack upon civilians has ever been brought before the courts of law in such a manner as to be fully considered and determined. Probably upon such an argument it would be found that the order of a military superior would justify his inferiors in executing any orders for giving which they might fairly suppose their superior officer to have good reasons. Soldiers might reasonably think that their officer had good grounds for ordering them to fire into a disorderly crowd which to them might not appear to be at that moment engaged in acts of dangerous violence, but soldiers could hardly suppose that their officer could have any good grounds for ordering them to fire a volley down a crowded street when no disturbance of any kind was either in progress or apprehended. The doctrine that a soldier is bound under all circumstances whatever to obey his superior officer would be fatal to military discipline itself, for it would justify the private in shooting the colonel by the orders of the captain, or in deserting to the enemy on the field of battle on the order of his immediate superior. I think it is not less monstrous to suppose that superior orders would justify a soldier in the massacre of

Ch. VII. unoffending civilians in time of peace, or in the exercise of inhuman cruelties, such as the slaughter of women and children, during a rebellion. The only line that presents itself to my mind is that a soldier should be protected by orders for which he might reasonably believe his officer to have good grounds. The inconvenience of being subject to two jurisdictions, the sympathies of which are not unlikely to be opposed to each other, is an inevitable consequence of the double necessity of preserving on the one hand the supremacy of the law and on the other the discipline of the army.

Happily the employment of military force for the suppression of a riot is a matter of rare occurrence in this country. When there is reason to fear any tumult with which the common police establishment cannot deal, the course usually taken is to swear in special constables. [1] The acts now in force for that purpose authorise any two justices for any county, &c., on being satisfied upon the oath of any one witness, that any tumult, riot, or felony has taken place, or may be reasonably apprehended within their jurisdiction, to nominate as special constables any persons willing to act as such, and to administer to them an oath to do their best to cause the peace to be kept, and offences to be prevented. Such persons have all the powers of constables. If necessary, all persons may be required to act as special constables, and are liable to be fined £5 if they refuse to serve or to appear when summoned to be sworn in.

These provisions are older than the acts by which police were established throughout the country, and are now seldom resorted to, as bodies of undisciplined men are apt to do more harm than good in cases of riot. On one memorable occasion, however (April 10, 1848), the swearing in of a vast number of special constables in London and elsewhere, as an answer to threats of revolutionary disturbance, was of much use, as a proof to demonstration of the fact that the great bulk of the population were at that time opposed to any resort to violence for political objects.

[1] 1 & 2 Will. 4, c. 41, amended by 5 & 6 Will. 4, c. 43. See also 1 & 2 Vic. c. 80, as to special constables on railroads, canals, and public works, and 5 & 6 Will. 4, c. 76, s. 83 (the Municipal Corporations Act).

MARTIAL LAW.—The extreme remedy which can be em- CH. VII. ployed in the case of rebellion is a proclamation of martial law and operations consequent upon it. The law upon this subject was much discussed in reference to the cases of General Nelson and Mr. Eyre, who were prosecuted for murder in causing Mr. Gordon to be executed by martial law for his alleged complicity in an insurrection of negroes which took place in 1865 at Morant Bay in Jamaica. The opinion of the late Mr. Edward James and myself was taken as to the legal meaning and effect of a proclamation of martial law. I drew the opinion and we both signed it. Nothing which took place in the proceedings which followed altered my view, and I may add that the charge delivered by Lord Chief Justice Cockburn to the grand jury at the Central Criminal Court followed almost precisely the statement of the law given in this opinion. [1] I accordingly reprint the material part of it with a few slight changes as representing what, upon the fullest inquiry, I believe to be the law upon this subject.

[2] The expression "martial law" has been used at different times in four different senses, each of which must be carefully distinguished from the others:—

1. In very early times various systems of law co-existed in this country—as the common law, the ecclesiastical law, the law of the Court of Admiralty, &c. One of these was the law martial, exercised by the constable and marshal over troops in actual service, and especially on foreign service.[3]

2. The existence of this system in cases of foreign service or actual warfare appears to have led to attempts on the part of various sovereigns to introduce the same system in time of peace on emergencies, and especially for the punishment

[1] Lord Blackburn charged the Grand Jury of Middlesex in one of the proceedings against Mr. Eyre on the subject in terms which, so far as they relate to the common law of England, do not greatly differ from what is here stated (see Mr. Finlason's report of R. v. Eyre, 68-73). I am not sure, however, that I should altogether agree with the view taken by Lord Blackburn of the effect of the Petition of Right.

[2] The case and opinion will be found in Forsyth's *Constitutional Law*, p. 551. Mr. Finlason published a *History of the Jamaica Case*, and other works connected with the subject.

[3] As to this see the "Statutes and Ordinances to be keped in time of Warre." —*Black Book of the Admiralty*, i. 282, &c. See also an essay on the "Laws of War," by Professor Mountague Bernard, in the *Oxford Essays* for 1856.

CH. VII.   of breaches of the peace.   [1] This was declared to be illegal by
———   the Petition of Right, as I shall show more fully immediately.

3. When standing armies were introduced, the powers of
the constable and marshal fell into disuse, and the discipline
of the army was provided for by annual Mutiny Acts,
which provided express regulations for the purpose. These
regulations are now contained in the Army Discipline Act,
1879 (42 & 43 Vic. c. 33), amended by 44 & 45 Vic. c. 57,
and annually brought into force.   [2] They form a code, which
is sometimes called martial, but more properly military, law.

4. Although martial law in sense (1) is obsolete, and in
sense (2) is declared by the Petition of Right to be illegal,
the expression has survived, and has been applied to a very
different thing, namely, to the common law right of the
Crown and its representatives to repel force by force in the
case of invasion or insurrection, and to act against rebels as
it might against invaders.

The provisions of the Petition of Right (3 Chas. 1, c. 1) upon
Martial Law are contained in ss. 7, 8, 9, 10. These sections
recite that commissions under the Great Seal had lately
been issued to certain persons to proceed in particular cases
" according to the justice of martial law;" and that thereby
persons had been put to death who, if deserving death, ought
to have been tried in the ordinary way, whilst others, pleading
privilege, had escaped. Such commissions are then declared
to be " wholly and directly contrary to the said laws and
" statutes of this your realm," and it is provided that henceforth no commissions of like nature may issue forth to any
person or persons whatsoever.

The commissions themselves explain the nature of the
system which the Petition of Right prohibited. Three,
which were issued shortly before it passed, are given in 17
Rymer's *Fœdera* (pp. 43, 246, 647). They are dated respectively 24th November, 1617; 20th July, 1620; 30th
December, 1624. The first is a commission to certain persons
for the government of Wales and the counties of Worcester,

[1] See Hallam's *Constitutional History*, vol. i. p. 240, seventh edition, ch. v.
near the beginning. See Vol. III. p. 109.
[2] Grant *v.* Gould, 2 H. Blackstone, 69.

Hereford, and Shropshire. It directs them to call out the array of the county, and then proceeds to direct them to lead the array—

" As well against all and singular our enemies, as also
" against all and singular rebels, traytors, and other offenders
" and their adherents, against our Crown and dignitie, within
" our said principalitie and dominions of North Wales and
" South Wales, the marches of the same, and counties
" and places aforesaid, and with the said traytors and rebells
" from tyme to tyme to fight, and them to invade, resist,
" suppresse, subdue, slay, kill, and put to execution of death,
" by all ways and means, from tyme to tyme, by your
" discretion.

" And further to doe, execute, and use against the said
" enemies, traytors, rebells, and such other like offenders
" and their adherents afore-mentioned, from tyme to tyme
" as necessities shall require, by your discretion, the law
" called martiall lawe according to the law martial, and of
" such offenders apprehended or being brought into subjection,
" to save whom you shall think to be saved, and to slaye,
" destroye, and put to execution of death, such and as many
" of them as you shall think meete, by your good discretion,
" to be put to death."

The second empowers Sir Robert Maunsell to govern the crews of certain ships intended for the suppression of piracy, and gives him "full powers to execute and take away their " life, or any member, in form and order of martial law."

The third is a commission to the Mayor of Dover, and others, reciting that certain troops, then at Dover, were licentious, and empowering them—

" To proceed according to the justice of martial law against
" such soldiers with any of our list aforesaid, and other dis-
" solute persons joining them, or any of them, as during
" such time as any of our said troops or companies of
" soldiers shall remain or abide there, and not be transported
" thence, shall, within any of the places or precincts afore-
" said, at any time after the publication of this our com-
" mission, commit any robberies, felonies, mutinies, or other
" outrages or misdemeanours which, by the martial law,

CH. VII. " should or ought to be punished with death, and by such
" summary course and order as is agreeable to martial law,
" and as is used in armies in time of war, to proceed to the
" trial and condemnation of such delinquents and offenders,
" and them cause to be executed and put to death according
" to the law martial, for an example of terror to others,
" and to keep the rest in due awe and obedience."

The distinctive feature in all these commissions is, that
they authorise not merely the suppression of revolts by
military force, which is undoubtedly legal, but the subsequent
punishment of offenders by illegal tribunals, which is the
practice forbidden by the Petition of Right. The course
taken by a lieutenant-general and his provost-marshal in
the reign of Queen Elizabeth illustrates this. In 1569
the Earls of Northumberland and Westmoreland had risen
and besieged and taken Barnard Castle, and committed
other acts of open treasonable warfare. The rising took
place and was suppressed in the course of the month of
December. The Earl of Sussex received from the Queen
a commission, evidently similar to the one already cited,
and appointed Sir George Bowes his provost-marshal. Sir
George Bowes made a circuit through Durham and Yorkshire, between the 2nd and 20th January, 1589, and executed
at various places 600 persons.[1]

As to the legal character of such punishments, Lord Coke
observes (3rd Inst. c. 7, p. 52), " If a lieutenant, or other that
" hath commission of martial authority in time of peace, hang
" or otherwise execute any man by colour of martial law, this
" is murder, for this is against Magna Charta, c. 29." [2]

These authorities seem to show that it is illegal for the
Crown to resort to martial law as a special mode of punishing
rebellion.

Some authorities look in the other direction. In 1799,
an act of the Irish Parliament (39 Geo. 3, c. 11) was
passed, the effect of which was to put the parts of the
country which were still in rebellion under military

---

[1] Sharpe's *Memorials of the Rebellion*, No. 1569, pp. 99, 113, 121, 133, 140,
143, 153, 163.
[2] See too Hale, *Hist. Common Law*, 34.

command, according to a system therein described. The preamble states that the rebellion had already been suppressed, and it sets forth that on the 24th May, 1798, Lord Camden did, by and under the advice of the Privy Council, issue his orders to all general officers commanding his Majesty's forces, to punish all persons acting, ordering, or in any way assisting in the said rebellion, according to martial law, either by death or otherwise, as to them should seem expedient, and did by his proclamation ratify the same. It further goes on to recite, that "by the " wise and salutary exercise of his Majesty's undoubted " prerogative in executing martial law for defeating and " dispersing such armed and rebellious force, and in bringing " divers rebels and traitors to punishment in the most speedy " and summary manner, the peace of the kingdom has been " so far restored as to permit the course of the common law " partially to take place," &c. And in the body of the Act (section 6) there is contained a proviso that "nothing in " this Act shall be construed to abridge or diminish the " undoubted prerogative of his Majesty for the public " safety to resort to the exercise of martial law against open " enemies or traitors."

There is a similar recital in the act known as the Insurrection Act, 3 & 4 Will. 4, c. 4 (A.D. 1833) ; s. 40 of this act provides that none of its provisions "shall be construed " to take away, abridge, or diminish the undoubted pre-" rogative of his Majesty for the public safety to resort " to the exercise of martial law against open enemies or " traitors."

It is impossible to suppose that such declarations as these should operate as a repeal of the Petition of Right as regarded Ireland, though the language of the two Acts appears to be conflicting. As, however, it merely declares an "un-" doubted prerogative of the Crown," it cannot refer to what the Petition of Right expressly denied to exist, and therefore it must probably be construed to mean only that the Crown has an undoubted prerogative to attack an army of rebels by regular forces under military law, conducting themselves as armies in the field usually do. This construction is strength-

CH. VII. ened by the fact that traitors are coupled with open enemies. Now, the force used against an invading army is used for the purpose, not of punishment, but of conquest, and thus the words in the Irish Act would mean only that the Crown has an undoubted prerogative to carry on war against an army of rebels as it would against an invading army, and to exercise all such powers as might be necessary to suppress the rebellion and to restore the peace and to permit the common law to take effect.

As soon, however, as the actual conflict was at an end it would be the duty of the military authorities to hand over their prisoners to the civil powers. This was affirmed by the case of [1] Wolfe Tone, who, having been captured when the French surrendered, was sent up to Dublin barracks, tried by court-martial and sentenced to death. The Court of King's Bench immediately granted a habeas corpus, and directed the sheriff to take into custody the provost-marshal and officers in charge, and to see that Mr. Tone was not executed. No doubt many military executions took place during the Irish rebellion, but an Act of Indemnity was passed in respect to them, and it must always be remembered that by the laws of war (which are a branch of morals rather than of law proper, and prevail not over soldiers, but only between contending armies) many severities may be justified, such as refusal of quarter and the putting to death of soldiers who have surrendered at discretion; and thus, in a war like that of 1798, much might be done which might pass under the name of martial law, but which in reality would be no more than incidents of ordinary warfare conducted with unusual rigour.

Another argument is drawn from the Annual Mutiny Acts. They contain a declaration that "no man can be forejudged " of life or limb, or subjected to any punishment within this " realm by martial law, in time of peace." This has been construed to imply that in times of war or disturbance martial law is legal. As to this, however, it must be remembered that in its original meaning, the phrase "martial " law" included what we now understand by military law,

[1] 27 *St. Tr.* 624, 625.

and that one principal object of the commissions, declared to CH. VII. be illegal by the Petition of Right, was the creation of military tribunals without Parliamentary authority. Hence the words " in peace," which were not in the first Mutiny Act, probably mean that standing armies and military courts were, in time of peace, illegal, except in so far as they were expressly authorised by Parliament.

The whole doctrine of martial law was discussèd at great length before a Committee of the House of Commons, which sat in the year 1849 to inquire into certain transactions which had taken place at Ceylon. Sir David Dundas, then Judge Advocate-General, explained his view at length, and was closely examined upon it by Sir Robert Peel, Mr. Gladstone, and others. The following answers, amongst others, throw much light on the subject :—

" 5437. The proclamation of martial law is a notice, to " all those to whom the proclamation is addressed, that there " is now another measure of law and another mode of pro- " ceeding than there was before that proclamation.

" 5459. If a governor fairly and fully believes that the " civil and military power which is with him, and such " assistance as he might derive from the sound-hearted part " of the Queen's subjects, is not enough to save the life of " the community and to suppress disorder, it is his duty " to suppress by this (*i.e.* by martial law) or any other " means.

" 5476. *Q.* (Sir Robert Peel). A wise and courageous man, " responsible for the safety of a colony, would take the law " into his own hands, and make a law for the occasion rather " than submit to anarchy? *A.* I think that a wise and " courageous man would, if necessary, make a law to his " own hands, but he would much rather take a law which " is already made ; and I believe the law of England is, that " a governor, like the Crown, has vested in him the right, " where the necessity arises, of judging of it, and being " responsible for his work afterwards, so to deal with the " laws as to supersede them all, and to proclaim martial " law for the safety of the colony.

" 5477. (In answer to Mr. Gladstone). I say he is

CH. VII.   " responsible, just as I am responsible for shooting a man on
——   " the king's highway who comes to rob me. If I mistake
           " my man, and have not, in the opinion of the judge and
           " jury who try me, an answer to give, I am responsible.

           " 5506. My notion is, that martial law is a rule of necessity,
           " and that when it is exercised by men empowered to do
           " so, and they act honestly, rigorously, and vigorously,
           " and with as much humanity as the case will permit, in
           " discharge of their duty, they have done that which every
           " good citizen is bound to do."

Martial law has, accordingly, been proclaimed in several colonies, viz. at the Cape of Good Hope, in Ceylon, in Jamaica, and in Demerara.

The views thus expressed by Sir David Dundas appear to me to be substantially correct. According to them the words, " martial law," as used in the expression " proclaiming martial " law," might be defined as the assumption for a certain time, by the officers of the Crown, of absolute power, exercised by military force, for the purpose of suppressing an insurrection or resisting an invasion. The "proclamation" of martial law, in this sense, would only be a notice to all whom it might concern that such a course was about to be taken. I do not think it is possible to distinguish martial law, thus described and explained, from the common law duty which is incumbent on every man, and especially on every magistrate, to use any degree of physical force that may be required for the suppression of a violent insurrection, and which is incumbent as well on soldiers as on civilians, the soldiers retaining during such service their special military obligations. Thus, for instance, I apprehend that if martial law had been proclaimed in London in 1780, such a proclamation would have made no difference whatever in the duties of the troops or the liabilities of the rioters. Without any such proclamation the troops were entitled, and bound, to destroy life and property to any extent which might be necessary to restore order. It is difficult to see what further power they could have had, except that of punishing the offenders afterwards, and this is expressly forbidden by the Petition of Right.

I may sum up my view of martial law in general in the CH. VII.
following propositions :—

1. Martial law is the assumption by officers of the Crown
of absolute power, exercised by military force, for the suppression of an insurrection, and the restoration of order and
lawful authority.

2. The officers of the Crown are justified in any exertion
of physical force, extending to the destruction of life and
property to any extent, and in any manner that may be
required for the purpose. They are not justified in the use
of cruel and excessive means, but are liable civilly or
criminally for such excess. They are not justified in inflicting punishment after resistance is suppressed, and after the
ordinary courts of justice can be reopened.

The principle by which their responsibility is measured is
well expressed in the case of [1] Wright *v.* Fitzgerald. Wright
was a French master of Clonmel, who, after the suppression
of the Irish rebellion in 1798, brought an action against
Mr. Fitzgerald, the sheriff of Tipperary, for having cruelly
flogged him without due inquiry. Martial law was in full
force at that time, and an Act of Indemnity had afterwards
been passed, to excuse all breaches of the law committed in
the suppression of the rebellion. In summing up, Mr. Justice
Chamberlain, with whom Lord Yelverton agreed, said :—
" The jury were not to imagine that the legislature, by
" enabling magistrates to justify under the Indemnity Bill,
" had released them from the feelings of humanity, or per-
" mitted them wantonly to exercise power, even though it
" were to put down rebellion. They expected that in all cases
" there should be a grave and serious examination into the
" conduct of the supposed criminal, and every act should show
" a mind intent to discover guilt, not to inflict torture. By
" examination or trial he did not mean that sort of examination
" and trial which they were now engaged in, but such ex-
" amination and trial—the best the nature of the case and
" existing circumstances should allow of. That this must
" have been the intention of the legislature was manifest from
" the expression ' magistrates and all other persons,' which

[1] 27 *St. Tr.* 765.

Сн. VII.   " provides that as every man, whether magistrate or not, was
———   " authorised to suppress rebellion, and was to be justified
           " by that law for his acts, it is required that he should not
           " exceed the necessity which gave him that power, and that
           " he should show in his justification that he had used every
           " possible means to ascertain the guilt which he had punished;
           " and, above all, no deviation from the common principles of
           " humanity should appear in his conduct."

Wright recovered £500 damages, and when Mr. Fitzgerald applied to the Irish Parliament for an indemnity, he could not get one.

3. The courts-martial, as they are called, by which martial law, in this sense of the word, is administered, are not, properly speaking, courts-martial or courts at all. They are merely committees formed for the purpose of carrying into execution the discretionary power assumed by the Government. On the one hand, they are not obliged to proceed in the manner pointed out by the Mutiny Act and Articles of War. On the other hand, if they do so proceed, they are not protected by them as the members of a real court-martial might be, except so far as such proceedings are evidence of good faith. They are justified in doing, with any forms and in any manner, whatever is necessary to suppress insurrection, and to restore peace and the authority of the law. They are personally liable for any acts which they may commit in excess of that power, even if they act in strict accordance with the Mutiny Act and Articles of War.

[1] PRELIMINARY INQUIRY.

Before the establishment of justices of the peace, cases of public importance were inquired into before the Privy Council, as I have already observed; but there seems to have been no preliminary inquiry at all in regard to common offences, except in the single case of the coroner's inquest. The justice of the peace was at first little more than a constable on a large scale, whose power even to issue a warrant for the

———
[1] For the present law on this subject, and on incidental procedure, see *Dig. Crim. Proc.* ch. xiii.—xvii., arts. 99-140.

apprehension of suspected persons was acquired by practice, CH. VII.
and was not derived from express parliamentary authority.
In early times the formal accusation was often, perhaps
usually, the first step in the procedure, and the prisoner was
not arrested until after he had been indicted. This may
still occur under the existing law, but such an occurrence
is not usual. In almost every case in the present day a
suspected person appears before a justice. Witnesses are
then examined, he is either discharged, bailed, or imprisoned till trial, and is then indicted and tried.

The earliest instance that occurs of any sort of preliminary inquiry into crimes with a view to subsequent proceedings is the case of the coroner's inquest. Coroners,
according to [1] Mr. Stubbs, originated in the year 1194, but the
first authority of importance about their duties is to be
found in Bracton. [2] He gives an account of their duties so
full as to imply that in his day their office was comparatively
modern. The Statute de Officio Coronatoris (4 Edw. 1,
st. 2, A.D. 1276) is almost a transcript of the passage in
Bracton. It gives the coroner's duty very fully, and is to
this day the foundation of the law on the subject. The
following are its main provisions:—" A coroner of our Lord
" the King ought to inquire of these things if he be certified
" by the King's bailiffs or other honest men of the country;
" first he shall go to the places where any be slain, or
" suddenly dead, or wounded, or where houses are broken, or
" where treasure is said to be found, and shall forthwith
" command four of the next towns, or five, or six [*i.e.* the
" reeve and four men from each] to appear before him in
" such a place: when they are come thither the coroner
" upon the oath of them shall inquire in this manner, that
" is, to wit, if they know where the person was slain, whether
" it was in any house, field, bed, tavern, or company, and

---

[1] *Const. Hist.* i. 505. For present law, see *Dig. Crim. Proc.* ch. vii. arts.
43-60, as to appointment and removal of coroners, as to inquests, procedure, &c., arts. 207-232.

[2] Bracton, lib. iii. (*De Corona*) ch. v. Sir T. Twiss discusses the question
whether Bracton copied from the statute or the statute from Bracton, and
gives reasons in support of the latter view in the introduction to vol. ii.
of his edition of Bracton, p. lxi. The Statutum Walliæ contains provisions
substantially identical with those of 4 Edw. 1.

" who were there. Likewise it is to be inquired who were
" culpable either of the act or of the force, and who were
" present, either men or women, and of what age soever
" they be, if they can speak or have any discretion, and how
" many soever be found culpable in any of the manners
" aforesaid, they shall be taken and delivered to the sheriff,
" and shall be committed to the gaol."

If any one is found guilty of the murder, the coroner is
immediately to value his property [1] "as if it were to be
" immediately sold," and is to deliver it to the township
which is to answer for it to the justices.

The statute contains important provisions as to appeals
which I pass over for the present. It is silent as to the
course to be taken where houses are broken, though the
opening words of the statute refer to such cases. In practice
the coroner's duties have been confined to cases of suspicious death and treasure trove.

The coroner's duties in respect of inquiries into the cause
of suspicious deaths have hardly varied at all from the days
of Edward I. to our own, except as regards the method of
summoning jurors, and witnesses, and other details. The
statute book contains a variety of provisions as to matters of
secondary importance connected with inquests. The only
ones which need here be mentioned are the statute of Philip
and Mary (1 & 2 Phil. & Mary, c. 13, s. 5, 1554), which
required a coroner to " put in writing the effect of the evidence
" given before him being material," and to bind over the
witnesses to appear at the trial of the person accused. This
act remained in force till 1826, when it was superseded
by 7 Geo. 4, c. 64, s. 4, which provides that every coroner
upon any inquisition before him taken whereby any one
is indicted for manslaughter or murder, or as an accessory
to murder before the fact, shall put in writing the evidence
given to the jury before him, or as much thereof as shall
be material, and shall have authority to bind over the
witnesses to give evidence at the trial, and certify and
return the depositions and inquisition to the court before
which the person indicted is to be tried. The inquisition

[1] " Sicut statim vendi possunt."

of the coroner always was and still is a formal accusation
of any person found by it to have committed murder or
manslaughter, or to have found and concealed treasure, and
a person may be tried upon such an inquisition without any
further accusation.

It is singular that, with the law as to coroners in full
operation since 1276, no duties of the same sort should have
been imposed on the justices of the peace appointed forty-
eight years afterwards, in 1324.

Whatever may have been the reason, the fact is certain
that no allusion is made to the holding of any sort of preliminary inquiry by justices in any statute passed before
the statutes of Philip and Mary already casually referred to.
It is probable, however, that from the very earliest times
magistrates would make a more or less formal inquiry before
they took steps towards the arrest or bail of a suspected
person, and it is not at all improbable that the two statutes in
question may have given legal sanction to a practice which
had grown up without express statutory authority. The
statutes were as follows. By the 1 & 2 Phil. & Mary,
c. 13 (1554), it is enacted that, when any person arrested for
manslaughter or felony, or suspicion of manslaughter or felony,
being bailable by the law, is brought before any two justices,
they are " to take the examination of the said prisoner and
" information of them that bring him of the fact and cir-
" cumstances thereof, and the same or as much thereof as
" shall be material to prove the felony shall be put in writing
" before they make the bailment." The examination and bailment are to be certified to the court, and " all such as do de-
" clare anything material to prove the said murder " (murder is
not mentioned in the earlier part of the act), " manslaughter,
" offences, or felonies, or to be accessory or accessories to the
" same as is aforesaid " (it is remarkable that the word
" witnesses " is not used) " are to be bound over to appear
" to give evidence at the court of gaol delivery." This act was
confined to the case of prisoners admitted to bail. It was
followed in the next year (1555) by an act (2 & 3 Phil. &
Mary, c. 10), which recites that it " does not extend to such
" prisoners as shall be brought before any justice of peace

Ch. VII. " for manslaughter or felony, and by such justices shall be
" committed to ward for the suspicion of such manslaughter
" or felony and not bailed, in which case the examination
" of such prisoner and of such as shall bring him is as
" necessary or rather more than where such prisoner shall
" be let to bail." The act then goes on to re-enact, with
respect to cases in which the prisoners are committed, the
provisions of the act of the preceding year as to prisoners
bailed.[1]

These statutes continued to be in force till the year 1826,
when they were repealed, and re-enacted, and extended to
misdemeanour by 7 Geo. 4, c. 64, ss. 2 & 3, and this act
was in its turn repealed and re-enacted in a more elaborate
form, with some important variations, by 11 & 12 Vic. c. 42
(1848), which is known as Sir John Jervis's Act.

The important provisions of Sir John Jervis's Act upon the
subject of the preliminary inquiry are these. [2] The witnesses
are to be examined in the presence of the accused person, and
he is to be at liberty to cross-examine them. The depositions
are to be written down and signed by the magistrate and by the
witnesses.   After all the witnesses have been examined, the
justice is to say to the accused, " Having heard the evidence,
" do you wish to say anything in answer to the charge? You
" are not obliged to say anything unless you desire to do so,
" but whatever you say will be taken down in writing and
" may be given in evidence against you at your trial."
Whatever he says is then taken down and returned with the
depositions. [3] The accused person is then to be asked whether
he wishes to call any witnesses, and if he does, they must be
examined and cross-examined, and their depositions must be
taken in the same manner as those of the witnesses for the
prosecution.   [4] If the evidence is in the opinion of the
justices not sufficient to put the accused person on his trial,
they are to discharge him. If they think it " raises a strong
" or probable presumption of " his " guilt," they are to
commit him for trial or admit him to bail. [5] The accused is

---

[1] The historical reason for these enactments will be found below, p. 236.
[2] 11 & 12 Vic. c. 42, s. 17. See *Dig. Crim. Proc.* art. 109, &c.
[3] 30 & 31 Vic. c. 35, s. 3.   [4] S. 25.   [5] S. 27.

entitled to copies of the depositions, and his right to be represented by counsel or by a solicitor is incidentally assumed in [1]one section of the act, and is, I believe, never disputed in practice.

A comparison of these provisions with those of the acts of Philip and Mary shows several changes of the utmost importance in one of the most important parts of criminal procedure.

Speaking generally, the difference between the procedure established in the sixteenth century and the procedure of the nineteenth is that under the first the magistrate acts the part of a public prosecutor, whereas under the second he occupies the position of a preliminary judge. This appears in every detail. Under the acts of Philip and Mary the accused person is to be examined. This meant that he was to be fully questioned as to all the circumstances connected with his supposed offence. Under the act of Victoria he can be asked no questions at all, though he is invited to make any statement he pleases, being cautioned that it will be taken down and may be given in evidence against him. Under the statutes of Philip and Mary the examination of the witnesses and the recording of their depositions was intended only for the information of the court. The prisoner had no right to be, and probably never was, present. Under the statute of Victoria the witnesses are to be examined in the prisoner's presence, and may be cross-examined by him, his counsel, or his attorney. Under the statute of Philip and Mary the depositions were to be returned to the court, but there is evidence to show that the prisoner was not allowed even to see them. Under the statute of Victoria he is entitled to a copy of them. In all these particulars the change is uniformly in the same direction. The object of the earlier statute is to expose and detect a man assumed to be guilty. In the later statute, the object is a full inquiry into his guilt or innocence.

One circumstance must here be mentioned, which makes a distinction of considerable importance between the preliminary criminal procedure of our own country and that of all the countries which used the civil law. I refer to the absence

[1] S. 17.

CH. VII.   of the use of torture as a means of collecting evidence whilst
           the prisoner was in custody. It was never recognised as a
           part of the law of England, and its illegality was made the
           subject of much boasting by some of the earliest panegyrists
           of English institutions, and in particular Fortescue, Smith,
           and Coke. There is, however, proof that it was practised
           for the purpose of obtaining evidence under Henry VIII. and
           his three children, and also during the reigns of James I. and
           Charles I., and that not only in political cases but also in
           the case of common crimes. The proof of this is given in
           Jardine's *Reading on Torture*, in the appendix to which work
           there are printed fifty-five letters taken from the Council
           books, the first dated 5th November, 1551, and the last
           21st May, 1640, authorising or otherwise relating to the use
           or the threat of torture in a variety of instances. In how
           many cases it may have been used without such authority,
           and when the practice began, no one can now even guess with
           any plausibility. Why torture was not employed in this as
           well as in other countries it is difficult to say. Probably the
           extremely summary character of our early methods of trial,
           and the excessive severity of the punishments inflicted, had
           more to do with the matter than the generalities of Magna
           Charta or any special humanity of feeling. People who, with
           no sort of hesitation, hanged a man who could not read, or who
           being able to read had married a widow, simply because
           twelve of his neighbours, reporting the village gossip, said he
           had stolen a dress worth two shillings, cannot be called
           scrupulously humane. If their conscience had declined to
           hang him till they had tortured him into a confession capable
           of being verified independently, they would perhaps have been
           a little more humane, though this certainly admits of a
           doubt.[1]

           However this may be, it is still possible to give evidence
           of the manner in which the old system of preliminary
           investigations worked. In several of the trials reported
           under the Stuarts, the justice who had got up the case

           ---

           [1] The subject is fully described in Mr. Lea's *Superstition and Force*,
           Philadelphia, 1878, 371-522. According to Mr. Lea, torture was gradually
           introduced throughout the Continent in the course of the fourteenth, fifteenth,
           and sixteenth centuries. It was connected with the revival of the Roman law.

was the principal witness against the prisoner, and detailed at
length the steps which he had taken to apprehend him. The
following are instances :—

[1] In 1664 Colonel Turner was tried for a burglary, together
with his wife and three of his sons. The principal witness
was Sir Thomas Aleyn, an alderman of the city. He
said : " Mr. Francis Tryon" (the person robbed) "put me
" on the business to examine it. I went and examined the
" two servants—the man and the maid. Upon their examina-
" tion I found they had supped abroad at a dancing-school and
" had been at cards." . . . "The man confessed he had been
" abroad twenty or thirty times at Colonel Turner's house at
" supper about a year since. The maid denied they had
" been there at all; but it is true the man's saying he supped
" there (though it was false) was the first occasion of sus-
" picion against Colonel Turner. When I had examined
" these two, I went to the examination of Turner, where he
" was all that day, where at night? He told me at several
" places and taverns, and in bed at nine of the clock, and
" was called out of his bed ; but having myself some suspicion
" of him, I wished him to withdraw. I told Tryon that I
" believed, if he was not the thief, he knew where the things
" were." Aleyn afterwards charged Turner ; "but he denied
" it, but not as a person of his spirit, which gave me some
" cause of further suspicion." He afterwards searched
Turner's house unsuccessfully ; but next day received information from one of the other aldermen which enabled
him to track Turner into a shop in the Minories, where he
found him in possession of money which he believed to be
part of the stolen property. He pressed him to account for
it, took him to Tryon, managed matters so as to induce him
to admit to Tryon, upon Tryon's engaging not to prosecute,
that he knew where the property was, and, after all sorts
of manœuvres, got him to cause his wife to give up a number
of Tryon's jewels, and finally committed him and her to
Newgate. In short, he acted throughout the part of an
exceedingly zealous and by no means scrupulous detective
armed with the authority of a magistrate. [2] He detailed in

[1] 6 *St. Tr.* 619, 630.   [2] *Ib.* 572-575.

CH. VII. court the whole of his proceedings, which were very ex-
peditious. "Thursday," said one of the judges, "was the
"robbery, Friday he was examined, Saturday the money was
"brought, and that night the jewels were brought and he
"committed."

In the famous case of [1] Count Coningsmark and his alleged
agents, who were tried for the murder of Mr. Thynne, a
similar part was taken by Sir John Reresby, the committing
magistrate. Just as he was going to bed, "Mr. Thynne's
"gentleman came to me to grant a hue and cry, and soon
"after the Duke of Monmouth's page to desire me to come
"to his master at Mr. Thynne's lodging, sending his coach
"to fetch me." Reresby immediately went to Mr. Thynne's
and granted warrants to search for several suspected persons.
At last a Swede was brought before him who confessed that he
served a German captain who had had a quarrel with Thynne.
Upon information obtained from the Swede, "having searched
"several houses till six o'clock in the morning, having been
"in chase almost the whole night, I personally took the
"captain at the house of a Swedish doctor in Leicester
"Fields, I going first into the room." Other suspected
persons being afterwards arrested were brought to this house
and [2] examined, and finally were committed for trial to the
Old Bailey, after being examined on several occasions before
the King in Council.

Other cases are mentioned in Reresby's memoirs in which
he took a similar part. [3] For instance, under the date of 6th
of July, 1683, after referring to the Rye House Plot, he
says: "Six Scotchmen being stopped at Ferry Bridge, by
"directions from the Secretary, coming from London towards
"Scotland, and being but slightly examined by the justice
"of the peace, I caused them to confess much more to me,
"which I transmitted to the Secretary, as also the examina-
"tion of another of that nation, who was sent to York Castle,
"and proved a very dangerous rogue."

[4] In 1681, George Busby was tried at Derby assizes for being

---

[1] 9 *St. Tr.* 1, and the *Memoirs of Sir John Reresby*, pp. 235-241.
[2] 9 *St. Tr.* pp. 122-124.
[3] *Memoirs*, p. 281.   [4] 8 *St. Tr.* 525.

a Popish priest. The chief witness against him was Mr. Gilbert, a magistrate of the county, who gave a long account of the manner in which he went on several occasions to the house where he suspected Busby to be. On one occasion he took " a crimson damask vestment, wherein was packed a " stole, a maniple of the same (as the Papists call them), an " altar-stone, surplice, and a box of wafers, mass books, and " divers other Popish things." All these he took to Derby assizes and showed them to the judge, who directed them to be burnt, but Mr. Gilbert " entreated his favour that I might " send them again to the same place for two or three days to " make the priest more confident." He went back accordingly and made a most elaborate search, having a singular series of conversations with people in the house, till at last he took the prisoner in a curiously contrived hiding-hole, near some chimneys, and carried him to Derby, " where after " I had taken his examination, I made a mittimus and com- " mitted him to Derby gaol."

I do not think any part of the old procedure operated more harshly upon prisoners than the summary and secret way in which justices of the peace, acting frequently the part of detective officers, took their examinations and committed them for trial. It was a constant and most natural and reasonable topic of complaint by the prisoners who were tried for the Popish Plot that they had been taken without warning, kept close prisoners from the time of their arrest, and kept in ignorance of the evidence against them till the very moment when they were brought into court to be tried.

This is set in a strong light by the provisions of the celebrated act " for regulating of trials in cases of treason and misprision of treason" (7 & 8 Will. 3, c. 3), and those of [1]s. 14 of the Act of Union with Scotland (7 Anne, c. 21). The first of these acts provides that every person accused of high-treason shall have a true copy of the whole indictment delivered to him five days at least before he is tried. The second extends the time for the delivery of the copy of the indictment to ten days before the trial, and enacts that at the same time that the copy of the indictment is delivered

[1] In the Revised Statutes.   In other editions it is s. 11.

"a list of the witnesses that shall be produced on the trial
"for proving the said indictment, and of the jury, mentioning
"the names, professions, and place of abode of the said
"witnesses and jurors, be also given." This was considered as
an extraordinary effort of liberality. It proves, in fact, that even
at the beginning of the eighteenth century, and after the experience of the state trials held under the Stuarts, it did not occur
to the legislature that, if a man is to be tried for his life, he
ought to know beforehand what the evidence against him is,
and that it did appear to them that to let him know even
what were the names of the witnesses was so great a favour
that it ought to be reserved for people accused of a crime
for which legislators themselves or their friends and con-
nections were likely to be prosecuted. It was a matter
of direct personal interest to many members of parliament
that trials for political offences should not be grossly unfair, but they were comparatively indifferent as to the fate
of people accused of sheep-stealing, or burglary, or murder.

It is probable, however, that the practice of the magistrates
varied, and that where there was no particular reason, political
or otherwise, for keeping a prisoner in the dark, he was
allowed, during the interval between the commitment and
trial, to see his friends and make such preparation for his trial
as he could. In some remarks [1] by Sir John Hawles (Solicitor-
General in the reign of William III.), on the trial of Colledge,
the Protestant joiner, it is said that in murder and all other
crimes, the prisoner is always permitted to advise with counsel
before his trial, and that all persons are allowed in such cases
to have free and private access to him, and the usage followed
in the political trials of the seventeenth century is strongly
reflected upon. This irregular and unsystematic good nature
may have been sufficient in practice to prevent the infliction
of gross injustice upon persons capable of making their
complaints heard, but till the year 1849 prisoners certainly
had no legal right to know beforehand what evidence was
to be given against them. I will give a single illustration
of this, and in giving it, I may observe that it is not so
easy as it might be expected to be, to discover accounts of

[1] 8 *St. Tr.* 723-726, 732.

routine proceedings which are not recorded, and do not become the subjects of judicial decision, though they are more important than many others of which this cannot be said.

John Thurtell was tried on the [1] 6th and 7th Jan. 1824, and executed on the 9th, for the murder of William Weare, on the 24th Oct. 1823. In the *Times* newspaper, Oct. 31, 1823, there is a statement that the magistrates' investigation commenced at 10.30 p.m. "The prisoners were not brought " into the room, it being thought best to keep them ignorant " of the entire evidence against them, at least for a short time." Thurtell was then called in and asked many questions by Mr. Noel, the solicitor for the prosecution. Hunt (Thurtell's accomplice) was afterwards separately examined, which led to his making a full confession. The examinations taken before the magistrates were published in the newspapers, and [2] Mr. Justice J. A. Park made the following observations upon the subject in his charge to the grand jury:—

"These depositions he understood (for he repeated he knew " nothing of the fact himself) had already appeared very " copiously and even with notes and comments in the public " press. Now it appeared to him that the first fault (and he " had no doubt it was most unintended, and in noticing it he " did not mean to wound the feelings of any individual)—it " appeared to him that the first fault originated with the " magistrates in allowing any persons to enter into their " private apartments for the purpose of taking notes of their " proceedings. He held there was a vast difference between " the inquisitorial and the judicial power of the magistrates; " where the magistrate was acting judicially his conduct was as " open to the inspection and judgment of the public as that of " himself and that of his learned brothers on the bench ; to " such publicity he had no objection, for he could wish every- " thing he said as a judge to be heard and fairly canvassed " by the public. [3] He knew he erred sometimes, because he

---

[1] Mr. Chitty moved in arrest of judgment that the proceedings were void because part of the trial took place on the Feast of the Epiphany.

[2] The charge is published in the *Times*, Dec. 5, 1823, also in two printed accounts of the trial which appeared at the time, one of which is in the Inner Temple library. Both of them appear to be in substance reprints from the *Times*.

[3] This observation is too characteristic to have been invented, and so guarantees the authenticity of the report.

CH. VII. " was human, and nothing that was human could escape
————— " without error. But when a magistrate was acting inqui-
" sitorially, when he was taking an inquisition for blood, were
" these proceedings fit to be known and published to the
" world ? He was bound to investigate and inquire—ought
" his inquiries and investigations to be conducted in a
" private or public manner ? The statute law of the land
" prescribed the course to be pursued upon such an occa-
" sion for more than 200 years " (269 years). " There was
" a statute of Philip and Mary which stated that deposi-
" tions before magistrates should be taken in writing in
" order that they might be transmitted to the judges
" who were to try the offence under the commission of
" oyer and terminer for the county. He appealed to the
" experience of every gentleman who heard him, and he
" knew what his own experience as judge had taught him,
" whether the constant course was not to transmit them
" to the judge, taking care that the accused should not
" have an opportunity of seeing them. The prosecutor or
" his solicitor might have access to them, but not the party
" accused. For what would be the consequence if the
" latter had access to them ? Why, that he would know
" everything which was to be produced in evidence against
" him—an advantage which it was never intended should
" be extended towards him."

The first alteration made in this state of things was effected in
1836 by the Prisoners' Counsel Act (6 & 7 Will. 4, c. 114, s. 4),
which provided that all persons under trial should at their trial
have a right to inspect all depositions taken against them.
In 1849, by 11 & 12 Vic. c. 42, s. 27, it was provided that
the accused should be entitled to a copy of the depositions.
This change was probably due to a growing sense of the
unfairness of the law. Probably, too, the establishment of
a regular police force by the steps already detailed may
have put the magistrates in a new position in fact before
the change was embodied in the statute law. As a regular
force was established, first in the towns and then in the
country by which charges of crime were investigated, however imperfectly, the magistrates would naturally assume a

more and more judicial position. The inquiry before the magistrates is now essentially judicial. It may indeed admit of a doubt whether it is not too judicial, and whether it does not tend to become a separate trial. This tendency was certainly encouraged by the power given by 30 & 31 Vic. c. 35, to the prisoner to call witnesses before the magistrates, and to have them bound over to appear at the trial and to have their expenses allowed. The power was conceded because it was thought hard that a man should be prevented by poverty from producing witnesses. This may have been a good reason for the act, and it has had some collateral advantages, but it has made the law more elaborate than it was.

In the course of the last century a change has taken place in the position of magistrates parallel to and closely connected with the change in the position of constables.

The management of local public business of all kinds, and especially of that part of it which consists in the administration of justice, has happily been at all times, as it still continues to be, a matter of honourable ambition and interest to large numbers of persons well qualified for the purpose by education and social standing. No one, however, can be expected to devote the whole of his time to the duties of a magistrate unless he is paid for it, and in places where the population is very dense, there is so much business that it cannot be efficiently done except by persons who give their whole time to it. Moreover, as the law becomes more and more elaborate, and the standard of judicial-proof rises, special knowledge is continually becoming more and more necessary for the proper discharge of the duties of a magistrate.

The force of these considerations has been recognised by slow degrees, and so strong are the attractions of the voluntary system, that up to this time the magistrates are unpaid in nearly all the counties, and in most of the cities and boroughs. But a different system has been introduced in the metropolitan district, and in some other parts of the country, by the following steps.

Throughout a great part of the eighteenth century the

CH. VII. business of magistrates in that part of London which was
not included in the City was carried on by magistrates who
were paid almost entirely by fees. What the fees precisely
were, and by what law their exaction was justified, I am not
able to say, nor is it worth while to inquire. One or two
curious memorials of the state of things which then existed
will be worth mentioning by way of introduction to the later
legislation on the subject.

Writing in 1754, [1] Henry Fielding says of his career as a
magistrate : ' By composing instead of inflaming the quarrels
" of porters and beggars (which I blush when I say has not
" been universally practised), and by refusing to take a
" shilling from a man who most undoubtedly would not have
" had another left, I reduced an income of about £500 a
" year of the dirtiest money upon earth to little more than
" £300, a considerable proportion of which remained with
" my clerk; and indeed, if the whole had done so, as it
" ought, he would be but ill paid for sitting almost sixteen
" hours in the twenty-four in the most unwholesome as well
" as nauseous air in the universe, and which hath in his case
" corrupted a good constitution without contaminating his
" morals."

He observes in a footnote : " A predecessor of mine used
" to boast that he made £1,000 a year in his office, [2] but how
" he did this (if indeed he did it) is to me a secret. His
" clerk, now mine, told me I had more business than he had
" ever known there; I am sure I had as much as any man
" could do. The truth is, the fees are so very low when any
" are due, and so much is done for nothing, that, if a single
" justice of peace had business enough to employ twenty
" clerks, neither he nor they would get much by their labour.
" The public will not therefore think I betray a secret when
" I inform them that I received from the government a
" yearly pension out of the public service money."

He afterwards says that he resigned the office to [3] his

---

[1] Introduction to *Journal of a Voyage to Lisbon*, *Works*, xii. p. 230, edition
of 1775.

[2] This reads like an insinuation that he took bribes.

[3] This brother was John Fielding, well known for many years as the blind
justice. Henry Fielding's son, William Fielding, was also a London magis-

brother, who had always been his assistant. It was by a rare CH. VII.
accident indeed that such a man as Fielding found himself
in such a position. Men of genius are exceptions every-
where, but a magistrate ought at least to be, as in these days
he is, a gentleman and a man of honour. It was not so in
the last century in London. [1] A characteristic account of the
"trading justices" was given to the Committee of 1816, by
Townsend, a well-known Bow Street runner, who at that
time had been in the police thirty-four years or more, *i.e.*
since 1782 : " At that time before the Police Bill took
" place at all, it was a trading business; and there was
" Justice This and Justice That. Justice Welch in Litch-
" field Street was a great man in those days, and old Justice
" Hyde, and Justice Girdler, and Justice Blackborough, a
" trading justice at Clerkenwell Green, and an old iron-
" monger. The plan used to be to issue out warrants and
" take up all the poor devils in the street, and then there
" was the bailing of them, 2*s.* 4*d.*, which the magistrates
" had; and taking up 100 girls, that would make, at
" 2*s.* 4*d.*, £11 13*s.* 4*d.* They sent none to gaol, the bailing
" them was so much better."

These scandals led to the statute, 32 Geo. 3, c. 53,
which authorised the establishment of seven public offices
in Middlesex and one in Surrey, to each of which three
justices were attached. The fees were to be paid to a
receiver. No other Middlesex or Surrey justices were to
be allowed, under heavy penalties, to take fees within the
jurisdiction of the new magistrates. The justices were to be
paid by a salary of £400 apiece.

This experiment proved highly successful. The numbers,
the salaries, and the jurisdiction, both in point of locality
and in point of authority, of the metropolitan stipendiary
magistrates have been repeatedly raised. They are now
regulated by the [2] acts referred to in the note; the effect of
which is that the Queen has power to establish in the

trate. He gave evidence before a Commitee of the House of Commons in
1816, when he said he had been fifty years in the commission for Westminster.
[1] Report of 1816, pp. 139, 140.
[2] 2 & 3 Vic. c. 71, ss. 1 & 3 ; 11 & 12 Vic. c. 42, s. 31 ; 38 & 39 Vic. c. 3
(as to salary).

CH. VII.   Metropolitan District [1]thirteen police courts, with any
number of magistrates up to twenty-seven, the chief magistrate with a salary of £1,800 a year, and the others with
salaries of £1,500. They must be barristers of seven years'
standing. Each is a magistrate for Middlesex, Surrey, Kent,
Essex, and Hertfordshire, and the chief magistrate is also
a magistrate for Berkshire. The success of the experiment
in London led to the introduction of a similar state of things
in other large towns.

Stipendiary magistrates may be appointed ([2]under 5 & 6
Will. 4, c. 76, s. 99) in any borough on a bye-law, to be
made by the Council and approved by the Secretary of State,
fixing the amount of salary which the magistrate is to
receive. Similar powers are given, by 26 & 27 Vic. c. 97,
to local boards having authority over a district containing
more than 25,000 inhabitants.

Even in towns, however, the majority of the magistrates
are unpaid. In the City of London the Mayor and Aldermen are magistrates by charter, and there are also magistrates by charter in the 88 small corporations not brought
under the Municipal Corporations Act. In boroughs under
the Municipal Corporations Act [3](5 & 6 Will. 4, c. 76) the
mayor for the time being is a justice of the peace *ex officio*,
as also is the recorder (s. 104), if there is one ; (s. 57) and
the Queen has power (s. 98) to nominate as many other
justices as she thinks fit from persons resident within seven
miles of the borough.

The general result is that the business of holding the preliminary inquiry and committing or bailing the prisoner is, in
the metropolitan district and in many large towns and
populous districts, in the hands of trained lawyers, who act as
preliminary judges ; that in municipal boroughs it is in the
hands of the mayor, an elected officer, and a number of
other justices nominated by the Crown, but unpaid ; that in

---

[1] There are at present eleven, viz. : 1, Bow Street. 2, Clerkenwell. 3,
Lambeth. 4, Marlborough Street. 5, Marylebone. 6, Southwark. 7,
Thames. 8, Westminster. 9, Worship Street. 10, Hammersmith and
Wandsworth. 11, Greenwich and Woolwich.

[2] After January 1, 1883, under 45 & 46 Vic. c. 50, s. 161.

[3] After January 1, 1883, 45 & 46 Vic. c. 50, s. 155.

the City of London it is vested by charter in the Mayor and
Aldermen; in boroughs not under the Municipal Act in a
variety of officers appointed under the provisions of charters
and private acts; and that in the rest of the country it
is in the hands of the local gentry, appointed by the
Crown and exercising their office gratuitously.

DISCHARGE, [1] BAIL, OR COMMITTAL.

The next step to the preliminary inquiry held by the
magistrates is the discharge, bail, or committal of the suspected person. Little need be said of the law as to the
discharge or committal of the suspected person. It is
obvious that, as soon as justices of the peace were erected
into intermediate judges, charged to decide the question
whether there was or was not ground for the detention of
a suspected person, they must have acquired, on the one
hand, the power of discharge, and, on the other, the power
of committal. The whole object of the preliminary inquiry
was to lead to the one or the other result, and the history
of the preliminary inquiry is in fact the history of the steps
which led to the determination of this question in a judicial
manner. The law of bail has a separate independent history.

The right to be bailed in certain cases is as old as the law
of England itself, and is explicitly recognised by our earliest
writers. When the administration of justice was in its
infancy, arrest meant imprisonment without preliminary inquiry till the sheriff held his tourn at least, and, in more
serious cases, till the arrival of the justices, which might be
delayed for years, and it was therefore a matter of the utmost
importance to be able to obtain a provisional release from
custody. The right is recognised in curt and general terms
by Glanville. [2] He says: " Cum quis itaque de morte regis
" vel de seditione exercitus infamatur aut certus apparet
" accusator aut non. Si nullus appareat certus accusator
" sed fama solummodo publica accusat; tunc ab initio salvo
" accusatus attachiabitur vel per plegios idoneos, vel per
" carceris inclusionem." If there is a determinate accuser—

---

[1] *Dig. Crim. Proc.* arts. 136-140. [2] Lib. xiv. c. 1.

CH. VII. " is qui accusatur ut prædiximus per plegios salvos et secu-
" ros solet attachiari aut si plegios non habuerit in carcerem
" detrudi. In omnibus autem placitis de feloniâ solet accu-
" satus per plegios dimitti præterquam in placito de homi-
" cidio ubi ad terrorem aliter statutum est." [1]Bracton refers
to bail in many places, but the most general passage in
his treatise *De Corona* which I have noticed [2] is to the effect
that the sheriff ought to exercise a discretion in regard to
bailing accused persons, having regard to the importance of
the charge, the character of the person, and the gravity of
the evidence against him.

These very ancient authorities are somewhat general in
their language, but it is still possible to trace the history of
the law relating to bail from the beginning of the reign of
Edward I. to our own days.

The sheriff was the local representative of the Crown, and
in particular he was at the head of all the executive part of
the administration of criminal justice. In that capacity he,
as I have already shown, arrested and imprisoned suspected
persons, and, if he thought proper, admitted them to bail.
The discretionary power of the sheriff was ill defined, and
led to great abuses, which were dealt with by the Statute
of Westminster the First (3 Edw. 1, c. 12, A.D. 1275). This
statute was for 550 years the main foundation of the law of
bail. It recites that sheriffs and others " have taken and kept
" in prison persons detected of felony, and incontinent have let
" out by replevin such as were not replevisable, and have kept
" in prison such as were replevisable because they would gain
" of the one party and grieve the other." It also recites,
" that before this time it was not determined which persons
" were replevisable and which not, but only those that were
" taken for the death of man [3]or by commandment of the
" king, or of his justices, or for the forest." It then proceeds
to enact that certain prisoners shall not be replevisable either
" by the common writ or without writ ;" that others shall

---

[1] In cases of treason, ii. 261 ; homicide, ii. 283 ; treasure trove, ii. 287 ;
rape, ii. 289 ; wounding, ii. 288 ; and see 293.   [2] P. 302.
   [3] Coke labours to show that this means " by a court of justice," through
which alone the king can act (*2nd Inst.* p. 186), and see 2 Hale, *P. C.* 131.
This may be very sound constitutional doctrine, but it seems to make nonsense of the alternative " or of his justices."

" be let out by sufficient surety, whereof the sheriff will be
" answerable, and that without giving ought of their goods."

The persons not to be bailed (apparently in addition to the
four classes referred to in the recital) are (1) prisoners outlawed ; (2) men who had abjured the realm (and so admitted
their guilt) ; (3) approvers (who had confessed) ; (4) such
as be taken with the manour ; (5) those which have broken
the king's prison ; (6) thieves openly defamed and known,
and such as are appealed (accused) by approvers ; (7) such
as are taken for felonious arson ; (8) or for false money ; (9)
or for counterfeiting the king's seal ; (10) or persons excom-
municate taken at the request of the bishop ; (11) or for
manifest offences ; (12) or for treason touching the king himself. On the other hand, the persons to be bailed are (1)
persons indicted of larceny by inquests taken before sheriffs
or bailiffs by their office, *i.e.* at sheriffs' tourns or courts leet ;
(2) or of light suspicion (I suppose wherever indicted) ; (3)
or for petty larceny that amounteth not above the value of
12*d.* if they were not guilty of some other larceny aforetime ;
(4) guilty of receipt of felons, or of commandment, or of
force, or of aid in felony done (*i.e.* accessories before or
after a felony) ; (5) guilty of some other trespass for which
one ought not to lose life nor member, *i.e.* misdemeanours in
general ; (6) a man appealed by a prover after the death of
the prover (if he be no common thief nor defamed). The
statute does not say distinctly whether persons arrested on
suspicion (for instance by hue and cry) were to be bailed or
not. It applies to persons [1] " rettes " (which is translated
" detected ") of felony, as having been wrongfully let out by
the sheriffs. Whether the word implied that the prisoner
had been indicted, or whether it meant only in a general
sense charged, or whether its use invested the sheriffs with a
discretion, I cannot say.

The way in which the later statutes are framed seems to
favour the supposition that the justices at all events could in
the first instance admit to bail only persons indicted before

---

[1] Mr. Stubbs, in his glossary, says, "*Retare, Rettare,* to accuse, from the
" Norse *rett,* an imputation or accusation." It soon ran into *rectatus* from a
reminiscence of *rectum.*

CH. VII. them in their sessions. However this may have been, the Statute of Westminster determined what offences were bailable or not for five centuries and a-half. The last statute which regulates the sheriffs' power of bailing is 23 Hen. 6, c. 9 (A.D. 1444). This statute requires the sheriffs in certain cases to bail, in terms which seem to imply that their refusal to do so had become a well-known abuse. It should be read in connection with c. 7 of the same statute, which recites many statutes forbidding persons to hold the office of sheriff for more than a year, states that they have been frequently disregarded, confirms them, and renders a sheriff liable to a penalty of £200 to be sued for by a common informer if he disobeys its provisions.

Between 1275 and 1444, however, the sheriffs' powers had been to a great extent transferred to the justices of the peace in whom the power of admitting prisoners to bail was vested by a series of statutes. The 4 Edw. 3, c. 1 (1330), provided that persons indicted or taken by the keepers of the peace should not be let to mainprise by the sheriffs. The statute of 34 Edw. 3, c. 1 (1360), gave the justices power to bail in very general terms. The statute 1 Rich. 3, c. 3 (1485) recites that many persons have been daily arrested and imprisoned, some for malice and "sometimes of a light suspicion," and accordingly empowers "every justice of the peace to let such "persons to bail and mainprise in like form as though the "said person were indicted thereof of record before the same "justices in their sessions." This looks as if the statute of Edward III. applied only to persons indicted at the sessions. The statute of Richard III. remained in force for three years only. By 3 Hen. 7, c. 3 (1486), it was recited that persons not mainprisable were "oftentimes let to bail and mainprise by "justices of the peace against due form of law, whereby many "murderers and felons escaped." It was enacted therefore that the power of bailing should be exercised only by two justices, who should let prisoners to bail till the next sessions or gaol delivery, and "certify the same at the next general sessions "of the peace, or next general gaol delivery." By the same statute it was provided that "every sheriff, bailiff of franchise, "and every other person having authority or power of keeping

" of gaol or prisoners for felony," should certify the names
of all prisoners in their custody to the next court of gaol
delivery, " there to be calendered before the justices." These
measures formed a part of the rigorous administration of
justice by which Henry VII. restrained the disorders arising
from the Wars of the Roses. They are contained in the
statute of which the act relating to the Star Chamber (3 Hen·
7, c. 1), already noticed, formed a part. They show how
great was the power committed to the justices, and what
grievous consequences might follow from its abuse. Under
the earlier law, any one justice of the peace might let any
offender to bail on any security, and as there was nothing to
warn the courts of oyer and terminer that this had been done,
the result might be, and often was, the complete impunity of
the offender. To require the presence of two justices on the
occasion was probably some, though no very great, security.

The system established by the statute of Philip and Mary
already referred to (Phil. & Mary, c. 13), was much more stringent. It was, in fact, the origin of the preliminary inquiry
which has come to be in practice one of the most important
and characteristic parts of our whole system of procedure,
but it was originally intended to guard against collusion between the justices and the prisoners brought before them. It
recites that until the making of the statute of Henry VII. " one
" justice of the peace in the name of himself and one other of
" the justices his companion not making the said justice party
" nor privy unto the case wherefore the prisoner should be
" bailed hath oftentimes by sinister labour and means set at
" large the greatest and most notable offenders such as be not
" replevisable by the laws of this realm; and yet the rather
" to hide their affections in that behalf have signed the cause
" of their apprehension to be but only for suspicion of felony
" whereby the said offenders have escaped unpunished." It
then provides that, whenever a prisoner is bailed, the depositions of the witnesses are to be taken and returned to the
court. Justices omitting this duty are to be fined.

The fact that this act was intended primarily as a security
against malpractices of the justices, and that the improvement
which it introduced into the administration of justice was

CH. VII. not its principal object, even if it was distinctly intended, explains some singularities in the act. It explains the circumstance that the first statute was confined to cases in which prisoners were bailed. If a man was committed to prison, there was no fear of the justices unduly favouring him; and therefore no need for special precautions against such favour. It also explains the circumstance that London and other corporate towns and the county of Middlesex were excepted from the act. In a great town where there were aldermen or other magistrates by charter, and a considerable population, the danger of collusion would be less than in the country.

[1] These statutes assume that the question who is bailable and who not is settled by the statute of Edward I. though there are some inconsistencies between them, especially as to bail in cases of homicide, to which I need not refer. [2] Numerous statutes, relating to particular offences, were passed in the seventeenth and eighteenth centuries, but no general provision on the subject was made till 1826, when the statute of 7 Geo. 4, c. 64, was passed, being one of the first attempts to consolidate the criminal law. It repealed all the statutes above referred to, so far as they relate to bail, and made other provisions on the subject which were in their turn superseded by those of 11 & 12 Vic. c. 42, s. 23, which are now in force. [3] This enactment provides that the committing justice may in his discretion, admit to bail (or commit to prison without bail, though the alternative is not expressly mentioned) any person charged with felony, or with [4] any one of the

[1] 2 Hale, *P. C.* 138-140.
[2] For them see 7 Geo. 4, c. 64, s. 32, the repealing clause.
[3] Under this act a single justice may act. Under the Act of 7 Geo. 4, c. 64, a complicated arrangement was made, not necessary to be noticed.
[4]   1. Assault with intent to commit felony.
    2. Attempt to commit felony.
    3. Obtaining or attempting to obtain property by false pretences.
    4. Misdemeanour in receiving property stolen or obtained by false pretences.
    5. Perjury or subornation of perjury.
    6. Concealment of birth of a child.
    7. Wilful or indecent exposure of the person.
    8. Riot.
    9. Assault in pursuance of a conspiracy to raise wages.
    10. Assault upon a police officer in the execution of his duty.
    11. Neglect or breach of duty as a peace officer.
    12. Any misdemeanour for the prosecution of which costs may be allowed

misdemeanours mentioned in the note. The short result is that the justice may in his discretion either bail or refuse to bail any person accused either of felony or of any common misdemeanour except libel, conspiracies other than those named, unlawful assembly, night poaching, and seditious offences. In these cases, and in misdemeanours [1] created by special acts, bail cannot be refused. [2] In cases of treason no bail may be taken except by order of a Secretary of State or by the High Court. The statute contains a series of provisions,[3] to which a general reference is sufficient, as to admitting to bail, after committal, persons who, in the opinion of the committing magistrate, ought to be bailed if they can find sufficient sureties.

Such is the history of the existing state of the law as to the bailing by justices of persons accused or suspected of crimes, but in order to make the history complete, it is necessary to mention shortly a branch of law which has

out of the county rate. The principal statute in force on the subject of costs at the time when 11 & 12 Vic. c. 42 was passed (*i.e.* in 1848) was 7 Geo. 4, c. 64, s. 23, which empowered the court to allow costs in cases of prosecution for ten specified misdemeanours, viz. all those mentioned in 11 & 12 Vic. c. 42, s. 23, with the exception of concealment of the birth of a child. Probably, therefore, there were in 1848 some provisions in force enabling the court to give costs in cases of misdemeanour other than those mentioned in 11 & 12 Vic. c. 42, s. 23. I have not, however, thought it worth while to examine into this minutely. In any event, I suppose the words under consideration contained in 7 Geo. 4, c. 64, are meant to apply to all misdemeanours, the costs of which may be allowed by the court under the law in force for the time being, though they do not say so distinctly. Several statutes have been passed since 1848 which have this effect. By 14 & 15 Vic. c. 55, s. 2, the act of George IV. is extended to the following misdemeanours :—

1. Unlawfully and carnally knowing and abusing any girl being above the age of ten (now twelve) and under the age of twelve (now thirteen) years.

2. Abduction of girls under sixteen.

3. Conspiring to charge any person with felony or to indict any person of felony.

4. Conspiring to commit any felony.

By 24 & 25 Vic. c. 96, s. 121 (larceny), c. 97, s. 77 (malicious injuries to properties), c. 98, s. 54 (forgery), c. 100, s. 77 (offences against the person), the court may allow the expenses of prosecutions for misdemeanours punishable under those acts. There is a more special provision of the kind in the Coinage Act, 24 & 25 Vic. c. 99, s. 42.

[1] This subject will be treated hereafter. Great numbers of misdemeanours are created by way of sanction to the provisions of particular administrative measures, such as the Lunacy Laws, the Merchant Shipping Acts, &c.

[2] 11 & 12 Vic. c. 47, s. 23 (at the end).

[3] Ss. 23 & 24. The act is a most useful one, but it is drawn in a manner calculated to drive the reader to despair. The principle on which its arrangement is based is that of the accidental association of ideas, and the style is to the last degree verbose and drawling.

CH. VII. become obsolete. In our own time there is practically no
reason to fear that justices under a legal duty to admit a man
to bail will refuse to do so. It was otherwise with the sheriffs
of earlier times. Not only did the vagueness of the law
itself leave a wide and ill-defined discretion in their hands,
but their power was so great that even in plain cases
they were often disposed to set it at defiance. Hence
royal writs requiring them to do their duty were necessary;
and of these there were several, the most important of
which were the writ *de homine replegiando*, the writ *de
manucaptione*, and the writ *de odio et atiâ*. These writs
issued out of the chancery to the sheriff or coroner. If
the first writ was not obeyed, a second writ, which was called
an "alias," was issued, and if that was not obeyed, a third,
called a "pluries." The final remedy was an attachment
under which the sheriff or other officer was imprisoned for
his disobedience. He might be fined for delaying till an
"alias" and "pluries" issued. [1] The writ *de homine replegiando* was confined (at least after 3 Edw. 1) to cases in
which a person was imprisoned before trial for an offence
bailable under the Statute of Bail (3 Edw. 1), though it also
applied to cases in which a person was unlawfully detained by
any one not having legal authority to detain him. In such
cases the sheriff might return that the person detained had
been "eloigned" (*elongatus*, carried to a distance where he
could not be found), and upon such a return a writ might
issue requiring the sheriff to take the captor "in withernam,"
that is, to imprison the captor till he produced the person so
detained. The writ "de manucaptione" (of mainprise) was
appropriated to cases in which a person had been taken on suspicion of felony and had tendered "manucaptors" or "main-
pernors" who had been refused. The difference between bail
and mainprise is long since obsolete. It is thus described by
Hale: [2] "Bail and mainprise are used promiscuously often-
"times for the same thing, and indeed the words import
"much the same thing, for the former is *traditus J. S.* and

---

[1] There were various forms of it, one for common offences, another for
forest offences. See FitzHerbert, *De Naturâ Brevium*, and see also 2 Hale,
Pleas of the Crown.

[2] 2 Hale, *P. C.* 124.

" the other is *manucaptus per J. S.* But yet in a proper and
" legal sense they differ. 1. Always mainprise is a recog-
" nizance in a sum certain, but bail is not always so. 2.
" He that is delivered per manucaptionem only is out
" of custody; but he that is bailed is in supposition of
" law still in custody, and the parties that take him to
" bail are in law his keepers, and may reseize him to
" bring him in." The difference between the use of the
two writs is described in [1]Hale, but is to me very obscure.

The writ *de odio et* [2]*atiâ* was confined to cases of
homicide, and has an odd history, as it was in itself a
singularly clumsy procedure. When a person was imprisoned on a charge of homicide, says [3]Bracton, "Fieri
" solet inquisitio utrum hujusmodi imprisonati pro morte
" hominis culpabiles essent de morte illâ vel non, et
" utrum appellati essent odio vel atya." If the person
imprisoned was found guilty, he was not to be admitted to
bail. If, however, the inquest said, "quod per odium et
" atyam, et contineatur causa in inquisitione quo odio vel
" qua atya diligenter erit causa examinanda, cum sint plures,
[4]" &c., et ballivi qui non sine causæ cognitione in hujusmodi
" inquisitionibus prætendunt non causam ut causam, et si
" sufficiens fuerit causa per ballium dimittatur." This curious
passage seems to imply that even in the infancy of our
law questions arose as to malice similar to those which
have given so much trouble in our own days. It obviously was not every sort of hatred or malice in the
prosecutor which would entitle the prisoner to be bailed.
The cause of it was to be considered. It is probable
that the "causa" which was to be diligently examined
was the evidence of the guilt of the accused man, and that
"odium et atya" were mere legal figments by which the
presence or absence of reasonable cause of suspicion was
obscurely denoted. If a man hated another because he
had been seen committing a murder, his hatred would
be no reason why he should not prosecute the criminal.

[1] 2 Hale, *P. C.* 140.
[2] Malice. "Ex Anglo-Saxonico forte 'hatung' unde Anglis 'hate' et
"Germanis 'Haet' . . . vel potius a Greco ἄτη " (Ducange).
[3] Bracton, ii. pp. 292-296.   [4] I suppose sheriffs and coroners.

CH. VII. If the prosecutor was unable to assign any cause for the prosecution, it would be not unnatural to say that he must hate the person imprisoned. If there was evidence malice was immaterial. If there was no evidence malice was inferred. Hence, the sufficiency of the evidence, being the real point, was inquired into under pretence of inquiring into the malice. But, however this may have been, it is at all events clear that the effect of the writ was to cause a preliminary trial to take place in cases of homicide, the result of which determined whether the accused should be admitted to bail or imprisoned till he was finally tried. If he was found to have been accused by malice, he was admitted to bail on finding twelve sureties, [1] "qui manucapiant habendi " eum ad primam assisam et coram justitiariis nostris ad " respondendum de morte B."

The writ *de odio et atiâ* is referred to in [2]Magna Charta. Foster is of opinion (upon grounds which to me seem just) that it was abolished by 6 Edw. 1, c. 9 (the Statute of Gloucester), in 1278. Coke says in one place that it was abolished by the general words of 28 Edw. 3, c. 9, and revived by 42 Edw. 3, c. 1, in which I think he was mistaken; elsewhere he contradicts this opinion, saying that it was abolished by the Statute of Gloucester. At all events it has been obsolete for centuries.[3]

These writs, which issued to the sheriff and the coroner, can never have been of the first importance, and must have gone into disuse at an early period ([4]though there are a few instances of them in comparatively modern times), as from the earliest times [5] the superior courts and the lord

---

[1] Bracton, ii. 295-297.

[2] " Nihil detur vel capietur de cetero pro brevi inquisitionis de vita vel membris, sed gratis concedetur et non negetur."—Stubbs, *Charters*, p. 301. Magna Charta, art. 36.

[3] See on this writ, 2 Hale, *P.C.* 148 ; Coke, *2nd Inst.* 421, on Magna Charta, c. 26, p. 315, on the Statute of Gloucester, c. 9. See also Foster, 284-285.

[4] See *e.g.* the case of Witmore for kidnapping in 1682, 8 *State Trials*, 1347, and two records of *de homine replegiando* printed at pp. 1350-1385. See also some remarks in Selden's argument in the case of the writ of *habeas corpus* moved for on behalf of Hampden and others, 3 *St. Tr.* 95. In the case of Lord Grey of Werke, a writ *de homine replegiando* was issued to force him to produce his sister-in-law, Lady Henrietta Berkeley, whom he had seduced. See 9 *St. Tr.* 184.

[5] The Courts of Common Pleas and Exchequer had originally to issue the writ under a fiction to the effect that the person requiring it was privileged

chancellor had the right of issuing the writ of habeas corpus, which answered in a simpler and more direct way all the purposes of the other writs.

The history of the writ of habeas corpus, regarded as a protection against wrongful imprisonment, hardly falls within the scope of a history of the criminal law. It is well known, and is associated with the most stirring period of our history. I need not therefore refer to it on the present occasion. The power of the superior courts to bail in all cases whatever, even high-treason, has no history. I do not know, indeed, that it has ever been disputed or modified. It exists in the present day precisely as it has always existed from the earliest times. The only matters connected with it which need be noticed here are some of the provisions in the Habeas Corpus Act of 1679 (31 Chas. 2, c. 2). This act provides that any person committed to prison "for any crime unless for treason "or felony plainly expressed in the warrant of commitment," may obtain a writ of habeas corpus from the lord chancellor or any judge of the common-law courts. The writ being served on the gaoler, and certain conditions being complied with it as to expenses, a return must be made to the writ within three days. Upon the return, the judge is required to admit the prisoner to bail.

In the 11 & 12 Vic. c. 42, no notice is taken of the Habeas Corpus Act, so that it seems that, although in many cases of misdemeanour the committing magistrate may refuse bail, a judge who knows nothing of the case is absolutely required to bail any misdemeanant who takes out a writ of habeas corpus. There is indeed an obscure proviso which perhaps might be held to meet such a case as the end of s. 2, but the act is as ill-drawn as it is celebrated.

or was to be sued in the court from which the writ issued. See 2 Hale, *P.C.* 144 ; but by 16 Chas. 1, c. 10, s. 6, the Common Pleas obtained original jurisdiction in the matter and by 31 Chas. 2, c. 2, all the three courts are empowered to grant the writ.

CHAPTER VIII.

HISTORY OF THE LAW OF CRIMINAL PROCEDURE CON-
TINUED.—FORMS OF ACCUSATION AND TRIAL—APPEALS—
ORDEALS—TRIAL BY JURY.

CH. VIII.   THE subject of the present chapter is the history of the
———   methods of accusation and trial which have prevailed in
England. These are private and public accusations, and trial
by battle, by ordeal, by jury, and by the Star Chamber and
similar courts of which I have [1] already spoken.

ACCUSATION BY A PRIVATE ACCUSER—APPEALS.

Accusation and trial are so closely connected that for
practical purposes they are most conveniently considered
together.

Since the Norman Conquest there have been [2] three modes
of trial in criminal cases, namely, trial by ordeal, trial by
battle, and trial by jury; and there have been also three
modes of accusation, namely, appeal or accusation by a
private person, indictment or accusation by a grand jury,
and informations which are accusations either by the
Attorney-General or by the Master of the Crown Office.

---

[1] *Supra*, ch. vi.

[2] If compurgation is counted there have been four, but compurgation in
criminal cases hardly survived the Norman Conquest, though some traces of
it remained in the hundred and manor courts. In the ecclesiastical courts it
lasted till 1640, as will appear hereafter. In the form of "wager of law" in
civil cases it maintained a nominal existence till the year 1834, when it was
abolished by 3 & 4 Will. 4, c. 42, s. 13. Probably the last case in which
it was actually put in force was King v. Williams (2 B. and C. 538, 1824). In
this case on an action of simple contract the defendant prepared to bring eleven
"compurgators, but the plaintiff abandoned his action." Much information
on this subject is to be found in Pike's *History of Crime*. The references are
collected in the Index.

The history of these modes of accusation and trial may be conveniently related under one head.

The history of appeals or accusations by a private person and trial by battle go together, as trial by battle was an incident of appeals.

The fact that the private vengeance of the person wronged by a crime was the principal source to which men trusted for the administration of criminal justice in early times is one of the most characteristic circumstances connected with English criminal law, and has had much to do with the development of what may perhaps be regarded as its principal distinctive peculiarity, namely, the degree to which a criminal trial resembles a private litigation. In very early times this showed itself in the circumstance that the law of appeals formed the most, or nearly the most, important and prominent part of the criminal law. An elaborate account of the procedure connected with them fills a large part of the book of Bracton, *De Corona*, and also a considerable part of the first book of Britton, which relates mainly to the same subject. Each of these authors, but particularly Bracton, goes into the subject with great minuteness, Bracton in particular having a separate chapter upon each different kind of appeal and mixing it up with definitions of the various offences as to which appeals might be brought, forms of writs to sheriffs, and much other matter which has now altogether lost its interest.

The following was the substance of the process according to which appeals might be made in cases of treason, homicide, breach of the, peace and wounding (*de pace et plagis*), mayhem, breaches of the peace by false imprisonment, robbery, arson, and rape. The appeal was made before the coroner or before more coroners than one. The appellor was required to make a minute and strictly formal statement before the coroner as to the nature of the offence, [1] setting forth a great variety of particulars as to the time, place, and circumstances of the offence, in order that the appellee might be enabled to defend himself. This statement was enrolled by the coroner, and the appellor appears to have been held

[1] Brac. 424-33.

CH. VIII. to it strictly in all subsequent stages of the proceedings. The next step was to secure the appearance of the appellee, the process for which was to publish the appeal at five successive county courts. If he did not appear at the fifth the consequence was outlawry. There were elaborate rules as to this, and as to the counter process of inlawry, by which the effect of outlawry was taken off, and the appellee was permitted to defend himself.

If the appellee appeared before the justices he might avail himself of any one of a great variety of pleas or exceptions, which are detailed at great length in Bracton. [1] He states the following as "ista generalis exceptio et prima":—"Si "secta non fuerit bene facta, quia qui appellare voluerit et "bene sequi, debet ille, cui injuriatum erit, statim quam "cito poterit hutesium levare, et cum hutesio ire ad villas "vicinas et propinquiores et ibi manifestare scelera et in-"jurias perpetratas." There were, however, many other exceptions, one of which is introduced in the middle of the chapter without any special notice, but which must, if it really prevailed, have made appeals comparatively unimportant. [2] "Cadit appellum ubi appellans non loquitur de "visu et auditu," but there is reason to think that if this was the law in Bracton's time it ceased to be so afterwards.

[3] If the appellee did not plead, or not adequately, battle was waged between the parties, but the judges were bound, *ex officio*, to inquire (it is not clearly stated how) into the circumstances of the case, and not to allow the battle if the case was such that there were against the appellee [4] "pre-"sumptiones quæ probationem non admittunt in contrarium, "ut si quis cum cultello sanguinolento captus fuerit super "mortuum, vel a mortuo fugiendo, vel mortem cognoverit "coram aliquibus qui recordum habeant, et hujusmodi tales." If the appellee was defeated before the stars appeared he was hanged. If he was victorious or defended himself till the stars appeared he was acquitted of the appeal, [5] but inasmuch as the appeal was considered to raise a presumption of his guilt he was to be tried by the country as if he had been indicted.

---

[1] Bracton, ii. 425.　　[2] *Ib.* p. 434.　　[3] *Ib.* p. 442.
[4] *Ib.* p. 452.　　　　　[5] *Ib.* p. 448.

There are some variations from this in [1] Britton's *Account* CH. VIII.
of Appeals, which was written about 1291, in the time of
Edward I., and no doubt the practice must have varied, but
it would not be worth while to go minutely into the subject.
[2] In Hawkins's *Pleas of the Crown* is to be found an elaborate
account of the law as it stood when all but practically obsolete. I may however observe that the plea of want of fresh
suit was taken away by the Statute of Gloucester (6 Edw. 1,
c. 9) in 1278, which allowed the appellor to sue within a
year and a day.

The principal points in the history of appeals are as
follows :—Appeals in cases of treason were properly (it seems)
brought in Parliament. I have already given an account of
them and of the manner in which they came to be abolished
by statute, 1 Hen. 4, c. 14. That statute applies only to
appeals of treason within the realm. Appeals for treasons
done out of the realm were not affected by it, but were to
be brought before the constable and marshal. [3] Such an
appeal actually was brought by Lord Rea against David
Ramsey in the year 1631, and combat was ordered upon it,
but the king revoked his letters patent to the constable and
marshal, and the matter came to an end.

Appeals in cases which were not capital, and in particular
appeals for blows, for wounds, and false imprisonment, merged
in actions of tort for damages for those causes. Appeals of
mayhem lingered a little longer, but became obsolete.

Appeals of robbery and larceny lasted longer, because at
Common Law the restitution of property feloniously taken
could be awarded only when the thief or robber was convicted on an appeal, but this was altered by 21 Hen. 8,
c. 11, which gave a writ of restitution to the true owner upon
the conviction of the felon on an indictment.

Appeals of arson seem to have been discontinued at a very
early time.

[1] 1 Britton (by Nicholls), 97–125.
[2] Bk. ii. ch. xxiii. vol. ii. p. 223–281, ed. 1824. The book was written
early in the eighteenth century.
[3] 3 *St. Tr.* 483–519. Some other cases of trial by combat in civil cases are
referred to in the notes to this case. One of the combatants in the last case
of trial by battle in a civil action was Lilburn, the father of John Lilburn,
known under Charles I. and Cromwell as " Free-born John."

CH. VIII.　Of appeals of rape it is only necessary to say that they seem to have differed less than other appeals from indictments, and that the offence at which some early statutes on the subject were levelled seems to have included what we should describe as abduction with intent to marry as well as what we describe as rape.

Hence the only appeals which can be said to have had any definite history and to have formed a substantial part of the criminal procedure of the country were appeals of murder. It seems that appeals continued to be the common and established way of prosecuting murder till the end of the fifteenth century. Indeed, they were viewed with so much and, according to our notions, such strange and unmerited favour that in 1482 (22 Edw. 4) they were made the subject of an act of judicial legislation of an almost unexampled kind. [1] FitzHerbert has this note on the subject : "Note that all the justices of each bench say that " it is their common opinion that, if a man is indicted of the " death of a man, the person indicted shall not be arraigned " within the year for the same felony at the king's suit, and " they advise all legal persons (touts hōēs de ley) to execute " this point as a law without variance, so that the suit of " the party may be saved." This resolution, in which the judges, openly and in the plainest words, assumed legislative power, was apparently acted upon to the great injury of the public, and it was found necessary six years afterwards to repeal it by statute. This appears from the recitals and provisions of 3 Hen. 7, c. 1, to which I have already referred in connection with the Court of Star Chamber. This act recites that "murders and slayings of the king's " subjects do daily increase, that the persons in towns where " such murders fall to be done will not attach the murderer" as by law they ought, and that " it is used that within the " year and a day after any death or murder had or done the " felony should not be determined at the king's suit for " saving of the party's suit" (the appeal), "wherein the " party is oftentimes slow, and also agreed with, and by the " end of the year all is forgotten, which is another occasion of

[1] Corone, No. 44, H. 22 Edw. 4.

" murder. And also he that will sue any appeal must sue in
" proper person, which suit is long and costly that it maketh
" the party appellant weary to sue." As a remedy it is provided
that indictments for murder shall be tried at once, and that
an acquittal on an indictment shall be no bar to an appeal.

The effect of this provision seems to have been that the
indictment, which did not involve trial by battle, was
usually tried first, and its result was practically conclusive, unless the prisoner was acquitted under circumstances which greatly dissatisfied the parties concerned.
This state of things continued till the year 1819, though
the resort to an appeal became less and less common
as time went on. [1] There are, however, some specimens
of appeals of murder reported in the *State Trials,* [2] and
an attempt to abolish them by statute was successfully
resisted in the years 1768 and 1774. The last appeal
of murder ever brought was the case of [3] Ashford *v.*
Thornton. Thornton, being strongly suspected of having
murdered Mary Ashford, was tried for that offence and
acquitted at Warwick Assizes, and an appeal was brought by
her brother. On the 2nd November, 1818, the appellant
read his count (the equivalent of an indictment) in the
Court of King's Bench, charging Thornton with his sister's
murder Thornton then pleaded, " Not guilty, and I am
" ready to defend the same with my body ; " " and thereupon
" taking his glove off he threw it upon the floor of the court."
The appellant then counter-pleaded that Thornton ought not
to be permitted to wage battle, because the circumstances
(which are set out in detail in the counter-plea) were such as
to show that he was guilty. The appellee replied, setting
out circumstances which he regarded as establishing an alibi
in his favour. To this there was a demurrer. Upon this
issue was joined, and an argument took place, in which [4] all

---

[1] In Spencer Cowper's case, 13 *St. Tr.* 1190, as also the cases of Bambridge
and Corbet, 17 *St. Tr.* 395-7.   In Bigby *v.* Kennedy, 5 *Bur.* 2643, a careful report is given of the proceedings in an appeal on account of their
rarity.
[2] See an account of this in Horne Tooke's defence on his prosecution for
libel in 1777.   20 *St. Tr.* 716, 717.   [3] 1 Bar. and Ald. 405.
[4] Mr. Chitty and Sir N. Tindal argued the case.   It will be found that
practically Bracton is the great authority.

CH. VIII. the authorities on the subject are reviewed. The Court decided that the result of the authorities was that the appellee had a right to wage his body, unless circumstances practically inconsistent with his innocence appeared, and that such did not appear from the matter put upon the pleadings to be the case. The result was that no further judgment was given, the appellant not being prepared to do battle. The proceedings ended by Thornton's arraignment on the appeal, to which he pleaded *autrefois acquit*.

This proceeding led to the statute 59 Geo. 3, c. 46, by which all appeals in criminal cases were wholly abolished.

It is probable that the commonest and most important form of appeal was that of appeal by an approver. The nature of this proceeding was as follows :—[1] If a person accused of any crime, but especially of robbery, chose to plead guilty and to offer to give up his accomplices he was handed over to the coroner, before whom he confessed his guilt and accused a certain number of other persons, and the king might " grant him life and limb if he would deliver the " country from a certain number of malefactors either by his " body " (*i.e.* by killing them upon battle waged) " or by the " country " (*i.e.* convicting them before a jury), " or by " flight." If he failed to fulfil the conditions imposed on him he was hanged on his own confession. If the person accused was a man of good character, the conditions of the proceeding were made less favourable to the approver than they otherwise would have been.

If the approver fulfilled the stipulated condition and disposed of the prescribed number of accomplices he had to abjure the realm [2] " in regno remanere non poterit etiam si " velit plegios invenire."

ACCUSATIONS BY PUBLIC REPORT—ORDEALS—TRIAL BY JURY.

I have already described the manner in which public accusations were made before the Conquest. I now come to the procedure subsequent to the Conquest.

---

[1] Bracton, 523, &c.   [2] *Ib.* 532.

Glanville mentions the subject very slightly. [1] In his short chapter on criminal proceedings he describes the procedure adopted in the case of each particular crime separately, but he seems in all cases to recognize the distinction between an accusation by a definite accuser and an accusation by public report alone.

The silence of Glanville upon this subject is, however, of the less importance, because we have still [2] the text of the Assize of Clarendon (1164) and that of the Assize of North-ampton (1176), which constitute the legislation of Henry II. upon this subject.   The Assize of Northampton was a republication of the Assize of Clarendon, with some altera-tions and additions intended to make the system established by it more rigorous.   Its provisions are as follows :—" If any " one is accused before the justices of our Lord the King of " murder or theft or robbery, or of harbouring persons com-" mitting those crimes, or of forgery or of arson, by the oath of " twelve knights of the hundred, or, if there are no knights, " by the oath of twelve free and lawful men, and by the oath " of four men from each township of the hundred, let him go " to the ordeal of water, and if he fails let him lose one foot. " And at Northampton it was added for greater strictness of " justice " (*pro rigore justitiæ*) " that he shall lose his right " hand at the same time with his foot, and abjure the realm, " and exile himself from the realm within forty days.   And " if he is acquitted by the ordeal let him find pledges and " remain in the kingdom unless he is accused of murder or " other base felony by the body of the country and the lawful " knights of the country ; but if he is so accused as aforesaid, " although he is acquitted by the ordeal of water, neverthe-" less he must leave the kingdom in forty days and take his " chattels with him, subject to the rights of his lords, and he " must abjure the kingdom at the mercy of our Lord the " King.   This assize is to apply from the time of the Assize " of Clarendon to the present time, and from the present " time as long as our Lord the King pleases in cases of " murder and treason and arson, and in all the aforesaid

---

[1] Glanville, book xiv.
[2] Stubbs, *Charters*, 143, 150.

" matters, except small thefts and robberies done in the time
" of war, as of horses and oxen, and less matters."

The system thus established is simple. The body of the
country are the accusers. Their accusation is practically
equivalent to a conviction subject to the chance of a favourable termination of the ordeal by water. If the ordeal fails,
the accused person [1] loses his foot and his hand. If it
succeeds, he is nevertheless to be banished. Accusation
therefore was equivalent to banishment at least.

We have still some evidence as to the kind of cases in
which the ordeal was inflicted. It is to be found in the
Rotuli Curiæ Regis for the reigns of Richard I. and John,
said by Sir F. Palgrave to be the oldest judicial records in
existence. The following illustrations (amongst others) are
published by Sir F. Palgrave in his [2] *Proofs and Illustrations.*

" *Roll of the Iter of Stafford in* 5 *John.*—One Elena is
" suspected by the jurors because she was at the place where
" Reinalda de Henchenhe was killed, and because she was
" killed by her help and consent. She denies it. Let her
" purge herself by the judgment of fire ; but as she is ill, let
" her be respited till she gets well."

" Andrew of Bureweston is suspected by the jurors of the
" death of one Hervicus because he fled for his death, there-
" fore let him purge himself by the judgment of water."

" *Roll of the Iter of Wiltshire,* 10 *Rich.* 1.—The jurors
" say that Radulphus Parmentarius was found dead with his
" neck broken, and they suspect one Cristiana, who was
" formerly the wife of Ernaldus de Knabbewell, of his death,
" because Radulphus sued Cristiana in the ecclesiastical court
" for breach of a promise of marriage she had made to him,
" and after the death of her husband Ernaldus, Reginald, a
" clerk, frequented her and took her away from Radulphus,
" and Reginald and Cristiana hated Radulphus for suing her,

---

[1] This was the common punishment for robbery in India under native rule.
I have myself seen men in Lahore whose hands (as they said themselves) had
been cut off by Runjeet Singh for theft. In the *Life of Thomas,* a Baptist
missionary at Calcutta, there is an account of the punishment of fourteen
dacoits in the neighbourhood of Calcutta, each of whom had his hand and
foot cut off on the 15th February, 1789, on the western bank of the Hooghly,
opposite Calcutta.—Lewis's *Life of Thomas,* p. 18.
[2] Palgrave, clxxxv.—clxxxviii.

" and on account of that hatred the jurors suspect her and
" the clerk of his death. And the country says it suspects
" her. Therefore it is considered that the clerk and Cristiana
" appear on Friday, and that Cristiana purge herself by fire."
It is impossible to say how long the system of ordeals
lasted. In the *Mirror* there is a list of 155 abuses in the
law of which the author complains. The 127th is—" It is
" an abuse that proofs and purgations be not by the miracle
" of God where other proof faileth." [1] The *Mirror* was
written in the reign of Edward I., so that it appears probable
that ordeals fell into disuse in the course of the thirteenth
century, [2] probably in consequence of the decrees of the
Lateran Council of 1216.

The system of accusation which led up to, and to use a
modern legal expression " sounded," in ordeal, was the origin
of the grand jury of later times, and of our own days. In
my chapter on the History of the Criminal Courts, [3] I have
given Bracton's description of the justices' eyre, as it existed in
the time of Henry III., and have shown that the accusation of
suspected persons was only one of its multifarious duties, which
were of such magnitude and variety that they may properly
be said at that time to have consisted of a general superintendence over all the local details of the executive government.
By degrees the old system of convening something like a
county parliament, in which every township was represented
by its reeve and four men, fell into disuse, and the sheriffs
fell into the habit of summoning only a sufficient number
of *probi et legales homines* to form a grand jury and as
many petty juries as might be needed for the trial of the
civil and criminal cases to be disposed of. The law upon
the subject of the number and qualifications of the men to be

[1] Palgrave, cxiii.
[2] The last reference to the system which I have met with is in one of the
trials for the Popish Plot. Gavan, one of the five Jesuits who were tried and
executed upon the evidence of Oates in 1679, begged to be allowed "to put
" himself upon the trial of ordeal" (7 *St. Tr.* 383), alleging that "in the be-
" ginning of the Church it was a custom, and grew to a constant law," that
a person accused of a capital offence should be allowed to do so when there was
only the accuser's oath against his denial. It is odd that Gavan should have
supposed that judgment by ordeal was a specially ecclesiastical mode of proceeding, when, in fact, its abolition was due to the ecclesiastical legislation on
the subject.   [3] *Supra*, p. 102.

CH. VIII. put upon the pannels formerly was, and to some extent still is, singularly vague. In practice at the assizes the grand jury for counties is always composed of the county magistrates, whose names are called over by the officer of the court until twenty-three at most have appeared. The magistrates, however, have no special legal right or duty in the matter. Any '' good and lawful men '' of the county may serve, no special qualification being required, though there are some disqualifications.[1] There is no historical interest in the enactments which have been made upon this subject. The grand jury to the present day accuses every person who is put on his trial before any court of criminal jurisdiction which tries prisoners by a jury. The most interesting point connected with their operations is to trace out, if possible, the manner in which the powers of the petty jury grew up, and the way in which they were exercised.

The origin of petty juries seems now to be pretty clearly determined. Various institutions having more or less resemblance to petty juries are to be found in different ages and countries, but the following points connected with their history in England are clear beyond dispute, and are those which it really concerns us to know.

When trial by ordeal was abolished and the system of accusation by grand juries was established, absolutely no mode of ascertaining the truth of an accusation made by a grand jury remained. Trial by battle could apply only in cases where there was an individual accuser, in other words in cases of appeals ; and thus an accusation by a grand jury became practically equivalent to a conviction. This led to the introduction of trial by jury as we understand it, by the following steps. In the first place, the usual mode of determining questions of fact known to and practised by the Normans was the inquest. An inquest was a body of persons representing a certain number of townships or other districts. The township being represented by the four men and the reeve. They were convened by the representative of the

---

[1] The law relating to petty juries is now regulated by statute in most though not in all particulars (see 6 Geo. 4, c. 50, and some later acts, especially 33 and 34 Vic. c. 77). As to grand juries, see *Dig. Crim. Proc.* ch. xxii. arts. 184-188.

royal authority, such as a justice, a sheriff, or a coroner, as the case might be, and answered upon oath the particular matters proposed to them. The most important instances of inquests which can be cited are those by whose report were drawn up Domesday Book and the Hundred Rolls, to which I have already referred.

The manner in which the inquests informed themselves of the particular facts to which they swore has not been recorded. Probably they would be warned beforehand of the matters to which they were to depose, and would make local inquiries. Possibly they took evidence on the spot. [1] In one of the passages I have quoted from the Hundred Rolls for another purpose, a complaint is made of the misbehaviour of a local noble, who threatened a person in order to deter him from giving evidence before the inquest, but upon these matters we are left to conjecture, and it is probable that different methods would be employed on different occasions and for different purposes. Be this however as it may, one point is clear. The inquest were the witnesses in contemplation of law. It was by their oath, and not by the oath of their informants, that the fact to be proved was considered to be established, and the only form of perjury known to the law of England as a crime till comparatively modern times was that form of perjury which was committed by giving a false verdict, and which was punished by the process known as an attaint.

The introduction of the inquest into the administration of justice took place apparently by steps. It was first introduced in what were in earlier days the commonest and most important of civil causes, namely, trials held in order to determine the right to land. In these cases, as in private accusations of crime, the mode of trial after the Norman Conquest was by battle, but in the reign of Henry II. was introduced what was called the "Great Assize." This form of trial is thus described by [2] Glanville : "Now the Great " Assize is a royal benefit indulged to the people by the " clemency of the prince on the advice of the nobles, whereby " life and property are so wholesomely cared for that men

---

[1] *Ante*, p. 130.   [2] Glanville, ii. 7, p. 35.

" can avoid the chance of the combat and yet keep what-
" ever right they have in their freeholds. And thereby they
" can avoid the last penalty of unexpected and premature
" death, or at least of that perpetual infamy, that horrible
" and shameful word (craven) which sounds sadly in the
" mouth of the conquered. This constitution arises from
" the highest equity, for the right which can scarcely be
" proved by battle after many and long delays is more con-
" veniently and speedily acquired by the benefit of this
" constitution. The Assize does not admit of as many
" essoigns as the combat, as will immediately appear, and by
" this both the labour of men and the expense of the poor
" are spared. Besides, this institution has in it more equity
" than trial by combat in proportion as more weight is to be
" allowed in judgment to many fit witnesses than to one
" alone."

In the following chapters the nature of the institution is
described :—[1] The defendant " put himself on the assize,"
whereupon trial by combat was stayed, [2] and four knights
were summoned to return twelve knights of the vicinage to
say (ad recognoscendum) by their oaths [3] which of the parties
had most right to the land. These recognitors were obviously
witnesses, as appears from the [4] account given of their proceedings when they met. Upon their assembly it is said
either all will know where the right is, or some will and
others will not, or all will not. If some or all are ignorant,
and say so on their oaths, they are to be excluded. If some
are on one side and some on the other, "adjiciendi sunt alii
"donec duodecim ad minus in alterutram partem acquieverint."
It is also said that they were to swear to matters within their
own knowledge, or "per verba patrum suorum et per talia
" quibus fidem teneantur habere ut propriis." [5] Severe
punishment was provided for those who swore falsely. [6] If
the claimant could not find twelve persons to swear to his
right he was thrown back on the remedy by combat.

Even before the abolition of ordeals it seems to have been

---

[1] Glanville, c. 8.   [2] *Ib.* c. 11.
[3] " Quis eorum scilicet an tenens an petens majus jus habeat in suâ de-
"mandâ " (Glanville, c. 14).
[4] *Ib.* c. 17.   [5] *Ib.* c. 19.   [6] *Ib.* c. 21.

not very unusual for persons accused of crimes by what CH. VIII.
answered to the present grand jury to purchase from the
king the privilege of going before a petty jury, which was
to determine finally on his guilt or innocence. [1] Sir F.
Palgrave gives several instances of this. When ordeals were
discontinued it is probable that petty juries would come into
general use, and such appears to have been the case.

Bracton's account of the proceedings before justices is exceedingly full, but it is so discursive that it is by no means
easy to be sure as to its meaning. It appears, however, to
be as follows: [2] First, the justices are to give a charge to
the persons appearing before them, and after various consultations and explanations a kind of grand jury, consisting
of four knights from each hundred, is to be sworn to answer
to what is required of them. They are to give a schedule
of suspected persons, whom the sheriff is forthwith to seize
and cause to appear before the justices "ut justitiarli de iis
"faciant justitiam." After stating this Bracton goes to
other subjects, but returns at last to the question of public
accusations. [3] In a passage too long to extract at length he
gives the following account of the procedure:—[4] When a man
is indicted the justice is to examine the twelve who indict
him (this must mean the grand jury) as to their means of
knowledge. Whereupon "Dicet forte aliquis vel major pars
"juratorum quod ea quæ ipsi proferunt in veredicto suo
"didicerunt ab uno ex conjuratoribus suis," and this being
followed up the report may at last be traced, "ad aliquam
"vilem et abjectam personam et talem cui non erit fides
"aliquatenus adhibenda." What is to happen in this case
is not stated, but it is observed that on account of the
possibility of false and malicious accusations the accused
person may object to individuals or townships. At last twelve
persons are to be sworn and [5] "secundum eorum veredictum

[1] *Proofs and Illustrations*, clxxvi., clxxvii., and clxxxvi., No. 17. A person
appealed of robbery, "affert domino regi unam marcam argenti pro habendâ
"inquisitione per legales milites utrum culpabilis sit inde necne . . . oblatio
"recipitur. Juratores dicunt quod revera contencio fuit inter gardinarium
"prædicti Roberti, Osmund nomine, et quosdam garciones, sed Ranulfus" (the
prisoner) "non fuit ibi nec malecredunt eum de aliquâ roberiâ vel de aliquo
"malo facto eidem." [2] Bracton, ii. 234-241.
[3] *Ib.* c. xxii. pp. 450-462. [4] *Ib.* p. 454. [5] *Ib.* p. 456.

CH. VIII. " aut sequitur deliberatio aut condemnatio." " The justices
_____ " are to observe this form of inquisition by the country
" generally in all inquests to be made of the death of a man,
" when any one puts himself on the inquest either willingly
" or from caution, or by necessity, in all crimes greater or less ;
" but the justices can, if they think it expedient on a neces-
" sary cause, and if a great crime lies hid, and the jurors wish
" to conceal the truth from love, or hatred, or fear, separate the
" jurors from each other and examine them separately to
" disclose the truth sufficiently."

The difficulty is to ascertain from these passages whether
they speak of two juries or of only one. I am disposed to
think that they refer to two, as two distinct occasions are
mentioned in which the jurors swear. It must be admitted
that the matter is left in great doubt, but whatever may
have been the truth on this subject, it is obvious that in
Bracton's time the jury were not only witnesses, but witnesses
who might be and habitually were examined and cross-
examined by the justices.

Bracton's work is supposed by Sir H. Twiss to have
been written before 1258. Britton, who took Bracton's
work to a great extent as a foundation for his own, [1]wrote,
it is supposed, about 1291-2. In his time there certainly
were two juries, and each was composed of witnesses. [2] The
proceedings of the grand jury are first described much as
Bracton describes them, though more succinctly. [3] The
persons indicted are then to be called upon, and if necessary
compelled, to put themselves on their country or to plead
guilty. Then comes [4] a passage obviously founded upon the
one just quoted from Bracton, which leaves no doubt as to
the functions of the petty jury: " And afterwards let the
" jurors be charged of what fact they are to speak the truth,
" and then go and confer together and be kept by a bailiff."
. . . "If they cannot all agree in one mind let them be
" separated and examined why they cannot agree ; and if the
" greater part of them know the truth and the other part
" do not, judgment shall be according to the opinion of the

[1] Nicholls' *Britton*, lxix.   [2] Britton, 22-26.
[3] *Ib.* 26-31.   [4] *Ib.* 31, 32.

"greater part. And if they declare upon their oaths that
"they know nothing of the fact, let others be called who do
"know it; and if he who put himself on the first inquest
"will not put himself on a new jury, let him be remanded
"back to penance till he consents thereto. We will also
"that if any man who is indicted of a crime touching life
"and limb and perceives that the verdict of the inquest on
"which he has put himself is likely to pass against him,
"desires to say that any one of the jurors is suborned to
'condemn him by the lord of whom the accused holds his
"land, through greediness of the escheat or for other
"cause by any one else, the justices thereupon shall carefully
"examine the jurors whether they have reason to think that
"such slander is true. And often a strict examination is
"necessary, for in such case inquiry may be made how the
"jurors are informed of the truth of their verdict; when
"they will say by one of their fellows, and he peradventure
"will say that he heard it told for truth at the tavern or
"elsewhere by some ribald or other persons unworthy of
"credit, or it may be that he or they by whom the jurors
"have been informed were intreated or suborned by the
"lords or by the enemies of the person indicted to get him
"condemned, and if the justices find this to be the fact, let
"such suborners be apprehended and punished by imprison-
"ment and fine. And if the jurors are in doubt of the matter
"and not certain, the judgment ought always in such case to
"be for the defendant."

There is, however, evidence that though the jurors were
themselves the witnesses by whose evidence the prisoner's
fate was decided, other witnesses might be and sometimes were called upon criminal trials. [1] Witnesses are expressly mentioned in the *Leges Henrici Primi* as taking part
in trials. Moreover [2] one of the entries reprinted by Sir F.
Palgrave from the records of the eyre of Gloucester in the fifth
year of Henry III. is as follows: " William, son of Matilda,
"was taken and imprisoned at Gloucester for the death of
"William Blund, whom he killed; and Nicholas Church, John,

---

[1] *Leges H. P.* v. " *De Causarum Proprietatibus.*"—Thorpe i. p. 505.
[2] Palgrave, *Proofs and Illustrations*, clxxxvii. 21.

" the son of Melisent, Walter de Havena, Walter Smith, and
" Richard de Herdeshelt, and several others who were present
" when he was killed, testified that they saw when he killed
" him, and that they immediately upon the fact took him
" still holding in his hand the stick with which he killed
" him, and besides the four next townships testify to the
" same thing; and besides . . . . and Dionysia, the wife of
" William Blund, appealed him of the aforesaid death as seen
" by her; and besides twelve jurors say that he is guilty.
" And he defends himself against all. But because he was
" taken still holding the stick in his hand with which he
" killed him, and all with one voice say he is guilty, it is
" adjudged that he cannot defend himself, and therefore let
" him be hanged."

In this case there were five witnesses, four townships, and
a jury, by all of whom the accused was said to be guilty.

It is not my intention to try to trace out in detail the
history of trial by jury. The authorities already given show
with sufficient clearness how it originated, but the steps by
which the jury ceased to be witnesses and became judges of
the evidence given by others cannot now be traced without
an amount of labour out of proportion to the value of the
result. I will, however, state the very little which I am able
to say upon the subject. As appears by the passage quoted
above from Glanville, the process which took place when a
jury said that they, or some of them, were ignorant on the
matter to which they were to swear, was what was called
" afforcement." That is, new witnesses were added until the
number required was made up. This process was well
exemplified by the [1] practice, which was followed when deeds
or charters which had been attested by witnesses were to be
proved. The witnesses were, it seems, a kind of assessors
to the jury, and this was the origin of what, till very modern
times indeed, was an inflexible rule of evidence that the
attesting witnesses to a written document must in all cases
be called or accounted for. As the juries became less

---

[1] Bracton, i. 298-300 ; *Fortescue de Laudibus*, ch. xxxii., and Selden's
note ; Brooke's *Abridgment Testmoignes*. As to the modern law, see my *Digest
of the Law of Evidence*, articles 66 and 67, and note xxviii.

numerous and transactions more complicated, this clumsy
system would naturally lead up to the system now in use, by
which the jury judge of the evidence of the witnesses.

One step which would naturally conduce to this result has
left behind it traces which are still distinguishable. The
juries in early times seem to have been accustomed not
only to give general verdicts of guilty, or not guilty, but to
answer questions as to specific facts from which the judgment
followed as a legal consequence. A remarkable instance
occurs in the [1] *Year-book*, 30 & 31 Edw. 1 (1303). "It was
"presented by the twelve of Y, that Hugo" committed a
rape. Hugo was brought to the bar by Brian and Nicholas.
The justice (his name is not given) told them to stand back,
as the prisoner could not have counsel against the king,
wherefore " præcipimus ex parte regis quod omnes narra-
"tores qui sunt de consilio vestro recedant." Hugo was
then asked what he had to say to the charge against him ?
He replied that he was a clerk. The justice replied that he,
having married a widow, was " bigamus," and had so lost his
privilege. Hugo said that his wife was not a widow when he
married her " *Justiciarius*: Hoc debet statim sciri, et hone-
" ravit duodecim si Hugo, &c., qui dixerunt quod ipsa fuit
" vidua quando dominus Hugo contraxit cum eâ. Sed notan-
"dum quod, &c." (*i.e.* the jurors), "de novo non fuerunt
"jurati quia prius jurati." Hugo was then required to
answer further. He objected that he was a knight and his
jurors were not his equals, not being knights. " Et nomina-
"bantur milites." He was asked if he challenged any of
them. He said he would not consent. The judges could
take what inquest they pleased. The justice said in that
case he must be put to his penance, and he had better plead.
Hugo then asked to have his challenges heard. The justice
agreed, but Hugo said he could not read, and asked for
counsel. [2] The justice asked how he could claim clergy if
he could not read ? He was refused counsel, but allowed to
be prompted by a person who could read. He then made

---

[1] Published by direction of the Master of the Rolls in 1863. The case
referred to is in Appendix ii. p. 529–532.
[2] Upon this, " Hugo stetit inpace quasi confusus. *Justiciarius*: Non sitis
" stupefacti, modo est tempus loquendi."

CH. VIII. his challenges, which were allowed. The justice then repeated the charge to the jury, ending thus : " Ideo vobis injungimus "in virtute sacramenti utrum dominus Hugo dictam mu-"lierem rapuit vel non nobis dicatis. *Duodecim :* Nos "dicimus quod ipsa rapiebatur vi per homines domini "Hugonis. *Justiciarius :* Fuitne Hugo consentiens ad "factum vel non? *Duodecim :* Non. *Justiciarius :* Cogno-"verunt ne eam carnaliter. *Duodecim :* Sic. *Justiciarius :* "Muliere invitâ vel consentiente? *Duodecim :* Consentiente. "[1] Credo quod deberet hic quod tamen post defuit. *Justi-*"*ciarius :* Domine Hugo quia ipsi vos acquietant nos vos "acquietamus."

In the case of Berkeley, tried in Parliament for the murder of Edward II., [2] already referred to for another purpose, the jury were questioned in like manner in detail, and gave specific answers. Other instances of the same kind might be alleged.

It is obvious that if the same jury had to answer to facts which might have no connection with each other (as whether Hugo was *bigamus,* and whether he had committed rape), they would have to rely upon evidence given by others, and not upon their own knowledge, and it is also obvious that when a variety of questions arose, more or less connected with and dependent upon each other, it would be the most convenient course to explain to them how the law stood, and to take from them a general verdict. In such a case as Hugo's, for instance, a modern judge would say, " before you "can return a verdict of guilty, you must be satisfied not "only that the fact took place, but that the woman did not "consent; if you are not satisfied as to either point you will "acquit the prisoner." Whenever this stage was reached our present system would be established in principle.

[3] I have found one case in which an inquest of office set forth the reasons which led them to find that one of the king's tenants was a minor at a given date. The reasons are that several knights and squires on the inquest remem-

---

[1] This seems to be a remark of the reporter, indicating that something was left out.
[2] *Ante,* p. 147.   [3] 2 *Rot. Par.* 291a, 292b (1366).

bered the child's father coming to the siege of Calais, and
saying, he had just had a son born; that the then abbot
of St. Augustine at Canterbury was about a month before
his death godfather to the child; and that the date of the
abbot's death was fixed by the date of the *congé d'élire* to the
Chapter for a new abbot, and that a Sir Johan Freebody,
who was treasurer to Thomas Daldon, the other godfather
of the child, charged Daldon, in an account bearing a
certain date, with a silver cup and ewer for a christening
present to the child. In this instance the inquest acted
partly on their own knowledge and partly on facts proved
by witnesses.

Whatever inferences may be drawn from the scattered
illustrations and broken hints which are to be found on the
subject in the Rolls and the Year-books, it is abundantly
clear that trial by jury as we now know it, was well established, at least so far as civil cases were concerned, in all its
essential features, in the middle of the fifteenth century.
This is put beyond all question by the full account given
of the subject in Fortescue, *De Laudibus Legum Angliœ*, which
must have been written between 1460 and 1470. After
describing at full length the preliminaries of the trial, he says
that the record and the issue having been read to the jury,
[1] "Each of the parties by themselves, or their counsel in
" presence of the court, shall declare and lay open to the jury,
" all and singular, the matters and evidences whereby they
" think they may be able to inform the court concerning the
" truth of the point in question, after which each of the parties
" has a liberty to produce before the court all such witnesses
" as they please or can get to appear on their behalf, who
" being charged upon their oaths shall give in evidence all
" that they know touching the truth of the fact concerning
" which the parties are at issue." He afterwards speaks of
the jurors themselves as "well acquainted with all the
" facts which the evidences depose, and with their several
" characters." [2] In reference to criminal trials Fortescue
does not mention witnesses at all. He dwells upon the power
of the prisoner to challenge thirty-five jurors peremptorily.

[1] Fortescue, c. xxvi. p. 89 (Amos's edition).   [2] *Ib.* c. xxxvii. p. 92, 93.

Ch. VIII. An innocent man need fear nothing, because "none but
"his neighbours, men of honest and good repute, against
"whom he can have no probable cause of exception, can find
"the prisoner guilty." Nor can a guilty person escape.
"Such a man's life and conversation would be restraint and
"terror sufficient to those who should have any inclination
"to acquit him." [1] The prince argues with his chancellor
in such a way as to imply that though the jury were
witnesses, other witnesses were or might be called. "Wit-
"nesses cannot even bring about such a wicked device"
(as a conviction based on perjury), "when what evidence
"they give in must be in open court, in the presence and
"hearing of a jury of twelve men, persons of good character,
"neighbours where the fact was committed, apprised of
"the circumstances in question, and well acquainted with
"the lives and conversations of the witnesses, especially as
"they be near neighbours, and cannot but know whether
"they be worthy of credit or not. It cannot be a secret to
"every one of the jury what is done by or amongst their
"neighbours. I know of myself more certainly what is
"a-doing at this time in Berry where I reside, than what is
"doing in England, neither do I think it possible that such
"things can well escape the observation and knowledge of
"an honest man as happen so near to his habitation, even
"though transacted with some kind of secrecy."

[2] Further on the prince objects that he fears the law of
England as to juries is repugnant to Scripture. "It is
"written in your law that the testimony of two men is true."
"That in the mouth of two or three witnesses every word
"may be established." [3] The chancellor replies to this,
that in various obvious cases the rule supposed to be laid
down in Scripture cannot apply, and that the prince misap-
prehends it, but his most important remark is that "the
"law of England never decides a cause only by witnesses
"when it can be decided by a jury of twelve men."

These passages show, I think, with sufficient clearness that

---

[1] Fortescue, c. xxviii. p. 100. The work is in the form of a conversation
between Fortescue and Prince Edward, the son of Henry VI.
[2] Ib. c. xxxi. p. 111, &c.   [3] Ib. c. xxxii.

by the middle of the fifteenth century the fundamental CH. VIII.
principles of trial by jury in criminal cases had been
established to a great measure, though not entirely.

It is always difficult to find definite illustrations of the
working of rude and obsolete institutions, but I am able to
offer two which I think will throw some light upon the nature
of trial by jury in its early and rude form.

The first is taken from a curious tract, called [1]*Halifax and
its Gibbet-law*, which contains not only a full account of the
gibbet-law of Halifax (said by Sir F. Palgrave to be the last
vestige of the law of infangthief), but also what purports to
be a report of the last case in which it was put in force.

Halifax, it is stated, is part of the duchy of Lancaster and
the manor of Wakefield, and lies within the forest of Hardwick. It has an ancient custom " that if a felon be taken
" within their Liberty with goods stolen out of or within the
" Liberty or Precincts of the said Forest either handhabend,
" backberand, or confessand, cloth or any other commodity of
" the value of thirteen-pence-halfpenny, that they shall after
" three markets or meeting-days within the town of Halifax
" next after such his apprehension, and being condemned he
" shall be taken to the gibbet and there have his head cut off
" from his body." This statement is intelligible though not
very grammatical. [2] The author justifies the wisdom and
humanity of the custom at length on grounds which are
not convincing, but his account of the details of the

---

[1] *Halifax and its Gibbet-law placed in a true light, together with a
description of the town, the nature of the soil, the temper and disposition
of the people, the antiquity of its customary law, and the reasonableness thereof,
with* (many other things) ; Halifax (no date, but apparently published about
the middle of the last century. In the catalogue of the bookseller from
whom I bought it, it is said to be written by " Dr. Samuel Midgley." The
report of the trial is a hundred years subsequent to the trial, but it is
hardly likely to have been forged.

[2] Here is one of his arguments. " It is a received maxim that the common
" law is grounded upon reason, and so is undeniable. Now by the common
" law it is felony and death for any person to steal a thing which is above the
" value of twelvepence, on a verbal proof: surely then it must needs pass
" undeniable that it ought to be felony and death to him that steals anything
" above the value of thirteen-pence-halfpenny, more especially ought it to be
" so where the person is remarkably known and taken in the fact, that the
" goods are brought in for evidence against him " (the bricks are there to this
day, therefore deny it not), " and the truth thereof confirmed by his own
" confession ; this is a matter of fact which cannot be denied by any prudent
" and considering person."

CH. VIII. procedure is extremely curious, and carries us back to remote antiquity. There were seventeen townships and hamlets in the liberties, who chose the most wealthy and best-reputed men for their juries. When a felon was arrested, he was brought before the bailiff of the lord of the manor of Wakefield. The bailiff had a gaol in which he detained the prisoner. He then issued a summons to the constables of four several towns to require four frith burghers from each of those towns to attend at a time and place fixed. " At which " time of appearance both the felons and the prosecutors are " brought before them face to face, and the thing stolen " produced to their view," . . . " and if upon examination they " do find that the felon is not only guilty of the goods stolen, " but also do find the value of the goods stolen to be of the " value of thirteen-pence-halfpenny or above, then is the " felon found guilty by the said jury: grounding that their " verdict upon the evidence of the goods stolen and lying " before them, together with his own confession, which in " such cases is always required, and being so found guilty " is by them condemned to be beheaded according to ancient " custom." After conviction the felon was sent to prison for a week or thereabouts. There were three market-days in every week, and he was exposed publicly at each in the stocks with the goods on his back or by him, after which he was executed by the gibbet, a primitive guillotine, of which a cut is given in the frontispiece. It seems that the rule that the prisoner must be taken " confessand" was considered to be satisfied if he could not give a satisfactory account of his possession of the stolen goods, " and doth refuse when asked " to tell where he found it or how he came by the same; nor " doth produce any witness to testify for him how he came " by such things, but seeks to evade the truth of the matter " by trivial excuses, various reports, and dubious stories."

In illustration of the custom there is given "a true and " impartial narrative of the trials of Abraham Wilkinson, " John Wilkinson, and Anthony Mitchell," in April, 1650, which was the last instance in which the custom was put in force.

At the complaint and prosecution of Samuel Colbeck, John

Fielden, and John Cutforth, "these above-said felonious per- CH. VIII.
"sons" were, "about the latter end of April," 1650, taken into
the custody of the chief bailiff of Halifax, who forthwith issued
his summons to the constables of Halifax, Sowerby, Warby,
and Kircoat, requiring them to attend, each with four men
from his constabulary, at the high bailiff's house in Halifax,
on the 27th April, "to hear, examine, and determine," the
cases.

Sixteen jurors (the names are given) accordingly came to
the bailiff's house, where "in a convenient room" they were
brought face to face with the prisoners and the goods. The
bailiff then delivered a short charge in these words: " Neigh-
"bours and friends, you are summoned hither according to
" the antient custom of the forest of Hardwick, and by virtue
" thereof you are required to make diligent search and inquiry
" into such complaints as are brought against the felons
" concerning the goods that are set before you, and to make
" such just, equitable, and faithful determination betwixt
" party and party as you will answer it to God and your own
" consciences," which said, the several informations were
brought in and alleged against them in manner and form
following : —

"The information of Samuel Colbeck of Warby.

" The informant saith and affirmeth that upon Tuesday,
" the 19th of April, 1650, he had feloniously taken from
" his tenters by Abraham Wilkinson, John Wilkinson, and
" Anthony Mitchell, sixteen yards of russet-coloured kersey,
" part of which cloth you have here before you, and of which
" you are to inquire of its worth and value, and take their
" confession here before you."

The information of Cutforth related to the colts ; and the
information of Fielden to certain cloth as to which he said
(*inter alia*) that one Mrs. Gibson said that Abraham Wilkinson delivered it to her. To this Wilkinson said that "he
" did not confess the aforesaid piece to Gibson's wife, but
" saith that he was by and present when John Spencer, a
" soldier in Chesterfield, did deliver the said piece unto
" Gibson's wife."

" Thereupon some debates arising amongst the jurymen

" touching Abraham Wilkinson's reply to the last information,
" after some mature consideration the jury, as is customary
" in such cases, did adjourn themselves unto the 30th day of
" April, resolving that day fully to give in their verdict. And
" accordingly on the said 30th of April they met together
" again at the bailiff's house, together with the informers,
" felons, and stolen goods, some whereof were placed before them
" in the room, and the rest in such convenient places where
" the jury might view them. And after a full examination
" and hearing of the whole matter, they with united consent
" gave in their verdict in writing in the words following :—

" An inquisition taken at Halifax, the 27th and 30th days
" of April, 1650, upon certain informations hereunto annexed.

" To the complaint of the said Samuel Colbeck, &c.

" We, whose names are hereunto subscribed, being sum-
" moned and empanelled according to ancient custom, do find
" by the confession of Abraham Wilkinson of Warby, within
" the liberty of Halifax, being apprehended and taken, that
" he, the said Abraham Wilkinson, took the cloth in the in-
" formation mentioned, with the assistance of his brother,
" John Wilkinson." They then describe the cloth, and value
it at nine shillings.

The information of Cutforth as to the colts is dealt with
in a similar way. It begins : " We, the aforesaid empanelled
" jury, do find by the free confession of Anthony Mitchell that
" John Wilkinson did take the black colt of John Cutforth's
" from Durker Green, and that himself and Abraham Wilkin-
" son were there present at the time, and also that Anthony
" Mitchell himself did sell the aforesaid colt to Simeon
" Helliwell." . . . . " Likewise, we find by the confession of the
" aforesaid Anthony Mitchell that Abraham Wilkinson did
" take the grey colt of Paul Johnson's from off Durker Green
" aforesaid, and that John Wilkinson was with his brother
" Abraham Wilkinson when he took him, and that the said
" Anthony Mitchell was by and present when Abraham
" Wilkinson did stay and bridle the grey colt. Also he con-
" fesseth that himself and John Wilkinson did leave the said
" colt with George Harrison." The colts were valued at
forty-eight shillings and three pounds respectively.

After these proceedings follows " the determinate sentence," CH. VIII.
which recites the principal matters found, and then goes on:
" By the ancient custom and liberty of Halifax, whereof the
" memory of man is not to the contrary, the said Abraham
" Wilkinson and Anthony Mitchell are to suffer death by
" having their heads severed and cut off from their bodies
" at Halifax gibbet, unto whioh verdict we subscribe our
" names, the 30th April, 1650."

They seem to have been executed accordingly.

I have given a full account of this strange proceeding, not
only on account of its great curiosity, but because its details
illustrate many obscure points in the ancient law. This trial
took place, it must be recollected, under the Commonwealth,
and only three years before a comprehensive scheme for re-
forming the law, to be hereafter noticed, was brought before the
Barebones Parliament ; but at every point it displays traces of
the earliest form of our judicial institutions. The townships
are represented each by four men, who are brought up by the
constable, who represented and succeeded to the reeve. The
bailiff charges them to inquire, much as a justice might have
charged the inquest in Bracton's day. Obviously they must
have questioned the prisoners in order to " take their confes-
" sions." When Abraham Wilkinson contradicts a statement
ascribed to him, they adjourn for three days, probably to make
local inquiries. After the adjournment they talk it all over
again with the prisoners and get further confessions. Probably they may have gone in the interval to Durker Green
and questioned Simeon Helliwell and George Harrison, and
seen other places and persons, and it seems that in some way
or other their inquiries were favourable to John Wilkinson,
who seems to have been acquitted, notwithstanding Mitchell's
confessions, which implicated him. Lastly, the juries not
only find all the facts in detail, but they, like the suitors of
the old County Courts, are the judges, and the bailiff merely
registers their sentence. On the other hand, the informations
and the inquest were obviously drawn up by a lawyer, who
probably was the bailiff, and this shows how great an authority
he might come to have over the deliberations of jurors, and
also how the jury held that intermediate position between

CH. VIII. modern witnesses and modern jurors which I have tried to
sketch. Lastly, the case shows how liberally the stewards
and jurors of franchise courts would be likely to construe the
restrictions laid upon the right of "infangthief" by the rule
that the criminal ought to be handhabend or backberand,
and even "confessand."

There is nothing whatever to show that either Abraham
Wilkinson or Anthony Mitchell was taken "handhabend or
"backbarend," unless those words include every case in which
the goods were taken and produced before the jury, and in
which there was evidence that the prisoner took them. As
for "confessand," it seems probable that the prisoner's confessions consisted only in unsatisfactory answers and alleged
admissions to persons other than the jurors.

The second illustration is taken from an institution still in
full vigour—the Court of the Liberty of the Savoy, the proceedings of which will help us to realize the nature of the
ancient trial by jury, and to understand how they dispensed
with witnesses. The manor and honour of the Savoy lies
immediately to the west of the place where Temple Bar
formerly stood, and extends for some distance westwards
along the bank of the river, as far (I believe) as the middle
of Cecil Street. It is divided into four wards, and has a
court leet which meets twice a year, within a month after
Easter, and a month after Michaelmas. Special courts can
be held if required. The court consists of the [1] steward, who
presides, and eight burgesses, two from each of the four wards
of the manor. A jury for the year, consisting of sixteen, is
annually elected at the court. The steward fixes the day, and
the bailiff summons the burgesses and the jury, as well as a
proper number of residents to be sworn in as jurymen for the
year following. The jury are called over, and absentees,
if any, having been fined, are sworn; the form of oath
being the same as that which is administered to a grand
jury at Assizes and Quarter Sessions. They then make their
presentments, which are in writing, and are signed by the

[1] My old and valued friend, Mr. S. B. Bristowe, Q.C., formerly M.P. for
Newark, and now Judge of the Nottingham County Court, is the steward, and
to him I owe the curious information in the text.

jury. These presentments are brought about as follows:— If any inhabitant thinks that a neighbour's house is unsafe, or that a house is disorderly, or the like, he complains verbally or otherwise to the foreman of the jury for the time being. The foreman calls the jury together, and they satisfy themselves in any way they please as to the matter complained of. They then give notice to the party complained of, and if the nuisance is not abated to their satisfaction the matter is embodied in the form of a presentment, which is given in at the court day to the steward. The steward inspects the presentment to see if it is in proper form and relates to a matter within the jurisdiction of the court, and if he approves of it (he informs me that he never has occasion to disapprove) and if the jury think that the party presented ought to be fined, four of their number are appointed affeerers, and they "affeer" or settle the fine. The finding of the jury is thus conclusive upon the facts, although they hear no evidence, examine no witnesses, and go through nothing in the nature of a trial. The leet jury thus represents that stage in the history just related at which ordeal and purgation had fallen into disuse, and the substitute for them had not been discovered.

I have been favoured with a copy of the presentments at a court held on the 26th April, 1880. The most important of them states in language of the simplest and most untechnical kind, that in October, 1879, the attention of the jury was called to a certain disorderly house kept by a person named, that thereupon they gave that person notice to discontinue her business within a week, that she did so, but afterwards returned and carried on the same business. The jury accordingly present that the woman named does carry on the business in question and that her house is a common nuisance, and they "therefore amerce the said —— in the "sum of £50," which said "amercement is affeered by A. B. "C. and D."

This instance actually existing amongst us appears to me to throw great light upon the manner in which trial by jury originated. It is an institution fit for a small precinct where every one knows every one and can watch and form an opinion upon what goes on. In the few streets which form the liberty

CH. VIII. of the Savoy, such an institution is, I have no doubt, as useful and efficient as it is curious. If it were extended to a large town or county it obviously could not be worked at all.

Even in the Savoy it would probably not be permitted to continue if it involved a result more serious than a money fine, or was applied to offences less easy of proof than keeping disorderly houses, and other common nuisances or petty offences. In the case in question the steward made an estreat directed to the bailiff requiring him to raise the £50, and the bailiff returned that the person concerned had no goods within the jurisdiction.

If after this she continued her misconduct, she would have to be indicted at the Quarter Sessions, when she might be imprisoned, though on the other hand she would be entitled to trial by a petty jury.

CHAPTER IX.

HISTORY OF THE LAW OF CRIMINAL PROCEDURE CONTINUED.
—LEGAL INCIDENTS OF A CRIMINAL TRIAL—INDICT-
MENT AND INFORMATION—ARRAIGNMENT, TRIAL, AND
VERDICT.

HAVING in the last chapter given an account of the various Chap. IX. forms of accusation and trial which have finally merged into trial by jury, I propose in the present chapter to give an account of the legal incidents of a criminal trial. These are the indictment or information, the arraignment of the prisoner, and his trial down to the verdict and judgment.

INDICTMENTS.—The indictment was originally an accusation presented by the grand jury upon their own knowledge, whereby some person was charged with a crime. This, however, has long ceased to be the case, and indictments are now drawn and proved in the following way :—

When a person is committed for trial, some one, as often as not a police-constable, is bound over by the magistrate to prosecute, and the depositions are sent to the clerk of assize if the case is to be tried at the assizes, or to the clerk of the peace if it is to be tried at the Quarter Sessions. A solicitor is in practice almost always employed by the prosecutor, and he as a rule instructs the clerk of assize or clerk of the peace to draw the indictment, the depositions serving as instructions. The prosecutor, however, may, if he prefers it, have his indictment drawn by counsel or by his own solicitor, and counsel are often instructed for this purpose if the case presents any peculiarity. The indictment being drawn has endorsed upon it the names of the witnesses, and the solicitor for the prosecution takes it and them to the grand jury-room, to which he is admitted or not as the grand jury think proper. The grand jury sit by themselves and hear the witnesses one at a time, no one else being present except the solicitor for the prosecutor if he is admitted. The name of each witness examined before the .grand jury is initialled by the foreman ; and when they have heard enough to satisfy themselves that a *primâ facie* case is or is not made out against the prisoner, they endorse upon the indictment " a true bill," or " no true bill," as the case may be (in the days of law Latin the endorsements were " Billa Vera," or " Ignoramus "), and come into court and hand the indictments to the clerk of assize or clerk of the peace, who says, " Gentlemen, you find " a true bill," or "no true bill " as the case may be, " against " A. B. for felony or misdemeanour." If the finding is " no true bill," the matter drops and the prisoner is discharged, though he is liable to he indicted again. If the finding is " a true bill," the trial proceeds and the "bill" becomes an indictment. As an indictment must be found by a majority of the grand jury, and as it must also be found by twelve grand jurors at least, grand juries are generally composed of twenty-three persons, so that the smallest possible majority may consist of twelve. They may, however, consist of any number not less than twelve.

The indictment is the foundation of the record in all criminal cases, and is indeed the only document connected with the trial which in all cases is in writing. It is in the form of a statement upon oath by the grand jury that the prisoner committed the offence with which he is charged. This assertion in former times went a long way (as I have already shown), to his conviction. At present, however, it is a mere accusation. It is now a far simpler document than it would have been in early times, or even early in the present reign. I cannot say when it was first enacted that indictments should be in writing. [1] It is said by Reeve that a statute to that effect

---

[1] *Hist. of Eng. Law*, i. 424. The only act of the sort I can find is 13 Edw. 1, c. 13, which applies only to indictments taken by sheriffs in their tourns. See, too, 1 Edw. 3, s. 2, c. 17.

was passed under Edward I., but however this may be, I CHAP. IX.
think it is clear that the form of indictments, and the
extreme strictness with which rules respecting them have
been observed, were derived principally from the laws
relating to appeals. As I have already stated, the utmost
strictness and particularity was required of the appellor
in the statement of his case, which was enrolled before
the coroners, and variances between the allegations so
made and those made before the justices were fatal.
Elaborate provisions are contained in Bracton for comparing the two sets of statements together, and for
settling the relative authority of the rolls kept by different
coroners if they varied, and of the rolls kept by the
sheriffs.

The history of indictments is a branch of the history
of the law of special pleading. It would extend this work
beyond all limits if I were to attempt to enter upon this
subject at length. It is enough to say that in all common
cases the pleadings in a criminal trial have always consisted,
and still consist, of an indictment engrossed on parchment, and a plea given by the accused person orally in open
court, of guilty or not guilty. The requisites of an indictment at common law differed hardly at all from the earliest
times till our own, indeed the only statutes which much
affected them up to the year 1827 were what was called the
Statute of Additions (1 Hen. 5, c. 5), which provided that
the names of the defendants should be followed by a statement of "their estate or degree or mystery, and of the towns,
" hamlets, or place, and counties, in which they were," and
the 4 Geo. 2, c. 26, which enacted that all indictments should
be in English. Subject to these alterations an indictment
under George IV. was what an indictment under Edward
III., and probably under Edward I., had been. Its requisites were, and subject to modern amendments, still are,
as follows:—

It consists of a commencement, a statement, and a conclusion. The conclusion by recent legislation has ceased
to be of importance, but the rules as to the venue and
the statement are still important, and each is curious.

T 2

THE VENUE.—The venue is in this form—

| Hampshire to wit; | } | The jurors for our Lady the Queen upon their oaths, present, &c. |
| *or,* Central Criminal Court to wit; | } | |

or,
County of the Town of Nottingham to wit;

The object of this beginning is to show that the court has jurisdiction over the offence to be tried, and the venue accordingly refers to the local area over which, by the commission under which it sits, the court has jurisdiction. Thus in the three examples given, the first shows that the court is sitting under commissions of Oyer and Terminer and gaol delivery for one of the counties. The second, that the court is sitting for the district over which the Central Criminal Court has jurisdiction, extending over all Middlesex, the City of London, and parts of several neighbouring counties. The last, that the court is sitting under commissions of Oyer and Terminer and gaol delivery, for the county of the town of Nottingham. The jurisdiction of the court, and the knowledge of the grand jury by which it is informed are supposed to be co-extensive. The Queen sends her commissioners to learn what crimes have been committed in a given county. The grand jury from their local knowledge give the required information. It is true that the High Court of Justice and the courts by which peers are tried for felony have jurisdiction wherever the crime may have been committed, but their jurisdiction arises only upon an indictment found by a grand jury for the body of the county, or upon an impeachment in the nature of an indictment found by the House of Commons. The Queen's Bench Division of the High Court of Justice might sit in any county in England, or try at Westminster or elsewhere offences brought before it by *certiorari* from any such county, but in all cases it would have to try indictments found by a grand jury of the county in which the crime was committed. In short, the theory of trial by the neighbourhood (*vicinetum— visne—venue*) has been inflexibly adhered to, though it has

been subjected to many exceptions. It was originally carried
out so far, that at common law, and down to the passing in
1548 of the statute 2 & 3 Edw. 6, c. 24, if a man was
wounded in one county and died in another, the person who
gave the wound was indictable in neither, " for that," to
quote the preamble of the statute referred to, " by the custom
" of this realm, the jurors of the county where such party
" died of such stroke, can take no knowledge of the said
" stroke, being in a foreign county," . . . . " ne the jurors
" of the county where the stroke was given cannot take
" knowledge of the death in another county." The preamble
goes on to say, " And also it is a common practice amongst
" [1] errant thieves and robbers in the realm, that after they
" have robbed or slain in one county, they will convey their
" spoil or part thereof so robbed and stolen, unto some of
" their adherents into some other county," . . . . " who
" knowingly receiveth the same, in which case, although the
" principal felon be after attainted in one county, the acces-
" sory escapeth by reason he was accessory in another county,
" and that the jurors of the said other county by any law
" yet made can take no knowledge of the principal attainder
" in the first county." It is difficult to understand how such
defects as these should have been permitted to continue as
long as they did, but there were many others, which, if
rather less obvious, were quite as discreditable. Thus,
for instance, there are crimes as to which it is generally impossible to prove where they were committed. The county in
which a man committed a forgery would usually be unknown.
It would generally be extremely difficult to say where a
conspiracy was formed, the existence of which was inferred
from acts done in different places, and so of many other cases.
[2] The result is that in a large number of statutes by which
offences are defined, special provisions are made as to the place
in which the venue may be laid. The only general interest attaching to these exceptions is that they prove that the general
principle which requires so many exceptions must be wrong.

Other inconveniences of the general doctrine are shown

[1] This shows the meaning of the expression an " arrant rogue,"—a rogue
who wandered about the country, a rogue, so to speak, in eyre.

[2] *Dig. Crim. Proc.* art. 244, and ch. ix. and x.

by another class of exceptions, arising not from the nature of particular crimes, but from uncertainty as to the place where they are committed ; such are crimes committed on a journey or on the boundary of a county. These cases are provided for by 7 Geo. 4, c. 64, ss. 12 and 13, under which a person charged with a crime committed during a journey in any conveyance by land or water, may be indicted in any county over which the conveyance passed during the journey, and a person charged with a crime committed within 500 yards of the boundary between two counties, may be indicted and tried in either.

In cases of theft the law of venue was found so inconvenient that a doctrine was invented before the time of [1] Hale, that if a man steals property and carries it from place to place he goes on stealing it as long as he keeps possession of it, and so may be indicted in any county into which he conveys it. This doctrine has been made the subject of several subordinate refinements, which it is unnecessary to mention.

A rule which requires eighteen statutory exceptions, and such an evasion as the one last mentioned in the case of theft —the commonest of all offences—is obviously indefensible. It is obvious that all courts otherwise competent to try an offence should be competent to try it irrespectively of the place where it was committed, the place of trial being determined by the convenience of the court, the witnesses, and the person accused. Of course, as a general rule, the county where the offence was committed would be the most convenient place for the purpose.[3]

Before leaving this matter I may refer to a few statutes

[1] Hale, P. C. 507.   [2] Dig. Crim. Proc. art. 82.
[3] In the Draft Code for 1879 provision was made for obtaining this object by section 504. "Jurisdiction of Courts.—Every court competent to try offences "triable in England or Ireland, as the case may be, shall be competent to try "all such offences wherever committed, if the accused is found or apprehended "or is in custody within the jurisdiction of such court, or if he has been com- "mitted for trial to such court or ordered to be tried before such court, or "before any other court the jurisdiction of which has by lawful authority "been transferred to such first-mentioned court under any act for the time "being in force : Provided that nothing in this act shall authorise any court "in England to try any person for any offence committed entirely in Ireland, "or any court in Ireland to try any person for any offence committed entirely "in England, or any court either in England or Ireland to try any person for "any offence committed entirely in Scotland. No proceeding before any "court shall be held invalid only because it took place in any other district "than the one in which the court ought to have sat, unless it is made to "appear affirmatively that the accused was actually prejudiced thereby."

by which the rules as to the local jurisdiction of the ordinary CHAP. IX.
courts are varied.

[1] Many cities and towns are counties in themselves. Most, but not all, of these are also county towns in which the assizes are held for the county in which they are situated. For instance, York is a county in itself, and is also the county town for the East and North Ridings of Yorkshire. Hull is a county in itself, but no assizes are now or have for a great length of time been held there.

With regard to all cities and towns which are counties in themselves it is [2] enacted (1) that indictments for offences committed in them may be preferred before the grand jury of the next adjoining county, and (2) that indictments found by the grand juries of such counties of towns or cities, and inquisitions found by the coroners there, may be ordered by the court having jurisdiction to be tried in the next adjacent county.

Hull being adjacent to both Yorkshire and Lincolnshire, and Newcastle to both Northumberland and Durham, it is directed that for this purpose Hull shall be deemed to be adjacent to Yorkshire, and Newcastle-on-Tyne to Northumberland.

This act does not apply to London.

It is further [3] enacted, that when a person is committed for any offence not triable at Quarter Sessions to the gaol of any county of a city or town corporate for which no separate commission has been issued since [4] 1846, the trial should be

---

[1] The following is, I think, a complete list. The towns whose names are printed in ordinary type are also assize towns for the counties in which they are situated. The towns whose names are italicised are not. Of these Bristol is the only one for which separate commissions of Oyer and Terminer and gaol delivery are now issued. *Bristol, Canterbury,* Chester, *Coventry,* Exeter, Gloucester, Lincoln, *Litchfield,* Norwich, Worcester, York, Caermarthen, Haverfordwest, *Hull,* Newcastle-on-Tyne, Nottingham, *Poole, Southampton.* Before the act referred to in the text was passed, the separate jurisdictions of counties of cities was a great abuse, as commissions of gaol delivery for such counties were issued only at long intervals. This is noticed by Howard in his *State of the Prisons in England and Wales* (fourth edition, 1792, p. 15). He says that "at Hull they used to have the assize but once in seven years. Peacock, "a murderer, was in prison there near three years; before his trial the principal "witness died, and the murderer was acquitted. They now have it once in "three years."

[2] 38 Geo. 3, c. 52, ss. 2, 3, 9; and see 51 Geo. 3, c. 100, s. 1, and 5 & 6 Will. 4, c. 76, superseded by 45 & 46 Vic. c. 50, s. 188.

[3] 14 & 15 Vic. c. 55, s. 19.

[4] Five years next before the passing of this act, *i.e.* Aug. 1, 1851.

at the next adjoining county, as defined in the Municipal Corporations Act, 1835 (5 & 6 Will. 4, c. 76), Schedule C. The Queen's Bench Division of the High Court of Judicature is said to have power at common law to order a change of venue if a fair trial cannot be had in the county where a crime is committed, but I do not think this power has ever been exercised in fact. On the occasion of the trial of the notorious William Palmer for poisoning, an act (19 Vic. c. 16, 1856) was passed enabling the Court of Queen's Bench to make an order for the trial of any indictment at the Central Criminal Court. The act is very elaborate. It is seldom put in force.

In 1862 a soldier shot his officer, I think at Aldershot, and various persons having contended that the minds of soldiers would be greatly impressed if the punishment of such offences were a little more speedy, an act (25 & 26 Vic. c. 65) was passed, drawn on the model of the act last mentioned. It provides that if any person subject to the Mutiny Act commits murder or manslaughter on any other such person he may be ordered to be tried at the next session of the Central Criminal Court.

This is a singular illustration of the capricious casual character of English legislation. I never heard of the act being put in force. It is elaborate enough to have set the whole law of venue on a rational footing five times over.

[1] THE STATEMENT.—The statement sets out all the ingredients of the offence with which the defendant is charged, namely, the facts, circumstances, and intent which constitute it. These matters must be set forth with certainty, and without repugnancy, and the defendant must be directly and positively charged with having committed the offence. The name of the defendant must be correctly set forth, also his rank in life and his occupation (by the Statute of Additions, but it does not matter whether they are or not). Moreover, the name of the party injured, and if the offence relates to property, the name of the owner of the property must be stated correctly, or if he is unknown the fact that he is

---

[1] See *Dig. Crim. Proc.* ch. xxx. arts. 242-253. The chapter referred to is somewhat differently arranged from the statement in the text. I have followed in the text the usual arrangement.

unknown must be stated. At common law, every material CHAP. IX. fact, that is every fact which formed an ingredient in the offence, had to be alleged to be done at a particular place and time. This was called the "special venue," and was usually effected by introducing the words "then and "there" after every averment subsequent to the first, and in very early times it was necessary that the special venue should show that the act to which it applied was done in the town, hamlet, or parish, manor, castle, forest, or other place whence the jurors were to come who were to try the case—a singular illustration of the extent to which the jurors were originally regarded as witnesses.

All the facts and the intent constituting the offence were also to be stated with certainty,—that is to say, with a degree of detail and specification regulated by circumstances. [1] Coke explains what is meant by certainty. There are three degrees of certainty :—Certainty to a certain intent in every particular. Where this is required the court will presume the negative of everything which the pleader has not expressly affirmed, and the affirmative of everything which he has not expressly negatived. In other words the pleader must expressly exclude every conclusion against him. The lowest degree of certainty is certainty to a common intent, and where this is required the court will presume in favour of the pleader every proposition which by reasonable intendment (i.e. according to the common use of language) is impliedly included in the pleading, though not expressed.

Between these there is a third degree of certainty, called " certainty to a certain intent in general," which cannot be otherwise described than by saying that it does not require quite so much explicit statement as certainty to a certain intent in every particular, and that it requires more than certainty to a common intent. It is this middling kind of certainty tnat is required in indictments. It is said that, where it is required, everything which the pleader should have stated, and which is not either expressly alleged or by

[1] Co. Litt. 303a, and see Long's case, 5 Rep. 121a. The explanation or expansion of Coke's language is given in Archbold, 57. *Dig. Crim. Proc.* arts. 242, 243.

CHAP. IX. necessary implication included in what is alleged, must be presumed against him. Words, however, are in this case construed rather less artificially and technically than in the case of certainty to a certain intent in every particular. As an illustration, written instruments had to be set out verbatim, and chattels had to be described correctly. If a man were charged with stealing a sheep, that would be held to mean a living sheep and not the dead body of a sheep. A boot must not be called a shoe, and money originally had to be described as so many pieces of the current gold or silver or copper coin of the realm called sovereigns, shillings, or pence, as the case might be.

There are besides certain technical words which must be used in charging certain crimes. The words " murder," " ravish," " steal, take, and carry away," or, in the case of cattle, " drive or lead away," and " burglariously " cannot be replaced by any equivalents.

There are some other rules as to the drawing of indictments, of which I need only mention one. Indictments must not be double. No one count ought to charge more than one offence.

THE CONCLUSION.—Formerly the rule was that the indictment must conclude, if it was for an offence at common law, with the words "against the peace of our Lady the " Queen," to which are always added, in fact, though they are not essential, "her crown and her dignity." If the offence was by statute the proper ending was "against the form of the statute (or statutes) in that case made or provided." When indictments were in Latin the form used always was " contra formam statut'," and it was held that "statut'" would do equally well whether it [1] ought to have been "statuti" or "statutorum." After the 4 Geo. 2, c. 26 (1730), which required indictments to be in English, this convenient ambiguity became unlawful, and it was necessary to say either " the statute" or " the statutes." At last it was enacted (14 & 15 Vic. c. 100, s. 24) that no objection should be

---

[1] This act came into force in 1733. It was repealed by 42 & 43 Vic. c. 59, schedule 1, but it has not been contended that the common law has revived, though none of the words in s. 4 (4) seems to meet the case quite plainly. I suppose, however, that the rule that indictments must be in Latin would in case of need be held to be an " usage," " practice," or " procedure."

taken on the ground that it ought to have been either " statute " instead of " statutes," or " statutes " instead of " statute." Indeed it is now unnecessary to have " a proper " and formal conclusion " at all.

These were, and to some extent still are, the leading requisites as to the contents of an indictment. In order to appreciate the matter fully it must be remembered that, subject to some [1] few exceptions, it is necessary to prove the averments of an indictment as they are laid, so that if a man is indicted for the murder of John Smith, and is proved to have murdered James Smith, this is a fatal " variance," and he is entitled to be acquitted, unless the defect is amended, though he might afterwards be indicted again for the murder of James. The effect of the two rules that an indictment must contain certain averments, and that each averment must be proved as laid, was, before late alterations, to introduce into the administration of justice an element of arbitrary uncertainty not unlike that which the Roman augurs introduced into Roman public affairs by their supposed knowledge of the omens. To give one instance where a thousand might be given. [2] A man who had from mere wantonness stabbed a lady whom he met in St. James' Street, was indicted under a statute of George I. (6 Geo. 1, c. 23, s. 11), for " maliciously assaulting her with intent to cut her clothes," which was then a capital felony. The indictment stated that on the 18th January, 1790, at, &c., Williams assaulted Ann Porter with intent to cut her clothes, and that Williams on the said 18th January, 1790, at, &c., did [*then and there* was here omitted] cut the clothes of the said Ann Porter, to wit, a silk gown and a pair of stays, and a silk petticoat and a linen petticoat, and a linen shift. It was objected that it did not appear from this that the assault

---

[1] It was never necessary to prove the special venue as laid, but it was enough if the fact stated was shown to have happened within the jurisdiction of the court. For instance, in an indictment against an Indian official for receiving presents, a fact which happened at, say, Madras, had to be alleged to have happened to wit, at Bow, in the County of Middlesex, but inasmuch as the court had by statute jurisdiction over acts done at Madras it was sufficient to prove that the offence really did happen at Madras and not at Bow.

[2] Williams's case, 1 Leach, 529 (A.D. 1790). The picturesque part of the story is to be found in the *Newgate Calendar*, iii. 161, which contains an account of " Renwick Williams, commonly called the Monster." His peculiar title to infamy was his taste for stabbing in various places women whom he did not know.

and the cutting the clothes were all one act, and that as far as the indictment went the assault might have been in the morning and the cutting of the clothes in the evening, which flaw would have been avoided by inserting the words " then and there," between " did " and " cut," and this objection was held to be fatal.

I do not think that anything has tended more strongly to bring the law into discredit than the importance attached to such technicalities as these. As far as they went their tendency was to make the administration of justice a solemn farce. Such scandals do not seem, however, to have been unpopular. Indeed, I have some doubt whether they were not popular, as they did mitigate, though in an irrational, capricious manner, the excessive severity of the old criminal law.

There was a strange alternation in the provisions of the law upon this subject, by which irrational advantages were given alternately to the Crown and to the prisoner. In favour of the prisoner it was provided that the most trumpery failure to fulfil the requirements of an irrational system should be sufficient to secure him practical impunity for his crime.[1] On the other hand, in favour of the Crown, it was provided that the prisoner should not be entitled to a copy of the indictment in cases of felony, but only to have it read over to him slowly, when he was put up to plead, a rule which made it exceedingly difficult for him to take advantage of any defect. But then again, any person might point out such a flaw, and it was in a sort of way the duty of the judge as counsel for the prisoner to do so. On the other hand, some flaws were, and others were not, waived, by pleading to the indictment.

In short, it is scarcely a parody to say, that from the earliest times to our own days, the law relating to indictments was much as if some small proportion of the prisoners convicted had been allowed to toss up for their liberty.

In practice this system is to a great extent a thing of the past. Legally it is still in full force except so far as it has been relaxed by a few specific sections of acts of parliament.

---

[1] I say practical impunity because the chance of his being indicted a second time and of the prosecution being able to prove that the flaw in the first indictment was such that he had never been legally in peril, and so could not plead *autrefois acquit*, was not great.

The following are the practically important sections :—

By 7 Geo. 4, c. 64 (1826), ss. 14—18 inclusive, it is enacted that the property of a number of articles (as to which it is difficult to say to whom they belong), may in any indictment be laid in particular persons, *e.g.* the property in things provided for the repair of a county bridge, may by s. 15 be laid in the inhabitants of the county, and none of them need be named. These provisions have saved a great deal of petty trouble.

By s. 19 misnomers and wrong additions, or the want of an addition, are rendered practically unimportant.

By 9 Geo. 4, c. 15 (1828), variances between allegations in indictments as to the contents of documents written or printed, and the documents proved on the trial, may be amended in cases of misdemeanour, and are therefore rendered unimportant. This is extended to felonies by 11 & 12 Vic. c. 46, s. 4 (1848) The acts applied only to the superior courts, and their provisions were extended to the Courts of Quarter Sessions in 1849, by 12 & 13 Vic. c. 45, s. 10.

In 1851 an act was passed which went further in the way of removing technicalities, but it did so by an enumeration of them, so technical and minute, that no one could possibly understand it who had not first acquainted himself with all the technicalities which it was meant to abolish. This is 14 & 15 Vic. c. 100. Section 1 enables the court to amend many specified variances between the indictment and the evidence, and especially all variances in the descriptions of either persons or things, and in the ownership of property. The effect of this is, that if a man is indicted for stealing a sheep the property of James Smith, and is proved to have stolen a lamb the property of John Smith, the court may amend the indictment if it thinks it not material, *i.e.* if it thinks that the prisoner has not been misled. This has practically relaxed very greatly the rule about "certainty to a certain " intent in general," already referred to.

By ss. 5 and 18 it was provided that documents might be described by their common names without setting out copies, and that bank-notes might be described as money, and it was

CHAP. IX.   provided that it should be no variance to prove a theft, &c., of coin in an indictment for stealing, &c., a bank-note. By s. 23 special venues were abolished. By s. 24 it was provided that indictments were not to be held bad for the want of any one of fifteen specified formal phrases such as " as appears by the record," " with force and arms," " against the peace," &c. Some of these are noticeable as matter of curiosity. For instance, the want of " the averment of any matter unneces- " sary to be proved," was in effect declared to be no longer a defect. This did away with the statements that the crime was committed by a person " not having the fear of God " before his eyes," and " at the special instigation of the " devil." By s. 25 it was provided that every objection in respect of any formal defect patent on the face of the indict- ment must be taken before plea, and the court was empowered to amend any such defect. The result of this was to make such defects unimportant, as they can now be noticed only under such circumstances that they can be at once amended.

[1] The effect of these complicated and narrowly guarded amendments was to leave the greater part of the law relating to indictments in a blurred half-defaced condition, like a slate the greater part of the writing on which has been half rubbed out. They added greatly in one sense to the intricacy of the law, for nothing can be more intricate than a system of unwritten rules qualified by numerous written exceptions. For instance, it was formerly enough to know what was meant by a special venue. Now, if the law is to be fully understood, you must both know what a special venue was, and what effect was produced by its abolition. It was once enough to know what is meant by certainty to a certain intent in general, and to know that it is required in all the averments in an indictment, but to this there ought now to be added a knowledge of the many exceptions to that rule introduced by statute. Practically no one takes the trouble to learn the law so elaborately. A general impression has been produced that quibbles about indictments have come to

---

[1] *Dig. Crim. Proc.* ch. xxx. gives as accurate a statement of this as I could make. See especially the rule as to certainty, art. 242, the exceptions, art. 243. The rules and exceptions as to descriptions in art. 246, as to ownership, art. 249, as to powers to amend, art. 250.

an end. It has ceased to be the fashion to make them, and if
they are made they do not succeed. This is practically
convenient, but, on the other hand, it is a very slovenly state
of things.

Besides the provisions to which I have referred, a certain
number of special provisions have been made as to indictments for particular offences. Thus, it was formerly necessary
upon an indictment for murder, to set out in minute detail
all the circumstances of the crime, and it was usual to vary
the details in different counts, so as to meet possible variations
in the proof. Thus, in one count it would be stated that A
made an assault upon B with a knife which A held in his
right hand, and gave B one mortal wound in the breast, of
such a length and depth, of which B languished for so many
days, " and languishing did live," and on such a day did die.
Another count would vary this by alleging that the knife was
held in the left hand. A third, that it was held in the hand
without saying either right or left, and so on. These
variations extended the indictment to an enormous length,
and made it [1] grotesque beyond belief. By 24 & 25 Vic.
c. 100, s. 6, re-enacting an earlier act, it was enacted that it
should be sufficient in indictments for murder to charge
generally that the defendant did feloniously, wilfully, and of
his malice aforethought, kill and murder the deceased.

So in indictments for forgery, it used to be necessary not
only to allege an intent to defraud, but to specify the person
intended to be defrauded. This was often a matter of great
difficulty, and numerous counts were introduced, each of
which specified a different person as having been intended
to be defrauded. Now by 24 & 25 Vic. c. 98, s. 44, it is
enough to allege in general terms an intent to defraud. It
would be foreign to my purpose, however, to enumerate every
statutory provision of this sort. It is enough to say, that

---

[1] I have been informed that in the case of Daniel Good, who murdered a
maidservant at Roehampton and burnt her body afterwards so as to leave the
precise manner in which the crime was committed uncertain, the indictment
contained nearly seventy counts, the last averring (which was no doubt true)
that the woman was murdered by means to the said jurors unknown. It must
be remembered in reference to this that the clerks of assize and other officers
who drew indictments were paid by fees, and that each count in an indictment
was charged for separately.

CHAP. IX. though a good many convenient exceptions to the old rigour of the law have been made, enough of it still remains to make criminal pleading intricate and technical to the last degree. I will give a few illustrations of this.

The rule of pleading which requires all the elements of a crime to be set out in an indictment, still in full force, in cases in which no statutory exception applies, causes extreme intricacy and elaboration in indictments. For instance, an indictment for perjury must set forth the following matters : First, the jurisdiction of a competent tribunal. Secondly, the taking by the defendant of an oath duly administered. Thirdly, that the truth of the matter deposed to became and was a question material to the decision of the matter before the court. Fourthly, that the defendant swore such and such matters relating to it (these averments are called assignments of perjury). Fifthly, that each matter assigned as perjury is false in fact. To give a copy of such an indictment would be tedious, but the following is a much abridged skeleton of one.

The jurors for our Lady the Queen present that at ([1] to put it shortly) the assizes held on the 20th July, 1880, at York, before such a judge, B was indicted for the murder of C, which indictment came on to be tried before a jury duly sworn, and upon the trial thereof A " took his corporal oath " on the Holy Gospel of God," that the evidence which he should give should be the truth, the whole truth, and nothing but the truth, and upon the trial it became a material question whether at mid-day, on the 1st March, 1880, A saw B at Westminster Hall, in the City of Westminster, and A " falsely, corruptly, knowingly, wilfully, " and maliciously" swore that he did see B at mid-day, on the 1st March, 1880, at Westminster Hall, in the City of Westminster, whereas in truth and in fact, A did not see B at mid-day, or at any other hour on the said first day of March, 1880, at Westminster Hall, aforesaid, " and so the " jurors aforesaid, upon their oath aforesaid, say that the said " A, on the said 20th July, 1880, before the said Sir E. F.,

---

[1] A number of particulars as to the commission under which the court sits would in practice be set forth.

"so being such judge as aforesaid, by his own act and consent,
"and of his own most wicked and corrupt mind, in manner
"and form aforesaid, falsely, wickedly, wilfully, and corruptly,
"did commit wilful and corrupt perjury against the peace of
"our Lady the Queen, her crown, and her dignity."

This form tells one story three times over, namely, once in
averring materiality, again in assigning perjury, and for a
third time, in negativing the truth of the assignments of
perjury. It adds nothing to what any one would learn from
the following statement:—"The jurors for our Lady the
"Queen present, that at the assizes held at York, before such a
"judge, on such a day, B was indicted for the murder of C,
"and that A upon the trial of that indictment committed
"perjury by swearing that he saw B, at mid-day, on the
"1st March, 1880, at Westminster Hall, in the City of West-
"minster, which statement was material to the indictment
"under trial, and was false to the knowledge of A."

An indictment for false pretences is also an intricate
matter, as the nature of the pretence must be set out and
its falsehood averred in such a way as to repeat the story
twice : thus, "A did falsely pretend to B that A had been
"sent to B by C for £5 which C wanted to borrow of B, by
"means of which said false pretence A did obtain from B
"£5, whereas in truth and in fact A was not sent to B by C
"for £5 which C wanted to borrow of B or for any other sum
"of money whatever." Moreover, the rule that averments
must be proved as laid makes it necessary to vary the
description of the false pretence in a variety of ways, so
that one at least may correspond with the evidence. The
operation of these rules frequently swells indictments for
obtaining goods by false pretences to a length at once
inconvenient and absurd.

Perjury and false pretences afford perhaps the commonest
illustrations of the bad effects produced by the rules of
special pleading still in force as regards indictments, but
there is another rule which has never been made the subject
of any statutory qualification, and which is the cause of much
greater prolixity, obscurity, and expense. This is the rule
that indictments must not be "double." That is that each

CHAP. IX. count must charge one offence and no more. A policeman tries to apprehend a burglar who fires a pistol in his face and gives him a serious wound in the mouth, knocking out a front tooth. This act is an offence under 24 & 25 Vic. c. 100, s. 18, and might, though in practice it would not, be made the subject of the following counts:—

(1) Wounding with intent to maim.

(2) Wounding with intent to disfigure.

(3) Wounding with intent to disable.

(4) Wounding with intent to do some grievous bodily harm other than those above specified.

(5) Wounding with intent to resist lawful apprehension.

(6) Wounding with intent to prevent lawful apprehension.

(7) Wounding with intent to resist lawful detainer.

(8) Wounding with intent to prevent lawful detainer.

(9—16 inclusive) Causing grievous bodily harm with each of the eight intents before stated.

(17—24 inclusive) Shooting at the policeman with each of the eight intents before mentioned.

Another count might be added under s. 14 for shooting with intent to murder, and another under s. 15 for attempting to murder otherwise than in the five ways specified in s. 14. These would make in all twenty-six different counts for a single act.

This is an illustration of the principal cause of the enormous length and intricacy of indictments. Indictments for fraudulent misdemeanours sometimes consist of more than a hundred counts, differing from each other almost imperceptibly by minute shades of meaning and expression. No one ever reads them except the clerk who compares the draft with the engrossed copy. The draftsman draws one count as a pattern of the class, and directs the counts to be varied by a short note such as I have given. The judge never looks at the indictment unless his attention is directed to some particular point. The counsel look at abstracts like the one just given, which [1] show the sense of the indictment. No

---

[1] I have heard of a very eminent special pleader who, when he had drawn a specially long indictment, used to "shuffle his counts," so that his opponent might find it, humanly speaking, impossible to understand what the indictment did and did not contain. The short illustration I have given will

undefended prisoner would get the least information from it, and the document is of infinitely less use as a record of the transaction than a short and simple one would be.

To complete the specification of the causes why indictments are still intricate and technical documents, notwithstanding such efforts as have been made at their improvement, I must mention the [1]rule as to what is called the joinder of counts, that is as to including more charges than one in the same indictment. The rule is that you may theoretically join in the same indictment any number of counts for felony, and any number of counts for misdemeanour. But a count for a felony can in no case be joined with a count for a misdemeanour. One reason of this rule was that when felonies were in almost every case punishable by death it would have been absurd to join a charge which if established would involve capital punishment with a charge which would at most involve fine and imprisonment. Another reason is that the incidents of trials for felony and misdemeanour differ. It would be obviously inconvenient, if not impracticable, to indict a man for two offences for one of which he might challenge twenty jurors peremptorily, whilst he had no right to challenge on the other. There is, however, a further distinction. The right to charge any number of felonies in the same indictment is subject to the [2]doctrine of election—a doctrine introduced simply by the practice of the courts. This doctrine is that if it should appear, either upon the face of an indictment or when the evidence is given, that the different counts in an indictment for felony relate to more transactions than one, and are not different ways of describing the same transaction, the court will compel the prosecutor to confine his evidence to one of the transactions. No such rule applies to misdemeanours. The result of this is that counts charging any number of misdemeanours each charged in any number of different ways may be included in a single

show how confusing this would be If, for instance, counts charging wounding with various intents, were mixed up just as it happened with counts charging causing grievous bodily harm and counts charging shooting, the patience of most men would break down before they had ascertained precisely what the indictment charged.

[1] *Dig. Crim. Proc.* arts. 236-241.   [2] *Ib.* art. 240.

CHAP. IX. indictment, and this is the cause of the enormous prolixity of indictments for mercantile frauds and of the trials which ensue upon them. I have known cases in which indictments on the Fraudulent Debtors' Act have charged each of ten or twelve acts in each of ten or twelve ways.

The defects of this system need no remark, and as to the manner in which they might be removed, it will be enough to refer to the Draft Code prepared in 1878-9 by the Criminal Code Commissioners. An account of this and of some other proposals of theirs for the simplification of criminal procedure will be found [1] below.

An information differs from an indictment, so far as the rules of pleading are concerned, only in the circumstance that it is a formal statement made by the Attorney-General that the defendant is guilty of a misdemeanour instead of being a formal statement upon oath by a grand jury that the person accused is guilty of felony or misdemeanour.

[2] If a person is indicted when he is not in custody a certificate of the indictment may be procured by the prosecutor from the officer of the court before which the indictment is found, and upon the production of the certificate to a magistrate a warrant for the apprehension of the person accused must be issued, and upon his identification the person accused must be committed for trial. If he cannot be apprehended he may (in theory) be [3] outlawed, which in cases of treason and felony has the effect of a conviction. Outlawry, however, has gone completely out of use. The principal importance of it was that it involved, as indeed [4] it still involves, forfeiture, but forfeitures have not in practice been exacted (except in very exceptional cases) in modern times, and for other purposes outlawry is useless. The effect of extradition treaties is that a criminal can be arrested for most of the graver offences in almost any part of the world, and if a man is driven from his native country and cannot be found elsewhere there is no use in obtaining a formal conviction against him.

Notwithstanding all the pedantry and technicalities by

[1] Pp. 511-513.
  Ib. art. 233.
[2] *Dig. Crim. Proc.* arts. 193-194.
[4] 33 & 34 Vic. c. 23, s. 1.

which the law relating to indictments was disfigured, it ought
to be said that they had at least one valuable feature. The
rule that the indictment must set out all the elements of the
offence charged, was some sort of security against the arbitrary multiplication of offences and extension of the criminal
law by judicial legislation in times when there were no
definitions of crimes established by statute, or indeed by any
generally recognised authority. If, for instance, it had been
lawful to indict a man in general terms, say for high treason,
and if the judges had had to say what constituted high treason,
the law might have been stretched to almost any extent. The
necessity for setting forth that the prisoner imagined the
death of the king, and manifested such imagination by such and
such overt acts, was a considerable security against such an
extension of the law, though, as the history of the crime of
treason will show, it was not a complete one. The same
principle was illustrated by indictments for libel in the latter
part of the last century, and even in our own days instances
may be found in indictments for conspiracy in which laxity
of pleading might have had serious consequences to the
accused. The fact is that looseness in the legal definitions
of crimes can be met only by strictness and technicality in
indictments, and that indictments may be reduced with
safety to perfect simplicity as soon as the law has either been
codified or reduced to certainty by authoritative writings
which practically supply the place of a code.

In concluding the subject of indictments and informations,
I must say something of the right to prefer them. Indictments, as I have already shown, are, properly speaking,
accusations made by the grand jury, who are called together
to acquaint the court before which they are assembled with
the crimes committed in their district. Any one, however,
may appear before them with a bill or draft indictment and
witnesses to prove its truth. Theoretically, or at least according to the earliest theory upon the subject, the court does
not look beyond the grand jury. The result is that in this
country any one and every one may accuse any one else,
behind his back and without giving him notice of his intention to do so, of almost any crime whatever. Till very lately

CHAP. IX.   the word "almost" ought to have been omitted, but in 1859 one of those small reforms was made which are characteristic of English legislation. In that year it was provided by [1] 22 & 23 Vic. c. 17, that no person should indict another for perjury, subornation of perjury, conspiracy, obtaining money by false pretences, keeping a gambling house, keeping a disorderly house, or any indecent assault, unless he is permitted to do so by a judge or the Attorney or Solicitor General, or unless he is bound over to prosecute by a magistrate. These provisions were extended to libels by 44 & 45 Vic. c. 60, s. 6. It is impossible to give any reason why the limitation so imposed on a dangerous right should not be carried much further, indeed it obviously ought to be imposed on all accusations whatever. It is a monstrous absurdity that an indictment may be brought against a man secretly and without notice for taking a false oath or committing forgery but not for perjury; for cheating but not for obtaining money by false pretences; and for any crime involving indecency or immorality except the three above specified, namely, keeping gambling houses, keeping disorderly houses, and indecent assaults. There are many such offences (rape, for instance, and abduction) which are quite as likely to be made the subject of vexatious indictments intended to extort money. The Criminal Code Commissioners of 1878-9 recommended that this act should be applied to all indictments whatever, and that the power of secret accusation, which came into existence only by an accident, should be altogether taken away.

[2] CRIMINAL INFORMATIONS.—The right to prefer a criminal information is restricted, both as regards the offences for which and the persons by whom it may be preferred. It may be preferred only for misdemeanours, and only by the Attorney or Solicitor General, or by the Master of the Crown Office acting under the orders of the Queen's Bench Division, upon a motion made in open court.

Two conflicting accounts are given of the origin of criminal informations. One view of the subject is stated in the case of [3] R. v. Berchet and others (1689), in

---

[1] See, too, 30 & 31 Vic. c. 35, ss. 1 & 2.
[2] For present law, see *Dig. Crim. Proc.* ch. xxiii. arts. 195-206.
[3] 1 Showers, 106-121.

an elaborate argument which Sir B. Shower intended to
deliver on the question whether a criminal information
would lie at the suit of a private person for a riot. The
argument refers to a great number of records of informations from the reign of Edward I. to the Revolution which
show that throughout the whole of that period the king's
officers exercised the right of putting persons on their trial
for all sorts of misdemeanours in the Court of King's Bench
without any indictment by a grand jury. Such a course was
certainly taken before the Council Board and the Court of
Star Chamber, as I have already shown, and it thus appears
that from the earliest times the king accused persons of
offences not capital in his own court by the agency of his
immediate legal representatives without the intervention of
a grand jury.

The other view is advanced in [1] Earbery's case, which
also contains an undelivered argument. According to
this view criminal informations are only a vestige of one
of the provisions by which Henry VII. increased the
stringency of the administration of criminal justice at
the beginning of his reign. In 1494 an act was passed
(11 Hen. 7, c. 3) which authorised the Courts of Assize
and Quarter Sessions, "upon information for the king to
"hear and determine all offences and contempts (saving
"treason, murder, and felony) committed by any person
"against the effect of any statute made and not repealed."
This act was the one under which Empson and Dudley
earned their obscure infamy. It was repealed in the year
1509 (1 Hen. 8, c. 6). In the interval between 1494 and
1509 informations were common, but they were afterwards
disused except in the Court of Star Chamber, till they
were revived in the time of Charles I., when an information was filed against Elliot, Hollis, and others, for words
spoken in Parliament, the object of that mode of procedure
being to avoid the unpopularity of a Star Chamber prosecution. After the abolition of the Court of Star Chamber, it is
said there was another interruption in the use of informations
till the reign of Charles II., during which they were not

[1] 20 *St. Tr.* 856.

CHAP. IX. very common. After the Revolution they became common, and were regulated by statute. It would be impossible to determine which if either of these accounts is true, without a full examination of the rolls; but for practical purposes the inquiry is of little importance, as no one in the present day would question the legality of criminal informations. For upwards of 200 years they have been in use, and they have been recognised and regulated by several acts of parliament. Whatever may have been its origin, the power to file criminal informations in the Court of King's Bench was used, not merely by the Attorney and Solicitor General in cases of public importance, but also by the Master of the Crown Office, who appears to have lent his name to any one who wished to use it. Thus all private persons were able to prosecute criminally any person who had offended them by any act which could be treated as a misdemeanour, without the sanction of a grand jury. This led to abuses in the way of frivolous malicious prosecutions, in which the defendants recovered no costs. This abuse was effectually remedied by 4 Will. & Mary, c. 18 (A.D. 1692), which enacts that the Master of the Crown Office shall file no criminal information " without express order to be given " by the said Court in open court" and upon certain conditions as to costs. The practical result of this statute has been to make a motion for a criminal information practically equivalent to a proceeding before magistrates in order to the committal of the accused. It is usually resorted to in cases of a grave public nature, as, for instance, where a person holding an official position is libelled and wishes to have, not only a speedy remedy for the wrong done to him, but the opportunity of justifying his conduct and character upon affidavit.

The power of the law officers of the Crown to file criminal informations is, or rather was, commonly exercised in the case of offences likely to disturb the public peace or the established order of things. Such offences are, however, now more frequently prosecuted by indictments. Throughout the latter part of the last and the beginning of the present century the hardships to which defendants were or were said to be exposed upon criminal informations were the subject of frequent complaints, and [1] some legislation took place on CHAP. IX. the subject to which it is needless to refer in detail.

PLEAS.—The next step to the indictment is the arraignment, or calling of the accused person to the bar to plead to the charge made against him. There are now only four pleas in bar which an accused person can make, namely, not guilty, guilty, autrefois acquit, and autrefois convict. The only case in which a special plea can be pleaded is upon trials for libel, as to which some remarks will be made in reference to that offence. The plea of not guilty puts the prosecutor upon the proof of everything necessary to prove the prisoner's guilt. The plea of guilty admits everything and supersedes all further proceedings. The pleas of autrefois acquit and convict simply allege a previous acquittal or conviction for the same offence as the one charged in the indictment. A pardon might also be pleaded, and if a peer of parliament were arraigned for felony before any court other than the House of Lords or the Court of the Lord High Steward, or if a person were arraigned, e.g. for murder before a Court of Quarter Sessions, he might plead to the jurisdiction, but in practice such pleas are never heard of.

Nothing more need be said here of the effect of these pleas, but some matters of considerable historical interest are connected with the subject of pleading in criminal cases. For reasons which it is now difficult to represent clearly to the mind, it seems to have been considered in early times that criminals accused of felony could not be properly tried unless they consented to the trial by pleading and " putting themselves on the country." The prisoner was first required to hold up his hand, and having done so, or having otherwise owned himself to be the person indicted, the substance of the indictment was stated to him, and he was asked the question, " How say you, are you guilty or not " guilty ? " If he said, " Not guilty," the answer was, " [2] Culprit, how will you be tried ? " to which the prisoner had

---

[1] See 60 Geo. 3, and 1 Geo. 4, c. 4, " An Act to prevent delay in the administration of justice in cases of misdemeanour."

[2] Blackstone gives a curious account of the word " culprit." The word, he says, was coined out of two abbreviations used in taking notes in the indictment for making up the record, if necessary. When the prisoner pleaded

CHAP. IX. to reply, "By God and my country." Sacramental importance was attached for centuries to the speaking of these
words. If a prisoner would not say them, and even if he
wilfully omitted either "By God" or "by my country," he
was said to stand mute, and a jury was sworn to say whether
he stood "mute of malice" or "mute by the visitation of
"God." If they found him mute by the visitation of God
the trial proceeded. But if they found him mute of malice,
if he was accused of treason or misdemeanour, he was taken
to have pleaded guilty, and was dealt with accordingly. If
he was accused of felony, he was condemned, after much exhortation, to the *peine forte et dure*, that is, to be stretched,
naked on his back, and to have "iron laid upon him as
much as he could bear and more," and so to continue, fed
upon bad bread and stagnant water on alternate days, till he
either pleaded or died. This strange rule was in force till
the year 1772, when it was abolished by 12 Geo. 3, c. 20,
which made standing mute in cases of felony equivalent to
a conviction. In 1827 it was enacted, by 7 & 8 Geo. 4, c. 28,
s. 2, that in such cases a plea of not guilty should be
entered for the person accused. [1] A case in which pressing
was actually practised occurred in 1726, when one Burnwater,
accused at Kingston Assizes of murder, refused to plead, and
was pressed for an hour and three quarters with nearly four
hundredweight of iron, after which he pleaded not guilty,
and was convicted and hanged. In 1658 Major Strangeways
was pressed to death in about ten minutes, a wooden frame
and weights being placed anglewise over his breast, and
several [2] persons standing on the frame to hasten his death.

"not guilty," the clerk of assize wrote on the indictment the two words *non
cul.* ; for "*non*" or "*nient culpable*" not guilty. The officer of the court
then joined issue on behalf of the king by saying that the prisoner was guilty
and that he (the officer) was ready to prove it. The note which was made of
this was "cul.," for "culpable," guilty ; and "prit.," which was the abbreviation for "*paratus verificare*," the two abbreviations making "cul. prit." In
the present day, for some reason which I do not pretend to understand, as
soon as a prisoner pleads "not guilty" the clerk of assize writes on the indictment the word "puts." Does this mean "puts himself on the country,"
or can it in any way be connected with the old "prit"? The forms used in
court are all very old and mostly extremely curious. They are preserved all
the more carefully because they are mere forms the significance of which is
not usually understood by those who use them. The derivation of "culprit"
given in dictionaries is "culpatus." (See Johnson's *Dictionary* by Latham ;
Skeat's *Etymological Dictionary* and *Imperial Dictionary.*

[1] Pike's *History of Crime*, ii. 195, 283.   [2] Were they guilty of murder?

The object of refusing to plead was that as in that case there CHAP. IX.
was no conviction, no forfeiture took place, and the property
of the accused person was thus preserved for his heir.

This practice of the "*peine forte et dure,*" as it was called,
is one of the most singular circumstances in the whole of the
criminal law. [1] Its origin probably is to be found in the
times when ordeals were abolished and petty juries introduced.
As I have already observed, to be tried by an inquest instead
of being tried by ordeal was at first an exceptional privilege, for which money was paid to the king. The ordeal
being abolished, it is possible that it was thought hard to
put a man to death upon a bare accusation without any kind
of trial, and that it appeared to be contrary to the nature of an
inquest to appoint a jury to try the prisoner unless he applied
for it. If, therefore, an accused person said nothing at all, the
court felt embarrassed. They could not put him to death upon
what was felt with increasing distinctness to be a mere accusation. They could not make an inquest pass upon him without
his consent. They determined accordingly to extort his consent

Mr. Pike produces some evidence to show that in the
early part of Edward I.'s reign, people who refused to put
themselves on their trial were executed, but this practice was
opposed to the statute 3 Edw. 1, c. 12 (A.D. 1275), which
provided that "notorious felons" (*felouns escriez*), "and
" which openly be of evil name and will not put themselves
" in inquests of felonies that men shall charge them with
" before the justices at the king's suit, shall have strong and
" hard imprisonment, as they which refuse to stand to the
" common law of the land. But this is not to be understood
" of such prisoners as be taken of light suspicion." According
to [2] Barrington this meant that the prisoner who refused to
plead was to be starved till he did, but not tortured, and
he quotes in proof of it a pardon granted in the reign of
Edward III. to a woman who "pro eo quod se tenuit
" mutam," was put " in arctâ prisonâ," and there lived
without eating or drinking for forty days, which was
regarded as a miracle. [3] The case which I have already

[1] This was pointed out, I think, for the first time in Pike's *History of Crime*,
i. 210, &c.   [2] *Observations on the Statutes*, p. 83.
[3] *Year-Book*, 30 & 31 Edw. 1, p. 531. *Supra*, p. 260.

CHAP. IX referred to of the trial of Hugo for rape, in 1303, also favours
this view, for when Hugo refused to plead the justice said to
him, " Si vos velitis legem communem refutare vos portabitis
" pœnam inde ordinatam.   Scilicet uno die manducabitis
" et alio die bibebitis ; et die quo bibitis non manducabitis, et
" e contra ; et manducabitis de pane ordeaceo et non salo et
" aqua, &c."   Nothing seems to have been said about pressing
to death.   There is a passage in [1] Britton to the same effect.
Indeed the rule as to eating and drinking on alternate days
implies that pressing was an innovation.   A man could
not be subjected to such a process for days together.   The
practice of pressing to death was, according to [2] Barrington,
introduced in the reign of Henry IV., the object being to get
on with business, which would be impossible if the Assize
Court had to go on sitting till an obstinate prisoner was tired
of bread and water on alternate days.   The practice was
afterwards supplemented by tying the thumbs with whip-
cord, a milder form of torture which might render pressing
unnecessary.

The whole law of England presents no more characteristic
incident than this.   It exemplifies the extreme scrupulosity
of its founders, their occasional and rather capricious indifference to the infliction of pain, the power of tradition and
practice to vary even the plain meaning of a statute, and the
astonishing tenacity of legal forms.   Ordeals were abolished
about 1215, yet the question of the officer of the court,
" Culprit, how will you be tried ? " and the prisoner's answer,
" By God and my country," preserved the memory of them
down to the year 1827.   " By God " no doubt once meant
" by ordeal," " my country" always meant the inquest or
jury, and the " and " marks the period at which " by God "
became a merely conventional phrase, preserving, though used
in a different sense, the memory of an extinct institution.

[1] 1 Britton, 26 (by Nicholls). " Et si il ne se veulent aquitter si soint mis a
" leur penaunce jekes antant qe il le prient.   La penaunce soit tele qe et
" soint dechancez et sauntz ceijnture et saunz chaperon en pyer liu de la
" prisoun sur la neuve terre assiduelment jour et nuyt et qe il ne mangeusent
" for qe pagn de orge ou de bien et qe il ne beyvent mie le jour qe il mange-
" runt et le jour qe il beyvent ne mangerunt mie et qe il ne beyvent for qe
" del eur et il soint en fyrges " (i.e. fers).
[2] P. 84.   A man was compelled to plead by having his thumbs tied at the
Old Bailey in 1734.

There must have been a time when the prisoner answered, "by God," if he had not bought a licence to have a jury, and meant to go to the ordeal, and "by my country" if he had, and so avoided the ordeal.

[1] IMPANNELING THE JURY.—The prisoner having pleaded, the next step is that of impanneling the jury by whom he is to be tried. It follows· from what I have already said as to the origin of trial by jury that the impanneling of the jury was in very ancient· times equivalent to the choice of the witnesses by whom matters of fact were to be determined. The old law of evidence consisted perhaps mainly, at all events largely, of rules by which certain classes of witnesses were rendered incompetent, and the rules, whatever they were, as to challenging jurors, must have been in fact rules whereby the parties were enabled to exclude testimony, though we cannot now say how far the fact that a man was successfully objected to as a juryman operated to prevent him from giving those who were sworn the benefit of any evidence he might have it in his power to give.

The right of challenge is mentioned by Bracton incidentally and in very general terms. In the passage already commented upon he says, [2] "Cum igitur procedendum sit de hujusmodi " ad inquisitionem ut ad judicium securius procedatur, et ut " periculum et suspicio tollatur justitiarius dicat indictato " quod si aliquem ex duodecim juratoribus suspectum habeat " illum justa ratione amoveat. Et illud idem dicatur de " villatis ut si capitales inimicitiæ fuerint inter aliquos ipsorum " et indictatum vel si ob cupiditatem terræ habendæ, ut " predictum est, qui omnes amovendi sunt ex justâ suspicione " ut inquisitio absque omni suspicione procedat."

There are also references to challenges of jurors in the passages already quoted from Britton. Without following out the subject minutely, the following may be stated as the broad final result: The prisoner was allowed to challenge peremptorily, i.e. without showing cause, any number of jurors less than thirty-five, or three whole juries. When or why he acquired this right it is difficult to say. Neither Bracton nor Britton mention it, and it is hard to reconcile it

---

[1] *Dig. Crim. Proc,* arts. 274-282.   [2] ii. 454.

CHAP. IX. with the fact that the jurors were witnesses. A man who might challenge peremptorily thirty-five witnesses could always secure impunity. It probably arose at a period when the separation between the duties of the jury and the witnesses was coming to be recognised. The earliest statute on the subject, 33 Edw. 1, st. 4 (A.D. 1305), enacts "that " from henceforth, notwithstanding it be alleged by them " that sue for the king that the jurors of those inquests, " or some of them, be not indifferent for the king, yet such " inquests shall not remain untaken for that cause, but if " they that sue for the king will challenge any of those " jurors, they shall assign of the challenge a cause certain." This says and implies nothing at all as to the party's right of peremptory challenge, but implies that before that time the king had an unlimited right of peremptory challenge, and this, though it may seem harsh, is intelligible when we remember that the jurors were witnesses. It would obviously be right that the prosecutor should choose his witnesses, otherwise the jury might know nothing of the matter.

Be this how it may, a right to challenge thirty-five jurors peremptorily did undoubtedly, before Fortescue wrote, accrue to prisoners accused of felony, for he describes and boasts of it, and that right remained unaltered till 25 Hen. 8, c. 3 (1533), when the number was limited to twenty in all cases except treason. The acts of Edward I. and Henry VIII. were repealed and re-enacted by 6 Geo. 4, c. 50. s. 29, which is still in force.

There were at one time considerable doubts, which were not finally decided till our own time, as to the manner in which the rights of the Crown and the prisoner were to be regulated. The effect of various decisions on the subject is this: When, which rarely happens, the right of peremptory challenge is to be exercised in the strictest way, the following course is taken: The officer of the court calls over the whole pannel, so that both parties may know what jurymen answer to their names. The jurors who answer are then called, and the prisoner, as "each comes to the book to be " sworn," must challenge him either peremptorily or for cause. If the prisoner does not challenge the juror the

Crown may direct him to stand by without assigning any CHAP. IX.
cause. When the whole pannel has been gone through, if
twelve have not been sworn, the men ordered to stand by
must be recalled, and if the prisoner does not challenge either
peremptorily or for cause, the Crown must show its cause of
challenge. In other words, the prisoner has twenty peremptory challenges, and the Crown has none, but the prisoner may
be compelled to exhaust all his challenges before the Crown
is called upon to show cause for its challenges. [1] If a very
large number of jurors is returned, the effect of this is to give
the Crown what is nearly equivalent to a right of peremptory
challenge. This, speaking practically, is a matter of hardly
any importance in quiet times in England. In the course of
my experience I do not remember more than two occasions on
which there were any considerable number of challenges.

When a challenge is made its truth is tried either by two
persons named by the sheriff, or if any jurymen have been
sworn, then by the two last sworn.

A challenge to the array is also possible, though very
uncommon. It occurs when it is alleged that the sheriff has
made up the pannel unfairly.

[2] THE HEARING.—The jury being sworn, the trial proceeds.
It consists of the following steps. The prisoner is given in
charge to the jury by the officer of the court. The counsel
for the Crown states his case and calls his witnesses to prove
it. If the prisoner calls no witnesses, or calls witnesses to
character only, the counsel for the Crown may (unless the
prisoner is undefended by counsel) at the end of his evidence
sum up its effect to the jury. The prisoner, or his counsel,
then makes his defence, and calls his witnesses. If he
calls witnesses, the counsel for the Crown has a right to
reply, and if the Attorney or Solicitor General prosecutes in
person, he has a right to reply whether the prisoner calls

---

[1] Suppose, *e.g.* 150 jurymen are on the pannel. The prisoner challenges
twenty peremptorily. The Crown makes 130 stand by. The 130 are then
called, and the prisoner challenges for cause. It is hardly likely that he will
be able to allege a definite cause of challenge against more than a few ; say,
however, that he challenges twenty more for cause. There still remain 110
as to whom the Crown must show cause. The Crown shows no cause, and the
first twelve are sworn. Obviously ninety-eight remain whom the Crown has
practically challenged peremptorily. [2] *Dig. Crim. Proc.* arts. 283-300.

witnesses or not. The judge then sums up the evidence. The jury return their verdict. If they acquit the prisoner, he is discharged. If they convict him, he is asked in cases of felony what he can say why judgment should not be passed upon him, and unless he says something in arrest of judgment, he is sentenced.

Criminal trials as we know them, are the result of a long series of changes which occurred between the reign of Queen Mary, when the earliest trials of which we have detailed accounts took place, and down to our own time. These changes can be understood only by a study of the trials themselves, and by experience of the proceedings of the existing courts of justice. I have thought it best to treat this matter apart from the legal incidents of a trial ; and, accordingly, what I have to say upon it will be found in Chapters XI. and XII., the first of which traces the development of criminal trials through a period of about 200 years, whilst the second describes contemporary trials. I mention the matters above referred to here in order to preserve the continuity of this chapter.

THE VERDICT.—In relation to the verdict of the jury two matters only require notice, namely, the rule that the jurors must be unanimous, and the right of the jury to return whatever verdict they think right without being subject to be punished at the will of the court.

The rule which required unanimity is, I think, easily explained historically, and easily justified on grounds of expediency. The historical explanation appears from the passages already quoted from Bracton, Britton, and other early authorities. The jurors were required to be unanimous because they were witnesses, and the rule was that twelve witnesses, or persons taken as witnesses, must swear to the prisoner's guilt before he could be convicted.

The justification of the rule, now that the character of the jury has changed from that of witnesses to that of judges of fact, seems to me to be that it is a direct consequence of the principle that no one is to be convicted of a crime unless his guilt is proved beyond all reasonable doubt. How can it be alleged that this condition has been fulfilled so long as some of the judges by whom the matter is to be determined do in CHAP. IX. fact doubt? It has been often suggested that after a certain time the verdict of a minority should be taken, as for instance, that the verdict of eleven should be taken after one hour, and that of nine after three hours. Such proposals appear to me to be open to the objection that they diminish the security provided by trial by jury in direct proportion to the occasion which exists for requiring it. If a case is easy you require unanimity. If it is difficult you accept a small majority. If very difficult a still smaller one. My own opinion is that trial by jury has both merits and defects, but that the unanimity required of the jurors is essential to it. If that is to be given up, the institution itself should be abolished. There is a definite meaning in the rule that criminal trials are to be decided by evidence plain enough to satisfy in one direction or the other a certain number of representatives of the average intelligence and experience of the community at large, but if some of the members of such a group are of one opinion and some of another, the result seems to be that the process has proved abortive and ought to be repeated. If the rule as to unanimity is to be relaxed at all, I would relax it only to the extent of allowing a large majority to acquit after a certain time.

It is a remarkable illustration of the vagueness of the criminal law upon points which one would have thought could not have remained undecided, that till very modern times indeed it was impossible to say what was the law as to cases in which the jury could not agree, and it was possible to maintain that it was the duty of the presiding judge to confine them without food or fire till they did agree. It was, however, solemnly determined in 1866 in [1] the case of Winsor v. R. that in any case regarded by the judge as a case of necessity the jury may be discharged and the prisoner committed and tried a second time, and that a judge is justified in regarding a case in which the jury are unable to agree after a considerable length of time as a case of necessity. One result of this decision has practically been to

[1] L. R. 1 Q. B. 289, and Cam. Sc. 390.

CHAP. IX. obviate the objections usually made to the rule requiring unanimity in jurors, all of which turned on the notion that the law required the jury to be starved into giving a verdict. Every authority bearing on the subject is referred to in the argument. [1] By the Jurors Act of 1870, juries may be allowed when out of court a fire, and refreshments to be procured at their own expense.

The right of the jury to return a verdict according to their own consciences, and without being subjected in respect of it to any penal consequences was finally established by [2] Bushell's case in the year 1670. In some earlier instances and particularly in the celebrated case of Sir Nicholas Throckmorton in 1554, the jurors were imprisoned and heavily fined for acquitting the prisoner. This, however, was regarded as a great stretch of power even in those days. Sir Thomas Smith says—[3] "If they" (the jury) "do pronounce " not guilty upon the prisoner against whom manifest witness " is brought in the prisoner escapeth ; but the twelve not " only rebuked by the judges but also threatened of punish-" ment, and many times commanded to appear in the Star " Chamber or before the Privy Council for the matter. But " this threatening chanceth oftener than the execution thereof, " and the twelve answer with most gentle words they did " it according to their consciences and pray the judges to be " good unto them as they did as they thought right and as " they accorded all, and so it passeth away for the most part." He then refers to cases in which the jurors had been fined— no doubt having in his mind Throckmorton's case, and adds, " But these doings were even then of many accounted very " violent, tyrannical, and contrary to the liberty and custom " of the realm of England."

Anciently, it may be, though the contrary seems as probable, jurors who returned a corrupt verdict in criminal cases were liable to what was called an attaint at the suit of the

---

[1] 33 & 34 Vic. c. 77, s. 23.
[2] 6 *St. Tr.* 999. In a case very similar to Bushell's, which happened a few years before, Kelyng, C.J., fined the jury. His account of the matter is long and very curious. See edition of 1873, pp. 69-75. This matter was not printed in the old edition.
[3] *Commonwealth of England*, p. 211.

king, though not at the suit of the party. The attaint was a
remedy for a corrupt verdict in civil cases, and was tried by a
jury of twenty-four, who, if they thought proper, might convict
the first jury of a false verdict. The first jury were thereupon
subjected to what was called the [1] "villain judgment," namely,
imprisonment, infamy, and various forfeitures. This is referred
to with applause by [2] Fortescue in the middle of the fifteenth
century. It is spoken of by [3] Smith late in the sixteenth
century as being in his time hardly known. Hale says somewhat faintly, speaking late in the seventeenth century of
perverse acquittals in criminal cases: [4] "I think in such
" cases 'the king may have an attaint.'" And [5] Lord
Mansfield said in 1757, "The writ of attaint is now a mere
" sound in every case." In 1825, attaints were abolished
by 6 Geo. 4, c. 50, s. 60.

The attaint (whether it ever really applied to criminal cases
or not) deserves notice as one of the many proofs which may
be given of the fact that jurors were originally witnesses.
Perjury by a witness was not a crime known to the law of
England till the reign of Queen Elizabeth. The only form of
that offence which was punished in the early stages of our
legal history was the perjury of jurors, which made them
liable to an attaint.

JUDGMENT.—The verdict of the jury is followed by the
judgment of the Court, which may be either that the prisoner
be discharged or that he suffer punishment. This matter
I do not propose to consider at length in this place, the
importance of the subject of legal punishments and their
history being such as to deserve separate consideration.

---

[1] *3rd Institute*, 222.   [2] Ch. xxvi.
[3] Bk. iii. ch. 2.   " Attaints be very seldom put in use."
[4] 2 Hale, *P. C.* 310.
[5] Bright *v.* Eynon, 1 Burr. 393.   See, too, Barrington on the *Statutes*,
100, 459.

CHAPTER X.

HISTORY OF THE LAW OF CRIMINAL PROCEDURE CONTINUED.
[1] PROCEEDINGS BY WAY OF APPEAL.

CHAP. X.   HAVING in the preceding chapters described the proceedings
connected with a criminal trial from the apprehension of the
suspected person to the judgment, I proceed to give an
account of the manner in which the judgment of the court
may be called in question.

It is a characteristic feature in English criminal procedure
that it admits of no appeal properly so called, either upon
matters of fact or upon matters of law, though there are a
certain number of proceedings which to some extent appear
to be, and to some extent really are, exceptions to this rule.

The first of these exceptions is a writ of error. It is a
remedy applicable to those cases only in which some irregularity apparent upon the record of the proceedings takes
place in the procedure.

In order to explain this it is necessary to describe what is
meant by the record. As I have already observed the only
document connected with a trial necessarily put into writing is
the indictment. Upon this the clerk of assize or other officer
of the court makes certain memoranda, showing the plea of the
prisoner and the verdict of the jury. He also keeps a minute
book in court in which he makes a note of the names of the
jurors by whom different sets of cases are tried, an abstract
of the indictments, and a memorandum of pleas, verdicts, and
sentences. This is a mere private memorandum book having
no legal authority, and kept merely for the purposes of
the officer who keeps it. He is under no obligation to

[1] *Dig. Crim. Proc.* arts. 301-315.

keep it. No form is prescribed in which it is to be kept, and CHAP. X. it never becomes in any way a public record. In all cases, however, except an infinitesimally small number, it is the only record kept of criminal trials, and nothing more meagre, unsatisfactory, and informal can well be conceived. If, however, it becomes necessary (to use the technical expression) "to make up the record," it becomes the foundation of a history of the proceedings, set out with pedantic and useless minuteness and detail. The record in cases of felony, says [1]Chitty, "states the session of Oyer and Terminer, the " commission of the judges, the presentment by the oath of " the grand jurors by name, the indictment, the award of the " capias or process to bring in the offender, the delivery of the " indictment into Court, the arraignment, the plea, the issue, " the award of the jury process, the verdict, the asking the " prisoner why sentence should not be passed upon him, " and the judgment."[2] All this matter is stated with the utmost elaboration and detail, and the special matter which is of real importance and on which error is to be assigned comes in in its place in the midst of a quantity of matter which is of no sort of practical use. As the record takes no notice either of the evidence or of the direction given by the judge to the jury the grossest errors of fact or of law may occur without being in any way brought upon the record, and as the writ of error affirms that there is error *on the record*, no error which is not so recorded can be taken advantage of by those means.

The history of writs of error in criminal cases is given by Lord Mansfield in [3]Wilkes's case. It is shortly this. Till the third year of Queen Anne writs of error in all such cases were issued entirely as a matter of favour, and were the means by which the Crown when so minded caused a conviction to be reversed. The defendant brought his writ of error. The Attorney-General admitted that there was error. The court accepted his admission and the conviction was set

---

[1] 1 *Cr. Law.* 719.

[2] In Orton's case the main question was whether cumulative punishment could be awarded for two offences charged in separate counts of the same indictment. The record was a parchment roll of monstrous size, setting forth together with much other wholly unimportant matter, every order made by the court for the adjournment of the trial to the next sitting. [3] 4 Burr. 2550.

CHAP. X. aside. But in the third year of Queen Anne's reign the court
held, on the one hand, that in cases of misdemeanour writs
of error ought to be granted as a matter of justice if there
was probable ground to think that there actually was any
error in the proceedings, and that if the Attorney-General
refused to grant his fiat for the issue of such a writ they
would direct him to grant it : they held on the other hand,
that when the writ was issued they would not be contented
with the Attorney-General's admission of error, but would
judicially determine whether error existed or not. In cases
of felony and treason, however, the issue of a writ of error
was and always continued to be exclusively matter of favour.
In more modern times this distinction has practically passed
into oblivion. A writ of error still issues upon the fiat of the
Attorney-General, but it is never refused when any point
which can be regarded as arguable arises, whether in cases of
felony or of misdemeanour, and when such a case does arise
it is always judicially decided as a matter of course, whether
error exists or not.

Writs of error are for the reasons above given so limited
in their application that they are but rarely used.

[1] Besides writs of error motions for new trials are permitted
in some cases of misdemeanour, namely, cases of misdemeanour
tried before the Queen's Bench Division in the exercise of
its original jurisdiction, or sent down by that division to be
tried at the Assizes on the Nisi Prius side If a misdemeanour is tried before Commissioners of Oyer and
Terminer at the Assizes or at the Quarter Sessions, the
Queen's Bench Division will not after verdict remove the
case by *certiorari*, with a view to granting a new trial.
If the parties wish to have the possibility of applying
for a new trial, or to have a special jury, their course
is to apply for a *certiorari* before the case comes on to be
tried. If the court is satisfied that questions of difficulty
are likely to arise they will issue a *certiorari*, and either
have the case tried before the Queen's Bench Division at
Westminster, or send it down to be tried as a Nisi Prius
record at the Assizes or in the City of London. When the

[1] Chitty, *C. L.* 653—660.

case is so tried a new trial may be moved for on the ground
of misdirection, that the verdict was against the evidence, or
on other grounds on which new trials are moved for in
civil cases. According to Chitty, the first instance of such
a new trial was in the year 1655.

[1] One case only has occurred in which a new trial was
granted for felony, and that case was afterwards disapproved
of and not followed by the Judicial Committee of the Privy
Council in R. v. Bertrand (L. R. 1 P. C. 520). It is very
remarkable that in the argument upon R. v. Scaife, no
notice was taken of the novelty of the proceeding.

[2] When the jury return an imperfect special verdict in any
criminal case a new jury may be summoned and the matter
reheard (by a proceeding called a *venire de novo*). Special
verdicts are verdicts in which the jury not wishing to decide
upon the law find the facts specially, referring it to the court
to say whether upon those facts the prisoner is or is not guilty
of the crime for which he is indicted.

Special verdicts have now gone almost entirely out of use,
having been superseded by the establishment of a court
called the Court for Crown Cases Reserved. The history of
this court is as follows. From very early times a practice
had prevailed that a judge before whom any criminal case
of difficulty arose at the Assizes or elsewhere, should respite
the execution of the sentence or postpone judgment, and
report the matter to the other judges. The question reserved
was argued before the judges by counsel, not in a court of
justice but at Serjeant's Inn of which all the judges were
members. If they thought that the prisoner had been improperly convicted he received a free pardon. If not, the
sentence was executed or judgment was passed. No judgment was delivered and no reasons were given in such cases,
the whole proceeding being of an informal kind. When a
case was tried at the Quarter Sessions no means for questioning the result existed. [3] In 1848 this informal tribunal
was erected into a court called the Court for Crown Cases
Reserved. It consists of all the judges; but five, of whom

[1] R. v. Scaife, 17 Q. B. 238 (1851). [2] Chitty, C. L. 654.
[3] 11 & 12 Vic. c. 78.

CHAP. X. the [1]Lord Chief Justice must be one, are a quorum. If,
however, the five judges differ, the minority are not bound
by the decision of the majority, but any one of them may
require the matter to be referred to the whole body of
fifteen. This course was taken in the well-known case of
R. v. Keyn. It is obviously extremely inconvenient, and it
may be doubted whether those who framed the statute
intended it to be taken. Any judge or chairman, or
recorder of a Court of Quarter Sessions, may state a case
for the opinion of the court "as to any question of law
" which shall have arisen at " any "trial," either committing
or bailing the prisoner in the meanwhile. The court hears
the case argued, delivers judgment, and may either reverse
the judgment (if any) or confirm it, or direct the court by
which the case was stated to give judgment. This court can
determine questions of law arising at the trial, but cannot
take notice of questions of fact, and it is absolutely in the
discretion of the presiding judge at a trial whether he will
or will not reserve a point for its decision.

The result of the whole is that a provision, sufficient though
intricate and technical, is made for the decision of questions
of law arising at the trial by courts in the nature of appellate
tribunals ; but it must be added that the criminal law is now
for the most part so well settled and understood that this
is a matter of little practical importance. Writs of error
[2]are of rare occurrence, and the Court for Crown Cases Reserved sits only three or four times a year for a day, or more
often half a day, at a time, and probably does not determine
twenty cases a year.

It is a much more important circumstance that no provision whatever is made for questioning the decision of a
jury on matters of fact. However unsatisfactory such a

---

[1] Till the abolition of those offices the Lord Chief Justice of the Common
Pleas, or the Lord Chief Baron of the Exchequer, or the Lord Chief Justice of
the Queen's Bench, was to be one of the judges.
[2] The writ of error in Orton's case, decided in March, 1881, and the
writ of error in Bradlaugh v. R. in 1878, are the only writs of error in
criminal cases which have been decided for a considerable time. I could
never understand upon what ground it was thought necessary to grant a
writ of error in Orton's case. No one of the three courts before which the
matter came felt the smallest doubt upon any of the points raised in it.

verdict may be, whatever facts may be discovered after the CHAP. X. trial, which if known at the trial would have altered the result, no means are at present provided by law by which a verdict can be reversed. All that can be done in such a case is to apply to the Queen through the Secretary of State for the Home Department for a pardon for the person supposed to have been wrongly convicted.

This is one of the greatest defects in our whole system of criminal procedure. To pardon a man on the ground of his innocence is in itself, to say the least, an exceedingly clumsy mode of procedure ; but not to insist upon this, it cannot be denied that the system places every one concerned, and espe- cially the Home Secretary and the judge who tried the case (who in practice is always consulted), in a position at once painful and radically wrong, because they are called upon to exercise what really are the highest judicial functions with- out any of the conditions essential to the due discharge of such functions. They cannot take evidence, they cannot hear arguments, they act in the dark, and cannot explain the reasons of the decision at which they arrive. The evil is notorious, but it is difficult to find a satisfactory remedy. The matter has been the subject of frequent discussion, and it was carefully considered by the Criminal Code Commission of 1878—9. I have nothing to add to the following obser- vations which occur in their *Report* as to the reforms which seem to be required in regard to the whole matter of appeals in criminal cases.

After describing the different forms of appeal now in use much as I have described them above, though in other words, [1] the *Report* proceeds : " It seems to us that in order to form " a complete system these various forms of proceeding ought " to be combined. For this purpose we propose, in the first " place, to constitute a single Court of Criminal Appeal " closely resembling the Court for Crown Cases Reserved, " but with two important differences. We propose that, as " in other courts, the minority should be bound by the " majority. A court composed of fifteen judges is incon- " veniently large. If on a point of importance a court of

[1] Pp 38—40.

" five should be divided, it might be desirable that a further
" appeal should be possible. We accordingly propose that
" the court should have power to permit an appeal to the
" House of Lords.

" We do not interfere with the present practice as to trials
" in the Queen's Bench Division, and we propose that in the
" case of such trials the Queen's Bench Division should be
" the Court of Appeal, and that it should have power to give
" leave to appeal to the House of Lords.

" As to the power to appeal and the cases in which an
" appeal should lie, the Draft Code proposes to make consider-
" able changes in the existing law as regards both matter of
" law and matter of fact. With regard to matter of law, the
" judge has at present absolute discretion as to reserving or
" not reserving questions which arise at the trial and do not
" appear on the record. This we think ought to be modified.
" We propose accordingly that the judge shall be bound to
" take a note of such questions as he may be asked to
" reserve, unless he considers the application frivolous. If
" he refuses to grant a case for the Court of Appeal, the
" Attorney-General may in his discretion grant leave to the
" person making the application to move the Court of Appeal
" for leave to appeal, and the court may direct a case to be
" stated. The court on hearing the case argued may either
" confirm the ruling appealed from, or grant a new trial, or
" direct the accused to be discharged ; in a word, it may act
" in all respects as in a civil action when the question is one
" of law, and that on the application of either side. This in
" some ways is favourable, and in others unfavourable, to
" accused persons. By the existing law the prisoner's right
" to appeal on a point of law is, generally speaking, subject
" to the absolute discretion of the judge ; but if he is per-
" mitted to appeal, and if the court above decides in his
" favour, the conviction is quashed, although in a civil case
" he would gain nothing but a right to a new trial. Under
" section 542 the prisoner would be able to appeal, with the
" leave of the Attorney-General, against the will of the
" judge, but if he succeeded he would in many cases only
" obtain a new trial. If the matter appealed upon was a

" mere irregularity, immaterial to the merits of the case, the
" Court of Appeal would have power to set it right. All
" this would diminish the value of the right of appeal to
" prisoners, though it would increase its extent. It must be
" observed, too, that the right of appeal on questions of law
" is given equally to both sides. The Commissioners as a
" body express no opinion on the expediency of this. If it
" is thought proper to confine the right to the accused, the
" alteration of a few words in the section would affect that
" object. In dealing with appeals upon matter of law little
" is wanted beyond an adaptation of the existing law.

" It is more difficult to provide in a satisfactory way for an
" appeal upon matters of fact. It is obvious that the only
" practicable means of giving such an appeal is by permitting
" convicted persons to move under certain circumstances for a
" new trial, either on the ground that the verdict was against
" the evidence, or on the ground that the verdict has been
" shown to be wrong by facts discovered subsequently to the
" trial. If the ground on which a new trial is sought for is
" that the verdict was against the evidence, the case is com-
" paratively simple. In such cases the judge before whom
" the case was tried ought to have power to give leave to
" the convicted person to apply to the Court of Appeal for a
" new trial. If the convict had an absolute right to make
" such an application, it would be made whenever the convict
" could afford it. By making the leave of the judge who
" tried the case a condition for such an application, such
" motions would be practically confined to cases in which the
" judge thought the jury had been harsh towards the prisoner
" However, when the application was made the Court of
" Appeal could deal with it as in civil cases.

" A much more difficult question arises in relation to cases
" which occur from time to time, where circumstances throw-
" ing doubt on the propriety of a conviction are discovered
" after the conviction has taken place. It these cases it was
" provided by [1] the bill that the Secretary of State should
" have power to give leave to the person convicted, to apply

---

[1] This was a Draft Code prepared by me, and introduced into Parliament
by Sir John Holker in 1878.

" to the Court of Appeal for a new trial. Upon the fullest
" consideration of the subject we do not think that such an
" enactment would be satisfactory. In such a case the Court
" of Appeal must either hear the new evidence itself, or have
" it brought before it upon affidavit. In the former case the
" court would substantially try the case upon a motion for a
" new trial, and this is opposed to the principle of trial by
" jury. In the latter case they would have no materials for
" a satisfactory decision. It is impossible to form an opinion
" on the value of evidence given on affidavit and *ex parte*
" until it has been checked and sifted by independent inquiry.
" Such duties could not be undertaken by a Court of Appeal.
" If the Secretary of State gave leave to a convict to move
" the Court of Appeal for a new trial on evidence brought
" before the court by affidavit, the only well-ascertained fact
" before the court would be that the Secretary of State
" considered that there were grounds for such an application.
" This would make it difficult to refuse the application. The
" Secretary of State would be responsible only for granting
" leave to move the court for a new trial. The court, in
" granting a new trial, would always in fact take into account
" the opinion indicated by the Secretary of State's conduct.
" It must also be remembered that a court of justice in de-
" ciding upon such applications would, in order to avoid
" great abuses, be obliged to bind itself by strict rules,
" similar to those which are enforced in applications for new
" trials in civil cases on the ground of newly-discovered
" evidence. Such applications cannot be made at all after
" the lapse of a very short interval of time, and are not
" granted if the applicant has been guilty of any negligence ;
" and this stringency is essential to the due administration of
" justice and to the termination of controversies. It would
" be unsatisfactory to apply such rules to applications for new
" trials in criminal cases. No matter at what distance of
" time the innocence of a convicted person appeared probable,
" —no matter how grossly a man (suppose under sentence of
" death) had mismanaged his case, it would be impossible to
" refuse him a fresh investigation on the ground of such lapse
" of time or mismanagement. Cases in which, under some

"peculiar state of facts, a miscarriage of justice takes place,
"may sometimes though rarely occur; but when they occur it
"is under circumstances for which fixed rules of procedure
"cannot provide.

"Experience has shown that the Secretary of State is a
"better judge of the existence of such circumstances than a
"court of justice can be. He has every facility for inquiring
"into the special circumstances; he can and does, if neces-
"sary, avail himself of the assistance of the judge who tried
"the case, and of the law officers. The position which he
"occupies is a guarantee of his own fitness to form an
"opinion. He is fettered by no rule, and his decision does
"not form a precedent for subsequent cases. We do not see
"how a better means could be provided for inquiry into the
"circumstances of the exceptional cases in question. The
"powers of the Secretary of State, however, as to disposing
"of the cases which come before him are not as satisfactory
"as his power of inquiring into their circumstances. He
"can advise Her Majesty to remit or commute a sentence;
"but, to say nothing of the inconsistency of pardoning a man
"for an offence on the ground that he did not commit it,
"such a course may be unsatisfactory. [1] The result of the
"inquiries of the Secretary of State may be to show, not
"that the convict is clearly innocent, but that the propriety
"of the conviction is doubtful; that matters were left out of
"account which ought to have been considered; or that too
"little importance was attached to a view of the case the
"bearing of which was not sufficiently apprehended at the
"trial; in short, the inquiry may show that the case is
"one on which the opinion of a second jury ought so be
"taken. If this is the view of the Secretary of State, he
"ought, we think, to have the right of directing a new trial
"on his own undivided responsibility. Such a power we
"accordingly propose to give him by section 545.

"With respect to the materials to be laid before the Court
"of Appeal we propose to abolish the present record. It
"is extremely technical and gives little real information.

---

[1] As an illustration of these remarks, see the case of Smethurst at the end of
Vol. III.

" Instead of it, we propose that a book to be called the Crown
" Book should be kept by the officer, which should record in
" common language the proceedings of the court. In prac-
" tice the record is hardly ever made up, and if it is necessary
" to make it up, the officer's minute-book affords the only
" materials for doing so. Our proposal is practically to
" substitute the original book for the record which is made
" up from it, and is merely a technical expansion of the
" original.

" We also propose that the Court of Appeal should have
" power to call for the judge's notes, and to supply them if
" they are considered defective by any other evidence which
" may be available,—a shorthand writer's notes for instance.
" We consider the statutory recognition of the duty of the
" judge to take notes as a matter of some importance. Upon
" the subject of appeal there is not much difference between
" the Draft Code and the Bill. The provisions of the former
" are more simple."

CHAPTER XI.

HISTORY OF CRIMINAL TRIALS IN ENGLAND FROM
1554—1760.

IN the earlier chapters I have given the history of each of CHAP. XI.
the steps in the prosecution of criminals from the first moment when a person is suspected down to the final conclusion
of the proceedings. I have, however, intentionally omitted
all but the most cursory notice of the actual trial by which
the guilt or innocence of the suspected person is determined.
In attempting to relate its history 1 shall adopt a somewhat
different method from that which I have hitherto followed.
Instead of treating separately the history of the opening
speech of the counsel for the Crown, the prisoner's defence,
the examination of the witnesses, and the judge's summing
up, I shall give an account of characteristic trials or groups
of trials from the reign of Queen Mary, when the earliest
trials of which we have detailed reports took place, till the
reign of George III., when the system now in force was
established in all its main features.

It may be said that the matter of which I now propose to
treat belongs rather to history proper than to law; but the
great interest of English criminal law lies in the circumstance that it has been closely connected with several of
the turning-points of English constitutional history, and the
proceedings have been recorded in the *State Trials* with
such completeness and authenticity as to give to [1] that great

---

[1] The *State Trials* contain thirty-three volumes, royal 8vo., averaging, I
suppose, from 600 to 700 pages, in double column and small type. The collection extends from the earliest times to the year 1822, the last trials reported
being those of Thistlewood and his associates for the Cato Street Conspiracy. I

CHAP. XI. collection the character of a judicial history of England. The
principal groups of trials of which accounts have been preserved illustrate the gradual development of the system
which at present exists. They will be found to throw
light on every part of it.

One large class of cases, namely, trials for heresy and
other ecclesiastical offences, I pass over for the present, as I
propose to notice some of them in a separate chapter. I may
observe, however, that the reports of some of them are the
earliest detailed reports which we possess of any criminal
proceedings.

BAGA DE SECRETIS.

By way of introduction to the first group of trials of which
we have detailed reports, I will say a few words of the traces
which still exist of those which occurred during the preceding
seventy-seven years, namely, between 1477 and 1544. There
are no reports, properly so called, of criminal trials during
this period, but a remarkable, though in some respects dis-
appointing, document exists, which I refer to on account
rather of its curiosity than on account of any positive information upon criminal procedure which it contains. It is a
translation of part of the contents of the *Baga de Secretis* for
the reigns of Edward IV., Henry VII., and Henry VIII.
The contents of this bag consist of indictments for a great
variety of offences tried in the Court of King's Bench in
the years mentioned, the earliest occurring 19th May, 1477,
and the latest 13th January, 1547. In our own times the
names of the witnesses always appear on the back of the
bill, but this practice was not then adopted, and the documents referred to contain no other indication of the nature of
the evidence, or of the management of the trial, than can be

think no more important addition to the materials for the history of our own
times could be made than a continuation to the present day. The great trials
which have occurred during the last sixty years have been unequalled in excellence, and, to say the least, have been equal in interest to any of those of
former times. The trials of the Bristol rioters, the trial of O'Connell in
1844, the trials for treason-felony in England and Ireland in 1848, many
of the trials for conspiracy, the trial of Bernard for the Orsini plot, the
various proceedings against Governor Eyre, the Fenian trials subsequent
to 1865, and very many more, are parts, not only of the legal, but also
of the political and general history of England which ought to be carefully
preserved.

found in the terms of the indictments. These, however, are CHAP. XI. not quite so barren as such documents would be at present. Some of them are so detailed and circumstantial as to show that evidence must have been carefully taken before the indictment was sent before the grand jury, and the contents of these are very curious. For instance, part of [1] the indictment against Lord Warwick for high treason, by conspiring with Perkin Warbeck in the Tower against Henry VII., runs as follows:—" The Earl and Cleymound, on the said 2nd " August, 14 Henry VII., being in the chamber of the Earl " in the Tower of London, the said Cleymound, in order to " comfort the said Peter, then being in a chamber in the " Tower under their chamber, by assent of the said Earl " knocked upon the vault of the said chamber to the intent " that the said Peter might hear the Earl and Cleymound, and " Cleymound said to the said Peter, ' Perkin, be of good " ' cheer and comfort,' and further showed to him that he " had a certain letter, directed to the said Peter, which he " had received from one James, a clerk of Flanders, which " letter he, Cleymound, would, as he promised, deliver to the " said Peter the following day," and so on, with many further details.

[2] The indictment against the Duke of Buckingham, 13th May, 1521, is even more detailed and circumstantial. Here is a specimen :—" The Duke, in order to carry his inten- " tion " (to depose the King) " into effect did, on the 24th " day of April, 4 Henry VIII., lead one John Delacourt, late " of Thornbury, in the county of Somerset, to one Nicholas " Hopkins, a monk of the Carthusian Priory of Henton, who " pretended to have knowledge of future events by certain " revelations which he feigned to have had, in order that the " Duke might have further knowledge thereof from the said " Nicholas." It then proceeds to set out the particulars of various negotiations between the Duke and Father Nicholas.

There is one case in which it is still possible to compare the indictment with the evidence given at the trial. This is the case of Sir Thomas More, who was tried on the 1st July. 1535, for denying the King's supremacy. A report of the

---

[1] *Baga de Sec.* p. 216.   [2] *Ib.* p. 230.

CHAP. XI. trial itself is given in the *State Trials*. It is taken principally
from the *Life of Sir Thomas More* by his great-grandson,
but it contains some matter which is not to be found either
in that work or in Hall's *Chronicle*, or in Lord Herbert's
Life of Henry VIII., which works are also referred to. In
particular the account in the *State Trials* says (I know not
who is supposed to be speaking, but I suppose More,
the great-grandson) :—" The indictment was very long,
" but where to procure a copy of it I could never learn;
" it is said in general it contained all the crimes that
" could be laid to the charge of any notorious malefactor,
" and Sir Thomas professed it was so long that he could
" scarce remember the third part of what was objected
" therein against him." To judge from the abstract, which
fills a folio page, the indictment was not at all long. It
began by setting forth the substance of 26 Hen. 8, c. 1,
which enacts that Henry VIII. and his successors, kings
of this realm, "shall be taken, accepted, and reputed the
" only supreme head on earth of the Church of England." It
then sets out the substance of c. 13 of the same statute, which
makes it high treason " if any person maliciously hath wish or
" desire, by words or writing, to deprive the king of his
" dignity, title, or name of his royal estate." It then avers
that More, traitorously imagining and attempting to deprive
the king of his title as supreme head of the Church, did,
when examined before Cromwell and others, whether he
accepted the king as supreme head on earth of the Church
of England, refuse to answer directly, saying : " I will not
" meddle with any such matters, for I am fully determined to
" serve God, and to think upon his passion, and my passage
" out of this world."

Further, it sets out a letter written by More to Fisher, and
a statement made by More upon examination at the Tower,
in each of which he said that the statute was like a two-
edged sword, that if he answered one way he should offend
his conscience, and if he answered the other, lose his life.

Lastly, it sets out a conversation between More and Rich,
the king's Solicitor-General, in which, after some introductory
matter, More said that if a statute made the king supreme

head of the Church, the subject cannot be obliged, because CHAP. XI.
his consent cannot be given for that in Parliament. In the
report in the *State Trials* it is said that Rich swore to the
conversation as laid in the indictment. To this it is said Sir
Thomas replied: "If I were a man, my lords, that had no regard
" to my oath, I had had no occasion to be here at this time, as
" is well known to everybody, as a criminal; and if this oath,
" Mr. Rich, which you have taken be true, then I pray I may
" never see God's face, which, were it otherwise, is an impre-
" cation I would not be guilty of to gain the whole world."
The account proceeds: "More, having recited in the face of
" the court all the discourse they had together in the Tower
" as it truly and sincerely was," added bitter reproaches against
Rich, saying, amongst other things: " You always lay under
" the odium of a very lying tongue, a great gamester, and of
" no good name and character either here " (in Westminster
Hall) " or at the Temple." More was convicted and executed.

¹ Lord Campbell has spoken in terms of almost passionate
indignation of this trial. He adopts absolutely, and with no
evidence whatever, More's statement that Rich committed
perjury. It is impossible to have any decided opinion as to
the details of a conversation held nearly 350 years ago; but
even assuming the correctness of the partial and unlawyerlike
report of the proceedings which remains, there are some
reasons to think that Rich's evidence was substantially
true. First, the reporter does not give More's own account
of the conversation. This looks as if it differed only in
detail from Rich's. Secondly, More's oaths and his
vehemence against Rich look as if Rich had, at all events,
told some truth. Thirdly, there can be no doubt that
More did think the Act of Supremacy wrong, and beyond
the competency of Parliament, for in arrest of judgment
he said that the indictment "is founded upon an Act of

¹ Campbell's *Chancellors*, ii. 59—63. This delightful writer, and most
powerful and impressive of judges, seems to me to be in his biographies as
impressible by topics of prejudice as a common juryman. More's genius and
the beauty of his character make it impossible for Lord Campbell to see
anything but perjury and oppression in his trial; yet, after all, why is it
unlikely that he should have unintentionally expressed an opinion which
he held so strongly that the terms in which he moved in arrest of judgment
were an act of high treason within the statute?

CHAP. XI. "Parliament directly repugnant to the laws of God and his "Holy Church." Fourthly, More laid great stress upon the argument that, even if Rich spoke the truth, "it cannot in "justice be said that they were spoke maliciously." As far as the law goes, I think the word "malicious" in the statute could mean no more than seriously—meaning what was said— the meaning being regarded by the legislature as in itself bad. Whether it was, under all the circumstances of the time, expedient to make the denial of the king's supremacy high treason is a question on which I have no opinion for want of study; but I cannot see that More's trial was in itself unfair, though no doubt it was grossly indecent that the principal witness should also act as counsel for the Crown, as Lord Campbell says Rich did, though the fact is not mentioned in the report to which he refers.

[1] The indictment against Anne Boleyn is more concise, but the charges in it are specific and pointed, though [2] they do not enter into details. They alleged that she committed adultery with five specified persons on five separate occasions, time and place being assigned in each instance. As to the proceedings at the trial itself, nothing appears beyond a formal record of the verdict. The indictments against Katharine Howard and her various adulterers enter into greater detail. There are six indictments, relating to offences committed in Yorkshire, Middlesex, Lincolnshire, the City of Lincoln, Surrey, and Kent, respectively. One only (the Yorkshire indictment) is fully abstracted. It enters into a certain amount of detail, especially as to Lady Rochford's acting as a "common procuress" between them.

I.—1554—1637.

The first group of trials which I shall consider are those which took placed betweeen 1554 and 1637, the first being the

---

[1] *Baga de Sec.* p. 244.

[2] I have not referred to the original, but the abstract suggests a possibility that it may contain some details omitted from the abstract from regard to decency. It says that the Queen "did falsely and traitorously procure, by "means of indecent language, gifts, *and other acts therein stated*, divers of "the King's doctors and familiar servants to become her adulterers."

trial of Sir Nicholas Throckmorton, and the last being the proceedings in the Star Chamber which led to its abolition. [1] The report of the trial of Throckmorton is the earliest which is full enough to throw much real light on the procedure which then prevailed. All the trials which took place during this period seem to have followed much the same course, and to have been conducted in the same manner.

The cases of which reports remain were, for the most part, of great political importance, and were accordingly, during the early stages of the procedure, under the charge not of the justices of the peace, but of the Privy Council, and especially of the judges who were members of it, and the law officers of the Crown. The suspected person, having been arrested, was kept in confinement more or less close according to circumstances, and was examined in some cases before the Privy Council, in some cases by the judges, and in some instances by torture. The evidence of other persons, and more especially the evidence of every one who was suspected of being an accomplice, was taken in the same manner. When the case was considered ripe for trial the prisoner was arraigned and the jury sworn, after which the trial began by the speeches of the counsel for the Crown. There were usually several counsel, who, in intricate cases, divided the different parts of the case between them. The prisoner, in nearly every instance, asked, as a favour, that he might not be overpowered by the eloquence of counsel denouncing him in a set speech, but, in consideration of the weakness of his memory, might be allowed to answer separately to the different matters which might be alleged against him. This was usually granted, and the result was, that the trial became a series of excited altercations between the prisoner and the different counsel opposed to him. Every statement of counsel operated as a question to the prisoner, and indeed they were constantly thrown into the form of questions, the prisoner either admitting or denying or explaining what was alleged against him. The result was that, during the period in question, the examination of the prisoner, which is at present scrupulously, and I think even pedantically, avoided, was the

[1] 1 *St. Tr.* 395.

very essence of the trial, and his answers regulated the production of the evidence; the whole trial, in fact, was a long argument between the prisoner and the counsel for the Crown, in which they questioned each other and grappled with each other's arguments with the utmost eagerness and closeness of reasoning. The judges occasionally took part in the discussion; but, in the main, the debate was between the parties. As the argument proceeded the counsel would frequently allege matters which the prisoner denied and called upon them to prove. The proof was usually given by reading depositions, confessions of accomplices, letters, and the like; and this occasioned frequent demands by the prisoner to have his " accusers," *i.e.* the witnesses against him, brought before him face to face, though in many cases the prisoners appear to have been satisfied with the depositions. When the matter had been fully inquired into by this searching discussion, the presiding judge "repeated" or summed up to the jury the matters alleged against the prisoner, and the answers given by him; and the jury gave their verdict.

I will give an account of a few of the most remarkable trials as specimens.

Sir N. Throckmorton was tried for high treason in 1554, [1] the charge against him being that he compassed and imagined the Queen's death, and levied war against her, and adhered to her enemies; the alleged fact on which the charge was founded being a conspiracy with Wyat before his rising.

The trial took place on the 17th April, 1554. [2] The Court sat probably from 8 A.M. till 2, or, at any rate, some time before 3 P.M., as at their rising they adjourned till 3, and the jury gave their verdict at 5. The trial would seem accordingly to have lasted altogether for about six hours. It consisted almost entirely of a verbal duel between Throckmorton and the counsel for the Crown, namely, Serjeant Stanford, who, I suppose, may have been the author of Stanford's *Pleas of the Crown*, and Griffin, the Attorney-General. [3] Stanford took by

---

[1] The copy of the indictment is very imperfect. 1 *St. Tr.* p. 869.
[2] In Fortescue's time the judges usually sat from 8 to 11.
[3] He was probably the Prime Serjeant, who, if there were such a personage-

far the most conspicuous part in the proceedings. He began CHAP. XI.
by asking Throckmorton if he had not sent Winter to Wyat
in Kent to confer about taking the Tower of London
and about Wyat's rising? Throckmorton said he had told
Winter that Wyat wanted to speak to him; but that he said
nothing on the matters stated, and challenged Stanford to
prove what he alleged. Stanford read Winter's " confession,"
and offered to call Winter to swear to it. Throckmorton said
that, for the sake of argument, he would admit the "con-
"fession " to be true, and pointed out that certain parts of it
were highly favourable to him, and that no part of it showed
anything criminal on his part. Some matters he explained in
answers to questions from the judges and the Attorney-
General.

Stanford then read the confession of Cuthbert Vaughan,
which, if true, proved that Throckmorton had given Vaughan
much information as to the designs of Wyat's confederates.
The Attorney-General offered to produce Vaughan to swear
to his confession. To which Throckmorton replied, " He that
" hath said and lied will not, being in this case " (*i.e.*, under
sentence of death), "stick to swear and lie." Vaughan, however, was called, swore to the truth of his confession, and, in
answer to a question from Throckmorton, said he was only a
common acquaintance, and that Wyat had given him a letter
of introduction to Throckmorton. Upon this Throckmorton
said, "If you have done with Vaughan, my lord, I pray you
"give me leave to answer." The Chief Justice replied,
"Speak, and be short." Throckmorton thereupon insisted
on the improbability of his placing so much confidence in a
common acquaintance, and appealed to Sir R. Southwell (one
of the Commissioners by whom he was tried, and before
whom, as a Privy Councillor, Vaughan had been examined
to confirm him in saying that Vaughan had varied in his
evidence, and in particular that he had vouched a witness
who had not been examined and a document which had
never been produced. He also insisted that Vaughan ought
not to be believed, because his only hope of escape from his

in these days, would take precedence of the law officers. In most of the
cases referred to the Prime Serjeant is leading counsel for the prosecution.

own sentence of death was to accuse some one else. The judges hereupon asked if he meant to say that Vaughan's deposition was totally false. Thereupon Throckmorton admitted that much of it was true; but he denied the specially damaging parts of it, and explained a variety of matters which were specifically pointed out to him. Throckmorton's own "confession" was then read by Stanford. It admitted in substance that he had discussed with several persons the scheme of the marriage between Queen Mary and Philip II., of which he and they strongly disapproved; but it went no further. A deposition of the Duke of Suffolk was next read, on which Throckmorton remarked that it stated only what the Duke said he had heard from his brother, Lord Thomas Grey, who "neither hath said, can say, nor will say "anything against me." Certain statements, very remotely connected with the subject, made by one Arnold, were then referred to. They mentioned a man named FitzWilliams. Throckmorton, seeing FitzWilliams in court, desired that he might be sworn as a witness. FitzWilliams offered himself to be sworn, but, upon the Attorney-General's application, the Court refused to hear him, and ordered him out, one of the judges saying, "Peradventure you would not be so ready in a "good cause." Finally it was said that Wyat had "grievously "accused" the prisoner, to which Throckmorton replied, "Whatsoever Wyat hath said of me in hope of his life, he "unsaid it at his death." One of the judges owned this, but added that Wyat said that all he had written and confessed to the Council was true. Throckmorton replied, "Master Wyat said not so. That was Master Doctor's "addition." On this another Commissioner observed that Throckmorton had good intelligence. He answered, "God "provided that revelation for me this day, since I came hither; "for I have been in close prison these fifty-eight days, where "I heard nothing but what the birds told me which did fly "over my head,"—an assertion which was probably false. After this Throckmorton objected, that his case was not brought within 25 Edw. 3, as no overt act of compassing the Queen's death was proved against him; but at the most, procurement by words only of levying war. The judges put

various difficulties in his way, refusing to have the statutes
read, and, [1] in at least one instance, misconstruing their
language grossly when Throckmorton quoted them. They
held however, certainly in accordance with all later
authorities, that in treason there are no accessories,
all being principals. Nothing can exceed the energy, in-
genuity, presence of mind, and vigour of memory which
Throckmorton showed, or is reported to have shown, throughout every part of the case, and especially in the legal argument. The Attorney-General is reported to have appealed
to the Court for protection. " I pray you, my lords that be
" the Queen's Commissioners, suffer not the prisoner to use
" the Queen's learned counsel thus. I was never interrupted
" thus in my life, nor I never knew any thus suffered to talk
" as this prisoner is suffered. Some of us will come no more
" to the bar, an we be thus handled."

The Chief Justice summed up, "and," says the reporter
(who, no doubt, was very favourable to Throckmorton),
" either for want of good memory or good will, the prisoner's
" answers were in part not recited, whereupon the prisoner
" craved indifferency, and did help the judge's old memory
" with his own recital." After the summing up, Throckmorton made to the jury a short, earnest, pathetic address,
full of texts. He begged the Court to order that no one,
and in particular none " of the Queen's learned counsel be
" suffered to repair to them." Whereupon two serjeants
were sworn to attend them for that purpose. After a deliberation of two hours the jury acquitted him. They were committed to prison for their verdict, and eight of them (four
having submitted and apologised) were brought before the
Star Chamber in October (six months and more after the trial),
and discharged on the payment by way of fine of £220 apiece,
and three, who were not worth so much, of £60 apiece.
" This rigour was fatal to Sir John Throckmorton, who was
" found guilty upon the same evidence on which his brother
" had been acquitted."

[1] " Proveably attainted by open deed by *people of like condition.*" People
of like condition, according to Bromley, C.J., means " your accomplices in
" treason—traitors like yourself "—which Throckmorton naturally called " a
" very strange and singular understanding."

CHAP. XI.   The next trial to which I will refer is that of [1] the Duke of
Norfolk in 1571. He was tried for high treason by imagining
the death and deposition of Queen Elizabeth ; the overt act
being an endeavour to marry Mary, Queen of Scots, knowing
that she claimed title to the Crown as against Queen Elizabeth. He was also charged with being concerned in various
other treasonable enterprises, which are set out at great length
in the indictment. The case was tried before the Court of
the Lord High Steward, consisting of twenty-six Lords Triers.
The proceedings, though not so animated as those in Throckmorton's case, followed much the same course. Serjeant
Barham conducted the greater part of the prosecution.
After opening the case, he urged the Duke to confess that he
knew that Mary claimed the crown of England. He admitted that he knew it, "but with circumstance," that is,
subject to explanation. Barham contested the value of the
explanation, and many depositions were read, on the bearing
of which the Duke on the one side, and Barham on the
other, argued, questioned each other, and exchanged explanations at great length. Here is a single specimen :—

" *Serjeant* : Now for the matter of taking the Tower.
" *Duke* : I deny it. *Serjeant* : Was it not mentioned unto
" you in the way when you came from Titchfield, by one that
" came to you and moved you a device between you and
" another for taking the Tower ? *Duke* : I have confessed
" that such a motion was made to me, but I never assented
" to it. *Serjeant* : You concealed it ; and to what end
" should you have taken the Tower but to have held it against
" the Queen by force ? " &c.

After Barham had finished the part of the case which he
was to manage, other charges were enforced in the same way
by the Attorney-General, and others again by the Solicitor-
General. After which " Mr. Wilbraham, the Attorney of
" the Wards," made a speech ending with a burst of patriotic
eloquence as to how under circumstances the English would
have beaten certain Walloons. On this the reporter observes,
" This point Mr. Attorney spoke with such a grace, such
" cheerfulness of heart and voice, as if he had been ready to

[1] 1 *St. Tr.* 957—1042.

" be one at the doing of it, like a hearty true Englishman, a CHAP. XI.
" good Christian, a good subject, a man enough for his
" religion, prince, and country." After this Wilbraham, like
his leaders, had an argument at length with the prisoner, who
was thus expected to deal successively with no less than
four eminent counsel.

Some of the Duke's observations throw much light
on the position of a prisoner in those days. At one point
he said, " There is too much for me to answer without book ;
" for my memory is not so good to run through everything,
" as they do that have their books and notes lying before
" them. Therefore, I pray you, if I forget to answer to any-
" thing, remind me of it." The Duke, like Throckmorton,
argued with much reason that no overt act of compassing
the Queen's death had been proved against him, and quoted
some authorities, and in particular Bracton. The Attorney-
General was indignant at his audacity. " You complained
" of your close keeping that you had no books to provide for
" your answer: it seemeth you have had books and counsel;
" you allege books, statutes, and Bracton. I am sure the
" study of such books is not your profession." The Duke
humbly said, " I have been in trouble these two years; think
" you that in all this time I have not had cause to look for
" myself? " The Duke was convicted and executed.

Many other trials in Queen Elizabeth's time were conducted in the same way. I may mention those of [1] Cam-
pion and other Jesuits in 1581, those of [2] Abington and
others in 1586, that of [3] Lord Arundel in 1589, and a
very remarkable one of [4] Udale, for felony in writing the
libel called Martin Marprelate in 1590. In Udale's case
there was really no evidence, or hardly anything which
could by courtesy be called evidence, except the fact that
when examined before the Privy Council he would not deny
having written the book; and that when the judge who
tried him offered to direct an acquittal if he would only
say he did not write it, he refused to do so.

Under James I. the character of the procedure remained

[1] 1 St. Tr. 1049—1088.   [2] Ib. 1141—1162.   [3] Ib. 1253.
[4] Ib. 1271—1315.

CHAP. XI. unchanged, as may be seen by reference to the cases of
[1] Raleigh in 1603, the trials for the [2] Gunpowder Plot in
1606, and those of [3] Overbury's murderers in 1615.
The trials of [4] Lord Somerset and [5] Sir Jervase Elwes
are perhaps the best illustrations of the old procedure.
Each affords a striking instance of the importance which
then attached to the examination of the prisoner. [6] The
argument between Lord Somerset and the different counsel
and members of the court is exceedingly curious and minute,
but its effect cannot be given shortly. Elwes, who was
Lieutenant of the Tower, and had delivered the Countess of
Somerset's poisons to Overbury, defended himself on the
ground that he did not know what they were, though he
admitted that he knew that at one time one of the subordinate
agents had thoughts of committing the crime. [7] He defended himself with so much energy and skill that he might
perhaps have escaped had not Coke, the presiding judge,
cross-examined him as to some expressions in his letters
which he was unable to explain, [8] and (which is even more
at variance with our modern views) produced against him,
after his defence had been made, a "confession" by one
Franklin, who had made the confession privately and not
even upon oath before Coke himself, at five o'clock that
morning, before the court sat. The "confession," if true, no
doubt proved Elwes's guilt beyond all doubt, but put upon
him as it was at the very last moment, when he had no
opportunity to inquire about it, or even to cross-examine
Franklin without inquiry, it is not surprising that "he knew
"not what to answer." If Elwes's dying speech is rightly
reported, he confessed his guilt at the gallows, and, without making any complaint on the subject, ascribed its
discovery to Coke. [9] "I displeased God, being transported
"with over-much pride of my pen; which obsequious quill
"of mine procured my just overthrow upon the knitting of
"my Lord Chief Justice's speech at my arraignment, by
"reason of two or three passages at the bottom of my

---

[1] 2 *St. Tr.* 1—60.   [2] *Ib.* 159—359.   [3] *Ib.* 911—1022.
[4] *Ib.* 965—1022.   [5] *Ib.* 936.   [6] *Ib.* 992—994.
[7] *Ib.* 939—940.   [8] *Ib.* 941.   [9] *Ib.* 946.

"letter subscribed with my own hand, which I utterly had
"forgotten, because I felt not my sin."

Of all the trials which I have mentioned, however, that of Raleigh is by far the most remarkable. He was accused of treason by conspiring with Lord Cobham to make Arabella Stuart Queen of England through the agency of the Archduke of Austria and his ambassador. The whole evidence against Raleigh was a "confession" or examination of Cobham before the Privy Council, and a letter which he wrote afterwards. Both in the confession and in the letter, Cobham charged Raleigh with this plot by obscure allusions and implications, and with no details. Some few trifling bits of hearsay were proved, I suppose by way of corroboration. For instance, [1] Dyer, a pilot, swore that he accidentally met some one in Lisbon, who said that Cobham and Raleigh would cut King James's throat before he could be crowned. The extreme weakness of the evidence was made up for by the rancorous ferocity of Coke, who reviled and insulted Raleigh in a manner never imitated, so far as I know, before or since in any English court of justice, except perhaps in those in which Jefferies presided.[2] The trial is extremely curious, but its great interest in a legal point of view lies in the discussion which occupied most of it on Raleigh's right to have Cobham called as a witness. He knew that Cobham had retracted his confession, and he had actually received from him a letter saying, "I protest upon my salva- "tion I never practised with Spain by your procurement. "God so comfort me in this my affliction as you are a good "subject, for anything I know." For these reasons, and also

---

[1] 2 St. Tr. 25.

[2] Ib. 26 :—"Att.: Thou art the most vile and execrable traitor that "ever lived. Raleigh : You speak indiscreetly, barbarously, and uncivilly. "Att. : I want words sufficient to express thy viperous treasons. Raleigh : "I think you want words, indeed, for you have spoken one thing half a dozen "times. Att. : Thou art an odious fellow. Thy name is hateful to all the "realm of England for thy pride. Raleigh : It will go hard to prove a measur- "ing cast between you and me, Mr. Attorney. Att. : Well I will now make "it appear that there never lived a viler viper upon the face of the earth "than thou." In the case of Wraynham before the Star Chamber for slander- ing Lord Bacon, Coke said, "Take this from me, that what grief soever "a man hath, ill words work no good, and learned counsel never use them." —2 St. Tr. 1073. As to Raleigh's trial viewed historically, see Gardiner's Hist. of Eng. i. 93-109.

CHAP. XI, because as he said he felt sure that Cobham would not venture to state openly and on oath what he had confessed before the Council, Raleigh earnestly pressed for his production. He put his demand partly on two statutes of Edward VI. (1 Edw. 6, c. 12, s. 22, and 5 & 6 Edw. 6, c. 11, s. 11). The first act provides that no one is to be indicted, arraigned, or convicted of treason unless he be accused by two sufficient and lawful witnesses. The second act is to the same effect, but uses the words "lawful "accusers," which [1] Coke himself afterwards interpreted as meaning witnesses, "for other accusers have we none in "the common law." It also provides that the accusers shall, at the time of the arraignment, be brought in person before the accused. Of these statutes Coke declares that they were grounded on the common law, which "herein is grounded upon the law of God, expressed "both in the Old and New Testament ' in ore duorum vel "' trium testium,' &c." [2] In Raleigh's trial, Coke insinuated that these statutes were no longer in force, and [3] Chief Justice Popham expressly said that they were repealed, adding, "It sufficeth now if there be proofs made either "under hand or by testimony of witnesses, or by oaths." As for having Cobham produced in court, Lord Salisbury (Robert Cecil) said that the commissioners ought to know from the judges whether Raleigh had a right to demand his production, or whether it was matter of favour? Upon this the following remarkable statements were made :—

[4] "*Lord Chief Justice:* This thing cannot be granted, for "then a number of treasons should flourish : the answer "may be drawn by practice whilst he is in person. *Justice* "*Gawdy :* The statute you speak of concerning two wit- "nesses in case of treason is found to be inconvenient ; "therefore by another law it was taken away. *Raleigh :* "The common trial of England is by jury and witnesses. "*Lord Chief Justice:* No, by examination : if three con- "spire a treason and they all confess it, there is never a "witness, yet they are condemned. *Justice Warburton :* "I marvel, Sir Walter, that you, being of such experience

[1] 3rd Inst. 25—26.   [2] 2 St. Tr. 14.   [3] Ib. 15.   [4] Ib. 18.

" and wit, should stand on this point: for so many horse-
" stealers may escape, if they may not be condemned without
" witnesses. If one should rush into the king's privy chamber
" whilst he is alone and kill the king (which God forbid), and
" this man be met coming with his sword drawn all bloody,
" shall not he be condemned to death? My Lord Cobham
" hath perhaps been laboured in that, and to save you, his old
" friend, it may be that he will deny all that he hath said?"

The result was that Cobham was not produced, and that
Raleigh was convicted and executed on the 29th October,
1618, just fifteen years after his trial. The avowed reason
for keeping back Cobham was that, if called, he would have
withdrawn what he had said. It is right, however, to observe
that in the letter which he wrote he made one charge against
Raleigh which may probably have been true. "Raleigh," he
said, "was to have a pension of £1,500 a year for which he
" promised that no action should be against Spain, the Low
" Countries, or the Indies, but he would give knowledge
" beforehand." The Chief Justice asked Raleigh what he
said to this. Raleigh replied, "I say that Cobham is a base,
" dishonourable, poor soul;" and he then produced the letter
already quoted, in which Cobham withdrew all his accusations.
He did not, however, deny the charge about the pension.

Of Coke's share in this matter nothing need be said
except that it was infamous; but the observations of the
judges as to the right of the prisoner to have the witness
produced before him face to face, and their assertion that the
statutes of Edward VI. had been repealed, and that the trial
at common law was by examination and not by a jury and
witnesses, are extremely curious. That the judges of that
time were subservient to the Crown must be admitted;
that they would venture to put forward as undoubted
law and ordinary practice that for which there was no sort
of colour of law is most improbable. The explanation
which I should be inclined to put upon the opinions just
quoted is as follows. The meaning of the assertion that
the statutes of Edward VI. had been repealed was, that by a
statute of Philip and Mary (1 & 2 Phil. & Mary, c. 10) it
was enacted that for the future all trials for treason " shall

" be had and used only according to the due order and course
" of the common law." The statutes requiring two witnesses
in treason were regarded as an innovation upon the common
law, and were thus considered as being repealed implicitly by
the Act of Philip and Mary. The rule as to the two witnesses
seems to have been construed as referring to the trial by witnesses as it existed under the civil law, which seems to have
been regarded in England as a trial in which two eye or
ear-witnesses to the fact constituting the crime itself were
required—a condition so difficult of fulfilment that it was
in practice supplemented by torture, a confession so obtained being regarded as sufficient for a conviction. With
this trial by witnesses trial by jury was frequently contrasted
(as, for instance, by [1] Fortescue, *De Laudibus Legum Angliæ*);
and the opinion seems to have prevailed that if a trial by
witnesses according to all the rigour attributed to the civil
law was not to be insisted upon, the only alternative was that
the jury should form their opinion as they could, whether
upon their own knowledge or upon any sort of materials
which might be supplied to them, of which materials the
examination of the accused would probably be the commonest
and most natural. It should be observed that the remarks
of the judges, and especially the illustration given by Judge
Warburton as to a murder being proved by the fact that the
prisoner was seen with a bloody sword in his hand leaving
the room where the murder was committed immediately
after the crime, show that the judges of that day recognised
no distinction between different kinds of evidence, except the
distinction between the evidence of an eye-witness to the
actual crime and everything else. They seem to have
thought that if the evidence of two such eye-witnesses was
dispensed with, no other line could be drawn. There was no
reason why the most remote and insignificant hearsay should
not be admitted even as to the contents of written documents, or why the prisoner should not be convicted solely
on the impression derived by the jury from the way in which
he sustained his examination. The only rules of evidence as

---

[1] Chapters xxi.—xxvii. pp. 37—60 ; and see 28 Hen. 8, c. 15. As to
the trial of pirates, *post*, Vol. II. p. 18.

to matters of fact recognised in the sixteenth century seem
to have been the clumsy rules of the mediæval civil law,
which were supposed to be based on the Bible. If they were
set aside, the jury were practically absolute, and might decide
upon anything which they thought fit to consider evidence.
On the other hand, as the prisoner had no counsel, no books
no means of procuring evidence, and no right to give it if he
did procure it, the jury were practically in the hands of the
court, especially as there was a possibility (as Throckmorton's case showed) of their being fined if they gave an
unwelcome verdict."

Before leaving these trials I may make an observation on
the judges.   Most of the trials to which I have referred were
before Commissioners of Oyer and Terminer.   Such commissions are still addressed not only to the judges who are to
go on circuit and to the Queen's Counsel who on occasion
sit for them, but also to a number of distinguished persons
who are probably not aware that they are included in the
commission.   This is a mere relic of what was once an important matter.   In the sixteenth century the lay commissioners took a prominent part in the trials.   In Raleigh's
case, for instance, there were eleven commissioners, of whom
four were judges and seven laymen.   Lord Salisbury (Robert
Cecil) and Lord Henry Howard, especially the former, took a
prominent part in the trial.   [2] Cecil in particular got into a
dispute with Coke, who " sat down in a chafe, and would speak
" no more until the Commissioners urged and entreated him."

I now pass from the proceedings before the Courts of
Common Law to those which took place before the Star
Chamber.

I have already given some account of the history and of
the jurisdiction of that court.   I will now notice some of the
cases which led to its abolition.   Its function as a criminal
court was to try cases of misdemeanour which were not, or
were supposed not to be, sufficiently recognised or punished
at the common law.   Its procedure was founded upon an information, generally by the Attorney-General, who drew up
a charge like a Bill in Chancery against the defendant.   The

[1] *Commonwealth of England*, 212.   [2] 2 *St. Tr.* 26.

CHAP. XI. defendant put in his answer also in the form of an Answer in Chancery. He might be examined upon interrogatories, and was liable to be required to take what was called the *ex officio* oath. This was an oath in use in the Ecclesiastical Courts, by which the person who took it swore to make true answer to all such questions as should be demanded of him. The evidence of witnesses was given upon affidavit. When the case was ripe for hearing it came on for argument much in the way in which cases are argued in the Chancery Division of the High Court The parties appeared by counsel; the information, answer, and depositions were read and commented upon; and finally each member of the court pronounced his opinion and gave his judgment separately—a point worth noticing because it stands in marked contrast to the practice of the modern Judicial Committee of the Privy Council, which in a certain sense represents the Star Chamber.

The Star Chamber proceedings reported in the *State Trials* leave a singular impression on my mind. As far as the mere management in court of the different cases went, it cannot be denied that they are for the most part calm and dignified, though the strange taste and violent passions of the time give them occasionally a grotesque appearance; but the severity of the " censures " or sentences is in these days astonishing. A few instances may be mentioned. In 1615 [1] Sir John Hollis and Sir John Wentworth were prosecuted " for traducing the public justice." Weston had been hanged for the murder of Sir Thomas Overbury, to whom he had administered poison. Wentworth and Hollis went to Weston's execution, where Wentworth asked Weston whether he really did poison Overbury, and pressed him to answer, " saying he desired to know, that he might pray with him." Hollis " was not so much of a questioner," but, " like a kind " of confessor, wished him to discharge his conscience and " satisfy the world." Hollis moreover, when the jury gave their verdict, said, " If he were on the jury, he would " doubt what to do." It is difficult to see how this could be regarded as in any sense criminal conduct; but it seems to have been thought that Wentworth's question

[1] 2 *St. Tr.* 1022.

and Hollis's remarks remotely implied that Weston's guilt CHAP.
might perhaps be not absolutely certain, notwithstanding his conviction. Lord Bacon (then Attorney-General)
developed this view of the subject at length, and with
characteristic grace, calmness, and power. The defendants
excused themselves in a polite manner ; Sir John Hollis
observing that " Mr. Attorney had so well applied his
" charge against him that, though he carried the seal of a
" good conscience with him, he would almost make him
" believe he was guilty." As for what he had said to Weston,
he was there " carried with a general desire which he had to
" be at the execution as he had done in many like cases
" before." It was a common thing on such occasions to
question the person about to be executed, and he had only
followed his usual practice. Coke pronounced sentence. He
referred to Abimelech, to cases of poisoning in the Year-books,
as to which he remarked that "from Edward III. to 22
" Henry VII. (which was a great lump of time) no mention
" is made of poisoning any man." As to going to executions,
he said that " ever since he was a scholar and had read those
" verses of [1] Ovid, *Trist.* iii. 5, ' Ut lupus et vulpes instant mori-
" entibus et quæcumque minor nobilitate fera est,' he did
" never like it, and he did marvel much at the use of Sir
John," to whom he applied, "with a little alteration," Virgil's
line, " Et quæ tanta fuit Tyburn tibi causa videndi."
Finally by way of "censure" Sir John Hollis was fined
£1,000 and Sir John Wentworth 1,000 marks, and each
was imprisoned a year in the Tower.

[2] In 1632 Mr. Sherfield was prosecuted before the Star
Chamber for breaking a glass window in St. Edmond's Church
in Salisbury. He admitted that he had done so, but justified his
conduct on the ground that the window " was not a true re-
" presentation of the Creation; for that it contained divers
" forms of little old men in blue and red coats, and naked in
" the head, feet, and hands, for the picture of God the Father,
" and the seventh day he therein hath represented the like

---

[1] *Tristia*, iii. 5, 35, 36. The first line is both incorrect and imperfect.
It is " Ut lupus et *turpes* instant morientibus ursi."
[2] 3 *St. Tr.* 519.

" image of God sitting down taking his rest, whereas the
" defendant conceiveth this to be false." The window contained many other inaccuracies. Eve, for instance, was represented as being taken whole out of Adam's side, whereas in fact
a rib was taken and made into Eve. Besides, as to the days,
" he placed them preposterously, the fourth before the third,
" and that to be done on the fifth, which was done on the sixth
" day." For these reasons the defendant made eleven holes
in the window with his pikestaff, and, said one of the witnesses,
" the staff broke and he fell down into the seat and lay
" there a quarter of an hour groaning." For this, after a
long and decorous discussion, Sherfield was fined £500.

[1] Mr. Richard Chambers, a merchant of London, who had a
dispute with some under officers at the Custom House, was
summoned before the Privy Council at Hampton Court, where
he said to the Council, " that the merchants are in no part of
" the world so screwed and wrung as in England ; that in
" Turkey they have more encouragement." For this little
bit of grumbling, directed solely against under officers, he
was fined £2,000, and required to make a written sub-
mission or apology, which he refused to do. For his refusal
he was imprisoned for six years.

These proceedings, were sufficiently severe, but those which
made the Court utterly intolerable and brought about its
abolition were the sentences upon libellers, and the proceedings connected with them. The best known of these may be
shortly noticed.

[2] In 1632 William Prynne was informed against for his
book called *Histrio Mastix*. Prynne's answer was, amongst
other things, that his book had been licensed, and one of the
counsel, Mr. Holbourn, apologised, not without good cause,
for his style. [3] " For the manner of his writing he is
" heartily sorry, that his style is so bitter, and his impu-
" tations so unlimited and general." The book certainly
was a bitter and outrageous performance, and it is probable
that a moderate sentence upon the author would, at the time,
have been approved. His trial was, like the other Star
Chamber proceedings, perfectly decent and quiet, but the

[1] 3 *St. Tr.* 373.   [2] *Ib.* 561.   [3] *Ib.* 572.

sentence can be described only as monstrous. He was sen- CHAP. XI.
tenced to be disbarred and deprived of his university degrees;
to stand twice in the pillory, and to have one ear cut off each
time; to be fined £5,000; and to be perpetually imprisoned,
without books, pen, ink, or paper. One of the Court, [1] Lord
Dorset, was as brutal in his judgment as Prynne in his book.
" I should be loth he should escape with his ears, for he may
" get a periwig which he now so much inveighs against, and
" so hide them, or force his conscience to make use of his un-
" lovely love-locks on both sides; therefore I would have
" him branded in the forehead, slit in the nose, and his ears
" cropt too."

Five years after this, in 1637, Prynne, Bastwick, and
Burton, were tried for libel, and were all sentenced to the
same punishment as Prynne had received in 1632, Prynne
being branded on the cheeks instead of losing his ears.

The procedure in this case appears to me to have been as
harsh as the sentence was severe, though I do not think
it has been so much noticed. In cases of treason and felony
no counsel were allowed to prisoners in the sixteenth and
seventeenth centuries, indeed in cases of felony they were
not allowed to address the jury for the prisoner till 1837.
The rule was otherwise in misdemeanours, and by the practice of the Star Chamber defendants were not only allowed
counsel, but were required to get their answers signed
by counsel. The effect of this rule, and probably its object
was, that no defence could be put before the Court which
counsel would not take the responsibility of signing—a
responsibility which, at that time, was extremely serious.
If counsel would not sign the defendant's answer he was
taken to have confessed the information. Prynne's answer
was of such a character that one of the counsel assigned to
him refused to sign it at all, and the other did not sign it till
after the proper time. Bastwick could get no one to sign
his answer: Burton's answer was signed by counsel, but was
set aside as impertinent. Upon the whole, the case was taken
to be admitted by all the three, and judgment was passed on
them accordingly. There is something specially repugnant

[1] 3 *St. Tr.* 585.

to justice in using rules of practice in such a manner as to
debar a prisoner from defending himself, especially when the
professed object of the rules so used is to provide for his defence.   It ought, however, in fairness to be admitted that the
course taken made no practical difference to the defendants,
as they neither could, nor did they wish to deny that they
were the authors of the books imputed to them, and the books
spoke for themselves.   They were asked at the final hearing
whether they pleaded guilty or not guilty, although the Court
took the matter of the information as admitted.   I suppose
this was to give them an opportunity of disavowing the
publication, if they were so minded, but this is only a
conjecture.

The last Star Chamber case to which I will refer is noticeable, amongst other reasons, because it illustrates the intense
unpopularity of one of the principal points in the procedure,
both of the Star Chamber and of the Ecclesiastical Courts, from
which, the Star Chamber probably borrowed it.   This was
what was known as the *ex officio* oath, already mentioned.
In the Common Law Courts [1] this oath is still in constant use
without objection, in interlocutory proceedings, but in the old
Ecclesiastical Courts and in the Star Chamber it was understood to be, and was, used as an oath to speak the truth on the
matters objected against the defendant—an oath, in short
to accuse oneself.   It was vehemently contended by those who
found themselves pressed by this oath that it was against the
law of God, and the law of nature, and that the maxim "*nemo
"tenetur prodere seipsum*" was agreeable to the law of God, and
part of the law of nature.   In this, I think, as in most other
discussions of the kind, the real truth was that those who
disliked the oath had usually done the things of which they
were accused, and which they regarded as meritorious actions,
though their judges regarded them as crimes.   People always
protest with passionate eagerness against being deprived
of technical defences against what they regard as bad
laws, and such complaints often give a spurious value to
technicalities when the cruelty of the laws against which

[1] Under the name of the "voir" (vrai) "dire."   "You shall true answer
"make to all such questions as shall be demanded of you."

they have afforded protection has come to be commonly CHAP. XI.
admitted.

Be this as it may, the extreme unpopularity of the *ex officio*
oath is set in a clear light by the case of John Lilburn. Lilburn wrote an account of the proceedings against him which
is probably substantially accurate and is extremely lively and
circumstantial. [1] He was committed to the Gatehouse "for
" sending of factious and seditious libels out of Holland into
" England." He was afterwards ordered by the Privy
Council to be examined before the Attorney-General, Sir
John Banks. He was accordingly taken to the Attorney-
General's chambers, [2] "and was referred to be examined by
" Mr. Cockshey his chief clerk; and at our first meeting
" together he did kindly entreat me, and made me sit down by
" him, put on my hat, and began with me after this manner.
" Mr. Lilburn, what is your Christian name ? " A number of
questions followed, gradually leading up to the matter complained of. Lilburn answered a good many of them, but at
last refused to go further, saying, " I know it is warrantable
" by the law of God, and I think by the law of the land, that
" I may stand on my just defence, and not answer your inter-
" rogatories, and that my accusers ought to be brought face
" to face, to justify what they accuse me of." He was afterwards asked by the Attorney-General to sign his examination,
but refused to do so, though he offered to write an answer of
his own to what might be alleged against him. [3] Some days
after he was taken to the Star Chamber office that he might
enter his appearance. He replied that he had been served
with no subpœna, and that no bill had been drawn against him.
" One of the clerks said I must first be examined and then
" Sir John" (the Attorney-General) "would make the bill."
Lilburn thought the object of the examination was to get
materials for a bill, and accordingly when the head of the
office tendered him the oath "that you shall make true answer
" to all things that are asked you," he refused to do so, saying, first, " I am but a young man and do not well know what
" belongs to the nature of an oath." Afterwards he said he
was not satisfied of the lawfulness of that oath, and after

---

[1] 3 *St. Tr.* 1315—1368.   [2] *Ib.* 1317.   [3] *Ib.* 1320.

CHAP. XI. much dispute absolutely refused to take it. After about a fortnight's delay he was brought before the Star Chamber, where the oath was again tendered to him and he again refused it on the gronnd that it was an oath of inquiry for the lawfulness of which he had no warrant. [1] Lilburn had a fellow prisoner, "old Mr. Wharton," said in one part of the case to have been eighty-five years of age. When asked to take the oath Wharton refused, and began to tell them of the bishops' cruelty towards him, and that they had " had him in five several prisons within these two years for " refusing the oath." On the following day they were brought up again. Lilburn declared, on his word and at length, that the charges against him were entirely false, and that the books objected to were imported by another person with whom he had no connection. [2] " Then," said the Lord Keeper, " thou art a mad fellow, seeing things are thus that thou " wilt not take the oath and answer truly." Lilburn repeated that it was an oath of inquiry and that he found no warrant in the word of God for an oath of inquiry. " When I named " the word of God the Court began to laugh as though they " had had nothing to do with it." Failing with Lilburn, the Court asked Wharton whether he would take the oath, where-upon getting leave to speak, " he began to thunder it out " against the bishops, and told them they required three " oaths of the king's subjects, namely, the oath of church- " wardenship, and the oath of canonical obedience, and the " oath *ex officio*, which, said he, are all against the law of " the land, and by which they deceive and perjure thousands " of the king's subjects in a year." " But the Lords, wonder- " ing to hear the old man talk after this manner, commanded " him to hold his peace, and to answer them whether he would " take the oath or no. To which he replied, and desired " them to let him talk a little, and he would tell them by " and by. At which all the Court burst out laughing; but " they would not let him go on, but commanded silence (which " if they would have let him proceed, he would have so pep- " pered the bishops as they never were in their lives in an " open Court of judicature)." As both absolutely refused to

[1] 3 *St. Tr.* 1322.   [2] *Ib.* 1325.

take the oath they were each sentenced to stand in the
pillory, and to pay a fine of £500, and Lilburn to be whipped
from the Fleet to the pillory, which stood between Westminster Hall Gate and the Star Chamber. Lilburn was whipped
accordingly, receiving, it was said, upwards of 500 lashes, and
was made to stand in the pillory for two hours after his whipping. In May, 1641, the House of Commons resolved "that the
" sentence of the Star Chamber given against John Lilburn
" is illegal, and against the liberty of the subject: and also
" bloody, cruel, barbarous, and tyrannical."

It is difficult to say how far the cases reported in the
State Trials can be regarded as fair specimens of the common
course of the administration of criminal justice, as it is not
unnatural to suppose that in cases in which the Government
were directly interested prisoners might be treated more harshly
than in common cases. The only report of a trial for a
common offence given in the *State Trials* before the year 1640,
is that of an appeal of murder tried at the King's Bench bar,
in the 4th Charles I. (1628). The report is published in 14
St. Tr. 1342, from the papers of Serjeant Maynard. The
evidence given seems to have been with one strange exception, similar to the evidence which would be given in the
present day on a trial for murder. It was proved that one
Jane Norkott was found lying dead in her bed in a composed
manner, the bed clothes not disturbed, and her child in bed.
Her throat was cut and her neck broken. There was no
blood on the bed, but much at two distinct and distant places
on the floor, and a bloody knife was found sticking in the
floor, the point towards the bed and the haft from the bed.
These facts clearly proved that the case was one of murder,
and not (as was supposed at first) of suicide. Mary Norkott,
the mother of the deceased, Agnes Okeman, her sister, and
Okeman, her brother-in-law, deposed at the inquest that they
slept in an outer room through which her room was entered,
and that no stranger came in in the night. Upon this singularly weak evidence they were suspected of murder, though a
coroner's jury at first returned a verdict of *felo de se*. After
thirty days the body was disinterred and a second inquest
held. Probably (though that is not stated) they found a

CHAP. XI. verdict of murder against the defendants, who were tried at Hertford assizes and acquitted. The judge, being dissatisfied with the verdict, recommended that the infant child should be made plaintiff in an appeal of murder against its father, grandmother, aunt, and uncle, and the appeal was tried accordingly. On the trial it was sworn that when the body was disinterred at the second inquest "the four defendants were " required, each of them, to touch the dead body. Okeman's " wife fell upon her knees and prayed God to show tokens of " her innocency. The appellant " (*sic*, but as the appellant was a baby this seems strange; probably it should be "appellees") " did touch the dead body, whereupon the brow of the dead, " which before was of a livid and carrion colour, began to " have a dew or gentle sweat arise on it, which increased by " degrees till the sweat ran down in drops on the face, the " brow turned to a lively and fresh colour, and the deceased " opened one of her eyes and shut it again ; and this opening " the eye was done three several times; she likewise thrust " out the ring or marriage finger three times and pulled it in " again, and the finger dropped blood on the grass." These occurrences, which I believe (some allowance being made for exaggeration and inaccurate observation) are not unnatural effects of decomposition, seem to have excited the greatest astonishment in Court, but Serjeant Maynard does not say how the judge dealt with them in his charge or what was the result of the proceedings. If they are regarded as miraculous, they have the defect of being wholly uncertain in their meaning, for it is impossible to say whether they attested the innocence of Elizabeth Okeman or her guilt, or that of any, and if so of which, of the other persons concerned.

In the absence of reports of particular trials I may refer to a striking description of trials in general by Sir Thomas Smith, Secretary of State to Queen Elizabeth, which occurs in his *Commonwealth of England*, written during the author's embassy to France, with special reference to the difference between the institutions of France and England, and the Common and the Civil Law.

The following is his description of a trial at the Assizes :

[1] Smith's *Commonwealth*, ch. xxv. pp. 183—201.

Having described the preliminary proceedings and the fixing
of the circuits he describes the Courts themselves.   " In the
" town house or in some open common place there is a tribu-
" nal or place of judgment made aloft.   Upon the highest
" bench there sit the judges which be sent down in commis-
" sion in the midst.   Next them on each side the justices of
" the peace according to their degree.   On a lower bench
" before them the rest of the justices of the peace and some
" other gentlemen or their clerks.   Before these judges and
" justices there is a table set beneath, at which sitteth the
" custos rotulorum, or keeper of the writs, the escheator, the
" under sheriff, and such clerks as do write.   At the end
" of that table there is a bar made with a space for the in-
" quests, and twelve men to come in when they are called,
" behind that space another bar, and there stand the
" prisoners which be brought thither by the gaoler all
" chained together."   The introductory proceedings, including the various proclamations and the taking of the pleas,
the challenges and swearing of the jury, are next fully
described.   They are identically the same as those which
now obtain, the very words of the proclamations having
remained almost unchanged.   The prisoner having pleaded
not guilty, and the jury having been sworn, the crier " saith
" aloud, If any can give evidence or can say anything against
" the prisoner, let him come now, for he standeth upon his de-
" liverance.   If no man come in, then the judge asketh who
" sent him to prison, who is commonly one of the justices of
" the peace.   He, if he be there, delivereth .up the examina-
" tion which he took of him " (under the Acts of Philip and
Mary), " and underneath the names of those whom he
" hath bound to give evidence : although the malefactor hath
" confessed the crime to the justice of the peace, and that it
" appear by his hand and confirmation, the twelve men will
" acquit the prisoner, but they which should give evidence
" pay their recognizances.   Howbeit this doth seldom
" chance except it be in small matters and where the justice
" of·the peace who sent the prisoner to the gaol is away."
This curious passage gives a different impression from
the reports of cases in the State Trials.   The juries in the

cases I have referred to showed little inclination to acquit
prisoners who had confessed or had been accused by the
confessions of others; but Sir Thomas Smith's account clearly
implies that, if the witnesses did not appear, the examination
of the prisoner was read, and he probably may (though this
is not stated) have been further examined upon it. In such
cases as Smith refers to, in the present day the judge would
direct an acquittal.

To resume Smith's account, "If they which be bound to
" give evidence come in, first is read the examination which
" the justice of the peace doth give in " (it is likely that the
prisoner would be questioned upon it, but this is not mentioned),
" then is heard (if he be there) the man robbed, what he can
" say, being first sworn to say the truth, and after the con-
" stable, and as many as were at the apprehension of the
" malefactors, and so many as can say anything being sworn
" one after another to say truth. These be set in such a place
" as they may see the judges and the justices, the inquest
" and the prisoner, and hear them and be heard of them all.
" The judge, after they be sworn, asketh first the party robbed
" if he know the prisoner, and biddeth him look upon him:
" he saith Yea. The prisoner sometimes saith Nay. The
" party pursuyvant giveth good ensignes, *verbi gratiâ*, I know
" thee well enough ; thou robbedst me in such a place, thou
" beatedst me, thou tookest my horse from me, and my purse;
" thou hadst then such a coat, and such a man in thy company.
" The thief will say No, and so they stand a while in alterca-
" tion. Then he " (I suppose the prosecutor) " telleth all that
" he can say: after him likewise all those who were at the ap-
" prehension of the prisoner, or who can give any indices or
" tokens, which we call in our language evidence against the
" malefactor. When the judge hath heard them say enough,
" he asketh if they can say any more. If they say No, then
" he turneth his speech to the inquest. Goodmen (saith he),
" ye of the inquest, ye have heard what these men say against
" the prisoner. You have also heard what the prisoner can
" say for himself. Have an eye to your oath and to your duty,
" and do that which God shall put in your minds to the
" discharge of your consciences, and mark well what is said.

" Thus sometimes with one inquest is passed to the number CHAP. XI " of two or three prisoners. For, if they should be charged " with more, the inquest will say, My lord, we pray you charge " us with no more; it is enough for our memory. Many " times they are charged with but one or two." The jury then retire to consider their verdicts, and are confined " with " neither bread, drink, meat, nor fire. If they be in doubt " of anything that is said, or would hear again some of them " that gave evidence, to interrogate them more at full, or if " any that can give evidence come late, it is permitted that " any that is sworn to say the truth may be interrogated of " them to inform their consciences." Finally the verdict is returned ; the prisoner, if found guilty, and his offence is clergyable, prays his clergy. If he can read he gets it. If not, or if his offence is not clergyable, the judge passes sentence : " Law is thou shalt return to the place from whence " thou camest; from thence thou shalt go to the place of " execution. There thou shalt hang till thou be dead. " Then he saith to the sheriff, Sheriff, do execution."

Several observations arise on this striking passage. Smith makes no mention of counsel; he says nothing explicitly of the prisoner's defence, and he seems to attach little or no importance to the judge's summing up. On the other hand, the whole account assumes that the common course was to call witnesses face to face, though [1] expressions occur which imply that depositions might be used instead ; on what conditions is not stated. From the account given of the reading of the prisoner's examination as a first step, and of the "altercation" between him and the prosecutor, I should infer that the prisoner's defence was made, not in a set speech as at present, but by fragments in the way of argument and "altercation " with the prosecutor and the other witnesses. This would agree with and illustrate the reports in the State Trials already referred to. Upon this view the only difference

[1] " It will seem strange to all nations that do use the Civil Law of the " Roman Emperors that for life and death there is nothing put in writing " but the indictment only. All the rest is done openly in the presence of the " judges, the inquest, and the prisoner, and so many as will or can come " so near as to hear it, and all *depositions* and witnesses given aloud, that " all men may hear from the mouth of the *depositors* and witnesses what is " said."—P. 196.

CHAP. XI. between the trials which are fully reported and the routine described by Smith would be that in the more important cases the examination of the prisoner would be conducted by counsel, whereas in less important cases it would usually consist of a debate between the prisoner and the prosecutor and the other witnesses, the judge of course interfering as he saw fit.

Upon the whole it may be said that the criminal trials of the century preceding the civil war differed from those of our own day in the following important particulars :—

(1) The prisoner was kept in confinement more or less secret till his trial, and could not prepare for his defence. He was examined, and his examination was taken down.

(2) He had no notice beforehand of the evidence against him, and was compelled to defend himself as well as he could when the evidence, written or oral, was produced on his trial. He had no counsel either before or at the trial.

(3) At the trial there were no rules of evidence, as we understand the expression. The witnesses were not necessarily (to say the very least) confronted with the prisoner, nor were the originals of documents required to be produced.

(4) The confessions of accomplices were not only admitted against each other, but were regarded as specially cogent evidence.

(5) It does not appear that the prisoner was allowed to call witnesses on his own behalf; but it matters little whether he was or not; as he had no means of ascertaining what evidence they would give, or of procuring their attendance. In later times they were not examined on oath, if they were called.

This last rule appears to us so extraordinary, that it is necessary to explain how it came about.

[1] Barrington, in his *Observations on the Statutes*, says, " The " denying a felon to make his defence by advocate, and the " not permitting his witnesses to be examined upon oath till " the late statute, seem to have been borrowed from the " Roman law, which is indeed the more severe upon the " criminal as he is not permitted to produce any witnesses in " his favour ; and Montesquieu gives this as a reason why

[1] *Observations on the Statutes*, pp. 89, 90.

"perjury is a capital offence in France, though not in CHAP. XI.
England." [1] Barrington quotes from the journals of the
House of Commons, Thursday, June 4, 1607, a paper " de-
" livered to and read by Mr. Speaker, declaring the manner
" of proceeding in Scotland for point of testimony upon
" trials in criminal cases, for satisfaction of some doubts.

" In criminal causes by the civil law there is no jury called
" upon life and death, and therefore the judges admit wit-
" nesses in favour of the pursuer, but none in favour of the
" defender, because in all cases (either criminal or civil) no man
" can be admitted to prove the contrary of his own accusa-
" tion, for it is his part who relevantly alleges the same to
" prove it. As, if A accused B for breaking his stable and
" stealing his horse such an hour of the night, the pursuer
" may be well admitted to prove what he hath alleged; but
" the defendant can never be admitted to prove that he
" was alibi at that time, for that would be contrary to
" the libel, and therefore most unformal. In Scotland we
" are not governed by the civil law, but *ordanes* (ordinaries
" probably), and juries are to pass upon life and death much
" the same as here, which jury, as it comes from the neigh-
" bourhood where the fact was committed, are presumed to
" know much of their own knowledge, and therefore they are
" not bound to examine any witnesses except they choose to
" do it on the part of the pursuer; but this is not lawful to
" be done in favour of the defendant. It is of truth the
" judge may either privately beforehand examine *ex officio*
" such witnesses as the party pursuer will offer to him; and
" then, when the jury is publicly called, he will cause these
" depositions to be read, and likewise examine any witnesses
" which the pursuer shall then desire, but never in favour of
" the defender."

The same subject is discussed at length in [2] Hume's
Commentaries. "Of old," he says, "the panel was con-
" fined to a very narrow and disadvantageous field by the
" received maxim of the law against admitting any defence

[1] The paper is not printed in the *Journals*, but the House had then before it
a question as to giving Scotch courts jurisdiction over Englishmen charged
with border offences. See Gardiner, *Hist. of Eng.* i. 320-321.
[2] ii. 70 (edition of 1800).

"that was contrary to the averment of the libel—a maxim
"which sounds strange in our ears, but is taught in the
"writings of many foreign lawyers, and seems to have
"found reception formerly into the practice of other nations
"as well as ours. The meaning of it was this: for instance,
"in a case of murder, if the libel charged that the panel
"gave the deceased a mortal wound, of which wound he
"languished for some days and thereof died, it was in vain
"for the panel to allege, for he could not be allowed to
"prove, that in truth the man died of some other ailment.
"By the same rule, as little could the panel allege a casual
"rencounter, or self-defence, or great and sudden provocation,
"if the libel set forth that the slaughter was done by lying
"in wait or on challenge to fight a single combat."

    "The sort of argument, as far as I can collect it, by which
"our lawyers justified so strange a restriction of the panel's
"proof, was to this purpose, that the accuser had set forth
"certain facts and qualities in his libel, and must establish
"these with evidence to be used in his prosecution; that if
"he failed to prove them the panel must be acquitted, of
"course, for that reason only, though there were no evidence
"on his part at all; and that, on the other hand, if the
"prosecutor proved his libel, it could serve to no purpose,
"but to occasion perjury, to admit a contrary proof on the
"part of the panel, whose witnesses, if they contradicted
"what had already been proved by those for the prosecution,
"must be swearing falsely, which it was the business of the
"Court to deny them an opportunity of doing. ' *Quando*
"' *delictum est plene probatum*' (says the commentator Baldus)
"' *per testes affirmantes, non est admittenda contraria probatio*
"' *per testes negantes.*' In like manner Sir George M'Kenzie,
"' To admit contrary probations,' says he, ' were to open a
"' door to perjury.' And much to the same purpose the
"pleadings in cases which were actually under trial. ' This
"' alledgiance being direct contrair to the libel cannot be
"' admitted. Besides that the pursuer offering to prove the
"' libel as it stands, his probation, as it has the preference
"' to it, cannot be reargued by a contrary proof; for seeing
"' the law both of God and man has so far established

" ' the credit of two witnesses to hold their concurring
" ' testimony undoubtedly true, there can no proof be ad-
" ' mitted of facts contrary to the nature of those established
" ' by their joint testimony. More especially considering
' ' that witnesses verifying a crime against a person accused
" ' thereof are less to be suspected (particularly at the instance
" ' of the public) of partiality than any that can possibly be
" ' adduced by the parties accused.' In short, the notion of
" a conjunct probation of the libel and defences before the
" assize was thought too dangerous to be admitted: the
" prerogative of proving, and the choice of the witnesses,
" were to be given to one of the parties only; and on the
" evidence taken by that party the issue was entirely to
" depend. To mention but one instance of so notorious a
" point of practice : in the case of William Sommerville, who
" was indicted for the murder of his mother" (in 1669), "a
" great part of the debate turns on this point,—To whom
" should the prerogative of probation be given ? Should
" the prosecutor be allowed to prove that the woman died
" of the injuries libelled, or the panel to prove that she
" died from other causes. The Court were of opinion for the
" prosecutor; the defences were repelled, and the libel alone
" was remitted to an assize." In course of time it appears an
exception was made as to alibis, though Sir George M'Kenzie
did not altogether like it. He thought the judges ought to
hold a preliminary inquiry about an alibi, and dismiss the
libel if it was proved. Thus "contrary probations" would
be avoided, and the plan of cutting one trial into two
" seems to be our law, and more just and Christian than
" *conjunct probations* are." This strange rule was not absolutely given up in Scotland till 1735. In France the same
practice prevailed much later. Montesquieu, in *L'Esprit des
Lois* (Book xxix. ch. xi.), comparing the law of France and
England as to perjury, says, " En France l'accusé ne produit
" point ses témoins, et il est très rare qu'on y admette ce
" qu'on appelle les faits justificatifs. En Angleterre l'on
" reçoit les témoignages de part et d'autre." Noticing that
in England perjury was not, though in France it was, capitally
punished, and that torture was practised in the one country

and not in the other, he observes that the three things go together. " La loi Française ne craint pas tant d'intimider " les témoins ; au contraire en cas on demande qu'on les " intimide ; elle n'écoute que les témoins d'une part, ce " sont ceux que produit la partie publique, et le destin de " l'accusé dépend de leur seul témoignage."

I have quoted these passages at length, not only on account of their curiosity, but because they seem to me to throw much light on the spirit of the old criminal procedure. The true reason for the rule as to restricting the defence is obvious. It increased the power of the prosecution, and saved trouble to those who conducted it. It was in complete harmony with the other points in which the trials of the sixteenth century formed a contrast to those of our own day. In the present day the rule that a man is presumed to be innocent till he is proved to be guilty is carried out in all its consequences. The plea of not guilty puts everything in issue, and the prosecutor has to prove everything that he alleges from the very beginning. If it be asked why an accused person is presumed to be innocent, I think the true answer is, not that the presumption is probably true, but that society in the present day is so much stronger than the individual, and is capable of inflicting so very much more harm on the individual than the individual as a rule can inflict upon society, that it can afford to be generous. It is, however, a question of degree, varying according to time and place, how far this generosity can or ought to be carried. Particular cases may well be imagined in which guilt, instead of innocence, would be presumed. The mere fact that a man is present amongst mutineers or rebels would often be sufficient, even in our own days, to cost him his life if he could not prove that he was innocent.

In judging of the trials of the period in question we must remember that there was no standing army, and no organised police on which the Government could rely ; that the maintenance of the public peace depended mainly on the life of the sovereign for the time being, and that the question between one ruler and another was a question on which the most momentous issues, religious, political, and social, depended

In such a state of things it was not unnatural to act on a different view as to the presumptions to be made as to guilt and innocence from that which guides our own proceedings.

Suspected people, after all, are generally more or less guilty, and though it may be generous, for the reason already given, to act upon the opposite presumption, I do not see why a Government not strong enough to be generous should shut their eyes to real probabilities in favour of a fiction. This principle must be admitted, and the procedure of the period in question must be judged in the light of it, before it can be fairly criticised. I think such criticism would not be wholly unfavourable to it. The trials were short and sharp; they were directed to the very point at issue, and, whatever disadvantages the prisoner lay under, he was allowed to say whatever he pleased; his attention was pointedly called to every part of the case against him, and if he had a real answer to make he had the opportunity of bringing it out effectively and in detail. It was but seldom that he was abused or insulted.

The general impression left on my mind by reading the trials is that, harsh as they appear to us in many ways, the real point at issue was usually presented to the jury not unfairly. In Raleigh's case, for instance, the substantial question was, Do you, the jury, believe that Raleigh was guilty because Cobham said so at one time, although it is admitted that he afterwards retracted what he said? In our days such evidence would not be allowed to go before a jury, and, if it were, no jury would act upon it; [1] but it is quite a different question whether, in fact, Cobham did let out the truth in what he said against Raleigh.

It is very questionable to me whether Throckmorton was not privy to Wyat's rising, and there can be no reasonable doubt that the Duke of Norfolk intrigued with Queen Mary in a manner which meant no good to Elizabeth, whether his conduct amounted technically to high treason or not. In a word, admit that the criminal law is to be regarded as the weapon by which a Government not very firmly established

[1] This matter is fully examined in Mr. Gardiner's *History of England*, i. pp. 96-108 ; see in particular pp. 106-7.

CHAP. XI. is to defend its existence, admit also that a person generally suspected of being disaffected probably is disaffected, and that, even if he has not done the particular matters imputed to him, he has probably done something else of the same sort, finally remember that the political contests of the sixteenth and seventeenth centuries turned upon the bitterest and the most deep-seated differences which exist amongst men, and that they appealed to the strongest of human passions, and the inference will be that the trials to which I have referred were conducted on intelligible principles, and that, the principles being conceded, their application was not unfair, though the punishments inflicted were no doubt extremely severe.

These trials should be compared not to the English trials of later times, but to those which still take place under the Continental system. It will appear hereafter that the criminal procedure of modern France cannot be said to contrast advantageously with that of the Tudors and early Stuarts, so far as concerns the interests of the accused, and the degree in which the presumption of his innocence is acted upon in practice.

Of course our modern English criminal procedure is greatly superior to that of our ancestors, but there is a common tendency to depreciate past times instead of trying to understand them. The consideration and humanity of our modern criminal courts for accused persons, are due in a great degree to the fact that the whole framework of society, and especially the Government in its various aspects—legislative, executive, and judicial, is now immeasurably stronger than it ever was before, and that it is accordingly possible to adjust the respective interests of the community and of individuals with an elaborate care which was formerly impracticable.

The part of the early criminal procedure which seems to me to have borne most hardly on the accused was the secrecy of the preliminary investigation, and the fact that practically the accused person was prevented from preparing for his defence and from calling witnesses. I am by no means sure that the practice of examining the prisoner pointedly and minutely at his trial was not an advantage to him if he was innocent; and I doubt whether the absence of all rules of evidence, and the habit of reading depositions instead of CHAP. XI having the witnesses produced in court, made so much difference as our modern notions would lead us to believe. The one great essential condition of a fair trial is that the accused person should know what is alleged against him, and have a full opportunity of answering either by his own explanations or by calling witnesses, and for this it is necessary that he should have a proper time between the trial and the preparation of the evidence for the prosecution. The management of the trial itself is really a matter of less importance. It will appear, as we go on, that the trial was improved first, and the preliminary procedure afterwards, and it will also appear that the improvement of the trial did little good whilst the preliminary procedure remained unaltered.

II.—1640—1660.

The trials which took place between the meeting of the Long Parliament and the Restoration illustrate that part of our history which, for obvious reasons, has aroused the strongest party feelings. The only matter on which I have to observe is the effect which it produced on the administration of criminal justice. With some obvious qualifications, this was almost wholly good. The qualifications are those which are inseparable from the administration of justice in a revolutionary period. The judicial proceedings of such a period cannot, in the nature of things, be regular, because no system of government can make provision for its own alteration by main force. A forcible revolution implies a new departure, and new institutions based upon the will of the successful party, and necessitates acts which involve a greater or less departure from legality. This was no doubt the case to a considerable extent in the English Civil Wars. In some of the impeachments which formed the turning-points in the struggle between the King and the Parliament, and particularly in the attainder of Strafford and the execution of Laud, the law was, to say the least, violently strained. The trial and execution of Charles I. was a proceeding which cannot be criticised at all upon strictly legal grounds. The establishment of the High Court of Justice which tried not only Charles I., but many of his adherents, without a jury, and sentenced them to death, was in itself a greater departure from the ordinary practice of English criminal justice than the Star Chamber. It supplies the only case (so far as I know) in English history in which judges sitting without a jury (other than the members of courts-martial) have been entrusted with the power of life and death. Nevertheless, after making every allowance on these points, it must be remarked that, from the year 1640 downwards, the whole spirit and temper of the criminal courts, even in their most irregular and revolutionary proceedings, appears to have been radically changed from what it had been in the preceding century to what it is in our own days. In every case, so far as I am aware, the accused person had the witnesses against him produced face to face, unless there was some special reason (such as sickness) to justify the reading of their depositions. In some cases the prisoner was questioned, but never to any greater extent than that which it is practically impossible to avoid when a man has to defend himself without counsel. When so questioned, the prisoners usually refused to answer. The prisoner was also allowed, not only to cross-examine the witnesses against him if he thought fit, but also to call witnesses of his own. Whether or not they were examined upon oath I am unable to say.

These great changes in the procedure took place apparently spontaneously, and without any legislative enactment. This, no doubt, favours the view that the course taken in the political trials of the preceding century either really was or else was regarded as being illegal. If they were, the word illegal must have been construed in a sense closely approaching to unjust or immoral. I know of no precise, clear authority for the proposition that a prisoner is entitled to have the witnesses against him examined in his presence, or that he is entitled to call witnesses or examine them upon oath till long after the Revolution; and I have given my reasons for thinking that nothing of the kind was involved in the original institution of trial by jury, though it is probable that

in cases in which the Government were not directly interested, the practice may have come to prevail. Looking at
the matter in a purely legal point of view, it is difficult to say
that the one practice was more legal than the other; but
there is no doubt that the later practice was not only more
humane, but more conducive to the discovery of truth than
the earlier one, and in the seventeenth century this was
enough, not only to establish its legality, but also to establish
the fact, supposed to be essential to its legality, that it
formed a part of the "good old laws of England." The
belief in a golden age of law in some indefinite past time
has been common in this country from immemorial antiquity.
After the Norman Conquest it was supposed to have existed
under Edward the Confessor or King Alfred, and the halo
which surrounded their names was afterwards transferred
to "the common law of England," which was sometimes
called by the more attractive title of "common right." It
is impossible to study the proceedings of the seventeenth
century without perceiving that the line between what was
legal, in the strict sense of the word, and what was morally
just was then far less strongly drawn than it is now. It was,
indeed, impossible that it should not be so. The whole, or
all but the whole, of the law relating to procedure was unwritten. Coke's Third Institute was the principal authority
as to the criminal law, and the little which he says on the
subject is fragmentary and incomplete. Besides this, the
whole policy of the Parliamentary party was to represent
their proceedings as being justified by law, and that of their
opponents as being illegal and oppressive. That the law
itself might be oppressive was an admission which they could
never afford to make. As far as I can form an opinion as to
what really was the law, I should say that some of its
leading principles, especially the two well-known phrases of
Magna Charta were on their side. On many other points,
the law, properly so called, was either absolutely silent or
vague and uncertain. In some it may have been opposed to
them. Their case, accordingly, was that all express law,
which they thought just, was law in a transcendent sense;
that whatever they considered just, though not expressly

enacted, was also law ; and that express laws which they considered unjust were to be explained away according to their views of justice. This way of looking at the subject is strikingly expressed by Keble, who acted as Lord President of the High Court of Justice at the trial of Love. [1] " There " is no law in England but is as really and truly the law of " God as any Scripture phrase, that is by consequence from " the very texts of Scripture : for there are very many con- " sequences reasoned out of the texts of Scripture : so is the " law of England the very consequence of the very Decalogue " itself; and whatsoever is not consonant to Scripture in the " law of England is not the law of England, the very books " and learning of the law : whatsoever is not consonant to " the law of God in Scripture, or to right reason which is " maintained by Scripture, whatsoever is in England, be it " Acts of Parliament, customs, or any judicial acts of the " Court, it is not the law of England, but the error of the " party which did pronounce it; and you, or any man else at " the bar, may so plead it."

I will now give a few illustrations of the points to which I have referred. [2] The proceedings upon the impeachment of Lord Strafford may stand as an example of the proceedings by impeachment, which were the great legal weapon of the Parliamentary party in their struggle. The most interesting questions connected with the trial I must pass over, but I may make a few remarks on its more technical aspects.

Strafford was accused on the 11th November, 1640. He was at once committed to custody, and on the 25th November twenty-eight articles of impeachment were delivered in against him. He delivered answers in detail to each charge, and each charge was heard severally and successively. The trial lasted from March 22nd to April 19th, when the impeachment was discontinued, and the bill of attainder substituted for it. The bill received Charles's assent on the 10th

---

[1] 5 *St. Tr.* 172. The grammar of this passage is not very plain, but its general sense is obvious. It would be easy to multiply illustrations.

[2] There is a compressed account of the proceedings in 3 *St. Tr.* 1381—1536, to which I refer as being sufficiently full for my purpose. The trial itself fills a folio volume in Rushworth. See too Mr. Gardiner's *Fall of the Monarchy*, ii. pp. 100-180.

May, and Strafford was executed on the 12th. The different CHAP. XI. charges were opened by different managers, and upon each charge witnesses were called, and the prisoner was heard in his own defence. The effect of this was that he underwent as many trials as there were articles in the impeachment. He does not appear to have been questioned directly and in set terms; but such a mode of procedure practically amounted to questioning, and the mode of procedure by articles and detailed written answers to each had the same effect.

I may here observe that the practice pursued in Strafford's case of putting in a detailed answer to detailed articles of impeachment was followed in most cases of Parliamentary impeachment down to and including the impeachment of Lord Macclesfield in 1724. [1] On the impeachment of Warren Hastings an answer to each charge was put in, and the reading of the charges and answers occupied two days. Hastings's counsel, [2] however, strenuously objected to the evidence on each charge being taken, and to the defence being made, separately, and they carried their point. In the case of Lord Melville, [3] the answer amounted merely to a general plea of not guilty, and the whole of the evidence against him was given before he was called upon for his defence.

So far as the mere procedure went, the management of Strafford's impeachment seems to have been conspicuously fair, though it must not be forgotten that he was tried before a tribunal (the House of Lords) which was far from being unfavourable to him, and which was at the time extremely jealous of any invasion by the Commons of their privileges. Every fact alleged against him was made the subject of proof by witnesses produced in court, some of whom [4] he successfully cross-examined. In some instances, also, rules of evidence were recognised and enforced. [5] Thus, one of the charges against him was, issuing a warrant to Savile to quarter soldiers upon the lands and houses of certain persons, in order to extort money from them. An attempt was made to prove this by the production of a copy of the

---

[1] See *Annual Register* for 1788.
[2] Mill's *History of British India*, v. 57.
[3] 29 *St. Tr.* 622.
[4] See *e.g.* 3 *Ib.* 1422.
[5] *Ib.* 1393 and 1434.

CHAP. XI. warrant. Strafford objected, alleging that the original ought
to be produced. The Lords upheld this objection, but admitted secondary evidence of the original in a manner which
would not at present be considered regular.

The most curious point in the proceedings in reference to
evidence arose upon the notes of what was said to have
passed at the Council Board (as taken by Sir Henry Vane
the father). He deposed that Strafford had advised the King
to bring over the Irish army to subdue England. No other
person present on the occasion heard any such statement
made, and Sir Henry Vane himself spoke with some slight
hesitation. The original notes had been delivered up to
Charles I. and had been destroyed by him. It was contended
by and for Strafford, first, that Vane was mistaken, and, next,
that if he spoke the truth, he was only a single witness. In
consequence of this, Pym declared that he had a copy
privately made by young Sir Henry Vane of the notes
made by his father at the Council, which young Vane had
copied when entrusted by his father for another purpose
with the keys of his papers. These notes, it was maintained, when established by young Vane's evidence, would
be equivalent to a second witness. According to our
modern view, the utmost use to which the original notes,
if produced, could have been put would have been to refresh the memory of the person by whom they were taken.
The view suggested by Pym was not, however, insisted upon.
In fact, this matter was the turning point of the trial.
Legally, if the words were spoken, which must for ever
remain in doubt, it seems to me that they could not upon
any theory whatever amount to treason.

On the substantial merits of the conduct of Parliament
towards Strafford it is not my intention to express any
opinion. The bill of attainder clearly shows on the one
hand a consciousness that the prosecutors had failed to prove
that Strafford was guilty of treason, and, on the other, a determination to assert, or to go as near as they could to asserting,
that he was guilty of that crime. It seems to me that the
real question is, whether Strafford's conduct had been so
criminal, and whether his life was so dangerous to the State,

that Parliament would have been justified in passing a bill
enacting simply, and without any recital, that he should be
put to death. If so, the introduction into the bill of recitals
of a doubtful character (for I cannot call them absolutely and
unquestionably false) ought to be regarded simply as an
attempt to disguise the harshness of the proceeding. If not,
the proceeding itself was unjustifiable. Hallam thinks
that the fifteenth article of the impeachment approached
more nearly to a charge of treason than any other.
The article charges in substance that Strafford taxed
certain towns in Ireland in an arbitrary way, and
caused the sums to be levied by quartering troops on the
inhabitants till they paid the money. This is described as
treason by levying of war, and also as treason under two
Irish Acts, one of the reign of Edward III. and the other of
the reign of Henry VI. One of these Acts (7 Hen. 6)
provides that "whosoever shall cess men of war in His
"Majesty's dominions, shall be thought to make war against
"the King," and be punished as a traitor. The Act of
Edward III. is similar. The words of the Act of Henry VI.
do undoubtedly cover Strafford's conduct, but each of these
Acts appears to have been directed against the exactions and
oppressions of private persons, and not against the oppressive execution of legal process by public authority; and
Lord Strafford showed that it had been a common practice
with his predecessors to levy taxes and enforce the execution
of judgments as he had done. Besides this, it was very
doubtful whether the Acts in question had not been repealed.
[1] Hallam lays little stress upon the Irish Acts, but contends
that "it cannot be extravagant to assert" that if a military
officer were to levy taxes by quartering troops on inhabitants
"in a general and systematic manner, he would, according
"to a warrantable construction of the statutes, be guilty of
"the treason called levying of war against the King." He
thinks, however, that there was no evidence that Strafford
did act in a general and systematic way, and this, no doubt,
is true. Whether such an interpretation "could be extra-
"vagant" it is difficult to say, and it must be admitted that

[1] *Const. Hist.* ii. 107.

it might be said to be " warrantable " by reference to some of
the cases which have been decided upon the 25 Edw. 3 ;
but, however that may be, I think it is at least equally clear
that it would not be correct. The abuse of military power to
the oppression of the subject is no more the same thing as
an attempt to subvert the established Government by force,
than perjury which misleads is the same thing as bribery
which corrupts a judge.

The proceedings against King Charles I. form a remarkable illustration of the contrast which exists between the
administration of justice before and after the Long Parliament and the Civil War. He was, as is known to every
one, condemned principally for refusing to plead to the
charges made against him by the High Court of Justice, and
this was nearly the only step in the whole of his career in
which he was not only well advised, but perfectly firm and
dignified in his conduct. If he had pleaded he would, of course,
have been convicted. The Court, however, did not put their
sentence solely on that ground. They took evidence to satisfy
their consciences, and there are few stranger documents than
[1] the depositions of the witnesses who would have been called
against him if he had pleaded, and whom the Court thought
it necessary to hear. They prove his presence at the different
battles, and the fact that people were killed there, just as witnesses in the present day would prove the facts about any
common case of theft or robbery. For instance : " Samuel
" Morgan, of Wellington, in the county of Salop, felt-maker,
" sworn and examined, deposeth, that he, this deponent, upon
" a Monday morning in Keynton field, saw the King upon the
" top of Edge Hill, in the head of the army ; . . . . and he
" saw many men killed on both sides, at the same time and
" place." " Gyles Gryce . . . saw the King in front of the
" army in Naseby Field, having back and breast on." Also,
he " saw a great many men killed on both sides at Leicester,
" and many houses plundered."

The punctilious and almost pedantic formality of providing
such witnesses for the purpose of proving such facts is characteristic, and shows how deeply men's minds had been

[1] 4 *St. Tr.* 1101—1113.

impressed with the importance of proceeding upon proper and CHAP. XI.
formal evidence in criminal cases.

None of the trials under the Commonwealth are more
remarkable than two prosecutions of [1] John Lilburn, who had
suffered so severely at the hands of the Star Chamber. The
trial in 1649 was for publishing pamphlets denouncing the
Parliament and Cromwell, in contravention of [2] acts of May
and July, 1649, which made it treason to "maliciously and
" advisedly publish by writing, printing, or openly declaring
" that the said Government is tyrannical, usurped, or unlaw-
" ful." That Lilburn had published the pamphlets, and that
the pamphlets did in express words assert that the Government
was tyrannical, was proved beyond all possibility of doubt;
but he was acquitted; "which," says Clarendon, "infinitely
" enraged and perplexed Cromwell, who looked upon it as a
" greater defeat than the loss of a battle would have been."
It is difficult to give an idea, in any moderate compass, of the
trial which ended in this manner, but it was on many
accounts remarkable. Lilburn, who had been nicknamed
"Freeborn John" on account of his continual brags about
freeborn Englishmen, Magna Charta, and the good old laws
of England, entered, on each of his trials, into a regular battle
with the Court, and appealed to the jury for protection. He
began by refusing to plead, or even to hold up his hand,
until he had made a [3] long speech upon all sorts of topics
which the Court was weak enough to listen to without inter-
rupting him. He then got into an almost endless discussion
as to pleading not guilty. He meant to say that he did not
wish by pleading to waive any objections which might lie to
the indictment and that he did wish to have a copy of the indictment and counsel assigned to him, to see whether or not it

---

[1] Besides the Star Chamber prosecution already noticed Lilburn was tried
for his life four times, namely (as he said), first in London in 1641, "before
" the House of Peers;" next at Oxford for levying war against the King at
Brentford (where he had been taken prisoner), when his life was saved by the
Parliament's threat to treat the Cavalier prisoners as he might be treated;
again for high treason in 1649, and again for felony in returning from
banishment in 1653. Of his first and second trials on capital charges there
are no reports. There is an account of the third trial in 4 *St. Tr.* 1269, and
of the fourth in 5 *Ib.* 407. The last, which was written by Lilburn himself, is left incomplete.

[2] Printed in 4 *St. Tr.* 1347—1351.   [3] *Ib.* 1270—1283.

CHAP. XI. was open to any objection.　He urged these contentions with such pertinacity, and managed to introduce so many collateral topics into the discussion, that the whole day was spent in it. The Court showed, as it seems to me, little either of firmness or dignity in the manner in which they discussed the subject, and argued with the prisoner.　They told him, time after time, that he was not entitled to what he demanded, but they shrank apparently from saying, as, the charge being treason, they undoubtedly might have done, that if he did not plead directly guilty or not guilty, they would pass judgment on him. One point in the discussion is curious enough to be noticed specifically.　On one occasion, when he was pressed to plead, Lilburn said, " By the laws of England, I am not to answer " to questions against or concerning myself."　To this Keble, who was first on the commission, replied, " You shall not be " compelled ; " and he afterwards added, " The law is plain, " that you are positively to answer guilty or not guilty."　To which Lilburn replied, " By the Petition of Right, I am not " to answer any questions concerning myself."　I cannot understand what Lilburn can have been thinking of in this observation, for there is not a word in the Petition of Right which bears upon the subject, but his argument shows how strong the popular feeling was on the subject of questioning prisoners.　After infinite wrangling Lilburn was got to plead not guilty, after which the trial proceeded with interruptions and wrangling at every instant.　The printing of the books was proved, and the prisoner was asked on several occasions whether he owned them to be his.　He uniformly replied that the Petition of Right taught him to answer no questions about himself, [1] " and I have read of the law to be practised by " Christ and his apostles."　At last, after endless " struggling," as Lilburn calls it, he arrived at his defence, which, stripped of the innumerable quibbles and topics of grievance in which he wrapped it up, amounted to this, that the Act under which

---

[1] In answer to one question he said, " I am upon Christ's terms.　When " Pilate asked him whether he was the Son of God, and adjured him to tell " him whether he was or no, he replied, ' Thou sayest it.'　So say I, thou Mr. " Prideaux " (the Attorney-General), " sayest it, these are my books.　But· " prove it."　Lilburn did not perceive what an astonishing saying he was putting into Christ's mouth, who, according to his view, refused to admit that he was the Son of God, and called upon Pilate to prove it.　(4 *St. Tr.* 1342.)

he was indicted was bad and tyrannical, that he was a better CHAP. XI.
patriot than those who prosecuted him, and had done and
suffered much in the popular cause ; and that [1] "The jury by
" law are not only judges of fact but of law also ; and you
" that call yourselves judges of the law are no more but
" Norman intruders ; and in deed and in truth, if the jury
" please, are no more but ciphers to pronounce their ver-
" dict." This, no doubt, was the point which secured his
acquittal.

Lilburn was afterwards banished by Act of Parliament,
and it was provided that if he returned from his banishment
he should be guilty of felony. He did return, and [2] his trial
on that occasion was even more stormy than the earlier
one. His own account of its "furious hurley burleys"
is very curious, as far as it goes. He performed the feat
which no one else ever achieved, of extorting from the Court
a copy of his indictment in order that he might put it before
counsel and be instructed as to the objections which he might
take against it. His substantial defence on that occasion also
was, that the Act applied to him was tyrannical, and that the
jury were judges of the law apparently in such a sense,
that they need not put it in force unless they approved of it.
He was acquitted again, and [3] the jury were examined before
the Council of State as to their reasons for their verdict. Many
of them refused to answer, but several of them said that they
regarded themselves as judges of the law as well as of the
fact, whatever the judges might say to the contrary.

Such incidents as the acquittals of Lilburn are defeats
which every revolutionary Government is exposed to if their
proceedings are disapproved of by any considerable section of
the community; and parallels to Lilburn's trial might be
found in many of the political prosecutions which took place
under Louis Philippe. When an ancient and well-established
system of government has been overthrown by force, that
which is established in its place can hardly expect to have its
laws supported and carried into execution merely as law,
and apart from the personal opinion which jurors may have
of their justice. Even under the quietest and best-established

[1] 4 *St. Tr.* 1379.　　　[2] 5 *Ib.* 407.　　　[3] *Ib.* 445—450.

CHAP. XI. Governments it not unfrequently happens that a jury will
refuse to enforce the law if they think it hard in a particular
case.   Instances of this have occurred even in our own times.

In further illustration of the remarks already made as to
the character of the trials under the Commonwealth, I may
refer to the [1] trial of Colonel Morris, for treason, at the York
Assizes, in 1650, and to the trial [2] of Love, for treason, by
the High Court of Justice.   An unfair advantage is said to
have been taken of Morris in disallowing one of his challenges
on a very technical ground, but, otherwise, each trial is fair
and patient enough, and conducted in a manner closely
resembling our modern practice.

Few trials are reported in the *State Trials* during the
Commonwealth for offences not connected with politics, but I
may mention one on account of the way in which it illustrates
the absence of rules of evidence in the seventeenth century.
[3] In 1653, Benjamin Faulconer was tried for perjury before
the Commissioners for sequestrations and compositions of the
Royalists' estates.   He had made statements the effect of
which was that the estates of Lord Craven were sequestrated.
Upon this he was [4] indicted for perjury by the Craven
family, in the Upper Bench, as the Court of King's Bench
was then called.   Many witnesses were called to prove the
falsehood of the matter sworn, after which [5] others were called
to show that Faulconer was a man of bad character.   They
testified to his having drunk the devil's health in the street
at Petersfield ; to his having used bad language and been
guilty of gross immorality ; and, lastly, to his having been
committed on suspicion of felony and having " a common
" name for a robber on the highway."   As Faulconer's evidence
had been accepted and acted upon by Parliament, it is
unlikely that he should have been treated at his trial with
any special harshness.   It would seem, therefore, that at this
time it was not considered irregular to call witnesses to prove
a prisoner's bad character in order to raise a presumption of
his guilt.

---

[1] 4 *St. Tr.* 1250.   [2] 5 *Ib.* 43.   [3] 4 *Ib.* 323.
[4] It is remarkable that the indictments do not aver the materiality of the
matter sworn.
[5] 4 *St. Tr.* 354—356.

III.—1660—1678.

The reigns of Charles II. and James II. form perhaps the CHAP. XI.
most critical part of the history of England, as the whole
course of our subsequent history has been determined by the
result of the struggles which then took place. At every
critical point in those struggles a leading part was played by
the courts of criminal justice, before which the contending
parties alternately appeared, charged by their adversaries
with high treason, generally on perjured evidence, and before
judges who were sometimes cowardly and sometimes corrupt
partisans.

The history of the most important of these proceedings
has been so often related that I should not feel justified,
even if my space allowed me, in attempting to go into their
circumstances minutely ; but there is still room for some observations upon them from the merely legal point of view.
I do not think that the injustice and cruelty of the most
notoriöus of the trials—the trials for the Popish Plot, or
those which took place before Jeffreys—have been in any
degree exaggerated. The principal actors in them have
incurred a preeminent infamy, in mitigation of which
I have nothing to say, but I am not sure that their
special peculiarity has been sufficiently noticed. It may be
shortly characterised by saying that the greater part of
the injustice done in the reigns of Charles II. and
James II. was effected by perjured witnesses, and by the
rigid enforcement of a system of preliminary procedure
which made the detection and exposure of perjury so difficult as to be practically impossible. There was no doubt a
certain amount of high-handed injustice, and the disgusting
brutality of Jeffreys naturally left behind it an ineffaceable
impression ; but, when all this has been fully admitted, I
think it ought in fairness to be added that in the main
the procedure followed in the last half of the seventeenth
century differed but little from that which still prevails
amongst us ; that many of the trials which took place—
especially those which were not for political offences—were

CHAP. XI. perfectly fair ; and that even in the case of the political trials the injustice done was due to political excitement, to individual wickedness, and to the harsh working of a system which, though certainly defective in admitting of the possibility of being harshly and unjustly worked, was sound in many respects.

The number of the trials reported during these reigns is so great (they fill seven volumes of the *State Trials*) that it is necessary to notice them in groups, and to pass over unnoticed many curious details.

The first set of trials after the Restoration are [1] those of the regicides in 1660, to which may be added the trial of Sir H. Vane the younger in 1662. Of the trials of the regicides there is little or nothing to be said from the legal point of view. That they had compassed and imagined the death of the King, and had (as the indictment averred) displayed that compassing and imagination by cutting off his head, admitted of no doubt at all, and it was equally plain that this was treason within the 25 Edw. 3. Their real defence was that Charles had in fact ceased to reign, and that they acted under the authority of those who, for the time being, were in fact the rulers of the country; but the very point of the Restoration and of the prosecution was that this defence was not sufficient, that the civil war had been a successful rebellion, that the proceedings of the part of the House of Commons which exercised the powers of Parliament in 1649 were, so to speak, a rebellion upon a rebellion, and that the execution of Charles was a combination of treason and murder. As a practical proof of this, Denzil Hollis and the Earl of Manchester—who had been two of the six members arrested by Charles I.—and Annesley, who was a member expelled by Pride, were members of the Commission of Oyer and Terminer, which tried Charles's judges. Hollis and Annesley took an active part in the proceedings. [2] Hollis in particular rebuked Harrison vehemently when he alleged the authority of Parliament for what he had done.

---

[1] 5 *St. Tr.* 947—1364.

[2] *Ib.* 1078. "You do very well know that this that you did, this "horrid, detestable act which you committed, could never be perfected by "you till you had broken the Parliament. . . . Do not make the Parliament

The facts were so plain, and the views of the subject, taken CHAP. XI.
by the Court and the prisoners respectively, so diametrically
opposed to each other, that the legal interest of the trials is
small. The prisoners did not dispute the facts; many of
them avowed and justified what they had done, particularly
Harrison, Scroop, and Carew. [1]Cook, who had been Solicitor-
General at the King's trial, defended himself elaborately and
ignominiously, on the ground that, though excepted by name
from the Act of Oblivion, he had not within its true meaning "been instrumental" in taking away the life of Charles.
The words were, "sentencing, signing, or being instrumental,"
which, he argued, must mean being instrumental in the same
way as a person who sentenced or signed. "Observe it is
"not said being any other ways instrumental." "I have
"been told," he said, "that those that did only speak as
"counsel for their fee, who were not the contrivers of it, the
"Parliament did not intend they should be left to be pro-
"ceeded against." .... "I must leave it to your" (the jury's)
"consciences, whether you believe that I had a hand in the
"King's death, when I did write but only that which others
"did dictate unto me, and when I spoke only for my fee."

By this mean line of defence he had no chance (as he ought
to have known) of saving his life, and he only exposed himself to the crushing and unanswerable retort of Sir Heneage
Finch (his successor in the office of Solicitor-General), [2]"He
"that brought the axe from the Tower was not more
"instrumental than he."

The least intrinsically important of the trials of the regicides, that of [3]Hulet, has some legal interest, as it shows
how loose the rules of evidence then were. Hulet was accused of having been the actual executioner of Charles. He
was tried, I think, quite fairly; but was convicted on such
insufficient evidence that the judges procured a reprieve for
him. The evidence against him consisted almost entirely
of hearsay, and of evidence of his own admissions. On the
other hand, he was allowed to call several persons who said

"to be the author of your black crimes." Annesley said something to the
same effect, though in gentler language, to Carew.—Pp. 1056, 1057.
[1] 5 St. Tr. 1077—1115 (see especially 1097, 1098).
[2] Ib. 1100.   [3] Ib. 1185—1195.

CHAP. XI. they heard Brandon, the hangman, admit that he had done
it. [1] Such evidence would, under the present rules of evidence,
be excluded.

In the case of the trials of the regicides, as in several
subsequent cases, the judges held a consultation, at which
[2] the law officers of the Crown were present, in which they
came to a number of resolutions as to points of law which
might arise upon the trial. One of these has some general
interest. "It was resolved that any of the King's counsel
"might privately manage the evidence to the Grand In-
"quest, in order to the finding of the bill of indictment,
"and agreed that it should be done privately : it being
"usual in all cases that the prosecutors upon indictments are
"admitted to manage the evidence for finding the bill, and
"the King's counsel are the only prosecutors in the King's
"case, for he cannot prosecute in person." One of the resolutions deserves to be reprinted on account of its extraordinary pedantry. "The compassing of the King's death
"being agreed to be laid in the indictment to be 29th
"January, 24 Car. I., and the murder on the 30th of that
"same January, it was questioned in which king's reign the
"30th of January should be laid to be,—whether in the reign
"of King Charles I. or King Charles II.; and the question
"grew because there is no fraction of the day ; and all the acts
"which tended to the King's murder until his head was
"actually severed from his body were in the time of his own
"reign, and after his death in the reign of Charles II. And
"although it was agreed by all except Justice Mallett that
"one and the same day might in several respects and as to
"several acts be said to be entirely in two kings' reigns . . . .
"yet because Justice Mallett was earnest that the whole day
"was to be ascribed to King Charles II., therefore it was
"agreed that in that place no year of any king should be
"named, but that the compassing of the King's death should
"be laid on the 29th January, 24 Car. I., and the other

---

[1] See Stobart v. Dryden, 1 M. & W. 615.
[2] *i.e.* the Attorney and Solicitor-General and their King's counsel, "there
"being then no King's serjeant but Serjeant Glanvil, serjeant to the late
"King, who was then old and infirm."—Kelyng's *Reports*, quoted in 5 *St.
Tr.* 971—983. I think that after the Civil War the King's serjeants, in England
at least, were entirely superseded by the Attorney- and Solicitor-General.

" acts tending to the murder and the murder itself laid to be
" ' *tricesimo mensis ejusdem Januarii*,' without naming the year
" of any king, which was agreed to be certain enough."

The [1] trial of Sir Henry Vane in 1662 appears to me to
have been a cruel and revengeful proceeding, as the treason
alleged and proved against him [2] consisted exclusively in his
having acted in the ordinary routine of government, and
especially as a member of the Council of State from the execution of Charles downwards, and in particular in his having
kept Charles II. out of possession of his kingdom. These
acts were clearly within the spirit of the famous act of
11 Hen. 7, c. 1, and it was difficult to bring them within
the letter of the 25 Edw. 3. It is remarkable that in
this case the Court held that no bill of exceptions can be
tendered in criminal cases—a memorable resolution, the effect
of which has been to restrict anything in the nature of an
appeal in criminal trials to those few and rare instances in
which some error has taken place in the procedure which
would be entered on the record.

Between the trials of the regicides and the trials for the
Popish Plot (1660–1678) several trials of great constitutional
importance took place. One of them was the case of
Messenger and others, who were tried at the Old Bailey
for high treason in levying war against the King. I shall
refer to it in connection with the history of the law of
treason. Another and a far more important one was [3] the
trial of Penn and Meade for a tumultuous assembly, and the
proceedings which arose out of it against Edward Bushell.
The tumultuous assembly consisted in Penn's preaching a
sermon in Gracechurch-street. The account of the trial was
written by the prisoners, and naturally gives them the best
of the argument on every occasion. If the account is correct,
they both showed remarkable presence of mind and vigour of
language; but I cannot help thinking that a good many of

[1] 6 *St. Tr.* 119—202. Vane's real offence was no doubt his conduct at
Strafford's trial.
[2] *Ib.* 148, 149.
[3] *Ib.* 951. This trial was in 1670. A similar case in which the jury were
fined and questioned by Kelyng, C.J., is reported in Kelyng, p. 69, first
edition of 1873.

CHAP. XI. their retorts were recollections of what they ought to have said. Whether actually made or not, the remarks of Penn and Meade throw light on the temper of their time and class on several legal subjects. The meeting having been sworn to, the Recorder asked Meade if he was there, to which [1]Meade replied, "It is a maxim in your own law, '*Nemo tenetur* "'*accusare seipsum*,' which, if it be not true Latin, I am sure "it is true English, that no man is bound to accuse himself. "And why dost thou offer to ensnare me with such a ques- "tion? Doth not this show thy malice? Is this like unto "a judge that ought to be counsel for the prisoner at the "bar?" Afterwards Penn asked the Recorder, "Let me "know upon what law you ground my indictment. *Re-* "*corder :* Upon the common law. *Penn :* Where is that "common law? *Recorder :* You must not think that I am "able to run up so many years and over so many adjudged "cases which we call common law to answer your curiosity. "*Penn :* The answer, I am sure, is very short of my question ; "for if it be common law it should not be so hard to pro- "duce." The Court and the prisoners by degrees got into a dispute so hot that [2] the Lord Mayor is said to have told Meade he "deserved to have his tongue cut out," and both he and Penn were removed into the "Bale Dock," which they describe as "a stinking hole," out of court. The jury would find no other verdict than that Meade was not guilty, and Penn "guilty of speaking in Gracechurch-street." According to Penn, the jury were shamefully reviled and locked up for the night, "till seven o'clock next morning (being the 4th "instant), vulgarly called Sunday." Ultimately they re- turned a verdict of not guilty as to both, though not (if the report is correct) till the Recorder had expressed his admira- tion for the Spanish Inquisition, and the Mayor had said he would cut Bushell's (the foreman's) throat as soon as he could. The jury were fined forty marks apiece for their verdict, and sentenced to be imprisoned till they paid it. Bushell and his fellow-jurors obtained a writ of *habeas corpus.* The return to the writ was that they were imprisoned for con-

---

[1] 6 *St. Tr.* 987.
[2] The trial was before the Mayor, the Recorder, and five aldermen.

tempt of court in acquitting Penn and Meade "contra legem
"hujus regni Angliæ, et contra plenum" (*sic*) "et manifestum"
(*sic*) "evidentiam, et contra directionem Curiæ in materia
"legis." But the judges who heard the argument (ten out
of twelve) decided that the discretion of the jury to believe
the evidence or not could not be questioned, and the jurymen
were accordingly discharged from custody without paying their
fines. This is the last instance in which any attempt has
ever been made to question the absolute right of a jury to
find such a verdict as they think right. I am not certain,
however, that the case of a jury persisting in convicting a
prisoner without evidence, or on evidence clearly insufficient
in law to sustain the conviction, might not, if it ever arose,
give rise to considerable difficulty.

A trial which has been little noticed, but which, if it had
been treated as a precedent, would have been of momentous
importance, took place at Aylesbury assizes in 1665, before
Lord Chief Justice Hyde. [1] One Keach, of Winslow, in Buckinghamshire, wrote a tract containing what were then known
as Anabaptist doctrines. It maintained that infants ought
not to be baptized, that Christ would reign on earth permanently for a thousand years, and some other matters. For
this he was indicted for "maliciously writing and publishing
"a seditious and venomous book, wherein are contained damn-
"able positions contrary to the Book of Common Prayer."
Keach was convicted, and sentenced to a fortnight's imprisonment and to stand twice in the pillory. The judge's conduct
on the bench, as reported, was in every respect disgraceful.
The indictment is not given in the report. It might have been
drawn under the Licensing Act (13 & 14 Chas. 2, c. 33, s. 2),
which provides that no person shall presume to print any
heretical book or pamphlet, wherein any doctrine or opinion
is asserted or maintained contrary to the Christian faith, or
the doctrine or discipline of the Church of England. This
would make such a publication a misdemeanour. Whether
the indictment was at common law or under the statute does
not appear. If the book was treated as a libel indictable at
common law, and not as, at most, an ecclesiastical offence, the

[1] 6 *St. Tr.* 701.

CHAP. XI. case was an unheard-of extension of the criminal law. I am not aware that this bad example was ever followed.

A considerable number of trials for ordinary crimes unconnected with politics are reported in the *State Trials* during this period. I may particularly refer to [1] the trial of Colonel Turner, his sons and his wife, for burglary and robbery, in 1664, [2] that of Hawkins, for theft, in 1669; the trials for murder of [3] Lord Morley, in 1666, and [4] Lord Pembroke, in 1678, and the trial of [5] the witches in Suffolk, in 1665.

The trial of the Turners is extremely curious as an [6] illustration of the manners of the time; but in a legal point of view its chief interest depends on its forming a very perfect illustration of the way in which, at that time, a complicated trial for a common offence was conducted. It is indeed the earliest instance, so far as I know, of a full report of such a trial.

No counsel seem to have been employed; at least none are mentioned. The first witness called was the magistrate who had investigated the case and committed the prisoner (Sir Thomas Aleyn, an alderman). Being asked in general terms to "tell his knowledge to the jury," he made a speech describing all his proceedings and inquiries, and stating the information he had received from various people of whom he made inquiries; far the greater part of what he said would by the present rules of evidence be inadmissible. The gist of it was, that suspecting Turner he examined him the day after the robbery, and having received further information next day (all of which he stated at full length), examined him further, searched his house, and, partly by promises of favour, got him to restore a great deal of the stolen property (£1,000 in cash, and jewels worth £2,000 and upwards). The prosecutor and various other witnesses to the facts were then called, and in particular Sir Thomas Chamberlain, another alderman, who had been concerned in inquiring into the case. When all the evidence had been given, Lord Chief

[1] 6 *St. Tr.* 566.　　[2] *Ib.* 922.　　[3] *Ib.* 770.　　[4] *Ib.* 1310.　　[5] *Ib.* 647.

[6] Turner was an old Cavalier officer. His speech at the scaffold lasted two hours. It is an extraordinary performance, full of an infinity of things which he said to spin out the time, in hopes of the arrival of a pardon. He said, for instance, "I was a constant Churchman; it is well known to my parish- "ioners I never durst see a man in the church with his hat on. It troubled "me very much."—6 *St. Tr.* 626.

Justice Hyde shortly and very clearly [1] summed up the whole
matter to Turner, saying, "I would propose this to you, to
" make your defence touching your charge ;" and he ended by
saying, "Laying all this together, unless you answer it, all the
" world must conclude that you are one that did this robbery."
Turner [2] made a long speech in answer to this, and called
witnesses. He was questioned at intervals, and [3] on one occasion at considerable length, on his statement, in such a way
as to set in a clear light its glaring improbability, but not, as
it seems to me, harshly or unfairly. The questioning, in
short, was no longer what it had been in the days of Elizabeth
and James I.,—the very essence of the trial. It was used as
the natural way of getting at the truth, and was by no means
in all cases a disadvantage to the prisoner. It served rather to
call his attention to the matter against him, and so to bring
out his defence, if he had one.

The defence was followed by the summing-up of the judges.
Lord Chief Justice Hyde said, amongst other things, to the
jury, [4] " You take notes of what hath been delivered " (which
seems as if he did not). " I have not your memories : you are
" young." If fully reported, the summing-up was not very
remarkable in any way.

The trials of Hawkins for theft, and of the Suffolk witches,
are the only cases in the *State Trials* tried by Hale. I cannot say that either of them justifies his extraordinary reputation. Hawkins was a Buckinghamshire clergyman, accused
by an Anabaptist parishioner of stealing two rings, an apron,
and £1 19s. in money. The report is by the prisoner himself. If correct, it shows that the charge against him was
the result of the grossest perjury and conspiracy founded
upon base personal malice. In the case itself there is
nothing very remarkable, except that the prosecutor (who

[1] 6 *St. Tr.* 593—594. This summary gives the history of the case, which
is very intricate, in a very few words.
[2] His wife interrupted · him in a very grotesque way (603—604). He
apologized for her, observing for one thing that he had had "twenty-seven
" children by her—fifteen sons and twelve daughters."
[3] 6 *St. Tr.* 605—610, and especially 610.
[4] *Ib.* 612. The practice of taking notes, now universal amongst the judges,
was of slow growth. See Colledge's case; 8 *St. Tr.* 712 ; Cornish's case, 11 *Ib.*
437 ; the Annesley case, 17 *Ib.* 1419, *note.* A passage already referred to in
Throckmorton's case is to the same effect.

CHAP. XI. seems to have acted as counsel, there being no counsel for
the Crown) was allowed to give evidence to show that
Hawkins had committed two other thefts wholly unconnected with the one for which he was being tried, which,
[1] said Hale, "if true, would render the prisoner now at the bar
" obnoxious to any jury." Hale, after expressing his opinion
that the case was perfectly clear, and the prosecutor " a very
" villain,—nay, I think thou art a devil," and after the jury
had declared they were fully satisfied of Hawkins's innocence,
appears to have given an elaborate charge to the jury.

[2] The trial of the Suffolk witches, in 1665, is curious, not
only as one of the last specimens in England of an odious
superstition, but because it seems that rules of evidence
founded, one would have thought, on the most obvious common
sense were altogether unknown to, or at least unrecognised
by, the most famous judge of his time.

Two women, Rose Cullender and Amy Duny, were indicted
for bewitching several children, who were considered too young
to be called as witnesses. The evidence came in substance to
this—that each of the women had a quarrel with some of the
parents of the children said to be bewitched ; that afterwards
the children had fits ; that in their fits they threw up crooked
pins, and declared that the two prisoners were tormenting
them, and that they saw their apparitions. Some other incidents were alleged, almost too puerile to relate, *e.g.* "a
" little thing like a bee flew upon the face " of one of the
children, whereupon she " vomited up a twopenny nail with
" a broad head," and said, " The bee brought this nail and
" forced it into her mouth." This was proved, not by the
child, but by her aunt, who seems not to have been asked
the most obvious questions, such as whether when she saw
the bee it was carrying the nail, and, if so, how, and as to
the child's opportunities of getting the nail and putting it
in her mouth. A quantity of nonsense of this sort having
been proved, it is satisfactory to find that [3] " Mr. Serjeant
" Keeling " (probably as *amicus curiæ*) " seemed much un-
" satisfied with it, and thought it not sufficient to convict
" the prisoners; for, admitting that the children were, in

[1] 6 *St. Tr.* 950.   [2] *Ib.* 687.   [3] *Ib.* 697.

" truth, bewitched, yet " (said he) " it can never be applied
" to the prisoners upon the imagination only of the parties
" afflicted ; for, if that could be allowed, no person what-
" soever can be in safety." This view of the matter was
encountered by the famous Dr. Brown, the author of *Religio
Medici,* [1] " who, upon view of the three persons in court, was
" desired to give his opinion what he did conceive of them ;
" and he was clearly of opinion that the persons were be-
" witched, and said that in Denmark there had been lately
" a great discovery of witches, who used the very same way
" of afflicting persons by conveying pins into them, and
" crooked as these pins were, with needles and nails. And
" his opinion was that the devil in such cases did work upon
" the bodies of men and women upon a natural foundation
" (that is) to stir up and excite such humours superabound-
" ing in their bodies to a great extent, whereby he did in
" an extraordinary manner afflict them with such distem-
" pers as their bodies were most subject to, as particularly
" appeared in these children ; for he conceived that these
" swooning fits were natural, and nothing else but that they
" call the mother, but only heightened to a great excess by the
" subtlety of the devil cooperating with the malice of those
" we term witches, at whose instance he doth these villanies."

Fortunately, perhaps, for Dr. Brown, the art of cross-
examining experts was in those days uninvented. Some
slight experiments were tried with the children, who professed to be insensible, but to know when one of the witches
touched them. They performed this feat successfully in court ;
but, some persons being sceptical, the experiment was performed again in a different place, in the presence of several
persons of distinction, chosen by the judge, of whom Serjeant
Keeling was one. On this occasion one of the children was
blindfolded, and the witch brought to her ; but another
person was made to touch her, " which produced the same
" effect as the touch of the witch did in the court ; whereupon
" the gentlemen returned, openly protesting that they did
" believe the whole transaction of this business was a mere
" imposture." Hale, however, although he might, and I

[1] 6 *St. Tr.* 697.

CHAP. XI. think ought, to have told the jury that there was nothing which could possibly be called evidence to connect the prisoners with the supposed offence, treated the matter not only with gravity, which indeed was his duty, but with that misplaced and misunderstood impartiality which is one of the temptations of a judge better provided with solemnity, respectability, and learning than with mother-wit. His obvious duty was, first, to see that the case was one in which two poor old women's lives were put in jeopardy by the stupid superstition of ignorant people; next, to save them from their danger by insisting on the point put forward by Keeling, and on the proof of fraud given by the experiment tried in court. He did neither of these things. He told the jury that [1] "he " would not repeat the evidence unto them, lest by so doing " he should wrong the evidence on the one side or the other. " Only this he acquainted them, that they had two things to " inquire after. First, whether or no these children be be- " witched? Secondly, whether the prisoners at the bar were " guilty of it? That there were such creatures as witches he " had no doubt at all; for, first, the Scriptures affirmed so " much; secondly, the wisdom of all nations had provided " laws against such persons, which is an argument of their " confidence of such a crime. And such hath been the judg- " ment of this kingdom, as appears by the Act of Parliament " which hath provided punishments proportionable to the " quality of the offence; and desired them strictly to observe " their evidence, and desired the great God of heaven to " direct their hearts in this weighty thing they had in hand; " for to condemn the innocent, and to let the guilty go free, " were both an abomination to the Lord." The poor old women were both convicted and hanged.

[2] A trial for witchcraft took place seventeen years afterwards (in 1682), before Judge Raymond, in which three poor old creatures confessed their guilt, and were hanged. [3] Roger North has some remarks on this, which do honour to his good sense and feeling. " These were two miserable old " creatures that one may say, as to sense or understanding, " were scarce alive, but were overwhelmed with melancholy

---

[1] 6 *St. Tr.* 700, 701.   [2] 8 *Ib.* 1017.   [3] *Lives of the Norths*, i. 266, 267.

" and waking dreams, and so stupid as no one could suppose
" they knew either the construction or consequence of
" what they said. All the rest of the evidence was trifling.
" I, sitting in court the next day, took up the file of the
" informations taken by the justices, which were laid out
" upon the table, and against one of the old women read
" thus : 'This informant saith he saw a cat leap in at her
" ' (the old woman's) window when it was twilight. And this
" ' informant further saith that he verily believeth the said
" ' cat to be the devil, and further saith not.' The judge
" made no such distinctions as how possible it was for old
" women, in a sort of melancholy madness, by often thinking
" in pain and want of spirits, to contract an opinion of them-
" selves that was false ; " . . . " but he left the point upon the
" evidence fairly (as they call it) to the jury, and they con-
" victed them both." He proceeds to give an account of the
dexterity and quiet good sense with which Lord Keeper
Guildford tried such a case, and procured the acquittal of a
poor old man. One remark in it must not be omitted. " It
" is seldom that a poor old witch is brought to trial on that
" account, but there is at the heels of her a popular rage
" that does little less than demand her to be put to death ;
" and if a judge is so clear and open as to declare against
" that impious, vulgar opinion that the devil himself has
" power to torment and kill innocent children, or that he is
" pleased to divert himself with the good people's cheese,
" butter, pigs, and geese, and the like errors of the ignorant
" and foolish rabble, the countrymen (the triers) say their
" judge hath no religion, for he doth not believe witches ;
" and so, to show they have some, hang the poor wretches.
" All which tendency to mistake requires a very prudent,
" moderate carriage in a judge, whereby to convince rather
" by detection of the fraud than by denying authoritatively,
" such power to be given to old women."

The impression made upon my mind by these trials is,
that when neither political nor religious passions or preju-
dices were excited, when the matters at issue were very
plain and simple, when the facts were all within the
prisoner's knowledge, and when he was not kept in close

CHAP. XI. confinement before his trial, and was able to consult counsel, and to procure witnesses if he had any, trials were simple, fair, and substantially just, though little or no protection against perjury was afforded ; but when any of these conditions was not fulfilled, the prisoner was at a great disadvantage. There were practically no rules of evidence. The witnesses were allowed to make speeches, in which they introduced every sort of irrelevant matter which might prejudice the jury against the prisoner. The prisoner had no counsel. He was, indeed, allowed to cross-examine, but cross-examination was hardly understood at all, and every one who has any experience of the matter knows that to cross-examine on bare speculation, and without previous knowledge of what the witness is going to say, is likely to do even a good case more harm than good. The result was that if the Court were prejudiced, if the prisoner was kept in close confinement up to his trial, and if perjured witnesses were called against him, he was practically defenceless. The character of the procedure is well illustrated by the argument constantly used by the [1]judges to justify the rule which deprived prisoners of counsel on matters of fact. It was, that in order to convict the prisoner, the proof must be so plain that no counsel could contend against it. In the very commonest and simplest cases there is some truth in this, if it is assumed that the witnesses speak the truth ; but if the smallest complication is introduced, if the facts are at all numerous, if the witnesses either lie or conceal the truth, an ordinary man, deeply ignorant of law, and intensely interested in the result of the trial, and excited by it, is in practice utterly helpless if he has no one to advise him. A study of the *State Trials* leads the reader to wonder that any judge should ever have thought it worth while to be openly cruel or unjust to prisoners. His position enabled him, as a rule, to secure whatever verdict he liked, without taking a single irregular step, or speaking a single harsh word. The popular notion about the safeguards provided by trial by jury, if only " the good old laws of England " were observed, were, I think, as fallacious as the popular conception of those

[1] See *e.g.* Coleman's case, 7 *St. Tr.* 14.

imaginary good old laws. No system of procedure ever devised will protect a man against a corrupt judge and false
witnesses, any more than the best system of police will
protect him against assassination. The safeguards which the
experience of centuries has provided in our own days are, I
think, sufficient to afford considerable protection to a man
who has sense, spirit, and, above all, plenty of money; but
I do not think it possible to prevent a good deal óf injustice
where these conditions fail. In the seventeenth century,
rich and powerful men were as ill off as the most ignorant
labourer or workman in our own day; indeed, they were
much worse off, for the reasons already suggested.

The importance of these remarks will be illustrated by the
trials during the next period to which I have to refer.

IV.—1678—1688.

The ten years immediately preceding the Revolution are,
perhaps, the most important in the judicial history of
England. In them occurred the trials for the Popish Plot,
the Meal Tub Plot, and the Rye House Plot, the trials connected with the Duke of Monmouth's rebellion, and the trials
which led to the Revolution itself, of which the trial of the
seven bishops was by far the most important. The proceedings of the criminal courts have never before or since been
of so much general importance, and for the first time we have
reports of the cases which appear to have been thoroughly
well taken by [1] good shorthand writers. The result is that
it is still possible to follow with minute accuracy every word
of the proceedings.

Nearly every topic connected with the trials for the Popish
Plot has been so fully discussed that it will be unnecessary
to say more than a very few words by way of introduction
to the subject.

The story of Oates, brought out by degrees as he gained
experience of the public passion and credulity, was this:—

---

[1] The first instance I know of in which a shorthand writer's evidence
appears to have been given is in the trial of Sir Patience Ward for perjury in
1683, when Blaney, a shorthand writer, was called to prove the words sworn.
He was severely cross-examined by Jeffreys and others.—9 *St. Tr.* 317—320.
He was called in many subsequent trials, *e.g.* in Oates's trial for perjury.

The Catholics had for many years had a plan for introducing Popery into this country, and destroying Protestantism
by force.   The principal parties to this scheme were the
Jesuits in Spain and France.   They held a correspondence
with Jesuits and others in England, Coleman being one
of the chief correspondents.   They also held "consults"
at various places in order to concert measures for this
purpose.   One of these was held on the 24th April, 1678,
at the "White Horse" tavern.   It was there determined that
Charles II. should be murdered by Pickering and Groves, or
failing that, and failing also "four ruffians procured by Dr.
"Fogarty," he was to be poisoned by Sir George Wakeman, the
Queen's physician.   A great army was also to be raised by
some means, and introduced into England to massacre the
Protestants; and a number of commissions, signed by "the
"General of the Society of Jesus, Joannes Paulus d'Oliva, by
"virtue of a brief from the Pope, by whom he was enabled,"
were brought over to England, and were distributed by Mr.
Langhorn, a barrister in the Temple, to a number of distinguished persons, who, upon the success of the scheme, were
to receive all the high offices of State.   This scheme was
known to a number of influential Catholics, who held
"consults" on it in different parts of the country.

The following dates are material.

[1] On the 29th September, 1678, Oates made his first dis-
coveries to the Council.   [2] The same evening a warrant was
issued by the Council to seize Coleman's papers; and they
were accordingly seized by Bradley, their officer.

[3] On the 12th October, 1678, Sir Edmundbury Godfrey
was murdered.

[4] On the 28th November, 1678, Coleman was tried for high
treason, and convicted.

On the 17th December, 1678, Ireland, Pickering, and Grove
were tried for treason.

On the 5th February, 1679, Green, Berry, and Hill were
tried for the murder of Sir E. Godfrey.

---

[1] Extract from Burnet, printed in 6 *St. Tr.* 1408.
[2] Evidence of Bradley in Coleman's case, 7 *Ib.* 33.
[3] Trial of Green, Berry, and Hill, for his murder, *Ib.* 189, &c.
[4] *Ib.* 1.

On the 13th June, 1679, Whitehead and four other Jesuits Chap. XI. were tried for treason.

On the following day Langhorn was tried for treason.

On the 18th July, 1679, Sir G. Wakeman was tried for treason.

On June 23, 1680, Lord Castlemaine was tried for treason.

Finally, on the 30th November and the following days, 1680, Lord Stafford was tried for treason.

Other trials of minor interest were connected with the subject, but these were the most important. They ranged, as will be seen, over a little more than two years.

It would be superfluous to discuss minutely the value of Oates's statements. No one accustomed to weighing evidence can doubt that he and the subordinate witnesses, Bedloe, Dugdale, Turberville, and Dangerfield, were quite as bad and quite as false as they are usually supposed to have been. Their evidence has every mark of perjury about it. They never would tie themselves down to anything, if they could possibly avoid it. As soon as they were challenged with a lie by being told that witnesses were coming to contradict them, they always shuffled and drew back, and began to forget. Great part of what they said was in itself monstrous and incredible, and as they succeeded in one murder after another they assumed an air of self-complacent arrogance which rouses indignation even after the lapse of two centuries. The cowardice of Scroggs, who allowed such a wretch as Oates to assume an air of authority in the Court of King's Bench, without reminding him that, if his story was true, he was himself a traitor, liar, and hypocrite, who ought not to dare to look honest men in the face, is almost as disgusting as the impudence which brought that cowardice to light. In short, the common judgment on the whole subject appears to me right; but something remains to be said on the light which these transactions throw on the administration of criminal justice both then and now.

That the trials for the Popish Plot resulted in a dreadful series of failures of justice may be taken as admitted. The important questions are, Who or what was to blame for them? How far is it possible to guard against the recurrence of such

Chap. XI. failures of justice? and To what extent are we secured against them now? In order to answer these questions I will enter a little more fully into the evidence and procedure upon these trials. The general state of affairs is described in a few words, as follows, by [1] Mr. Green:—"The treaty of Nime-" guen not only left France the arbiter of Europe, but it left " Charles the master of a force of 20,000 men levied for the " war he refused to declare, and with nearly a million of " French money in his pocket. His course had roused into " fresh life the old suspicions of his perfidy, and of a secret " plot with Lewis for the ruin of English freedom and " English religion. That there was such a plot we know; " and the hopes of the Catholic party mounted as fast as the " panic of the Protestants."

Such was the state of feeling when Oates told his story. Immediately after it had been told, the papers of Coleman (the secretary of the Duchess of York) were discovered. [2] They consisted of drafts, in Coleman's own writing, of letters sent in 1675 to Père la Chaise (Louis XIV.'s confessor), which Coleman had the incredible folly to preserve or overlook when he destroyed other papers, thus giving every one the impression that these were the least important parts of his correspondence. The letter contained the following passages:—"We have here a mighty work upon our hands, " no less than the conversion of these kingdoms, and by that, " perhaps, the utter subduing of a pestilent heresy which has " domineered over a great part of this northern world a long " time. There were never such hopes of success since the " death of our Queen Mary as now in our days. When God " has given us a prince who has become (may I say a miracle?) " zealous of being the author and instrument of so glorious " a work." . . . . . . "That which we rely upon most, " next to God Almighty's providence and the favour of " my master the Duke, is the mighty mind of his most " Christian Majesty." A few days after this, Sir Edmund-bury Godfrey was murdered, probably (as Lord Macaulay

---

[1] *Short History of the English People*, 635.

[2] As to their seizure, see evidence of Bradley, Boatman, and Lloyd, 7 *St. Tr.* 33—35. The letters are printed in full, 35—58. The passage quoted is at p. 56.

thinks) by Papists. It was in this state of things that the [1]trial of Coleman for high treason took place. His conviction was, beyond all question, caused mainly by the letter quoted, and by other letters of a similar character; but partly also by the panic produced by Godfrey's murder, which was about a fortnight after Coleman's arrest, and about six weeks before his trial. The two witnesses, who by this time were universally admitted to be necessary in cases of treason (the views which prevailed in Raleigh's case having become inconsistent with the whole course of the procedure), were found in [2]Oates and Bedloe. Oates said (amongst many other things) that Coleman was, in his hearing, informed of the determination of the Jesuits to kill the King, and that he (Oates) [3]discussed with Coleman the project of bribing Wakeman to poison Charles; that Coleman took copies of certain instructions given by Ashby (a Jesuit) as to murdering the King and raising an insurrection, in order to forward copies all over the country; and he was allowed to say unreproved, [4] "I could give other evidence, but will not, "because of other things which are not fit to be known "yet." [5]Cross-examination in those days was very imperfectly understood; but Oates was obliged to admit that when he first saw Coleman before the Council he did not know him, and it seemed extremely doubtful whether he ever really charged him before the Council with the matters to which he swore at the trial. [6]Bedloe swore to a variety of treasonable speeches of Coleman's, and to having himself carried letters, which he said were treasonable, from Coleman to Père la Chaise. Coleman's defence was feeble in the extreme, as was the case with most of the prisoners. He said that Oates and Bedloe were great liars. He also said that, as Oates would not fix himself to particular days, he would not contradict him by proving an *alibi*. He apologised for his letters. He began in a feeble way to make some remarks on the improbabilities of the charge; on which Scroggs rudely interrupted him :—[7] "What a kind and way of talking is

---

[1] 7 *St. Tr.* 1—78.
[2] Oates's evidence, p. 18; Bedloe's, p. 30. They were frequently recalled.
[3] 7 *St. Tr.* 21. [4] *Ib.* 21. [5] *Ib.* 25. [6] *Ib.* 31—33. [7] *Ib.* 60.

CHAP. XI. " this! You have such a swimming way of melting words
" that it is a troublesome thing for a man to collect matter
" out of thee," &c.   Finally he was convicted and executed.

The [1] trial of Ireland, Pickering, and Grove took place on
the 17th December.   They were the persons who were said
to have undertaken to murder Charles II.   The evidence
against them was that of Oates and Bedloe, wholly uncorroborated by any other witnesses whatever.   They repeated
what they had said before, fixing the prisoners with the
scheme of murdering Charles.   Bedloe [2] swore that there
was a meeting, at which Ireland was present, " at the end of
" August or beginning of September," to consult as to the
assassination ; but, guessing that he was to be contradicted,
he refused to pledge himself as to the time, beyond saying
that it was " in August."   Ireland had probably heard that
something to this effect had been stated at Coleman's trial,
and had done what he could to provide witnesses to show
that through the whole of August he was in Staffordshire.
[3] He did call one or two such witnesses, but he said that his
imprisonment had been so short that he could send for no
one ; and on calling his first witness he observed, " It is a
" hundred to one if he be here, for I have not been permitted
" so much as to send a scrap of paper."   All the prisoners
were convicted and executed.

The next of the trials was [4] that of Green, Berry, and
Hill, for the murder of Godfrey.   This was a very curious
trial.   The principal witness was Prance, who described in
minute detail how the prisoners enticed Godfrey into a
yard adjoining Somerset House (then the palace of Queen
Catharine); how he was murdered there, and how his body
was concealed, first in a neighbour's house, and afterwards in
Somerset House itself, until it was carried into the fields
where it was afterwards found.   [5] According to his own account, Prance was consulted before the murder, was present

---

[1] 7 *St. Tr.* 79—143.   [2] *Ib.* 109.
[3] *Ib.* 121, &c. On Oates's second trial for perjury in 1685, Ireland's absence
from London through August and part of September was proved by a great
number of witnesses, who traced all his movements from day to day, giving,
by the way, a singularly vivid and authentic account of the life of country
gentlemen in the Long Vacation in 1678.   [4] 7 *St. Tr.* 159.
[5] *Ib.* 169.   As to his recantation, see pp. 176, 177, 209.

at the completion of the murder, though not at the whole of
it, and helped to conceal the body. Prance, before giving his
evidence, retracted and reasserted it more than once. In
some circumstances of his story he was confirmed by independent witnesses. In one very important one, as to the
temporary disposal of the body, he was contradicted. One
of the persons accused gave somewhat confused evidence of
an *alibi*. [1] Bedloe swore that he had been a party to a conspiracy of Jesuits to murder Godfrey, and that after the
murder he saw the body dead in Somerset House. Upon
two rather important collateral points Prance was corroborated. He said that Green, one of the prisoners, inquired for
Godfrey at Godfrey's house, and this was corroborated by
[2] Godfrey's servant; and he also gave [3] an account of a meeting
he had at Bow with certain priests and two of the prisoners,
which was [4] to some extent corroborated by witnesses and by
the admissions of the prisoners when questioned. They were
all convicted and executed.

The trial of the five Jesuits (Whitehead, the Provincial of
the Jesuits in England, Harcourt, Fenwick, Gavan, and
Turner) on the 13th June, 1679, and that of Langhorn, the
barrister, on the following day, may be noticed together, as
much the same facts were proved by the same witnesses.
The witnesses in each case were Oates, Dugdale, and Bedloe.
The substance of their evidence was that the Jesuits had
been guilty of the treasonable conspiracy sworn to in the
earlier cases, and that Langhorn was also a party to it, acting
as a sort of registrar of their resolutions, and in particular
receiving and distributing a number of commissions issued
by the General of the Jesuits to a variety of persons of
distinction in England.

In each case the witnesses were contradicted in several
particulars. The principal contradiction was that, whereas
Oates swore that he was at a " consult " of the Jesuits at
the " White Horse " tavern on the 24th April, 1678, he was in
truth on that day, and for a long time before and afterwards,
at St. Omers. [5] As many as sixteen witnesses were called on

[1] 7 *St Tr.* 179.   [2] Elizabeth Curtis, *ib.* 186.
[3] *Ib.* 174, 175.   [4] *Ib.* 187—191.   [5] *Ib.* 359—379.

CHAP. XI. this point; and there were some other contradictions quite as
circumstantial, and nearly as important. The witnesses were
faintly contradicted by [1] some witnesses who spoke of having
seen Oates in London about that time, but much of their
evidence was hearsay and uncertain. In each case the
prisoners were convicted and executed. [2] Oates was afterwards (in 1685) convicted of perjury on much the same evidence. It is curious to contrast the manner in which Jeffreys
spoke of his evidence on different occasions. As Recorder
of London, he sentenced the five Jesuits in 1679. He then
said:—[3] "Your several crimes have been so fully proved against
" you, that truly I think no person that stands by can be in
" any doubt of the guilt: nor is there the least room for the
" most scrupulous man to doubt of the credibility of the
" witnesses that have been examined against you; and sure I
" am you have been fully heard, and stand fairly convicted
" of those crimes you have been indicted for."

In 1685, as Lord Chief Justice, he ended his summing-up
in Oates's trial for perjury thus:—[4] "And sure I am if you
" think these witnesses swear true, as I cannot see any colour
" of objection, there does not remain the least doubt but that
" Oates is the blackest and most perjured villain that ever
" appeared upon the face of the earth."

[5] The trial of Sir George Wakeman, the Queen's physician,
and three other persons, Marshal, Rumney, and Corker, took
place on the 18th July, 1679. They were charged with
treason in taking part in the plot. Wakeman was to have
poisoned the King; Marshal and Rumney were to have paid
£6,000 towards the purpose of the plot; and Corker was
to have assisted. On this occasion [6] Oates swore that he saw
a letter from Wakeman to Ashby, a Jesuit, most of which
was about "how he should order himself before he went to
" and at the Bath;" but besides this, "in his letter Sir George
" Wakeman did write that the Queen would assist him to
" poison the King." Oates said that a day or two afterwards
he saw Wakeman write another letter, which he perceived
was in the same hand as the treasonable letter. He also

[1] 7 *St. Tr.* 396, &c.   [2] 10 *Ib.* 1079.   [3] 7 *Ib.* 488.
[4] 10 *Ib.* 1226.   [5] 7 *Ib.* 591.   [6] *Ib.* 619—621.

swore that being at Somerset House on treasonable business CHAP. XI. with several Jesuits, he stayed in an outer room whilst they went to see the Queen in an inner room, and that he heard " a woman's voice say that she would assist them in the pro- " pagation of the Catholic religion with her estate, and that " she would not endure these violations of her bed any longer. " and that she would assist Sir George Wakeman in the poisoning " of the King." Fortunately for himself, Sir George Wakeman had not written the letter for Ashby himself, but had dictated it to his servant, [1] Hunt. Ashby took it (apparently under the name of Thimbleby) to Chapman, an apothecary at Bath, who read it and tore off and kept the prescription. Hunt proved that the prescription was in his handwriting; and [2] Chapman proved that the body of the letter was in the same hand as the prescription, that it said nothing about murdering the King, and that so far from prescribing a milk diet, as Oates said it did, it prescribed a different kind of treatment; a milk diet he added would have been inconsistent with Bath water. [3] It was also proved that when Oates was before the Privy Council he had said upon hearsay that Wakeman had had a bribe to poison the King. Wakeman had denied it, and Oates had been asked whether he knew any more against Sir G. Wakeman; to which he replied, " God forbid that I should say anything against Sir G. " Wakeman, for I know nothing more against him." There was other evidence in the case which I need not notice. The prisoners were all acquitted.

[4] Lord Castlemaine (who, being an Irish peer, was tried in England as a commoner in the King's Bench) was tried June 23, 1680. Oates was the principal witness against him, and swore he had seen letters in the prisoner's handwriting about " the design," which, said Oates, meant the treasonable design he had deposed to on other occasions. Oates was to some extent corroborated by Dangerfield, a person if possible more infamous than himself. Dangerfield's competence as a witness was objected to on the ground of his infamy, he having been convicted of felony and burnt in the hand; but as he had been pardoned, he was admitted as a witness. The records,

---

[1] 7 *St. Tr.* 648.   [2] *Ib.* 645—647.   [3] *Ib.* 651.   [4] *Ib.* 1067.

CHAP. XI. however, were admitted against his credit, and [1] it appeared that he had been burnt in the hand for felony, pilloried as a cheat, and convicted on three indictments for coinage offences. A record was also produced which showed that Oates had accused a man at Dover of an odious offence, and that the prisoner had been acquitted. He was contradicted on another point besides. This so much shook the credit of the witnesses that Lord Castlemaine [2] was acquitted.

The last of the trials for the Popish Plot which I shall mention was that of [3] Lord Stafford before the House of Lords. It was much the longest (it lasted five days) and also much the fullest of all. The whole story of the plot was gone into at immense length. Stafford's participation in it rested principally on the evidence of one Turberville. He and the other witnesses were contradicted. The witnesses who contradicted them were contradicted, and the contradictions even went one step further. Thus Dugdale swore against Lord Stafford. Many witnesses were called by Lord Stafford to prove that Dugdale was unworthy of credit. Witnesses were called by the prosecution to set up his character, and especially Southall, a coroner and magistrate who received his evidence originally. Lastly, Lord Ferrers was called by Lord Stafford to testify that Southall "is counted a very pernicious man " against the Government." The prisoner was ultimately convicted by fifty-five votes against thirty-one. He was afterwards executed.

The result is that in two years, and in connection with one transaction, six memorable failures of justice, involving the sacrifice of no less than fourteen innocent lives, occurred in trials held before the highest courts of judicature under a form of procedure closely resembling that which is still in force amongst us. It is a matter of great importance to consider how far this is to be ascribed to individuals, how far it was due to defects inherent in the system under which it occurred, and how far the defects in the system have been remedied.

---

[1] 7 *St. Tr.* 1102.

[2] He was proceeded against for treason in 1689, in going as ambassador to Rome in James II.'s reign, 12 *St. Tr.* 897.

[3] 7 *Ib.* 1294.

The first point to be referred to is the influence of popular passion over the administration of justice. The effect of this may be traced more or less in all the trials for the Popish Plot, though it is fair to say in different degrees. That there actually was a Popish plot, in the sense of a conspiracy, of which the King was the principal member, to bring in the Roman Catholic religion, is undoubtedly true; indeed it is probable that, if the real relations between Louis XIV. and Charles II. had been known then as they are known now, the Revolution would have been antedated by ten years. It is, I think, highly probable that a certain number of desperadoes of infamous character did connect themselves with the Catholic party, and were in the habit of indulging in wild schemes and wild talk about the reestablishment of their religion. Worse men than Oates, Bedloe, Dugdale, Dangerfield, and Turber-ville never lived in the world; but all of them were more or less conversant with the Catholics, and Oates did pass a considerable time amongst the Jesuits both in Spain and in France. Lord Macaulay's reasons for believing that Godfrey was murdered by men of this stamp appear to me unanswer-able. It ought, moreover, to be remembered that in April, 1679, [1] a desperate attempt to murder Arnold, a Monmouth-shire justice who had made himself conspicuous by his anti-Popish zeal, was actually made in London by one Giles, and all but succeeded. The impression left on my mind by the trial of Green, Berry, and Hill certainly is that Prance, though an infamous liar (he afterwards pleaded guilty to perjury on this trial), was a party to the murder, though he put it upon innocent persons. I should think it not at all improbable that Oates himself was the murderer or the contriver of the murder. This would account for Prance's retractations, and for the extremely minute, coherent account he gave of the transaction. His knowledge of the circum-stances, as to which he was corroborated, showed that he was connected with and knew the movements of priests and others whom, in the then state of public feeling, he could accuse with plausibility. In these circumstances it is not surprising that a panic should have been produced which

[1] See the trial of Giles, 7 *St. Tr.* 1129.

CHAP. XI. predisposed juries to believe any revelations which might be made by pretended accomplices.

These considerations fully explain, and to a considerable extent palliate, the conduct of the jurors who convicted Coleman and the persons accused of the murder of Godfrey; and perhaps the same may be said of the jurors who tried Grove, Ireland, and Pickering, though this is more doubtful, as their guilt depended entirely on the evidence of accomplices as to words spoken. For the jurors who convicted the five Jesuits and Langhorn, in the face of the witnesses who contradicted Oates on the principal point in his evidence, it is difficult to admit any excuse whatever; for to say that their verdicts represented the furious bigotry which led the juries of that time to reject the evidence of all Roman Catholics is to condemn them. The acquittals of Wakeman and Lord Castlemaine were creditable as far as they went; but, in my opinion, the worst verdict given by any jury was a venial error in comparison with the injustice of the fifty-one peers who convicted Lord Stafford. The first panic had long subsided at the time of the trial. After his evidence on Wakeman's and Lord Castlemaine's trials, Oates ought never to have been believed again. The only witnesses who pretended to fix Lord Stafford with treason were, according to their own evidence (which in many points was contradicted), accomplices swearing to words spoken. To give a single illustration, [1] Dugdale swore that on the 20th or 21st September, 1678, Lord Stafford offered him £500 to kill the King. Lord Stafford called a witness who brought Dugdale to him on the occasion in question, explained every circumstance connected with the interview, and declared that he was present at the whole of it, and that nothing of the sort was said; and this witness was materially corroborated as to part of his evidence by another. The general accuracy of this evidence was not disputed, but it was suggested as possible that Lord Stafford and Dugdale might have been alone together for a moment, in which the offer might have been made. It is humiliating to think that English noblemen should have convicted one of their own number of high treason because a man who, by his

[1] 7 *St. Tr.* 1343—1346, and see 1386—1391 and 1500.

own account, was a traitor and a murderer in intention, charged him with having taken advantage of their being alone together for a moment to say, " I will give you £500 to kill the King."

Passing from the jurors to the judges and counsel, it must be admitted, in the first place, that Scroggs, who presided at all the trials, was guilty of some misbehaviour which compares unfavourably even with the brutality of Jeffreys. His summings-up in the cases of [1] Ireland, Pickering, and Groves, and in the trial of the five Jesuits, can be described only as infamous. The first is full of attacks on the Roman Catholics, disgusting in the mouth of a judge on a capital trial, and the second is such a speech for the prosecution as no counsel in the present day would make. Besides this, he continually checked and sneered at the prisoners when on their trial. I must, however, say in justice to Scroggs that, disgusting as his manner was, I am not prepared to say that he strained the law as it then stood. What strikes a modern lawyer as the most questionable thing done by him occurred on the trial of Ireland, Pickering, and Grove. Two leading Jesuits, Whitehead and Fenwick, were indicted with them and were given in charge to the jury and tried. [2] At the end of the case it appeared that there was only one witness against them. Upon this Scroggs discharged the jury of them and recommitted them ; and they were afterwards tried and executed for the same treason. Whitehead urged that he had been given in charge once, and ought not to be tried again; but the whole Court held, without hesitation, that there was nothing in the objection. The whole law upon this subject was elaborately considered a few years ago, [3] in R. v.

---

[1] 7 *St. Tr.* 131—134 and 411—415. Here is a specimen of Scroggs's attacks on the Roman Catholics :—'This is a religion that quite unhinges all " piety, all morality, and all conversation, and to be abominated by all man- " kind. They eat their God, they kill their King, and saint the murderer."

[2] 7 *St. Tr.* 119, and see the subsequent proceedings at p. 315.

[3] L. R. 1 Q. B. 289. In 2 Hale, *P. C.* p. 295, the following passage occurs ; after noticing some ancient authorities against the discharge of the jury, he says : " But yet the contrary course hath for a long time prevailed at " Newgate. Nothing is more ordinary than after the jury is sworn and "charged with a prisoner and the evidence given, yet if it appears to the " Court that some of the evidence is kept back, or taken off, or that there " may be a fuller discovery, and the offence notorious, as murder or burglary,

CHAP. XI. Winsor, when it appeared, from many authorities, that the
practice had fluctuated.

It should also be observed that, whatever may have been
his motives, Scroggs did turn against Oates and Bedloe,
and did powerfully help in their final exposure and dis-
comfiture by the acquittal of Sir George Wakeman and Lord
Castlemaine, to each of which results he contributed vigorously.
This is usually attributed to subserviency to Charles II., but
it was conduct good in itself, and required courage. [1] He was,
indeed, proceeded against both before the Privy Council and
in Parliament on this subject, and ran a considerable risk of
impeachment.

Some points connected with the conduct of the judges in
these cases deserve more notice than, so far as I am aware,
they have received. Two of the trials connected with the
plot were conducted with conspicuous fairness and decency.
One of them was the trial of Giles for the attempt to murder
Arnold, the Monmouthshire magistrate—an act extremely
like the murder of Sir E. Godfrey, except in the point that it
did not succeed. In this trial the presiding judge. was
Jeffreys, who sat as Recorder of London. The other was the
trial of Lord Stafford. I do not think that even in our own
times a prisoner could be treated with greater tenderness,
consideration, and courtesy. The presiding judge was [2] Lord
Nottingham, who acted as Lord High Steward on the occasion;
yet this most courteous and humane proceeding ended in what
I think must be regarded as by far the most inexcusable of all
the verdicts given in connection with the Popish Plot.

I do not think much censure attaches to the counsel for
the Crown for their conduct in these trials. They were undoubtedly zealous, and they did not abstain from the popular
topics as to Roman Catholics, Jesuits, the doctrine of equivo-
cation, and the like, but I know of no behaviour on the part

"and that the evidence, though not sufficient to convict the prisoner, yet
"gives the Court a great and strong suspicion of his guilt, the Court may
"discharge the jury of the prisoner, and remit him to the gaol for further
"evidence ; and accordingly it has been practised in most circuits of England,
"for otherwise many notorious murders and burglaries may pass unpunished,
"by the acquittal of a person probably guilty, where the full evidence is not
"searched out or given."

[1] 8 *St. Tr.* 163.
[2] He was Lord Chancellor at the time, and his title was Lord Finch.

of any one of them which can be fairly compared to that of
Coke on the trial of Raleigh.

One great leading cause of the result of these trials is, I think, to be found in the defects of the system of criminal procedure which was then in full vigour, and which, even to this day, is in force, theoretically though not practically, to a greater extent than is generally supposed to be the case. The prisoner was looked upon from first to last in a totally different light from that in which we regard an accused person. In these days, when a man is to be tried, the jury are told that it is their first duty to regard him as being innocent till he is proved to be guilty, and that the proof of his guilt must be given step by step by the prosecution, till no reasonable doubt can remain upon the subject. This sentiment is both modern and, in my opinion, out of harmony with the original law of the country. No one can be brought to trial till a grand jury has upon oath pronounced him guilty, as the form of every indictment shows. "The jurors "for our Lady the Queen, upon their oaths, present that A, "wilfully, feloniously, and of his malice aforethought, did kill "and murder B." Why should a man be presumed to be innocent when at least twelve men have positively sworn to his guilt? In former days, as I have already shown, the presentment of a grand jury went a long way towards a conviction, and a man who came before a petty jury under that prejudice was by no means in the same position as a man against whose innocence nothing at all was known. In nearly every one of the trials for the Popish Plot, and, indeed, in all the trials of that time, the sentiment continually displays itself, that the prisoner is half, or more than half, proved to be an enemy to the King, and that, in the struggle between the King and the suspected man, all advantages are to be secured to the King, whose safety is far more important to the public than the life of such a questionable person as the prisoner. A criminal trial in those days was not unlike a race between the King and the prisoner, in which the King had a long start and the prisoner was heavily weighted.

The following were the essential points in the proceedings

CHAP. XI. which establish this view.　First, the prisoner as soon as he was committed for trial might be, and generally was, kept in close confinement till the day of his trial.　He had no means of knowing what evidence had been given against him.　He was not allowed as a matter of right, but only as an occasional, exceptional favour, to have either counsel or solicitors to advise him as to his defence, or to see his witnesses and put their evidence in order.　When he came into court he was set to fight for his life with absolutely no knowledge of the evidence to be produced against him.　Any one who has ever acted as an advocate knows what it is to be called upon to defend a man at a moment's notice.　Under such circumstances, a modern barrister has usually at least a copy of the depositions.　To defend a prisoner efficiently is a task which makes considerable demands on the readiness, presence of mind, and facility of comprehension of a man trained to possess and use those faculties.　That an uneducated man, whose life is at stake, and who has no warning of what is to be said against him, should do himself justice on such an occasion is a moral impossibility.　But this was what was required of every person tried for high treason in the seventeenth century.　None of the prisoners tried for the Popish Plot, except Lord Stafford and Sir George Wakeman, defended themselves even moderately well.　Langhorn, who was a barrister, lost his head so completely that he did not cross-examine Oates as to the arrangement of his chambers, which was said to be such that Oates could not possibly have heard and seen what he said he heard and saw there—a circumstance on which Scroggs afterwards relied as a justification of his conduct in disbelieving Oates.　When an experienced lawyer defended himself so feebly, it is not surprising that inexperienced persons should have been utterly helpless.

That the prisoner's witnesses were not permitted to be sworn was even in those days considered as a hardship, and the jury were told in all or most of the trials to guard against attaching too much weight to it.　The advantage which that state of the law gave to fraudulent defences, which might be set up without any risk of a prosecution for perjury, seems to have been stupidly overlooked.　It was also a common topic of complaint that prisoners had no copy of the indict- ment against them, or of the pannel of jurors ; but I think the importance of these matters was overrated. A copy of the indictment would only have enabled prisoners to make little quibbles, which the judges would have overruled, and would have been right in overruling; and a copy of the pannel is of no real use to a prisoner. If the sheriff wishes to pack a jury, he must be very clumsy if he does not provide a sufficient number of partial jurors, free from any legal objection, to allow for thirty-five peremptory challenges. If, on the other hand, he is fair, one juryman is practically as good as another. The real grievance was keeping the prisoner in the dark as to the evidence against him. Theoretically this grievance still exists, though practically it has long since been removed. As the law still stands, a bill might be sent before a grand jury without notice to the person accused. The bill being found, the person accused might be arrested merely on proof of his identity ; he would not be taken before a magistrate, and until he was put in the dock to take his trial he would have no legal right to know who were the witnesses against him, or what they had said, or even to have a copy of the indictment.

These defects in the system of trial in the seventeenth century, I own, strike me as being almost less important than the utter absence which the trials show of any conception of the true nature of judicial evidence on the part of the judges, the counsel, and the prisoners. The subject is even now imperfectly understood, but at that time the study of the subject had not begun. I do not think any writer of the seventeenth century has anything of importance to say about it. Hale tells a trifling anecdote or two about mistaken convictions, the result of which is that in trials for murder the body of the person murdered ought to be proved to have been seen after death; but he obviously knew nothing at all of the theory of the subject. It is stated in various places in the *State Trials* that people ought not to be convicted on hearsay, and it was an established rule, regarded as highly important, that there must be two witnesses in treason ; but, subject to these small rules, the opinion of the time seems to have been that if a man came and swore to anything whatever, he ought to be believed unless he was directly contradicted. The greater part of the evidence given in the trials for the Popish Plot consists of oaths by Oates, Bedloe, and others, that they heard this man or that say he would kill the King, or that they read letters to the same effect, which, upon mentally comparing them with letters written by the accused, they perceived to be in the same handwriting.

The remarks which in the present day would occur upon such evidence, and which seem to us almost too obvious to be made, are that it would be wholly unsafe to act upon it, even if it were given by witnesses who were not accomplices. To convict any man of treason simply because two persons swore that on two separate occasions he made separate treasonable overtures to them, there being no corroboration whatever of their statement, would put every honest man's life at the mercy of every pair of villains in the country. If the evidence were given by accomplices, the jury would be told to pay no attention to it unless it was corroborated by independent evidence; but this does not seem to have occurred to the judges and juries of the seventeenth century. The judges continually say that no doubt accomplices are bad men, but that if their evidence is not taken crimes will not be discovered; and the juries seem to have thought (as they very often still think) that a direct unqualified oath by an eye- or ear-witness has, so to speak, a mechanical value, and must be believed unless it is distinctly contradicted. This is strongly illustrated by the circumstance that the objections made by the accused persons to the evidence against them almost always took the form of objections addressed to the court to the competency of the witnesses and not of objections to their credit addressed to the jury. If the court regarded a man as "a good" (*i.e.* a competent) "witness," the jury seem to have believed him as a matter of course, unless he was contradicted, though there are a few exceptions. [1] In Lord Castlemaine's case, for instance, Dangerfield's evidence was left to the jury, though he had been previously convicted

[1] 7 *St. Tr.* 1110.

of " six great enormous crimes." They were, however, told they need not believe him, and they did not.

The most remarkable illustration of these remarks is to be found in the trial of the [1] five Jesuits. Fenwick objected that the evidence against him was entirely composed of accounts of the contents of letters not produced. " All the evidence that is " given comes but to this : there is but saying and swearing. " I defy them to give one probable reason to satisfy any " reasonable man's judgment how this can be." Upon this Scroggs observed: " Mr. Fenwick says to all this, here " is nothing against us but talking and swearing ; but for " that he hàth been told (if it were possible for him to learn) " that all testimony is but talking and swearing, for all " things, all men's lives and fortunes, are determined by an " oath, and an oath is by talking, by kissing the book and " calling God to witness to the truth of what is said."

I think that Fenwick was right as to what the law, or rather the practice of juries, ought to be, and that Scroggs was right as to what it actually was and, to a certain extent, still is. It is true that juries do attach extraordinary importance to the dead weight of an oath. It is also true, so at least I think, that a consideration of the degree to which circumstances corroborate each other, and of the intrinsic probability of the matter sworn to, is a far better test of truth than any oath can possibly be, and I should always feel great reluctance to convict a prisoner on the uncorroborated testimony of a single witness to words spoken, or to any other isolated fact which, having occurred, leaves behind it no definite trace of its occurrence.

The principle that the uncorroborated evidence of an accomplice is not to be acted upon, which is now well established, though it cannot be said to have the force of a positive rule of law, seems to have been unknown, and was at all events systematically disregarded and even disavowed in the seventeenth century. If observed, it would have prevented every one of the unjust convictions referred to.

The inference suggested by studying the trials for the

[1] Whitbread, Harcourt, Fenwick, Gavan, and Turner, 7 *St. Tr.* 311, 358, 411.

Popish plot is not so much that they show that in the seventeenth century judges were corrupt and timid, or that juries were liable to party spirit in political cases, as that they give great reason to fear that the principles of evidence were then so ill understood, and the whole method of criminal procedure was so imperfect and superficial, that an amount of injustice frightful to think of must have been inflicted at the assizes and sessions on obscure persons of whom no one ever has heard or will hear. A perjurer in those days was in the position of a person armed with a deadly poison which he could administer with no considerable chance of detection. What the political trials of the seventeenth century really did was to expose men of high rank and conspicuous position to the calamities which must have been felt by thousands of obscure criminals without attracting even a passing notice. The truculence of Jeffreys, the time-serving cowardice of Scroggs, and the fierce prejudice of some of the jurors were, so at least we must hope, exceptional; but the light which these trials throw on what must have happened in the common routine of the administration of criminal justice is a far more serious matter.

In some matters to which the public would perhaps attach more importance than professional persons, the rules of evidence in the seventeenth century were administered in a way which might be regarded as more favourable to the prisoner than our modern practice. Evidence was not confined to the issue with anything like the modern strictness. For instance, prisoners were allowed to prove almost anything by way of discrediting a hostile witness. On the other hand, cross-examination to credit was practically unknown, though the judges appear to have varied and to have been at times partial in their practice in relation to this matter. When Oates was tried for perjury, he was stopped as soon as he asked a witness any question tending " to ensnare him." In our times this practice has been reversed. A witness may be cross-examined to his credit to any extent, but the rule is that his answer must be taken, and that if he swears falsely the remedy is to indict him for perjury. This, however, was not established till comparatively modern times.

I do not think that the power or danger of perjury has been by any means removed since Oates's time. I am not sure that it has been as much diminished as we are accustomed to believe. Cross-examination will no doubt defeat it in some cases. If Oates and the others had been cross-examined with what would now be considered even a moderate degree of skill, they could scarcely have been believed, and they must either have exposed themselves to contradiction or have forfeited all credit by forgetting everything upon which they could be contradicted; but practice and time are essential to the efficiency of cross-examination, and without proper instructions to the cross-examiner it is to the last degree dangerous to a prisoner's interests. In the seventeenth century the judges seem to have done most of the cross-examination; the prisoner could have no instructions,[1] and it was a rule that trials must be finished at a single sitting.

It must, however, be admitted that under particular circumstances no really effectual protection against perjury ever has been or ever can be devised. If all the circumstances except one are consistent either with guilt or innocence, and that one circumstance depends on the testimony of a single alleged eye- or ear-witness to an act done or words spoken, of which no assignable trace remains, it is impossible to prevent or detect perjury.[2] Suppose, for instance, there is a violent riot, and many persons are present merely as innocent bystanders, how

---

[1] Lord Stafford's trial before the House of Lords lasted for five days; but in Lord Delamere's trial before Jeffreys, as Lord High Steward, Jeffreys refused to adjourn for the night, saying that he greatly doubted whether or not he had power to do so. The right of the court to adjourn in cases of treason or felony was not fully established till the treason trials of 1794. In Scotland in 1765, in the case of Nairne and Ogilvie, the court sat forty-three hours (19 *St. Tr.* 1326), never rising. An objection was taken to the conviction on the ground that the jury rose for about half an hour for refreshment; this, however, was overruled.

[2] In the case of R. *v.* Lyons and eight others, tried at the Old Bailey, in February, 1863, for piracy and murder, the evidence showed that the prisoners, who were sailors on the ship *Flowery Land*, mutinied, murdered the captain and mate, scuttled the ship, and went off in a boat. When the captain was killed, the carpenter, Andersen, a Norwegian, was knocked down with a hand-spike. He swore that one of the prisoners, Marcelino, afterwards said to him, "Me strike you." This was the only evidence of Marcelino's connection with the crime. He was nevertheless convicted; but he afterwards received a free pardon, as it was thought that a Norwegian's impression of what a Spaniard said in broken English was not evidence sufficiently weighty to justify a capital conviction.—59 *C. C. C. Sessions Papers*, 275, 286.

can one such bystander defend himself against a witness who falsely swears that he saw him strike a blow or throw a stone, or that he heard him encourage others to do so ?

The observations which arose upon the trial for the Popish plot apply to the trials which took place between 1680 and 1688. All or most of them were conducted in the same way and upon the same principles of procedure, but they were in themselves so memorable that I will make a few observations upon some of the most important of them.

The first of the trials to be noticed is [1] that of Fitzharris, who was tried in 1681 for treason, in publishing a pamphlet accusing Charles II. and his brother of [2] "confederacy with " the Pope and the French to introduce Popery and arbitrary " government," and calling on the nation to " up all as one " man, look to your own defence e'er it be too late," with much other violent language to the same effect. He pleaded, first, that he was impeached for the same offence, and that the impeachment was still pending ; but this plea was [3] over-ruled on argument, the Court giving no reasons. This proceeding was severely and, I think, justly criticised. He was then tried, convicted, and executed. About the facts there was no doubt. Fitzharris had made a proposal to one Everard to write the pamphlet. Everard invited Fitzharris to his chambers in Gray's Inn, to give him instructions, and concealed people there to hear what passed. Fitzharris gave instructions at one meeting and corrected the draft at a second. The object with which the pamphlet was written was, according to Everard, to stir up a civil war in England, which would enable Louis XIV. first to gain Flanders, [4] " and " then we shall make no bones to gain England too." Fitz-harris's defence in substance was that the pamphlet was written by the orders of Charles II. ; that he meant to send it to the leading men of the exclusionist party, and to have it found in their possession as evidence against them to be used on occasion. [5] This seems, on the whole, to have been what he meant to suggest by a number of witnesses whom he called,

---

[1] 8 *St. Tr.* 243.　　[2] *Ib.* 333, and see 357.　　[3] *Ib.* 326.　　[4] *Ib.* 345.
[5] See some remarks by Sir J. Hawles, pp. 439—440 ; and see 378 for Fitz-harris's defence.

though he put the matter in rather a different way in his
defence, alleging that he drew Everard on to write the pamphlet in order to give information against him. Fitzharris was
executed. Hawles observes that both Whigs and Tories
" agreed he deserved to be hanged. The first thought it for
" their advantage to save him if he would confess; but the
" last thought it was fit to hang him for fear he would confess."
The question in respect of which his confession was hoped
and feared was apparently the degree in which the King and
other distinguished persons had really been his accomplices.
The trial is confusing, as Fitzharris only hinted at his defence,
and was obviously weak and timid. One point worth noticing
in the case is the manner in which he was hampered in his
defence. The Attorney-General (Sir R. Sawyer) strenuously
objected to his [1] solicitor assisting him in any way, and indeed
to his wife being by him. He had a copy of the pannel, with
crosses to show whom he was to challenge, which gave special
offence. Upon this [2] said Jeffreys, " God forbid but his
" memory should be helped in matters of fact, as is usual in
" these cases; but no instructions ought to be given him here."
It was also remarked that Mr. Fitzharris "had a perfect formal
" brief," and he was compelled after much discussion, as a sort
of compromise, to give the papers to his wife, who, however,
was allowed to stand by him.

[3] The trial of Stephen Colledge is next to be noticed. To
do justice to it would require more space than I can afford.
He was known as "the Protestant joiner," and was accused
of high treason by Dugdale and others, by way of a counter-
blast to the Popish plot. It was alleged that he had

---

[1] A solicitor occupied a low position in those days. "It is not the duty of
" a solicitor to bring papers; he was only appointed by the court to run of
" errands; he was not to advise or furnish with matter of defence " (p. 353),
said the Solicitor-General. The solicitor was inferior to the attorney, who, as
his name implied, represented his client. It is odd that "solicitor" should
have been regarded of late years as the more honourable title.

[2] 8 *St. Tr.* 332. "*Jeffreys:* I see it is a perfect formal brief. *Mrs. F.:* Must
" he have nothing to help himself? *F.:* In short, the King's counsel would take
" my life away without letting me make my defence. *A.-G.:* I desire not to
" take any papers from him if they be such as are permitted by law. *S.-G.:*
" My lord, his innocency must make his defence, and nothing else. *Jeffreys:*
" My lord, we are in your lordship's judgment, whether you will allow these
" papers. *L. C. J.:* Let us see the papers. *F.:* My lord, I will deliver it to
" my wife again. *L. C. J.:* Let it be so."

[3] 8 *St. Tr.* 549.

proposed to Dugdale to murder the King, but the London grand jury threw out the bill against him. Hereupon the witnesses swore that at the time of the Oxford Parliament he said at Oxford treasonable words in pursuance of his design. The bill was found by the grand jury of Oxfordshire, and after a long and memorable trial Colledge was convicted before Chief Justice North, afterwards Lord Keeper. On his way to the trial he was taken into a house and deprived of all the papers provided for his defence, although he had been allowed the use of pen, ink, and paper, and the assistance of counsel and solicitor, and to see his friends, by the express orders of the King in council. The papers seem to have been examined by the King's counsel, who were enabled to manage their case accordingly, not calling certain witnesses whom Colledge could have contradicted or cross-examined. This was one of the most wholly inexcusable transactions that ever occurred in an English court, and leaves a stain on the Lord Keeper's character which the many amiable points in it cannot efface. It must be owned, however, that it carried the principle that counsel were not to be allowed to a prisoner to its logical result. Many of the papers were returned to Colledge; but one, which the judges considered [1] "a most seditious libellous speech "to spit venom upon the Government in the face of the "country," and also instructions as to examining the witnesses, were kept from him, as the Chief Justice observed that to let him have them would be "to give you counsel "in an indirect way."

The vigour with which Colledge under these difficulties asserted his rights and defended himself through a sitting of twelve or thirteen hours was admirable. The evidence was much the same as in the Popish plot cases. Dugdale and others swore that he made treasonable proposals to them, and [2] other witnesses proved that he had spoken unfavourably of Charles II., and justified the Long Parliament of 1640—language which it was absurd to describe as treasonable. A mass of contradictory and defamatory evidence was brought against the witnesses for the prosecu-

---

[1] 8 St. Tr. 585.   [2] Ib. 616.

tion, and [1] Oates in particular contradicted Dugdale, getting
into a shameful altercation with him, in which Dugdale committed a perjury which was afterwards detected, and which prevented his reappearance as a witness. The trial became a fierce dispute, made up of contradiction upon contradiction, till every one was tired out. The counsel for the Crown, however, and particularly the Solicitor-General (Finch) and Jeffreys, made elaborate speeches, having the last word. [2] The Chief Justice summed up very shortly, saying, "For me to "speak out of memory, I had rather you should recur to "your own memories and your own notes," showing clearly that he had taken no notes. Colledge, indeed, pressed him to refer to his notes, which he refused to do. Colledge was convicted and executed.

The trial of Colledge may, I think, be put on a level with that of Lord Stafford in regard of the iniquity of the result. The behaviour of the judges, though not brutal, was singularly unfair to the prisoner and weak as against the counsel for the Crown.

The long list of political prosecutions which occurred at this time is varied by a memorable trial for a private crime, namely, the [3] trial of Count Coningsmark for the murder of Mr. Thynne. Thynne was a very rich country gentleman, then lately married to Lady Ogle. He was shot dead in his coach in Pall Mall by Boroski, a Pole, acting under the orders and in the company of Lieutenant Stein and Captain Vratz, two German officers; all three being, so to speak, retainers of Count Coningsmark. The substantial question in the case was whether the Count was or was not an accessory before the fact, as there was no question as to the guilt of the other three. Charles was known to be favourably disposed to the Count, and he was accordingly tried with conspicuous humanity and favour. Perhaps the most remarkable

---

[1] P. 641. Oates's evidence in this trial was curious in many ways. He deposed for one thing that he went to the Crown Tavern with Colledge, when, "We did, to divert ourselves till dinner came up, enter into a philosophical "discourse with one Mr. Savage." . . . "It was concerning the existence of "God, whether that could be proved by natural demonstration, and whether "or no the soul was immortal." He said that on that occasion no treason was talked, though one Smith swore the opposite.—P. 646—647.

[2] 712—714.   [3] 9 *St. Tr.* 1.

CHAP. XI. circumstance in the case is that the Lord Chief Justice (Pemberton), obviously as a favour to the prisoner, asked him [1] a long series of questions through the interpreter, drawing his attention to all the suspicious circumstances in the case, and asking. how he explained them. The counsel complained that the interpreter acted as an advocate. The Court said that the case was an extraordinary one, as none of the prisoners could speak English. The Count was acquitted, it has usually been said unfairly. I have little doubt that he was guilty; but I am not quite sure that it was positively proved that his friends and their servant did not go beyond their instructions.

Passing over with a bare reference the various angry and obviously partisan trials [2] connected with the election of the sheriffs of London, in 1682, I pass to the celebrated trials of Lord William Russell and Algernon Sidney for treason. [3] That both of these eminent persons had been engaged in a conspiracy for an insurrection there seems to be little doubt. There is no evidence that they were privy to the Rye House plot—Rumbold's scheme for killing Charles and James on their way from Newmarket; but they scarcely denied their participation in a conspiracy to levy war against Charles II. The witnesses against them were accomplices, namely, Lord Howard and, in Lord William Russell's case, Ramsey, who, as Hallam remarks, was an unwilling witness. Lord Howard was certainly swearing to save his own life, and he was permitted, after the manner which prevailed for many years after the trial, to tell his story in his own way, the result of which was that he made a long and elaborate speech. [4] It was proved by several witnesses that Lord Howard had on other occasions denied that Lord W. Russell was concerned in the plot. [5] Howard's explanation was that

[1] 9 St. Tr. 60—64.
[2] Pilkington and others for a riot, 9 St. Tr. 187 : Sir Patience Ward for perjury, Ib. 299. This last was a shameful case.
[3] Lord Macaulay's account of them is comprised in very few words. "Russell, who appears to have been guilty of no offence falling within the "definition of treason, and Sidney, of whose guilt no legal evidence could be "produced, were beheaded, in defiance of law and justice." Mr. Hallam is fuller, and I think fairer. See Const. Hist. ii. 457. Lord W. Russell's trial is in 9 St. Tr. 577.
[4] Ib. 619.   [5] Ib. 623.

on one occasion he did say what was alleged, out of regard to CHAP. XI. the Duke of Bedford. As to another occasion on which he was said to have sworn to what he said, he declared that what he swore to was, that he did not believe Lord W. Russell had any design to murder the King. In this he said he was "carrying his knife close between the paring and the apple." ¹ The prisoner's defence was so weak and hesitating, that it is difficult to doubt that the charge made against him was substantially true. It is remarkable that he objected to the introduction of hearsay evidence as tending to prejudice him, an objection which in those days was seldom taken, and which, indeed, was opposed to the practice of the courts. The jury were told, as they always were, that the prisoner was not to be convicted on such evidence. The conduct of the judges in this trial was, I think, moderate and fair in general. The Chief Justice's direction to the jury was more favourable to the prisoner than, according to precedents which are still binding, it ought to have been. ² He told them in substance that a conspiracy to levy war against the King was not an overt act of conspiring the King's death, unless the war to be levied was of such a nature as to expose the King to personal danger.

³ The trial of Sidney much resembled that of Russell. He was indicted for compassing and imagining the King's death. Three overt acts were charged as displaying this intention, namely,—(1) holding consultations amounting to a conspiracy to levy war ; (2) sending Aaron Smith to Scotland to invite certain Scotchmen to come and join in the conspiracy; (3) composing a treasonable libel, affirming amongst other things,

---

¹ "He once intended to have related the whole fact just as it was, but his "counsel advised him against it." . . . "He was a man of so much candour "that he spoke little as to the fact ; for since he was advised not to tell the "whole truth, he could not speak against that which he knew to be true though "in some particulars it had been carried beyond the truth."—Burnet, *Own Times*, ii. 172, 173.

² "The question before you will be whether upon this whole matter you do "believe my Lord Russell had any design upon the King's life, to destroy the "King, to take away his life, for that is the material part here. It is used "and given you (by the King's counsel), as an evidence of this, that he did "conspire to raise an insurrection . . . and to surprise the King's guard, "which, say they, can have no other end but to seize and destroy the King, "&c."—9 *St. Tr.* 636. Cf. Foster's *Discourse on Treason*, p. 197, where a wider doctrine is laid down. ³ *St. Tr.* 9818—1002.

CHAP. XI. that the King was subject to Parliament, and that "we may "therefore change or take away kings."

Lord Howard, if believed, proved the first, and less distinctly the second, overt act. He gave the same evidence as in Lord Russell's case, and was subjected to the same or similar contradictions. As to the third, the papers were undoubtedly found in the prisoner's study; [1] and three persons—Sheppard, who had seen him endorse bills; Cary, who knew his endorsements, and Cook, who cashed bills bearing his endorsement,— all proved his handwriting. This was evidence which in the present day, would be not only admissible, but practically conclusive. It seems, though it is not quite clear [2] on the report, that "some papers of his particular affairs" were produced for comparison. In later times, and down to 1854 (see 17 & 18 Vic. c. 125, s. 27, and 28 Vict. c. 18, s. 8), this method of proof was regarded as improper. But the law of evidence hardly existed in those days, and nothing can be more vague and loose than the way in which the matter was handled.

The most important points were these :—

(1) It was said that a conspiracy to levy war was not an overt act of treason by compassing the King's death. Much no doubt might be said in favour of this view ; but the law was otherwise interpreted, not only before, but after, Sidney's time, particularly in the case of Lord Preston and Ashton, who were tried by Chief Justice Holt.

(2) It was said that there was only one witness, whereas there should have been two. I do not think this objection was accurately taken. Assuming the possession and writing of the pamphlet to be an overt act of treason, it was proved by at least four witnesses, namely, one who found it on the prisoner's table, and three who swore it was his handwriting.

(3) It was said that the possession of the writing was not an overt act of treason, as it appeared only that the paper was in the prisoner's study, and not that he had published it, or that he meant to publish it, in furtherance of his design, and this I think was true; but, regard being had to the then state of the law, I do not think that the illegality of permitting the jury to treat the possession of the

[1] 9 St. Tr. 854.   [2] Ib. 854.

pamphlet as an overt act of treason was as clear as it would
be at present. [1] In 1663, Twyn, a printer, was executed
for treason, for printing a book much to the same effect as
Sidney's pamphlet. In Twyn's case no doubt there was a
much nearer approach to publication than in Sidney's; but
[2] Jeffreys's summing up (which is not very clearly reported)
seems to assume that the book was intended to be published
in connection with the conspiracy to make war on the King.
If it were so, I am not sure that it might not have amounted
to an overt act of a conspiracy to levy war, which was itself
held to be an overt act of imagining the King's death. By
a statute then in force, 13 Chas. 2. c. 1, it was enacted in substance that any declaration by writing, printing, or speaking
of an intention to compass the King's death, imprisonment,
or restraint, or to depose him, or levy war against him, should
be treason; but prosecutions were limited to six months after
the offence. There was no proof at all as to the time when
the pamphlet in Sidney's possession was written.

(4) Objections were taken to the indictment which I am
inclined to think were properly overruled.

(5) It was said that Jeffreys treated the prisoner brutally,
misled him as to the law, designedly interrupted him in his
defence, and summed up more like an advocate than a judge.
No doubt he disgraced himself; but I think he was right in
many of his remarks, and that Sidney did not understand
the law, and overrated the importance of various technicalities
on which he relied. When you have on the one side a
prisoner guilty of a crime which many people regarded, and
still regard, as an act of virtue, and on the other a judge
whose name is justly steeped in infamy, and when the judge
has to try the prisoner according to a law full of fiction and
uncertainty, obscure in some points, and irrational in others,
it is almost hopeless to do strict justice between them, and
it really is not worth the trouble to try to do so, for the
questions which would have to be determined for that purpose have long ceased to have any interest or importance.

I may, however, observe that the [3] grounds on which the

---

[1] 6 *St. Tr.* 514, and see Kelyng's *Reports*, p. 57.   [2] 9 *St. Tr.* 893.
[3] *Ib.* 695—696 and 996—997.

attainders of Russell and Sidney were reversed seem to me doubtful. They were in each case refusal of the challenge of jurors for want of freehold, and "partial and unjust "constructions of law" (unspecified). Any one who will read the arguments as to the question of the jurors will, I think, agree with me in saying that the law upon the subject was at that time utterly uncertain, there being no direct authority upon it till the question was settled by the Bill of Rights (1 Will. & Mary, st. 2, c. 2). This Act converted many doubtful propositions into law by saying that they were "antient rights and liberties," when all that could truly have been said was that it would have been well to act upon that supposition in the past and that for the future the matters stated should be held to be law. With regard to the "partial and unfair con-"structions of law," I have already spoken. In Sidney's case it was also said that "there was produced a paper found in the "closet of the said Algernon, supposed to be his handwriting, "which was not proved by the evidence of any one witness to "be written by him, but the jury was directed to believe it "by comparing it with other writings of the said Algernon." This recital is directly contradicted by the report of the trial. It is remarkable that the far stronger ground that there was no proof that he meant to publish the paper, or that it had any connection with the plot imputed to him, is not referred to. Perhaps the recollection of the 13 Chas. 2, c. 1, in force at the time of the trial explains the omission.

The trials of Russell and Sidney were followed by others which I must pass over with a very few words. Oates's trial for perjury was not, I think, unfair. Jeffreys treated him in parts of his defence with brutality, but Oates undoubtedly tried to bully the Court as he had done on former occasions. I cannot say that I think the sentence upon him too severe. To be flogged to death would have been an appropriate end for him; but though there are crimes which would justify the infliction of death by torture, it is wrong to pass such a sentence under false pretences. Perjury was not a capital crime, and ought not to have been treated as one.

Of the trials on the western circuit, after Monmouth's insurrection, little need be said, as they throw no light on the

ordinary administration of justice. I may, however, make CHAP. XI
one or two remarks on the case of Lady Lisle. It was cruel,
but legal, to sentence a woman to be burnt alive for harbouring two rebels for a night. The conviction was probably illegal
on the ground that Hicks, whom she harboured, had not been
convicted before her trial. Her attainder was reversed in
Parliament upon this ground, and [1] Foster, relying on the
authority of [2] Hale, treats this as good law. It can, no doubt,
be supported by some strong arguments, though others in the
contrary direction might be suggested; but the law was
vague. Hale gives no authority for his statement, and indeed
puts it forward in the second passage quoted only as his
opinion—" It seems to me." [3] I think that this is another of
the numerous instances in which there really was no definite
law at all, and in which the fact that a particular course was
taken by a cruel man for a bad purpose has been regarded
as proof that the course taken was illegal.

The conduct of Jeffreys in this trial· has made his memory
justly infamous; but there is one point in it on which a
remark arises. The most disgraceful part of the trial, or
rather the most notorious and glaring instance of brutality
which occurred in it, is the way in which the judge treated
the principal witness, Dunne, at whom he repeatedly [4] swore
and railed. It ought, however, to be said that Dunne was a
liar, and that, striking out the brutality and ferocity of his
language, Jeffreys's cross-examination was masterly, and not
only involved Dunne in lie after lie, but at last compelled
him to confess the truth. He wished no doubt, to save his
mistress's life, and kept back the essential part of the story
till he could face it out no longer.

Many other trials of this period I pass over unnoticed, though
they were of great interest. The case of Lord Delamere, who
was tried for high treason before Jeffreys, sitting as Lord

---

[1] P. 346.   [2] 1 Hale, *P. C.* 238, and 2 Hale, *F. C.*, 223.
[3] See Vol. II. p. 234-5.
[4] " Why, you impudent rascal." " But, you blockhead." " Why, thou
" vile wretch." " Jesus God, there is no sort of conversation nor human
" society to be kept with such people as these." " It seems that the saints
" have a certain charter for lying," &c.—11 *St. Tr.* 325—360. See Dunne's
confession of his falsehoods, 355—360. The whole passage deserves careful study
on many grounds.

CHAP. XI. High Steward with a jury of peers, deserves mention. The prisoner was clearly innocent, and proved his innocence, and was acquitted. The remarkable point in the case is that Jeffreys seems to have tried it with propriety and dignity. [1] A question arose on the trial whether the Court might adjourn till the next day. The lords triers obviously wished to do so. The judges, on being consulted on the lawfulness of an adjournment, refused to give an opinion ; and Jeffreys moderately and calmly refused to adjourn, considering it doubtful whether he had a right to do so.

The last of the trials to be noticed before the Revolution is the memorable case of the seven bishops. [2] Lord Macaulay's account of it is fuller and more lawyer-like than most of his notices of trials at this period, and I need only refer to it for the historical and picturesque elements of the case. In a legal point of view, the trial can be described only as chaotic. The four judges not only differed, but were obviously frightened, and would have been glad to get rid of the case on the technical ground that no publication was proved in Middlesex. Wrangles about the evidence and its effect, quarrels between the counsel, and occasional differences between the judges made up the greater part of the trial, and exhibited the administration of justice in a contemptible light. There was a total want of order, regularity, and dignity in the whole proceeding. The most curious part of it is, that all sides appear to have agreed that the falsehood of the matter alleged (the non-existence of the dispensing power) and the malice of the defendants must be left to the jury. The four judges gave contradictory directions. Wright, C.J., said, "I do take it to be a libel." Holloway, J., said he thought the bishops ought to be convicted, if the jury were " satisfied there was an ill intention of sedition or the like." Powell, J., said, " I cannot see, for my part, anything of " sedition, or of any other crime, fixed upon these reverend

---

[1] 11 *St. Tr.* 560—564.
[2] 12 *St. Tr.* 183. I think Lord Macaulay makes a little too much of Finch's interruption of the case, and a good deal too much of Somers's speech. He only repeated in a condensed shape what his leaders had said over and over again, besides I do not think the report can be more than an abridgment of what was really said.

" fathers;" and Allybone, J. said, "The Government here
" has published such a declaration as this that has been read,
" relating to matters of government, and shall or ought any-
" body to come and impeach that as illegal which the Govern-
" ment has done ? Truly, in my opinion, I do not think he
" should or ought." He added, " I think these venerable
" bishops did meddle with that which did not belong to
" them. They took upon them in a petitionary to contradict
" the actual exercise of the government, which, I think, no
" particular persons or irregular body may do." The result
is too well known to be noticed. Speaking merely as a lawyer,
I can only say that the law of libel at that time was so vague,
that it is difficult to say whether or not a perfectly modest
and respectful expression of the opinion that the king had
made a mistake was a libel. But I shall examine this
matter fully hereafter.

I have now completed what I had to say on the administration of criminal justice under the Stuarts after the Restoration. The most general observation which it suggests to me
is, that it brought to light and illustrated in the case of
eminent persons defects both in the law itself and in the
methods of procedure which must have produced a great
amount of obscure injustice and misery. There must have
been plenty of Oateses and Bedloes at the assizes and quarter
sessions who have never been heard of, and no doubt scores
or hundreds of obscure people suffered for common burglaries
and robberies of which they were quite as innocent as Stafford
was of the high treason for which he was convicted. There
certainly was, however, a considerable improvement in the
methods of trial during the seventeenth century. Prisoners
were not tortured (as they were in every other part of Europe) ;
witnesses were produced face to face, whom the prisoner could
cross-examine. The rules of evidence were beginning to be, to
some extent, though to a small extent, recognised and understood, and by the end of the century the evils of judicial
corruption and subserviency, and the horrors of a party warfare carried on by reciprocal prosecutions for treason alternately
instituted against each other, with fatal effect, by the chiefs of
contending parties, had made so deep an impression on the

CHAP. XI. public imagination, that a change of sentiment took place which from that time effectually prevented the scandals of the seventeenth century from being repeated. I have dwelt at length upon the second half of the seventeenth century because it was from its troubles and scandals that a better system arose, which has been by degrees improved into the one which is now administered amongst us.

V.—1688—1760.

The administration of criminal justice, after the Revolution, passed into quite a new phase. I should doubt whether much difference was made in the common course of justice, at the assizes and sessions, till very recent times; but from the Revolution to our own day political parties have been recognised parts of the body politic, and political differences have been treated as matters on which contending parties can differ without carrying their disputes to the deadly extremity of prosecutions for treason. There have been plenty of political trials since the Revolution, but from a variety of causes they have been conducted in most cases fairly, in some instances more or less unfairly, but never scandalously. The legislative result of the scandals of the seventeenth century upon criminal procedure was slight. The most important was the enactment that the judges should hold office, not at the pleasure of the Crown, but during good behaviour. This deeply affected the whole administration of justice. The changes in procedure were less important; and applied entirely to trials for high treason. As to them it was enacted, [1] in 1695, that persons indicted for high treason or misprision of treason should have a copy of the indictment five (afterwards extended to ten) days before trial, and be allowed to have counsel and witnesses upon oath; and that the treason should be proved by two witnesses, either both to one overt act, or each to one of two overt acts of the same kind of treason. [2] In 1708 the prisoner was also allowed to have a list of the witnesses and of the jury ten days before his trial. [3] In 1702 it was enacted that in cases of treason and felony

---

[1] 7 & 8 Will. 3, c. 3.   [2] 7 Anne, c. 27, s. 14.   [3] 1 Anne, st. 2, c. 9.

the prisoner's witnesses should be sworn, as well as the witnesses for the Crown. These were the only legislative changes which the scandals of the trials in the days of the later Stuarts produced; and nothing can set in a clearer light the slightness of the manner in which the public attention was then, or indeed till a far later time, directed to the defects of the criminal law.

Many of the trials which took place in the reigns of William III., Anne, George I., and George II. are deeply interesting on various accounts, and especially on account of the strong light which they throw, not only on the history, but still more on the manners of the time; but in a legal point of view they call for little remark. As time passes, the differences between our own days and those of the seventeenth century gradually pass away. From the first there is a complete absence of fierceness and brutality. At first there are [1] a few instances in which prisoners are questioned. For a considerable time the witnesses are allowed to tell their own story at length in their own way, and the restriction as to not swearing the prisoner's witnesses is kept up till the passing of the statute already referred to. I am not sure that the most striking feature in the political trials of the first part of the eighteenth century is not to be found in the fact that the reforms about giving prisoners indicted for treason a copy of the indictment, lists of jurors and witnesses, and the right to be defended by counsel, made in practice so very little difference. The truth is, that after the Revolution few, if any, prisoners were tried for high treason except people clearly proved to have committed what was held to be treason; and I do not think that counsel had learnt the art of defending prisoners zealously or impressively. For instance, a very poor defence was made in the famous cases of [2] Dammaree and others, who, for having taken part in a riot designed to pull down meeting-houses, were convicted of high treason by levying of war, though both the facts and the law were of such a nature as to give an opportunity for a great effort.

[1] See e.g. the trial of Harrison for the murder of Dr. Clench, in which the prisoner was questioned at some length by Holt, 12 *St. Tr* 859.
[2] 15 *Ib.* 522 611.

CHAP. XI.　The private trials which took place during this period were
of extraordinary interest, and set the manners of the time
before the reader with an authenticity and life which, in
my opinion, is more curious and entertaining than any
romance ever written.　To refer to a very few instances:
the [1] trials for piracy, common down to the reign of George
II., bring to light a chapter of history rapidly passing into
oblivion; the trial of [2] Hathaway as a cheat and impostor
marks the point at which witchcraft was coming to be recognised in its true light; [3] the trial of Beau Fielding for
bigamy is a more grotesque specimen of the manners of the
contemporaries of Swift and Addison and Steele than can be
found in any of their writings; the [4] two trials of Lord
Mohun for murderous duels, if indeed the first was not rather
a premeditated assassination, illustrate another side of the
life of the times.　[5] A whole series of prosecutions of the
officers of the Fleet Prison for the murder of prisoners by
barbarous ill-usage throws light upon another dark side of
the administration of justice in the eighteenth century.
Some of the trials again are, to me at least, much more
impressive than poetry or fiction; for instance, the [6] trial
of Mary Blandy at Oxford, in 1752, for poisoning her father,
and the [7] trial of a gang of smugglers at Chichester, in 1749,
for the murder of certain revenue officers.　In a legal point
of view little is to be said of these proceedings.　They were
all conducted fairly enough, and in a manner not essentially
different from that in which such trials would be conducted
at present.　One or two general observations, however, arise
upon the subject.

Hardly a trial of importance before the Revolution is
reported in which the Government is not interested directly
or indirectly.　Thus even in the case of Count Coningsmark,

---

[1] Major Stede, 15 *St. Tr.* 1231 ; Dawson, 13 *Ib.* 451 ; Green, 14 *Ib.* 1199 ;
Captain Kidd and others, *Ib.* 147 ; Captain Quelch and others, *Ib.* 1067.
　[2] *Ib.* 639.　　　　　　　　　　　　　　　　　　　[3] *Ib.* 1327.
　[4] In 1694 (12 *Ib.* 949) and in 1699 (13 *Ib.* 1033). This ruffian was killed in
a duel with the Duke of Hamilton in 1712, as the readers of Swift's *Journal*
and Mr. Thackeray's *Esm-nd* will remember.
　[5] See the trials of Huggins, Bainbridge, and Aston, in 17 *St. Tr.*
298—626.
　[6] 18 *Ib.* 1118.　　　　　　　　　　[7] Jackson and others, *Ib.* 1070.

whose crime had in itself no political importance, Charles II. let Reresby, the committing magistrate, see that he was favourable to the prisoner, and thus undoubtedly exercised a decisive influence upon the behaviour of the judges at the trial. But all through the period between 1688 and 1760 a feature presents itself in criminal trials which I believe to this day to be absolutely peculiar to this country and to countries which have sprung from it, and which has given its special colour and character to our whole method of procedure. In all other countries the discovery and punishment of crime has been treated as pre-eminently the affair of the Government, and has in all its stages been under the management of representatives of the Government. In England it has been left principally to individuals who considered themselves to have been wronged, the judge's duty being to see fair play between the prisoner and the prosecutor, even if the prosecutor happened to be the Crown. In my account of the growth of the system of criminal procedure I have given some of the reasons which account for this state of things, but I have little doubt that the scandals of the State trials before the Revolution, and the change in the position of the judges which was one of the consequences, were the principal historical causes of its prevailing.

A large proportion of the trials to which I have already referred might be cited as illustrations of this. I will mention by way of illustration some of the circumstances of two which are on other grounds very remarkable.

The first to be mentioned is the [1] trial of Spencer Cowper for the murder of Sarah Stout. Cowper was a man of rank and distinction. His brother, the first Earl Cowper, who was Chancellor in the reign of Queen Anne, was at the time of the trial member for Hertford, and his family were then, as now, one of the first in the county of Hertford. Spencer Cowper himself was made a judge in 1727, and at the time of his trial was a barrister on the home circuit. Sarah Stout was an unmarried Quakeress of twenty-six, the daughter of a wealthy father, who had died, leaving a widow, on whom,

---

[1] 13 *St. Tr.* 1105; and see Lord Campbell's *Life of Lord Cowper.*

however, the daughter was not dependent. She was intimate with both Spencer Cowper and his brother and their wives, who seem to have cultivated the society of the Stouts for electioneering purposes. The two Cowpers were both on the circuit, and Spencer Cowper at one time lodged with the Stouts. On the spring circuit of 1699 he intended to occupy lodgings which his brother had taken and would have to pay for, but having dined at the Stouts' was pressed by Miss Stout to sleep there, which he agreed to do. He afterwards supped there, and remained alone with her till near eleven. Miss Stout called in the servant, and in Cowper's presence ordered her to warm his bed, which she did. Whilst doing so she heard the house-door shut, and coming down found both Cowper and Miss Stout absent, and saw neither of them again though she sat up all night. Cowper soon afterwards, namely, at about eleven, called, according to several witnesses, at an inn about a quarter of a mile from the Stouts', and returned to his own lodgings a little after. Miss Stout was never seen alive again, but early next morning her body was found in a mill-stream entangled in some stakes. There was much evidence as to the exact position in which the body was found. All of it, to say the very least, is quite consistent with her having been washed down the stream for some distance and having been pressed slightly upwards by the force of the stream against the slope of the stakes. An inquest was held, and the jury returned a verdict that she had drowned herself whilst insane. It was proved that she had been in a melancholy state of mind.

Various rumours to the disadvantage of her character having got abroad, and the Quakers being dreadfully scandalised at the notion that one of their community should commit suicide under such circumstances, Cowper was indicted for murder, and tried at the following Hertford assizes. The case is extremely curious, both as supplying nearly the earliest instance of a trial depending largely on the evidence of experts, and as an early instance of the extent to which criminal trials in England are private litigations. The neighbourhood was divided into parties. The Stouts collected a body of doctors to establish the proposition thus

propounded by the counsel for the Crown:—"It is con-
" trary to nature that any persons that drown themselves
" should float upon the water. We have sufficient evidence
" that it is a thing that never was : if persons come alive
" into the water, then they sink ; if dead, then they swim."
There were also witnesses to prove the proposition that water
must be found in the stomach of a person who died of drowning, and that its absence was inconsistent with death so caused.
Miss Stout, it was said, floated, and her stomach contained
no water. On these grounds, and indeed on these grounds
only, it was asserted that she was murdered, and as Cowper
was last seen with her, it was inferred that he must have
murdered her. In our days such a case would not be
allowed to go to the jury ; but in 1699 it was pressed with
the utmost vehemence and pertinacity, not only against
Cowper, but against three other persons as to whom there was
no evidence whatever, except that they were at an inn at
Hertford that night, and were said to have had some conversation about Miss Stout which might be regarded as suspicious. Cowper defended himself with great tact and
vigour. He contradicted the evidence of the experts in a
way which still shows any one who reads the case that
he was fighting with a perfectly idle and ignorant superstition. He also contradicted the evidence as to the position
of the body when found. He also gave some, though I
think not strong, evidence of an *alibi;* and above all he
produced letters from Miss Stout to himself which seemed to
show that she had fallen passionately in love with him, and
he declared that when he refused her advances she rushed out,
and, as he supposed, drowned herself. He called many witnesses to show the state of mind in which she was at
the time.

The judge, Baron Hatsell, behaved with a languid indifference which even now raises a feeling of contempt. He
continually grumbled at the length of the trial. [1] " Do not
" flourish too much, Mr. Cowper." " Mr. Cowper, do you
" mean to spend so much time with every witness ? " He

[1] 13 *St. Tr.* 1151.

CHAP. XI. [1] ingenuously confessed that he could make nothing of the
medical evidence (which was quite easy if he had only given
his mind to it), and he modestly concluded his summing up
thus :—" I am sensible I have omitted many things ; but
" I am a little faint, and cannot repeat any more of the
" evidence."

The prisoners were all acquitted, but the matter did not
stop there. An appeal was brought, but it went off in a
wrangle too technical to be worth noticing. The case
excited great and widespread interest, and was the occasion
of numerous pamphlets. It would be difficult to find a
more remarkable specimen of the way in which a trial was
then, and may be still, a battle between private persons,
the one seeking with passionate earnestness the other's life,
and the other as desperately defending it ; the attitude of the
representative of the public being one of dignified indifference, slightly tempered in this particular case by impatience
and fatigue. On this last point I may observe that the rule
which prevailed then and long afterwards of finishing all
criminal trials in one day must often have produced cruel
injustice. Many of the cases I have referred to were tried
in a superficial, perfunctory way, and many of the judges
played their parts little better than Baron Hatsell. Few
judges are able to do justice to a complicated case after a
sitting of much more than eight hours, and it is still more
unusual for jurymen (quite unaccustomed to sustained attention, which involves a greater physical effort than those
who have not tried it might suppose) to be able to attend to
what is said, and to deliberate on it to any purpose, after ten
hours.

Many other instances of the peculiarity of English criminal
law, to which I am referring, might be given but I will confine myself to one which is remarkable, amongst other reasons,
because it has some resemblance to the famous case of

---

[1] " You have heard also what the doctors and surgeons said on the one side
" and the other concerning the swimming and sinking of dead bodies in the
" water ; but I can find no certainty in it, and I leave it to your consideration.
" The doctors and surgeons have talked a great deal to this purpose, and
" of the water going into the lungs or the thorax ; but, unless you have more
" skill in anatomy than I, you would not be much edified by it."—
13 *St. Tr.* 1188—1189.

Orton, namely the [1] trial of Elizabeth Canning for perjury, in 1754.

In 1753 Canning charged two women, Mary Squires and Susannah Wells, with having robbed her of her stays, and imprisoned her for a month in a house at Enfield Wash, to which house she was, according to her statement, taken by John Squires, the son of Mary, and another person unknown, the object being to induce her to become a prostitute. She escaped, she said, on the 29th January, and on the 31st went with a warrant to Enfield, where she found the prisoner and gave her in custody. In this story Canning was corroborated by one Virtue Hall, who said she was present on the occasion of the robbery, and saw John Squires bring Elizabeth Canning to his mother's house. Witnesses were called for Squires to prove that at the time in question she and her son John were at Abbotsbury, in Dorsetshire. The prisoners were convicted, and both were sentenced to death; but Virtue Hall recanted her evidence, and suspicion being aroused on these grounds as to the propriety of the verdict, Canning was prosecuted for perjury. Her trial excited the same sort of interest as that of Orton. Parties of Canningites and anti-Canningites were formed. The trial lasted seven days, which at that time was something unheard of. Numbers of witnesses were called, who traced the movements of Squires and the party of gipsies to which she belonged from place to place during the whole of the important period, giving vivid descriptions of every kind of country scene at which they had been present on their wanderings. They were traced on their travels through January, 1753, from South Parrot, in Dorsetshire, to Abbotsbury, Dorchester, Basingstoke, Bagshot, Brentford, and Enfield, which they did not reach till the 24th January. There they lodged with the woman Wells, and evidence was given that Wells's house and furniture were quite unlike the place in which Canning at first said she had been confined, though she pretended to identify them when it became necessary for her to fix upon some place as the scene of her alleged imprisonment.

---

[1] 19 *St. Tr.* 252. Fielding acted as committing magistrate in the case of Squires and Wells. He also advised upon the case as counsel—a strange mixture of functions according to modern ideas.

Such, shortly, were the leading points in the case for the prosecution. They are stated with admirable skill and clearness in the opening of Serjeant Davy, followed by Mr. Morton. The defence has almost greater interest. It deserves to be read and studied by all who care for questions of evidence; but I could not describe it without entering into details too minute to be stated here. Canning was convicted, and transported for seven years. The case gave rise to a great number of pamphlets, and is remarkable not only for the reasons I have already given, but because it is perhaps the first specimen to be found of those elaborately conducted criminal trials in which no time or expense is spared on either side, and in which all the characteristics of English criminal law are seen at their best.

From the middle of the eighteenth century to our own time there has been but little change in the character of criminal trials, and it is unnecessary to give further illustrations of them. The most remarkable change introduced into the practice of the courts was the process by which the old rule which deprived prisoners of the assistance o1 counsel in trials for felony was gradually relaxed. A practice sprung up, the growth of which cannot now be traced, by which counsel were allowed to do everything for prisoners accused of felony except addressing the jury for them. In the remarkable case of William Barnard, tried in 1758, for sending a threatening letter to the Duke of Marlborough, his counsel seem to have cross-examined all the witnesses fully, in such a way, too, at times, as to be nearly equivalent to speaking for the prisoner, " *e.g.* : " *Q.* It has been said he went away with a smile. Pray, " my Lord Duke, might not that smile express the conscious- " ness of his innocence as well as anything else ? *A.* I shall " leave that to the Great Judge."

On the other hand, at the trial of Lord Ferrers two years afterwards, the prisoner was obliged to cross-examine the witnesses without the aid of counsel and, what seems even harder, to examine for himself witnesses called to prove the defence of insanity which he set up.

Since the middle of the eighteenth century proceedings of

[1] 19 *St. Tr.* 815.   [2] *Ib.* 839.

the highest importance, and involving momentous changes in
the substantive criminal law, have been effected partly by
legislation, partly, though to a much smaller extent, by judicial
decisions. Of these I shall speak in my chapters on the different branches of the substantive law ; but I do not think that
the actual administration of justice, or the course of trials has
altered much since the beginning of the reign of George III.
Its general character has no doubt been affected to a considerable extent by the changes made in the law itself, by the
course of thought on legal and political, religious and moral
subjects, and by many other influences, but it can hardly be
said to have had any history of its own, and apart from its
connection with the current events of the time. The only
change which has made any great difference between the trials
of our own days and those of 120 years ago was made by [1] the
Act which allowed prisoners accused of felony to make their full
defence by counsel; and this, after all, has only put trials for
felonies, such as robbery or burglary, on the same footing
as trials for perjury, cheating, and other misdemeanours.
Indeed, if we have regard to the powers of cross-examination
which were conceded to counsel in the course of the eighteenth
century, the change was less important than it may at first
sight seem to have been.

The result of the history of the administration of criminal
justice in England which I have thus sketched—for it is a
slight though not, I hope, an incorrect sketch—may be thus
shortly summarized :—

Criminal justice was originally a rude substitute for, or
limitation upon, private war, the question of guilt or innocence, so far as it was entertained at all, being decided by
the power of the suspected person to produce compurgators
or by his good fortune in facing an ordeal. The introduction
of trial by combat, though a little less irrational, was in
principle a relapse towards private war, but it was gradually
restricted and practically superseded many centuries before
it was formally abolished.

Trial by jury originated in the adaptation to- the purpose

[1] 6 & 7 Will. 4, c. 114, s. 1.

of the administration of justice of the process commonly in use in the eleventh and twelfth centuries for obtaining information as to matters of fact, namely, collecting an inquest or body of persons supposed to be acquainted with the subject and taking their sworn statement about it. The members of the inquest were originally witnesses, and, even if they derived their knowledge from other witnesses, they, and not their informants, were responsible for the truth of their verdict. By slow degrees they acquired the character of judges of fact informed by witnesses. This process lasted from the first origin of juries in the twelfth or thirteenth centuries down to the sixteenth century, when we have the first fairly trustworthy records of actual trials.

Side by side with trial by jury during this period, a system was developing itself in the Star Chamber, and similar courts, of a trial by written pleadings, bills, answers, interrogatories, and affidavits, like those which were afterwards in use in the Court of Chancery in civil cases. It exercised a strong influence over trial by jury, and its effect can be traced in all the criminal proceedings which took place under the Tudors, James I. and Charles I. The administration of criminal justice at this time was also affected to a considerable extent by the civil law trial by witnesses, though, on the one hand, it never thoroughly adopted torture, which was practically an essential part of that system, nor did it, on the other, admit, except in the one case of treason, the necessity for two witnesses, which rendered torture necessary in countries where it prevailed.

The Civil Wars broke down this system, and gave to trial by jury an undisputed supremacy, which has now lasted for more than two centuries, in the administration of criminal justice; but the experience of the reigns of Charles II. and James II. showed, first, that juries might be quite as unjust and tyrannical as the Star Chamber; next, that they were equally likely to be unjust on any side in politics; and, lastly, that the true theory of judicial evidence was at that time not understood, and that, so far as it was understood, it had little influence upon verdicts.

Lastly, after the Revolution, a decisive victory having been

won by one of the great parties of the State, the administration of criminal justice was set upon a firm and dignified
basis, and so became decorous and humane; and as it was
mainly left in the hands of private persons, between whom
the judges were really and substantially indifferent, the
questions which were involved came to be fully and fairly
investigated, each party to the contest doing the best he
could to establish his own view of the case in which he was
interested. The rapid growth of physical science, and indeed of every branch of knowledge, which has been one great
characteristic of the history of the last two centuries, naturally influenced the administration of justice as well as other
things, and the final result of the long process which I have
been trying to describe seems to be that in criminal trials
questions of fact are investigated as nearly in the same spirit
as other matters of fact as the differences inherent in the
nature of the processes will admit. It would be interesting
to trace the steps by which this came about, but such an
inquiry belongs rather to the history of the rules of evidence
than to the history of the administration of criminal justice.
The last-mentioned history ends at the point at which the
present forms are fully established, and at which the process
carried on under them begins to develop itself, in accordance
with the general intellectual movement of the age.

CHAPTER XII.

[1] DESCRIPTION OF MODERN CRIMINAL TRIALS.

CH. XII. I PASS now to the consideration of modern criminal trials, by which expression I understand criminal trials as they now are, and as they have been for the last 120 years; for although some variations in the practice of the courts have taken place during that period, the resemblance between the proceedings of our own time and those of 1760 is so strong, that in reading the reports of the proceedings relating to Wilkes, Lord George Gordon, Tooke, Hardy, or Thelwall, a lawyer feels himself quite as much at home as when he reads the reports of contemporary trials in the newspapers of the day. I propose to give some account of each of the most important of the stages in the criminal trials which take place amongst us from day to day. In doing so I rely mainly upon the acquaintance with them which I have acquired by nearly thirty years' experience as a barrister and as a judge. During these thirty years nearly a quarter of the period which has elapsed since the beginning of George III.'s reign, no change in the procedure important enough to notice has taken place except the introduction of the second speech of the counsel for the prosecution, which I think of doubtful advantage.

The first step in the trial properly so called is the opening speech of the counsel for the Crown. He is expected to confine himself—except under very special and unusual circumstances—to a quiet account of the different facts to be proved, and of their bearing upon each other, and on the guilt of the prisoner. This statement is often of decisive importance,

---

[1] See *Dig. Crim. Proc.* arts. 283-300.

for it produces the first impression made upon the minds of
the judge and jury, the indictment being a neutral, formal
document, wholly unlike a Continental *acte d'accusation.*
It is pleasant to be able to say that, as a rule, subject
only to rare exceptions, extreme calmness and impartiality
in opening criminal cases is characteristic of the English
bar. It is very rare to hear arguments pressed against
prisoners with any special warmth of feeling or of language :
one reason for which no doubt is, that any counsel who
did so would probably defeat his own object. Apart,
however, from this, it is worthy of observation that
eloquence either in prosecuting or defending prisoners is
almost unknown and unattempted at the bar. The
occasion seldom permits of it, and the whole atmosphere
of English courts in these days is unfavourable to anything like an appeal to the feelings—though, of course,
in particular cases, topics of prejudice are introduced. This
characteristic of English courts has existed for a considerable
time. M. Cottu, who was sent by the French Government
in 1822 to inquire into the administration of criminal justice
in England, and who made an interesting report on the subject, thus describes the opening speeches of counsel :—
" [1] The plaintiff's counsel then lays before the jury a summary
" of the case, which is nothing but a more detailed and
" circumstantial repetition of the indictment, guarding him-
" self, however, from every sort of invective against the
" prisoner, and making no reflections on his depravity.
" Facts must speak ; the counsel is forbidden to excite feel-
" ings which must be called forth by them alone." This
description is as true now as it was sixty years ago. The
opening speech for the prosecution is followed by the examination of the witnesses, who are first examined in chief by
the counsel for the Crown, then cross-examined by the
counsel for the prisoner if he is defended by counsel, or by
the prisoner himself if he is not, and then re-examined by
the counsel for the Crown. The judge and the jury can also

---

[1] *On the Administration of Criminal Justice in England,* by M. Cottu
(English translation, 1822). The translation is not a good one. I have not
seen the original.

ask such questions as they may think necessary. The object
of examination-in-chief is to make the witness tell what he
knows relevant to the isssue in a consecutive manner and
without wandering from the point. The object of cross-
examination is twofold, namely, to prove any facts favourable
to the prisoner which may not have been stated by the witness when examined in chief, and to bring to light any
matter calculated to shake the weight of his evidence by
damaging his character, or by showing that he has made
inconsistent statements on former occasions, or that his
opportunities of observation, or his memory as to what passed,
were defective. The object of re-examination is to clear up
any matter brought out in cross-examination which admits
of explanation.

The main rule as to the manner in which the examination
of a witness must be conducted is, that leading questions,
that is questions which suggest the desired answer, must not
be asked by the side which calls the witness, and to which
he is presumed to be favourable, but that they may be
asked by the party against whom he is called and to
whom he is presumed to be unfavourable : in other words,
leading questions may not be asked in an examination-in-
chief, or in a re-examination, but they may be asked in cross-
examination.

This rule, however, is liable to be modified at the discretion
of the judge if the witness appears to be in fact unfavourable
to the party by whom he is called, and to be keeping back
matter with which he is acquainted. A common instance of
this is when a witness refuses or hesitates to state at the trial
what he stated in his depositions before the magistrate. The
great care bestowed upon the examination of the witnesses,
and the importance attached to such rules as these, are
characteristic features in an English trial; and though they
are sometimes carried to an apparently pedantic length,
there can be no doubt of their substantial value.

Their proper application requires experience and skill.
It is not easy to question a person in such a way as to
draw from him the knowledge which he possesses on a
given subject in the form of a continuous statement in the

order of time, the questions being so contrived as to keep
alive the attention and memory of the witness without being
open to the objection that they suggest the answer which
he is to give. The power of doing so can be acquired only
by experience joined with quickness of observation and
power of sympathy; and it may be compared, not inappro-
priately, to the management of a horse's bridle. The present
method of examining-in-chief must, to judge from the *State
Trials*, be at least as old as the beginning of the reign of
George III. In earlier times, as I have already observed,
the witness was allowed to tell his own story, and I have
little doubt that the present practice was introduced in order
to keep witnesses to the point, and as a consequence of the
recognition of the rule that all evidence must be confined
to the issue which, like other rules of evidence, found its
way from the civil into the criminal courts I should think
early in the eighteenth century.

The examination-in-chief is followed by the cross-examination. Cross-examination is a highly characteristic part of
an English trial, whether criminal or civil, and hardly any
of the contrasts between the English and Continental systems strikes an English lawyer so forcibly as its absence
in the Continental system. Its history may be collected
from the particulars given in the last chapter. So long as
prisoners were really undefended by counsel in serious
cases, their cross-examination of the witnesses against them
was trifling and of little or no importance, though they
did cross-examine to a greater or less extent. When they
were allowed to have counsel to cross-examine, but not
to speak for them, the cross-examination tended to become
a speech thrown into the form of questions, and it has ever
since retained this character to a greater or less extent.
Cross-examination is no doubt an absolutely indispensable
instrument for the discovery of truth, but it is the part of the
whole system which is most liable to abuse, and which, in my
opinion, ought to be kept most carefully and jealously under
control by the judge; but I do not think that the unfavourable criticisms often made upon it by unprofessional persons
are well founded.

    In discussing the subject of criminal trials and the procedure, as to evidence and otherwise, to be observed upon them, people are usually tempted to forget their real charactér. Cool, unexcited bystanders, often demand that a criminal trial should be conducted as quietly as a scientific inquiry, and are disgusted if any course is allowed to be taken which compromises the interests or character of third parties, or which leads to any sort of unseemly discussion. The truth is that litigation of all sorts, and especially litigation which assumes the form of a criminal trial, is a substitute for private war, and is, and must be, conducted in a spirit of hostility which is often fervent and even passionate. No man will allow himself to be deprived of character, or liberty, or possibly of life, without offering the most strenuous resistance in his power, or without seeking, in many cases, to retaliate on his opponent and his opponent's supporters. A trial of any importance is always more or less of a battle, and one object of the rules of evidence and procedure is to keep such warfare within reasonable bounds, and to prevent the combatants from inflicting upón each other, and upon third parties, injuries, the inflicting of which is not absolutely essential to the purposes of the combat. Such injuries, however, as are essential to the object in view must be permitted. Within its proper limits the battle must be fought with swords and not with foils. Unless this is clearly understood it is practically impossible to form a sound judgment upon the limits to be imposed upon cross-examination.

    These limits can hardly be defined with precision, nor do I think that it would ever be practicable to lay down rules upon the subject, which would not leave much to the discretion of the judge as well as to the honourable feeling of counsel. Some limits, however, may I think be described distinctly enough to answer many practical purposes.

    First, the difference between cross-examinations and examinations-in-chief, has reference rather to the question, What facts are relevant? than to the question, What proof must be given of a fact admitted to be relevant? In cross-examination the great object is to test the memory, the power of observation, and the good faith of the witness. Many matters are relevant to the probability of a witness's observing a fact correctly, and reporting it accurately, which are not relevant to the occurrence of the fact itself. It may thus often be proper to ask a witness under cross-examination whether at a given time he had not heard or done certain things, which might predispose him to take a prejudiced view of circumstances described, but which are quite irrelevant to the main facts to which he deposes.

Suppose, for instance, that a servant is charged with theft, and that a fellow-servant deposes to conduct which is at first sight suspicious, it may be very important to know whether the common master of both had set the one servant to watch the other, and had communicated to the one the suspicions which he entertained against the other. This would not be admissible upon the examination-in-chief, because the master's suspicion is not regarded as relevant to the guilt of the accused servant, but it may well be admitted in cross-examination, because it is relevant to the probable accuracy of the witness's observation.

Assuming, however, that the relevancy of the fact to be proved is not in question, its existence must be proved in precisely the same manner in the case of a cross-examination as in the case of an examination-in-chief. If, for instance, it is necessary to prove the contents of a document, the document itself, or such secondary evidence of it as the nature of the case permits or requires to be given, must be produced, whether it is proved in chief or upon cross-examination.

The most difficult point as to cross-examination is the question how far a witness may be cross-examined to his credit by being asked about transactions irrelevant to the matter at issue, except so far as they tend to show that the witness is not to be believed upon his oath.

No doubt such questions may be oppressive and odious. They may constitute a means of gratifying personal malice of the basest kind, and of deterring witnesses from coming forward to discharge a duty to the public. At the same time it is impossible to devise any rule for restricting the latitude which at present exists upon the subject, without doing cruel injustice. I have frequently

CH. XII.   known cases in which evidence of decisive importance was procured by asking people of apparent respectability questions which, when first put, appeared to be offensive and insulting in the highest degree. I remember a case in which a solicitor's clerk was indicted for embezzlement. His defence was that his employer had brought a false charge against him to conceal (I think) forgery committed by himself. The employer seemed so respectable and the prisoner so discreditable that [1] the prisoner's counsel returned his brief rather than ask the questions suggested by his client. The prisoner thereupon asked the questions himself, and in a few minutes satisfied every person in court that what he had suggested was true. I have in the same way heard of a woman, who seemed perfectly respectable, being compelled to admit that she had hidden in her servant's box articles which she charged the servant with stealing, and of a constable who was compelled by the late Serjeant Ludlow to confess that he had hidden forged bank-notes in the pocket of a man tried for being in possession of them. It is also to be remembered that cross-examination to credit may be conducted in very different ways. It is one thing to throw an insulting question coarsely and roughly in the face of a witness. It is quite another thing to follow up a point by questions justified by the circumstances. I remember an occasion when a most modest, respectable-looking woman swore to an alibi on the prisoner's behalf. She was cross-examined (without instructions) as follows :—Q. : Are you sure it was the same man ? A. : Oh, yes. Q. : Did you know him before ? A. : Yes, I knew him before (there was an expression in her eyes as she said this which led her questioner to go further). Q. : Did you know him well ? A. : Yes, well. Q. : Very well indeed ? A. : Yes. Q. : Did you live in the same house ? A. : Yes. Q. : Are you his wife ? A. : No. Q. : Do you live with him as his wife ? A. : Yes.

The most difficult cases of all are those in which the imputation is well founded, but is so slightly connected with the matter in issue that its truth ought not to affect the credibility of the witness in reference to the matter on which he

---

[1] The late Mr. Adams, afterwards Attorney-General for Hong Kong.

testifies. The fact that a woman had an illegitimate child at eighteen, is hardly a reason for not believing her at forty, when she swears that she locked up her house safely when she went to bed at night, and found the kitchen window broken open and her husband's boots gone when she got up in the morning.

Cases, however, may be imagined in which a real connection may be traced between acts of profligacy and a man's credibility on matters in no apparent way connected with them. Seduction and adultery usually involve as gross a breach of faith as perjury, and if a man claimed credit on any subject of importance, the fact that he had been convicted of perjury would tend to discredit him. No general rule can be laid down in matters of this sort. All that can be said is that whilst the power of cross-examining to a witness's credit is [1] essential to the administration of justice, it is of the highest importance that both judges and counsel should bear in mind the abuse to which it is liable, and should do their best not to ask, or permit to be asked, questions conveying reproaches upon character, except in cases in which there is a reasonable ground to believe that they are necessary.

There is another matter connected with cross-examination in which there is no room for doubt as to the duty of counsel, and as to the duty incumbent upon judges to enforce that duty stringently. The legitimate object of cross-examination is to bring to light relevant matters of fact which would otherwise pass unnoticed. It is not unfrequently converted into an occasion for the display of wit, and for obliquely insulting witnesses. It is not uncommon to put a question in a form which is in itself an insult, or to preface a question or receive an answer with an insulting observation. This naturally provokes retorts, and cross-examination so conducted ceases to fulfil its legitimate purpose, and becomes a trial of wit and presence of mind which may amuse the audience, but is inconsistent with the dignity of a court of justice, and unfavourable to the object of ascertaining the truth. When such a scene

---

[1] As illustrations of such examinations see the cross-examination of Lutterloh by Dunning in 1781 (21 *St. Tr.* 746—54) and the cross-examination of Castles, the spy, by Sir C. Wetherell in 1817 (32 *St. Tr.* 284).

Ch. XII. takes place the judge is the person principally to blame.
He has a right on all occasions to exercise the power
of reproving observations which are not questions at all,
of preventing questions from being put in an improper form,
and of stopping examinations which are not necessary for any
legitimate purpose.

I have already given the history of cross-examination in
general. The history of cross-examination to credit is a
separate matter. As I have shown in the chapter on trials the
practice of the court in the seventeenth century was to allow
great latitude in calling witnesses to discredit witnesses for the
Crown by showing almost any sort of disgraceful conduct on
their part, but witnesses were not allowed to be discredited
by cross-examination. By degrees this practice was reversed and the modern rule substituted for it. The rules
upon the subject are stated in my *Digest of the Law of
Evidence*, Articles 129—133. The history of these rules
is curious. In the seventeenth century, as I have already
shown, evidence defaming a witness was permitted, but
he was not allowed to be cross-examined as to his character. By degrees cross-examination as to character came
into use, but evidence defaming a witness's character was
allowed at the same time. The most modern and most remarkable instance of this which I can cite occurred in the
trials for the Irish rebellion of 1798. [1] On the trial of the
Sheares, Captain Armstrong, the principal witness against
them, was accused of disloyalty, of holding atheistical opinions,
and of cruelty in the suppression of rebellion, and this having
been denied on cross-examination several witnesses were
called to prove it. On the [2] trials of Byrne, M'Cann, and
Oliver Bond, Reynolds was the principal witness. In cross-
examination questions were asked him suggesting that he
had poisoned his mother-in-law and committed other gross
offences. He denied the imputations made against him, and

---

[1] 27 *St. Tr.* Cross-examination of Armstrong, 314—319. Evidence in contradiction, 347—358.

[2] *Ib.* See Reynolds's examination and cross-examination in Byrne's case,
469—479; and see the evidence of Eleanor Dwyer, p. 499. Most of the
witnesses against Reynolds, however, confined themselves to the general assertion that he was not to be believed on his oath. They gave their reasons on
cross-examination. This is the modern practice.

witnesses were called to prove some of them. This is no
longer allowed on account of its obvious inconvenience and
unfairness. It is inconvenient because a trial so conducted
has a tendency to swell to unmanageable dimensions. It is
unfair because it puts the witness on his trial for every act
of his life without notice. The modern rule accordingly is
that when defamatory questions are asked the witness's
answer must be taken, though he may be indicted for perjury if he swears falsely. He may, however, be impeached
by witnesses who will swear in general terms that he is not
worthy of credit on his oath, and if such witnesses are asked
why they say so they can answer that they know the imputa-
tation which he denied on oath to be true in fact. Such
evidence is now very rarely given. I can remember only one
case in which it decided the issue of a trial. That case
occurred very lately in a trial before me for rape. The
prosecutrix in that case was shown in the manner just
described to be a person on whom it was impossible to rely,
and the jury stopped the case.

[1] The rules as to the relevancy of facts and as to the
proof of relevant facts, are, speaking generally, the same in
relation to criminal as in relation to civil proceedings, for
the manner in which a fact is to be proved has no necessary
connection with the use to which it is to be applied when it
has been proved. If it is necessary to show that a man is
dead the fact must be proved in the same way, whether it is
proved in a criminal trial for murder or on the trial of a
civil action for the recovery of an estate. Moreover the
principles which determine whether or no a given fact is
either in issue or is or is not relevant to the issue, are the same
whatever may be the nature of the issue. Some of the more
detailed rules of evidence, however, apply exclusively, and
others most frequently to criminal cases, and as they give
much of its special character to an English criminal trial, I
will refer to the most important of them.

In the first place, I may mention the general presumption of
innocence which, though by no means confined to the criminal

---

[1] As to the rules of evidence in general see my *Digest of the Law of Evidence*
(4th edition, Macmillan).

Ch. XII. law, pervades the whole of its administration. This rule is thus
expressed in my [1] *Digest of the Law of Evidence,* " If the com-
" mission of a crime is directly in issue in any proceeding, civil
" or criminal, it must be proved beyond all reasonable doubt.

"The burden of proving that any person has been guilty of
" a crime or wrongful act is on the person who asserts it,
" whether the commission of such act is or is not directly in
" issue in the action."

This is otherwise stated by saying that the prisoner is
entitled to the benefit of every reasonable doubt. The
word "reasonable" is indefinite, but a rule is not
worthless because it is vague. Its real meaning, and I
think its practical operation, is that it is an emphatic
caution against haste in coming to a conclusion adverse to a
prisoner. It may be stated otherwise, but not, I think, more
definitely, by saying that before a man is convicted of a crime
every supposition not in itself improbable which is consistent
with his innocence ought to be negatived. But I do not
know that "improbable" is more precise than "reasonable."
It is also closely connected with the saying that it is
better that ten guilty men should escape than that one innocent man should suffer—an observation which appears to me
to be open to two decisive objections. In the first place, it
assumes, in opposition to the fact, that modes of procedure
likely to convict the guilty are equally likely to convict
the innocent, and it thus resembles a suggestion that soldiers
should be armed with bad guns because it is better that
they should miss ten enemies than that they should hit
one friend. In fact, the rule which acquits a guilty man is
likely to convict an innocent one. Just as the gun which
misses the object at which it is aimed is likely to hit an object
at which it is not aimed. In the second place, it is by no
means true that under all circumstances it is better that ten
guilty men should escape than that one innocent man should
suffer. Everything depends on what the guilty men have
been doing, and something depends on the way in which
the innocent man came to be suspected. I think it probable
that the length to which this sentiment has been carried

[1] Article 94.

in our criminal courts is due to a considerable extent to the
extreme severity of the old criminal law, and even more to
the capriciousness of its severity and the element of chance
which, as I have already shown, was introduced into its
administration. In the report already quoted, [1] M. Cottu
remarks that the English, " not thinking it for the advantage
" of the public to punish every crime committed lest the
" effect of example should be weakened by the frequency
" of executions, they reserve the full measure of their severity
" for the more hardened offenders, and dismiss unpunished
" those whose guilt is not proved by the most positive testi-
" mony. [2] They are indifferent whether among the really
" guilty such be convicted or acquitted. So much the worse
" for him against whom the proofs are too evident, so much
" the better for the other in whose favour there may exist
" some faint doubts ; they look upon the former as singled out
" by a sort of fatality to serve as an example to the people,
" and inspire them with a wholesome terror of the vengeance
" of the law; the other as a wretch whose chastisement
" heaven has reserved in " (? for) " the other world." He adds
that none of the English with whom he was in company
" ever positively expressed such a sentiment, but they act as
" if they thought so." There may be some exaggeration
in this, but the sentiment here described is not altogether
unlike the practical result to be expected from the maxim,
" Timor in omnes pœna in paucos," a sentiment not unnatural
when the practice and the theory of the law differed so widely
as they did sixty years ago. It was natural that a convicted
prisoner should be looked upon as a victim, chosen more or
less by chance, when the whole law was in such a state that
public sentiment would not permit of its being carried even
proximately into effect.

I know of only four rules of evidence which can be said to
be peculiar to criminal proceedings.

1. The first and by far the most important is the rule that
the prisoner and his wife are incompetent witnesses. The
history of this rule is as follows :—The husbands or wives of

---

[1] Cottu's *Report*, p. 91, &c.
[2] This clumsy sentence is obviously the fault of the translator.

CH. XII. prisoners, were never, so far as I know, compelled to testify against their wives or husbands. But down to the Civil Wars, as I have already shown, the interrogation of the prisoner on his arraignment formed the most important part of the trial. Under the Stuarts questions were still asked of the prisoner, though the extreme unpopularity of the *ex officio* oath, and of the Star Chamber procedure founded upon it, had led to the assertion that the maxim, "*Nemo tenetur accusare seipsum*," was part of the law of God and of nature (to use the language of the day), an assertion which was all the more popular because it condemned the practice of torture for purposes of evidence, then in full use both on the Continent and in Scotland.

Soon after the Revolution of 1688, the practice of questioning the prisoner died out, and as the rules of evidence passed from the civil to the criminal courts, the rule that a party was incompetent as a witness, which (subject to evasion by bills of discovery in equity) prevailed in civil cases till [1] 1853, was held to apply to criminal cases. This, however, was subject to two important qualifications. First, the prisoner in cases of felony could not be defended by counsel, and had therefore to speak for himself. He was thus unable to say, as counsel sometimes still says for him, that his mouth was closed. On the contrary his mouth was not only open, but the evidence given against him operated as so much indirect questioning, and if he omitted to answer the questions it suggested he was very likely to be convicted. This was considerably altered by the act which allowed prisoners accused of felony the benefit of counsel. The counsel was always able to say, " My client's mouth is closed. If he " could speak he might say so and so." Within the last few years, however, counsel have been allowed to make any statement they please as from their clients, and in [2] some instances prisoners have been allowed to make such statements themselves, though such a course has been held to give the prosecutor a right to reply. Counsel still often allege by way of grievance that their clients' mouths are closed; but no one who is acquainted with the law can believe

---

[1] It was repealed by 16 & 17 Vic. c. 83.
[2] Especially by Cave, J., in the winter circuit of 1882. I have done the same.

it, nor ought judges to allow such a statement to pass uncontradicted.

Secondly, the statutes of Philip and Mary already referred to, repealed and re-enacted in 1826 by 7 Geo. 4, c. 64, authorized committing magistrates to " take the examina-" tion " of the person suspected. This examination ([1] unless it was taken upon oath, which was regarded as moral compulsion), might be given in evidence against the prisoner.

This state of the law continued till the year 1848, when by the 11 & 12 Vic. c. 42, the present system was established, under which the prisoner is asked whether he wishes to say anything, and is warned that if he chooses to do so what he says will be taken down and may be given in evidence on his trial. The result of the whole is that as matters stand the prisoner is absolutely protected against all judicial questioning before or at the trial, and that, on the other hand, he and his wife are prevented from giving evidence in their own behalf. He is often permitted, however, to make any statement he pleases at the very end of the trial, when it is difficult for any one to test the correctness of what is said.

This is one of the most characteristic features of English criminal procedure, and it presents a marked contrast to that which is common to, I believe, all continental countries. It is, I think, highly advantageous to the guilty. It contributes greatly to the dignity and apparent humanity of a criminal trial. [2] It effectually avoids the appearance of harshness,

---

[1] See my *Digest of the Law of Evidence*, Art. 23, and note xvi.

[2] The contrast is described by M. Cottu in a singular passage, p. 103—4. " The courts of England offer an aspect of impartiality and humanity which " ours, it must be acknowledged, are far from presenting to the eyes of the " stranger. In England everything breathes an air of lenity and mildness, " the judge looks like a father in the midst of his family occupied in trying " one of his children " (an extraordinary position certainly for a man to be placed in). " His countenance has nothing threatening in it. According to " an ancient custom flowers are strewed upon his desk and upon the clerk's. " The sheriff and officers of the court wear each a nosegay." . . . . " Every-" thing among us, on the contrary, appears in hostility to the prisoner. He " is often treated by the public officers with a harshness, not to say cruelty, at " which an Englishman would shudder. Even our presiding judges, instead " of showing that concern for the prisoner to which the latter might appear " entitled from the character of impartiality in the functions of a judge, " whose duty is to direct the examination, and to establish the indictment, " too often becomes a party against the prisoner, and would seem sometimes " to think it less a duty than an honour to procure his conviction."

not to say cruelty, which often shocks an English spectator in a French court of justice, and I think that the fact that the prisoner cannot be questioned [1] stimulates the search for independent evidence. [2] The evidence in an English trial is, I think, usually much fuller and more satisfactory than the evidence in such French trials as I have been able to study.

On the other hand, I am convinced by much experience that questioning, or the power of giving evidence, is a positive assistance, and a highly important one, to innocent men, and I do not see why in the case of the guilty there need be any hardship about it. It must be remembered that most persons accused of crime are poor, stupid, and helpless. They are often defended by solicitors who confine their exertions to getting a copy of the depositions and endorsing it with the name of some counsel to whom they pay a very small fee, so that even when prisoners are defended by counsel the defence is often extremely imperfect, and consists rather of what occurs at the moment to the solicitor and counsel than of what the man himself would say if he knew how to say it. When a prisoner is undefended his position is often pitiable, even if he has a good case. An ignorant uneducated man has the greatest possible difficulty in collecting his ideas, and seeing the bearing of facts alleged. He is utterly unaccustomed to sustained attention or systematic thought, and it often appears to me as if the proceedings on a trial, which to an experienced person appear plain and simple, must pass before the eyes and mind of the prisoner like a dream which he cannot grasp. I will give an illustration of what I mean, which many years ago impressed me deeply.

A number of men, six or seven, I think, were indicted at Lincoln on three separate charges arising out of the same set of facts. The indictments charged, wounding A, with

---

[1] During the discussions which took place on the Indian Code of Criminal Procedure in 1872 some observations were made on the reasons which occasionally lead native police officers to apply torture to prisoners. An experienced civil officer observed, "There is a great deal of laziness in it. It is far "pleasanter to sit comfortably in the shade rubbing red pepper into a poor "devil's eyes than to go about in the sun hunting up evidence." This was a new view to me, but I have no doubt of its truth.

[2] See the trials at the end of this work.

intent to do him grievous bodily harm, wounding B, with the same intent, and being to the number of three or more on land armed by night for the purpose of poaching. The facts were that a gang of poachers had fallen in with certain keepers and their assistants, and that A and B, two of the keepers' party were severely beaten and, indeed, nearly murdered. [1] On the first and second indictments some of the party were convicted of unlawfully wounding A and B respectively. On the third indictment all were convicted of night poaching. At the first trial they hardly defended themselves at all, though one of the party slightly cross-examined the leading witnesses for the Crown. One witness said that a dog which he saw with the poachers was white, and another said that it was red. The prisoners pointed out this small difference in a feeble helpless way, without showing that it was at all important, and they were at once convicted on the minor charge of unlawful wounding. As I considered this verdict insufficient the other indictments were tried. On the second trial, as I was informed, the prisoners appeared to understand what was going on much better, and some of them defended themselves with a good deal of energy. On the third trial they fully understood the whole matter and brought out their real defence. The defence was that on the night in question two different parties went out poaching, one with a white dog and the other with a red dog, that they set out together and returned together, but that the fray took place between the keepers and one only of the parties of poachers, and that the evidence confused together the white dog party and the red dog party. The judge who tried the case was so much impressed by the defence, which the jury would not believe, that he made, and caused to be made, independent inquiries, which finally resulted in a grant of free pardons to several of the prisoners. Others were clearly guilty, and, indeed, admitted their guilt. If these men could have been questioned, I think all the innocent members of the party would have been acquitted at once.

The following is another instance which struck me much. I

[1] I was counsel for the crown, but I was not present at the second and third trials, though I was present at the first, and was fully informed at the time of all that happened at the other two.

heard of it on unquestionable authority, though I was not myself present on the occasion:—A man was indicted at a Court of Quarter Sessions for stealing a spade. The evidence was that the spade was safe overnight and was found in his possession next day, and that he gave no account of it. He made no defence whatever, and was immediately convicted. When called upon to say why sentence should not be passed upon him, he replied in a stupid way, "Well, it is hard I should be sent to gaol for this spade, when the man I bought it of is standing there in court." The chairman caused the man referred to to be called and sworn; the jury, after hearing him, recalled the verdict they had given, and the man was acquitted at once.

These are specimens of a considerable number of cases which have led me to form an opinion, that when a wrong conviction does occur in an English criminal court, it is usually caused by treating a poor and ignorant man as if he were rich, well advised, and properly defended. If money enough is to be had to procure the services of skilful counsel and solicitors, and to provide all the evidence which may be required, the presumption that every point is taken which can be taken, and that matters passed over are passed over advisedly, is probably true, and I think nothing can be fairer or more completely satisfactory than a great criminal trial so conducted. A poor and ill-advised man, on the contrary, is always liable to misapprehend the true nature of his defence, and might in many cases be saved from the consequences of his own ignorance or misfortune by being questioned as a witness. I do not think that any evil would ensue to the wealthy and well-advised from being placed in the same position.

The practice suggested would also make it impossible for prisoners to play a trick upon the court which is sometimes practised at present, and which causes great embarrassment. A prisoner, let us suppose, has a defence to offer which he considers doubtful and dangerous. He accordingly keeps it to himself, and takes his chance of an acquittal on the weakness of the case for the crown. After conviction and sentence he brings out his real defence. This, especially in capital cases, is extremely embarrassing. It is hard to hang a man because he or his advisers have not been candid, and it is also hard to hang a man whose real defence was not put before the jury. In such cases, accordingly, informal inquiries have to be made, which are seldom satisfactory, and often cause failures of justice. If the prisoner was questioned, this result would be generally avoided.[1]

The propriety of making the parties competent witnesses in civil cases is no longer disputed. It is difficult to say why the same rule should not apply to criminal cases also. One objection to the admission of such evidence rests upon the false supposition that a witness is to be believed because he is sworn to speak the truth. The proper ground for admitting evidence is not that people are reluctant to lie but that it is extremely difficult to lie minutely and circumstantially without being found out.

If prisoners are to be made competent witnesses, I think they ought to be competent to testify as well before the magistrate as before the judge. No greater test of innocence can be given than the fact that as soon as he is charged, and whilst there is still time to inquire into and test his statements, a man gives an account of the transaction which will stand the test of further inquiry.

Some precautions might properly be observed in admitting such evidence. If the prisoner did not offer his testimony it would be hard to allow the prosecution to call him. The fact of his refusing to testify would always have its weight with the jury. By leaving him to be examined in chief by his own counsel and cross-examined by the counsel for the crown the danger of placing the judge in a position hostile to the prisoner would be avoided. I should regard this as so important an object that unless it could be fully secured I should prefer to maintain the existing law as it stands. The following provision upon this subject was introduced into the Draft Criminal Code of 1879, though the Commissioners were divided in opinion as to its policy :—

" [2] EVIDENCE OF THE ACCUSED.—Every one accused of any

---

[1] As an instance, I may refer to the recent case of Lamson, hanged for poisoning his brother-in-law. [2] See *Report*, p. 37, s. 523.

" indictable offence shall be a competent witness for himself
" or herself upon his or her trial for such offence, and the wife
" or husband as the case may be of every such accused person
" shall be a competent witness for him or her upon such
" trial: provided that no such person shall be liable to be
" called as a witness by the prosecutor, but every such witness
" called and giving evidence on behalf of the accused shall
" be liable to be cross-examined like any other witness on any
" matter though not arising out of his examination-in-chief:
" provided that so far as the cross-examination relates to the
'" credit of the accused, the court may limit such cross-
" examination to such extent as it thinks proper, although
" the proposed cross-examination might be permissible in the
" case of any other witness."

　　2. Another set of rules peculiar to criminal trials are [1] the
rules relating to evidence of confessions. These extremely

---

[1] The rules as to confessions are thus stated in my *Digest of the Law of
Evidence*: " Article 21.—*Confessions Defined.*—A confession is an admission
" made at any time by a person charged with a crime, stating or suggesting
" the inference that he committed that crime. Confessions, if voluntary, are
" deemed to be relevant facts as against the persons who make them only.

　　" Article 22.—*Confessions caused by Inducement, Threat, or Promise, when
'" Irrelevant in Criminal Proceedings.*—No confession is deemed to be volun-
" tary if it appears to the judge to have been caused by any inducement, threat,
" or promise, proceeding from a person in authority, and having reference to
" the charge against the accused person, whether addressed to him directly or
" brought to his knowledge indirectly ; and if (in the opinion of the judge)
" such inducement, threat, or promise, gave the accused person reasonable
" grounds for supposing that by making a confession he would gain some
" advantage or avoid some evil in reference to the proceedings against him.
" A confession is not involuntary only because it appears to have been caused
" by the exhortations of a person in authority to make it as a matter of
" religious duty, or by an inducement collateral to the proceeding, or by
" inducements held out by a person not in authority.　The prosecutor,
" officers of justice having the prisoner in custody, magistrates, and other
" persons in similar positions, are persons in authority.　The master of the
" prisoner is not as such a person in authority, if the crime of which the
" person making the confession is accused was not committed against him.
" A confession is deemed to be voluntary if (in the opinion of the judge) it is
" shown to have been made after the complete removal of the impression pro-
" duced by inducement, threat, or promise which would otherwise render it
" involuntary.　Facts discovered in consequence of confessions improperly
" obtained, and so much of such confessions as distinctly relate to such facts,
" may be proved.

　　" Article 24.—*Confession made under a Promise of Secrecy.*—If a confession
" is otherwise relevant, it does not become irrelevant merely because it was
" made under a promise of secrecy, or in consequence of a deception practised
" on the accused person for the purpose of obtaining it, or when he was
" drunk, or because it was made in answer to questions which he need not
" have answered, whatever may have been the form of those questions, or
" because he was not warned that he was not bound to make such confession,
'" and that evidence of it might be given against him."

detailed and elaborate rules were developed by a series of CH. XII.
judicial decisions within the last century (Warickshall's
case, 1 Leach, 263, decided in 1783, is one of the earliest on
the subject), from the general proposition that "confessions
" ought to be voluntary and without compulsion." The rule
is stated almost in these words in the sixth edition of Gilbert
on the *Law of Evidence,* published in 1801, p. 123. [1]A vast
number of cases have since been decided by which every
branch of the rules given below is established. It would
be difficult to give a stronger illustration of the way in
which the law of England is gradually made by judicial
decisions than is afforded by the growth of this rule. I cannot here go into detail upon the subject, but I may observe
in general that the character of the decisions has varied
considerably. At one time the courts were disposed to take
almost any opportunity to exclude evidence of confessions,
almost anything being treated as an inducement to confess.
In 1852, however, the law was considerably modified by the
decision in the case of [2]R. *v.* Baldry, since which time the
disposition has been rather the other way.

The general maxim, that confessions ought to be voluntary,
is historically the old rule that torture for the purpose of
obtaining confessions is, and long has been, illegal in England.
In fact it cannot be said that it ever was legal, though it
seemed at one time as if it were likely to become legal.

3. Another rule peculiar to criminal cases is [3]the exception
to the rule respecting hearsay evidence which renders dying
declarations as to the cause of death admissible in trials for
murder or manslaughter. I believe this rule as now limited
to be about 100 years 'old. The earliest emphatic statement

---

[1] They are collected in Taylor, *On Evidence,* 769—809, and elsewhere.
[2] 2 Den. 430. The latest cases are R. *v.* Jarvis, L. R. 1 *C. C. R.* 96, and
R. *v.* Reeve, *ib.* 364.
[3] The rule is thus stated in my *Digest of the Law of Evidence :*—" Article
" 26.—*Dying Declaration as to the Cause of Death.*—A declaration made by
" the declarant as to the cause of his death, or as to any of the circumstances of
" the transaction which resulted in his death, is deemed to be relevant only
" in trials for the murder or manslaughter of the declarant ; and only when
" the declarant is shown, to the satisfaction of the judge, to have been in
" actual danger of death, and to have given up all hope of recovery at the
" time when his declaration was made. Such a declaration is not irrele-
" vant merely because it was intended to be made as a deposition before a
" magistrate, but was irregular.

CH. XII.   of it commonly quoted is to be found in [1]Woodcock's case, decided in 1789 by Lord Chief Baron Eyre. This case refers to a decision in 1720 by Lord Chief Justice King, and to the case of [2]R. v. Reason and Tranter, decided in 1722. That case, however, says nothing as to any limitation on the rule. A series of cases from 1678 to 1765 show that during that period declarations of deceased persons as to the cause of their death were admitted even though the declarants had hopes of recovery when they were made. In the [3]trial of Lord Pembroke for the murder of Mr. Cony in 1678, evidence was given of many statements made by the deceased as to the cause of his death; they must have been made when he hoped to recover, as he said he should demand satisfaction for the injury done him. In the case of [4]Lord Ferrers, tried in 1760, evidence was given as to what Johnson, the steward, said about Lord Ferrers having shot him, without any question being asked as to his hopes of recovery at the time. Lord Mansfield was one of the peers present on this occasion, and took a leading part in the proceedings. Again, in the trial in 1765 of [5]Lord Byron for the murder of Mr. Chaworth, evidence was given by Mr. Cæsar Hawkins, the surgeon, of what Mr. Chaworth said about the transaction, without any such preliminary inquiry as to his expectation of recovery as would now be made. It certainly appeared from the evidence that he was aware of his danger but not that he had no hopes of life.

The rule is in many ways remarkable. It has worked, I am informed, ill in India, into which country it has been introduced together with many other parts of the English law of evidence. I have heard that in the Punjab the effect of it is that a person mortally wounded frequently makes a statement bringing all his hereditary enemies on to the scene at the time of his receiving his wound, thus using his last opportunity to do them an injury. A remark made on the policy of the rule by a native of

---

[1] Leach, 502. It is singular that Warickshall's case, which contains the earliest statement of the modern law as to confessions, should have been decided by the same judge a few years before. The language used in each case is rather rhetorical and inflated.   [2] 1 St. Tr. 449.
[3] 6 St. Tr. 1325.   [4] 19 Ib. 918.   [5] Ib. 1205-6.

Madras shows how differently such matters are viewed in different parts of the world. "Such evidence," he said, " ought never to be admitted in any case. What motive for " telling the truth can any man possibly have when he is " at the point of death ? "

4. Lastly, evidence as to the character of the accused person is admitted in criminal cases as a sort of indulgence, though character is usually treated as irrelevant. Before the Norman Conquest (as I have already shown) the character of the accused decided the question whether he was to be allowed to make his purgation by compurgators or was to be sent to the ordeal. In later times the character of the accused must have weighed with the jury who acted as witnesses. Under the Stuarts (as I have shown) evidence was freely given of particular crimes or misconduct, unconnected with the matter in issue, committed by the prisoner. Evidence of his good character was also admitted. An early, perhaps the earliest, instance of this is to be found in [1] the trial of Colonel Turner for burglary in 1664. The report does not give the evidence of the prisoner's witnesses, but he must have called such witnesses, for Lord Chief Justice Hyde said in summing up : " The witnesses he called in point of reputation that I must " leave to you. I have been here many a fair time. Few " men that come to be questioned but shall have some come " and say—He is a very honest man, I never knew any hurt " by him; but is this anything against the evidence of " the fact ? "

All through the eighteenth century evidence of character was given on behalf of the prisoner as it is now. Perhaps the most remarkable recorded instance of-it occurred in the [2] trial of Mr. Arthur O'Connor for high treason in 1798, when Lord Moira, Mr. Erskine, Mr. Fox, Lord Suffolk, Mr. Sheridan, Mr. Michael Angelo Taylor, Mr. Grattan, and Mr. Whitbread, were called, and " many other gentlemen equally respectable " were tendered to give evidence as to his character for loyalty. Great importance must have been attached to this evidence as the prisoner gave up the advantage of being defended by Erskine for the sake of calling him as a witness.

[1] 6 St. Tr. 613.　　　　　　　[2] 27 Ib. 31—53.

CH. XII.   The whole of the law as to witnesses to character was
———   greatly discussed in the case of [1] R. *v.* Rowton, decided in 1863,
in which it was decided by all the judges that if evidence
of good character was given for the prisoner evidence of bad
character might be given against him, and by eleven judges
against two (Erle, C. J., and Willes, J.) that evidence of
character means evidence of reputation as opposed to evidence
of disposition. The decision settled the law, but in practice
it is impossible to act upon it, and it may be doubted whether
it is desirable to try to do so. The facts in R. *v.* Rowton set
this in so clear a light that comment upon them seems to me
superfluous. The prisoner took pupils, and was convicted
of committing an indecent assault upon one of them. He
called witnesses who gave him "an excellent character as a
moral and well-conducted man." Thereupon a witness was
called to contradict this evidence, who was asked, "What is
" the defendant's general character for decency and morality
" of conduct?" He was allowed to answer, "I know nothing
" of the neighbourhood's opinion, because I was only a boy
" at school when I knew him, but my own opinion, and the
" opinion of my brothers, who were also pupils of his, is that
" his character is that of the grossest indecency and the most
" flagrant immorality." This was held to be a ground for
quashing the conviction, so that the case expressly decides
that if a man gains a reputation for honesty or morality by
the grossest hypocrisy he is entitled to give evidence of it,
which evidence cannot be contradicted by people who know
the truth.

     The examination of the witnesses having been completed
if the prisoner is defended by counsel, and if no witnesses
(except witnesses to character) are to be called for the defence,
the counsel for the Crown may sum up the evidence. His
right to do so was given by 28 Vic. c. 18, s. 2, which was
passed in 1865. The theory was that matters might come out
in evidence which ought to be explained and commented upon
by the counsel for the Crown before the defence was made.
I doubt the advantage of the change. It adds a speech where
there is already speaking enough.

[1] L. & C. 520.

This is followed by the defence. It is a highly character-istic part of an English criminal trial.

[1] M. Cottu observes, in reference to the mildness with which prisoners are prosecuted in England: "It is true that the " liberty of defence, very differently understood in France " from what it is in England, forces us to a much more " rigorous prosecution; it would be almost impossible to " convict a prisoner considering the latitude which our laws " give to the defence, were the prosecution confined within " the limits prescribed in England, that is, were it forbidden " to question the prisoner and his accomplices."

No one at all acquainted with the subject would admit that English barristers are in any degree inferior, either in courage, or in independence, or in resource, to any body of professional men in the world, but it is unquestionably true that the history of English advocacy in criminal cases is far calmer than the history of French advocacy in recent times. Collisions between the Bench and the Bar are exceedingly rare, and when they do occur they arise rather out of individual faults of temper on the one side or the other than from any struggle as to matters of principle, or any attempt on the part of the Bar to prevent the application to the case of the law laid down by the judge.

Several observations arise both upon the history and the causes of this state of feeling. For a great length of time the Bar had no opportunity of defending their clients at all, except in cases of misdemeanour. Misdemeanours of importance on public grounds were usually tried before the Star Chamber, and the discretion of that court was so wide and its decisions so little capable of being checked by any power except Parliament, that there was practically no opportunity for the Bar to say anything of importance. From the Civil Wars to the Revolution of 1688, prisoners in cases of treason and felony had no counsel. Their defences, in cases of misdemeanour, were not very impressive. The only case to the contrary which occurs to me is the case of the seven bishops, which was in every way so exceptional that no inference as to the common course of justice can be drawn from it.

[1] P. 104.

Since the Revolution the following affirmations with respect to the Bar and the defence of prisoners may fairly be made. In the first place there always has been and still is a degree of sympathy and fellow-feeling between the Bench and the Bar which I believe to be peculiar to this country, and which has had and still has most important, and, as I (naturally) consider, most beneficial effects upon the administration of justice. The judges are simply barristers who have succeeded in the profession [1] of which they still are members, and they carry to the Bench the professional habits and ways of thought acquired in the course of a professional lifetime, beside which they are naturally upon terms of intimacy with the senior members of the profession. This gives them an influence in the administration of justice which those who have neither felt nor exercised it can hardly appreciate. The judges can hardly fail to understand the un-written rules and sentiments which determine the duties of counsel, and when they do understand them and apply them fairly, they have the sentiment of the profession on their side. These sentiments are to a surprising extent on the side of the existing law. The number of barristers who try to evade its application or who wish to see it defeated by an appeal to prejudice is small. The action of a judge who warns counsel that he is going beyond the limits assigned to him either by trying to intimidate a jury or by attempting to induce them to break the law from motives of prejudice, or by making suggestions which the evidence does not warrant, is never in my experience unpopular amongst those with whom the judge wishes to be on good terms, namely, the members of his own profession. The barrister's province is singularly well defined. It is to say for his client whatever upon the evidence it is by law open to him to say, and which he thinks likely to be advantageous. The judge's province is equally well defined.

---

[1] In former times judges when dismissed from the Bench returned to prac-tice at the Bar, and I know of no legal reason why if a judge resigned his office he might not resume his practice. The judges are now Benchers of their respective Inns. As members of Serjeant's Inn they formed a domestic tribunal having the authority of a Court of Appeal over the Inns of Court. The present judges of the Queen's Bench Division had been on an average nearly twenty-eight years at the Bar before they were raised to the Bench.

It is to prevent mis-statements of law and of fact and attempts CH. XII. to intimidate or mislead the jury. Again, though the form of the law is clumsy, its substance is on almost every subject so minute and complete that there can be little doubt as to the point at which a barrister begins to mis-state it or to ask the jury to transgress it. Finally, the whole legal profession is a pre-eminently manly one. It is a calling in which success is impossible to the weak or timid, and in which every one, judge or barrister, is expected to do his duty without fear or favour to the best of his ability and judgment.

I am no doubt prejudiced in favour of a system in the administration of which great part of my life is passed, but it seems to me that the result of this state of things has been in the past, and is in the present, eminently satisfactory. Even in times of vehement political excitement the Bench and the Bar have hardly ever been brought into collision, though neither has as a rule failed in its special duty, and though on particular occasions the result of the criminal trials conducted by their agency has been of the highest political importance.

The following are a few instances of this :—

Throughout the eighteenth century counsel were allowed to speak in cases of treason and misdemeanour only. No case of treason which gave rise to any point of much constitutional importance occurred before the trial of Lord George Gordon for the riots of 1780. In the trials for the rebellions of 1715 and 1745, there was no room for doubt as to either the law or the facts. The points connected with the trial of Lord George Gordon I shall consider more fully [1] hereafter, but the matter relevant to the present subject is that Erskine's famous speech in his defence does not in any single instance go beyond the line I have tried to draw as that which limits the duty of an advocate. His whole defence is based upon a view of the law which differs from that which was afterwards laid down by Lord Mansfield mainly in style. The statements of the law made by the advocate and the judge are in substance identical. Nearly the same may be said of the trials for high treason in 1794, and something not unlike it

[1] Vol. II., pp. 273, 274.

may be observed as to the famous trials for libel which led to Fox's Libel Act. Erskine was by far the most popular and effective advocate who ever appeared at the English Bar, but the more his speeches are studied the more distinctly will it be seen that he was essentially on the side of the law, and that though fearless and independent [1] he was hardly ever brought into collision with the judges.

If time and space permitted it would not be difficult to trace this state of things down to our own times. Strong illustrations of it might be drawn from the trials of the Chartists in 1841, 1842, and 1843, from some of the trials of a later date for trade conspiracies, and from a long series of Irish trials extending from those which arose out of the rebellion of 1798 to those which arose out of the abortive rising of 1848. As a general rule counsel on all these occasions have taken the law as they found it, and have not attempted to induce juries to break it.

Few stronger proofs are to be found of the simplicity of English taste in the matter of making speeches than the exceedingly prosaic character of speeches in defence of prisoners. Even when the circumstances of crimes are pathetic or terrible in the highest degree, the counsel on both sides are usually as quiet as if the case was an action on a bill of exchange. This way of doing business is greatly to be commended. It is impossible to be eloquent in the sense of appealing to the feelings without more or less falsehood, and an unsuccessful attempt at passionate eloquence is of all things the most contemptible and ludicrous, besides being usually vulgar. The critical temper of the age has exercised an excellent influence on speaking in the courts. Most barristers are justly afraid of being laughed at and looking silly if they aim at eloquence, and generally avoid it by keeping quiet.

The defence is followed by the examination of the prisoner's witnesses, if any, the summing-up of his counsel, and the reply of the counsel for the Crown, if he is entitled to a reply.

---

[1] The famous scene between him and his old tutor, Buller, at the trial of the Dean of St. Asaph is no doubt something of an exception. See Vol. II. p. 331.

But upon these matters I need add nothing to what I have CH. XII.
already said.

The trial concludes by the summing-up of the judge.

This again is a highly characteristic part of the proceedings, but it is one on which I feel it difficult to write. I think, however, that a judge who merely states to the jury certain propositions of law and then reads over his notes does not discharge his duty. This course was [1]commoner in former times than it is now. I also think that a judge who forms a decided opinion before he has heard the whole case, or who allows himself to be in any degree actuated by an advocate's feelings in regulating the proceedings, altogether fails to discharge his duty, but I further think that he ought not to conceal his opinion from the jury, nor do I see how it is possible for him to do so if he arranges the evidence in the order in which it strikes his mind. The mere effort to see what is essential to a story, in what order the important events happened, and in what relation they stand to each other must of necessity point to a conclusion. The act of stating for the jury the questions which they have to answer and of stating the evidence bearing on those questions and showing in what respects it is important generally goes a considerable way towards suggesting an answer to them, and if a judge does not do as much at least as this he does almost nothing.

The judge's position is thus one of great delicacy, and it is not, I think, too much to say that to discharge the duties which it involves as well as they are capable of being discharged, demands the strenuous use of uncommon faculties, both intellectual and moral. It is not easy to form and suggest to others an opinion founded upon the whole of the evidence without on the one hand shrinking from it, or on the other closing the mind to considerations which make against it. It is not easy to treat fairly arguments urged in an unwelcome or unskilful mannner. It is not easy for a man to do his best, and yet to avoid the temptation to choose that view of a subject which enables him to show off his special

---

[1] It was followed, to take one instance in a thousand, by Lord Mansfield in Lord George Gordon's case.

gifts. In short, it is not easy to be true and just. That the problem is capable of an eminently satisfactory solution, there can, I think, be no doubt. Speaking only of those who are long since dead, it may be truly said that to hear in their happiest moments the summing-up of such judges as Lord Campbell, Lord Chief Justice Erle, or Baron Parke, was like listening not only (to use Hobbes's famous expression) to "law living and armed," but to the voice of Justice itself.

CHAPTER XIII.

HISTORY OF LEGAL PUNISHMENTS.

HAVING in preceding chapters described the whole of the procedure in criminal cases up to the end of the trial, I propose in this chapter to give the history of the various punishments inflicted by law for different offences.

The verdict of the jury is followed by the judgment of the court, which is either acquittal or condemnation. A acquittal does not entitle the prisoner to be instantly discharged, though, as a fact, he usually is so discharged. [1] In strictness, when a man is committed to gaol to be tried, he is liable to be detained till the end of the sittings of the next commission of gaol delivery or Oyer and Terminer, when, if he is not indicted, he is entitled to be discharged upon bail, unless it is proved upon oath that the witnesses for the Crown could not be produced, or without bail if he is tried and acquitted or if he has not been indicted and tried at the second sitting after his committal.

If the prisoner is convicted he is sentenced usually at once.

The judgments which may be pronounced are as follows :— Death, penal servitude, imprisonment with or without hard labour, detention in a reformatory school, subjection to police supervision, whipping, fines, putting under recognizances. The history of these punishments is perhaps the most curious part of the history of the criminal law.

I shall consider first the history of the punishment of

---

[1] 31 Chas. 2, c. 2, s. 6 (the Habeas Corpus Act, 1679).

CH. XIII. death and of benefit of clergy, and the history of the punishments which by degrees were substituted for death. I shall
then consider the history of other punishments, especially
those. inflicted at common law for misdemeanours.

As I have already observed, the punishments inflicted for
what we now call treason and felony, varied both before the
Norman Conquest, and for some time after it. At some
periods it was death, at others mutilation, and it is remarkable that under William the Conqueror the punishment of
death was almost entirely replaced by mutilation. Hoveden
says that Henry I. " firmissimâ lege statuit quod fures latro-
" cinio deprehensi suspendantur," but he quotes no authority,
and he did not write till perhaps fifty years after Henry's
time.   [1] The *Leges Henrici Primi* speak of some kinds of
theft as being capitally punished, and imply that other
crimes were capital.   Mutilation, however, is the punishment mentioned in the Assizes of Clarendon and Northampton in the time of Henry II.

Capital punishments were [2] certainly in use in Richard I.'s
time.   In the reigns of Henry III. and Edward I. there is
abundant evidence that death was the common punishment
for felony ; and this continued to be the law of the land as to
treason and as to all felonies, except petty larceny and
mayhem, down to the year [3] 1826, subject to the singular and
intricate exceptions introduced by the law relating to the
benefit of clergy.

Of this branch of the law, Blackstone characteristically
remarks that the English legislature, [4] " in the course of a
" long and laborious process, extracted by noble alchemy rich
" medicines out of poisonous ingredients."

According to our modern views it would be more correct to
say that the rule and the exception were in their origin
equally crude and barbarous, that by a long series of awkward
and intricate changes they were at last worked into a system

---

[1] " Furtum probatum et morte dignum " is mentioned as one of the crimes
which " mittunt hominem in misericordiâ regis " (Thorpe, i. 518). So " De
" furto autem, et de hiis quæ sunt mortis, faciat," &c., p. 561.
[2] A record is quoted by Sir F. Palgrave of the 10th Richard I. in which a
woman was sentenced to be burnt for murder.—*Proofs and Illustrations,*
clxxxv. (11).   [3] See 7 & 8 Geo. 4, c. 26, ss. 6, 7.
[4] 4 *Bl. Com.* p. 364 (2nd edition).

which was abolished in a manner as clumsy as that in which Ch. XIII. it was constructed.

[1] The history of the subject falls naturally into three heads, namely, first, the history of the privilege itself, next the history of its gradual extension to all persons whatever, and lastly, the history of the exclusion from it of a large number of offences. The two processes last mentioned to some extent overlapped each other, but it is obvious that as the privilege ceased to be confined to a comparatively small class of persons, it would be necessary to confine it to a comparatively small number of offences.

Privilege of clergy consisted originally in the right of the clergy to be free from the jurisdiction of lay courts, and to be subject to the ecclesiastical courts only, and it might be compared to the privilege which European British subjects in India still possess of being tried in some cases by tribunals different from those by which natives would be tried in similar cases, and also to the privilege claimed by British and other foreign subjects in Turkey, in Egypt, and in China, of being tried before their own courts.

The following is Bracton's account of it, "[2] When a clerk of " whatever order or dignity is taken for the death of a man " or any other crime, and imprisoned, and an application is " made for him in the Court Christian by the ordinary " . . . . " the prisoner must be immediately delivered up without " making any inquisition. He must not, however, be set at " liberty and allowed to wander about the country, but is to " be safely kept, either in the bishop's prison, or in the King's " prison if the ordinary wishes, till he has duly purged

---

[1] The subject is described at full length and with the greatest technical minuteness of detail by Hale (2·*P. C.* 323—390). Blackstone (4 *Com.* 358) has given (principally from Hale) an account of the subject as it stood in his time ; and an account of the law as it stood in 1826, just before benefit of clergy was abolished, is given in 1 Chitty's *Criminal Law,* 666—90. Hale's account of the law is rendered prolix and intricate by the necessity under which he lay of referring to a number of minute and capricious distinctions which in his time applied to the law relating to accessories and principals and to the varied provisions of the statutes relating to particular crimes, as to cases ended by conviction, by indictment, by appeal, by standing mute, by pleading guilty, or by challenging more than twenty jurors. Blackstone was placed under the same difficulty, though to a smaller extent.

[2] Br. *De Cor.* ch. ix. II. 298.

CH. XIII. "himself from the accusation laid upon him, or has failed to "purge himself, for which he ought to be degraded."

Ecclesiastical purgation is thus described, "[1] The trial was "held before the bishop in person, or his deputy, and by a "jury of twelve clerks, and there first the party himself was "required to make oath of his own innocence; next there was "to be the oath of twelve compurgators, who swore they "believed he spoke the truth; then witnesses were to be "examined upon oath, but upon behalf of the prisoner only, "and lastly, the jury were to bring in their verdict upon oath, "which usually acquitted the prisoner, otherwise, if a clerk, "he was degraded or put to penance." Probably this strange proceeding might be justified by the singular notions which prevailed in the civil law as then understood as to [2] evidence. The burden of proof was on the clerk who had to make his purgation, and it might be thought as improper to allow evidence to be given against him by the king, as to allow evidence to be produced against the king, when the burden of proving guilt lay on him. However this may have been, the claim of the ordinary in Bracton's time went so far as to require that the clerk should be delivered up to him as soon as he was imprisoned on suspicion of any crime whatever.

In the course of the three centuries which followed Bracton, this claim was considerably restricted by the legislature.

The Statute of Westminster the First (3 Edw. 1, A.D. 1275) [3] was interpreted to mean that the prisoner must be indicted before he could be claimed, and afterwards in the reign of Henry VI. it was settled by the practice of the courts that a clerk must be convicted before he could claim his clergy This was at once an advantage to the prisoner, who had the chance of being acquitted, and a restriction on the privilege of the clergy as a separate order in the state, as it subjected them to the lay tribunals.

In the next place the courts exercised a discretion in de-

---

[1] R. v. Burridge (1735); 3 Peere Williams, 447. See, too, Searle v. Williams, Hobart, 288, p. 291 (1620); Staundforde, *Purgacion*, 138. Hobart speaks of purgation as "turning the solemn trial of truth by oath into a "ceremonious and formal lie."

[2] See p. 335, *sup.*; also p. 349, &c.   [3] 2 Hale, 377.

livering the clerk to the ordinary. He might be delivered either
to make his purgation, or " absque purgatione," in which latter
case he was to be imprisoned in the bishop's prison for life.

The privilege was originally confined to those who had
"habitum et tonsuram clericalem," but in 1350, by the
25 Edw. 3, st. 3 (called the statute *pro clero*), it was
enacted that "all manner of clerks, as well secular as reli-
" gious, which shall from henceforth be convict before the
" secular justices . . . shall from henceforth freely have and
" enjoy the privileges of Holy Church." The "secular
" clerks " here mentioned were, [1] it is said, " persons not strictly
" in orders, but assistants to them in doing Divine offices,
such as Doorkeepers, Readers, Exorcists, and Sub-deacons, and
the statute is said to have been passed because " the said pre-
" lates have grievously complained, praying thereof remedy."
It seems, however, that whether by the construction given to
this statute or otherwise, the courts extended the privilege to
every one who could read, whether he had the clerical dress
and tonsure or not. This apparent extension of the privilege greatly diminished its value to the clergy as a distinct
caste, but considerable traces of the old clerical view of the
subject remained for centuries. The most important and
least amiable of them was that all women (except, till the
Reformation, professed nuns) were for centuries excluded
from the benefit of clergy because they were incapable
of being ordained. Another exception, which may almost be
called grotesque, was that " bigamus " was excluded from
clergy. This is recognised by two statutes, 4 Edw. 1, c. 5 (1276),
and 18 Edw. 3, c. 2 (1344). " Bigamus " was not a bigamist
in our sense of the word, but a man who " hath married two
" wives or one widow." By the last-mentioned statute the
bigamy was to be tried in the ecclesiastical court. This strange
rule was repealed in 1547 by 1 Edw. 6, c. 12, s. 16, which
allows clergy to " bigami," " although they or any of them
" have been divers and sundry times married to any single
" woman or single women, or to any widow or widows, or
" to two wives " (? at once) " or more."

---

[1] Lord Holt in Armstrong *v*. Lisle. Kelyng, p. 143 (edition of 1873);
old edition, p. 99.

CH. XIII.   In 1487 (4 Hen. 7, c. 13) it was enacted that every
person convicted of a clergyable felony should be branded on
the brawn of his thumb with an M if his case was murder,
and a T if it was theft, and that if any person claimed clergy
a second time (which fact the brand would prove), he should
be denied it if he was not actually in orders, or if, being
actually in orders, he failed within a day to be assigned by
the judge to produce either his letters of orders or a certificate of his ordination from the ordinary. This distinction
was abolished by [1] 28 Hen. 8, c. 1, s. 7, in 1536, but it
was considered to be revived by 1 Edw. 6, c. 12, s. 14
(A.D. 1547), which also gave every peer of the realm ("though
"he cannot read") a privilege equivalent to, though not
identical with, benefit of clergy. The peer was to be " ad-
"judged, deemed, taken, and used for the first time only to
"all intents, constructions, and purposes as a clerk convict,"
and was to be "in case of a clerk convict which may make
"purgation, without any burning in the hand, loss of inherit-
"ance, or corruption of his blood." When benefit of clergy
was abolished in 1827, by 7 & 8 Geo. 4, c. 28, this act
was overlooked, and upon the occasion of Lord Cardigan's
trial in 1841 it was doubted whether, if he were convicted,
he would not be entitled to the benefit of it, notwithstanding
the act of 1827. The question was finally set at rest by
4 & 5 Vic. c. 22, which provided that peers accused of
felony should be liable to the same punishment as other
persons, and repealed the act of Edward VI.

By the 18 Eliz. c. 7, ss. 2, 3 (1576), purgation was
abolished, and it was enacted that persons taking the benefit
of clergy should be discharged from custody subject to a
power given to the judge to imprison them for any term not
exceeding a year.

In 1622, by 21 Jas. 1, c. 6, women obtained a privilege
analogous to that of clergy in the case of larceny of goods
worth more than 1s. and not more than 10s.; and in 1692, by 4
Will. & Mary, c. 9, they were put on the same footing as men.

In 1705, by 5 Anne, c. 6, the necessity for reading was
abolished.

---

[1] Made perpetual by 32 Hen. 8, c. 3, s. 8.

In 1717 it was enacted by [1] 4 Geo. 1, c. 11, that persons CH. XIII guilty of clergyable larcenies should be liable to be transported for seven years instead of being branded or whipped.

In 1779, by 19 Geo. 3, c. 74, s. 3, branding was practically abolished, though the words of the act are not absolute.

Shortly, the form which the law relating to benefit of clergy had assumed at the beginning of the eighteenth century was this :—

All felonies were either clergyable or not.

Every one charged with a clergyable felony was entitled to benefit of clergy for his first offence, and clerks in orders were entitled thereto for any number of offences.

Benefit of clergy consisted in being excused from capital punishment, but the person who claimed it was, till 1779 (unless he was a peer or a clerk in orders), branded in the hand, and might be imprisoned for a term not exceeding one year. If his offence was larceny he might be transported for seven years. This result had been reached by the long series of changes above described.

The great importance of benefit·of clergy in the history of the criminal law consists in the fact that the existence of the privilege determined the form taken by our legislation on the whole subject of legal punishments for serious common offences. The number of felonies at common law was but small. In Coke's *Third Institute* only seven are mentioned, namely homicide (in its two forms of murder and manslaughter), rape, burglary, arson, robbery, theft, and mayhem. All of these except petty larceny (stealing things worth less than twelvepence) and mayhem were punished with death, and were originally subject to the privilege of clergy.

The result of this was to bring about for a great length of time a state of things which must have reduced the administration of justice to a sort of farce. Till 1487 any one who knew how to read might commit murder as often as he pleased, with no other result than that of being delivered to the ordinary to make his purgation, with the chance of being delivered to him "absque purgatione." That this should have been the law for several centuries seems hardly credible,

---

[1] And see 6 Geo. 1, c. 23.

CH. XIII. but there is no doubt that it was. Even after 1487 a man who could read could commit murder once with no other punishment than that of having M branded on the brawn of his left thumb, and if he was a clerk in orders he could till 1547 commit any number of murders apparently without being branded more than once.

The claim of the clergy to exemption from the jurisdiction of the lay courts was however never admitted to its full extent by the common law. [1]It is said that high treason against the king was never clergyable, and this is confirmed by the words of the statute *de clero* (25 Edw. 3, st. 3, A.D. 1350) which extends benefit of clergy to "any treason or "felonies touching other persons than the king himself or his "royal majesty."

[2] There were also two forms of felony which were excluded from benefit of clergy at common law, namely, "Insidiatio "viarum, et depopulatio agrorum," or highway robbery and wilful burning of houses.

These, however, appear, according to Hale, to have been the only exceptions to benefit of clergy till the reign of Henry VII., when a statute was passed, 12 Hen. 7, c. 7 (1496), depriving of clergy laymen committing petty treason by "prepensedly murdering their lord, master, or sovereign "immediate." The act is drawn in a singular manner. The preamble recites that whereas "abominable and wilful pre- "pensed murders be by the laws of God and of natural reason "forbidden, and are to be eschewed, yet not the less, many "and divers unreasonable and detestable persons lacking "grace, wilfully commit murder," . . . . "in trust to eschew the "peril and execution of the law by the benefit of their clergy." It then goes on to state that in particular one Grame had then lately murdered his master Tracy, and provides that Grame is to be drawn and hanged as if he were no clerk, and that similar offenders shall for the future be treated in the same way.

In 1512, another statute (4 Hen. 8, c. 2) was passed, depriving persons of clergy who committed murder in churches highways, &c.

In 1531 (23 Hen. 8, c. 1, ss. 3, 4) every one convicted

[1] 2 Hale, 350.   [2] *Ib.* 333.

of petty treason, or "for any wilful murder with malice pre- "pensed," or for robbing churches, chapels, or other holy places, or of certain kinds of robbery or certain kinds of arson, was excluded from clergy, except clerks in orders, who, however, were to be imprisoned for life, unless (a somewhat impotent conclusion) they could find two sureties in 20*l.* each for their good behaviour.

In 1536 (28 Hen. 8, c. 15) piratical offences were excluded from clergy. There was a question whether clergy was not restored in these cases by 1 Edw. 6, c. 12, and [1]Hale was with some doubt of opinion that it was restored in some cases which might be described as piratical, but that in cases which we should now describe as piracy by the law of nations clergy was not restored, if it ever existed (which he denies).

In 1547 ([2]1 Edw. 6, c. 12 s. 10) benefit of clergy was taken away in all cases of murder, cases of burglary and housebreaking, in which any person was in the house at the time and was put in fear, highway robbery, horse stealing, and robbing churches. The necessity for using the word "murdravit" in an indictment (which was so essential that murderavit was a fatal flaw) was based on this statute. If the indictment was "felonice et ex malitiâ suâ præcogitatâ "interfecit," or "felonice murdravit," it was an indictment for manslaughter only which was clergyable. What an indictment for "murderavit" would have amounted to I do not know.

In 1565 (8 Eliz. c. 4) clergy was taken away in cases of "felonious taking of any money, goods, or chattels from the "person of any other privily without his knowledge." But this was interpreted to mean above the value of a shilling.

In 1576 (18 Eliz. c. 7) rape and burglary were excluded from clergy, [3] but the part of the statute which relates to burglary was very unskilfully adapted to the statutes of Edward VI. and Philip and Mary.

In 1597 (39 Eliz. c. 9) abduction with intent to marry,

[1] 2 H. P. C. 369—71.
[2] 4 & 5 Phil. & Mary, c. 4. applied to accessories in these cases.
[3] See 2 Hale, 360—4.

which by 3 Hen. 7, c. 2 was a clergyable felony, was deprived of the benefit of clergy.

Finally, by 22 Chas. 2, c. 5 (1671) stealing clothes off the racks, and stealing the king's stores were deprived of clergy.

These are all the cases enumerated by Hale in which clergy was taken away from common law crimes down to his time, but many statutory felonies had also been created which, for the sake of brevity, I have not noticed. These statutes, as well as those which I have noticed, were worded in all sorts of ways. A trial might end, it must be remembered, either by the accused person standing mute and being pressed to death, or by his challenging too many jurors and being hanged, or by his pleading guilty, or by his being convicted and pardoned, or by his being convicted and attainted. If a statute taking away clergy did not expressly mention all these possible cases, and take away clergy in all of them, both from the principal and from his accessories both before and after, clergy remained in every omitted case. Hence questions arose on the special wording of every statute, as to whether it ousted an offender of clergy not only if he was convicted, but if he pleaded guilty, if he stood mute, &c., and similarly as to his accessories. Hardly any branch of the law was so technical and so full of petty quibbles as this. The detailed statement of them makes a large part of Hale nearly unreadable. They were abolished by two successive statutes, 3 Will. & Mary, c. 9, s. 2 (A.D. 1691), which enacted that if any person were convicted of a felony, excluded from benefit of clergy " by virtue of any former statute," if convicted or attainted, the exclusion should extend to cases in which they stood mute, challenged too many jurors, or were outlawed. This was extended to accessories by 1 Anne, st. 2, c. 9, and by 7 Geo. 4, c. 64, s. 7, to all statutory felonies subsequent to the act of William and Mary, or afterwards to be created.

All this legislation shows that the early criminal law was extremely severe, that its severity was much increased under the Tudors, but that it varied little from the time of Elizabeth to the end of the seventeenth century. Before noticing the legislation of the eighteenth century on this subject, it will be

desirable to sum up what has been said. The result of it is as
follows:—Towards the end of the seventeenth century the following crimes were excluded from benefit of clergy, and were
thus capital whether the offender could read or not: high
treason (which had always been so), petty treason, piracy,
murder, arson, burglary, housebreaking and putting in fear,
highway robbery, horse stealing, stealing from the person
above the value of a shilling, rape and abduction with intent
to marry. In the case of persons who could not read, all
felonies, including manslaughter, every kind of theft above
the value of a shilling, and all robbery were capital crimes.
It is difficult, if not impossible, to say how this system
worked in practice. No statistics as to either convictions or
executions were kept then, or till long afterwards. A few
vague generalities, with here and there a piece of positive
evidence are all that I at least can refer to. I will mention
one specimen of each. There are still preserved at Exeter
Castle many of the depositions and other records of the
Courts of Quarter Sessions, held there from the latter part of
the reign of Elizabeth—they begin in 1592. From these
materials Mr. Hamilton has compiled a *History of the Quarter
Sessions from Elizabeth to Anne.* The following is one result
at which he arrives, " [1] At the Lent Assizes of 1598, there
" were 134 prisoners, of whom seventeen were dismissed with
" the fatal S. P., it being apparently too much trouble to
" write *sus. per coll.* Twenty were flogged; one was liberated
" by special pardon and fifteen by general pardon; eleven
" claimed benefit of clergy and were consequently branded and
" set free, ' *legunt uruntur et deliberantur.*' At the Epiphany
" Sessions preceding there were sixty-five prisoners, of whom
" eighteen were hanged. At Easter there were forty-one
" prisoners, and twelve of them were executed. At the Mid-
" summer sessions there were thirty-five prisoners and eight
" hanged. At the Autumn Assizes there were eighty-seven on
" the calendar and eighteen hanged. At the October Sessions
" there were twenty-five, of whom only one was hanged.
" Altogether there were seventy-four persons sentenced to be
" hanged in one county in a single year, and of these more

[1] Hamilton's *History of Quarter Sessions*, pp. 30—1.

"than one-half were condemned at Quarter Sessions." Mr. Hamilton gives[1] a copy of the calendar for the Midsummer Sessions for 1598. It appears that five persons were convicted of sheep-stealing. John Capron was sentenced to death. Stephen Juell, Andrew Penrose, and Anthony Shilston had their clergy. Gregory Tulman was flogged. In Tulman's case the sheep was probably valued at less, or charged in the indictment as being of less value, than a shilling. If the average number of executions in each county was only twenty, or a little more than a quarter of the number of capital sentences in Devonshire in 1598, this would make 800 executions a year in the forty English counties. The number of executions was notoriously very great. A remarkable illustration of this is afforded by the remark with which Coke concludes his *Third Institute*. " What a lamentable case it is to see so many Christian men " and women strangled on that cursed tree of the gallows, " insomuch as if in a large field a man might see together all " the Christians that, but in one year throughout England " come to that untimely and ignominious death, if there were " any spark of grace or charity in him, it would make his " heart to bleed for pity and compassion." He then points out three remedies : education, laws to set the idle to work, and "that forasmuch as many do offend in hope of " pardon, that pardons be very rarely granted." This contrasts oddly with the philanthropic tone of the preceding extract.

When all the restrictions upon benefit of clergy had been taken off at the beginning of the eighteenth century, so that women were entitled to it as well as men, and those who could not read, as well as those who could, the punishment for all the common offences became slight. If a man was not hung he was discharged, or at most imprisoned for a year without hard labour, though under circumstances likely to injure both his health and his morals. At the same time the rapidly increasing trade and wealth of the country brought to light the great defects in the criminal law as it then stood, and especially the crudity and meagreness of its

[1] *History of Quarter Sessions*, p. 33.

provisions, of which I shall give a fuller account in relating Ch. XIII. the history of the substantive law.

I do not think, however, that these defects were recognised as such. The fact that the revolutions of the 17th century had been conducted with an almost superstitious respect for law, and that the party opposed to the encroachments (as they said) of royal power, had always taken their stand upon what they called the good old laws of England, and the fact that the law was professedly based upon what were regarded as the highest standards of truth and goodness, had surrounded the law with a degree of veneration, which, in these days, it is not easy to understand, but which is represented probably with little exaggeration in the courtly and, indeed, reverential language of Blackstone, who scarcely ever misses an opportunity of extolling the system which he describes, though he may [1] " occasionally find room to " remark some particulars that seem to want revision and " amendment."

Hence, the alterations made in the criminal law by the legislation of the eighteenth century preserved its form and did not greatly alter its substance. The benefit of clergy having been extended at the beginning of the century to all persons whatever, it was in the course of the century taken away from a great variety of offences. This in some cases simply extended the old law relating to women and to illiterate persons to all persons whatever. Sheep-stealing, for instance, though clergyable, was from the earliest times a capital felony if the sheep stolen was over one shilling in value ; and, as [2] Mr. Hamilton tells us, one man was hanged for it, and two had their clergy at the Exeter Midsummer Sessions in 1598. By [3] the 14 Geo. 2, c. 6 (1741), and

---

[1] 4 Bl. *Com.* 3.

[2] *Hist. Quarter Sessions*, p. 33. Mr. Hamilton observes as to the value of sheep in James I.'s time the King was entitled to have sheep at 6s. 8d. a-piece. . . . It is probable that the average price of sheep at that time was nearer that given by Justice Shallow, "A score of good ewes may be " worth £10."

[3] The first of these Acts applies to "sheep and other cattle." The second defines "cattle" to mean "bull, cow, ox, steer, bullock, heifer, calf, and "lamb, as well as sheep, and no other cattle whatever." It is curious that pigs have never met with any special recognition or protection from the law, nor, I think, donkeys or mules.

CH. XIII. 15 Geo. 2, c. 34 (1742) all sheep-stealers were deprived of benefit of clergy. The process, however, was carried much beyond removing benefit of clergy from offences formerly clergyable. The severity of the criminal law was greatly increased all through the eighteenth century by the creation of new felonies without benefit of clergy. In the second edition of the [1] *Commentaries*, published in 1769, Blackstone says that "among the variety of actions which men are daily "liable to commit no less than 160 have been declared by "Act of Parliament to be felonies without benefit of clergy." This passage has often been quoted, but it must be observed that the number of capital offences on the statute-book is no test of its severity. A few general enactments would be much more severe than a great number of special ones. A general enactment that grand larceny should be excluded from benefit of clergy would have been infinitely more severe than fifty acts excluding the stealing of fifty different sorts of things from the benefit of clergy. By a great number of statutes the forgery of different specified documents was made felony without benefit of clergy. Different statutes provided, for instance, for the forgery of Exchequer bills, South Sea bonds, certain powers of attorney, &c. The real severity of a single general Act about forgeries would have been much greater than that of these numerous scattered provisions, each of which went to swell the number of capital offences. Moreover, the 160 offences mentioned by Blackstone might probably be reduced by careful classification to a comparatively small number. For instance, I know not how many offences of the 160 are included in what was known as the Black Act (9 Geo. 1, c. 27, 1722). This Act provided, amongst other things, that if any persons armed or having their faces blacked, or being otherwise disguised, should appear in any forest, &c., or in any warren or place where hares or rabbits were usually kept, or in any high road, open heath, common, or down, or should unlawfully and wilfully hunt, wound, kill, destroy, or steal any red or fallow deer, &c., they should be guilty of felony, without benefit of clergy. The part of this provision which I

4 *Com.* 18.

have quoted creates [1] fifty-four capital offences, for it forbids
three classes of persons to do any one of eighteen acts.
However, after making all deductions on these grounds, there
can be no doubt that the legislation of the eighteenth century in criminal matters was severe to the highest degree,
and destitute of any sort of principle or system. In practice
the punishment of death was inflicted in only a small proportion of the cases in which sentence was passed. The
persons capitally convicted were usually pardoned conditionally on their being transported either to the American or
afterwards to the Australian colonies for life or for a long
term of years. These conditional pardons were recognised by
the Habeas Corpus Act (31 Chas. 2, c. 2, ss. 13, 14), and used
to be granted by the king through the Secretary of State
upon the recommendation of the Judges of Assize. This
being thought circuitous and dilatory, it was enacted in 1768
(8 Geo. 3, c. 15) in substance that Judges of Assize should
have power to order persons convicted of crimes without the
benefit of clergy to be transported for any term they thought
proper, or for fourteen years if no term was specially
mentioned.

The result of all this legislation as to the punishment of
death was in the reign of George IV. as follows :—All
felonies except petty larceny and mayhem were theoretically
punishable with death, but clergyable felonies were never
punished with death, nor were persons convicted of such
felonies sentenced to death. When asked what they had to
say why sentence should not be passed upon them, they "fell

---

[1] The classes of persons are : (1) Persons armed, (2) persons with their
faces blacked, (3) persons otherwise disguised.   The 18 acts are :—
    (1) Appearing in a forest.
    (2)   ,,   ,,   warren.
    (3)   ,,   ,,   place where hares are kept.
    (4)   ,,   ,,   ,,   ,,   rabbits ,,
    (5)   ,,   ,,   high road.
    (6)   ,,   ,,   open heath.
    (7)   ,,   ,,   common.
    (8)   ,,   ,,   down.
    (9) Unlawfully hunting
    (10)   ,,   wounding
    (11)   ,,   killing   any red deer.
    (12)   ,,   destroying
    (13)   ,,   stealing
    (14—18) Same as to fallow deer.

CH. XIII.   "upon their knees and prayed their clergy," upon which they were liable to imprisonment for not exceeding a year, or in some cases to whipping, or in the case of petty larceny, or grand larceny not excluded from clergy, and in some other cases to seven years' transportation.

A great number of felonies had been excluded from benefit of clergy in the course of the eighteenth century, and when a person was convicted of such an offence he had to be sentenced to death, but the judge might order him to be transported instead, and such an order had all the effects of a conditional pardon.

It came to be considered that to pass sentence of death in cases in which it was not intended to be carried out was objectionable, and accordingly in 1823 an act (4 Geo. 4, c. 48) was passed which authorized the court in cases of capital convictions for any felony except murder to abstain from actually passing sentence of death, and to order it to be recorded, which had the effect of a reprieve.   The act is still in force, but as in cases of murder sentence of death [1] must be passed, and practically no other felony is capital, it is hardly ever acted upon.

This state of the law excited great philanthropic indignation, and was completely altered by the first set of Acts passed for the reform of the criminal law.   They were conceived in a spirit totally different from that of our earlier legislation. The following were their most important provisions :—In 1827 (7 & 8 Geo. 4, c. 28) benefit of clergy was abolished by s. 6. Standing alone this would have made every case of stealing above the value of a shilling punishable by death.   It was therefore provided by s. 7 that no one convicted of felony should suffer death unless for felonies excluded from benefit of clergy, or made punishable by death by some statute subsequently passed.   In order to meet the case of acts made felony in general terms it was provided that in such cases the

---

[1] The repealed statute, 6 & 7 Will. 4, c. 30, s. 2, seems to have extended (4 Geo. 4, c. 48) to cases of murder, but (24 & 25 Vic. c. 100 s. 2) had the effect stated in the text.   I remember a case in which Mr. Justice Wightman ordered sentence of death to be recorded upon a conviction for murder.   The prisoner, though not quite mad enough to be acquitted, was obviously too mad to be hanged.   I have met with cases in which I wished I had a similar power.

punishment should be seven years' transportation or two years' CH. XIII.
imprisonment, with or without whipping in the case of males.
Section 9 provided that in case of a second conviction for
felony the offender should be liable to transportation for
life, imprisonment up to four years, and public or private
whipping once, twice, or thrice. In all such cases the court
was authorised to direct that the imprisonment should be
with hard labour. This section replaced the old rule that
privilege of clergy could be had once only. It is still in
force, though seldom acted on, as certain provisions in the
Larceny Act have practically superseded it.

The Act of 1827 was followed by several others which were
intended to form the nucleus of a criminal code, and to re-
place the fragmentary and yet indiscriminate legislation of the
eighteenth century by laws in which punishments were more
carefully adjusted to offences. Each of them retained the
punishment of death in a considerable number of cases. The
first of them was 7 & 8 Geo. 4, c. 29, "for consolidating
"and amending the laws relating to larceny." This Act
re-enacted the punishment of death in the following instances, namely, robbery either by force, or by threats to
accuse of an infamous crime (ss. 6—9), sacrilege (s. 10),
burglary (s. 11), housebreaking and stealing or putting in
fear any person in the house, stealing to the value of 5*l.*
in a dwelling-house (s. 12), and stealing horses, sheep, and
other cattle (s. 25).

[1] By the 7 & 8 Geo. 4, c. 30, which consolidated the law
as to malicious injuries, the punishment of death was
retained in cases of arson, riotously demolishing houses,
&c., destroying ships in certain cases, and exhibiting false
signals.

In the following year (1828) an Act was passed for consolidating the law relating to offences against the person (9 Geo.
4, c. 31). [2] By this Act death was retained as the punishment of murder; attempts to murder by poisoning, stabbing,
shooting, &c.; administering poison to procure abortion;
sodomy; rape; and connection with a girl under ten.

In 1830 was passed 11 Geo. 4, and 1 Will. 4, c. 66,

[1] Ss. 2, 8, 9, 10, 11.   [2] Ss. 3, 11, 12, 13, 15, 16.

consolidating the law relating to forgery. [1] This Act retained the punishment of death for forging the great seal (which was treated as high treason), public securities, wills, bills of exchange, and promissory notes, making false entries in certain public books of accounts, and forging transfers of stocks.

Each of these Acts repealed and re-enacted a number of Acts passed at various times, but principally in the eighteenth century, excluding particular offences from benefit of clergy, and punished the offences created by those statutes with terms of transportation varying in their maximum length from life to seven years, the court having power to sentence the offender in the alternative to imprisonment with or without hard labour, and in some cases with or without whipping.

The number of cases in which the punishment of death was retained under the Acts of George IV. was considered excessive, and it has since been greatly reduced, though by slow degrees. The history of this legislation is curious, as it traces the gradual growth of a sentiment very characteristic of our generation. It is as follows:—In 1832 the punishment of death was abolished, by 2 & 3 Will. 4, c. 62, in the case of stealing horses, sheep, and other cattle. In 1835 it was abolished in cases of letter-stealing (which was capital under 52 Geo. 3, c. 143, and had not been included in the consolidation Act of 1827), and in cases of sacrilege in which it had been reimposed by that Act. This was effected by [2] 5 & 6 Will. 4, c. 81.

In 1837 several acts were passed which abolished the punishment of death in other cases.

By 7 Will. 4, and 1 Vic. c. 84 capital punishment was abolished in all cases of forgery.

By chapter 85 the punishment of death was modified in regard to attempts to murder by confining it to cases of administering poison or inflicting bodily injury dangerous to life with intent to murder; it was abolished in respect of the other offences made capital by 9 Geo. 4, c. 31, with the

---

[1] Ss. 2—6, inclusive.

[2] A clerical error in this Act ("act" for "acts") made it doubtful whether any punishment at all could be awarded in cases of letter-stealing and sacrilege. It was set right by 6 & 7 Will. 4, c. 4.

exception of murder, rape, abusing girls under ten, and sodomy, as to which the provisions of that act were left unaltered.

By chapter 86 the punishment of death in cases of burglary was confined to burglary accompanied with actual violence to any person in the house.

By chapter 87 the punishment of death in cases of robbery was confined to cases accompanied by "stabbing, cutting, or wounding."

By chapter 88 the punishment of death in cases of piracy was confined to piracy accompanied by an assault with intent to murder, or by stabbing, cutting, or wounding, or by any act by which the life of any person on board is endangered.

By chapter 89 the punishment of death was abolished in all cases of injury to houses and ships, except only the case of setting fire to a dwelling-house, some persons being therein.

By chapter 91 the punishment of death was abolished in the case of offences against the Riot Act, rescuing persons going to execution, seducing soldiers from their allegiance, administering seditious oaths, slave-trading, and certain forms of smuggling accompanied with violence.

In 1841 by 4 & 5 Vic. c. 38, the punishment of death was abolished in cases of rape and abusing children under ten.

By the [1] Consolidation Acts of 1861 the punishment of death was abolished in cases of robbery with violence, attempts to murder, arson of dwelling-houses, and sodomy.

The only offences now punishable with death are treason, murder, piracy with violence, and setting fire to dockyards and arsenals.

The manner in which the punishment of death has been inflicted for many centuries has been and still is hanging, though in early times beheading was also common, not only as a favour to persons of rank, but as a mode of executing common criminals.[2]

---

[1] 24 & 25 Vic. ss. 96, 97, 98, 99, 100.

[2] A curious proof of this occurs in the Parliament Rolls for 1314 (8 Edward II.). The land of a person who had been beheaded escheated to the King, and the writ stated that he had been hanged. Upon which "concordatum est "per consilium quod consuetum breve de escaeta non mutetur, et quod illum "verbum 'suspensus,' &c., habeat locum in omni casu quando aliquis "mortem patitur pro felonia per ipsum commissa. Ita quod sive fuerit

The only exceptions to the general rule were the punishment of treason, which, in the case of men, was hanging,
drawing (this anciently meant dragging the offender along
the ground at the tail of a horse), and quartering; and in the
case of women, burning; and heresy, which was also punished
by burning. [1] In Henry VIII.'s time poisoning was declared
to be treason, punishable by boiling to death; and it seems
that three or four persons were so boiled, but this Act was
repealed by the 1 Edw. 6, and it is remarkable as supplying the single instance in which death by torture has been
authorised in England as a punishment for any offence except treason and heresy. As to the punishment of treason,
[2] in 1283, at a kind of Parliament held at Shrewsbury, David,
the last native Prince of Wales, was sentenced to be hanged,
drawn, and quartered, and to have his bowels burnt. [3] In

" decollatus, sive alio modo pro felonia per ipsum facta moriatur illud verbum
" 'suspensus' locum habeat" (1 *Rot. Par.* 293*a*—296*b*). So in 31 Hen. 3,
upon an appeal for murder, "Duodecim juratores dicunt quod prædicti
" Albinus et Ricardus" (said to have been murdered) "fuerunt latrones de
" bobus et vaccis, et cum latrocinio capti unde fuerunt in sesinâ *et ideo fuerunt*
" *decollati* " (Palgrave, *Proofs and Illustrations*, clxxxvii.). There are several
references in the Year-books to decapitation as a punishment for flight. See
3 Edw. 3, it. North. FitzHerbert, *Corone*, 346. "It was presented that a
" thief indicted was taken and led towards the gaol by four of the town, and
" when they came to a church two went in to hear mass, and two stayed out-
" side to guard the prisoner. The prisoner fled; the two followed and raised
" the hue and cry, whereby the town rose and followed the felon till they
" beheaded him, because they could not otherwise take him. The justices
" charged the town which ought to have taken him for an escape" (les justiez
ag. le pur eschape ss le vill' q̃ luy duit aū amesñ), "and the twelve said he
" was never out of their sight; the justices said that he escaped by the fault
" of their guard, and this was a case of escape. *Louth* said that when a thief
" is beheaded in pursuing him for a robbery the act can be justified, and this
" is more accordant to reason than it is to behead a man who flies, having
" been indicted and being under guard, for honest men are sometimes indicted,
" so that the law should be more favourable to them than to the others" (*i.e*
robbers followed by hue and cry). This seems to be the meaning of the
passage, but the wording is rather confused. Cf. FitzHerbert, *Corone*, 290
and 328, which seem to relate to the same case.

[1] *3rd Institute*, p. 48.

[2] *Ante*, p. 146. Lingard, iii. 196, and see Stubbs, *C. H.* ii. 216. The
sentence as quoted by Lingard (iii. 196) from a chronicler, is "to be drawn to
" the gallows as a traitor to the king who made him a knight, to be hanged
" as the murderer of the gentleman taken in the Castle of Hawarden; to have
" his bowels burnt because he had profaned by assassination the solemnity of
" Christ's passion; and to have his quarters dispersed through the country
" because he had in different places compassed the death of his lord the
" king." Cumulative punishments were inflicted on Lord Cobham and afterwards on Friar Forrest, each being half hanged as a felon and half burnt as a
heretic.

[3] See 2 *Rot. Par.* 3, 4. The form of the sentence in this case is, "Con-
" sideratum est quod prædictus Thomas Comes pro prædicta prodition

the time of Edward II., Thomas of Lancaster was sentenced
to be hanged, drawn, and beheaded, but on account of his
high birth was pardoned all but the beheading. Burning
continued till 1790 to be the punishment inflicted on
women for treason, high or petty (which latter included
not only the murder by a wife of her husband, and the
murder of a master or mistress by a servant, but also
several offences against the coin). Burning in such cases was
abolished by 30 Geo. 3, c. 48. In practice, women were
strangled before they were burnt; this, however, depended
on the executioner. In one notorious case a woman was
actually burnt alive for murdering her husband, the executioner being afraid to strangle her because he was caught
by the fire. In the reign of George II. an act was passed
which was intended to make the punishment for murder more
severe than the punishment for other capital crimes. This was
25 Geo. 2, c. 37, which provided that a person convicted
of murder should be executed on the next day but one after
his sentence (unless he was tried on a Friday, in which case
he was to be hanged on the Monday). He was to be fed on
bread and water in the interval, and his body, after death,
was either to be dissected or to be hung in chains. The
judge, however, had power to respite or to remit these
special severities. Under this act murderers were usually
anatomized, but sometimes gibbeted. By the 2 & 3 Will.
4, c. 7, s. 16 (for the regulation of schools of anatomy), it
was enacted that the bodies of murderers should no longer
be anatomized, but that the sentence should direct that they
should either be hung in chains or be buried in the prison.
Several persons were gibbeted under this act, but by the 3 &
4 Will. 4, c. 26, s. 2, it was enacted that the bodies of murderers should no longer be hung in chains, but that the sentence
should direct that they should be buried in the precincts of
the prison in which they should last have been confined
before their execution, and this direction is repeated in

" trahatur, et pro prædictis homicidiis, depredationibus, incendiis, et roberiis,
" suspendatur et pro predicta fugâ in hac parte decapitetur " In each of
the cases referred to above as to beheading, the persons were taken whilst
running away, and were probably there and then put to death.

CH. XIII. 24 & 25 Vic. c. 100, s. 2, which is now in force. These provisions distinguish English law in a marked manner from the continental laws down to the end of the last century. In most parts of the Continent breaking on the wheel, burning, in some cases quartering alive and tearing with red-hot pincers, were in use, as well as simpler forms of death. English people, as a rule, have been singularly reckless (till very lately) about taking life, but they have usually been averse to the infliction of death by torture.

Such is the history of the punishment of death as inflicted by the law of England. The subject is so trite that I feel reluctant to discuss it, but I am also reluctant to pass it over without shortly stating my own opinion upon it. My opinion is that we have gone too far in laying it aside, and that it ought to be inflicted in many cases not at present capital. I think, for instance, that political offences should in some cases be punished with death. People should be made to understand that to attack the existing state of society is equivalent to risking their own lives.

In cases which outrage the moral feelings of the community to a great degree, the feeling of indignation and desire for revenge which is excited in the minds of decent people is, I think, deserving of legitimate satisfaction. If a man commits a brutal murder, or if he does his best to do so and fails only by accident, or if he ravishes his own daughter (I have known several such cases), or if several men acting together ravish any woman, using cruel violence to effect their object, I think they should be destroyed, partly in order to gratify the indignation which such crimes produce, and which it is desirable that they should produce, and partly in order to make the world wholesomer than it would otherwise be by ridding it of people as much misplaced in civilized society as wolves or tigers would be in a populous country. What else can be done with such people? If [1] William Palmer had not been hanged in 1856, he would probably have been alive at this day, and likely to live for many years to come. What is the use of keeping such a wretch alive at the public expense for, say, half a century?

[1] See his case at the end of Vol. III.

If by a long series of frauds artfully contrived a man has shown that he is determined to live by deceiving and impoverishing others, or if by habitually receiving stolen goods he has kept a school of vice and dishonesty, I think he should die.

These views, it is said, are opposed to the doctrine that human life is sacred. I have never been able to understand distinctly what that doctrine means, or how its truth is alleged to be proved. If it means that life ought to have serious aims and to be pervaded by a sense of duty, I think the doctrine is true, but I do not see its relation to the proposition that no one ought ever to be put to death. It rather suggests the contrary conclusion as to persons who refuse to act upon it. If it means only that no one ought ever to be killed, I do not know on what grounds it can be supported. Whether life is sacred or not, I think there are many cases in which a man should be ready to inflict, or, if necessary, to suffer death without shrinking.

As, however, these views are at present unpopular and peculiar, and in the present state of public feeling on the subject it is useless to discuss this matter at length, no good purpose is served by making specific proposals which no one would entertain; but I may remark that I would punish with death offences against property only upon great deliberation, and when it was made to appear by a public formal inquiry held after a conviction for an isolated offence that the criminal really was an habitual, hardened, practically irreclaimable offender. I would on no account make the punishment so frequent as to lessen its effect, nor would I leave any doubt as to the reason why it was inflicted. I suspect that a small number of executions of professional receivers of stolen goods, habitual cheats, and ingenious forgers, after a full exposure of their career and its extent and consequences, would do more to check crime than twenty times as many sentences of penal servitude. If society could make up its mind to the destruction of really bad offenders, they might, in a very few years, be made as rare as wolves, and that probably at the expense of a smaller sacrifice of life than is caused by many a single shipwreck or colliery explosion; but, for this purpose, a change

CH. XIII. of public sentiment would be necessary, of which there are at present no signs.

In relating the history of the punishment of death I have also related by anticipation the greater part of the history of the punishment of transportation. The punishment was unknown at common law, though in [1] one case exile was at common law a consequence of crime. This happened when a criminal took sanctuary and confessed his crime. Upon this he was allowed to leave the kingdom, taking an oath of abjuration, as it was called, which bound him never to return; but sanctuary and abjuration were both abolished by 1 Jas. 1, c. 25, and 20 Jas. 1, c. 18. [2] The earliest instances of transportation as a punishment seem to have occurred in the reign of Charles·II., when pardons were granted to persons capitally convicted conditionally on their being transported for a number of years—usually seven. This practice was recognised, as I have observed, by the Habeas Corpus Act, and greatly extended by subsequent legislation, and particularly by the Act of 1768. It was first legalized as a substantive punishment by the Act of 4 Geo. 1, c. 11, already mentioned. In the course of the eighteenth and the early part of the present century an immense number of Acts were passed by which various terms of transportation, with alternative terms of imprisonment, and power, in some cases alternative and in others cumulative, to order whipping more or less frequently, were allotted to particular offences. This legislation was guided by no principle whatever, and was utterly destitute of any sort of uniformity. Its result is given in the [3] fifth and sixth Appendices to the *Fourth Report of the Criminal Law Commissioners.* They contain lists of all the felonies not at that time punishable by death,

---

[1] Chitty, *Crim. Law,* 789 ; 2 Hale, *P. C.* 68.

[2] In the "Directions for Justices of the Peace" (prefixed to Kelyng's *Reports,* which were published in 1664), the twelfth direction is "that such "prisoners as are reprieved with intent to be transported be not sent away "as perpetual slaves, but upon indentures between them and particular "masters to serve in our English plantations for seven years, and the three "last years thereof to have wages that they may have a stock when their time "is expired, and that an account be given thereof and by whom they are "sent, and of their arrivals."—Kelyng's *Reports,* 3—4.

[3] Dated 8th March, 1839. See App. v. pp. 10—64; App. vi. pp. 64—101.

and of all statutory misdemeanours, classified according to Cʜ. XIII
their punishments. There are thirty-eight classes of felonies
and ninety-six classes of misdemeanours. The extreme
intricacy of this classification is thus accounted for. In the
case of an offence punishable by transportation the enactment
providing for its punishment might, and generally did, contain
the following matters :—

(1) A maximum term of transportation.

(2) Intermediate terms of transportation.

(3) A minimum term of transportation.

(4) A maximum alternative term of imprisonment with
or without hard labour.

(5) A minimum alternative term of imprisonment.

(6) Power to inflict whipping, publicly or privately, and
once or more than once.

(7) Power to inflict solitary confinement during a certain
part of the term of imprisonment.

These seven elements of punishment were combined and
varied in all imaginable ways.

In their [1] Seventh Report the Criminal Law Commissioners
refer to many instances of these capricious variations. They
say, for instance, "In seventeen different classes of cases the
" sentence may be transportation for life ; in two the punish-
" ment is absolute without any alternative. In another,
" power is given to transport for any other term without
" fixing any minimum term of transportation or any
" alternative term of imprisonment. Of the fourteen other
" classes in one only is the minimum of transportation fifteen
" years." . . . "In one case only is the minimum term of
" transportation ten years. We find fifteen varieties in
" punishments where the maximum is transportation for a
" term of fourteen or fifteen years. The instances in which
" the punishment of transportation for seven years may be
" inflicted present twenty-three varieties."

The only point worth special notice in this state of the law
is the wide though capriciously restricted discretion left to
the judge: In regard to the great majority of offences the
judge was able to give as little punishment as he pleased. In

[1] 11 March, 1843, pp. 100—103.

CH. XIII. some few the punishment was absolute.   In many a greater or less minimum punishment was inflicted of necessity.

This was to a great extent remedied in the year 1846 by an Act (9 & 10 Vic. c. 24, s. 1), which provided that in all cases where any court is (*i.e.* was then) empowered to pass a sentence of more than seven years' transportation it should have power to pass instead sentence of transportation for any term not exceeding seven years, or sentence of imprisonment with or without hard labour for any term not exceeding two years.

Far the greater part of the criminal law relating to felonies has been recast and re-enacted since the reports to which I have been referring, and though the varieties in punishment are still considerable, and perhaps not always of obvious utility, they are greatly diminished. There is only one [1] common case in which a minimum punishment is still retained. The maximum punishments are penal servitude for life, for fourteen years, for ten years (in a very few cases), for seven years, and for five years. The alternative punishments in all cases are imprisonment for a term not exceeding two years with or without hard labour. Whipping may be added in a very few cases of crimes by adults, and in a larger number of cases of crimes committed by boys under sixteen.

The punishment of transportation was gradually abolished between 1853 and 1864, principally on account of the objection of the colonies to receive the convicts sentenced to it, and [2] penal servitude or imprisonment and hard labour on public works was substituted for it. The Penal Servitude Acts authorize the carrying out of the sentence in any part of Her Majesty's dominions, and under those Acts criminals were kept in confinement at Bermuda and in Gibraltar till very lately. The difference between the two punishments is thus rather a difference in name than in fact, indeed the provisions of the Act which regulated

---

[1] The case of unnatural offences, for which the minimum punishment is ten years' penal servitude.

[2] 16 & 17 Vic. c. 99 (1853), 20 & 21 Vic. c. 3 (1857), 27 & 28 Vic. c. 47 (1864). The Act as to transportation is 5 Geo. 4, c. 54.

transportation (5 Geo. 4, c. 84) are still in force as regards CH. XIII.
prisoners under sentence of penal servitude. A singular
variation in the scale of punishment produced by the
change from transportation to penal servitude deserves
notice. The common minimum term of transportation
was seven years, but when that punishment was commonly
inflicted imprisonment might in many cases be inflicted
for three, four, and even [1] seven years, so that the break
between a sentence of imprisonment and a sentence of
transportation was not necessarily a long one. When penal
servitude was substituted for transportation imprisonment
had been rendered both [2] more severe and shorter than
it had formerly been, so that with hardly an exception the
maximum punishment permissible was two years' hard
labour. At first the minimum term of penal servitude was
three years, so that the break between the longest term of
imprisonment and the shortest term of penal servitude was
not longer than would be proportional to the greater severity
of the former punishment. In 1864, however, the minimum
term of penal servitude was raised to five years, at which it
still remains, so that at present no sentence can be passed
intermediate in severity between two years' imprisonment
and hard labour (which, however, is considered so severe that
sentences are usually restricted, except in very peculiar cases,
to eighteen months) and five years' penal servitude.

The history of the punishment of imprisonment presents
some features of interest. Imprisonment is as old as the law
of England, and from very early times enactments were made
as to the provision of gaols. One of the earliest occurs in
the seventh chapter of the Assize of Clarendon (A.D. 1166),
[3] which is as follows:—" Et in singulis comitatibus ubi non
" sunt gaiolæ fiant in burgo vel aliquo castello regis de
" denariis regis et bosco ejus si prope fuerit, vel de alio bosco
" propinquo, per visum servientium regis, ad hoc ut vice
" comites in illis possint illos qui capti fuerint per ministros

---

[1] Seven years' imprisonment is still lawful in cases of perjury.
[2] The great increase in the severity of imprisonment was by making the
confinement in all case separate. The present Act on the subject is 28 & 29
Vic. c. 126, s. 17.   [3] Stubbs, *Charters*, p. 144.

" qui hoc facere solent et per servientes suos custodire."
This, no doubt, is the origin of the use as prisons of large
numbers of ancient castles, some of which are still used for
that purpose, as, for instance, at Norwich, Cambridge, and
York. These were the original common gaols, but they were
far from being the only prisons in the country. Nearly every
court had its own particular prison. Thus the Marshalsea was
specially the prison of the Marshal of the Court of King's
Bench. The Fleet was the prison of the Star Chamber and
of the Court of Chancery, but besides and apart from these,
there were in many places franchise prisons. The right of
keeping a gaol in and for particular districts was a franchise
which the king granted to particular persons as he granted
other rights connected with the administration of justice,
such as the right to execute writs (*retorna brevium*).

In this as in many other cases, the discharge of the legal
duty of keeping prisoners in custody was paid for, not by
salaries, but by fees, which were levied on the prisoners; and
as prisoners accused of crime were, as a rule, poor and
wretched to the last degree, fees had to be extorted from
them by all kinds of oppression and cruelty. A remarkable
illustration both of the manner in which particular prisons
came into existence, and of the horrible abuses to which the
system was liable, is to be found in the [1] proceedings, recorded
in the seventeenth volume of the *State Trials*, against
Huggins, Bambridge, Corbett, and Acton, for a series of
murders by cruel treatment, said to have been committed by
them in the Fleet and the Marshalsea.

The first matter [2] published is a report of a Committee of
the House of Commons upon the gaols, and especially upon
the Fleet. The Committee reported that the Fleet prison
was [3] an ancient prison, and had been used to receive prisoners
committed by the Star Chamber. It afterwards became a prison
for debtors and for contempts of the Courts of Chancery, Exchequer, and Common Pleas only. In the 3rd Elizabeth (1561)
the office of warden was granted in fee simple to Sir Jeremy

---

[1] 17 *St. Tr.* 297—618.   [2] 17 *St. Tr.* 297—310.
[3] It must have been very ancient if it really gave its name to *Fleta*,
which was written in Edward I.'s time.

Whichcot and his heirs for ever. The patent was at last set aside, as it descended to persons unable to execute it, and a grant for life was made to Baldwin Leighton, in consideration of the expense to which he had been put in repealing the former patent. Afterwards Huggins got a grant of it for his own and his son's life, "by giving £5,000 to the late Lord "Clarendon." Huggins, "growing in years, and wishing to "retire from business," sold his and his son's interest to Bambridge and Corbett for £5,000. The rest of the report relates to the horrible cruelties which, in order to make their speculation succeed, Huggins and Bambridge exercised on a variety of prisoners. These cruelties are more particularly described in seven trials for murder and one trial for theft, which are reported in the *State Trials*, and which show the horrible results which such a system not unnaturally produced.

The report of the Committee above referred to was made in 1729, and the trials took place in that year and in 1730. In 1729 an act was passed (2 Geo. 2, c. 22) which was intended to remedy the mischiefs thus exposed. It was, however, a most imperfect measure, and the prisons of England continued for many years afterwards to be in an infamous condition. The first great step made towards their reformation was taken in consequence of the labours of Howard, which began in 1773, when he was sheriff of Bedfordshire. Finding his own gaol in a disgraceful condition on account of the gaoler's being paid by fees, Howard proposed that the gaoler should be paid by a salary, but his brother magistrates refused to agree to this unless a precedent could be found for such a payment. Howard travelled through the whole of England in search of a precedent, and found that none existed. His attention was thus directed to the shameful state of the prisons. After employing himself for several years in collecting information on the subject, for which purpose he travelled all over Europe and part of Asia, his labours resulted in a series of acts of Parliament, the most important of which were 22 Geo. 3, c. 64, passed in 1782, and 24 Geo. 3, c. 54, passed in 1784. The first act applies to the discipline of houses of correction, and the

CH. XIII. second to the building, repairing, and government of county gaols. These acts were of the greatest importance, and recognised many excellent principles, but in practice they left many evils undisturbed. The subject, however, is not so closely connected with criminal law as to justify me in going at any length into the details. It is enough to say that from Howard's time to the present day the attention of the legislature has been specially directed to the whole subject of prison management and discipline. There have been three principal acts passed in relation to it, namely, 4 Geo. 4, c. 64, passed in 1823; the 28 & 29 Vic. c. 126, passed in 1865 (which repealed the Act of 4 Geo. 4), and the 40 & 41 Vic. c. 21—the Prison Act of 1877—which is now the principal Act on the subject. These Acts (there are very many others relating either to particular prisons or to matters connected with prison administration) at first established a distinction between common gaols (of which one was to be provided for every county, and which were to be used principally for the purpose of the confinement of prisoners of all sorts, debtors as well as criminals), and houses of correction, which were to be used principally for the purpose of punishing convicted criminals. The distinction, however, was not maintained, as statutes creating crimes usually provided that the sentence of imprisonment might be carried out either in a common gaol or in a house of correction. Each of the Consolidation Acts of 1861 contains such a clause. The Act of 1865 considerably simplified this state of things, abolishing, for one thing, the distinction between common gaols and houses of correction, directing that imprisonment should in all cases be " separate," which in practice means much the same as solitary, and laying down other regulations tending to make the punishment of imprisonment and the discipline of prisons more uniform than they used to be.

The Prison Act of 1877 lessened the number of prisons, and gave to the Home Secretary and to certain Prison Commissioners appointed on his recommendation extensive powers for their management. It would be foreign to my purpose to enter into details on these matters. It is enough to say that since the Act of 1865 solitary confinement, which before that Act passed was allowed to be inflicted only for a short part of the whole term of imprisonment, is now, under the name of separate confinement, inflicted in all cases as the regular and appointed mode of punishment.

Shortly to sum up the whole matter, the history of the punishment of death and of the punishments substituted for it is as follows :—

Death was at common law the punishment of all felonies except petty larceny and mayhem. But a large class of persons were exempted from it by the law as to benefit of clergy, which at first applied to the clergy only, then to all men who could read, except the husbands of second wives or widows, and at last to all persons whatever.

On the other hand, when benefit of clergy was extended to all persons, it was taken away from many crimes. This was done to a considerable extent under the Tudors, and to a much greater extent in the eighteenth century, but during that century pardons conditional on transportation were granted in the great majority of cases of capital convictions.

In the reign of George IV. benefit of clergy was abolished and capital punishment was abolished as regards most of the offences which had been excluded from clergy, but the number of offences subject to it was still considerable.

By successive steps, the last of which was taken in 1861, the law was reduced to its present state.

Transportation, having been introduced as a condition of pardon in the case of crimes excluded from clergy, was made a substantive punishment by a great number of statutes passed in the 18th and the early part of the 19th century, but penal servitude was substituted for it between 1853 and 1864.

Imprisonment with hard labour was introduced as a punishment alternative to transportation and penal servitude.

One other consequence of treason and felony remains to be noticed. This is corruption of blood and forfeiture of property. The effect of corruption of blood was that descent could not be traced through a person whose blood was corrupted. Also his real property escheated to the lord of the fee or to the king.   The personal property of a traitor or felon was forfeited not by his attainder, but by his conviction.

These incidents of treason and felony have their source in the feudal theory that property, especially landed property, was held of a superior lord upon the condition of discharging duties attaching to it, and was forfeited by the breach of those conditions.   They have no history at all, but prevailed from the earliest time till the year 1870, when they were abolished by 33 & 34 Vic. c. 23 s. 1, except in the case "of "forfeiture consequent upon outlawry."   Some of the provisions by which they were replaced appear to me exceedingly objectionable.   It is provided by section 2 that upon a conviction for felony and a sentence of twelve months' imprisonment or upwards or imprisonment with hard labour for any term the convict shall forfeit "any military or naval office "or any civil office under the Crown or other public employ-"ment, or any ecclesiastical benefice, or any place, office, or "emolument in any university, college, or other corporation "which he may hold, and also any pension or superannuation "allowance or emolument" to which he is entitled.   I think that the question whether a person should on account of a conviction of felony followed by a sentence of imprisonment and hard labour, be deprived of official employment or ecclesiastical perferment, should be left to his official or ecclesiastical superiors.   I do not see why an officer in the army who in a moment of irritation strikes a blow which kills a man and is convicted of manslaughter, should lose his commission because the judge sentences him to imprisonment with hard labour; nor do I think that in considering the sentence the judge ought to be obliged to take into account the fact that a sentence of hard labour will necessarily cost the offender his commission.   The matter seems to me to be one for the military authorities, just as the question whether a barrister should be disbarred upon a conviction is a question for the Benchers of his Inn.

To deprive a man of a pension or superannuation allowance, which is in reality deferred pay earned by work done, is to keep up the principle of forfeiture of property as a punishment for crime in a special class of cases when it has been given up in all others. Two officers of a bank are convicted of a forgery for which each is sentenced to a year's hard labour. One is a retired Indian civilian with a pension of £1000 a year; the other has bought a life annuity of the same amount out of his savings in a profession. Why is the one to lose his pension and the other to keep his annuity? The pension is just as much property as the annuity. It is part of the consideration for which many years of labour were given. Apart from this why when removing an admitted grievance keep up a perfectly irrational distinction between the punishment of felons and the punishment of misdemeanants? Suppose that two other persons—directors of the same bank—had fraudulently misappropriated its funds in concert with the two forgers, but by means amounting only to misdemeanour. If they held pensions or commissions they would forfeit nothing, even if they were sentenced to penal servitude. Surely this is highly unjust. It seems to me that the whole act, except the section which abolishes forfeiture, should be repealed. If its provisions are not wanted in cases of misdemeanour they are not wanted at all. They are practically a dead letter in cases of felony.

I now pass to the punishments provided by law for misdemeanours. As I have already said, they varied in an even more remarkable manner than the punishments for felonies, as in 1839 there were no less than ninety-six classes of them. I will notice only the most important.

A large number of misdemeanours were created by statute at different times, but especially in the eighteenth and nineteenth centuries, which differ in no essential respect from the common crimes distinguished as felonies. For instance, to obtain goods by false pretences, to misappropriate securities intrusted to the offender as an agent, solicitor, or banker, and to commit many other fraudulent or mischievous acts are, as far as moral guilt is concerned, on a level with theft. They have been punished by transportation and imprisonment with or without hard labour in exactly the same way as felonies, and what I have already said of those punishments applies equally to both classes of offences.

But apart from these statutory punishments there are

Cʜ. XIII. punishments appointed by the common law, both for misdemeanours at common law and also for those statutory
misdemeanours for which no punishment is provided by
statute.   These are fine and imprisonment and whipping.
Whipping has never been formally abolished for common law
misdemeanours, though I believe it has never in modern
time been inflicted except under the provisions of some
statute.

The statutory rules as to the amount of the fines and the
length of the imprisonment which the court may impose, are
vague to the last degree. I know, indeed, of two only.
The first is the provision of [1] Magna Carta, ch. 20, " Liber
" homo non amercietur pro parvo delicto, nisi secundum
" modum delicti, et pro magno delicto amercietur secundum
" magnitudinem delicti salvo contenemento suo ; et mercator
" eodem modo salva mercandisa sua ; et villanus eodem modo
" amercietur salvo wainagio suo." The second is the provision
of the Bill of Rights (1 Will. & Mary, sess. 2, c. 2), " that ex-
" cessive bail ought not to be required, nor excessive fines
" imposed, nor cruel and unusual punishments inflicted." No
doubt the floggings to which Oates and some others were sentenced were the " cruel punishments " which Parliament referred to, and the fine of £40,000 to which John Hampden
(the grandson of the celebrated Hampden) was sentenced
in 1684, would be one of the " excessive fines." The severest
sentence for a common law misdemeanour that I am aware of
since the Revolution, was passed upon one Hales for forging
a promissory note in 1729. He was to stand twice in the
pillory, to be fined fifty marks, be imprisoned for five years,
and find security for his good behaviour for seven years.

The pillory was abolished in all cases except perjury in
1816 (56 Geo. 3, c. 138), and was abolished absolutely in
general terms and without exception in 1837 by 7 Will. 4,
and 1 Vic. c. 23.

There were, and in a sense still are, certain exceptional
misdemeanours, mostly of a political, or ecclesiastico-political
kind, which theoretically subject the offender to punishments
so severe that they are never inflicted. It is said that for

[1] Stubbs, *Charters*, 299.

misprision of treason an offender must be imprisoned for life CH. XIII.
and forfeit his property. [1] There are a variety of offences
of an ecclesiastical kind such as "depraving" the Book of
Common Prayer, and a minister obstinately refusing to use
the said Common Prayer, for which the offender must for a
third offence be imprisoned for life. There are also some
offences for which the penalty of a "præmunire" is incurred.
[2] This is said to involve imprisonment for life, or during
pleasure, exclusion from the queen's protection, and forfeiture of property. These, however, are little more than
monuments of past times, devoid of any interest except
by way of antiquarian curiosity.

In concluding this chapter I may refer shortly to a branch
of the law which has been obsolete for ages, but which, when
it existed, was connected with benefit of clergy. I refer to
the law of sanctuary. In very early times a criminal who
took refuge in a church could not be taken from it, but was
allowed to take before a coroner an oath of abjuration. That
is to say, he admitted his guilt, and swore to leave the realm
for life at a place appointed for that purpose. In process of
time abjuration became obsolete, but various places came to
be privileged, and "sanctuary men" were allowed to live
there under regulations, some of which were imposed by
statute. The statutes of 27 Hen. 8, c. 19 (1537), & 32
Hen. 8, c. 12 (1540), show how this system worked. The
first statute enacts that sanctuary men are to wear badges, carry
no weapons, and to be to a certain extent under the control of
the governors of the sanctuaries. An abstract of the latter
statute, printed in the common edition of *The Statutes at
Large*, is as follows. It gives correctly the effect of the act as
printed in the *The Statutes of the Realm*. "All sanctuaries and
" places privileged which have been used for sanctuary shall
" be utterly extinguished, except parish churches and their
" churchyards, cathedral churches, and churches collegiate, and
" all churches dedicated, used as parish churches, and the
" sanctuaries to either of them belonging, and Wells in the

---

[1] The statutes are abstracted in my *Digest*, pp. 100, 101.
[2] Coke, 1*st Inst.* 130*a*. See offences in *Seventh Rep. C. C. and Com.*
p. 37 The Royal Marriage Act, 12 Geo. 3, c. 11, is, I think, the last Act
which subjects any one to this penalty.

" county of Somerset, Westminster, Manchester, Northampton,
" Norwich, York, Derby, and Lancaster. None of the said
" places shall give immunity of defence to any person which
" shall commit wilful murder, rape, burglary, robbery in the
" highway, or in any house, or in any church or chapel, or
" which shall burn wilfully any house or barn with corn. He
" that taketh sanctuary in any church, churchyard, &c., may
" remain there forty days, as hath been used, unless the coroner
" repair to him to take his abjuration, in which case he shall
" abjure to any of the foresaid privileged places, not being full
" of the number appointed to them, viz., above 20 persons,
" there to remain during life. If a privileged person, duly
" called to appear before the governor, shall make default
" three days, or if he commit any felony, he shall lose the
" benefit of sanctuary. A privileged person, abjuring to any
" of the aforesaid places, shall be conducted from constable
" to constable directly until he be brought to the governor
" of the said privileged place ; and if that place be full of
" his number then he shall be conducted to the next privileged
" place, and so to the next, &c., until, &c."

In 1623 sanctuary was abolished absolutely by 21 Jas. 1,
c. 28, s. 7, but in a modified form sanctuaries continued apparently in defiance of the law for another century, so far at
least as regards the execution of civil process.   This appears
from the acts of 8 & 9 Will. 3, c. 27, s. 15, which makes it
penal in sheriffs not to execute process in certain " pretended
" privileged places," such as Whitefriars and the Savoy ; and
9 Geo. 1, c. 28 (1722) and 11 Geo. 1, c. 23, which contain
provisions against resistance to process in " certain pretended
" privileged places " in the Mint and Stepney.[1]

---

[1] On Sanctuary, see Pike's *History of Crime*, ii. 252-5, and elsewhere.

CHAPTER XIV.

MANAGEMENT OF PROSECUTIONS.

THE only subject connected with procedure which remains to be treated is that of the manner in which criminal prosecutions are managed. This is a matter of the highest practical importance, though not of so much interest as some of the other topics which I have had to discuss.

In most countries the duty of making a preliminary investigation into the circumstances of an offence, collecting evidence for the trial, and managing the case in court, is in the hands of public officers. Throughout the Continent officers are to be found answering more or less to the French *Procureur Général, Procureur de la République,* and *Juge d'Instruction.* Even in Scotland the Procurator Fiscal and his officers have somewhat analogous duties, and in Ireland, where English law prevails with but slight variations, a system exists by which prosecutions are conducted principally by solicitors and counsel who represent the Crown. In England, and, so far as I know, in England and some English colonies alone, the prosecution of offences is left entirely to private persons, or to public officers who act in their capacity of private persons and who have hardly any legal powers beyond those which belong to private persons.

Incidentally this has already appeared in the course of this work, but I may now put together what has already been stated.

The police in their different grades are no doubt officers appointed by law for the purpose of arresting criminals; but they possess for this purpose no powers which are not also possessed by private persons. They are, indeed, protected in arresting innocent persons upon a reasonable suspicion that they have committed felony, whether a felony has in fact been committed or not, whereas the protection of a private person in such a case extends only to cases in which a felony has been committed, and they are, and private persons are not, under a legal duty to arrest when the occasion arises, but in other respects they stand upon precisely the same footing as private persons. They require a warrant, and may arrest without a warrant in the same cases. When they have arrested they are under precisely the same obligations. A policeman has no other right as to asking questions or compelling the attendance of witnesses than a private person has; in a word, with some few exceptions, he may be described as a private person paid to perform as a matter of duty acts which, if so minded, he might have done voluntarily.

When a prisoner has been arrested and is brought before a magistrate, the magistrate's duties are now entirely judicial. He hears the evidence, as a rule to which there are hardly any exceptions, in open court. He is provided with no means of making inquiries, though he can issue summonses for the attendance of witnesses if he is informed by others as to their knowledge, but it is no one's legal official duty to inquire into the matter. As a fact the duty is undertaken by the police, who, in cases of any importance, are usually authorised by the superior police authorities to instruct a solicitor, who, in some cases, instructs counsel to appear before the magistrates to prosecute. If, as is often the case, there is a private prosecutor, he can, and does, manage the whole matter, as he might manage any other action at law; he employs a solicitor who may or may not instruct counsel, and who takes the proofs of witnesses, brings them before the committing magistrate and the grand jury, instructs counsel at the trial, and, in a word, manages the whole of the proceedings just as he would in a civil cause.

The course pursued is precisely the same in all cases, and whoever may be the prosecutor. A prosecution for high treason, conducted by the Attorney-General, differs in no one

particular in matter of principle from the prosecution of a Ch. XIV.
servant by his master for embezzling half-a-crown.

No person has any legal power for the collection of evidence, or for its production before the magistrate, or in appearing before the court by which the matter is finally determined in the one case which the person placed in a corresponding situation has not in the other. When the Attorney-General conducts the most important State prosecutions before the Queen's Bench Division, he has (with one or two not very important exceptions) identically the same powers and duties as the youngest counsel at the bar on the prosecution of a petty thief at the Middlesex Sessions.

The Director of Public Prosecutions, when he has instituted a prosecution for the most serious offence, and one in which the whole country has a deep interest, has no other powers than a private person would have in respect of the prosecution of a fraud which affected no one but himself.

It is perhaps even more singular that the converse is true. Every private person has exactly the same right to institute any criminal prosecution as the Attorney-General or any one else. A private person may not only prosecute any one for high treason or a seditious conspiracy, but A may prosecute B for a libel upon C, for an assault upon D, or a fraud upon E, although A may have no sort of interest in the matter, and C, D, and E, may be altogether averse to the prosecution.

The rule of the French law, and I believe of most other continental countries, is that prosecutions having punishment for their object can be instituted only by public authority, but that a person injured by a crime may join in the prosecution as the *partie civile*, under certain rules.

The English system has no doubt its disadvantages, and is capable of being made to look extravagant by crude statements (like those just given) of the results which might follow from it if it were pushed to an extreme. It never is pushed to an extreme, however: first, because a jury as soon as the character of such a prosecution as I have suggested was exposed, would be certain to acquit, unless there were some extraordinary reason for sanctioning it; and secondly, because the result of such an acquittal would be an action

Сн. XIV. for malicious prosecution followed by a verdict for exemplary damages. Besides which, the management of a criminal prosecution is so expensive, so unpleasant, and so anxious a business, that no one is likely to undertake it without strong reasons.

On the other hand, no stronger or more effectual guarantee can be provided for the due observance of the law of the land, by all persons under all circumstances, than is given by the power, conceded to every one by the English system, of testing the legality of any conduct of which he disapproves, either on private or on public grounds, by a criminal prosecution. Many such prosecutions, both in our days and in earlier times, have given a legal vent to feelings in every way entitled to respect, and have decided peaceably, and in an authentic manner, many questions of great constitutional importance.

The unlimited power to institute prosecutions does not carry with it an unlimited control over them when they are instituted. When a charge has been made the maker of it is usually bound over to prosecute, and when a bill has been sent before the grand jury, the matter is entirely out of the original prosecutor's hands, and must run its course, unless the court before which it is to be tried sanctions the withdrawal of the charge, or unless the Attorney-General as the representative of the Crown, the nominal prosecutor, enters a *nolle prosequi,* which operates not as an acquittal, but as a stay of proceedings upon the particular case to which it refers.

I do not think that the existence of this state of the law can properly be regarded as the result of design. It seems rather to have been the effect of historical causes already referred to. One cause is no doubt to be found in the system of appeals or private accusations. They were in nearly every respect in the nature of civil actions, and were conducted like other private litigations. But another cause is to be found in the history of trial by jury. So long and so far as trial by jury retained its original character of a report made by a body of official witnesses of facts within their own knowledge, a criminal trial was a public inquiry, or rather a report upon a public inquiry, into the truth of CH. XIV. an accusation of crime, but when the jury assumed its present character the preparation of a case for trial consisted no longer in inquiries made by the jurymen themselves, but in the collection of evidence to be submitted to them. No direct express provision was ever made for this purpose, unless the appointment of justices of the peace is to be regarded in that light. Justices did no doubt concern themselves with the detection and apprehension of offenders and the collection of evidence against them to a greater extent and down to a later period than is commonly known, and to that extent they may be regarded as having for some centuries discharged more or less efficiently and completely the duties which in other countries are imposed upon public prosecutors. By degrees, however, their position became that of preliminary judges, and the duties which they had originally discharged devolved upon the police, who have never been intrusted with any special powers for the purpose of discharging them. It was thus by a series of omissions on the part of the legislature to establish new officers for the administration of justice as the old methods of procedure gradually changed their character, that English criminal trials gradually lost their original character of public inquiries, and came to be conducted in almost precisely the same manner as private litigations. Perhaps the strongest illustration of the length to which this process has gone is to be found in the way in which business is conducted before a coroner. The coroner was the predecessor of the justice of the peace, and it was his duty on the one hand to receive appeals or private accusations, and on the other to inquire into cases of homicide in the interest of the public. The inquiry was made originally by the reeve and the four men of a certain number of townships. It is now made by a jury before which witnesses may be, and are, summoned, but if the inquiry appears likely to result in a criminal charge, the inquest practically assumes the form of a litigation. The friends of the deceased and the suspected person are represented by advocates, and are entitled, or at all events permitted, to examine and cross-examine witnesses exactly as if the suspected person whom it is proposed to accuse was on his trial, and the coroner and jury occupy a position closely analogous to those of a judge and a jury, and very unlike the positions of persons holding an inquiry and pursuing their own independent investigations for the discovery of the truth.

One circumstance which practically left the whole business of originating and conducting prosecutions in private hands, and so gave to the whole procedure its character of a private litigation, was the fact that till about a century ago private persons had to pay all the costs of every prosecution. This was complained of by Lord Hale. [1] "It is," he said, "a " great defect in the law, to give courts of justice no power " to allow witnesses against criminals their charges therein, to " their great hindrance and loss." [2] Fielding in his essay on the causes of the increase of robberies, repeats and enforces this complaint. The extreme poverty of prosecutors, he says is one cause of the escape of offenders. "This I " have known to be so absolutely the case that the poor " wretch who hath been bound to prosecute was under more " concern than the prisoner himself. It is true the necessary " cost on these occasions is extremely small : two shillings, " which are appointed by Act of Parliament for drawing the " indictment, being, I think, the whole which the law requires, " but when the expense of attendance, generally with several " witnesses, sometimes during several days together, and often " at a great distance from the prosecutor's home . . . . are " summed up, and the loss of time added to the account, the " whole amounts to an expense which a very poor person " already plundered by the thief must look on with such horror " that he must be a miracle of public spirit " if he prosecutes. The first scheme for the remedy of this evil was [3] to provide by statute rewards for successful prosecutions. But this system was replaced by a more reasonable one authorizing the court to order payment of costs in cases of felony.

[1] Quoted by Fielding, *ubi infra.*   [2] *Works*, vol. x. p. 371—72.
[3] A list may be seen in Chitty's *Criminal Law*, 821—24. One of the rewards given was grotesque. If a man prosecuted certain kinds of felons to conviction he was entitled to a certificate (which was originally transferable once) freeing the holder from the obligation of holding certain parish offices. This was called a "Tyburn ticket," and in some parishes at particular times sold for a large sum.

Several statutes dealt with this subject successively. The first statute of importance was 18 Geo. 3, c. 19 (A.D. 1778), which was followed by 58 Geo. 3, c. 52 (A.D. 1818). The Acts now in force on the subject are 7 Geo. 4, c. 64, 14 & 15 Vic. c. 55, and the [1] five Consolidation Acts of 1861. The result of these statutes is that the court may allow costs to prosecutors in all cases of felony, and in all common cases of misdemeanour. The legislation on the subject is scattered, cumbrous, and in some points capricious, as the misdemeanours in respect of which costs may be given are chosen without much reference to principle. It would, however, be foreign to my purpose to go into minute detail on the subject.

In concluding this subject I may mention very shortly some particulars as to the different persons by whom criminal prosecutions are conducted in court, and as to the part which they take in the matter.

The highest in rank are the law officers of the Crown, the Attorney and Solicitor General.

The origin of these offices is, I believe, unknown, but it is obvious that the king must have been represented by counsel in his courts from the earliest time when counsel were employed at all in courts of justice ; and that they must have been employed from the very earliest times is obvious from the extremely minute and rigidly technical procedure which was inforced in the case of appeals. It has been conjectured that, as in old times the king had special attorneys or representatives in particular courts, as e.g. in the Court of Wards, the title of the Attorney-General means that the person who held it represented the king in all courts. This, however, seems to me doubtful. The expression " general attorney " meant no more than general agent or representative, and other persons besides the king had attorneys-general. Thus, in the Statute of Westminster the Second (A.D. 1283), 13 Edw. 1, c. 10, it is enacted that " such as 'have land in " divers shires where the justices make their circuit, and " that have land in shires where the justices have no " circuit, that fear to be impleaded and are impleaded of

[1] 24 & 25 Vic. cc. 96, 97, 98, 99, 100.
[2] *Dig. Crim. Proc.* arts. 316-331.

CH. XIV. " their lands in shires where they have no circuit, as before
" the justices at Westminster, or in the King's Bench, or
" before justices assigned to take assizes, or in any county
" before sheriffs, or in any court baron, may make a general
" attorney to sue for them in all pleas in the circuit of jus-
" tices, moved or to be moved for them or against them during
" the circuit, which attorney or attorneys shall have full
" power in all pleas moved during the circuit, until the plea
" be determined or that his master removeth."

This provision forms part of a statute introduced to prevent
suits from being brought behind the backs of defendants. It
shows that in very early times personal attendance in court
was necessary if a man meant to protect his interests, and
that persons who had much to lose had need of an attorney-
general to protect their interests. A curious instance of this
occurs in Shakespeare. In *Richard II.*, Act II. Sc. 1, York,
in attempting to dissuade Richard II. from confiscating
Bolingbroke's property, says :

" If you do wrongfully seize Hereford's rights,
" Call in the letters patent that he hath
" By *his attorneys-general to sue*
" *His livery*, and deny his offer'd homage,
" You pluck a thousand dangers on your head."

However this may be, [1] Mr. Foss gives a list of sixteen
" Attornati regis " who held office between 1277 and
1304. They were not originally the highest of the law
officers. Till the Civil Wars [2] the King's Serjeant usually
managed state prosecutions, and the proclamation made in
court when a batch of persons are arraigned for felony,
" Whoever can inform the Queen's Serjeant, the Queen's
" Attorney-General," &c. In early times before juries heard
evidence there could have been but little for the counsel for
the Crown to do in criminal trials, and neither Fortescue nor
Smith, in their accounts of the routine of criminal justice
take any notice of their interference, though the accounts of

---

[1] *Judges of England*, iii. 45.
[2] Blackstone (iii. 28) gives a table of precedence at the Bar, which begins
thus :—(1) The King's Premier Sergeant, (2) the King's Ancient Sergeant,
(3) the King's Advocate-General, (4) the King's Attorney-General, (5) the
King's Solicitor-General.

various trials in the sixteenth century show that at that time
the counsel for the Crown took an even more active and
prominent part in the proceedings than they do at present.

When by degrees criminal trials assumed their present
form all the counsel in the case on both sides found themselves practically on an equality. The Attorney-General has
no authority in court beyond that which his abilities and
eminence may give him, with the following exceptions:—
He can, by filing a criminal information, put a man on his
trial without sending a bill before a grand jury; he can stop
a prosecution by entering a *nolle prosequi*, and he has the
right to reply whether the prisoner calls witnesses or not.

Till the year 1879 the Attorney-General was the only
person who answered in any degree to the description of a
public prosecutor, but in that year an Act was passed for
the appointment of an officer called " the Director of Public
" Prosecutions " (42 & 43 Vic. c. 22). The Act confers no
power whatever on the Director of Public Prosecutions which it
required legislation to give, except powers of a very technical
kind (see ss. 5 and 6), and his duties seem to amount to little
else than those which the solicitor to the treasury used to
discharge when directed to take up a case for the government, and which any private solicitor might discharge for his
client. He is to "institute, undertake, or carry on criminal
" proceedings under the superintendence of the Attorney-
" General," and to give advice and assistance to " chief officers
" of police, clerks to justices, and other persons concerned in
" any criminal proceedings."

Though the law of England concedes to private persons a
control which in practice is almost unlimited over criminal
prosecutions, it nevertheless does not regard a criminal
prosecution as being to all intents a private action. Where
one person has a civil claim against another he can settle
it on such terms as he thinks proper, but he cannot do so
with respect to criminal proceedings. The law upon the
subject is by no means clear, but in general terms it is as
follows :—

1. The fact that the person injured by a crime has agreed
not to prosecute the criminal is no defence to the criminal.

Cɴ. XIV. In a civil proceeding it would be a good defence to any claim to allege that it had been compromised, but in criminal proceedings such a plea would not be permitted.

2. It is not quite clear whether an agreement not to prosecute an offender is in itself a crime. [1] It is commonly said to be a misdemeanour to agree not to prosecute a person for felony, but there is singularly little authority on the subject.

In ancient times it was an offence called " theft bote " to receive back stolen property upon an agreement not to prosecute the thief.

3. [2] It does not appear to be a misdemeanour to agree not to prosecute a person for misdemeanour, but such an agreement is generally speaking void, as being contrary to public policy. There probably is an exception to this in the case of misdemeanours in which the public have no substantial interest, as, for instance, the case of a common assault, or a libel on a private person.

[3] In some cases the court will, before passing sentence in a case of misdemeanour, allow the defendant and the person injured to come to terms, in consideration of which the court will pass a light or even a nominal sentence.

4. [4] It is an offence to compound a penal action without the leave of the court, and to take a reward corruptly for helping any person to recover goods stolen, or otherwise criminally obtained.

On the Continent a person injured by a crime may usually come in as what is called in French law the " partie civile " to a criminal proceeding. This is unknown in England, and till very lately it was considered that where a private person was injured by a felony the civil remedy was suspended till the felon was convicted. On the other hand, upon his convic-

---

[1] See my *Digest*, art. 158, p. 94. The reference there should be 1 Hale, 619, instead of 2 Hale, 619. The article goes a little beyond Hale's authority, but is founded on precedents of indictments given in Chitty. See too Archbold, 896.

[2] The fullest authority on this subject is Keir *v.* Leeman, 6 Q.B. 308, and same case in Cam. Scacc. 371.

[3] Russ. Cr. 293.

[4] See my *Digest*, articles 159 & 354(a), and 18 Eliz. c. 5, ss. 4 & 5, and 24 & 25 Vic. c. 96, s. 101.

tion the remedy ceased to be worth having, as his goods were CH. XIV.
forfeited. As forfeiture for felony has been abolished, this
last remark no longer applies, and the case of [1] Wells v.
Abrahams has thrown a good deal of doubt on the general
doctrine, by showing that even if the rule exists it is practically impossible to enforce it, unless special circumstances
make it necessary to do so in the public interest.

[1] L.R. 7 Q.B. 334 ; and see Osborne v. Gillett, L.R. 8 Ex. 89.

CHAPTER XV.

GENERAL AND COMPARATIVE VIEW OF ENGLISH AND FRENCH
CRIMINAL PROCEDURE.

Ch. XV.

Having related at length the history of the criminal courts, and of every step of the procedure pursued in them for the purpose of bringing criminals to justice, I propose in the present chapter to make some general observations upon the system and to point out such of the reforms, which it seems to me to require, as have not been discussed in earlier parts of the work. For this purpose I shall comment upon the provisions relating to procedure proposed to be made by the Draft Criminal Code of 1879; and, in order to set the special character of the whole system in as clear a light as possible, I shall compare or contrast it with the French *Code d'Instruction Criminelle.*

First, as to the English courts of justice. The only point of importance to be observed in connection with them is that though their history is intricate, and though their present condition displays some singular traces of their origin, they form a system of extreme unity and simplicity. There is, practically speaking, only one superior criminal court, judges from which sit four times every year either in or for every county in England, and twelve times a year in and for London and its neighbourhood.

There are numerous local Courts of Quarter Sessions, which sit for the trial of offences of less importance four times a year in every county and borough in England, and in some cases six times a year, and here and there even more frequently.

Some few little alterations as to these courts might be suggested. It would be easy, for instance, to have a single criminal court for all England, and so to supersede the necessity for issuing Commissions of Oyer and Terminer and Gaol Delivery, but this would make no real change either in the constitution or in the procedure of the courts. It would also be possible, and I think it would be desirable, to group the counties for assize purposes at all the assizes, as is now the practice at the spring and autumn assizes, but this is a very small matter. I know of no proposal worth mentioning for any alteration in the constitution of the [1] superior criminal courts, except such as relate to the institution of a Court of Criminal Appeal, as to which I have already expressed my opinion. The same observation applies to the Borough Courts of Quarter Sessions, in which Recorders appointed by the Crown are the judges. As to the County Courts of Quarter Sessions, though the magistrates who are the judges are appointed by the Crown, the chairmen are chosen by the magistrates from their own number. It has sometimes been doubted whether there ought not to be paid chairmen, being barristers. [2] In Middlesex there is such an officer. I should be sorry to see a general change in this matter, as a large proportion of the chairmen of Quarter Sessions whom I have known were judges quite good enough for their duties; but I think that power might be given to the justices of counties to appoint paid chairmen, being barristers of some standing, if the number of prisoners to be tried and the importance of the cases for trial required it. A small payment would be sufficient to secure the services, for such a purpose, of men of considerable professional eminence, as the position would be pleasant and a professional distinction, and as the work would not be great. The jurisdiction of the Courts of Quarter Sessions might also be increased with advantage. There can

[1] Whether the election of the Recorder of London by the Aldermen and the election of the Common Serjeant by the Common Council is a good arrangement, forming, as it does, the only exception of importance to the general rule that judges should not be elective, may be a question. All corporations mentioned in the Municipal Reform Act were deprived by it of the power of appointing their Recorders.
[2] See 7 & 8 Vic. c. 71 ss. 8-10, which empowers the appointment by the Crown of an assistant-judge and a deputy.

be no reason why they should not try cases of burglary, which in these days are generally little worse than common thefts, but it might be well to restrict them in respect of the sentence to be passed, say to seven or ten years' penal servitude, and to empower them to send cases which seemed to require a more serious punishment (as, for instance, when violence was used) to be tried at the assizes. A proposal to this effect was made in the Draft Code, s. 434.

Passing from the courts of justice to the procedure, I may observe in the first place that, as it now stands, it is from first to last distinguished by one characteristic feature. It has come by the steps already described to be preeminently litigious, and hardly at all inquisitorial. English criminal proceedings are from their very first institution and at every stage closely assimilated to proceedings for the prosecution of a civil action. This may seem not to apply to the preliminary steps in such proceedings—the arrest of the prisoner, his examination before the committing magistrate, and his imprisonment till he is tried. Even here, however, the resemblance is much stronger than would appear at first sight. The arrest and imprisonment of a person suspected of crime are precisely analogous to the law of arrest on mesne process, by which a defendant could, till recent times, be arrested and imprisoned till the trial of an action against him, or till he found bail. The proceedings before the magistrate are a great advantage to the suspected person, as in any case they give him notice of the case against him, and enable him to provide for his defence, and as they may lead practically (though not in theory) to his discharge and virtual acquittal. They put him in a position infinitely more favourable than that of a defendant in a civil action. The defendant in an action must put in a statement of defence, admitting, denying, or explaining every material fact alleged against him in the statement of claim. He must also make an affidavit of the documents in his possession bearing on the subject, give discovery of them to his antagonist, and answer interrogatories. He must in short completely disclose his defence, and to a considerable extent disclose the evidence by which he proposes to sustain his defence, before he comes to trial. CH. XV. A prisoner charged with crime is subject to no such necessity. He has an opportunity before he is committed for trial of saying whatever he pleases, but he cannot be asked a single question at any stage of the proceedings except the formal one, " Are you guilty or not guilty ? " and if he does not answer even that single question the omission to do so has no effect whatever, as a plea of not guilty is entered for him Besides this a prisoner cannot be detained in custody indefinitely in order to enable the prosecutor to get up the case against him. He can insist, under the Habeas Corpus Act, on being tried after one adjournment at most for which definite cause must be shown. Lastly, the trial which determines the question of his guilt or innocence is conducted precisely in the same manner as the trial of a civil action, subject only to the circumstance that the rule which rendered the parties to an action incompetent witnesses in civil cases has not in criminal proceedings been so far relaxed as to make the prisoner competent or compellable to give evidence. This single distinction between civil and criminal proceedings has been made or rather maintained in the supposed interests of the prisoner.

In the earlier chapters of this volume I have made such observations as occurred to me upon the different stages of criminal procedure. I will now, in order to give a general view of the whole subject, review that part of the [1] Draft Criminal Code of 1879, which related to procedure, noticing the changes which it proposed to make in the law as it then stood and still stands. This part of the Draft Code forms Title VII. of the Draft, and contains 125 sections divided into ten parts or chapters. It is arranged very nearly in the same order as the present volume, except that as it did not propose to make any alteration in the constitution of the existing criminal courts, ordinary or extraordinary, or in the constitution of the police establishment it takes no notice of those matters.

The first important alteration in the existing law of proce-

---

[1] The circumstances in which this bill originated are stated in the preface.

CH. XV. dure proposed to be made by the Draft Code was [1] the abolition of the distinction between felonies and misdemeanours. This was treated as a matter of procedure, because as the law now stands there is practically no distinction between the punishments allotted to felonies and misdemeanours, many misdemeanours (for instance, conspiracy to murder, frauds by trustees, perjury, and the obtaining of goods by false pretences) being punishable by penal servitude. Hence the practical importance of the distinction has reference entirely to matters of procedure, every part of which is more or less affected by it. A felon may in all cases be arrested without warrant, and is in no case absolutely entitled to be bailed, whereas a misdemeanant cannot be arrested without warrant except in cases specially provided for by statute, and is entitled to be bailed in all cases in which special statutory enactments do not modify his right. A misdemeanant has, and a felon has not, a right to a copy of the indictment. In an indictment for felony one offence only can practically be charged. In an indictment for misdemeanour any number of offences may be charged in different counts. There are, moreover, many distinctions as to the trial of felonies and misdemeanours. The only one of much practical importance is that a person accused of felony has, whereas a person accused of misdemeanour has not, the right of peremptory challenge.

This distinction with all its consequences the Commissioners proposed to abolish. In the definition of each particular offence there was contained a special provision deciding whether persons accused of it should be liable or not to summary arrest, and should or should not be bailable at discretion only. All trials were to be conducted in the same way; all provisions as to indictments were to apply to all offences alike; and as to challenges it was provided that persons indicted for treason should have thirty-five peremptory challenges; persons indicted for offences rendering them liable to death or penal servitude for life twenty, and all other persons six. The right to challenge is hardly ever made use of in the present day, but when it is it seems hard

[1] S. 431.

that a man indicted for theft should possess it, and that a man indicted for perjury, libel, or obtaining goods by false pretences should not.

The existing law as to the local jurisdiction of the courts was considerably altered by the Draft Code. The whole law of venue was swept away by s. 504, which gave every criminal court jurisdiction to try every offence over which it had jurisdiction, wherever it might be committed, subject only to the rule that English offences must be tried in England, and Irish offences in Ireland. In the same spirit the system of backing warrants was abolished, and a justice's warrant was made to run over the whole of England, or the whole of Ireland, an adaptation to England of the Irish practice.

With respect to proceedings to compel the appearance of suspected persons the Draft Code proposed a few alterations in the existing law.

By s. 437 power was given to justices to inquire into any suspected offence, although no person might be charged, by calling before them witnesses able to give material evidence and examining them upon oath. This power was originally given to justices in Ireland by the Peace Preservation Act of 1870 (33 Vic. c. 9, s. 13). A similar section is contained in the Prevention of Crime Act, 1882 (45 & 46 Vic. c. 25, s. 16). It is a power which obviously ought to exist in all cases, as it can inflict no hardship on any innocent person, and may frequently lead to the discovery of criminals. When a crime has been committed, and before any person has been arrested for it, many matters are noticed and remembered which are soon forgotten, but which may be found afterwards to be of great importance. Such inquiries can now be made only by policemen, who have no power to require any one to give the information, and no authority to put people upon their oaths. The power of holding such an inquiry ought to be part of the regular apparatus for the detection of crime. After all, it is only a speedier and less cumbrous form of doing what is done by coroners' inquests in cases of homicide. An attempt to introduce such a system was made by 30 & 31 Vic. c. 35, s. 6, but was defeated by amendments introduced in the passage of that measure through parliament.

No alteration of any great importance was proposed to be made in the proceedings before magistrates, but an alteration of great importance was proposed as to their position in the general system. As the law stands, as I have already explained at length, it is not necessary for a person wishing to accuse another of a crime to go before a magistrate at all, except in a few cases excepted (in 1859) from the general law by the Malicious Indictments Act (22 & 23 Vic. c. 17). It is thus legally possible that a man might be put upon his trial by an indictment found behind his back upon the evidence of witnesses whose names he would have no means of knowing before his trial. The Draft Code proposed to remedy this by extending the principle of the Malicious Indictments Act to all offences whatever, and by providing further that the verdict of a coroner's jury should no longer have the effect of an indictment, but should operate to bring the case before committing magistrates. The effect of this would have been that on the one hand every one brought to trial before a criminal court would know what was the evidence against him, and that on the other the mere fact that a magistrate, after hearing the evidence produced by the prosecutor, discharged the accused, would not put a stop to the proceedings, as the prosecutor would have a right to call upon the magistrate to bind him over to prosecute. He would then be entitled to send up an indictment on his own responsibility as he is at present. The power of the law officers to indict without going before a magistrate was reserved, and it was also provided that leave to do so might be given by the court or a judge. The grand jury would thus have ceased to be a body which designing persons could convert into an instrument of oppression, whilst it would have continued to afford a protection to the innocent (in my opinion, far from being superfluous) against the disgrace of being publicly accused and put upon their trial for offences which they have not committed. They would also continue to discharge, as they do at present, the function of preventing premature and abortive trials. It is by no means uncommon for offenders to be committed in cases in which the judge sees, though the

committing magistrate did not, that a link in the evidence is
wanting, or that the evidence itself is of such a nature that
the petty jury would be sure to acquit. In such cases it
is usual to advise the grand jury to throw out the bill, and in
this way open failures of justice are often prevented. This
is specially common in the case of crimes of a disgusting
nature imperfectly proved, the open trial of which is in itself
an evil, and by no means a small one.

The Draft Code proposed to sweep away completely all
the technicalities as to indictments, which have been half
effaced already. This was effected by a series of sections,
which stated shortly, but in positive terms, what the requisites of an indictment were to be, and then declared
negatively that no one of the old objections should be
made to them. The following sections speak for themselves,
and contain the gist of the proposed alterations:—

"SECTION 482.—FORM AND CONTENTS OF COUNTS.—Every
" count of an indictment shall contain and shall be sufficient
" if it contains in substance a statement that the accused has
" committed some offence therein specified. Such statement
" may be made in popular language without any technical
" averments or any allegations of matter not essential to
" be proved, and may be in the form I (2) in the first schedule
" hereto or to the like effect.

"Such statement may be in the words of the enactment
" describing the offence or declaring the matter charged
" to be an indictable offence, or in any words sufficient
" to give the accused notice of the offence with which he
" is charged.

"Every count shall contain so much detail of the circum-
" stances of the alleged offence as is sufficient to give the
" accused reasonable information as to the act or omission to
" be proved against him, and to identify the transaction
" referred to: Provided that the absence or insufficiency
" of such details shall not vitiate the count, but the Court
" may order an amendment or further particulars, as herein-
" after mentioned.

"A count may refer to any section or sub-section of
" any statute creating the offence charged therein, and in

" estimating the sufficiency of such count the Court may
" have regard to such reference.

" Every count shall in general apply only to a single
" transaction.

" SECTION 483.—OFFENCES MAY BE CHARGED IN THE
" ALTERNATIVE.—A count shall not be deemed objectionable
" on the ground that it charges in the alternative several
" different matters acts or omissions which are stated in the
" alternative in the enactment describing any offence or
" declaring the matters acts or omissions charged to be an
" indictable offence, or on the ground that it is double or
" multifarious : Provided that the accused may at any stage
" of the trial apply to the Court to amend or divide any such
" count on the ground that it is so framed as to embarrass
" him in his defence.

" The Court, if satisfied that the ends of justice require it,
" may order any count to be amended or divided into two or
" more counts, and on such order being made, such count
" shall be so divided or amended, and thereupon a formal
" commencement may be inserted before each of the counts
" into which it is divided."

Illustrations were given in the schedule of forms of the
kind of indictments which would have been drawn under this
system. They were as follows :—

I (1) *Heading.*

" In the (*name of the Court in which the indictment is*
" *found*).

" The jurors for Our Lady the Queen present that

" [*Where there are more counts than one add at the beginning*
" *of each count*] :

" ' The said jurors further present that '

I (2) *Charge.*

Examples of the manner of stating Offences.

" (*a*) *A.* murdered *B.* at   on

" (*b*) *A.* stole a sack of flour from a ship called the
at   on

"(c) A. obtained by false pretences from B. a horse a cart
" and the harness of a horse at   on

"(d) A. committed perjury with intent to procure the
" conviction of B. for an offence punishable with penal ser-
" vitude, namely robbery, by swearing on the trial of B. for
" the robbery of C. at the Court of Quarter Sessions for the
" West Riding of the county of York, held at Leeds on the
"   day of   1879; first, that he A. saw
" B. at Leeds on the   day of   ; secondly,
" that B. asked A. to lend B. money on a watch belonging to
" C.; thirdly, &c.

or

"(e) The said A. committed perjury on the trial of B. at a
" Court of Quarter Sessions held at Kilkenny on
" for an assault alleged to have been committed by the said
" B. on C. at Kilkenny on the   day of   , by
" swearing to the effect that the said B. could not have been
" at Kilkenny at the time of the alleged assault, inasmuch
" as the said A. had seen him at that time in Waterford.

"(f) A., with intent to maim disfigure disable or do
" grievous bodily harm to B., or with intent to resist the law-
" ful apprehension or detainer of A. [or C.], did actual bodily
" harm to B. [or D.].

"(g) A., with intent to injure or endanger the safety of
" persons on the North-Western Railway did an act calculated
" to interfere with an engine a tender and certain carriages on
" the said railway on   at   by [*describe*
" *with so much detail as is sufficient to give the accused reason-*
" *able information as to the acts or omissions relied on against*
" *him, and to identify the transaction.*]

"[1] (g) A. published a defamatory libel on B. in a certain
" newspaper, called the   on the   day of
"   A.D.   , which libel was contained
" in an article headed or commencing [*describe with so much*
" *detail as is sufficient to give the accused reasonable information*
" *as to the part of the publication to be relied on against him*],
" and which libel was written in the sense of imputing that
" the said B. was [*as the case may be*].

[1] (g) in the original. The lettering is wrong.

(*h*) " That *A.* without leave of Her Majesty did at [*Birken-* " *head*] equip, furnish, fit out, or arm, or attempt, or endeavour " to equip, furnish, fit out, or arm [*this is rendered sufficient* " *by Section* 483 *of the Code ; Section* 71 *renders it unnecessary* " *to proceed to state that they ' procured, aided, or assisted ' in the* " *equipment*] a ship called the ' *Alexandra*,' in order that it " might be employed in the service of a certain foreign " power called the Confederate States [*see Section* 484 *of the* " *Code*] against a foreign power called the United States, " with which Her Majesty was not then at war.

If these forms are compared with those to which I have referred in Chapter IX., the extent to which they would simplify the law will at once become apparent. The illustration marked (*h*) is the equivalent of the information in [1] R. *v.* Sillem, which contained ninety-five counts, charging separately all the combinations of the different operative words of the statute.

In order to prevent the prisoner from being embarrassed by the generality of indictments so drawn, the Code provided that he should be entitled to particulars of any statement which the court, after having regard to the indictment and to the depositions, believed to be really embarrassing. [2] Counts for different offences were allowed to be joined in all cases whatever, according to the present practice as to misdemeanours. An exception was made in regard to charges of murder, which, it was provided, were to be joined only with counts charging murder, so that if, as sometimes happens, a man set fire to a house, stole part of the property contained in it, and burned several persons to death, he might be charged in one indictment for the murder of all the persons burnt, the murder of each being charged in a separate count. He might also be charged in another indictment for arson and theft, the arson being charged in one count and the theft in another. This limitation upon the general rule was made because it was considered that on a trial for a capital crime the attention of the jury ought not to be diverted by any other inquiry, especially as the introduction of other charges might, under circumstances, invite a compromise. [3] The

[1] 2 Hurl. and Colt. p. 431.   [2] S. 493.   [3] S. 507.

prisoner was in all cases to be entitled to a copy of the indictment.

With regard to the place and mode of trial, the substance of the Draft Code was that accused persons should be brought before a justice having jurisdiction over the place where the offence was committed, and by him committed for trial to the court having jurisdiction over that place, but that this should be subject to a power in the Queen's Bench Division to direct a trial in any competent court. The court was also to have a right in every case to order a trial by a special jury.

The present law as to process to compel appearance on an indictment found was re-enacted in substance subject to only one alteration.—[1] outlawry was abolished. In the Draft Code of 1878 I proposed that for outlawry should be substituted a power to make a fugitive from justice a bankrupt, which would have involved the forfeiture of his property. The Commission of 1879 did not consider this necessary, but I doubt whether the omission was wise. It is true that under the provisions of extradition treaties offenders may in many cases be arrested abroad and brought back to England, but I do not see why, if a wealthy man committed treason or treasonable felony, he should be able to live in France with no other inconvenience than that of being unable to return to England. If a man will not answer to the laws of his country, I think he ought to forfeit the property which he holds under their protection. Forfeiture was expressly maintained in cases of outlawry by 33 & 34 Vic. c. 23, s. 1. The process of outlawry is practically obsolete, but bankruptcy is well understood; and if flying from justice were made an act of bankruptcy, it would operate as a severe check upon wealthy persons disposed to avoid justice.

Few alterations were suggested in the law relating to the actual trial, and those which were suggested were all in the direction of removing the few technical rules which still hamper the administration of justice.

The alterations proposed were as follows :—

First, with a view to the simplification of the process of appeal, it was proposed to abolish the present record, which is

[1] S. 501.

a document cumbrous and technical in the highest degree. For it was to be substituted a minute, to be made in a book to be called the Crown Book, kept for that purpose by the officer of the court, which would in every case record in a prescribed form all the essential parts of the proceedings, for the information of the Court of Appeal, if any appeal should take place. [1] The court was empowered to discharge the jury and adjourn the trial for the production of witnesses, but only in cases in which it appeared that the accused had been taken by surprise by the production of unexpected witnesses or that the prosecution had omitted to call witnesses whom they ought to have called. The jury of matrons in cases of pregnancy was abolished, and an examination by medical men substituted for it, and some minor matters which it is unnecessary to notice in detail, were provided for.

Of the proposal made for the examination of the prisoner I have already spoken, and I have also given an account of the alterations proposed as to appeals in criminal cases, as I thought that those proposals would be most naturally and easily considered in connection with a statement of the existing law and its history. One small alteration was not made which I think might be made with advantage. I think the judge ought to have a discretion to clear the court at the trial of indecent cases. At present it is usual to order boys and women to withdraw, but this is not in my judgment enough. The eagerness with which large numbers of men of all ages, especially young men and old men, press to hear cases which would make any decent person sick is revolting, is an insult to all good morals, and I am convinced does infinite mischief. All necessary publicity might be secured, and all possibility of perversions of justice by reason of the exclusion of public opinion might be avoided, by providing that persons having business in the court, and particularly reporters for newspapers, should not be excluded. The wholesome influences of public opinion would thus be retained, whilst the wretched creatures who gloat over the very worst forms of crime and vice would be prevented from turning what ought to be a school of virtue into a scene for the gratification of the lowest forms of vice.

[1] S. 525.

If these proposals had been, or if hereafter they should be, adopted, I think our system of criminal procedure would form a whole as complete, compact, and systematic as if it had been the work of a single mind. It would also have had the advantage of being passed, put together, and tested in every one of its constituent parts, by a succession of judges and legislators reaching back uninterruptedly to remote antiquity; and it would thus represent the experience of many centuries slowly accumulated and at last reduced to a definite, explicit system by a single statute.

No mere statement of such a system can give a full impression of its general character. In order to do this in a satisfactory manner it will be well to contrast it with what may be described as the great rival system of criminal procedure. The English system has extended itself not only over England and Ireland, but with variations over the whole of the North American continent; over all the English colonies, and in particular over Australia, the Cape of Good Hope, and New Zealand; and has formed the foundation of a system established throughout the Indian Empire, of which I shall give a full account in another part of this work.

The French *Code d'Instruction Criminelle* has served as a model for the legislation of a large part of continental Europe. It was the result of a different order of ideas from our own. It is enforced by a system of institutions widely different from ours; and though to a certain extent it has adopted our leading institution, trial by jury, a French jury occupies a position differing in many particulars from that of an English jury. In order to complete this chapter I will now proceed to give some account of French criminal procedure, comparing or contrasting it with our own.

The following is the organisation of the French criminal courts of justice. There are in France [1] twenty-six Courts of

[1] Agen; 2. Aix; 3. Ajaccio; 4. Amiens; 5. Angers; 6. Besançon; 7. Bordeaux; 8. Bourges; 9. Caen; 10. Dijon; 11. Douai; 12. Grenoble; 13. Limoges; 14. Lyons; 15. Montpellier; 16. Nancy; 17. Nîmes; 18. Orleans; 19. Paris; 20. Pau; 21. Poitiers; 22. Rennes; 23. Riom; 24. Rouen; 25. Toulouse; 26. Chambèry. Brussels and Liège were also the seats of Courts of Appeal, when they were established by the law of 27 Ventôse, An. VIII., and so were Colmar and Metz. These have ceased to be parts of France. Chambèry was added on the annexation of Nice in 1860 (Cours d'Appel, *Lois Usuelles*, p. 457). These courts have also been called *Cours Impériales* and *Cours*

CH. XV.   Appeal. [1] There are an indeterminate number of Courts of
——   First Instance. [2] There is in every *commune* one *juge de paix*
at least.   Others are divided between two or more.   These
are the French courts, from which are taken the Criminal
Courts as follows :—

[3] The *Cour d'Assises* is taken from each *Cour d'Appel*.   It
consists of three judges, one of whom is president.   In the
departments where the *Cours d'Appel* sit, all the judges are
members of the *Cour d'Appel*.   In the other departments the
president must be a member of the *Cour d'Appel*.   The other
two members may either be members of the *Cour d'Appel*
or presidents or judges of the Tribunal of First Instance for
the place in which the *Cour d'Assises* sits.

The *Cour d'Assises* sits in and for every department every
three months, but if need be they may sit more often.   The
Cours d'Assises try by a jury and [4] the proper subject of their
jurisdiction are *crimes* as distinguished from *délits*; but they
have also a special jurisdiction in some particular cases, and
if a case tried before them turns out to be a *délit*, or even a
police offence, they may deal with it.

[5] The *Tribunal Correctionnel* is the Tribunal of First Instance sitting as a criminal court.   It consists of three judges
taken from the Court of First Instance.   They try without a
jury, and have jurisdiction over *délits*, that is to say, over
offences which can be punished with more than five days'
imprisonment and more than 15 francs fine, but not with
death, *travaux forcés*, or *reclusion*.   The highest punishment
which they can inflict is five years' imprisonment, or, in cases
of a second conviction, ten years'.   They may also in many
cases try persons under sixteen for *crimes* punishable with
travaux forcés for not exceeding twenty years or *reclusion*.

Lastly, the *juges de paix* are judges in regard to police

Royales.   Most of them have three departments under their jurisdiction ; six,
namely Montpellier, Nancy, Nîmes, Poitiers, Riom, and Toulouse, have four
each ; one, Rennes, has five ; and Paris has seven.
  [1] Law of April 20, 1810, ch. 5.
  [2] *Code d'Instruction Criminelle*, pp. 141-142.   I refer to the Code as
C. I. C.
  [3] See *C. I. C.* pp 251-265.
  [4] *C. I. C.* p. 153 ; and see Hélie, *Prat. Crim.* i. pp. 434, 824.
  [5] *C. I. C.* pp. 179-181 ; and see Hélie, *Prat. Crim.* ii. pp. 187 188.

offences punishable with a fine not exceeding 15 francs, or CH. XV.
imprisonment not exceeding five days.

[1] If the *juge de paix* sentences any one to imprisonment
or to a fine of more than 5 francs, an appeal lies to the
Tribunal of Correctional Police; but it is not expressly stated
in the Code whether the defendant only or the prosecutor also
may appeal. The appeal suspends the execution of the sentence, and may, if either of the parties or the *Procureur
de la République* requires it, be by way of rehearing.

[2] An appeal lies from the Correctional Court to the Court
of Appeal in the case of all final judgments, and of such interlocutory judgments as have a direct bearing upon the final
judgment. [3] Either the defendant, the *partie civile*, the *Procureur de la République*, or the *Procureur-Général* may appeal.
[4] The appeal is heard as if it were a case brought before the
court in its original jurisdiction. [5] The court may dismiss the
defendant if it thinks that the facts proved constitute neither
a *contravention* nor a *délit* nor a *crime*. [6] If they think that
the offence was not a *délit*, but was a *contravention*, they may
inflict the proper punishment. [7] If they think the facts
amount to a *crime* they may take steps for the trial of the
case before the *Cour d'Assises*. [8] If they set aside the judgment on account of the violation or omission of forms prescribed by law under penalty of nullity, they may decide
upon the merits.

There is no appeal, properly so called, from the decisions
of a *Cour d'Assises*.

All the courts, the *Cours d'Assises* as well as the rest, are
subject to an appeal, as we should say, on matter of law only,
to the Court of Cassation. [9] This court sits at Paris, and is
composed of [10] three chambers, in each of which there are
sixteen judges. The leading principle as to its duties is
thus stated by [11] M. Hélie. "Il est de principe que la Cour

---

[1] *C. I. C.* 172-178.
[2] *C. I. C.* 199, *seq.*; Helie, *Prat. Crim.* i. p. 248, *seq.*
[3] *C. I. C.* 202. [4] *C. I. C.* 210, 190. [5] *C. I. C.* 212.
[6] *C. I. C.* 213. [7] *C. I. C.* 214. [8] *C. I. C.* 216.
[9] Roger et Sorel, *Lois Usuelles*, p. 414; Law 27 Ventôse, An. VIII.
[10] "La chambre des requêtes, la chambre civile, et la chambre criminelle."
—Roger et Sorel, p. 417; Law 15 Jan. 1826, art. i.
[11] *Prat. Crim.* i. p. 551.

" de Cassation ne peut, en aucun cas et sous aucun prétexte,
" connaître du fond des affaires, et que, lorsqu'elle casse les
" procédures et les jugements, elle doit renvoyer le fond aux
" tribunaux qui doivent en connaître. De là il suit que les
" arrêts portant cassation après avoir spécifié les limites de
" l'annulation, doivent ordonner le renvoi du procès aux juges
" qu'ils designent." To use the language of English law,
the Court of Cassation must either confirm the judgment
appealed against or order a new trial.

Such are the French courts. The general scheme of their
jurisdiction, and their relation to each other, has some points
of marked resemblance to our own. The *juge de paix* may
be compared to a police magistrate, the Correctional Tribunal
to a court of quarter sessions, the *Cours d'Assises* to our Assize
Courts, and the criminal chamber of the Court of Cassation
to our Court for Crown Cases Reserved, but this general
resemblance goes but a little way. Each of the courts in
question might be made the subject of a contrast to the
corresponding court in England much more striking than any
comparison between them could be. In the first place, the
whole system is far more systematic than our own, and bears
in every part of it the trace of having been formed upon one
general design. There is a neatness in the way in which the
tribunals of first instance and the courts of appeal are related
to each other, to the criminal courts derived out of them, and
to the Court of Cassation, which does not exist in our
institutions; but I am not sure that there is any special
advantage in this. If the English courts were described in
terms (so to speak) of the French courts, we should have to
say that there is one Court of Appeal in England, namely, the
High Court of Justice, that in each county and in every
borough having a separate court of quarter sessions there is a
correctional tribunal called the Court of Quarter Sessions,
and that there are also *juges de paix*, or justices of the peace,
in and for each county and borough—some paid, but mostly
unpaid; that the correctional tribunal is composed of all the
juges de paix in the county or borough who choose to attend at
the quarter sessions, and that each *juge de paix*, by himself or
in company with another, has jurisdiction to try all police cases.

Many observations might be made on the difference of the CH. XV.
position of judges in France and England. One is specially
characteristic and important—their comparative number.
The English Supreme Court of Judicature consists of the
Court of Appeal, in which there are five ordinary judges,
and four *ex officio* members—the Lord Chancellor, the Lord
Chief Justice of England, the Master of the Rolls, and the
President of the Probate Division (none of these, except
the Master of the Rolls, usually sits in the Court of Appeal).
The High Court of Justice consists of three divisions—the Chancery Division, with five judges; the Queen's Bench Division,
with fifteen, of whom the Chief Justice of England is one;
and the Probate, Divorce, and Admiralty Division, with two
judges, of whom the President of the Division is one. The
whole number of judges is thus twenty-nine, of whom nine
are members of the Court of Appeal. To these may be added
three paid judges of the House of Lords and two paid judges
of the Judicial Committee of the Privy Council, making up
the whole number to thirty-four—or two less than three-
fourths of the number of the Court of Cassation. Five of the
English judges are appellate judges only. The twenty-nine
others discharge not only all the duties of the Court of
Cassation, but most of the duties of the twenty-six French
courts of appeal, and in particular all the duties of all the
Cours d'Assises and many of the duties of the Courts of First
Instance. [1] By the law of April 20, 1810, the number of
judges in the *Cours d'Appel* is fixed as follows :—Paris, forty
to sixty, other courts twenty to forty. Taking thirty as the
average number of judges of a Court of Appeal, this would
give in all 810 judges for duties which in England are
performed by twenty-nine.

A [2] law of July 21, 1875, fixes the establishment of the
Tribunal of First Instance for the Seine as follows :—One president, eleven vice-presidents, sixty-two judges, fifteen supplementary judges—in all, eighty-seven judges. There are in the
Metropolitan District in England only eleven county courts in
all (counting the Lord Mayor's court as one), with a single
judge for each court. In the Tribunal of First Instance for the

---

[1] Roger et Sorel, *Lois Usuelles*, p. 469.　　　　[2] *Ib.* p. 493.

Department of the Seine there are more judges than there are county courts in all England and Wales. The largeness of the number of the French judges cannot but diminish very greatly their individual importance in comparison with that of English judges. Indeed, as will appear, the functions discharged by most of them in the actual management of criminal trials are of little importance. Some sort of analogy to this may be found in the number of persons included in our Commissions of Oyer and Terminer and Gaol Delivery almost entirely by way of compliment.

Passing from the constitution of the courts to their jurisdiction, the first remark which occurs is that our courts of summary jurisdiction have a much more extensive power than the French *juges de paix*. There is no definitely fixed limit to the authority of our stipendiary magistrates and justices in petty sessions. Their powers depend in every case on the statutes which create offences and give them jurisdiction for their punishment. There are many instances in which they may sentence offenders to six months' imprisonment and hard labour, some in which they may go as high as nine months, and [1] a few in which they may go as far as twelve months. They may also, in many cases, inflict heavy fines and forfeitures; as, for instance, £100 and £50 for offences against the law relating to explosive substances. Power to fine up to £10, £20, or £30, is given in almost innumerable cases. This is in marked contrast to the French law, which limits the *juge de paix* to imprisonment for not exceeding five days, and fine not exceeding 15 francs.

It may be observed that as there is an appeal from the *juge de paix* to the Tribunal of First Instance, so there is in many cases an appeal by statute from a conviction by a Court of Summary Jurisdiction to the Court of Quarter Sessions.

I now come to compare the Court of Quarter Sessions to the Correctional Tribunal. As far as regards the Constitution of the Courts the resemblance is greatest in the case of the Borough Courts of Quarter Sessions, as they, like the correctional tribunals, are held before professional judges,

---

[1] *E.g.* in the case of certain offences by convicts, under 34 & 35 Vic. c. 112, s. 7 (Prevention of Crimes Act, 1871).

namely, the Recorders and Deputy-Recorders of boroughs.
In the English courts, however, there is only one judge,
whereas in the French courts there must be at least three.
The County Quarter Sessions, with their volunteer judges
and chairmen are altogether unlike any French tribunal. In
the English courts there is a jury. In the French courts
there is none. As regards the extent of the jurisdiction of
the courts, the English Courts of Quarter Sessions may
(subject to certain specified exceptions) try any cases which
are neither capital nor punishable on a first conviction with
penal servitude for life, but on a second conviction they can
(theoretically) sentence to penal servitude for life. In practice
such sentences are exceedingly rare. The French courts are
limited to *délits*, and can pass no heavier sentence than five
years' imprisonment on a first conviction, or ten years on a
seeond.

The French correctional courts may thus be regarded as
having most of the jurisdiction of our Courts of Quarter
Sessions, and much of the jurisdiction of our Courts of Summary Jurisdiction. The right of appeal from a French
Correctional Court to the *Cour d'Appel* is unlike anything in
our Courts of Quarter Sessions. No appeal lies from their
decisions, which, no doubt, is a consequence of their trying
by a jury. Trial by jury is inconsistent with an appeal by
way of rehearing, though nut with an order for a new trial
before another jury.

The Courts of Assize, the Central Criminal Court, and the
Queen's Bench Division in its original jurisdiction, have
much in common, as far as jurisdiction goes, with the French
Cours d'Assises. They differ, however, in the circumstance
that they can, and not unfrequently do, try causes of small
importance, although their principal function is to try cases
of the more serious kind.

I now pass to the procedure followed in these various
courts in order to bring particular offenders to justice. The
first point to be noticed in connection with this subject is
the existence and organisation in France of a body to which
nothing at all analogous exists in England. I have already
explained at length and in detail in what sense it is true

that the administration of criminal justice in England is in the hands of private individuals, and I have pointed out that though a standing army for the suppression of crime has been established in England in the course of the present century, the police who constitute it can do hardly any single act for the suppression of crime or the apprehension and discovery of offenders which might not in case of need be done, and which indeed is not constantly done, in fact, by private persons.

This is diametrically opposed to the principles and practice of the French. The first article of the *Code d'Instruction Criminelle* is in these words, " L'action pour l'application des " peines n'appartient qu'aux fonctionnaires auxquels elle est " confiée par la loi. L'action en réparation du dommage " causé par un crime, par un délit, ou par une contravention " peut être exercée par tous ceux qui ont souffert de ce dom- " mage." The detection and punishment of crime is thus theoretically as well as practically regarded by the French as essentially a matter of public concern to be provided for by public officials appointed for that purpose. On the other hand, in every French criminal proceeding, from the most trifling to the most important, any person injured by the offence may make himself *partie civile*. In certain cases he may, by doing so, be made liable in damages to the accused. A French criminal trial may thus be also a civil proceeding for damages by the party injured by the crime, and at the same time an action by the accused for what we should call a malicious prosecution.

The French police accordingly is organised in a totally different manner from our own, and has very different duties. Section 8 of the *Code d'Instruction Criminelle* is as follows : " La police judiciaire recherche les crimes, " les délits, et les contraventions, en rassemble les preuves, " et en livre les auteurs aux tribunaux chargés de les " punir."

A complete body of persons is organised for this purpose. At the *Cours d'Appel* there is a staff of officers who act as public prosecutors and are described collectively as the *Ministère Public*. [1] The *Ministère Public* at the *Cours d'Assises* consists of the *Procureur Général*, and the *Avocats Généraux*, who are his substitutes. By Article 279 of the *Code d'Instruction Criminelle* it is enacted that " tous les officiers de police "judiciaire, même les juges d'instruction, sont soumis à la " surveillance du Procureur Géneral. Tous ceux qui d'après " l'article 9 du present code sont à raison des fonctions même " administratives appelés par la loi à faire quelques actes de "la police judiciaire, sont, sous ce rapport seulement soumis à " la même surveillance."

The officers of the judicial police are as follows :—

[2]In every *arrondissement* there must be a *Juge d'Instruction*, who is appointed to that office for three years by the President of the Republic, but is capable of being reappointed. He must be a judge or supplementary judge of the civil tribunal of the *arrondissement*, and more than one may be appointed if necessary. At Paris there are six. In every tribunal of first instance there is a *Procureur de la République* with substitutes who form the *Ministère Public* for that court. In the court of the *juge de paix* the commissary of police is the *Ministère Public*. The *juges de paix*, the *maire* and their *adjoints*, the commissaries of police, the gendarmerie, the *gardes champêtres*, and the *gardes forestiers* are also officers of the judicial police.

Their functions and the procedure adopted differ according to the nature of the offences to be inquired into.

[3]If the offence is a contravention of police, and if the offender is "en flagrant délit," or as our own law says, "found committing" the offence, or if he is "dénoncé par la clameur publique," the *gardes champêtres* or *gardes forestiers* may at once arrest him and take him before the *juge de paix* or the *maire* if he is liable to imprisonment.

[4] In other cases the *garde champêtre* or *forestier* draws up a *procès-verbal* for the purpose of recording the circumstances, the time of the supposed contravention and such proofs or evidence of it as they can find. A *procès-verbal* is a document unlike anything which we make use of in English procedure.

[1] *C. I. C.* 252.
[3] *C. I. C.* 16.
[2] *C. I. C.* 55 ; and see Hélie, p. 63.
[4] *C. I. C.* 16.

CH. XV.   It is thus defined by M. Hélie :—

[1] " Les procès-verbaux sont les actes dans lesquels les " officiers publics constatent les faits qualifiés par la loi " crimes, délits, ou contraventions, leurs circonstances, les " traces qu'ils ont laissées et tous les indices propres à en " signaler les auteurs." [2] A *procès-verbal* must be made within a short time, not precisely fixed, but differing in different cases, after the matters it records are observed. It must be written, signed and dated by the person who makes it. It must state the facts constituting any *délit* or *contravention* which it records, and the name, if possible, of the offender, and it ought to contain a list or description of any articles seized. In some cases it is, and in others it is not verified upon oath before a *juge de paix* or a *maire.* [3] A *procès-verbal* may be a mere *renseignement,* it may be *primâ facie* evidence of the matters stated, and this is the case with the *procès-verbaux* of *maires,* commissaries of police, *gendarmes, gardes champêtres* and *forestiers,* and many others. It may be evidence "jusqu'à l'inscription de faux," *i.e.* till legal means are taken to set it aside as being false. This is the case with the *procès-verbaux* of Custom House officers in some cases, and other executive officers of importance.

[4] When the *procès-verbaux* have been made, the party to whom they refer is either cited before the *juge de paix* or informed verbally, or indeed in any way, that his case is to be heard. If there is a citation there must be a day's notice. [5] The commissary of police acts as public prosecutor, the *juge de paix* as judge. [6] The hearing must be public and in the following order : The *procès-verbaux* are read by the [7] *greffier.* The witnesses summoned by the *Ministère Public* or the *partie civile* are heard ; the *partie civile* and the defendant are heard, and the defendant calls his witnesses ; the *Ministère Public* sums the matter up, and states its conclusions, after which the defendant " pourra proposer ses observations," as it is in all French trials a rule that the

---

[1] *Prat. Crim.* i. p. 146.

[2] *Ib.* pp. 147-148.

[3] *Ib.* p. 151.

[4] *C. I. C.* 21 and 137-154.

[5] *C. I. C.* 144.

[6] *C. I. C.* 153.

[7] In all French courts there is a greffier, who answers to our clerk of assize, clerk of the peace, and clerk to the magistrate.

accused shall have the last word. Finally the court gives judgment either at the hearing or at latest at the next hearing.

[1] The proceedings before a correctional court are very similar to those which take place before a *juge de paix*. The defendant may appear if he likes on a mere statement that his case is to be heard. If he does not appear he must be cited to appear by a citation stating the facts, which may be given either by the *partie civile* or by the *Procureur de la République* who in these courts acts as public prosecutor. [2] If a defendant is taken " en flagrant délit " he may be brought at once before the *Procureur de la République,* who is to interrogate him and take him at once before the tribunal " s'il y a lieu," that is, as it has been held if the defendant is a vagabond or a *repris de justice*. The court, however, even in this case will give three days' time to the defendant to prepare his defence if he asks for it. If the defendant is a person of good character and known domicile he is to be cited.

The proceedings before the court differ from those before the *juge de paix* principally in the circumstance that the defendant must be interrogated. This procedure differs from that which is followed in our courts of summary jurisdiction, to which it should be compared, principally in being more summary in cases other than those of *flagrant délit*. Where an offender is found committing an offence for which he may be imprisoned in a summary way, he is dealt with in France much as he is in England. In other cases there is this difference. In English courts of summary jurisdiction there must, as a rule, be a summons, and if the person summoned does not appear, a warrant may be issued for his apprehension. In the French police courts and correctional courts, a person who does not appear on citation may be tried in his absence [3] by default, but he has a right to set aside such a judgment by " forming opposition " to it within a certain time, in which case he has a right to be heard at the next sitting of the court.

[1] *C. I. C* p. 179-200.
[2] Hélie, *Prat. Cr.* i. p. 196, quoting law of May 26, 1863.
[3] *C. I. C.* 149, *seq.* and 185, *seq.*

I come now to the more careful and elaborate procedure which is followed in the case of *crimes*, though it may also be applied to the case of *délits* and *contraventions*. The summary methods already described are peculiar to the case of *délits* and *contraventions*.

There are various ways in which the first steps may be taken towards the commencement of serious criminal proceedings. They seem to be four in number, though they are not specifically distinguished in the *Code d'Instruction Criminelle*. All are more or less affected by the definition of *flagrant délit*, which is as follows:—[1] " Le délit qui se " commet actuellement, ou qui vient de se commettre est " un flagrant délit. Seront aussi reputé flagrant délit, le cas " où le prévenu est poursuivi par la clameur publique et celui " où le prevenu est trouvé saisi d'effets, armes, instruments, " ou papiers faisant presumer qu'il est auteur ou complice, " pourvu que ce soit dans un temps voisin du délit."

With regard to cases of *flagrant délit*, where the punishment involves any "peine afflictive ou infamante," any one is authorised, and indeed required, to arrest the offender at once. [2] " Tout dépositaire de la force publique, et même " toute personne, sera tenu de saisir le prevenu surpris en " flagrant délit, et de le conduire devant le Procureur de la " République sans qu'il soit besoin de mandat d'amener si " le crime ou délit emporte peine afflictive ou infamante." This resembles, as closely as the nature of the case permits, our law as to arrest without warrant in cases of felony and in other cases subjected to it by statute. When the prisoner is brought before the *Procureur de la République*, he is to be dealt with by him as if he had been brought before him otherwise.

In the second place, proceedings may begin by a "*dé-nonciation*," which is [3] defined by M. Hélie as " l'avis donné " au Ministère Public des crimes ou délits dont on a con-" naissance." [4] The *Code d'Instruction Criminelle* requires all constituted authorities, functionaries, and public officers who in the exercise of their functions come to know of a *crime*

[1] *C. I. C.* 41.   [2] *C. I. C.* 106.
[3] Hélie, *Prat. Cr.* i. p. 49.   [4] *C. I. C.* 29-31.

or *délit*, and all persons who have witnessed a violent attack (*attentat*) either upon the public safety or the life or property of an individual, to give notice of it to the *Procureur de la République*,[1] or to the *maire*, commissary of police, [2]*juge de paix*, or officer of gendarmerie, who are to [3] transmit the *dénonciation* to the *Procureur de la République*.

In the third place, any person injured by a *crime* or *délit* may make a complaint (*plainte*), and [4] constitute himself *partie civile* before a *juge d'instruction*.

In the fourth place when any of the officers of the judicial police have become aware of the fact that a crime has been committed they are empowered and required at once to take proceedings for the detection and apprehension of the criminal.

The principal officers by whom these duties are discharged are the *Procureur de la République* and the *Juge d'Instruction*. Their duties are similar, and the *Code d'Instruction Criminelle* seems to assume that the *Procureur de la République* will first appear upon the scene, and that he will be followed by the *Juge d'Instruction*[5] to whom, as well as to the *Procureur Général*, the *Procureur de la République* is bound to give notice of his proceedings, and upon whose appearance the matter will, to some extent, be taken out of his hands. To begin then with the duties of the *Procureur de la République* [6] in every case of *flagrant délit* punishable with death, *travaux forcés*, transportation, detention, *reclusion*, banishment, or civil degradation, he is bound at once to go to the place, to draw up the *procès-verbaux* necessary to ascertain and record the fact that the offence has been committed (*constater le corps de délit*), its nature, and the state of the place where it was committed, and to receive the declarations of the persons who were present or who have information to give. He must call before him all persons presumed to be in a state to give information, and take down their declarations in writing. He has a right to

[1] *C. I. C.* 50. [2] *C. I. C.* 48. [3] *C. I. C.* 54.
[4] *C. I. C.* 63, *seq.* [5] *C. I. C.* 22, 32.
[6] *C. I. C.* 32-47. "Lorsque le fait sera de nature a entrainer une peine "afflictive ou infamante." The punishments are those so described in the *Code Penal*, 7 and 8.

forbid any one to leave the house or place where the inquiry is going on under penalty of ten days imprisonment and 100 francs fine; he is to seize arms used in the crime, things acquired by it, and, " in short, everything which can be " of service for the manifestation of the truth." He is to question the suspected person on all these matters, and to make *procès-verbaux* of them. He may also search for papers and seal up all he finds. His *procès-verbaux* ought to be made in the presence of and countersigned by the commissary of police, the maire, or two citizens. He may arrest any suspected person against whom there are strong presumptions (*indices graves*), or if he does not appear may issue a warrant (*mandat d'amener*) against him. He may also summon experts, and in particular medical experts. The results of all these inquiries, and all *procès-verbaux*, papers, and other matters are to be transmitted by the *Procureur de la République* to the *Juge d'Instruction*.

[1] In any case in which the master of a house calls upon the *Procureur de la République* to record the commission in that house of any *crime* or *délit*, *flagrant* or not, the *Procureur de la République* has the same powers as he has in the case of *flagrant délit*.

[2] In cases where the *Procureur de la République* learns by any means that a *crime* or *délit*, not *flagrant*, has been committed, or that a person suspected of any *crime* or *délit* is in his arrondissement he is bound to call on the *Juge d'Instruction* to inquire into the matter, but cannot proceed himself in the manner just described.

I now come to the functions of the *Juge d'Instruction*. [3] In the first place, in all cases of *flagrant délit* or apparently requisition by the master of a house he may do himself all the acts which may be done by the *Procureur de la République* as already described, and he may call upon the *Procureur de la République* to be present, but not so as to delay operations in which he may be engaged. He is bound to examine all documents transmitted to him by the *Procureur de la République*, and may go over them again if he considers them incomplete.

[1] *C. I. C.* 46.   [2] *C. I. C.* 47.   [3] *C. I. C.* 59-60.

[1] By whatever means he becomes informed of a crime he must send for every one mentioned to him as having knowledge of the circumstances, and must examine them upon oath separately,[2] secretly, and in the absence of the accused. Their depositions are signed by the judge, by the *greffier* who takes them down, and by the witnesses themselves.

As to the manner in which the depositions are to be taken M. Hélie makes the following observation, [3] " Il est générale-" ment reconnu que le juge d instruction ne doit point procéder " vis-à-vis des temoins par forme d'interrogatoire, il doit les " entendre et recueillir leurs declarations, il doit à la fois main-" tenir dans le procès-verbal leurs expressions, leurs phrases, " en un mot l'originalité de la deposition. Il doit constater " les circonstances qui'impriment à chaque declaration un " caractère plus ou moins marqué de certitude."

The judge may search the house of the suspected person, or search for and seize documents or other things in the same way as the *Procureur de la République*.

[4] With respect to procuring the presence of suspected persons who have not been arrested by the *Procureur de la République*, the *Juge d'Instruction* may issue either a *mandat de comparution*, which answers to our summons, or a *mandat d'amener* which answers to our warrant. If the defendant is arrested in the manner described above by the *Procureur de la République*, [5] he is " en état de mandat d amener," till he is brought before the *Juge d'Instruction*. [6] When the suspected person appears before the *Juge d'Instruction* either upon a *mandat de comparution*, or upon a *mandat d'amener*, he must be interrogated in the case of a *mandat de comparution* at once ; in the case of a *mandat d'amener* within twenty-four hours. If his answers are satisfactory he is discharged, if not he is remanded under a *mandat de dépôt*. This *mandat de dépôt* may be changed into a *mandat d'arrêt* (which however can be issued only upon the requisition of the *Procureur de la République*), at any period

---

[1] *C. I. C.* 71-79.
[2] This is not stated in words in the Code, but the practice is so, and the Code does not prescribe publicity.
[3] *Prat. Crim.* i. 84.   [4] Hélie, *Prat. Crim.* i. 99-102.
[5] *C. I. C.* 45.   [6] *C. I. C.* 93.

of the instruction.   The principal difference between them is, that the *mandat d'arrêt* is definitive, the *mandat de dépôt* provisional.

The interrogatory of the accused by the *Juge d'Instruction* is one of the most characteristic parts of the French procedure, and it is certainly the part which is most opposed to our English notions. [1] It is mentioned in the slightest possible way in the *Code d'Instruction Criminelle*, and in such a manner as to give no idea of its importance. [2] M. Hélie gives a fuller account, it is as follows, " Tout inculpé " contre lequel une procédure est instruite doit être interrogé " par le Juge d'Instruction.   Ce n'est qu'en cas de flagrant " délit que cette formalité peut être remplie par le Ministère " Public et les officiers auxiliaires de la police judiciaire l'art " 40 *C. I. C.* et l'art 1 de la loi du 20 Mai 1863, sur les " flagrants délits attribuent dans ce cas reputé urgent, ce droit " exceptionnellement au Procureur de la République.   Mais " alors même le Juge d'Instruction qui peut refaire les actes " de cette procedure peut faire subir à l'inculpé un nouvel " interrogatoire.

" L'interrogatoire est à la fois un moyen de défense et " un moyen d'instruction.   Il a pour but d'entendre les ex- " plications de l'inculpé pour les vérifier, de consigner " ses dénégations ou ses aveux, de chercher dans ses dé- " clarations la vérité des faits.   De ce qu'il constitue un " moyen de défense, il suit qu'il est considéré comme une forme " essentielle de l'instruction, et que la procédure serait frappée " de nullité si elle était close sans que le prevenu eût été en- " tendu ou dûment appelé. *De ce qu'il constitue un moyen* " *d'instruction, il suit que le Juge peut la réitérer toutes les fois* " *qu'il le juge utile.*

It is important to add here though it is not noticed by M. Hélie, that article 613 of the code which forms part of a chapter relating to prisons contains the following provision.

" Lorsque le Juge d'instruction croira devoir prescrire à " l'égard d'un inculpé une interdiction de communiquer il ne

---

[1] Dans le cas de mandat de comparution il interrogera de suite : dans le cas de mandat d'amener dans les vingt-quatre heures au plus tard.—*C. I. C.* 93. This is the only mention made of the interrogatory.

[2] *Prat. Crim.* i. 97 *seq.*

"pourra le faire que par une ordonnance que sera transcrite "sur le registre de la prison. Cette interdiction ne pourra "s'étendre au-delà de dix jours, elle pourra toute fois être renou-"velée. Il en sera rendu compte au Procureur Général."

The result is that a suspected person may at the discretion of the *Juge d'Instruction* be put in solitary confinement for an indefinite time, during which he may be interrogated by the *Juge d'Instruction* as often as the latter pleases. No limit is provided as to the time during which the "instruction" may last.

[1] M. Hélie has some observations on the principles on which the interrogation should proceed which are creditable to him, but which to judge from such reports of French trials as I have seen do not appear to receive in all cases the degree of attention of which they are worthy. "Il est aujourd'hui "de principe que le Juge d'Instruction doit se borner dans "l'interrogatoire a poser loyalement et clairement toutes les "questions qui resultent de l'étude consciencieuse des faits, "qu'il doit s'abstenir de ces demandes captieuses ou sugges-"tives employées dans notre ancienne jurisprudence pour "surprendre le prevenu, et provoquer ses contradictions enfin "qu'il ne doit se servir d'aucun detour d'aucun artifice pour "obtenir des revelations. Il peut sans doute lui adresser, "quoique avec prudence et reserve, de sages exhortations, il "peut lui démontrer par un raisonnement simple, l'insuffisance "de ses réponses, mais il ne doit point substituer à l'examen "un combat où le plus faible doit necessairement succomber. "Le droit d'interroger n'emporte pas celui de débattre les "reponses et de leur dresser des embûches au moyen de "questions habilement tissues. Le juge ne cherche pas un "coupable mais seulement la verité." He adds, "La règle "légale est qu'il doit être interrogé avant la communication des "charges" (evidence), "que cette communication doit lui "être donnée ensuite, et qu'il doit alors être interrogé de nou-"veau et être mis à même d'y répondre." The interrogatory is secret, the accused is not allowed to have counsel present. What he says is taken down in the form of a narrative in the

---

[1] Hélie, *Prat. Crim.* 97. Compare the conduct of the *juge d'instruction* in the case of Léotade, Vol. III. pp. 475-477.

CH. XV. first person. [1] He may lay *mémoires* or written arguments before the *Juge d'Instruction*, but he has no legal right to see the
depositions of the witnesses or other evidence against him.
It is, however, usual to communicate to him in a final interrogatory all the evidence collected during the *instruction* that
he may discuss them and prepare his defence.

[2] The *Juge d'Instruction* is bound to keep the *Procureur de
la République* advised of all his proceedings, and the latter
may demand to see all the documents as they are drawn up,
but he must not keep them for more than twenty-four hours.
If the *Juge d'Instruction* goes to any place for the purpose
of his inquiry he must be accompanied by the *Procureur de
la République*.

When the *Juge d'Instruction* has completed his inquiries,
he must inform the *Procureur de la République* of the fact,
and he within three days must make such requisitions as he
thinks fit of the *Juge d'Instruction*.

[3] The *Juge d'Instruction* must deliver an interlocutory
judgment (*ordonnance*) on these requisitions. If the *Juge
d'Instruction* thinks that the facts proved do not amount to
an offence against the law, or that the probability of the
guilt of the accused is insufficient to put him on his trial,
the judgment may be that "il n'y a pas lieu de poursuivre,"
upon which the defendant is set at liberty.

If the offence is regarded as a *contravention* the prisoner
must, if in custody, be set at liberty, but sent before the
tribunal of police.

If the offence is a *délit* the prisoner must be sent before
the Correctional Court, and if the offence is one for which he
may be imprisoned, he must be kept in custody if he is in
confinement.

The *Procureur de la République* is to send the documents
to the Court before which the prisoner is sent, and that
Court disposes of the matter in the way already described.

If the *Juge d'Instruction* thinks that there is evidence
enough to put the accused on his trial for a *crime*, he must
order the documents in the case and a list of the exhibits

---

[1] *Prat. Crim.* 112.   [2] *C. I. C.* 61-62.
[3] *C. I. C.* 127-135; Hélie, *Prat. Crim.* 111-117.

(pièces servant à conviction) to be sent to the *Procureur Général* or the *Cour d'Appel.* Thereupon the *mandat d'arrêt* or *de dépôt* is continued until the Court of Appeal makes its order on the matter.

[1] The *Procureur de la République* or the *partie civile* may oppose the interlocutory judgment before the *chambre d'accusation,* but the prisoner is not allowed to do so unless the order has reference to his being admitted to bail and in some other rare cases.

[2] Every prisoner may, if both he and the *Procureur de la République* join in requesting it, be provisionally set at liberty on his undertaking to appear when required. In cases in which the maximum punishment is two years' imprisonment the prisoner has a right to be so set at liberty if he has a domicile, and has not been previously convicted of a crime or sentenced to a years' imprisonment. In cases in which the provisional liberation is not a matter of right the defendant may be held to bail.

This part of French Criminal Procedure is the part which differs most widely and most characteristically from our own, the *Procureur de la République* and *Juge d'Instruction,* their power of holding inquiries, drawing up *procès-verbaux,* examining suspected persons secretly, and without informing them even of the accusation or evidence against them, taking depositions behind their backs, and keeping them in solitary confinement till (whatever soft words may be used about it), every effort has been made to extort a confession from them, are contrasted in the strongest way with everything with which we are familiar, and which I have described, in detail, in the preceding chapters. To keep a man in solitary confinement and question him till he is driven into a confession is not the less torture because the process is protracted instead of being acute.

The instruction being completed the next step to be taken is the *mise en accusation.* This is the business of the *Chambre d'Accusation,* a body which answers roughly to our Grand Jury, though they differ widely, both in their constitution

[1] *C. I. C.* 135.　　　　　[2] *C. I. C.* 113.

CH. XV.   and in their functions. [1] The constitution of the *Chambre d'Accusation* is determined, not by the *Code d'Instruction Criminelle*, but by the laws which regulate the *Cours d'Appel*. By these laws the *Cours d'Appel* (then called *Cours Impériales*) are divided into three chambers, the Chamber for Civil Affairs, the Chamber of Accusation, and the Chamber of Appeals in Correctional matters. The Chamber of Accusation must consist of five judges at least, and in the ordinary course of things [2] sits once a week, but the *Procureur Général* may convene them when he thinks fit. The *Procureur Général* and his substitutes the *Avocats Généraux* form the *Ministère Public* of the *Cours d'Appel* as well as of the *Cours d'Assises*.

[3] When the *Procureur Général* has received the documents in any case of accusation of a crime from the *Juge d'Instruction*, he must make an oral or written report (in general in five days) to the *Chambre d'Accusation*. During this time the *partie civile* and the suspected person may write memoirs for the use of the *Chambre d'Accusation*. The *Procureur Général's* report must conclude by requisitions in writing addressed to the chamber. The written evidence must also be read to them.

The *Chambre d'Accusation* takes the whole matter into consideration and has power to direct a further inquiry upon any point which it thinks requires it. But they examine no witnesses, and none of the parties except the *Procureur Général* appears before them. They may not only consider the question whether there is a case made out by the *Ministère Public*, but also consider the question whether the accused has established what (in the Roman law sense of the word) is described as an exception, such as madness, prescription, or *chose jugée*, which is the equivalent of our pleas of autrefois convict or acquit. The Chamber of Accusation is in no way bound by the views of the *Juge d'Instruction*. They form their own opinion upon all the points which they consider to be raised by the inquiry, [4] and take cognizance of all offences which

---

[1] 20 Ap. 1810 ; 6 July 1810. Roger and Sorel, *Lois Usuelles*, pp. 468 and 473.   [2] *C. I. C.* 218.
[3] *C. I. C.* 217-222.   [4] *C. I. C.* 226-227.

are connected either by having been committed at the same time by several persons, or at different times and places in consequence of a previous agreement, or when one offence is committed to facilitate, complete, or prevent the discovery of another.

As the result of all these operations the *Chambre d'Accusation* may either discharge the suspected person, or make an order for the trial of the party by the *Cour d'Assises*, or other competent court, according as they consider the matter charged to amount to a *crime, délit,* or *contravention.* The one order is called an *arrêt de non-lieu* and the other an *arrêt de renvoi.* Each must be *motivé* that is, it must state in the case of the *arrêt de non-lieu* either that the matter charged does not amount to an offence or that the proof is insufficient, and in the case of the *arrêt de renvoi* that there is sufficient evidence of guilt, and that the fact charged is an offence against some specified penal enactment. In the case of an *arrêt de non-lieu* the suspected person must be set at liberty and cannot be prosecuted again for the same fact unless the *arrêt* was based upon insufficiency of the evidence and new evidence is discovered.

If an *arrêt de renvoi* is made the *Procureur Général* must draw up an *acte d'accusation.* This is usually drawn up by an *Avocat Général* and signed by the *Procureur Général.* It is based on the *arrêt de renvoi* and must not go beyond it.

[1] " L'acte d'accusation a pour objet de faire connaitre le " sujet de l'accusation, mais il n'en est point la base ; la seule " base de l'accusation est l'arrêt de renvoi. C'est cet arrêt " qui fixe la nature et les limites de l'accusation ; il est le " point de départ et la source unique de la procédure ultérieure " et des questions posées au jury." The *Code d'Instruction Criminelle* [2] says the act of accusation shall set forth (1) the nature of the offence which forms the base of the accusation (2) the fact and all the circumstances which can aggravate or diminish the punishment: the accused shall be named and clearly designated. The act of accusation shall end with the following *résumé.*

" In consequence N. is accused of having committed such a

[1] Hélie, *Pra!. Crim.* i. 297.　　　　　　[2] *C. I. C.* 241.

CH. XV.   "*meurtre*, such a theft, or such other crime with such and such
            "circumstances." M. [1] Hélie says that it is not a "plaidoyer."
It ought to be rigorously exact. It ought to be drawn up
with complete impartiality. It ought to be simple, clear and
precise, as it is not a literary work but an act of procedure.
In point of fact such of these actes as I have read, appear to
me to be the most ingenious of "plaidoyers." [2] They are like
the opening speeches of English counsel for the Crown, they
consist entirely of statements of fact, but the facts are so
arranged as to develop in the strongest way and set in the
clearest possible light everything which can be said against
the prisoner.   They are often drawn up with great literary skill and read like pungent and pointed abstracts of
French novels. Moreover they often give an account of the
character of the prisoner and of any discreditable incidents in his previous life. There is nothing in the written
proceedings in an English court which in any degree resembles
an *acte d'accusation*, though, as I have said, it has some
resemblance to the opening speech of the Counsel for the
Crown.

[3] The *acte d'accusation* and the *arrêt de renvoi* must be
notified to the accused, and a copy of each must be given to
him; and within twenty-four hours of this notification the
accused himself must be transferred from the prison in which
he had previously been confined to the *maison de justice*
attached to the court before which he is to be tried, [4] and the
documents and exhibits connected with the case are to be
taken to the office (*greffe*) of the court where the prisoner is
to be tried, unless he is to be tried at the place where the
Cour d'Appel sits, in which case they are already there.

I have already described the constitution of the *Cour
d'Assises*. Some remarks may now be made as to the powers
of its members. The President of the Court is not, like the
Lord Chief Justice, or other president of a division of the
High Court, *primus inter pares*, but has a position and powers
peculiar to himself. [5] He is nominated for each sitting either
by the *Premier Président* of the *Cour d'Appel*, or by the

---

[1] *Prat. Crim.* i. 297.   [2] See Vol. III. p. 509, for an instance.
[3] *C. I. C.* 249.   [4] *C. I. C.* 291.   [5] Hélie, *Prat. Crim.* i. 309-310.

Minister of Justice, commonly in practice by the Minister, CH. XV.
but the *Premier Président* may sit himself if he thinks
proper. [1] His special duties are defined by the *Code d'Instruction Criminelle.* He is intrusted with "la police de
l'audience," that is, the duty of keeping order; "la direction
des débats," that is, the general superintendence of the
proceedings subject of course to the express directions of
the law. In illustration of the nature of this power
[2] M. Hélie says it has been held that he may examine different accused persons separately, refuse to examine witnesses
as to the credit of one of their number, or to put questions
to them which he considers useless, or forbid the prisoner's
counsel to read to the jury the decisions of other juries in
analogous cases. These powers are similar to those which
an English judge possesses of deciding all questions of law,
including questions as to procedure which may arise in the
course of a trial, but more seems to be left to the discretion
of a president than is left to the discretion of our judges.

In addition to these powers the President [3] is "investi
" d'un pouvoir discretionnaire. En vertu duquel il pourra
" prendre sur lui tout ce qu'il croira utile pour découvrir la
" vérité, et la loi charge son honneur et sa conscience d'em-
" ployer tous ses efforts pour en favoriser la manifestation."
The next article specifies some of the most important of the
cases in which this power may be used. The President
" pourra dans le cours des débats appeler même par mandat
" d'amener et entendre toutes personnes ou se faire apporter
" toutes nouvelles pièces qui lui paraitraient, d'après les nou-
" veaux développements donnés à l'audience, soit par les ac-
" cusés, soit par les témoins pouvoir repandre un jour utile
" sur le fait contesté. Les temoins aussi appelés ne prêteront
" point serment, et leurs déclarations ne seront considereés
" que comme renseignements."

This discretionary power is bounded only by very general
rules. It ought to be so employed as to bear upon the
subject of the trial in progress. It ought not to be so
employed as to contradict the general law. The words which
enable the President to hear " all persons" permit him, how-

[1] *C. I. C.* 267-270.   [2] *Prat. Crim.* 324.   [3] *C. I. C.* 268.

CH. XV.   ever, to hear all witnesses who by law are prohibited from
————   testifying, or who on other grounds cannot be called by the
parties.

I now pass to the procedure at and immediately before
the trial itself.

[1] The President must interrogate the accused secretly
within twenty-four hours after the arrival at the office of
the papers and exhibits. This it is [2] said is " un acte
" d'instruction qui doit surtout constater ou la persistance
" de l'accusé dans ses précédentes déclarations, ou les modifications qu'il croit devoir y apporter."

This important act it is also said " ouvre enfin, en faveur
" de l'accusé l'exercice des droits de sa défense, et prepare
" en recueillant ses dernières déclarations écrites, l'instruc-
" tion orale de l'audience." This may be so, but it may
also be regarded in another light—that is to say, as an
advantage given to the President in the oral debate between
himself and the accused at the public hearing. On this
occasion the judge must ask the accused if he has counsel,
and if he has not he must nominate one for him " d'office."
[3] He must also inform the accused that he has five days in
which to move (as we should say) to quash the proceedings
(former une demande en nullité). [4] The prisoner's counsel
may communicate with the accused after the interrogatory,
and inspect all the documents and exhibits, and take copies
of such of them as they think proper. [5] The prisoner has a
right to one copy of the *procès-verbaux* recording the offence,
and of the depositions of the witnesses, gratuitously.

[6] A panel, as we should say, of thirty-six jurors and four
supplementary jurors is drawn by lot from [7] a general list of
persons qualified to serve as jurors, and of these thirty at
least must be present before the jury of twelve is formed.

[8] The list of jurors is notified to the accused the day before
the trial. When the day for the trial arrives all the names

---

[1] *C. I. C.* 266-293.   [2] Hélie, *Prat. Crim.* i. 344.
[3] *C. I. C.* 296.   [4] *C. I. C.* 302.
[5] *C. I. C.* 305.   [6] *C. I. C.* 388.
[7] The rules as to the qualifications of jurors and the formation of the general
list are contained in *C. I. C.* 381, *seq.*
[8] *C. I. C.* 395.

are put into a box and drawn out by chance. [1] As they
appear the accused or his counsel first, and then the *Procureur Général* either challenge or do not challenge until no
more than twelve names remain, or until twelve names are
unchallenged. [2] If an odd number of jurors appear, the
accused has one challenge more than the prosecution. If
the number is even, they have an equal number of challenges,
namely, the difference between the number of jurors who
appear and twelve, divided by two.

If the trial is likely to be long, two supplementary jurors
are chosen, who sit as jurors, but do not deliberate or give
their verdict unless any of the twelve are incapacitated by
illness or otherwise.

The trial before the *Cour d'Assises* is as follows. The
prisoner being introduced [3] without irons but guarded, the
president asks his name, profession, place of abode, and place
of birth. He then [4] warns, or ought to warn, the counsel
for the defence to say nothing against his conscience or the
respect due to the law, and to express himself with decency
and moderation. As this slightly absurd ceremony is not
commanded under the penalty of nullity it is commonly
omitted. It is indeed useless and disrespectful to the person
to whom it is addressed. The president then [5] swears the

---

[1] *C. I. C.* 399.

[2] *C. I. C.* 401. Suppose *e.g.* thirty-one jurors appear the two sides have
nineteen challenges between them, the prisoner ten and the prosecutor nine.
If thirty appears each has nine.

[3] "L'accusé comparaîtra libre, et seulement accompagné de gardes pour
" l'empêcher de s'évader." I know of no better illustration of the true meaning of " libre." A man being tried for his life, actually in prison and seated
between two gendarmes, is " libre " because he has no handcuffs on, and so he
is, free from handcuffs.

[4] *C. I. C.* 311.

[5] *C. I. C.* 312. The form of oath is, " Vous jurez et promettez devant Dieu
" et devant les hommes d'examiner avec l'attention la plus scrupuleuse les
" charges qui seront portées contre N ; de ne trahir ni les interêts de l'accusé
" ni ceux de la société qui l'accuse ; de ne communiquer avec personne jusqu'
" après votre déclaration ; de n'écouter ni la haine ou la mechanceté ni la
" crainte ou l'affection ; de vous décider d'après les charges et les moyens de
" defense, suivant votre conscience et votre intime conviction avec l'impartia-
" lité et la fermeté qui conviennent à un homme probe et libre."

Contrast this wordy, lengthy, tiresome formula with the words of our juryman's oath, which it seems to me impossible to improve and difficult even to
vulgarise :—" You shall judge and truly try and true deliverance make,
" between Our Sovereign Lady the Queen and the prisoner at the bar whom
" you shall have in charge, and a true verdict give according to the evidence.
" So help you God."

" Jurez et promettez devant Dieu et devant les hommes " is much jury, and [1] exhorts the accused to be attentive, which he is likely to be in any case. The *acte d'accusation* is then read, and the prisoner is to be thus addressed :—" Voilà de quoi " vous êtes accusé : vous allez entendre les charges " (evidence) " qui seront produites contre vous." This statement, if made (it is not necessary), is immediately falsified, for instead of hearing the evidence against him the accused is in practice interrogated himself.

It is a singular fact that throughout the *Code d'Instruction Criminelle* there is no reference to this process. Article 319 says, after several provisions as to the evidence of the witnesses: " Après chaque déposition le Président deman-" dera au témoin si c'est de l'accusé present qu'il a entendu " parler : il demandera ensuite à l'accusé s'il veut répondre "à ce qui vient d'être dit contre lui." This, if interpreted by English lawyers, would be held to indicate at least that the prisoner was not to be otherwise interrogated, but a totally different view has been taken in France. The following account of the matter is given by M. [2] Hélie : " Au-" cune disposition du Code ne prescrit en termes précis et " formels l'interrogatoire de l'accusé. De là on a pu induire " que dans son système, l'accusé ne doit pas nécessairement " subir cette forme de la procédure inquisitoriale, et qu'as-" sistant aux déclarations des témoins et ayant la faculté " de les discuter il n'est tenu de faire connaître ses explica-" tions, et son système de défense qu'après que ces déposi-" tions sont terminées. Ce système, qui est celui de la " procédure accusatoire, n'a point en général été admis dans " notre pratique. On a fait dériver l'interrogatoire du droit " que l'Article 319 reconnait, soit au président, soit aux juges " et aux jurés, soit aux parties elle-mêmes, de demander " à l'accusé après chaque déposition tous les éclaircisse-

---

less vigorous than " so help you God." " Examiner avec l'attention la plus " scrupuleuse " is inferior to " judge and truly try," and an abstraction like " la société qui l'accuse " is less impressive than " Our Sovereign Lady the " Queen." The " impartialité et la fermeté qui conviennent à un homme probe " et libre," would be better taken for granted. Moreover, from what are the jury "" libres " ? On the one hand, it is not necessary to say that they are not serfs ; on the other, they are liable to be fined up to 2,000 francs if they do not appear. The word is thus either insulting or inaccurate.

[1] *C. I. C.* 313. " Le président avertira l'accusé d'être attentif."
[2] *Prat. Crim.* i. 373.

" ments qu' il croira nécessaire à la manifestation de la
" vérité. Il est certain que l'interrogatoire, étant à la fois
" un moyen de défense et un moyen d'instruction, peut
" être employé dans l'instruction orale aussi bien que dans
" l'instruction écrite. Il suit de là que le magistrat qui
" adresse à l'accusé des questions, et lui demande des
" éclaircissements, a le droit de l'interpeller pour provoquer sa
" justification ou l'aveu de sa culpabilité ; il doit sans le
" presser ni le troubler, mais en le mettant à même de
" s'expliquer favoriser le libre développement de sa parole ;
" il doit chercher enfin avec la plus complète impartialité et
" uniquement la vérité. L'interrogatoire n'est ni une argu-
" mentation ni une lutte ; ce n'est point le débat ; son but
" principal est d'indiquer le système de la défense, et par
" conséquent de poser les termes du débat et les points qui
" doivent y être vérifiés." He adds that though the interrogatory is not essential, yet the president can interrogate the
accused either before or after the witnesses are heard, the
former being the common course. If there were any
doubt as to the legality of the interrogatory, I suppose it
would fall well within the discretionary powers of the
president.

Whatever may be the law on the subject, the fact unquestionably is that the interrogation of the accused by the
president is not only the first, but is also the most prominent,
conspicuous, and important part of the whole trial. Moreover, all the reports of French trials which I have seen, and
I have read very many, suggest that the views taken by
M. Hélie as to the proper object of the interrogatory, and
the proper method of carrying it on, are not shared by the
great majority of French Presidents of *Cours d'Assises.* [1] The
accused is cross-examined with the utmost severity, and with
continual rebukes, sarcasms, and exhortations, which no counsel
in an English court would be permitted by any judge who
knew and did his duty to address to any witness. This
appears to me to be the weakest and most objectionable part
of the whole system of French criminal procedure, except
parts of the law as to the functions of the jury. It cannot

[1] See *e.g.* Vol. III. p. 476.

CH. XV. but make the judge a party—and what is more, a party adverse to the prisoner—and it appears to me, apart from this, to place him in a position essentially undignified and inconsistent with his other functions. A man accused of a crime ought as such to be an object of pity and something approaching to sympathy on the part of all but those whose special duty it is to bring him to justice. This is the special duty of those who accuse him, and they are always keen enough to discharge it. The duty most appropriate to the office and character of a judge is that of an attentive listener to all that is to be said on both sides, not that of an investigator. After performing that duty patiently and fully, he is in a position to give a jury the full benefit of his thoughts on the subject, but if he takes the leading and principal part in the conflict—and every criminal trial is as essentially a conflict and struggle for life, liberty from imprisonment, or character, as the ancient trials by combat were—he cannot possibly perform properly his own special duty. He is, and of necessity must be, powerfully biased against the prisoner. That in the opinion of the French in general this has been the case with French judges appears to be indicated by the fact that by a very recent enactment they have been deprived of the right which they have hitherto possessed of closing the trial by a *résumé* which in some respects resembled our English summing-up.

[1] The *Procureur Général* states the case to the jury, and puts in the list of witnesses to be heard, of which list a copy must have been given to the accused twenty-four hours before the trial. "Il doit se borner à exposer les faits sans les discuter," says [2] M. Hélie; adding, "Toute discussion serait prémature " et donnerait à la défense le droit de répondre à l'instant " même." This part of the proceedings appears to be of little importance. The *Procureur-Général's* position in the *Cour d'Assises*, though in some respects analogous to that of an English counsel for the Crown, is in others contrasted to it. The *Ministère Public*, consisting of him and his substitutes, the *avocats généraux*, are part of the court. [3] " La

[1] *C. I. C.* 315.   [2] Hélie, *Prat. Crim.* i. 369.
[3] *Ib.* 318.

"Cour d'Assises" . . . "n'est constituée que par la présence
"d'un membre du Ministère Public.   La présence de ce
"magistrat à tous les actes de la procédure orale, à toutes les
"opérations de la Cour est donc nécessaire; et la nullité des
"débats serait encourue par le seul fait qu'un expert aurait
"été entendu, ou qu'un témoin aurait déposé en son absence."
[1] Whenever what the French call an "incident" arises in a
trial, that is to say, a question rendering necessary some
decision or act on the part of the court or president, the
Procureur Général has a right to make requisitions, to be heard
upon them, and to have a judgment from the court from
which he may appeal to the Court of Cassation.

[2] When the *Procureur Général* has made his statement the
witnesses are heard upon oath in an order decided on by the
Procureur Général. Witnesses in France are not examined
as with us, and they can hardly be said to be subject to cross-
examination.   [3] "Le témoin ne pourra être interrompu :
"l'accusé ou son conseil pourront le questionner par l'organe
"du président après sa déposition, et dire tant contre lui que
"contre son témoignage tout ce qui pourra être utile à la
"défense de l'accusé.   Le président pourra également
"demander au témoin et à l'accusé tous les éclaircissements
"qu'il croira nécessaires à la manifestation de la vérité.   Les
"juges" (*i.e.*, the two assessors to the president), "le Pro-
"cureur Général, et les jurés auront la même faculté, en
"demandant la parole au président.   La partie civile ne
"pourra faire de questions, soit au témoin, soit à l'accusé, que
"par l'organe du président."

[4] M. Hélie remarks upon this : "Les témoins doivent être
"*entendus* dans leur dépositions ; ils ne doivent pas être
"*interrogés*.   Cette règle resulte de tous les textes du Code.
"L'audition laisse parler le témoin comme il le veut ; elle
"reçoit sa déposition dans les termes où il la conçue, ou il a
"voulu la faire ; elle lui conserve sa spontanéité et sa liberté.
"La forme interrogative, qui n'est employée que vis-à-vis des
"prévenus, dirige, trop souvent les réponses des témoins et
"quelquefois les suggère ; elle les conduit, par les questions

---

[1] *C. I. C.* 276-278.   [2] *C. I. C.* 317.
[3] *C. I. C.* 319.   [4] Hélie, *Prat. Crim.* pp. 396-397.

"qu'elle pose, à des déclarations irréflechies ou embarrassées. "Le président peut, sans aucune doute, après la déposition "faite, demander au témoin tous les éclaircissements néces- "saires, toutes les explications qui doivent en compléter; "mais il doit le faire avec l'esprit de lui venir en aide, de lui "signaler les faits qu'il oublie, de lui rappeler le sujet de son "témoignage, et d'en écarter les additions superflues, et non "pour imprimer à ce témoignage un caractère que le témoin "n'a pas voulu lui donner, pour forcer le sens et la portée de "ses déclarations, pour enchaîner ses hésitations quelquefois "légitimes, et vaincre les doutes que son esprit conserve "réellement." M. Hélie's cautions would hardly have been given if his experience had not shown that they were necessary.

[1] The president must require the *greffier*, and the *Procureur Général* and the accused may call upon the president to require the *greffier*, to take a note of any variations between the evidence of the witnesses at the trial, and their deposi- tions made before the trial.

[2] The jury, the *Procureur Général*, and the judges (the president is not expressly mentioned), are expressly authorised to take notes of anything said by the witnesses which they consider important, "provided that the discussion is not "interrupted by it."

Taken together these provisions form a strong contrast to our English practice and principles. The whole of the English procedure proceeds upon what I cannot but regard as the true theory, that the only way by which oral testimony can be made full and relevant is by bringing it out by questions asked by the side which calls the witness, and that the only way in which it can be made tolerably trustworthy is by subjecting it in every detail to the severest possible adverse criticism. This with us is effected by cross-examinations in which the adverse party criticises everything said by the witness which he thinks he can shake, besides attacking, if he thinks it right, the character of the witness himself. Moreover our procedure is based upon the theory that all the facts should, as far as possible, be ascertained before they are discussed.

[1] *C. I. C.* 318.   [2] *C. I. C.* 328.

Under the French system the effect of each witness's CH. XV.
evidence is discussed as soon as it is given, and a highly
important, if not the principal, part of the discussion consists
in cross-examining the prisoner about it. The direct cross-
examination of the witness is confined to the president, who
has not those strong motives for doubting the witness's
truthfulness which alone make cross-examination really effective. The parties, and especially the prisoner, have to
cross-examine through him, and to cross-examine a witness
through a third person, who may probably be hostile or at
least indifferent to the cross-examiner, is as ineffectual as
it would be to carry on a fight by telling a proxy where to
strike. The fact that a trial is a combat must be realised
and carried out in every detail if the fight is to be fair. The
witnesses called against either side for the time being
the enemies of that side, and its representative should be
allowed to attack them hand to hand.

The provision as to the taking of notes is noticeable.
According to our practice, it is the indispensable duty of the
judge (though no law imposes it on him)[1] to take a careful
note of everything said by a witness ; and in order to do this
it is essential that the witness should be carefully and
deliberately questioned, and that he should not be allowed to
run on saying whatever he likes. If this were not done,
there would be endless disputes as to what the witness really
said, which disputes could never be decided. The provisions
of the French Code taken as a whole, suggest that the preliminary *instruction* must in practice settle what the witnesses are going to say at the trial ; and this is one of many
circumstances which leads me to think that the *instruction*
and the interrogatories to which the accused are subjected
form the real trial in France, and constitute in practice
the materials on which the jury have to decide.

There are some rules of evidence contained in the *Code
d'Instruction Criminelle*, as to the capacity of witnesses
to testify. Article 322 excludes the evidence of all

---

[1] This is, if not the most anxious, at all events the most fatiguing part of
a judge's duty. To take notes incessantly for eight or even ten hours is an
exertion which no one who has not known what it is could properly appreciate.

CH. XV.   the lineal ancestors and descendants, the brothers and sisters, the husband and wife of the accused, and also the evidence of such of the *dénonciateurs* as are entitled by law to any money recompense for their denunciation. They may, however, testify if none of the parties object, and even if the parties do object, the president, in virtue of his discretionary power, can hear them without oath, by way as it is said of *renseignement.* [1] Some other persons (as, for instance, some convicts) are incapacitated to the same extent.

These rules are of an altogether different kind from those which regulate trials in an English court. When closely examined, our rules of evidence will be found to be reducible to the following :—(1) Proof may be given of facts in issue, and relevant or treated as relevant to the issue, and of no others, with a few rare exceptions. There are careful and elaborate rules as to what does and does not constitute relevancy ; most of them are, more or less consciously, founded on the principle that the causes and effects of any given event are relevant to its existence. (2) When a fact may be proved at all, it must be proved by direct evidence, namely, if it is an event or occurrence, by the evidence of some person who perceived it by the use of his own senses ; if it is the existence of a document by the production of the document itself, or, under circumstances, a copy of it or statement as to its contents.

These leading rules, though qualified by important exceptions, are rigidly enforced in practice, and their enforcement gives to English trials that solid character which is their special characteristic. They seem to be quite unknown in French procedure. Witnesses say what they please and must not be interrupted, and [2] masses of irrelevant, and often malicious, hearsay which would never be admitted into an English court at all, are allowed to go before French juries and prejudice their feelings. The old rules of evidence which were in use before the Revolution, and were derived from the middle age version of the Roman law, were exceedingly technical and essentially foolish. They were accordingly abolished absolutely, and nothing was put in their place. The essentially scientific though superficially technical rules of

[1] Hélie, *Prat. Crim.* i. pp. 372-380.   [2] See *e.g.* Vol. III. p. 485.

evidence which give their whole colour to English trials, and which grew up silently and very gradually in our courts, seem to me to be just what is wanted to bring French trials into a satisfactory shape; but the evils of the old system were so strongly impressed on the authors of the *Code d'Instruction Criminelle*, that destruction was the only policy which presented itself to their minds.[1]

After the witnesses have been examined, the jury are addressed by the *partie civile*, the *Ministère Public*, and the prisoner, in succession. The *partie civile* and the *Ministère Public* reply, and the accused, or his counsel, or, indeed, both in succession, rejoin. There might thus be six, or counting the opening statement of the *Ministère Public* seven, or if the prisoner spoke as well as his advocate eight, speeches in one case, besides all the discussions at the end of each witness's evidence. The greatest possible number of speeches in an English trial would be four, supposing the prisoner to call witnesses, and to sum up as well as open their evidence, and so to give the reply to the crown.

A much wider field is open to French advocates in criminal trials than to English advocates, and French taste differs widely from our own as to the kind of speeches which should be made. This is due to many causes, some arising out of the difference between the characters of the two nations, but some from the difference between the laws in force in them.

---

[1] The strongest possible illustration of this is given by Article 342 of the *Code d'Instruction Criminelle*, which characteristically provides that, when the jury has retired, "le chef des jurés lui fera lecture de l'instruction suivante "qui sera en outre affichée en gros caractères dans le lieu le plus apparent de "leur chambre. 'La loi ne demande pas compte aux jurés des moyens par les- "'quels ils se sont convaincus ; elle ne leur prescrit point de règles desquelles "'ils doivent faire particulièrement dépendre la plénitude et la suffisance d'une "'preuve. Elle leur prescrit de s'interroger eux-mêmes dans le silence et le "'recueillement, et de chercher, dans la sincérité de leur conscience, quelle "'impression ont faites sur leur raison les preuves rapportées contre l'accusé, et "'les moyens de sa défense. La loi ne leur dit point :—*Vous tiendrez pour* "'*vrai tout fait attesté par tel nombre de témoins ;* elle ne leur dit pas non plus :— "'*Vous ne regarderez pas comme suffisamment établie toute preuve qui ne sera pas* "'*formée par tel procès-verbal, de telles pièces, de tant de témoins, ou de tant* "'*d'indices ;* elle ne leur fait que cette seule question, qui renferme toute la "'mésure de leurs devoirs :—*Avez-vous une intime conviction ?* " There is a great deal more of it, but as it does not matter whether these forms are gone through or not, they are probably important only as throwing light on the views of the authors of the *Code.* An English foreman reading to his colleagues a sermon of this sort would look and feel silly.

The *Procureur Général*, as I have observed, being something between counsel and judge, is allowed to say nearly
what he pleases. [1] "L'indépendance de la parole du Ministère
"Public dans le développement de ses requisitoires est une
"règle incontesté. Il a le droit de dire tout ce qu'il croit con-
"venable et nécessaire au bien de la justice, et le Président
"ne peut lui opposer aucune entrave. Il peut s'appuyer sur
"des renseignements qui lui sont fournis par des faits
"étrangers au procès, et faire connaître aux jurés les consé-
"quences légales de leur déclaration. Il peut produire tous
"les documents utiles à l'accusation, et il a été jugé même qu'il
"peut faire usage de déclarations reçues dans une autre affaire,
"et des déclarations écrites d'une instruction supplémentaire
"non communiqué à la défense. Cependant il est préférable de
"produire dans le cours des débats les pièces dont on veut se
"servir. Il ne faut pas transporter l'instruction dans le
"requisitoire et lui ôter la garantie de la contradiction."

The effect of this is that the *Procureur Général* may use
arguments to persuade the jury to convict the prisoner which
we should regard as wholly improper. For instance, in a
prosecution for an agrarian murder in Ireland, the counsel for
the Crown might, if he was in the position of a *Procureur
Général*, enlarge upon every kind of political and social topic,
read articles in newspapers which he thought likely to excite
the indignation of the jury, dwell upon the importance of
making examples, and point out the bad effects of the laxity
of former juries in acquitting when they ought to have convicted and the good effects which in cases alleged to be
analogous to the one being tried had followed from convictions.
He might also appeal to evidence alleged to have been given
in private in some other case, and read letters alleged to have
been intercepted since the prisoner's committal, in which it was
alleged that the prisoner was the agent of a secret society.
This last might be regarded as going a long way, but would
still be quite legal.

The counsel for the defence has a good deal of latitude,
though not quite so much as the Procureur Général. The
following [2] is strange to an English reader. "En ce qui

[1] Hélie, *Prat. Crim.* i. p. 449.   [2] *Ib.* p. 421.

"concerne les eroits de la défense il a été décidé que le
" président peut, sans fixer à l'avance la durée des plaidoiries,
" ² inviter les défenseurs à être brefs " (a valuable privilege),
" qu'il peut interdire à un accusé de présenter sa défense en
" vers, la sevérité des formes judiciaires repoussant cette forme
" de langage, qu'il peut interdire de citer les décisions de jury,
" dans les affaires analogues, qu'il peut également interdire la
" discussion dans la plaidoirie sur le fond de questions relatives
" à l'application de la peine. Mais le défenseur peut soutenir
" que les faits incriminés ne constituent pas le crime que
" poursuit l'accusation, par exemple, que l'homicide commis en
" duel n'est pas un meurtre, que la rétention d'une chose trouvée
" n'est pas un vol. Il peut quoique ce point soit contesté faire
" connaître aux jurés les conséquences légales de la déclaration
" qu'ils vont rendre. Il peut enfin soutenir et développer, non
" seulement les excuses légales, mais les faits d'atténuation qui
" résultent des débats, et qui peuvent motiver l'application
" des circonstances atténuantes."

Whether an English prisoner may put his defence into
verse is a question which has not yet arisen, and which
may be dealt with when it does arise, but the other points
mentioned are of great interest.

Whatever may be the law as to the prisoner's right to refer
to other cases, or to the consequences of the verdict, it is
hardly possible that the *Procureur Général* should be permitted to enter upon topics on which the prisoner is not to be
at liberty to reply, so that if these topics are once introduced,
their full discussion cannot be avoided, and this may easily
leave the question of guilty or not guilty to be lost sight of
in the discussion of general questions connected with or
suggested by the case.

The right of the counsel for the defence to address the jury
on questions of law, as for instance, whether killing in a duel
is *meurtre*, is one of the features in which the administration
of justice in France differs essentially from the administration

---

[1] English judges have the same right, but they do not always succeed.
" Mr. ——, this is the last day of term, and we have many cases in the
" paper." "In none of which has my client any interest whatever, my
" lord."

CH. XV. of justice in England. In England the judge's duty is to direct the jury in all matters of law, and any arguments of counsel upon the subject must be addressed to him and not to the jury. This is not only perfectly well established as matter of law, but it is as a fact acquiesced in by all whom it concerns. In France the principle that the court decides questions of law and the jury questions of fact only is if possible more strenuously asserted, as will appear immediately, than in England ; but in practice French juries habitually take the law into their own hands, and convict or acquit not in accordance with the judge's directions—for the judge as will be seen does not direct them—but according to their own views after hearing the *Procureur Général* and the prisoner's counsel. The result is that practically and especially in the case of crimes of violence done under the influence of passion, French juries decide with far more reference to momentary sympathy than to the definitions of the *Code Pénal*. Such a question as what constitutes *demence*, or self-defence, or the like is decided not by rules of law, but in each particular case by the verdict of the jury.

The power of the jury to return a verdict of guilty with extenuating circumstances, and thereby to prevent the Court from passing the extreme sentence allowed by law, and the right (which follows from it), of advocates to address themselves to the question of the existence of such circumstances, naturally introduces into the speeches of counsel an element almost unknown in English defences.

In practice these points taken together give to an advocate for the prisoner in France a far wider field for comment of all kinds than belongs to an English barrister. He can practically urge the jury on every kind of ground, general and special, to mitigate the law, or even to set it aside altogether, on the ground that they disapprove of it, either in general or in its application to the particular case, and this contention is constantly successful. For instance, a common, perhaps the commonest and most effectual argument in favour of *circonstances atténuantes* in capital cases, is declamation against capital punishment.

My own opinion is that in this matter the English practice

is in every way superior to the French. To put sentiment in the place of law, or to allow the administration of criminal justice to be overridden or interrupted by appeals to sentiment, is to deprive the criminal law of its most characteristic, most effective, and most wholesome attributes. It can never be a real terror to evil-doers and a real encouragement to the healthy indignation of honest men against criminals unless it is put in force inflexibly, and recognised and complied with even if the case is one in which much is to be said in mitigation of punishment. Murder should be called murder, though it may well be that the particular murderer ought not to be put to death. Whether he should or should not be put to death is a question on which I think the jury ought to have nothing decisive to say, though their expressed wish that a convict should be treated mercifully ought always to be considered by those in whose hands the power of showing mercy is vested.

After the speeches are concluded the President used, till the year 1882 to make a *résumé*. The [1] Code says: " Le " président résumera l'affaire. Il fera remarquer aux jurés " les principales preuves pour ou contre l'accusé. Il leur " rappellera les fonctions qu'ils auront à remplir." Of the *résumé* [2] M. Hélie says only that it should be short, "parce- " que la loi n'a voulu qu'un résumé," and that it should be absolutely impartial. It never was anything like so important as an English summing up, which in important cases includes a restatement to the jury of all the important points in the evidence. Practically, it is scarcely possible that after interrogating the accused not only on the whole affair at the beginning of the case, but in reference to every detail after the evidence of each witness, the President should sum up impartially.

Besides making his *résumé* the President is required by the [3] Code to state to the jury in writing the questions which they are to answer. In a technical point of view this is one of the most important parts, if not the most important part of the whole procedure, for the questions so proposed together with

---

[1] *C. I. C.* 336.　　　　[2] *Prat. Crim.* i. p. 425.
[3] *C. I. C.* 337-340.

Ch. XV.   the answers returned are a principal part of the materials on
which the Court of Cassation has to decide if there is an
appeal.

The subject is dealt with [1] in four short articles in the
Code which give no idea of the number and intricacy of the
questions connected with it.   [2] M. Hélie's exposition of these
matters fills more than thirty pages, some of the principal
points of which I will refer to.   It is a general principle
that the jury are to find all the facts, including the existence
of states of mind (*circonstances de moralité*) which collectively constitute the prisoner's guilt, and that the Court of
Assize (not the President) is to say what is the legal effect
of the facts found by the jury, and what the punishment to
be inflicted if they amount to a conviction.   The object of
the questions to each of which the jury must answer Yes or
No, is to constitute when taken with the answers a statement
of facts which will enable the Court to discharge their duty.
The result therefore of a French trial by jury is not to get a
verdict of guilty or not guilty, but to get the facts of the
case stated in a form analogous to a special verdict with us,
or to a special case in civil matters.

From this general theory result four general rules, first,
the questions must reproduce the operative words (*le dis-
positif*) of the *arrêt de renvoi* made by the *Chambre
d'Accusation*.   Secondly, the questions must dispose of all the
facts which, though not expressly found by the *arrêt de renvoi*,
are implied by it, and ought to have been included in it if the
other parts of the instruction had been fully studied.   But
the accusation must not go beyond the *arrêt de renvoi*, though
it may apply to facts not specifically stated in it if they are
" accessoires ou modificatifs de l'accusation principale."

The third rule is that questions may be asked as to the
commission of *délits* which are connected with the accusation,
although the *Cour d'Assises* deals in general only with *crimes*.
For instance if a man is accused of theft, as a vagrant or vagabond, questions may be asked as to vagrancy or beggary.   If
he is accused of *meurtre*, committed whilst poaching,
questions may be asked as to poaching ; if of fraudulent

[1] *C. I. C.* 337-340.   [2] *Prat. Crim.* i. 426-460.

bankruptcy connected with cheating, questions may be asked as to cheating.

The fourth rule is that the facts must be found by the jury, however authentic and conclusive may be the evidence given of them.

These rules have relation to the *arrêt de renvoi*, but apart from this it is also the duty of the President to put to the jury questions on all facts relevant to the accusation which are proved in the course of the trial. For instance, he may put to the jury the question whether a circumstance of aggravation (*e.g.* that a theft was committed at night) was proved, and the President decides *primâ facie* whether there is evidence of a circumstance of aggravation to go to the jury. If his decision is disputed, the Court has to settle the question.

Matters of excuse recognised as such by the law must be left to the jury if the accused requires it. Thus for instance provocation by blows is an excuse for *meurtre*, but drunkenness is not, nor is a provocation by words or threats. The jury may therefore be asked whether a man accused of *meurtre* was provoked by blows, but not whether he was provoked by words.

Matter which if true would modify the accusation by reducing the criminality to an offence of a lower grade than the one charged must be left to the jury. The principle has been stated as follows : "The jury ought to try the accusation as the trial (*les debats*) moulds it, and not as the written procedure establishes it." Hence if a fact is proved which is not, but ought to have been, stated in the *arrêt de renvoi* a question may be asked upon it. I suppose for instance that if a man were [1] charged with colouring money circulating in France, and it appeared that he did so in order to deceive as to the metal, the question whether he did so in order to deceive as to the metal, might be asked even if the *arrêt de renvoi* had omitted to state it. Secondly, the facts on the trial may come out otherwise than they did before the *Juge d'Instruction*. The president may put questions founded upon this. Thus if a man is accused of a complete offence

[1] *Code Pénal*, 133.

the jury may be asked whether there was a *tentative?* If he is accused of *meurtre* they may be asked whether 'he was guilty of striking or wounding ? Thirdly, if facts are proved at the trial which though distinct from, are accessory to the principal accusation, a question may be founded on them. For instance on a charge of robbery a question may be asked as to receiving, on a charge of infanticide a question as to the suppression of the *état civile* of a child. If, however, the facts are distinct from the accusation such a question cannot be asked. Suppose, *e.g.*, that if it incidentally appeared upon a trial, say for robbery, that the accused must on some other occasion have committed perjury, as by swearing in some other case that he was at a different place from that where the robbery was committed, questions could not be asked as to the perjury. The line between accessory facts and distinct facts is said to be at times hard to draw, which seems natural.

Besides the rules as to the subject-matter to which the questions put to the jury must refer, there are a variety of rules as to the form in which they must be put. [1] Every question must begin with " L'accusé est-il coupable ? " These words are considered as involving a criminal intention, and must apparently be used even if the definition of the crime given in the *Code Pénal* specifies the mental element of the crime. It is not enough to ask whether a man accused of theft has " frauduleusement soustrait la chose d'autrui." The question must be "Est-il coupable d'avoir frauduleusement " soustrait la chose d'autrui ? " On the other hand it is enough to ask whether a man " est coupable " of having passed bad money without asking if he knew the money was bad, as guilty knowledge is implied in the word " coupable."

It would be foreign to my purpose to attempt to enter at length into this subject. It is sufficient to say that there is a considerable degree of resemblance between the French rules as to the degree of minuteness with which the jury are to be questioned and the English law as to certainty in an indictment. The following observations of M. Hélie state the principle clearly and give an excellent illustration of it. " [2] La double ˜competence du jury et de la Cour d'Assises est

---

[1] Hélie, *Prat. Crim.* p. 440.   [2] *Ib.* p. 450.

" fondée sur le distinction du fait et du droit ; la loi a attri-
" bué aux jurés la déclaration des faits, et aux juges l'appli-
" cation de la loi. Les questions doivent donc être posées de
" manière à ne présenter aucune question de droit à résoudre
" aux jurés. Ils doivent être interrogés sur les faits qui
" sont les éléments de la qualification légale, et non sur
" cette qualification elle-même." The following illustration is given : " Dans une accusation de faux, le jury
" n'est point appelé à déclarer s'il y a faux et si l'écri-
" ture falsifiée est privée, commerciale ou publique, mais
" il doit déclarer si l'accusé a commis dans telle acte
" telle altération matérielle de nature à préjudicier à
" autrui, si l'écriture emane d'un officier public, et si
" elle constitue un acte du ministère de cet officier, si elle
" emane d'un commerçant, et si elle a pour objet une opéra-
" tion de commerce." The difficulty of clearly dividing
questions of fact from questions of law has, however, been
experienced in France as well as in England. Many common
names of crimes and many words used in describing the constituent parts of crimes involve a legal element. [1] " Il y a
" des cas où la separation du fait et du droit est très difficile.
" Dans une accusation de fausse monaie la question de savoir
" si les pièces contrefaites ont cours légal, circonstance con-
" stitutive, appartient au jury. Le jury est également com-
" petent pour statuer dans une accusation d'extorsion, sur la
" question de savoir si l'écrit extorqué opère obligation, dis-
" position, ou décharge "—" si l'accusé a commis un viol,
" une subornation de témoins, un complot, un attentat à la
" sureté de l'État." There are rules into which I need not
enter as to " complex questions " which are in some cases forbidden and others permitted. They have a resemblance to
the rule of English criminal pleading against duplicity in
the counts of an indictment. The object of these rules is
to get a direct yes or no from the jury upon every question
in the case. The effect of this if strictly applied must be to
make the catechism addressed to the juries exceedingly long
and intricate. Thus it is wrong to ask whether a *meurtre* has
been committed with premeditation and waylaying. The

---

[1] Hélie, *Prat. Crim.* i. p. 452.

premeditation and waylaying must be separated. This seems as if, upon a trial for assassination, the questions might be : Is A. guilty of having intentionally killed B. ? Is A. guilty of having formed a design before the act to make an attack on B.'s person ? Is A. guilty of having waited for B. in a place in order to kill him ? Is A. guilty of having waited for B. in a place in order to inflict upon him other acts of violence ?

It will be seen from all this that our own procedure, since the extremely technical but very skilful reforms which have been made in it, is considerably simpler than that of France. The leading difference between the two in reference to this particular matter is remarkable. Each system recognizes in the strongest way the principle that questions of law should be separated from questions of fact, and that the former should be decided by the judge and the latter by the jury. The English system is based upon the assumption that judge and jury will each perform their respective parts fairly and in good faith, that the judge will tell the jury what is the law applicable to the whole case, and that the jury will be guided by the judge's direction in finding their general verdict of guilty or not guilty. Both history and contemporary experience show that this system has in fact worked admirably, and does so still. The judge's direction, even if it is unpopular, is usually received by the jury as conclusive upon the law of the case. I could mention many instances in my own experience in which juries have found people guilty of murder and of other crimes in the face of the very strongest topics of prejudice, because the judge directed that the law required them to do so.

In cases in which the jury do go against the direction of the judge in point of law, the worst that can happen is that the law on that particular occasion is not carried into effect, which may be no great evil. It is an established principle in English law that the verdicts of juries are not precedents, and that they must not be referred to even in argument in other trials.

Under the French system elaborate and even intricate precautions are devised to keep apart the facts and the law, to leave the law for the court while the facts are for the jury, but in spite of these precautions the jury continually decide in the teeth of the law, and are in practice judges both of law and of fact. The court gives them no directions at all in point of law and never did so. It draws up for them a sort of catechism intended to raise legal points which the court can decide, but it is obvious that the questions will be answered according to the general view which the jury take of the law of the case and of the result which they wish to bring about, and that in the absence of any direction in point of law from the court, they will be guided principally by their own ideas on the subject, which may, and probably will, be extremely vague. I have found no trace in any part of the *Code d'Instruction Criminelle* of any provision for the information of the jury as to the law relating to the cases, except only the provisions described above as to the questions to be put to them. It is not surprising under these circumstances that they should take the law into their own hands as they notoriously do on many occasions ; and this is one principal reason why so large a number of French verdicts, especially in crimes of violence arising from passion, are so unsatisfactory and weak.

[1] The questions being drawn up are delivered in writing to the jury together with the act of accusation, the *procès-verbaux* which record the offence, and all the other papers in the case except the depositions of the witnesses. The effect of this can hardly fail to be to make them take as true the version of the facts given in the *acte d'accusation*, which contains a clear and easy narrative of them, difficult to correct by a recollection of the oral evidence, especially as a French jury cannot, as an English jury can and often does, appeal to the judge's notes to know what some particular witness said. They are told that if the majority thinks that there are extenuating circumstances they must say so expressly, and that they are to vote upon each question secretly. The foreman is required to read to the jury before they begin their deliberations the long formula, part of which I have quoted above, which is also to be written up in large letters in the room.

[1] *C. I. C.* 341-349.

CH. XV. The performance of this ceremony is practically optional, as its omission involves no consequences.

[1] The jury deliberate and then vote on each question proposed to them. [2] Each juryman has two tickets marked yes and no for each question. The tickets are counted and burnt after each vote, and the result yes or no is recorded on the margin of the paper of questions. The matter is decided by a bare majority, and the jury are expressly forbidden to state the number of the votes.

How these arrangements may be suited to France I do not venture to say. If they were applied to English trials I believe they would be most injurious. According to our experience a jury is a useful but a somewhat rough instrument, the duty of which in criminal trials is to say whether a prisoner is proved to be guilty beyond all reasonable doubt. If twelve people of the class from whence jurors are drawn say yes, he is guilty, he probably is so. If any of them doubt, even though they may be a minority, the proper course is to discharge them and have a new trial. In such cases there is no reason why the majority should be right. Many of the jury are men of little intelligence, and apt to follow any lead, so that the minority may probably be more intelligent and independent than the majority. I should say that if a jury were seven to five or even nine to three, there was a reasonable doubt in the case. I should also think that the rule that juries should vote by a secret ballot would be a direct inducement to impatience, and fatal to any real discussion of the matter.

There is one other point in which the English and French systems are strongly contrasted. This is the French system of *circonstances atténuantes* and the English system of recommendations to mercy. The finding of *circonstances atténuantes* by a French jury ties the hands of the Court and compels them to pass a lighter sentence than they otherwise would be entitled to pass. It appears to me to be as great a blot upon the French system as the way in which that system sets the judge in personal conflict with

[1] *C. I. C.* 345.
[2] Hélie, *Prat. Crim.* i. p. 466 ; Law 13 May, 1836 ; Roger et Sorel, 825.

the prisoner. It gives a permanent legal effect to the first impressions of seven out of twelve altogether irresponsible persons, upon the most delicate of all questions connected with the administration of justice—the amount of punishment which, having regard to its moral enormity and also to its political and social danger, ought to be awarded to a given offence. These are, I think, matters which require mature and deliberate consideration by the persons best qualified by their position and their previous training to decide upon them. In all cases not capital the discretion is by our law vested in the judge. In capital cases it is practically vested in the Secretary of State for the Home Department advised by the judge, and inasmuch as such questions always attract great public interest and attention and are often widely discussed by the press, there is little fear that full justice will not be done. To put such a power into the hands of seven jurymen to be exercised by them irrevocably upon a first impression is not only to place a most important power in most improper hands, but is also to deprive the public of any opportunity to influence a decision in which it is deeply interested. Jurymen having given their decision disappear from public notice, their very names being unknown. A secretary of state or a judge is known to every one, and may be made the mark of the most searching criticism, to say nothing of the political consequences which in the case of a secretary of state may arise from mistakes in the discharge of his duty.

On the other hand, our English system allows the jury to exercise at least as much influence on the degree of punishment to be inflicted on those whom they may convict as they ought to have. It is true that the recommendation to mercy of an English jury has no legal effect and is no part of their verdict, but it is invariably considered with attention and is generally effective. In cases where the judge has a discretion as to the sentence, he always makes it lighter when the jury recommend the prisoner to mercy. In capital cases, where he has no discretion, he invariably in practice informs the Home Secretary at once of the recommendation, and it is frequently, perhaps generally, followed by a commutation of the sentence. This seems to me infinitely preferable to the system of *circonstances atténuantes*. Though the impression of a jury ought always to be respectfully considered, it is often founded on mistaken grounds, and is sometimes a compromise. It is usual to ask the reason of the recommendation, and I have known at least one case in which this was followed first by silence and then by a withdrawal of the recommendation. I have also known cases in which the judge has said, " Gentlemen, you would hardly " have recommended this man to mercy if you had known " as I do that he has been repeatedly convicted of similar " offences." There are also cases in which the recommendation is obviously grounded on a doubt of the prisoner's guilt, and in such cases I have known the judge tell the jury that they ought to reconsider the matter and either acquit or convict simply, the prisoner being entitled to an acquittal if the doubt seems to the jury reasonable. This will often lead to an acquittal.

The French jurors bring their declaration into court when it is finished, and it is read for the first time in the absence of the accused, who is afterwards called in and hears it read by the President. If the prisoner is acquitted he is set at liberty at once, and [1] may recover damages from his *dénonciateurs* for calumny if they are private persons. The claim against the *dénonciateur* must be made before the *Cour d'Assises* if, before the case is over, the accused knows who the *dénonciateur* is.

[2] If the accused is convicted the *Procureur Général* calls for the application of the law. The accused may be heard upon this requisition. [3] If he can show that the facts proved by the declaration of the jury, which is conclusive as to their truth, do not amount to an offence known to the law " he is entitled to absolution." If not he must be sentenced.

An *arrêt d'absolution*, [4] it is said is usually pronounced when " la declaration de non-culpabilité n'est pure et simple, " lors qu'une déliberation de la Cour d'Assises est necessaire ' pour l'apprécier." As for instance in a case where the jury

[1] *C. I. C.* 358.   [2] *C. I. C.* 362.
[3] *C. I. C.* 364.   [4] Hélie, *Prat. Crim.* i. p. 481.

found the fact alleged, but declared that the accused acted CH. XV.
without fraud or criminal intention. If the prisoner is improperly "absous" the Court of Cassation may, upon an
appeal by the *Procureur Général*, set aside the order of absolution. If the appeal succeeds on the ground that the Court
denied the existence of a penal law still in force the order
may be pronounced absolutely. If it is pronounced on any
other ground it can be set aside only "in the interest of the
law," *i.e.* to avoid the establishment of a bad precedent, but
without prejudice to the interests of the parties absolved,
[1] so at least M. Hélie explains article 410. What is to
happen if the accused ought to have been "absous,' and
absolution was refused is not expressly stated. I suppose the
case would fall under the general rule and involve a new
trial.

A trial in the *Cour d'Assises* is subject to the following
incidents :—

1. [2] When it has once begun it must go on till it is finished;
subject to necessary adjournments for rest, unless a witness
fails to appear, in which case it may be adjourned till the next
session.

2. [3] If the prisoner is convicted, and the court is convinced
that the jury are mistaken on the merits, the court may
respite judgment, and adjourn the case to another session
to be tried before a new jury, but their decision is final.

3. [4] The accused may appeal to the Court of Cassation
upon any matter of law apparent upon the face of the proceedings, but the utmost result that can be obtained by this
appeal is a declaration of the nullity of the trial, and an
order for a new trial.

4. [5] If the accused is acquitted the public prosecutor may
appeal and have the order set aside but only " in the interest
"of the law," *i.e.* to prevent the establishment of a bad
precedent, and without prejudice to the acquitted person.

5. [6] A demand for review may be made before the Court of
Cassation in three cases :

---

[1] Hélie, *Prat. Crim.* i. p. 532.   [2] *C. I. C.* 353, 354.
[3] *C. I. C.* 352.   [4] *C. I. C.* 373, 408, *seq.*
[5] *C. I. C.* 409.   [6] *C. I. C.* 443.

(1). When after a conviction for homicide the person supposed to have been killed is found alive.

(2). [1] When inconsistent convictions have taken place.

(3). When a witness on whose evidence a person has been convicted has been himself convicted of false evidence given at the trial.

In either of these cases a new trial must be ordered before a different court.

These are the principal provisions of the *Code d'Instruction Criminelle* of sufficient general interest to be noticed in this place.

I have only one remark to add to those already made. The whole system from first to last bears upon it the clearest traces of being a compromise between two different systems. If the jury were left out the whole system would be symmetrical and harmonious. A crime is committed, a number of careful preliminary inquiries are made by subordinate officers under the general direction of a sort of judge-advocate who has to satisfy other official personages who are judges but not advocates: first, that the suspected person should be tried. and then that he is guilty. The prisoner is closely interrogated at every step in the proceedings, the evidence is sifted and arranged with the greatest care before it comes before the court. If the court had merely to satisfy itself and to declare its satisfaction or the reverse, the whole scheme would be harmonious, but either the jury or the judges are superfluous. The presence of the jury turns the judge into an additional advocate. The presence of the judge renders necessary a cumbrous apparatus for reserving points of law which after all leaves the jury in the position of being judges of the law to whatever extent they choose to act as such.

The English system, formed by very slow degrees and with absolutely no conscious adaptation of means to ends, is intrinsically more coherent and systematic than the French system. By the steps which I have traced in detail, trial by jury has come to be in substance an action in which the prosecutor is plaintiff and the prisoner defendant. The quarrel between

[1] See l'affaire Lesmer, Vol. III. p. 509.

the two is fought out before a tribunal consisting of the judge and the jury. After hearing all that is to be said on both sides, the judge repeats to the jury the evidence given on each side, indicates as far as he thinks proper his own view of the facts, and authoritatively lays down the law for their guidance. They ultimately decide the whole matter, fact and law, being guided in their decision by the judge's statement of the law but acting with perfect independence in their own sphere. Though our system of criminal procedure has many defects, and is extremely ill expressed, it possesses an internal organic unity which seems to me to be wanting in the system established by the *Code d'Instruction Criminelle*, though that document is, speaking generally, arranged with admirable perspicuity, and on a coherent systematic plan which contrasts very unfavourably for us with the mixture of statutes, decided cases, and common law which holds our code in suspension.

This comparison of French and English criminal procedure naturally suggests the question—Which of the two is the best? To a person accustomed to the English system and to English ways of thinking and feeling there can be no comparison at all between them. However well fitted it may be for France, the French system would be utterly intolerable in England. The substitution of a secret "instruction" for our open investigation before the committing magistrate would appear to us to poison justice at its source. An English judge would feel himself degraded if he were required or expected to enter into a personal conflict with the prisoner, and extort admissions from him by an elaborate cross-examination. All our notions of dignity, order, and calmness would be overthrown by the prolonged wrangle between the court and the prisoner renewed after every witness had made his statement. The practical abolition of cross-examination would in our eyes deprive the evidence of the strongest security for its truthfulness and accuracy, and the admission of unrestricted appeals to prejudice and sentiment on the part of the counsel on both sides in their addresses to the jury would appear to us to crown by feeble sentimentality a proceeding instituted secretly and carried on oppressively. The whole temper and spirit of the French and the English differs so widely, that it would be rash for an Englishman to speak of trials in France as they actually are. We can think of the system only as it would work if transplanted into England. It may well be that it not only looks, but is, a very different thing in France.

The only advantage which could be ascribed to it over our own system would be that of superior efficiency, and no doubt if it were true that it does, in fact, discriminate guilt from innocence and bring the guilty to justice more effectually than our own system, it would be necessary to admit that, at however high a price, its principal object had been attained. But is this the case? It can hardly be asserted that life and property are more secure in France than they are in England, but it would hardly fall within the province of this work to enter into a detailed inquiry on this subject. The best way of comparing the working of the two systems is by comparing trials which have taken place under them. For this purpose I have given at the end of this work detailed accounts of seven celebrated trials, four English and three French, which afford strong illustrations of the results of the two systems. It seems to me that a comparison between them shows the superiority of the English system even more remarkably than any general observations which may be made on the subject. In every one of the English cases the evidence is fuller, clearer, and infinitely more cogent than it is in any one of the French cases, notwithstanding which, far less time was occupied by the English trials than by the French ones, and not a word was said or a step taken which any one can represent as cruel or undignified.

Apart from the comparative merits of French and English criminal procedure, this appears to be the place for some observations on the positive value of trial by jury as practised and understood in England. It is perhaps the most popular of all our institutions, and has certainly been made the subject of a kind and degree of eulogy which no institution can possibly deserve. All exaggeration apart, what is its true value?

It may be regarded in several different lights.

The first question is, Are juries just? The second, Are they intelligent enough for the duties they have to perform?

The third, What are the collateral advantages of the institution? Upon each of these points it is necessary to compare juries to judges sitting without juries, for the choice lies
between these two tribunals. Our experience of trials by
judges without juries, in criminal as well as in civil cases, has
in the last two generations become very extensive. In the
first place, the judges of the Chancery Division of the High
Court are continually called upon to determine questions of
fact which in many instances are exactly like those which
are determined in criminal cases; as, for instance, where fraud
is alleged as a ground for setting a transaction aside. The
same is true of the county court judges and of the courts
of summary jurisdiction, which have extensive powers of
fine and imprisonment. Applications to the judges of the
Queen's Bench Division sometimes involve the determination
of similar questions. I have, for instance, known a case in
which the decision of the question whether a father should
be deprived of the custody of his child depended upon
the question whether he had committed a crime, which
question was tried and determined by a judge without a jury.
The trial of civil cases without juries has also become a
matter of everyday occurrence. Finally, in British India,
trial by a judge alone is in all criminal cases the rule, and
trial by jury the rare exception.

There is a considerable difference in the manner in which
cases are tried by judges sitting alone. In cases tried without
a jury by a judge of the High Court, notes are taken just as
if the case was tried by a jury; and in the case of an appeal,
they are forwarded to the Court of Appeal for their information. If serious criminal cases were to be tried by judges
without juries, I think that notes should be taken both by
the judge and, in capital cases, by a shorthand writer as well;
and I think the judge should give his reasons for his decision,
and that if he did not give them in writing they should be
taken down by a shorthand writer, and read and corrected by
the judge. In such cases I think there should be an appeal
both on the law and on the facts to the Court for Crown Cases
Reserved, or whatever court might be substituted for it.
In comparing trial by jury with trial by a judge without a

jury, I assume the establishment of such a form of trial as this.

First, then, as to the comparative justice to be expected of trials by jury and trials by a judge without a jury. Trial by a judge without a jury may, I think, be made, practically speaking, completely just in almost every case. At all events, the securities which can be taken for justice in the case of a trial by a judge without a jury are infinitely greater than those which can be taken for trial by a judge and jury.

1. The judge is one known man, holding a conspicuous position before the public, and open to censure and, in extreme cases, to punishment if he does wrong: the jury are twelve unknown men. Whilst the trial is proceeding they form a group just large enough to destroy even the appearance of individual responsibility. When the trial is over they sink back into the crowd from whence they came, and cannot be distinguished from it. The most unjust verdict throws no discredit on any person who joined in it, for as soon as it is pronounced he returns to obscurity.

2. Juries give no reasons, but judges do in some cases, and ought to be made to do so formally in all cases if juries were dispensed with. This in itself is a security of the highest value for the justice of a decision. An unskilled person may no doubt give bad reasons for a sound conclusion, but it is nearly impossible for the most highly skilled person to give good reasons for a bad conclusion; and the attempt to do so would imply a determination to be unjust which would be most uncommon.

3. From the nature of the case there can be no appeal in cases of trial by jury, though there may be a new trial. There can be an appeal where the trial is by a single judge. This may not, at first sight, be obvious, but it is a consequence of the circumstance that a jury cannot give their reasons. An appeal, properly so called, implies a judgment on the part of the court appealed from and an argument to show that it decided wrongly, which cannot be unless the reasons of the decision are known. If an appeal proper lay from the decision of a jury, and if it took the form of a

rehearing before a court of judges, trial by jury might as well be abolished.

4. Experience has proved that the decisions of single judges are usually recognised as just. There are very few complaints of the decisions either of magistrates or of county court judges on the ground of injustice. I never heard of a complaint of injustice in a trial by a judge of the High Court without a jury. Arbitrations, in which the arbitrator gives no reasons and is subject to no appeal, are not only common but are on the increase. This would scarcely be the case if confidence were not felt in the justice of arbitrators.

As to juries, experience no doubt has shown, and does continually show, that their verdicts also are just in the very great majority of instances, but I am bound to say I think that the exceptions are more numerous than in the case of trials by judges without juries.

In cases of strong prejudice juries are frequently unjust, and are capable of erring on the side either of undue convictions or of undue acquittals. They are also capable of being intimidated, as the experience of Ireland has abundantly shown. Intimidation has never been systematically practised in England in modern times, but I believe it would be just as easy and just as effective here as it has been shown to be in Ireland. Under the Plantagenets, and down to the establishment of the Court of Star Chamber, trial by jury was so weak in England as to cause something like a general paralysis of the administration of justice. Under Charles II. it was a blind and cruel system. During part of the reign of George III. it was, to say the least, quite as severe as the severest judge without a jury could have been. The revolutionary tribunal during the Reign of Terror tried by a jury.

There are no doubt some things to be set against this. It is often said in delicate terms that some degree of injustice is a good thing. The phrases in which this sentiment is conveyed are to the effect that it may sometimes be desirable that the strict execution of the law should be mitigated by popular sentiment, of which juries are considered to be the representatives. Whether it is a greater evil that a bad law

CH. XV.

should be executed strictly or capriciously is perhaps disputable, but it admits of no doubt that laws unfit to be strictly executed ought to be repealed or modified. Parts of the criminal law were no doubt formerly cruel and otherwise objectionable. I can understand, though I do not share, the sentiment which admires juries who perjured themselves by affirming a five-pound note to be worth less than forty shillings in order to avoid a capital conviction, or who refused to give effect to the old law of libel; but these are things of the past. I know of no part of our existing law which requires to be put in force capriciously. I see, for instance, no advantage in acquittals in the face of clear evidence for bribery, or for sending ships to sea in a dangerous condition, or for libels on private persons who happen to be disreputable and unpopular, or for frauds committed upon money-lenders, or for crimes committed by pretty women under affecting circumstances.

The cases commonly referred to as those which reflect the highest honour upon juries are—the trial of the seven bishops in 1688, the trials for libel in the last century, and the trials for treason in 1794. As to the trial of the seven bishops, their acquittal was, no doubt, right; but their conviction would have done no great harm, it would have merely hastened the Revolution, and given them a little martyrdom. Besides, if they had been tried by the presiding judges, they could not have been convicted, for the judges were two to two. In the case of libel, I think there can be no doubt that the alteration of a bad law was to some extent caused by the unwillingness of juries to enforce it, though (as will appear in a subsequent chapter) they were extremely capricious in their verdicts, and though the amendment of the law was due, after all, rather to Parliament than to the juries. In the case of the trials for treason in 1794, the case turned, not upon the law, but upon the evidence. I do not think that the prisoners would have been convicted if they had been tried by a judge without a jury. [1] Chief Justice Eyre's summing up was scrupulously fair, and cannot be said to have been calculated to procure a conviction. Even [2] Lord Eldon, not long

---

[1] 24 *State Trials*, p. 1293 *et seq.*
[2] Campbell's *Lives of the Chancellors*, ix. p. 197.

after the trial, said "the evidence was, in his opinion, so nicely
" balanced, that had he himself been on the jury he did not
" know what verdict he should have given." If so, he must
have given the prisoners the benefit of the doubt. I shall
refer more particularly to these matters elsewhere. It is
sufficient for the present purpose to observe that I think
that as a matter of history trial by jury has been less of
a bulwark against oppressive punishments than many of
the popular commonplaces about it imply.

The next point to consider is the comparative wisdom or
intelligence of judges and juries. I think that a judge ought
to be, and that he usually is, a man of far greater intelligence,
better education, and more force of mind, than any individual member of the juries which he has to charge, but it
must be remembered that there is a great difference between
jury and jury. The force and effect of evidence can hardly
be tested better than by the impression which it makes on
a group of persons large enough to secure its being looked
at from many different points of view and by people of
different habits of mind. But this advantage is obtained
only when all the jurors listen to the whole of the evidence;
and it continually happens that several of them are half asleep,
or listen mechanically, or think about something else, and
that when the verdict is considered they follow the lead of
any member of the jury who chooses to take the lead.
Again, as to experience, it is very unlikely that any judge
should have greater experience of the kind required upon
a criminal trial than all the twelve men in the jury-box put
together, unless indeed they are unusually stupid. A really
good special jury will usually consist of, or as a rule
contain, men in every respect as competent to judge
of the effect of evidence as any judge, and the probability
that they or some of them will possess experience bearing on
the case which has not come in the judge's way is considerable. I think that as far as skill and intelligence go it
would be impossible to have a stronger tribunal than a jury
of educated gentlemen presided over by a competent judge
I cannot, however, say much for the intelligence of small
shopkeepers and petty farmers, and whatever the fashion of

the times may say to the contrary, I think that the great bulk of the working classes are altogether unfit to discharge judicial duties, nor do I believe that, rare exceptions excepted, a man who has to work hard all day long at a mechanical trade will ever have either the memory, or the mental power, or the habits of thought, necessary to retain, analyse, and arrange in his mind the evidence of, say, twenty witnesses to a number of minute facts given perhaps on two different days. Jurors almost never take notes, and most of them would only confuse themselves by any attempt to do so, and I strongly suspect that a large proportion of them would, if examined openly at the end of a trial as to the different matters which they had heard in the course of it, be found to be in a state of hopeless confusion and bewilderment. I should be far from saying this of good special juries, but I think that the habit of flattering and encouraging the poor, and asserting that they are just as sensible and capable of performing judicial and political functions as those who from their infancy have had the advantages of leisure, education, and wealth, has led to views as to the persons qualified to be jurors which may be very mischievous. I think that, in all criminal cases of any considerable difficulty or importance, there ought to be at least a power to summon special juries. In short, I think a good judge and a good special jury form as strong a tribunal as can be had, but I think a judge without a jury would be a stronger tribunal than a judge and an average common jury.

There is a third point of view from which trial by jury must be considered, namely, its collateral advantages, and these, I think, are not only incontestable in themselves, but are of such importance that I should be sorry to see any considerable change in the system, though I am alive to its defects. They are these :—

In the first place, though I do not think that trial by jury really is more just than trial by a judge without a jury would be, it is generally considered to be so, and not unnaturally Though the judges are, and are known to be, independent of the executive Government, it is naturally felt that their sympathies are likely to be on the side of authority. The public at large feel more sympathy with jurymen than they do with judges, and accept their verdicts with much less hesitation and distrust than they would feel towards judgments however ably written or expressed.

In the next place, trial by jury interests large numbers of people in the administration of justice and makes them responsible for it. It is difficult to over-estimate the importance of this. It gives a degree of power and of popularity to the administration of justice which could hardly be derived from any other source.

Lastly, though I am, as every judge must be, a prejudiced witness on the subject, I think that the position in which trial by jury places the judge is one in which such powers as he possesses can be most effectually used for the public service. It is hardly necessary to say that to judges in general the maintenance of trial by jury is of more importance than to any other members of the community. It saves judges from the responsibility—which to many men would appear intolerably heavy and painful—of deciding simply on their own opinion upon the guilt or innocence of the prisoner. If a judge sums up for a conviction and the jury convicts, they share the responsibility with him and confirm his views by their verdict; and the same may be said if they follow his suggestion in acquitting. If they acquit when he suggests a conviction, he is spared from what is always a painful task—that of determining on the sentence to be passed. If they convict when he suggests an acquittal, he can, if he is decidedly of opinion that the prisoner is innocent, in practically all cases, procure a pardon; I think he ought to have a legal right to direct a new trial. On the other hand, he may not unfrequently feel that the jury have done substantial justice in overlooking some deficiency or weakness in the legal proof of the case which had occurred to his mind, and in this case the result is that, without any default on his part, a criminal meets his deserts, although the proof against him may not quite come up to the legal standard. I remember a case many years ago in which a surgeon was convicted of manslaughter for causing the death of a woman in delivering her of a child. The judge (the late Baron Alderson) summed up

strongly for an acquittal, remarking on the slightness of the
evidence that the man was drunk at the time ; but the jury
convicted him, well knowing that he was a notorious and
habitual drunkard.

For these reasons, the institution of trial by jury is so very
pleasant to judges that they may probably be prejudiced in
its favour. I think, however, that the institution does place
the judge in the position in which, with a view to the public
interest, he ought to be placed—that of a guide and adviser
to those who are ultimately to decide, and a moderator in
the struggle on the result of which they are to give their
decision. The interposition of a man, whose duty it is to
do equal justice to all, between the actual combatants and
the actual judges of the result of the combat, gives to the
whole proceedings the air of gravity, dignity, and humanity,
which ought to be, and usually is, characteristic of an
English court, and which ought to make every such court
a school of truth, justice, and virtue. In short, if trial by
jury is looked at from the political and moral point of view,
everything is to be said in its favour, and nothing can be said
against it. Whatever defects it may have might be effectually removed by having more highly qualified jurors. I think
that to be on the jury list ought to be regarded as an honour
and distinction. It is an office at least as important as, say, that
of guardians of the poor, and I think that if arrangements
were made for the comfort of jurors, and for the payment of
their expenses when on duty, men of standing and consideration
might be willing and even desirous to fill the position.

There is one further question connected with trial by jury
on which a few words may be said. This is the question :—
Which is right—the present system according to which skilled
witnesses are called by each side at the discretion of the parties
and are examined and cross-examined like other witnesses, or a
proposed system according to which such witnesses should be
appointed by the court and occupy a position more or less
resembling that of assessors ? The matter has been often discussed, especially by medical men. I have the strongest
possible opinion in favour of the maintenance of the present
system for the following reasons.

Our present system provides a definite place and definite rights and duties for the parties, the judge, the jury, and the witnesses. What room there is for any other person in the proceedings I do not see. It is impossible to say what an expert is to be if he is not to be a witness like other witnesses. If he is to decide upon medical or other scientific questions connected with the case so as to bind either the judge or the jury, the inevitable result is a divided responsibility which would destroy the whole value of the trial. If the expert is to tell the jury what is the law—say about madness—he supersedes the judge. If he is to decide whether, in fact, the prisoner is mad, he supersedes the jury. If he is only to advise the court, is he or is he not to do so publicly and to be liable to cross-examination? If yes, he is a witness like any other. If no, he will be placed in a position opposed to all principle. The judge and the jury alike are, and ought to be, instructed only by witnesses publicly testifying in open court on oath. It never would be, and never ought to be, endured for a moment that a judge should have irresponsible advisers protected against cross-examination. Again, suppose that some arrangement or other as to experts were devised by which they were to be not quite witnesses but something rather like it, what rule is to be laid down as to witnesses? Are the prisoner and the Crown to be allowed or to be forbidden to call them as at present? To forbid a prisoner to call a witness to say that in his opinion the symptoms of a given death were not those of poisoning would be an intolerable denial of justice; but if such witnesses are called, what becomes of the experts? When the jury have heard sworn witnesses, examined and cross-examined for the parties, what will they care, or what ought they to care, for the opinion of experts appointed by the Crown? Counsel would say with perfect truth, Listen to sworn testimony tested by cross-examination; what have you to do with people whose evidence, if evidence it is to be called, you are not allowed to test?

The truth is, that the demand for experts is simply a protest made by medical men against cross-examination. They are not accustomed to it and they do not like it, but I should say that no class of witnesses ought to be so carefully watched and so strictly cross-examined. There is one way in which medical men may altogether avoid the inconveniences of which they complain, and that is by knowing their business and giving their testimony with absolute candour and frankness. There have been, no doubt, and there still occasionally are, scenes between medical witnesses and the counsel who cross-examine them which are not creditable, but the reason is that medical witnesses in such cases are not really witnesses but counsel in disguise, who have come to support the side by which they are called. The practice is, happily, rarer than it used to be; but when it occurs it can be met and exposed only by the most searching, and no doubt unpleasant, questioning. By proper means it may be wholly avoided. If medical men laid down for themselves a positive rule that they would not give evidence unless before doing so they met in consultation the medical men to be called on the other side and exchanged their views fully, so that the medical witnesses on the one side might know what was to be said by the medical witnesses on the other, they would be able to give a full and impartial account of the case which would not provoke cross-examination. For many years this course has been invariably pursued by all the most eminent physicians and surgeons in Leeds, and the result is that in trials at Leeds (where actions for injuries in railway accidents and the like are very common) the medical witnesses are hardly ever cross-examined at all, and it is by no means uncommon for them to be called on one side only. Such a practice of course implies a high standard of honour and professional knowledge on the part of the witnesses employed to give evidence, but this is a matter for medical men. If they steadily refuse to act as counsel, and insist on knowing what is to be said on both sides before they testify, they need not fear cross-examination.

END OF VOL. I.

R. CLAY, SONS, AND TAYLOR, PRINTERS.

Lightning Source UK Ltd.
Milton Keynes UK
UKOW04f0237121213

222862UK00001B/25/P